Children's Writers' & Artists' YEARBOOK 2016

TWELFTH EDITION

The essential guide for children's writers and artists
on how to get published and who to contact

BLOOMSBURY
LONDON · OXFORD · NEW YORK · NEW DELHI · SYDNEY

Bloomsbury Publishing
An imprint of Bloomsbury Publishing Plc

50 Bedford Square	1385 Broadway
London	New York
WC1B 3DP	NY 10018
UK	USA

www.bloomsbury.com

BLOOMSBURY and the Diana logo are trademarks of Bloomsbury Publishing Plc

British Library Cataloguing-in-Publication Data
A catalogue record for this book is available from the British Library.

ISBN: PB: 978-1-4729-2495-7

2 4 6 8 10 9 7 5 3 1

Typeset by QPM from David Lewis XML Associates Ltd
Printed and bound in Great Britain by CPI Group (UK) Ltd, Croydon CR0 4YY

MIX
Paper from
responsible sources
FSC® C020471

To find out more about our authors and books visit www.bloomsbury.com. Here you will find extracts, author interviews, details of forthcoming events and the option to sign up for our newsletters.

Writers' & Artists' team
Editor Alysoun Owen
Articles Editor Virginia Klein
Listings Editors Lisa Carden, Rebecca Collins,
   Lauren Simpson
Editorial assistance Sophia Blackwell (poetry)
Database Manager Martin Dowling
Production Controller Ben Chisnall

About the *Yearbook*

The Editor welcomes readers to this edition of the *Children's Writers' & Artists' Yearbook.*

Last year, 2014, there was a significant rise in the sales of children's books in all their guises – hardback, paperback and e-books (see *Children's publishing: markets, news and trends* by Caroline Horn on page 15). Is this what some commentators are heralding as the dawn of a golden age for children's publishing? It certainly suggests that the campaigns and activities that for years have promoted reading and literacy have been effective (see the entries in the *Societies, prizes and festivals* section of this *Yearbook*, starting on page 375), that more young people are reading using a range of means to access their content, and that there is an extraordinary wealth of talent creating and publishing for children.

This *Yearbook* is proud once again to share advice from some of the most successful and accomplished writers and illustrators working in the UK today. Collectively they do a huge amount to share their passion with young readers and writers up and down the country, through school visits, literary festivals and campaigns to which they lend their support and, of course, through the worlds they conjure up in their words and pictures.

New to the *Yearbook* this year are articles written from the author's *and* the illustrator's perspective. Korky Paul, illustrator of the *Winnie the Witch* series (see *On being a storyteller: the illustrator's story*, page 258) and author Valerie Thomas (see *Picture books for children: the writer's story*, page 255) share their thoughts and experience. Collaboration of a different kind is explored by Steve Cole in *Playing with other people's toys: adventures in licensed publishing* (see page 127). Julia Golding takes adopting new voices and personalities one step further in *Who am I today? Writing under multiple pseudonyms* (page 182). Louise Jordan describes why – and how – she decided to start a new publishing business in *What publishers want: a new perspective* (page 21). The teenage market can be a challenging and rewarding one: Michelle Garnett, in *Writing for the teenage market* (page 327), considers the approach in the magazine sector. Frank Cottrell Boyce offers his tips on how to become a published writer in our *Foreword* on page xi.

In addition to the articles, the hundreds of listings in this guide are updated every year, providing details on who to contact across the book and wider media worlds.

Good luck as you explore the wonders of being a writer, a reader and an advocate for quality writing and illustration for children, from babies to young adults.

Alysoun Owen, Editor

We make every effort to contact all of the organisations and institutions listed in the *Yearbook* so they can update their information. To the best of our knowledge the websites, emails and other details are correct at the time of going to press.

Contents

More than a book

Writers & Artists online

The *Children's Writers' & Artists' Yearbook* is a highly regarded resource within the publishing and wider media industries. In response to the changing world of publishing and to the needs of writers and would-be writers, Writers & Artists also gives online support and information.

The Writers & Artists website (**www.writersandartists.co.uk**) provides up-to-the-minute writing advice, blogs, competitions and the chance to share work with other writers. Our editorial services offer guidance from experienced agents and editors on all stages in the development of a manuscript – from proposal, through the various editing phases, up to submission to an agent. To receive our regular newsletter, you can sign up at www.writersandartists.co.uk/register. The Writers & Artists listings service can be accessed at www.writersandartists.co.uk/listings.

Our free self-publishing comparison site (**www.selfpubcompare.com**) is aimed at writers who are interested in self-publishing their book but are not sure how to get started. It provides information, advice on options available to authors interested in self- or indie-publishing and an instant, independent set of results to meet each writer's specific self-publishing requirements.

Short story competition

If you write for adults as well as children, you may be interested in our Short Story Competition. This offers published and aspiring writers the chance to win a cash prize of £500 and a place on an Arvon residential writing course. The winning story will be published on the Writers & Artists website. To enter, submit a short story (for adults) of no more than 2,000 words, on the theme of 'Ageing' to competition@bloomsbury.com before 15 February 2016. For full details, including terms and conditions, visit **www.writersandartists.co.uk/competitions**.

You can find details of competitions for children's writing under *Children's book and illustration prizes and awards* on page 409.

ARVON runs three historic writing houses in the UK, where published writers lead week-long residential courses. Covering a diverse range of genres, from poetry and fiction to screenwriting and comedy, Arvon courses have provided inspiration to thousands of people at all stages of their writing lives. You can find out more and book a course online at **www.arvon.org**.

Praise for the *Yearbook*

'How to get published? 1. Write a good book.
2. Read a good book – this one.'
Charlie Higson

'Take the great advice that's in this *Yearbook*.'
David Almond

'... absolutely essential. If it were a person, it would
be your most knowledgeable and trusted confidant.'
Andy Stanton

'The *Children's Writers' & Artists' Yearbook* has two
great virtues: one is the wealth of information it contains
and the other is the impressive raft of advice and
notes on every aspect of the business.'
Quentin Blake

'The *Children's Writers' & Artists' Yearbook* is a
goldmine of invaluable information.'
Francesca Simon

'Whenever people ask me about how to get their
work for children published ... the first words
to come out of my mouth are always:
Children's Writers' & Artists' Yearbook.'
Michael Rosen

'Consult the excellent *Children's Writers' & Artists' Yearbook*
and get going!'
Jacqueline Wilson

'Stuffed full of useful facts to help you get writing
(and drawing).'
Liz Pichon

Foreword

Frank Cottrell Boyce is an award-winning author and scriptwriter. His children's books include *Millions* (*New York Times* bestseller and winner of the CILIP Carnegie Medal 2004), *Framed, Cosmic, Chitty Chitty Bang Bang Flies Again* and two further *Chitty Chitty Bang Bang* titles. In 2012 he won the *Guardian* Children's Fiction Prize for *The Unforgotten Coat* (Walker Books 2012). *Millions* was made into a movie by Oscar-winning director Danny Boyle. Frank has written scripts for *Doctor Who* and for a number of feature films, and also the script for the opening ceremony of the 2012 London Olympics. His most recent book is *The Astounding Broccoli Boy* (Macmillan Children's Books 2015).

Infallible spell for transforming yourself into a successful children's writer ... (it worked for me)

1 Acquire copy of current *Children's Writers' & Artists' Yearbook*.

2 Riffle pages. Inhale deeply of the fragrance of future fulfilment.

3 Place volume prominently on kitchen table or other work surface. You will remark an immediate alteration in the atmosphere. This alteration is caused by certain properties inhering in the vivid hues of its cover.

4 If working in a public space, insert Post-it notes and other bookmarks in profusion. Recall that the more attention the book attracts the more power it generates.

5 At certain intervals you may refresh the spirit by opening the book. Do not select the page. Allow the book to offer certain pages to your attention.

6 If the book offers you those pages on which are written the names of agents, consider all their descriptions to assay which ones reverberate most mellifluously in your heart. Seek out their addresses on Google Street View that you may see their doorways. Remember that each of these doorways is a portal to another, richer world. While you know not yet which doorway you will take, picture yourself walking through the door-way with your manuscript in hand (see note 1 below).

7 If the book offers you the pages describing festivals, then consider those festivals – the green rooms wherein great steaming buckets of latte stand next to towers of cupcakes, where the conversation is polished so that the very air doth seem to shine. See in your imagination, yourself bedecked with lanyard and shepherded by volunteers to the tent where eager children wait to hear you speak (see note 2).

8 If the book offers you the pages describing literary awards then inscribe in your imagination the name of your book beneath those of past winners (see note 3).

9 Before closing the volume always riffle and inhale. The air thus imbibed is of a special type and potency. It is called Inspiration.

10 Maintain these habits and observe these practices until your ends are obtained.

Notes

1 So you do have to write the book first.
2 Or you won't have anything to read out from.
3 And when you've written it, give it a title.

Before we walked on the Moon we had to spend hundreds of years imagining it. Before I became a writer I spent a lot of time pretending to be a writer. The ostentatious use of the *Writers' & Artists' Yearbook* (WAYB) in public places was a big part of that pretence. But it also helped me turn that pretence into a reality. I had never met a writer or indeed anyone who wanted to be one. The book showed me that it wasn't a 'dream' that somehow 'came true' but a job that involved work and meetings and word counts and layouts and invoices. All the pragmatic guidance it offered helped crystallise my thoughts and turn the dream into an ambition. When you think about it, that is magic.

Frank Cottrell Boyce

Books

Getting started

You just have! By buying or borrowing the *Children's Writers' & Artists' Yearbook* you have taken the first step towards a potential new career in the field of children's publishing. Alison Stanley gives the benefit of her experience for success in this expanding market.

Whether you want to write for magazines, television, write or illustrate books, adapt for radio, get published in the UK or overseas, find an agent, illustrate greetings cards, attend a festival, course or conference, or surf websites dedicated to children's literature, you will find the information on how to do it in this *Yearbook*.

But to help you on your way, here are ten top tips:

1. Read, read, read

• Read as many children's books as you can – picture books, young fiction, novels, teen reads, non-fiction, the classics, prize-winners – and find out what is being published … and what children like to read.

• Look at children's magazines and newspaper supplements as they will give you ideas about current trends. Read *Children's publishing: markets, news and trends* on page 15.

• Read reviews in national newspapers, read children's literary magazines such as *Books for Keeps* and *Carousel* (see *Magazines about children's literature and education* on page 337) and look at *Resources about children's books* (see page 99).

2. Get out and about

• Visit your local bookshop and browse in the children's section.

• Go to your library and talk to the children's librarian. Children's books are read by children but usually bought by adults – so find out what parents, teachers, librarians and other professionals are recommending for young people.

• Visit Seven Stories – National Centre for Children's Books (see page 385).

• If you have children, don't just go by what they are reading, ask their friends too – children have wide reading tastes, just like adults. Ask permission to sit in on their school 'storytime' (or a literacy hour or a guided reading session if educational publishing is what you are interested in).

• Go to a festival. There are many literature festivals held throughout the year and most have children's literary events (see page 419). All children's literature festivals will have a sprinkling of new and well-known authors and illustrators in attendance. Most will be accompanied by a representative from their publishing company, so you can see and hear the author/illustrator and even do a bit of networking with the publisher. You will also be guaranteed some fun. Festivals are also a useful way of seeing children's reactions to their favourite authors and books in an informal situation. See also *Children's authors at literature festivals* on page 31.

3. Watch, listen and … learn

• Familiarise yourself with children's media: watch children's television and listen to children's radio programmes (see the *Television, film and radio* section beginning on page 341), and check out the websites listed throughout the *Yearbook*. Look at children's character merchandising and greetings cards.

• Enrol on a creative writing course where you can meet others who also want to write for children. Or apply to do a postgraduate course in writing for young people, where you will be guided by published authors and other publishing professionals (see *Children's writing courses and conferences* on page 425).

4. Network

• Being an author or illustrator can be a lonely business – don't work in a vacuum. Talk to others of your discipline at festivals, conferences and book groups. Join the Federation of Children's Book Groups (see page 388), where you can network to your heart's content. Find out if there are any writer/illustrator groups in your area. If you are already published, join the Scattered Authors' Society (see page 404).

5. Never underestimate the job in hand

• Writing and illustrating for children is not an easy option. Many people think they can dash off a children's story and a few sketchy illustrations and that they will be good enough to publish. But if you have researched the marketplace you will realise that it is a hugely competitive area and you have to be talented, have something original to say, have a unique style … and know how to persevere in order to get your work published and out to a wider audience. For advice and inspiration on writing see *A writer's ten commandments* on page 122 and *My writing rules!* on page 124, and for illustration, see *Eight great tips to get your picture book published* on page 276.

6. Use your experiences

• Having your own children, or working in a child-related profession is helpful but shouldn't be relied on to bring you a new career as a children's writer or illustrator. (Never use this line when submitting a manuscript: 'I wrote this story for my children and they enjoyed it so please will you publish it?' Any story you write for your own children, grand-children, nieces, nephews, etc is likely to be enjoyed by them because children love attention.) Publishers will only want to take on something that has appeal for a wide range of children – both nationally and internationally – never forget that publishing is a business. However, do use your experiences in terms of ideas, especially the more unusual ones, like seeing your first alien fall from the sky!

7. Research catalogues and websites

• Look at publishers' catalogues and websites, not just to find out what they are publishing, but because many of them give guidance for new writers and illustrators. When submitting a manuscript or portfolio to a publisher, it is a good idea to let them know that you know (and admire!) what they already publish. You can then make your case about where your submission will fit in their list. Demonstrate to them that you mean business and have researched the marketplace.

8. Submit your material with care

• First decide whether to approach an agent or to go it alone and submit your material direct to a publisher (see *How to get an agent* on page 223, *What do agents* do *for their commission?* on page 227, *How to sell your book to an agent* on page 230, *Do you* have *to have an agent to succeed?* on page 235 and *Publishing agreements* on page 287 for the pros and cons of each approach.) Check that the agent or publisher you are thinking of approaching accepts (a) unsolicited material, and (b) is interested in the type of work you are doing. For example, don't send your potential prize-winning novel to an educational publisher, and don't send your ideas for a Guided Reading Series at Key Stage 1 to a 'trade' publisher without an educational list. And don't send your illustrations for a children's picture book to an agent who only deals with teenage fiction – there will be zero interest from them and you will be very disappointed.

Books

• Submit your work to the right publisher/agent and the right person within the company. Ring first to find out who the best person for your work might be, whether it be in a publishing company, an agency, a television production company or a children's magazine. Also ask whether they want a synopsis and sample chapters or the complete manuscript or, for artwork, a selection of illustrations or your whole portfolio.

• Presentation is important. For example, no editor will read a handwritten manuscript. It should be typed/word processed, using double spacing with each page clearly numbered. (Should an editor be interested in your work, it will be photocopied for all involved in the acquisition process to read. Photocopiers have a habit of chewing up pages and there's nothing worse than pages being missing at a crucial part of a novel.) If your manuscript is accepted for publication, the editor will want the text electronically.

• Self-publishing is an option, in either printed form or as an ebook. There are companies and individuals who can help you to produce a saleable product; see *What do self-publishing providers offer?* on page 203 and listings of providers start on page 206. *From self-publishing to contract* on page 196 and *An indie's journey to award-winning success* on page 200. And if you choose to go it alone, you may want to join *The Alliance of Independent Authors* (page 378).

• For illustrations, select work on a paper that can be easily photocopied – a white/cream background with no unusual textures for your first pitch (such as sandpaper or glass – yes, it really has happened!). And remember, publishers' photocopiers are notoriously bad at reproducing colour accurately, so if you are relying on the vibrancy of your colour to wow an art director, bear in mind that by the time they have been photocopied a few times for interested parties to see, the colours will not be the same. If your artwork is computer generated, send hard copies with your disk – it saves time when being shown around. See *Presenting your portfolio to a publisher* on page 273.

9. Identify your USP

• Ask yourself what the unique selling point (USP) of the material you are submitting for publication is. You may have an original authorial 'voice', you may have a particularly innovative illustration style or technique, or you may have come up with an amazingly brilliant idea for a series. If, after checking out the marketplace, you think you have something truly original to offer, then believe in yourself and be convincing when you offer it for publication.

10. Don't give up!

• Editors receive hundreds of manuscripts, and art directors receive hundreds of illustration samples every day. For a publisher, there are many factors that have to be taken into consideration when evaluating these submissions, the most important of which is 'If we publish it, will it sell?'. Publishing is a big business and it is ever more competitive. Even after an editor or art director has seen and liked your work, there are many other people involved before something is acquired for publication: the marketing manager, the publicist, the rights director, the book club manager, the sales director and, of course, the financial director. You will find this mantra repeated again and again in many of the articles in this book: *Have patience, keep at it.* If you believe in your 'product' eventually someone else will too. And meanwhile, keep perfecting your craft. After all, you are doing it because you enjoy it, aren't you?

Alison Stanley was a senior commissioning editor of children's fiction at Puffin Books and at HarperCollins Children's Books. As a freelancer, she commissioned more than 40 titles in the Collins *Big Cat* reading series and many articles for the first *Children's Writers' & Artists' Yearbook*.

See also...

Spotting talent

Publishers and literary agents are not looking for what *they* like but for what children will like. Barry Cunningham famously accepted the manuscript of the first *Harry Potter* book which – as everyone knows – turned out to be the first of an international bestselling series. He explains here what he is looking for when he reads a new manuscript.

I'm a fan: I love reading and I love great stories. My background is in sales and marketing, and for many years I travelled with Penguin the length and breadth of the country – on tours with authors like Roald Dahl, to schools with the Puffin Book Club or to lonely writers' festivals. It was during this time that I learnt the most important part of my trade – how children react to the books they love, the authors that they adore, and how they put up with the material that they are coerced into reading. Reluctant readers indeed!

So what I'm looking for is what *they* want, not what I like or what you think is good. More of this later.

First steps

All publishers get streams of brown envelopes – especially, like divorces, after Christmas or the summer holidays – when writers finally feel something must be done with that story they've been working on.

So, how do you get your manuscript read by a publisher? Firstly, find out what the publisher wants: A sample? The complete manuscript? Or perhaps, like us, they only accept submissions at certain times of the year. For most editors, first on the reading list are the submissions from agents, manuscripts recommended by other authors or by someone whose judgement they trust. So, if you know someone who knows someone – use the contact.

Next, know a little about the list you are submitting to: look at their catalogue or read some of their books. Let publishers know how much you like their publications (we all like those sorts of comments!) and how you think your novel might sit with the rest of their titles.

Then, write a short snappy synopsis – a page will do (I've had some that are as long as half the novel itself!). It should tell the publisher what the book is about, its characters and why they should read it. Also include a little bit about you, the author. Don't forget that. It can be almost as important as anything else in these days of marketing and personality promotion (no, you don't *have* to be a vicar or an ex-glamour model, but it does give an impetus to read on …).

I worked with a very famous editor in my first job who was talking one day about her regular advice to first-time writers. Her advice began with a simple question: 'Have you thought of starting at Chapter 2?' Strangely, I find myself repeating this regularly. Often I find the first chapter is tortured and difficult, before the writer relaxes into the flow of the story in Chapter 2. And often things improve if we start straight into the action, and come back and explain later. But more importantly, first novels often fail because the editor doesn't get past a poor opening section. Beginnings are crucial, because I know children won't persevere if the story has a poor start, either.

So what am I looking for?

Back to the heart of things … There are writers who know a lot about children – they might be teachers or parents – so does this mean they can write more relevantly for young people? There are authors who know nothing about modern children, don't even really like children – does this mean they will never understand what a child wants? There are 'crossover' books that don't appear to be for real children at all. There are books with children in them that aren't children's books. Confused?

To me it's simple. Books that really work for children are written from a child's perspective through an age-appropriate memory of how the author felt and dreamed and wondered. The best children's writers carry that childhood wonder, its worry and concern, or even its fear and disappointment, around with them. They have kept the child within alive – so writing is not a professional task of storytelling for tiny tots but a simple glorious act of recreating the excitement of childhood.

That's part one of what you need. Part two, in my view, is a concentration on your audience. I've worked with adult writers too and there is a difference here. Children's authors are creating for a distinctly different readership – they need to think in a more *humble* way than if their work was for their contemporaries. What I mean is that they have to be mindful of how their work will impact on children. Characters must have convincing voices, descriptions must be good enough for children to visualise, and authors must be aware of things like children's attention span when it comes to detailed explanations.

But perhaps even more important is an awareness of the emotional effect of a story on a child. We must always remember their hunger for hope and a bright tomorrow, the closeness and importance of relationships – how easily a world can be upset by parents, or loss of an animal or a friend – and the way in which action really does speak to children, for fantasy and adventure is part of the process of literally growing an imagination.

(If all this means nothing to you, and writing for children is just another category, then I don't think you should bother. That's not to say all this should operate consciously in the mind of the new writer – but that's what a publisher seeks, and that's what I'm looking for.)

Categories and concepts

Everyone has read about the older children's market, and its lucrative crossover into the kind of children's book that adults buy for themselves. I think this will continue to be a growing phenomenon – but the best books in the field will still be clear in their intent: not looking 'over their shoulder' at adults, but true to themselves and their subjects.

I'm sure fantasy will continue to hold a firm following – but with the best books based around character and not simply wild lands and strange people. Historical fiction is poised for a comeback for older children – showing the rich material and heritage we have in our shared everyday culture, as well as the 'big battles' of yore.

At last all kinds of young adult fiction has found a firm market and any number of clear voices: hard-edged, romantic, comic, or a wild mixture of all three! Both here and in the USA, the 13–18 age group is firmly established as a permanent adjunct to the children's market, buying for themselves thrillers, dystopian adventures and books that speak to crises and concerns.

But my favourite category is the most neglected – real stories and novels for 7–9 year-olds. This really was once the classic area of children's books, with the biggest names and the greatest longevity of appeal. Sadly, it has become the haunt of derivative series and boring chapter books. But there are clear signs of revival, and bestselling stories for this age group and the slightly older 9–12 category are coming thick and fast – it's a great area for new talent.

Picture books seem to have had a much quieter time lately and are, perhaps, awaiting a revival with some fresh creativity helped by new technologies and new interactions between readers and the page. The success of cartoon novels and graphic story treatments for older readers must also hint at a new market here.

Language and setting

It's often said that, like exams, children's books are getting easier, that the language is getting 'younger' while the plots are getting more sophisticated. I don't think this is true. Certainly, for all markets, dialogue is more important than ever – and less time is taken in description. Children are used to characters who say what they mean, and whose motivations and subtleties emerge in speech. But largely I think this makes for more interpretation and imagination. Descriptions now concentrate on setting and atmosphere, rather than telling us authoritatively what the hero or heroine feels. All to the good in my view, and something new writers for children should absorb.

Also welcome in contemporary children's books is the freeing up of the adult! These characters are no longer confined to small walk-on parts and 'parental' or 'villainous' roles. Nowadays, adults in children's novels are as well drawn as the children, sometimes as touchingly vulnerable people themselves. But as in life, the most potent and frightening image in any children's book remains the bad or exploitative parent.

International scope

Children's literature is truly one of our most glorious 'hidden exports'. British writers continue to be very successful around the world, particularly in the USA and Europe. It is worth remembering this – while setting is not so important as inspiration, obviously UK-centred plots, regional dialogue and purely domestic issues, if not absolutely necessary, are best avoided. But there is no need either – like a creaky old British film – to introduce 'an American boy' or mid-Atlantic slang to your work to appeal to another audience. This seldom works and is often excruciating!

The marketplace

The market still remains delightfully unpredictable. It is hopeless to look at last year's trends and try to speculate. The sound and timelessly good advice is to find your own voice and, above all, to write from the heart. If you can touch what moved you as a child or still moves the child within you, then there's your 'market appeal'. Whether it's aboard the frigate of your imagination or in the quieter, but equally dangerous seas of the lonely soul, skill and inspiration will win you your readership.

Oh, and finally, don't give up. As I once said to a certain young woman about a boy called Harry …

Barry Cunningham OBE was the editor who originally signed J.K. Rowling to Bloomsbury Children's Books. He now runs his own publishing company, The Chicken House (see page 42), specialising in introducing new children's writers to the UK and USA. Notable recent successes include James Dashner, Cornelia Funke, Dan Smith, Rachel Ward, Sophia Bennett, Janet Foxley and Lucy Christopher. The Chicken House and *The Times* jointly run an annual competition to find new writers; visit www.doublecluck.com or see page 415. Barry was awarded an OBE in 2010 for services to publishing.

See also...
- *Who do children's authors write for?*, page 119
- *What publishers want: a new publisher's perspective*, page 21

What makes a children's classic?

David Fickling describes how he chooses a story for publication and hints at how it is crafted into the final book.

This is a variation of the age old exam question, the general one you attempted in a hyperventilating panic as a last resort and with a plunging heart because the question you had swotted up on had been unaccountably and unfairly omitted. This was the make-weight question that looked deceptively easy but you knew was a trap. But you couldn't resist it because it looked like you could write *something*. It was really only meant for the brainiest, to sort them out from us goats. So, if you want a considered, deeply reflective and wonderfully good-humoured and, more to the point, *beautifully written* answer, then may I respectfully refer you to Italo Calvino and his essay *Why Read the Classics?*. Answers to all the 'whys' and most of the 'whats' are in there. Calvino offers 14 increasingly mysterious and connected answers in all, and each one is a gem. There is little more to be added by way of definition. By implication Calvino leads the reader onto '*How* do you write a classic?'. Of course the question asked of an editor is entirely different: 'How do you recognise a classic?', and that is the one I propose to attempt here in a deeply personal way with special reference to younger readers.

Recognising a good story

Recognition is everything. We publishers don't do much but recognise and act on the recognition. (The famous editor Maxwell Perkins just said we add enthusiasm.) 'No!' we say, 'We won't publish that'. Or 'Yes!' we say, 'I *love* this. Please please can we publish your story?' We are often wrong but at least we make a decision.

For good or ill, I am a potato print publisher. By which I mean that I do not analyse the decision (much) once it has been made. I am sent a story to consider for publication. I read the story (eventually). And if it moves me to laughter or tears or affects me in some other mysterious and powerful way and seems to be better than all the other things I am being asked to consider at that time, I say to myself 'Let's publish that'. In short, I *recognise* it. I *see* it, *make* it happen, *publish* it – 'there!' – like a potato print. I try to do all that as quickly as possible to the highest possible standard of manufacture. For the reader! Oh and I really like to meet the author, to see if we'll get on, and most of all to make sure they have tons of stories in them. There is really nothing in the world more exciting than meeting a writer with new stories to tell and a singing voice with which to tell them. And then to help bring those stories to readers. I am blessed.

A story is a whole thing in itself, like a melody, to which it is related. It must make sense in relation to itself. It is a wonderful pattern snatched out of the chaos. I try not to take it apart like a pocket watch fearing that I may not be able to reassemble it. It is not good if an author says back to you, 'Well if you know so much David, why don't you write it?'. As a young editor I once sent a five-page letter of quite brilliant, or so I thought, closely argued and typed editorial comments to an elderly experienced author who lived in Wales. My then boss received a sad note from his wife to the effect that Arthur (name changed) had been unfortunately taken to hospital after a heart attack. Nothing to do with David's letter of course, but … I have never since written such a letter even though I always write myself copious notes on a book. If I can, I boil those notes down to four or five practical points to say to the author in a relaxed way over lunch or a cup of coffee. Things 'said' can be more easily ignored, discarded, digested or given to the writer. Nowadays I never suggest that the author puts in any different ingredients. I never say, can we have some 'Tanks at the beginning' or could we have some 'Nude Women' or have you tried 'Vampires'? When I suggested to the late Jan Mark that she write about Japan, she reserved for me some choice language (not bad language, *choice*) that previously I had only heard her use about Tony Blair. Of course it was me that was interested in Japan, not Jan. I might venture something like, 'There seems to be something missing in chapter four, tho' I don't know what it is.' And the author might say, 'No there isn't, it's absolutely fine you fool'. To which I shall not demur. Or the author might say, 'Wow David, you are so right, you're a genius, we need some heavy artillery in there. I didn't tell you but I left out the pomegranates but now I am going to put them right back in. Thank you! Thank you!'. At this point my demeanour must be that of Beech the butler, or Jeeves. I may allow myself a raised eyebrow: 'Pomegranates' (*no inflection*). 'Very good sir. Will that be all?' P.G. Wodehouse contains in his butlers nearly all the editorial advice a good editor will ever need. The point here is that the story – however long – is the whole thing. I am interested in the whole thing and not just the parts.

When I was nine years old I can remember getting bored while reading the *Wind in the Willows* by Kenneth Graham, an acknowledged classic. The story seemed to be winging along quite merrily. I had been enjoying it. Mole, Rat, Badger and Toad were up and adventuring and then I came to Chapter Seven: *The Piper at the Gates of Dawn*. At that point the story gets interrupted by some long-winded poetical interlude (as it seemed to me at the time). Nowadays I am fond of poetical interludes. Not then. 'What was all that about?' my nine-year-old self asked. This is not to say my nine-year-old self was right. Recently I found myself editing the accumulated essays and articles of that amazing writer, Diana Wynne-Jones. Her young self was electrified by reading *Piper at the Gates of Dawn* at an even younger age and she believed reading and recognising the poetic brilliance of that chapter almost kick-started her career as a writer. My point is not about being correct but understanding all readers change over the course of their lives. My editorial point to Kenneth Graham would be this chapter may stop some readers and his answer could have been but it will inspire some too. I hope I would have said 'Okay, we'll leave it in.' Which brings me to the special circumstances in publishing for children. There really aren't any, apart from the fact that most of us are woefully bad at remembering what our minds were like when we were only seven years old. The single biggest error made by all of us publishers is to fail to empathise properly with the reader. Children suffer in particular.

I don't conduct research beforehand. I don't consult other people, unless they are members of the DFB editorial team. The DFB editorial team is like a gestalt mind, a hive mind. We are the editorial Borg. We always agree and no one can tell our opinions apart – in public. Behind the scenes we argue away like (polite) snarling dogs over a bone. Editors work well in teams. When I write 'I' I always mean 'We'. I certainly don't consult the accounts department, the marketing team, the sales department or the bookshop owner or anybody else in the book trade. I listen to them and respect them too, of course I do, but I don't consult them. I might pretend to consult them but I never really take any notice. (Please don't worry on my account as none of them ever bother reading this kind of article because they are usually too busy grappling with the appalling reality of sales figures.) But most of all, I *never* consult children. How much better it is to be told a wonderful story rather than be asked to choose one. Sometimes I feel I'm sailing against the world's prevailing wind. Children don't want to be asked. They want to be given. Actually all human beings want to be given stories and to learn how to give them to others. If a child likes something, you learn that very quickly. If they don't like something, you learn that quicker. They are the most honest audience on this Earth. Anybody who has read to five-year-olds and seen them peel off courteously to the sand pit will know this. Don't listen to all those comedians who talk about 'dying' in the clubs in Glasgow. They know nothing if they haven't 'died' in a nursery school. The test of a story for children is the intentness with which they listen and then how quickly they get their pencils out and start to write, draw or act their own stories. It is a guiding rule: Good stories promote creation, Classic stories promote a culture.

The editing secret

The point is, I have already made the decision to publish before the editorial stage, before any possibility of consultation, exulting inside myself as a reader. The recognition has already happened. I am in love. It's just a case of when not if.

It is in the editorial phase with the author where we check that the story is in as good a shape as it can be. This is really just another phase of the writer's work. It is the author who matters here, not the editor. This is the holy of holies, now, when classics are made. Editors may be useful in the early days, telling authors things they already know but haven't admitted to themselves or learned yet. Later on, good writers invariably know how to edit themselves. Then we editors are happy to be friends and supporters. This editorial phase is a secret, to be kept forever. The editing is important, not the editor. Any editing is like the scaffolding on a house: once the building is finished the scaffolding is taken away and forgotten. Once the story is published, that is how it is. Any new versions are new versions. The original story still stands and if we read it and loved it, we love it as we first read it. Were changes made? I am not saying. Was the first version different? None of your business! The author can talk about the building process if they want. The editor must never speak. It's not polite.

Another kind of group writing that is becoming more and more popular is where teams of writers get together to write stories. It happens a lot in films and television series, for example *The Simpsons*, etc. It has been done before: the great French storyteller Dumas had a lot of help. I admire this kind of writing but am not a practitioner. I like it because it raises the text and the reader's response above all other considerations. However, the set-up and the way of working needs to be established from the outset and all participants need to be given and to accept their due recognition as co-creators. This can be difficult, and besides, I suspect that there is always a presiding authorial mind that takes the decisions. For this reason I am happier with a clear editor/author demarcation. However it is written, the final version is the one to read.

Fairies and money

So you see it is not initially a matter of money, though the definition of Calvino's that most applies is No 6: 'A classic is a book that has never finished saying what it has to say'. And clearly, if that is the case then it need never go out of print. And it will keep making money for the author and the publisher forever – publisher heaven! A publisher's definition of a classic is a book that never stops selling. But this does *not* mean that everything that sells is a classic, nor that all classics sell immediately.

I have no desire to rehearse the reasons why money is in charge as it will be obvious to all of you: the huge agglomeration into mighty international corporations, the demise of the Net Book Agreement, the adoption of new technology, the internet, the withering of story value, as stories become 'loss leaders' for other more profitable products and thus we crazily sell the most desired books at a loss and the newest and least reader-tested books are priced highest. All this is driven by the insane, bonkers drumbeat of the vast corporations searching for double-digit growth forever ... In my experience the people who work within corporations are nicer and cleverer than those outside. But they have been 'taken' and are dancing under the hill with the fairies and cannot stop. When the corporation throws them out eventually, they are bemused and cannot remember where they have been or why. I have seen the sales graphs soaring into the future, and still they climb on and on, faster and faster. Speed is killing the book. Everything has to happen faster these days. Mark my words, there will be a crash. The fairies are powerful but they are no good with money. Put the sales graphs away. Stop consulting. Put the story horse before the sales cart and pile the sales in the back. Of course the sales are important. We need to earn a living. I *love* sales. Like everyone else, I want more. But the way to more is to make things; stop fiddling and checking and get writing and making.

It is the story that matters. When I read a text that is new and original and hits the mark, I know. You know. Everyone knows. You would be deaf and blind not to feel the thrill of it. It is like seeing the northern lights or hearing the horns of elfland and the trumpets of the seventh cavalry sounding together. Or it could be just hearing Christopher's voice in *The Curious Incident of the Dog in the Night-Time*, it is not loud but is so clear and it sounds as if it has always been there and never been heard before.

Why you might ask do I get to choose? Who do I think I am? What gives me the right? You do, dear reader. You do. Thank you. Oh, and a favour, please stop asking our very best storytellers to do so many things. Personal appearances, opening shops, writing reviews, giving quotes. Hush children! They are working. There will be a new story all in good time.

What makes a children's classic? Wait and see.

David Fickling is a children's book editor and publisher. He started his career with Oxford University Press in 1977, moving on to Transworld and then to Scholastic UK. In 1999, David formed his own imprint, the Oxford-based storyhouse David Fickling Books, which he then set up as an independent company in July 2013. DFB's successful fiction titles include Philip Pullman's *Lyra's Oxford*, Mark Haddon's *The Curious Incident of the Dog in the Night-Time*, John Boyne's *The Boy in the Striped Pyjamas*, Linda Newbery's *Set in Stone*, Jenny Downham's *Before I Die*, Simon Mason's *Running Girl* and four novels by the late Siobhan Dowd. In January 2012 David independently launched *The Phoenix Comic* to bring back totally joyful reading for girls and boys – because they love comics and they should have them by right!

See also...
• *Spotting talent*, page 5
• *Who do children's authors write for?*, page 119

Writing and the children's book market

Thousands of new children's titles are published in the UK every year. Chris Kloet suggests how a potential author can best ensure that their work is published.

The invoiced value of UK publishers'annual sales in 2014 remained flat (£4.3 billion), the same as in 2013. However, the children's sector was exceptionally strong in 2014, with an 11% rise in sales of children's books to £349 million.Yet it can be difficult for the first-time writer to get published. It is a diverse, overcrowded market, with many thousands of titles currently in print, available both in the UK and from elsewhere via the internet. Children's publishers tend to fill their lists with commissioned books in a variety of formats, both physical and digital, by writers they publish regularly. So they may have little space for the untried writer, even though they seek exceptional new talent. This is a selective, highly competitive, market-led business. Your work will be vying for attention alongside that of tried and tested children's writers, as well as titles from celebrities such as sports and television personalities, and the offerings for children and teenagers from established writers for adults, who seize the opportunity to widen their audience. Since every new book is expected to meet its projected sales target, your writing must demonstrate solid sales potential, as well as strength and originality, if it is to stand a chance of being published.

Is your work right for today's market? Literary tastes and fashions change. Publishers cater to children whose reading is now almost certainly different from that of your own childhood. In the present digital age, few want cosy tales about bunnies or magic teapots. Nor anything remotely imitative. Editors choose *original*, lively material – something witty, innovative and pacey. Witness the success of Jeff Kinney's quirky *Diary of a Wimpy Kid* series, with more than 150 million copies of the books in print. Actor/comedian David Walliams is the UK's fastest-growing children's author who also enjoyed similar popularity with a number of titles, such as *Demon Dentist* and *Gangsta Granny*. His books have sold over 4 million copies in the UK and have been translated into more than 40 languages. Editors look for polished writing with a fresh, contemporary voice that speaks directly and engages today's critical, tech-savvy young readers. These 'I want it and I want it now' children are used to multi-tasking via different platforms. Time poor, they are often easily bored.

Develop a sense of the market so that you can judge the potential for your work. Read widely and critically across the children's book spectrum for an overview, especially noting recent titles. Talk to children's librarians, who are expert in current tastes, and visit children's bookshops, both in the high street and online, and dedicated children's books websites. As you read, pay attention to the different categories, series, genres and publishers' imprints. This will help you to pinpoint likely publishers. Before submitting your typescript, ensure that your targeted publisher currently publishes in your particular form or genre. Request catalogues from their marketing department; check out their website. Consult the publisher's entry under *Children's book publishers UK and Ireland* (see page 39). Many publishing houses now stipulate 'No unsolicited MSS or synopses'. Don't spend your time and postage sending work to them; choose instead a publisher who accepts unsolicited work.

You might consider approaching a literary agent who knows market trends, publishers' lists and the faces behind them; see websites and *Children's literary agents UK and Ireland* on page 239 for current submission criteria. Most editors regard agents as filters and may prefer submissions from them, knowing that a preliminary critical eye has been cast over them. Self-publishing is also a possible option for fiction and some agents are offering 'concierge' services in this area.

Picture books

Books for babies and toddlers are often board books and novelties. Unless you are also a professional illustrator they present few opportunities for a writer. Picture books are aimed at children aged between two and five or six, and are usually 32 pages long, giving 12–14 double-page spreads, and illustrated in colour.

Although a story written for this format should be simple, it must be structured, with a compelling beginning, middle and end. The theme should interest and be appropriate for the age and experience of its audience. As the text is likely to be reread, it should possess a satisfying rhythm (but beware of rhymes). Ideally, it should be fewer than 1,000 words (and could be much shorter), must offer scope for illustration and, finally, it needs strong international appeal. Reproducing full-colour artwork is costly and the originating publisher must be confident of achieving co-productions with publishers overseas, to keep unit costs down. It is a tough field but it can be very rewarding. Lifetime sales of Julia Donaldson's numerous bestselling titles, including *The Gruffalo*, were worth a staggering £91.2 million in the UK.

Submit a picture book text typed either on single-sided A4 sheets, showing page breaks, or as a series of numbered pages, each with its own text. Do not go into details about illustrations, but simply note anything that is not obvious from the text that needs to be included in the pictures.

Younger fiction

This area of publishing may present opportunities for the new writer. It covers stories written for the post-picture book stage, when children are reading their first whole novels. Texts vary in length and complexity, depending on the age and fluency of the reader, but tend to be 1,000–5,000 words long.

A few publishers continue to bring out titles under the umbrella of various series, each targeted at a particular level of reading experience and competency, although now 'branded' author series are more usual. Categories are: beginning or first readers, developing or newly confident, confident, and fluent readers. Note that these are not the same as reading schemes published for the schools market and do not require such a restricted vocabulary. Stories for the bottom end of the age range are usually short, straight-through narratives illustrated throughout in colour, whereas those for older children are broken down into chapters and may be illustrated in black and white.

General fiction

Many novels for children aged 9–12+ are published as author 'brands'. The scope for different types of stories is wide – adventure stories, romance, fantasies, historical novels, science fiction, ghost and horror stories, humour, time travel and stories of everyday life. Generally, their length is 20,000–40,000 words. This is a rough guide and is by no means fixed. For example, J.K. Rowling's *Harry Potter* novels are 600–750+ closely printed pages.

Books

Stories for this age group are enjoying more popularity, as publishers seek to adjust the balance of their lists following an emphasis on the teenage novel. Some are available now in digital formats for various platforms, as indeed are interactive picture books for the youngest, although for most titles, electronic comes after the printed version.

Perhaps more than in other areas of juvenile fiction, the individual editor's tastes will play a significant part in the publishing decision, i.e they want authors' work which *they* like. They, and their sales and marketing departments, also need to feel confident of a new writer's ability to go on to write further books for their lists – nobody is keen to invest in an author who is just a one-book wonder.

When submitting your work it is probably best to send the entire typescript. Although some people advise sending in a synopsis with the first three chapters, a prospective publisher will need to see whether you can sustain a reader's interest to the end of the book.

Teenage fiction

Some of the published output for teenage (or Young Adult, YA) readers is published in series but increasingly publishers are targeting this area of the market with realistic romances and edgy novels about contemporary teenagers, which they publish as standalone titles. The vogue for post-apocalyptic dystopian fiction continues. Witness the success of *The Hunger Games* trilogy by Suzanne Collins and the *Chaos Walking* trilogy by Patrick Ness. Note the popularity of graphic novels for this age group, although the first-time writer is unlikely to find many opportunities here.

Non-fiction

There is a wide variety in the type of information books published for the young. Hitherto the province of specialist publishers catering for the educational market, the field now encompasses a range of presentations and formats, including electronic, which are attractive to the young reader. Increasingly, children who use the internet to furnish their information needs are wooed into learning about many topics via highly illustrated titles by publishers such as Usborne and Dorling Kindersley. In writing for this market, it goes without saying that you must research your subject thoroughly and be able to put it across clearly, with an engaging style. Familiarise yourself with the relevant parts of the National Curriculum. Ask publishers for any guidelines. You will be well advised to check that there is a market for your book before you actually write it, as researching a subject can be both time consuming and costly. Submit a proposal to your targeted publisher, outlining the subject matter and the level of treatment, and your ideas about the audience for your book.

Chris Kloet is Editor-at-Large at Walker Books. She has written and reviewed children's books and has lectured widely on the subject.

See also...

Children's publishing: markets, news and trends

Caroline Horn highlights the successes in the children's publishing over the last year.

The children's market is currently the success story of publishing and that seems unlikely to change given the plethora of reading conferences, festivals and children's events that now take place up and down the country. Along with the explosion in children's books, blogging and the emphasis in schools on reading for pleasure, these are all encouraging more books into the hands of young readers.

In 2014, UK consumers spent £453m on children's books, buying some 76m books (both in print and digital). Spending on children's books was up a massive 15% on 2013 (£395m), compared with a more modest 2% rise in spending on adult books to £1.7bn in 2014 (Source: Nielsen's UK Books & Consumers survey © Nielsen 2015).

According to the Publishers' Association, 2014 was the best year for children's literature since 2007 – when the final *Harry Potter* novel hit the shelves. The 2014 bestseller list for printed books was dominated by children's books, with seven out of the ten titles aimed at children and young people. In top place was *The Fault in Our Stars*, John Green's tale of a love affair between two teenage cancer patients, which was made into a film and sold more than 900,000 print copies in the UK. David Walliams's *Awful Auntie* was in second place with sales of over £7m, while Jeff Kinney's *Diary of a Wimpy Kid* also made the top ten. Both titles outsold the biggest-selling adult fiction titles of that year: Gillian Flynn's *Gone Girl* and Dan Brown's *Inferno*. There were also four books about the computer game Minecraft in the top ten.

This kind of growth is quite an achievement given the increasingly fragmented market which is making it harder than ever to get books into the hands of readers. While Waterstones and some supermarkets have increased the space dedicated to children's books, there are significantly fewer outlets selling books than there were a decade ago.

These days, book recommendations are far more likely to come via websites, bloggers, book groups, films and authors themselves than from a bookseller or a librarian, since the wave of bookshop closures we saw a decade ago is now being followed by a decline in libraries. Hundreds of libraries and trained librarians have already been lost to communities as austerity bites into local government services. In 2014 there were 337 fewer libraries than there had been in 2009/10, down from 4,482 to 4,145, a number that doesn't include all the mobile libraries that have also been lost. It is young families, children and the elderly who will be most affected by these losses. Ironically, as our libraries close as a result of government 'austerity', the same government's Education Department has been calling for schools to do more to encourage children to read for pleasure – by joining their local library.

Children's publishing also faces challenges from within. The world of publishing is changing rapidly and we haven't yet really seen where the evolution of ebooks, e-publishing and social media will take it. Publishers have been adapting for survival with moves and mergers. The merger of the publishing houses Random House and Penguin

Group in 2013 gave the new company, PRH, huge bargaining and cost-cutting powers and during 2014, its first year as a single entity, PRH's children's publishing output was slashed and budgets squeezed. In other moves, the Hachette Group has brought its seven imprints under one roof at Victoria Embankment, while HarperCollins has moved offices to south of the river, to join companies in its parent group News Corp.

So, where has that 15% growth in children's book sales come from? Some of it will actually have come from adult readers, people in their 20s and 30s who grew up reading *Harry Potter*, *Twilight* and *The Hunger Games* and who are still reading these kinds of books. The traditional wisdom in the industry has been that YA (Young Adult) publishing is where awards are to be had, not sales, but books like the *Twilight*, *Divergent* and *The Hunger Games* series have turned that perception on its head, with films of the books giving a massive boost to sales and ebooks encouraging more adults to try out these and other popular YA titles.

Industry experts estimate that more than 60% of Young Adult fiction is now bought for over-18s. The shift to ebooks has opened children's books to the 'crossover' market that publishers and authors have often aspired to, with books that have genuine appeal to adult readers as well as teenagers, such as John Green's *The Fault in our Stars*, Cassandra Clare's *Mortal Instruments* series and Patrick Ness's *Chaos Walking* trilogy. According to Nielsen's UK Books & Consumers survey ebook sales account for one quarter of YA volume sales, and it's growing, but these extra e-sales are just as likely to be adult as teenage purchases.

Publishers are now publishing quickly into ebook formats but Bloomsbury has taken this further with its Bloomsbury Spark digital YA list, launched at the end of 2013 to publish solely into ebooks. Digital editor Meredith Rich says, 'We started Bloomsbury Spark as an avenue to build our list in new directions with exciting authors and genres that Bloombury hasn't traditionally had before, including New Adult and Romance. Having Spark and the speed of ebooks lets us be innovative, flexible, and hit current market trends.'

The YA market is constantly changing and adapting, more quickly than any other part of the market. In the past four or five years we've moved on from the undead to dystopian, fantasy to grittier realism; young adults will quickly move on to the next trend, supported by a vibrant social media platform. The YA market is definitely where the buzz is, thanks in large part to the number of adult bloggers and reviewers in this space and on Twitter. This was supported by the timely launch of the annual Young Adult Literature Convention (YALC), the brainchild of Children's Laureate (2013–15) Malorie Blackman who dedicated her tenure to YA literature.

As for future trends, we can probably expect more romance around the corner, says Felicity Johnston, editor of the YA imprint, Indigo, at Orion. 'YA got quite dark for a while and there is a thirst now for lighter, romantic stories.' The film industry could already be on to this with Dreamworks' acquisition of *Eleanor & Park* by Rainbow Rowell, a quirky romantic story. Johnston also points to horror, which has been growing in 2014 and we may see more of that in the coming year or two.

Apart from its impact on sales, digital platforms and resources may also have had another impact on YA publishing; the trend towards younger authors with a growing body of YA authors being published in their teens and 20s. Veronica Roth was famously still at university when she sold *Divergent*; Taran Matharu's debut *The Novice* was published when he was 24 after attracting thousands of readers on Wattpad; Annabel Pitcher was successfully published aged 29 with her award-winning *My Sister Lives on the Mantlepiece*.

Today's young adults have a much better understanding of how publishing works and its possibilities. They also have resources at their fingertips that can help them get their books 'out there' to test out the market, says Naomi Greenwood, senior commissioning editor at Hodder Children's Books. 'Young people are so used to sharing their lives online that it will feel natural for them to use social media websites that are geared up for writing. They are happy to share their experiences and platforms like Wattpad democratise writing.'

Social media is becoming more significant in other areas of children's publishing too, especially in the picture book market where Waterstones' bookshelves are still dominated by Julia Donaldson and publishers have had to find other ways to help consumers to new picture book authors and illustrators. Many have developed their own online 'book club' for picture books, such as Walker Books' Picture Book Party (www.picturebookparty.co.uk) and Simon & Schuster's Picture Book Den (pages.simonandschuster.co.uk/picturebookden/main), but they also rely on bloggers and Twitter to help get the word out, for example The Book Sniffer (@maybeswabey), Picturebooks Blogger (@pbooksblogger), and children's books websites such as ReadingZone.com.

'There is a vibrant community of bloggers talking about picture books,' says Lara Hancock, editorial director at Simon & Schuster, while social media gives illustrators an opportunity 'to prolong the very short window picture books are given in bookshops'. While it is hard to enter the UK market as a debut writer/illustrator, there are lots of opportunities internationally for new names and that is encouraging more picture book publishing, although publishers remain cautious.

There is a broad range of subjects being published although with a unifying humour, says Hancock. 'Classic stories are being given a cool twist in fractured fairy tales and there are a number of feisty heroines about, for example in Anna Kemp and Sara Ogilvy's *The Worst Princess*, where the princess decides she doesn't need a prince.' Really strong picture book titles, like Yasmeen Ismail's *Time for Bed, Fred* or Sue Hendra's *Barry the Fish with Fingers* are also important, says Hancock, in telling the reader very quickly what the picture book is about.

In children's fiction, the traditional heartland of children's publishing, the quality of the books that make it on to the shelves is generally very high but, just now, it doesn't have the glamour of the YA market. That said, big names such as David Walliams and Jacqueline Wilson, and brands such as *Wimpy Kid* (Jeff Kinney) and *Tom Gates* (Liz Pichon) continue to ride high as the public become ever more cautious in their tastes.

Fantasy, adventure and mystery remain the strongest-selling genres in the children's market (Source: Nielsen's UK Books & Consumers survey © Nielsen 2015) and there are some strong new series making their mark. Jane Harris, publisher at Stripes Publishing, highlights Shane Hegarty's *Darkmouth*, Robin Stevens' *A Murder Most Unladylike* and *The Jolley-Rogers* by Jonny Duddle. Humour continues to be a huge seller for this age group, she adds, and, like other publishers, Stripes is always on the lookout for strong and original, laugh-out-loud, funny stories.

Another growing trend for this age group, says Harris, is the focus on the internal design of young fiction where the illustrations are an integral part of the books, with publishers building key author/illustrator partnerships. Philip Reeve and Sarah McIntyre (*Cakes in Space*, OUP 2014) are a great example of this, but many of the books for this age range now sport handsome internal illustrations. Even *Harry Potter* is now being published in illustrated editions.

Indeed, how books look across all ages is an increasing concern for publishers as they focus on making the printed book the format that people, and children, want to have. Aside from textbooks, children's literature is the only part of the book market where sales of paper books are still rising; hardback and paperback children's sales were up 10% last year, compared to an industry-wide decline of 5% as ebooks bit into physical sales.

In the children's market as a whole, ebook take-up has been relatively low, accounting for 14% of children's book purchases by volume in 2014, compared to the industry as a whole, where it is 35%. The bulk of children's ebook purchases were for YA books; ebooks only accounted for 5% of books bought for 0–12s (up slightly from 2% in 2013) (Source: Nielsen's UK Books & Consumers survey © Nielsen 2015). Parents are still reluctant for their children to spend more time on screens, even if that is in reading books, so children's ebook sales have risen only modestly – although further rises are expected. Just as in the adult market, however, the growth of ebooks and discounted online sales have impacted on authors' income and, unless they are in the very small band of very successful authors, it is becoming harder to make a living from writing for children.

Another effect of the reduced high-street presence of book shops is that authors, illustrators and poets have to work much harder in selling their books directly to children, through school and library events, festivals, etc. Paid events like these can help to offset the fall in income from books – but it does mean that authors will have less time to write and illustrate the books that they need to sell to make a living. However, with a number of routes available to writers to get their books seen by readers, publishers are also having to work harder to attract them to their stables and author care is becoming more integral to their message. As that 15% rise in sales shows, there have never been more opportunities to have your book published but, with so many more demands on the author, it has probably also never been harder to do so successfully.

Caroline Horn is Editor of www.ReadingZone.com.

See also...
- *Spotting talent*, page 5
- *What makes a children's classic?*, page 8
- *Children's authors at literature festivals*, page 31
- *Children's books: genres and categorisation*, page 35

Building a successful children's publishing list

Emma Blackburn gives a publisher's view on how to build a successful picture book list.

How wonderful it would be to know, instinctively, how to build a successful list, to be able to follow a prescribed formula safe in the knowledge that, having abided by the rules, success was waiting just around the corner. Imagine having that premonitory ability – to foresee trends, second-guess buyers and to know, without a shadow of doubt, what young children want to read, what their parents and grandparents want to buy for them, and what bookshop buyers want to stock. Imagine knowing, for sure, that your latest commission, the one for which you had such high hopes, *would* make the big time. Oh to be equipped with such foresight! I could become the Mary Portas of the children's picture book world – a one-woman rescue team, helping ailing picture book lists with my insightful trouble-shooting and breathtaking quick fixes. But, alas, I have no such superpower. Mary Portas may rest easy. Because, building (or trying to build) a successful list comes down to many things. In theory, it should be simple – produce the right books at the right time, market them well and get them into the hands of the right people. But what *are* the right books? What is the right time? And *how* can we get them into the hands of the right people?

The children's picture book charts continue to be dominated by the commercial might of big brands and key partnerships. Take, for example, the runaway success of Julia Donaldson's wonderful picture books, illustrated by Axel Scheffler and Lydia Monks. They currently occupy all the top picture book chart positions. What publisher wouldn't want a slice of that pie? The challenge lies in finding the next picture book bestseller or, better still, the next bestselling picture book series. But what exactly should we be looking for? Certainly humour would appear to work, rhyme too (at least for the UK market). At Simon & Schuster the success of Ben Cort and Claire Freedman's *Aliens Love Underpants* series shows how a successful picture book series can help to underpin the success of a list and shape its identity. The laugh-out-loud, rhyming picture books with a pants-based theme have developed a loyal following and their sales figures are enviable. The success of this series, supported by other commercial big-hitters, has helped to gain Simon & Schuster a reputation for publishing quality commercial picture books.

But establishing a brand is just half the battle. In a market where bestsellers and mass market appeal have become increasingly powerful, a brand's continued success requires a strategy for growth and development. Can the brand be taken into new formats? How many titles can the series sustain before consumer fatigue sets in? Are there any licensing opportunities? How about ebooks? Apps? Brand development and extension is a time-consuming business, but one that is undoubtedly crucial to the success of a list.

Introducing new talent

So what then of new talent? How can it compete with the big-hitters? Many publishers bemoan the difficulties of breaking debut talent in such a promotionally driven, bestseller-friendly market, and it is sadly true that getting new talent into the big budget promotional playground is, at best, challenging – and this, in turn, means that those books already featuring in key slots sell even more. A vicious circle? Perhaps. But any successful picture book list will endeavour to lead rather than follow trends, thereby keeping the market fresh, pushing boundaries and producing fresh and exciting new content for children.

Building talented debut authors and illustrators into the success stories of the future is a must. It's not easy, for sure, but the *right* book at the *right* time can succeed in getting to the *right* people. Take the author/illustrator team, Anna Kemp and Sara Ogilvie, for example. Their debut picture book for Simon & Schuster, *Dogs Don't Do Ballet*, sold well through all channels in the UK market, Sara was picked up as one of Book Trust's Best New Illustrators, and the partnership goes from strength to strength. And yet the book might not have been commissioned without their creative team's unshakeable belief in the project, and the support of both UK *and* international sales teams – a global approach to building a picture book list is essential. The high costs incurred in the production of full colour picture and novelty books mean that, more often than not, support from both established and emerging international markets is crucial in building economically viable print runs. But striving to achieve this support brings another batch of considerations for the commissioning editor. Will the subject matter 'travel'? Can rhyming texts ever work for international markets? Is the art style sympathetic to other countries' aesthetic sensibilities? And, yes, he/she may even ask such questions as, do squirrels even exist in Scandinavia? Whilst, on the surface, these may seem like laughable considerations, failure to understand the international market can, in fact, make or break a book. That's not to say, of course, that every book on a list will be successful internationally. There are times when a book will have a large enough home market to support its production costs and, in fact, occasionally, traction in the home market has led to take-up by international publishers further down the line.

Building a new picture book list

At Bloomsbury, the new-look picture book list is in its infancy but we will be creating a commercial, prize-friendly illustrated publishing list with global reach.

So, as the list continues to expand, I'm looking at the current strengths of our publishing and asking how we can develop these particular authors/illustrators/areas. I'm looking at gaps in our publishing and suitable projects to fill those gaps. I'm looking for the next picture book bestselling series – of course – but I'm equally on the lookout for talented new authors and illustrators. And I'm always looking for innovative and economical novelty formats.

Building a successful list has never been more challenging. Whilst the children's area of the business has by and large avoided the harshest effects of the economic crisis, mainly due to parents continuing to invest in their children, the uncertainty over the future of traditional bricks-and-mortar outlets remains unsettling. How can we open children's minds to new books and help chance discoveries of new authors without these? Add to this an ever-polarising market where big commercial books are king, and a burgeoning market for ebooks and apps, and there is much to challenge even the most strategically planned list. The good news, however, is that we are up for the challenge and that we will continue to publish books that children want (and that adults want to buy) in a format that they want. As our MD at Bloomsbury Children's says (or was it Kevin Costner?), 'If we build it, they will come.'

Emma Blackburn is Editorial Director of Illustrated Publishing at Bloomsbury Children's Books. She was previously Editorial Director of Picture Books at Simon & Schuster.

What publishers want: a new publisher's perspective

Louise Jordan set up Wacky Bee Books at the end of 2014. Here she shares her distinctive vision and experience of publishing for the 5–12 year-old market and offers advice to writers seeking success in this sector.

How it began

I've got a guilty secret. I don't like overly long books. Some children's books are long, but most aren't – and that suits me just fine. It's probably what attracted me to children's publishing. I don't like books that start with a map either. Or books that start with a family tree, or books that start with a cast list of characters. However, I do like books that start with a funny first line; I like books that start with Chapter One and not a prologue; and I like books with pictures.

That's how my publishing career started – writing stories with pictures. After working in the teenage magazine department at IPC, I signed up for a part-time course in writing for children at the City Literary Institute; I thought I wanted to write children's books. Then a job beckoned at Puffin, working as their reader, and my life took a very different turn. Same world, different perspective. In 1994 I launched the Writers' Advice Centre for Children's Books to help children's writers understand why publishers were rejecting them and what they could do about it. Over the years I became increasingly frustrated that some of my more talented writers were still falling through the publishing net despite expert help from me and my team. So I decided that if no one else was going to publish their books then I would, and Wacky Bee Books was born.

Creating a niche

While Wacky Bee was still in the planning stages, I heard Sam Arthur of NoBrow books speak at the London Book Fair on 'The Challenges of Creating a Children's Book Imprint'. He stressed the importance of finding a niche. The idea behind NoBrow was that this new publishing company wouldn't be offering anything highbrow or anything lowbrow, but 'everything in between'. This resonated with me because I was planning something similar for Wacky Bee. I didn't want to publish very short books (picture books) or very long books (for older children) but I did want to publish everything in between.

If you look around you will find that most publishers – other than the very big names – have created a niche for themselves in terms of what they publish. It's important for writers to get to grips with that niche and target their material accordingly. In the past many authors coming through my door at the Writers' Advice Centre had decided to self-publish for the simple reason that they had written something which didn't fit into the traditional slots created by the established children's publishing houses – young fiction for children aged 5–8 (approximately 1,000–10,000 words) or general fiction for the 8+ market (over 40,000 words). For the most part these authors had written something with suitable subject matter for the over-8s, but too short for most publishers.

At Wacky Bee I plan to change that traditional mindset. I've already confessed that I don't like long books and I don't see why children should be any different. Once a child reaches the age of eight or nine, why should they suddenly be expected to read adult-length books with no pictures? Officially, at Wacky Bee, we are publishing books for children aged 5–12 with our list dividing into two sections: 5–8 (Little Bee) and 8–12 (Big Bee) but unofficially I want the majority of our books to appeal somewhere between those two age-ranges. Reading-age boundaries are always going to be blurred. Our first title, *Geronimo, The Dog Who Thinks He's a Cat* is around 2,500 words; although it is labelled as a Little Bee, I hope that children younger than five will read about Geronimo and children older than eight will read about him too.

My ideal book would be a story that crosses our own boundaries and appeals to the 7+ market in terms of subject matter, but is no longer than around 25,000 words. And it will have pictures. All my books will have pictures, even if they're just at the chapter headings.

Diversity and inclusion

Look around you. Our society is hugely diverse. Books for children should reflect the world in which we all live. I'm not just talking about ethnicity – the term 'diversity' encompasses race and heritage, disability, gender and gender identity, sexual orientation, age, socio-economic status, religion and culture.

The hero in *Geronimo, The Dog Who Thinks He's a Cat* was originally called Angus. He was white, middle-class and probably lived an idyllic life, in a huge house out in the country somewhere. I loved Jessie Wall's story but I had to accept that, in its original form, it wasn't really a true reflection of the world most children live in today. Freelance editor and inclusion consultant, Beth Cox, took a look at the manuscript with her Inclusive Minds' hat on (see www.inclusiveminds.com) and made some suggestions. In the published book Angus has become Dylan, he is from a mixed-race family and lives a much more repre-sentative contemporary life than his original incarnation. Books for children have to be relevant and publishers are keen to find inclusive stories with a wide range of characters.

Finding a voice

Anyone who has received rejection letters from publishers will probably have come across the phrase 'it wasn't quite strong enough for us'. All publishers are looking for a strong writing 'voice'. It is what makes your story different; it's what makes your story original even if you are writing about well-worn subject matter; it's what jumps off the first page when the publisher first picks up your manuscript; it's a voice that says, 'Read me, love me, publish me – you won't be disappointed'.

Voice is something that can't be taught. You either have it or you don't. But there are tricks you can use to make your writing stronger. The most important of these is viewpoint. Readers are looking for a connection with a character – to see the world through their eyes, know what she knows, feel what she feels. Bouncing around from character to character will end up bouncing your reader right out of the story. So decide on your story idea, decide on whose story it is and then tell the story from that character's perspective.

Publishers want what they want

Since we opened up Wacky Bee to unsolicited submissions I have been shocked by how few would-be authors seem to pay attention to what we are actually looking for. There is clear information on our website, easily accessible from the home page, stating that any submission under 1,000 words is too short and anything over 50,000 words is too long, that manuscripts should be submitted as a Word attachment to an email, sent to the submissions@ email address, and that we are not publishing picture books for the under-5s or books for young adults. Yet this week I have been sent nine picture books, two books for young adults (both well over length) and a tottering pile of postal submissions. And it's only Tuesday!

Read the submission guidelines. Whatever it says in the submission guidelines is what that publisher wants. Be prepared for submission guidelines to be different depending on which publisher you are approaching. Some publishers *only* accept postal submissions, some publishers like a sample of the submission in the main body of the email, and some publishers don't accept unsolicited submissions at all.

Tailor your submission appropriately. It is important to exercise some common sense. Our first title is about a dog so we don't want more stories about dogs. Look at the books each publisher has on their lists and, in terms of subject matter, *don't* give publishers more of what they already have. Take time to do the research; trust me, it's time worth spending. If you get that very first step wrong then chances are your work will be thrown straight back at you, for no better reason than you didn't do what you were told.

Write funny

So back to our name, Wacky Bee. The *Oxford English Dictionary* defines 'wacky' as meaning 'funny or amusing in a slightly odd or peculiar way'. Humour is generally thought to be a very important element of books for 5-12 year-olds and I certainly want all Wacky Bee books to have funny bits. But that's not to say we are only interested in books about poo, bums and vomit – which is how some writers are interpreting the 'wacky' part of our name! We certainly don't want 'issue-driven' books either but nor do we want gratuitous revolt-ingness. Poo, bums and vomit have their place but not at the expense of 'story'.

There are many synonyms for 'wacky': zany, madcap, offbeat, quirky, outlandish, eccentric, idiosyncratic, surreal, ridiculous, nonsensical, crazy, absurd, insane, far out, fantastic, bizarre, peculiar, weird, odd and strange. All words which sum up most of the funny books out there at the moment. Is David Walliams' writing zany? Definitely. Is Jeff Kinney's writing quirky? Absolutely. Is Liz Pichon's writing absurd? Without doubt. 'Funny' books don't have to be laugh-out-loud, rolling-in-the-aisles, side-splittingly 'funny'. They can be so much more.

I'd say that my ideal book for Wacky Bee would be a younger version of John Green's *The Fault in our Stars* (Penguin 2012). Which is strange because that book isn't, on the surface, funny at all. It's a story about two terminally ill teenagers who fall in love and then die – or one of them does anyway. But it's also a book about two idiosyncratic protagonists who triumph in their own way against fantastic adversity. It is filled with quirky characters who aren't always very likeable but who redeem themselves in the end; it's a book where almost every other line made me laugh (which also meant that every other line made me cry). At the end I felt inspired and uplifted and that, somehow, I'd learned something and was a better person because of it. THAT'S the sort of book I'm looking for! Along with every other children's publisher.

Louise Jordan has worked in the children's publishing industry for over 20 years, first as a journalist and later as Head Reader for Puffin. In 1994 she helped found the Writers' Advice Centre for Children's Books (www.writersadvice.co.uk). She is the author of *How to Write for Children and Get Published* (Piatkus 2010). In 2014 she set up her own publishing imprint, Wacky Bee Books (www.wackybeebooks.com).

Marketing, publicising and selling children's books

Kirsten Grant introduces the world of marketing children's books and shares some practical tips and strategies that will help authors to market themselves and their books.

The children's book market

It is no surprise that the high street is suffering at the moment, with families struggling to make ends meet. But what *is* surprising is that children's books are currently experiencing a renaissance, in a market that is thriving and outperforming the adult market. And in addition, the vital importance of reading for pleasure as part of a child's development and future academic success is also a hot topic in schools at the moment.

Like never before, children's authors are writing 'must-have' books that children and young people are clamouring to read, retailers are devoting more space to children's and YA books instore and Hollywood directors are turning to bestsellers like John Green's *A Fault in our Stars* and *Paper Towns*, the *Insurgent* trilogy, *The Hunger Games*, *Diary of a Wimpy Kid*, *How to Train Your Dragon* and *Paddington* as source material for their latest blockbusters, driving an even bigger appetite for the original books.

Big authors are often talked about as 'brands' nowadays. They are household names and their publishers have made big ongoing investments in them in terms of time and money, and in some cases, the 'brand' has been diversified into different publishing formats, and even ranges of bestselling merchandise, such as *Charlie and Lola*, *The Gruffalo* or *The World of Eric Carle*.

So now is a great time to become a children's author – but if this is a career you are seriously considering, you should manage your expectations now as only a small percentage of authors hit the Big League. As the market has increased, publishers have become more rigorous and commercial, and they are managing their decreasing marketing and publicity budgets with military precision, meaning that only a small number of top-tier titles are treated to all-singing, all-dancing marketing and PR campaigns; and, unfortunately, the other titles have to fend for themselves. In this article, however, I hope to demystify the world of marketing children's books and share a number of practical tips and strategies that will help *you* do as much as you can to strengthen your position both for your sales and your future publisher.

The publishing process

Agents submit a manuscript to an editor, and if they feel that it is both right for the publisher's list *and* a commercially viable proposition, it is their job to then sell it to decision-makers across the business before it is acquired. When you or your agent are pitching your book to an editor, it is crucial to emphasise any good 'hooks' or existing platforms that you have, as publishers are keen to acquire authors nowadays who already have a profile or an existing fan-base.

Publishing is a democratic process, where a senior member of each team (editorial, design, sales, marketing, publicity and rights) needs to be on board before a manuscript is acquired. And by having buy-in from everyone in this way, it means that they are committed to making the book a success. Compared to newspaper or magazine publishing, the whole process is a 'slow burn' so patience is a necessary virtue – a fiction title usually takes about a year from acquisition to publication, and a picture book can take up to two years.

Who is your audience?

Over recent years, children's publishing has become much more like adult publishing. Previously, children's books were seen to need a slow burn, taking a long time to infiltrate consumer awareness. Now, they too follow the bestseller model, with a lot of pre-publication activity that seeks to attain the highest bestseller chart position on launch and then tries to maintain it in the chart for as long as possible.

The main difference between children's and adult books that will always remain however, is the target audience. In adult publishing, it is obvious that you directly target the readers themselves, whereas with children's books (depending on the age range of the book) there are multiple audiences, as the readers will very rarely be buying the books themselves. There are the 'gatekeepers' – teachers and librarians – the parents/grand-parents, and finally the readers themselves, who are inevitably the ones who drive demand for your books. So when publishers and authors are marketing and publicising children's books, it is important to ensure that each of these 'channels' is catered for and targeted directly, so that you have a 'multi-pronged attack'.

Marketing and publicity

People generally talk about these two departments in the same breath and, in very general terms, their principal role is to get your book out into the marketplace and talked about. Although they each do this in quite different ways, they work very closely together. Good marketing and publicity make children excited about books and reading and can help to bring the world of the book alive for its audience. It's a well-known fact that a consumer has to see or hear a publicity/marketing message an average of seven times before they take action.

In simple terms, the marketing team starts working on a book much earlier than the PR team, and they are responsible for 'the stuff that you pay for', such as designing and creating point-of-sale material for bookshops – posters and bookmarks, advertising, catalogues, websites and online activity. The marketing team will often create the 'look' of a campaign (based, of course, on the cover design), as well as straplines and the 'elevator pitch', where a book can be summed up in just a few short sentences – an important skill when you're trying to tell as many people as possible about a book.

The publicity team traditionally look after the 'free stuff', such as dealing with the media for press interviews, reviews and features, and sending out review copies. It also organises events such as author tours and launch parties (although there are fewer of those these days) and liaises with the organisers of literary festivals.

What can authors do?

Create a buzz

In the past ten years, children's authors have become celebrities for their fans and, unlike children of the '60s and '70s, authors are now directly accessible to their audience through author events and signings, author fan mail, social media and online marketing.

In recent years, there have been waves of book trends that have swept playgrounds nationwide, from *Harry Potter*, to vampires, to *Diary of a Wimpy Kid*. Pin-pointing exactly

Books

what starts these trends and predicting the next craze is very difficult, but that all-elusive playground buzz can certainly be influenced by a number of factors: great events, word of mouth, review coverage, online activity and the network of prizes (some of which are voted for by children, such as the Red House Children's Book Award, see page 414). And if this happens in tandem with nationwide publicity and marketing campaigns, the two things come together to create a buzz.

Build a relationship with your fan-base

Over the past five years, publishers have cottoned on to the fact that 'relationship marketing' makes a big difference to sales. If authors have an existing fan-base who they communicate with on a regular basis with news, updates, videos, interesting or funny anecdotes, competitions or a blog, then they have a ready-made audience of converts to promote news of a new publication. People are creatures of habit, for example if you read and liked a book by a particular author, you look out for new books by that author.

Online marketing

Reaching children directly has become both easier and more difficult at the same time. Traditional marketing channels, such as children's magazines and comics are ever-shrinking, and online marketing has become an increasingly important channel to promote children's books – so you should try to make the most of social media where you can, as this is how you will start to build up a fan-base.

Children nowadays are classed as 'digital natives', as they have grown up with digital technology and have a greater understanding of how to use it to maximum effect. They like being part of and connecting with an online community, are happy to promote and share your content for free and are used to picking up information and marketing messages in different ways – at school, on television, through advertisements and online. Online activity is also brilliant because the results are measurable, so you can actually see how many fans or followers you have and what works and what doesn't.

The two most important things you need to think about before creating an online profile for yourself, posting and commenting on Facebook, blogging or tweeting are:
• Content is King – and the target is to create interesting, 'sticky' content (which keeps people coming back) – which is where you, as an author come in, as that is what you *do*.
• You have to make a commitment to yourself (and your fans!) to keep up to date and make regular posts or comments – you should try to do it every day and soon it will become a habit that you might actually enjoy! It is crucial to think about your audience – who will read these posts? Make it relevant, keep it clean (we are talking about children's books after all!) and, most importantly, *engage* and listen to feedback. The best social media users ask their fans to participate and contribute, for example make a video, send a picture, answer a question. This will also give you an effective ready-made focus group, with your fans telling you what they think, want and don't want.

Create a website

Publisher's marketing budgets are being squeezed and squeezed, so they may only create a handful of microsites for authors in one year, as part of their digital strategy. But that shouldn't stop you from creating your own online profile. Nowadays, there are great, inexpensive websites like www.1and1.co.uk which allow you to create your own, tailored website for a small monthly fee.

Think carefully about your website before you create it:
• What do you want it to do?
• What do you think visitors will want to find when they visit it?
• How much time will you have to commit to it on an ongoing basis?

You should see your website as a living, breathing thing that needs to be nurtured, so there is no point in creating a blog, for example, if you don't update it regularly or a forum if you aren't going to moderate and post in it. Robert Muchamore (www.muchamore.com) is a great example of a children's author who created his own army of fans in this way, through news, competitions, teasers, rewards and even his own range of merchandise – and the fans loved it!

Twitter

Nowadays, lots of authors have Twitter accounts as a way of talking directly to their fans and/or their fans' parents. It's best not always to be on broadcast, so ask for the thoughts and opinions of others too. Don't just use it as a marketing channel to sell your latest book – of course, Twitter is a great way to let fans know you have a new book out, but try to be creative in the way you do this! Remember, your audience wants to find out more about you as a 'celebrity'.

Facebook

Children aren't allowed to be on Facebook under the age of 13, but this is also a great way of reaching parents, teachers and librarians. You can keep them up to date with your news and post extracts, teasers, events, photos, fan art and/or stories, trailers, covers, etc and respond to their questions or comments.

Outlets for selling children's books

Booksellers and librarians are critical 'gatekeepers' who can help you, as an author, to get your name out there, and I would advise you to get to know as many of your local contacts as you can. They are the filters of what's good, what's not, what works and what doesn't, and working with these key people and organisations is almost like pyramid selling – reaching targeted numbers of adults who then respond to the messages and feed them down to the children in their shops, classes or libraries, so it is essential to get them on your side. They have links throughout the local community and are very skilled at organising events with groups of children and recommending what they should read.

Bookshops

Naturally, publishers work closely with retailers of all sizes. Some publishers still maintain forces of sales reps who regularly visit small independents, whereas communication with high street chains and supermarkets is done at head office level. The high street chains tend to take a wider variety and number of titles, whereas supermarkets tend to focus on a small number of bestsellers, which they usually buy in very large numbers and sell at a discounted price.

Publishers spend huge chunks of their sales and marketing budget on securing instore promotional space, so driving as many consumers into shops as possible, through creative marketing tactics, author events, signings, competitions and price promotions is essential. It is worth remembering, though, that even the smallest bookshop can be integral in helping you to increase sales and in getting a word-of-mouth buzz going as, if they really get behind a title, 'hand-selling' is an extremely persuasive way of advising customers and is a real USP (unique selling point) for any bookshop.

Libraries

Libraries are critical in any grassroots campaign, as they work directly with children both at school and in their free time, making recommendations and feeding a child's 'reading habit'. They also organise interesting and creative initiatives to entice children into the library and keep them coming back, such as the Summer Reading Challenge (www.summerreadingchallenge.org.uk), to get children reading books voraciously over the summer holidays.

There are also a number of professional library organisations such as the Youth Libraries Group (YLG, see page 408) which runs the prestigious Carnegie and Kate Greenaway Medals for outstanding books for children (see page 411), and organises author events, workshops and presentations. YLG is an extremely influential group which can help you gain a great deal of awareness among children, although they also have close links with publishers, who will be able to introduce you to the right people at the right time.

Direct marketing to schools

One of the wonderful things about marketing children's books is that you always have new waves of children of a particular age ready to discover your work, and schools are the third in the triumvirate of essential places for children's authors to become familiar with. Authors such as Jacqueline Wilson and Jeremy Strong continue to be tireless in their endeavours to speak to children at events in schools all over the country and have reaped the rewards in sales and recognition.

Schools have become a key target for publishers, keen to spread news about new releases, as teachers are so influential in providing reading recommendations to children. Teachers can be a difficult-to-reach group as they are often very busy, but some publishers have a dedicated schools' sales force, who sell their publishing list directly into schools, while others use freelance reps to sell a limited selection from their list to schools.

Scholastic sells books directly to children in schools:

• **Scholastic Book Fairs** (www.scholastic.co.uk) are run in schools as a focus on literacy and give children who don't normally visit bookshops access to books. They are run all the year round and are perfect as a centrepiece to World Book Day or Children's Book Week in October. They consist of a number of large foldaway bookshelves on wheels containing up to 200 titles, which are ordered by a teacher, tailored to suit the school's needs and brought into the school for a select period of time. The shelves are then unfolded to create a pop-up bookshop to give children the opportunity to browse the shelves and discover new books and authors. And, in return for every book sold, teachers receive rewards of books and resources.

• **Scholastic Book Clubs** provide age-ranged leaflets containing a selection of books at pocket-money prices and children can discover books and authors either on their own or with their parents or teacher, and order their choice(s) via their teacher. Teachers receive back 20p in every £1 spent to spend on books for the class or library.

The annual World Book Day (www.worldbookday.com), which takes place on the first Thursday in March, has become a major way of celebrating books and reading in schools. Funded by National Book Tokens and a number of trade publishers and booksellers nationwide, it is a key time to get information about authors into schools, either via the resource pack (publishers can pay to include marketing materials), the website or a range of events and activities happening both on the day and throughout the rest of the month. It would be well worth your while contacting local schools, libraries and bookshops well in advance to offer your services as, not only will they be clamouring to have an author's involvement, but every child in the country receives a £1 book token which they can use either to get a free £1 World Book Day book or to get £1 off a book costing £2.99 or more, and it is well documented that footfall in bookshops and sales increase substantially throughout that period.

Apps, ebooks and e-readers

Keen to capitalise on this digital revolution in reading, publishers are running to keep up with the ever-changing digital market. More and more parents own e-readers, smartphones and tablets, which are perfect for children's books with their high-resolution screens, ease of use and ability to store texts.

Practically all children's books are now published simultaneously as ebooks and, despite the large costs involved, publishers are increasingly investing in the production of small numbers of apps, which boast a full multimedia experience, including animation and other appealing features, that are perfect for their target market. Some parents, however, are reluctant to trade a physical book for an ebook or app, as it is yet another screen for children to look at. Marketing for digital versions of books is done in a similar way to that of physical books, although the main difference is that they are purchased 'off the page' from a website such as a retailer website or the iTunes store (it is critical to get support from Apple if an app is going to be marketed through iTunes to enable it to get cut-through to the consumer).

Publicity

With the change in the market and the rise of the children's bestseller, children's authors have become media celebrities like never before. It's not unusual to see broadsheet features or television appearances by the likes of Julia Donaldson, Michael Morpurgo, Charlie Higson or Jacqueline Wilson, but at the same time there is generally less media space dedicated to children's book reviews than those for adults. So publicists have to be very creative and push all angles of an author's personality. And like pitching your book to an editor, you need to provide as many hooks as you can for your publicist, to help them secure that all-important piece of coverage.

Events

Children's authors have to be tireless about doing events in schools, libraries and the ever-increasing number of literary festivals throughout the year. In fact, for many authors, school events are their bread and butter, as schools generally pay for author visits, unless they are being funded by the publisher as part of an author tour (for recommended rates see www.societyofauthors.org/rates-and-guidelines). Avoid doing events at your peril, as being out and about in schools is a prime way to get yourself known and recognised, a great opportunity to listen to direct feedback and to get a word-of-mouth buzz going about your books.

As events have become such a valuable commodity, it is worth spending time thinking carefully about the structure of your event and how you can make it as lively, interesting and engaging as possible. You could also ask your publisher's publicity and marketing teams for input and advice.

Think about your audience – how will you immerse them in your books, engage them and hold their attention? How will you split up an hour (the usual time for an author event) and vary the content? This could include a reading, Q&A, interactive elements, visuals – for example a PowerPoint presentation or a video trailer. By creating an exciting 'experience' in this way, it will be easier for both you and your publicist to 'sell' your event to schools – and if one school or library has had a great experience, they are more likely to tell other teachers and librarians all about it.

It is also worth thinking about how your event can help teachers – how can they use it as a jumping-off point for a classroom activity, for example creative writing, etc?

As you can see, there are lots of things to think about when you are starting out as an author, to ensure that *yours* is the book that parents, teachers, booksellers and librarians are talking about. The main piece of advice I would give, though, would be to use your initiative and utilise all the channels at your disposal in an imaginative way – that will make people take notice. But above all, *be yourself and be consistent*, as your fans want to get to know *you* – and if, through your passion for what you do, you inspire children to develop a love of books and reading, there really can't be a bigger seal of approval.

Kirsten Grant is a freelance marketing consultant, an award-winning marketer, and former Marketing and Campaigns Director of Puffin Books, responsible for the marketing strategies for huge brands such as Roald Dahl, *Diary of a Wimpy Kid, The Very Hungry Caterpillar* and Puffin's 70th anniversary. Kirsten has been Director of World Book Day for four years, the book trade's biggest industry-wide celebration of books, authors, illustrators and reading for pleasure that has been running for 18 years (see page 424).

See also...

Children's authors at literature festivals

Festivals provide an excellent opportunity for readers to meet in person the creators of their favourite books. Nicolette Jones describes some of the many different approaches made by children's authors to entertain and captivate the attention of their audience.

Such roles as Children's Books Editor of *The Sunday Times* (which I currently occupy) and Director of the Young People's Programme at *The Sunday Times* Oxford Literary Festival (which I recently passed on to Andrea Reece) might both seem to be under threat. Literary criticism these days is a free-for-all through bookselling websites, blogs and social media. And authors can communicate with readers not only via their books, but individually, on websites and Facebook and Twitter. Yet the sheer volume of comment about books online can sometimes raise the value (I like to think) of edited, informed, identified voices to sift and discriminate. And literary events and festivals at which readers meet writers are flourishing, while the pressure on writers and illustrators to be performers as well as skilled practitioners of their craft has not let up.

Judging by ticket sales at literary festivals, the more we live our lives through screens, the more we are attracted by old-fashioned human contact. As with any friends you have never met, communicating by keyboard usually only stimulates the wish to meet in person. As well as the wish of the reader to meet the creator of the books they love, authors also find it rewarding to be face-to-face with their unknown readers. The experience for both sides is the opposite of the online/app/Facebook/Twitter experience – as different as going hiking is from looking at pictures of landscape: vital, immediate, active and in full Sensurround.

Stage presence

So what kind of encounters do festival programmers hope to orchestrate? Bloggers, critics and festival directors have in common a desire to encourage reading, to spread the word about good books, to inspire and stimulate and entertain. If the motive for scheduling an event is to encourage reading, the event has to be engaging and the author likeable. There is a place, of course, for prickly encounters between writers and readers, battling it out over ideas, and exposing authors to hostile responses to their work – that is an important part of intellectual debate. But in general that is not the aim of the children's programme of a literature festival. I was always looking not only for the creators of work I admired – so that the books purchased at the end of an event would not be a disappointment – but for the writers and artists who offered the best entertainment: who happened to have not only literary/artistic skill but also the completely separate quality of showmanship.

Publishers also look for this quality these days. They like authors and illustrators who can connect with audiences in person as well as on the page. Events in schools and libraries are a big part of the experience of publication. Many authors – Jacqueline Wilson is an example – built their readership principally by doing a great many of these. As a result, most of the potential participants who are put forward for festivals by publishers' publicists already have stage presence.

What is increasingly expected of festival participants is not merely a reading or a conversation, but a show, perhaps with PowerPoint pictures, or music, or costumes. If they are on a panel, or in discussion, they need to be fluent, funny and stimulating. Anecdotes, jokes, voices, props and ways to involve the audience are invaluable. At the Oxford Literary Festival (see page 422), successful examples of all these things have included Eoin Colfer's hilarious routine to rival any stand-up comedian, or Tamara McFarlane who came with a juggling clown on a unicycle. Professional actors, singers and musicians have been enlisted to do readings or accompany authors: with Michael Morpurgo, for instance, in his 'Mozart Question' concert, and a Matilda from the RSC's stage production performing at an event about Roald Dahl. Sometimes authors double up these skills themselves. Harriet Goodwin, author and a classically trained singer, filled a hall singing 'Blow the Wind Southerly' unaccompanied. Michelle Magorian, a former actor, read from *Goodnight Mister Tom* with distinct voices for all her characters. Louise Rennison recreated *ad hoc* on a platform her drama school audition in which she had to be an embryo. Sarah McIntyre and Philip Reeve learnt to play the ukele expressly to play and sing for their 'Oliver and the Seawigs' event – while Sarah is famous for the costumes, with extraordinary hats, that she makes. Kevin Crossley-Holland also adopted the costume – and the persona – of Merlin for an entire interview.

Great props I have also seen include Julia Golding's embroidered Round Table made by her mum and an assortment of helmets for children to wear, Cornelia Funke's costumes in character made by a prize-winning Hollywood designer, Louisa Young's box of storytelling objects, Christopher Lloyd's coat of many pockets, Frank Cottrell Boyce's homemade explosive (a film canister containing water and Alka-Seltzer, to illustrate suspense), a Tudor shift and doublet worn by *Horrible Histories* illustrator Martin Brown, and Caroline Lawrence's sponge on a stick (for cleaning Roman bottoms). Quizzes work too: have booked them about the Romans (Alex and Simon Scarrow), about the 1950s (prize from Ali Sparkes: a tin of spam) and about jungle survival skills (Andy Briggs's *Tarzan* books). For very young children, songs and movement and simple craft activities hold attention: Kristina Stephenson (Charlie Stinkysocks), for instance, is marvellous at these and what is more, gives away home-made sugar-crafted Wigglywoos to eat; Julia Donaldson dramatises her books with songs and audience participation, rather than reading them. Watching live drawing, from very skilled practitioners can be magical, too: Quentin Blake, Chris Riddell, Emily Gravett and Axel Scheffler have all amazed me.

The important thing is that all these performers have considered how to make an interactive entertainment above and beyond their own speaking skills. Some authors, of course, just talk, and hold you spellbound. Michael Morpurgo, Anthony Horowitz, Jacqueline Wilson, Philip Pullman and Michael Rosen are consummate examples. They all have years of experience, thousands of events behind them, and a huge repertoire of anecdotes. For less seasoned authors, the trick is to practise with audiences you can muster – at local schools, clubs, church halls, reading groups, libraries. Hone your talk and your skills by trying them out a lot, until you become the kind of performer who is sought after.

At the festival, my hope was that the audiences would feel they had witnessed something special and that the performers would also have a unique experience: every audience is different, with unexpected questions and responses. Children who are encouraged to draw at events take home their own creations. Obviously, everyone hopes that books are sold, but meeting readers is nourishing in ways that are beyond sales. True creativity is not motivated by commerce. For writers and artists, festivals also offer encounters with fellow practitioners: I have even seen book collaborations grow out of them. At their best, for everyone involved, the interactions between performers and the public can change lives. And above all, organisers hope – as reviewers do – that children will be enabled to find the books that hook them, and make reading a lifelong passion.

Reaching the stage

So how do you get to the platforms, once published? Your publicist should be the middle man or woman. It is unwise to approach festivals direct, principally because events need to command spectators, and it is rare for ticket sales to be automatic. Some festivals have a more captive audience than others. At Hay (see page 421), for instance, which takes place at half-term, many visitors come for a holiday and are prepared to try anything. This is also often true of Edinburgh (see page 420) and Cheltenham (see page 420), and increasingly at Oxford (see page 422), but in general in big towns and cities people may come to an event or two and then go home. In fact, small local festivals are often the ones with the most loyal audiences: Burnham Market, for example, or West Meon, or Headingley, where the festival is part of the social circuit.

But many festivals depend for ticket sales on a combination of big names and skilled marketing, working perhaps with schools to bring in large parties. But you can never assume that queues at the box office are a given. For programmers, part of the fun, as with reviewing, is to introduce the lesser known authors, especially those you believe have yet to achieve the fame they deserve, and often the best way of bringing them to attention is to pair them with a crowd-puller. This way, a big audience will get an unexpected chance to appreciate a new talent. Alternatively, if the author/artist is unknown the theme or nature of the event has to be appealing in itself.

The landmark festivals with big children's programmes are Oxford (March), Hay (June), Edinburgh (August), Bath (September/October; see page 419) and Cheltenham (October). Festivals with children's events include the Borders Book Festival in June (see page 419) and Ilkley in October (see page 421), for example. Some – such as Dartington, Charleston and Althorp – have no events specifically for children.

Festival alternatives

What of shy authors, then, or those with stage fright? The school/festival circuit is not for everyone. Some publishers offer training to help the uncertain to perform, but it is often better not to expose authors who are reluctant in public and unresponsive to media training than to let them alienate audiences. I have seen mumblers and ramblers who have talked their way out of book sales (though never at Oxford). Good publicists find ways of promoting books that play to authors' strengths: articles they can write, for instance, or one-to-one interviews for those nervous of the limelight.

The relationship between books and readers does not always, after all, have to be mediated by their creators. A connection with a book can be as powerful as a connection with a person, but does not need one to be involved, except as the consciousness expressed in the writing or illustration. When we judge the book, too, we are not judging the person. Even if, as a critic, you have had occasion to meet an author, any response to a book must be completely separate. As a festival director I sought people who projected well to an audience; as a reviewer I am only interested in these sorts of questions: does the book work, in its own terms? (That is, does it achieve what it sets out to do, not some idea I have of what I might like it to be.) Is the use of language skilled, apt, original? Is it convincing/moving/funny/suspenseful/imaginative/well-observed/true ...? And above all, is it likely to be a book that, for a certain child, at a certain stage of development as a reader, is just the book that they want to read? Or even, in fact, for an adult, because I believe, after decades of reading and studying English literature, that the difference between a good book and a bad book is greater than the difference between a children's book and an adults' book. I am with W.H. Auden, who said, reviewing C.S. Lewis: 'There are good books that are only for adults because they presuppose adult experience, but there are no good books that are only for children.' If a reader can be brought to one of those books, either through a review or an event, the reviewer's, and the festival director's, job is done.

Nicolette Jones is a writer, journalist and broadcaster who has worked for national newspapers and the book trade press. Specialising in literary and arts journalism, she is the children's books editor of *The Sunday Times* and was Director of the children's/YA programme at the Oxford Literary Festival 2010–13, and Consultant Director for 2014.

See also...
- *Marketing, publicising and selling children's books*, page 24
- *Children's literature festivals and trade fairs*, page 419

Children's books: genres and categorisation

When you walk into any high street bookstore or search online the range of children's books can seem overwhelming. Caroline Horn guides us through the maze of books and explains how publishers and booksellers categorise titles.

Retailers – both physical and online – generally organise their children's book displays according to age ranges, making it easier for buyers to go straight to the section they want, be it baby board books or children's fiction. This approach also reflects how publishers 'segment' their lists.

Categorising children's books according to age groups is helpful as these categories generally reflect children's interests and reading abilities at key stages in their development. A book's format and subject matter, the presence of illustrations, and the size of text and pagination signal the intended age of its reader. So, for example, toddlers and preschool titles comprise short, illustrated picture books while young fiction books are mainly black and white text with short chapters, large text and, increasingly, a smattering of black-and-white illustrations.

Large publishing houses will tend to cover the whole gamut of age ranges for children, from nought to young adult. They want their titles to win the loyalty of new parents from day one and to keep that loyalty all the way through to that child's teen years. Smaller, specialist publishers will often focus their lists on specific areas of children's publishing that reflect their in-house skills. Stripes Publishing, for example, is strong in junior fiction while Hot Key Books is known for its Young Adult fiction, books that appeal to readers aged 11 years plus.

Broadly speaking, children's books fit one of the following age groups: baby books (0–2 years), picture books (2–5 years), beginner readers (5–7 years), young fiction (6–8 years) and core fiction (8–11 years). Teen, or YA (Young Adult) titles, as this part of the industry is better known, are in the top age range, i.e. 12 years plus, and many readers at the top end of this age range are themselves adults; some 60% of YA books purchased are thought to be bought for adult readers. A more recent category, New Adult, has been introduced for older readers who are happy to have sexual content in the books they buy. Traditionally the sexual content in YA books is limited, but the success of *Fifty Shades of Grey* by E.L. James has opened the market to more explicit fiction. Non-fiction is also categorised according to age range and, often, national curriculum subject areas.

There are, though, always exceptions and children's varied abilities and interests will mean that young readers will often cross these age bands. This is why age guidance on books themselves – as shown on children's toys and clothing – is often absent. A nine-year-old boy with reading difficulties could, for example, find himself reading a title that he sees is recommended for a child aged six, and there's nothing more guaranteed to put off a child from picking up another book – ever! Lists have been developed by publishers like A&C Black (*White Wolves* series) and Barrington Stoke to fill the gap for titles that can be enjoyed by older readers who are still struggling to read fluently, and reluctant readers. In other cases, where perhaps an eight-year-old child has the reading ability of an 11- or

12-year-old, that child would probably struggle with the subject matter intended for older readers.

Age ranging

However, while there are very good reasons for not giving specific age recommendations on book covers, this has not helped parents and other book buyers who are struggling to find the right title for children. Publishers remain heavily reliant on the ability of booksellers, librarians or teachers to recommend the best book for individual children, although a limited number of fiction titles do now include an age guidance on the back cover, for example covering ages 5+, 7+, 9+, 11+ or 13+.

For those browsing online, very similar categories are used to those of physical bookshops. Amazon, for example, enables searches according to age ranges (0–2, 3–5, 6–8 and 9–11), as well as the type of book, such as picture book or pop-up book in the younger age ranges, while for older children you can search according to categories such as humour, themed or classic books. The more child-centred websites like Scholastic Book Club uses age-ranging to help narrow selections, and there is often a function to enable children to pick from an area of interest, either by subject (aliens, school, animals) or genre (humour, myths, thrillers etc).

Age ranging is the broadest tool publishers can use in categorising their lists but they will also build their lists' depth and range according to a variety of other factors, particularly genres that are popular such as romance, fantasy, adventure, horror, etc. Publishers will frequently revisit their lists to check where their 'gaps' are and look for new titles according to how well a particular genre is doing.

Recent developments in fiction

In recent years, the British and US markets for children's fiction has flourished thanks to authors such as David Walliams (*Awful Auntie, Demon Dentist*) and Liz Pichon (*Tom Gates*), while a growing body of adults as well as teenage readers are enjoying bestselling authors including John Green (*The Fault in our Stars*) and Veronica Roth (*Divergent* series).

While it was once hard to envisage any demand by adults for children's books prior to the *Twilight* (Stephenie Meyer) and *Hunger Games* (Suzanne Collins) series, many YA books are now bought to be read by adults and publishers will look closely at a title's potential for crossover appeal. After all, selling to adults as well as to teenagers instantly doubles a book's market. A few short years ago, publishers would create separate editions of books for adult and younger readers. David Fickling Books and Random House, for example, created distinct children's and adult covers for *The Curious Incident of the Dog in the Night-Time* by Mark Haddon and John Boyne's *The Boy in the Striped Pyjamas*, with identical text for both versions of each book. That rarely happens now, as so many YA books are already being bought by adults, but it has made publishers careful to use covers that are not defined by the age of the potential reader. The covers of Sarah J. Maas's *A Court of Thorns and Roses* (Bloomsbury) and Leslye Walton's *The Strange and Beautiful Sorrows of Ava Lavender* (Walker Books), for example, do not limit the readership to a particular age range.

The growing interest from adult readers and bloggers in YA fiction, as well as the number of authors wanting to write for young adults, means that YA fiction itself has really come of age, with publishers' YA lists flourishing and booksellers happily dedicating more space to this age range. This is also where the growth in ebooks has come in the children's market, with some 25% of YA book sales accounted for by ebooks (Source: Nielsen's UK Books & Consumers survey © Nielsen 2015).

Books are also sometimes categorised by author 'brand'. David Walliams, Jacqueline Wilson, Michael Morpurgo, and Julia Donaldson are all regarded as brands in their own right and, while they might write for many different age ranges, their titles will often be displayed together on an author's 'shelf' in bookshops. These key author 'brands' will regularly outsell adult bestseller titles and now take the biggest proportion of top ten places in the annual bestseller tables. Readers are also loyal to series – Liz Pichon's *Tom Gates* and Derek Landy's *Skulduggery Pleasant* series have shown how successful these can be.

At the younger end of the market, sales of the *Horrid Henry* series by Francesca Simon (Orion) encouraged publishers to develop more mass market series such as *Rainbow Magic* (Orchard Books) and the *Beast Quest* series (Orchard Books). Mass market series like these help to get 6–8 year-olds into the reading habit because they can recognise the books they have enjoyed and go back for more. Since young fiction books also tend to be relatively thin, a set of five or six books will help give them a presence on booksellers' shelves. Publishers are also turning to established picture book characters to help young fiction series stand out. Characters like Jonny Duddle's *Jolley Rogers* pirate family (from *The Pirates Next Door*) and Valerie Thomas's *Winnie the Witch* are now successful young fiction series.

The next 'big thing'

But publishers know that they would be unwise to focus exclusively on areas that are ahead in today's climate – children's books is a cyclical business and what works today could be out of favour a few months down the line. Dorling Kindersley's approach to production was key to driving non-fiction sales in the 1980s while Julia Donaldson and Axel Scheffler's *The Gruffalo* achieved a similar status for the picture book a decade ago. In today's climate, however, non-fiction is *struggling* while the fortunes of picture books, which were turned around by Julia Donaldson, have stagnated as the market is dominated by that single name. YA fiction, on the other hand, once the preserve of a dedicated but small band of readers, has been blown open with the advent of ebooks, blogging and blockbuster films like *The Hunger Games*. It only takes a new taste, design or development to flip sales up or down, and trends will have a huge influence on what is published into these markets. The dystopian trend in YA publishing, inspired by *The Hunger Games*, is on the wane with more romance and horror likely to take its place. Among younger readers, humour is what children are looking for, as well as the traditional adventure stories.

Demographics are also responsible for changing tastes and shifting emphasis in publishers' lists. The number of children aged under 12 years was falling, until a recent baby boom helped to grow the picture book market. The teen market is also growing and this partly accounts for the increasing interest in Young Adult books.

Publishers will regularly revisit and reshape their lists as a result of market changes like these. Egmont Press, a notable fiction publisher for younger readers, has in recent years strengthened its teen fiction list with an imprint for this age range, Electric Monkey, and created the 'Jelly Pie' brand for its funny books for younger readers. Traditional non-fiction publisher Raintree has moved into the fiction market with its imprint Curious Fox, reflecting the difficulties in growing the non-fiction market.

It goes without saying that writers need to know what areas a publisher specialises in before approaching them with manuscripts. A brilliant teenage title is likely to be rejected if the publisher's list does not include YA books. Still worse, an inexperienced publisher could take on a YA novel but let it fall into oblivion by failing to market it to the correct audience. That said, it is hard to second-guess what type of book publishers are looking for at any one time. A picture book publisher may still turn down a title, no matter how much they like it, or if they have over-commissioned in that area or if it is too similar to a title they are already publishing. Equally, even though booksellers' shelves are groaning with gritty realism, a book that stands out from the crowd will always find a home – publishers are continuously hunting for talented 'new voices'. In fact, 'debut author' has almost become a category in its own right as publishers strive to get unknown but promising authors into the hands of bloggers and booksellers.

It is also worth remembering that across the board, large publishing houses are reducing their children's output and that their lists are more structured and more focused than ever. If a company has filled the gap for a dragon fantasy for a ten-year-old reader, they won't be looking for any more. Another publisher, however, might be looking for exactly that.

Caroline Horn is editor of www.ReadingZone.com.

See also...
- *Writing for a variety of ages*, page 139
- *Writing for different genres*, page 134
- *Children's publishing: markets, news and trends*, page 15

Children's book publishers UK and Ireland

*Member of the Publishers Association or Publishing Scotland
†Member of the Irish Book Publishers' Association

Alanna Books
46 Chalvey Road East, Slough, Berks. SL1 2LR
tel (01753) 573245
email info@alannabooks.com
website www.alannabooks.com
Children's picture books. No unsolicited MSS.

Amgueddfa Cymru – National Museum Wales
Cathays Park, Cardiff CF10 3NP
tel 029-2057 3248
email books@museumwales.ac.uk
website www.museumwales.ac.uk
Head of Publishing Mari Gordon

Books based on the collections and research of Amgueddfa Cymru for adults, schools and children, in both Welsh and English.

Andersen Press Ltd
20 Vauxhall Bridge Road, London SW1V 2SA
tel 020-7840 8703 (editorial), 020-7840 8701 (general)
email anderseneditorial@randomhouse.co.uk
website www.andersenpress.co.uk
Managing Director Mark Hendle, *Publisher* Klaus Flugge, *Directors* Philip Durrance, Joëlle Flugge, Rona Selby (editorial picture books), Charlie Sheppard (editorial fiction), Sarah Pakenham (rights)

A leading children's publisher of picture books, fiction for 5–8 and 9–12 years and young adult fiction. Successes include the *Elmer* series by David McKee, the *Little Princess* series by Tony Ross, *Who's in the Loo?* by Jeanne Willis and Adrian Reynolds, *The Lonely Beast* by Chris Judge, *Out of Shadows* by Jason Wallace and *Liar & Spy* by Rebecca Stead. Founded 1976.

Will consider unsolicited MSS. Include sae and allow 3 months for response. For novels, send 3 sample chapters and a synopsis only. No poetry or short stories. Do not send MSS via email.

Anova Children's Books – see Pavilion Children's Books

Arcturus Publishing Ltd
26–27 Bickels Yard, 151–3 Bermondsey Street, London SE1 3HA
tel 020-7407 9400
email kate.overy@arcturuspublishing.com
website www.arcturuspublishing.com
Editorial Manager Kate Overy (children's)

Children's non-fiction, including activity books, 3D books, reference, education, geography, history and science. No unsolicited MSS.

Atlantic Europe Publishing Co. Ltd
The Barn, Bottom Farm, Bottom Lane, Henley-on-Thames, Oxon RG8 0NR
tel (01491) 684028
email info@atlanticeurope.com
website www.atlanticeurope.com
website www.curriculumvisions.com
Director Dr B.J. Knapp

Educational: children's colour illustrated information books, co-editions and primary school class books covering science, geography, technology, mathematics, history, religious education. Recent successes include the *Curriculum Visions* series and *Science at School* series. Founded 1990.

Submit via email to contactus@atlanticeurope.com with no attachments. No MSS accepted by post. Established teacher authors only.

Atom – see Hachette UK

Aurora Metro
67 Grove Avenue, Twickenham TW1 4HX
tel 020-3261 0000
email info@aurorametro.com
website www.aurorametro.com
Managing Director Cheryl Robson

Young adult fiction, drama (including plays for young people), non-fiction, theatre, cookery and translation. Submissions: send synopsis and 3 chapters as hard copy to: Neil Gregory, Submissions Editor at address above. Biennial Competition for women novelists, The Virginia Prize For Fiction. New imprint: Supernova Books publishes non-fiction titles on the arts, culture and biography.

Autumn Publishing (Autumn Group)
Deepdene Lodge, Deepdene Avenue, Dorking, Surrey RH5 4AT
tel (01306) 876361
email enquiries@autumnpublishing.co.uk
website www.autumnchildrensbooks.co.uk

Children's activity and learning books and character license ranges provide positive and fun experiences. The *Help with Homework* series helps to bridge the gap between school and home learning; also educational wallcharts, colouring, sticker and activity books, board books and picture story books. Formed in the late 1970s it is part of the Autumn Group, a division of the Bonnier Publishing Group.

Do not send unsolicited MSS. Email synopses/portfolios to autumn@autumnpublishing.co.uk. No responsibility is accepted for the return of unsolicited MSS.

Award Publications Ltd
The Old Riding School, The Welbeck Estate, Worksop, Notts. S80 3LR
tel (01909) 478170
email info@awardpublications.co.uk

Children's books: full-colour picture story books; early learning, information and activity books. No unsolicited material. Founded 1972.

b small publishing limited
27 Sladedale Road, London SE18 1PY
website www.bsmall.co.uk
Managing Director Catherine Bruzzone, *Publisher* Sam Hutchinson

Activity books and foreign language learning books for 2–12 years. Written in-house. No unsolicited MSS. Founded 1990.

Badger Learning*
Suite G06, Business & Technology Centre, Bessemer Drive, Stevenage, Herts. SG1 2DX
tel (01438) 791037
email info@badgerlearning.co.uk
website www.badgerlearning.co.uk
Publisher Susan Ross

Educational publishing for pupils and teachers across the curriculum, from Foundation Stage to Year 13, including books for reluctant readers, dual language books and science books for KS3–KS5. Founded 2001.

Barefoot Books Ltd
294 Banbury Road, Oxford OX2 7ED
tel (01865) 311100
email help@barefootbooks.com
website www.barefootbooks.co.uk
Owner, Co-founder & Ceo Nancy Traversy, *Co-founder & Editor-in-Chief* Tessa Strickland, *Group Operations Director* Karen Janson

Children's picture books, apps and audiobooks: myth, legend, fairytale, cross-cultural stories. See website for submission guidelines. Founded 1993.

Barrington Stoke
18 Walker Street, Edinburgh EH3 7LP
tel 0131 225 4113
email info@barringtonstoke.co.uk
website www.barringtonstoke.co.uk
Managing Director Mairi Kidd

Fiction for reluctant, dyslexic or under-confident readers: fiction for children 8–12 years with a reading

age of 8+, fiction for teenagers with a reading age of 8+, fiction for 8–12 years with a reading age of below 8, fiction for teenagers with a reading age of below 8, non-fiction for children 10–14 years with a reading age of 8+, fiction for adults with a reading age of 8+, graphic novels. Resources for readers and their teachers. Publishes approx. 70 titles a year and has over 350 books in print. Founded 1998.

No unsolicited MSS. All work is commissioned from well-known authors and adapted for reluctant readers.

BBC Children's Books – see Penguin Random House UK

A&C Black – see Bloomsbury Publishing Plc

Blackwater Press – see Folens Publishers

Bloomsbury Publishing Plc*
50 Bedford Square, London WC1B 3DP
tel 020-7631 5600
website www.bloomsbury.com
Founder & Chief Executive Nigel Newton, *Executive Director* Richard Charkin, *Group Finance Director* Wendy Pallot, *Non-executive Chairman* Sir Anthony Salz, *Non-executive Directors* Ian Cormack, Jill Jones, Stephen Page, *Group Company Secretary* Michael Daykin
Media enquiries Publicity Director, *tel* 020-7631 5670, *email* publicity@bloomsbury.com

A leading independent publicly-quoted publishing house with 4 worldwide publishing divisions: Bloomsbury Adult, Bloomsbury Children's & Educational, Bloomsbury Academic & Professional and Bloomsbury Information. It operates through offices in the UK, the USA (see page 71), India and Australia (see page 60). No unsolicited MSS unless specified below. The Bloomsbury Group includes the following: Absolute Press, Berg Publishers, The Continuum International Publishing Group Plc, Fairchild Books, Hart Publishing. Founded 1986.

Bloomsbury Children's & Educational Division
Managing Director Emma Hopkin, *Publishing Director & Editor-in-Chief* Rebecca McNally, *Education Publishing Director* Jayne Parsons
Editorial Directors Emma Blackburn (illustrated publishing), Ellen Holgate (fiction), Helen Diamond (educational resources), Saskia Gwinn (non-fiction)
Imprints include A&C Black, Andrew Brodie, Bloomsbury Activity Books, Bloomsbury Children's Books, Bloomsbury Education and Featherstone.

Children's. Bloomsbury Children's Books is a global publisher for children of all ages up to 16 years including titles such as the *Harry Potter* novels by J.K. Rowling, *Holes* by Louis Sachar and *The Graveyard Book* by Neil Gaiman. Recent highlights include *Throne of Glass* by Sarah J Maas; *The Wall* by William Sutcliffe; shortlisted for the Carnegie Medal; and *Lion* *in my Cornflakes* by Michelle Robinson and Jim Field, which won the inaugrual Sainsbury's Picture Book award. No unsolicited MSS; send a synopsis with 3 chapters. Bloomsbury Spark e-first list launched 2013: www.bloomsburyspark.com.

Educational. Publishes around 80 titles per year for readers 4–14 years including non-fiction, poetry and fiction. Publishes around 100 titles per year for teachers and practitioners in the areas of early years, music, teachers' resources and professional development. Recent fiction and poetry successes include, *Stars in Jars* by Chrissie Gittins, Tom and Tony Bradman's *My Brother's Keeper* and Terry Deary's *World War II Tales*. Recent non-fiction highlights include *My Silly Book of Side-splitting Stuff* by Andy Seed, winner of Blue Peter's Best Book with Facts award, *Steve Jobs* by Karen Blumenthaland publishing with the National Archive. Recent education titles include: *100 Ideas for Secondary Teachers: Outstanding Lessons* by Ross Morrison McGill; *Let's Do Spelling* by Andrew Brodie and *Continuous Provision: The Skills* by Alistair Bryce-Clegg.

No submissions by email. Look at recently published titles and catalogues to gauge current publishing interests. Much of the list is educationally focused and publishes in series. Allow 8–10 weeks for a response.

The Continuum International Publishing Group Ltd, part of Bloomsbury Academic & Professional Division
website www.bloomsburyprofessional.com
website www.bloomsburyacademic.com
Managing Director Jonathan Glasspool, *Publishing contacts*: Martin Casimir (Managing Director, Bloomsbury Professional: law, tax & accountancy); Kathryn Earle (Head of Visual Arts Publishing); David Barker (humanities)
Non-fiction including scholarly monographs and educational texts and reference works in education. Imprints: Burns & Oates, Continuum, Network Continuum, T&T Clark International, Thoemmes Press, Mowbray.

Education books include *Getting the Buggers to Write* and *Getting the Buggers to be Creative* by Sue Cowley.

Bodley Head Children's Books – see Penguin Random House UK

Boxer Books Ltd
101 Turnmill Street, London EC1M 5QP
email info@boxerbooks.com
website www.boxerbooks.com

No unsolicited MSS in any form unless via a recognised agency. Publishes innovative baby board books, picture books, young fiction and stunning story collections.

Bright Red Publishing
1 Torphichen Street, Edinburgh EH3 8HX
tel 0131 220 5804

email info@brightredpublishing.co.uk
website www.brightredpublishing.co.uk
Directors John MacPherson, Alan Grierson, Richard Bass

Educational publishing for Scotland's students and teachers. Founded 2008.

Brilliant Publications*
Unit 10, Sparrow Hall Farm, Edlesborough, Dunstable LU6 2ES
tel (01525) 222292
email info@brilliantpublications.co.uk
website www.brilliantpublications.co.uk
Managing Director Priscilla Hannaford

Practical resource books for teachers and others concerned with the education of children 0–13 years. All areas of the curriculum published, but specialises in modern foreign languages, art and design, developing thinking skills and PSHE. Some series of books for reluctant readers, aimed at children 7–11 years. No children's picture books, non-fiction books or one-off fiction books. See Manuscript Guidelines on website before sending proposal. Founded 1993.

The British Museum Press*
38 Russell Square, London WC1B 3QQ
tel 020-7323 1234
email publicity@britishmuseum.co.uk
website www.britishmuseum.org/publicity
Director of Publishing Rosemary Bradley

Award-winning illustrated books for children, young readers and families, inspired by the famous collections of the British Museum. Titles range across picture books, activity books and illustrated non-fiction. Founded 1973.

Andrew Brodie – see Bloomsbury Publishing Plc

Buster Books
16 Lion Yard, Tremadoc Road, London SW4 7NQ
tel 020-7720 8643
email enquiries@mombooks.com
website www.busterbooks.co.uk
Managing Director Lesley O'Mara, *Publishing Director* Philippa Wingate

Mainly non-fiction for 5–12 years. Publishes approx. 50 titles a year. Bestsellers include *The Creative Colouring Book*, *The Clever Kids' Colouring Book*, *Where's the Meerkat?*, and a wide selection of colouring, sticker and activity books.

Submit non-fiction with sae. Allow 1–2 months for response.

Cambridge University Press*
University Printing House, Shaftesbury Road, Cambridge CB2 8BS
tel (01223) 358331
email information@cambridge.org
website www.cambridge.org

Chief Executive Peter Phillips; *Managing Directors* Mandy Hill (academic), Michael Peluse (English Language Teaching), Hanri Pieterse (Cambridge Education)

For children: curriculum-based education books and software for schools and colleges (primary, secondary and international). English Language Teaching for adult and younger learners.

Anthropology and archaeology, art history, astronomy, biological sciences, classical studies, computer science, dictionaries, earth sciences, economics, engineering, history, language and literature, law, mathematics, medical sciences, music, philosophy, physical sciences, politics, psychology, reference, technology, social sciences, theology, religion. English language teaching, educational (primary, secondary, tertiary), e-learning products, journals (humanities, social sciences, science, technical and medical). The Bible and Prayer Book. Founded 1534.

Campbell Books – see Pan Macmillan

Candy Jar Books
Mackintosh House, 136 Newport Road, Cardiff CF24 1DJ
tel 029-21157202
email shaun@candyjarbooks.co.uk
email hayley@candyjarbooks.co.uk
website www.candyjarbooks.co.uk
Head of Publishing Shaun Russell, *Senior Publishing Coordinator* Hayley Cox

Non-fiction and fiction for children aged 7+. Will consider unsolicited MSS. Check website for submission details. Founded 2010.

Jonathan Cape Children's Books – see Penguin Random House UK

Carlton Publishing Group
20 Mortimer Street, London W1T 3JW
tel 020-7612 0400
email enquiries@carltonbooks.co.uk
website www.carltonbooks.co.uk
Chairman Jonathan Goodman, *Publisher* Sam Sweeney, Russell Mclean

No unsolicited MSS; synopses and ideas welcome, but no fiction or poetry. Founded 1992.

Carlton Kids (imprint)
Illustrated children's information books, with an emphasis on innovative formats and technologies such as augmented reality.

Caterpillar Books – see Little Tiger Group

Catnip Publishing Ltd
320 City Road, London EC1V 2NZ
tel 020-7138 3650
email liz.bankes@catnippublishing.co.uk
website www.catnippublishing.co.uk

Managing Director Robert Snuggs, *Commissioning Editor* Liz Bankes

New and previously published titles from picture books to teen fiction. Acquires new titles from overseas publishers, reissues out-of-print titles by top authors and commissions original fiction for 7–9, 9–12 years and young adult readers. Publishes 15–20 books a year. Recently published books by Pippa Goodhart, Jason Beresford, Berlie Doherty, Linda Newbery, Joan Lingard, Keris Stainton and Anne Booth. Founded 2005.

Will only consider agented submissions.

CGP
Coordination Group Publications, Broughton House, Broughton-in-Furness, Cumbria LA20 6HH
tel (01229) 715763
email jan.greenway@cgpbooks.co.uk
website www.cgpbooks.co.uk

Educational books centred around the National Curriculum, including revision guides and study books for KS1, KS2, KS3, GCSE and A level. Subjects include maths, English, science, history, geography, ICT, psychology, business studies, religious studies, child development, design and techology, PE, music, French, German, Spanish, sociology, 11+ and functional skills.

On the lookout for top teachers at all levels, in all subjects. Potential authors and proofreaders should email Jan Greenway with their name, subject area, level and experience, plus contact address, ready for when a project comes up in their subject area.

Chicken House
2 Palmer Street, Frome, Somerset BA11 1DS
tel (01373) 454488
email chickenhouse@doublecluck.com
website www.doublecluck.com
Managing Director & Publisher Barry Cunningham, *Deputy Managing Director* Rachel Hickman

Picture books, fiction for ages 7+ and young adult fiction. Publishes approx. 25 titles a year. No unsolicited MSS. See website for details of the annual *The Times*/Chicken House Children's Fiction Competition for unpublished writers. Successes include: *The Maze Runner* series by James Dashner.

The Children's Project Ltd
The Children's Project Ltd, PO Box 1200, Guildford GU2 9RA
tel 0845 094 5494
email info@childrensproject.co.uk
website www.socialbaby.com
Directors/Co-founders Helen Dorman, Clive Dorman

High-quality visual books that help parents and carers understand and communicate better with their children from birth. The Children's Project is dedicated exclusively to supporting the family and improved outcomes for children. It draws upon the experience and expertise of parents, health professionals and academics to provide up-to-date information in a form that is easily accessible to everyone – parents, carers and practitioners. No submissions. First books published 2000. Founded 1995.

Child's Play (International) Ltd
Ashworth Road, Bridgemead, Swindon, Wilts. SN5 7YD
tel (01793) 616286
email office@childs-play.com
website www.childs-play.com
Chairman Adriana Twinn, *Publisher* Neil Burden

Children's educational books: board, picture, activity and play books; fiction and non-fiction. Founded 1972.

Christian Education*
(incorporating RE Today Services and International Bible Reading Association)
1020 Bristol Road, Selly Oak, Birmingham B29 6LB
tel 0121 472 4242
email anstice.hughes@christianeducation.org.uk
website www.christianeducation.org.uk
website www.retoday.org.uk

Publications and services for teachers and other professionals in religious education including *REtoday* magazine, curriculum booklets and classroom resources. Also publishes Bible reading materials.

Chrysalis Children's Books – see Pavilion Children's Books

Claire Publications
Unit 8, Tey Brook Craft Centre, Great Tey, Colchester, Essex CO6 1JE
tel (01206) 211020
email mail@clairepublications.com
website www.clairepublications.com

Publisher and manufacturer of teachers' educational books and equipment, specialising in mathematics and literacy for children 5–15 years.

Classical Comics
PO Box 16310, Birmingham B30 9EL
tel 0845 812 3000
email info@classicalcomics.com
website www.classicalcomics.com
Managing Director Gary Bryant

Graphic novel adaptations of classical literature.

Collins Education – see HarperCollins Publishers

Colourpoint Creative Limited
Colourpoint House, Jubilee Business Park, 21 Jubilee Road, Newtownards, Co. Down BT23 4YH
tel 028-9182 6339
email sales@colourpoint.co.uk
website www.colourpoint.co.uk
Commissioning Editor Malcolm Johnston, *Marketing* Jacky Hawkes

Textbooks for Northern Ireland CCEA board. Educational textbooks for KS3 (11–14 years) KS3 Special Needs (10–14 years), GCSE (14–16 years) and A-Level/undergraduates (age 17+). Not primary. Subjects include biology, business studies, chemistry, English, geography, history, HE, ICT, Irish, LLW, MVRUS, PE, physics, politics, technology and design and RE. Founded 1993.

Short queries by email. Full submission in writing including details of proposal, sample chapter/section to show ability to connect with target age group, qualification/experience in the subject, full contact details and return postage. Textbooks, workbooks and electronic resources all considered.

Corner to Learn
Willow Cottage, 26 Purton Stoke, Swindon SN5 4JF
tel (01793) 421168
email neil@cornertolearn.co.uk
website www.cornertolearn.co.uk
Publisher Neil Griffiths

Books and learning materials aimed at teachers and parents with young children. Imprint: Red Robin Books (picture books).

Crown House Publishing Ltd
Crown Buildings, Bancyfelin, Carmarthen SA33 5ND
tel (01267) 211345
email books@crownhouse.co.uk
website www.crownhouse.co.uk
Chairman Martin Roberts, *Directors* David Bowman (managing), Glenys Roberts, Karen Bowman, Caroline Lenton, Cathy Heritage

IPA 2013 and 2014 Education Publisher of the Year with a large range of classroom resources and materials for professional teacher development. Also publish books on health and wellbeing, NLP, hypnosis, counselling, psychotherapy and coaching. Founded 1998.

Independent Thinking Press
Crown Buildings, Bancyfelin, Carmarthen SA33 5ND
tel (01267) 211345
email caroline@independentthinkingpress.com
website www.independentthinkingpress.com
Publishes the thoughts and ideas of some of the UK's leading educational innovators including world-class speakers, award-winning teachers, outstanding school leaders and classroom revolutionaries.

Dean – see Egmont UK Ltd

Dorling Kindersley – see Penguin Random House UK

Doubleday Children's Books – see Penguin Random House UK

Dref Wen

28 Church Road, Whitchurch, Cardiff CF14 2EA
tel 029-2061 7860
website www.drefwen.com
Directors Roger Boore, Anne Boore, Gwilym Boore, Alun Boore, Rhys Boore

Welsh language publisher. Original, adaptations and translations of foreign and English language full-colour picture story books for children. Also activity books, novelty books, Welsh language fiction for children 7–14 years, teenage fiction, reference, religion, audiobooks and poetry. Educational material for primary and secondary school children in Wales and England, including dictionaries, revision guides and Welsh as a Second Language. Publishes approx. 50 titles a year and has 450 in print. Founded 1970.
No unsolicited MSS. Phone first.

The Educational Company of Ireland

Ballymount Road, Walkinstown, Dublin 12, Republic of Ireland
tel +353 (0)1 4500611
email info@edco.ie
website www.edco.ie
Executive Directors Martina Harford (Ceo)

Educational (primary and post-primary) books in the Irish language. Publishes approx. 60–70 titles each year and has 600–700 in print. Ancillary materials include CD-Roms and CDs. Successes include *Sunny Street/Streets Ahead* Primary English Langue Programme, *Fonn 1, 2, 3* (Irish language publications for post-primary) and *Geo* (geography publication for post-primary). Trading unit of Smurfit Kappa Group – Ireland. Founded 1910.
Send an A4 page outlining the selling points and proposal, a draft table of contents and a sample chapter. Allow 3 months for response.

Educational Explorers (Publishers)

Unit 5, Feidr Castell Business Park, Fishguard SA65 9BB
tel (01348) 874890
website www.cuisenaire.co.uk
Directors M.J. Hollyfield, D.M. Gattegno

Educational. Recent successes include: mathematics: *Numbers in Colour with Cuisenaire Rods*; languages: *The Silent Way*; literacy, reading: *Words in Colour*; educational films. No unsolicited material. Founded 1962.

Egmont UK Ltd*

The Yellow Building, 1 Nicholas Road, London W11 4AN
email info@egmont.co.uk
website www.egmont.co.uk

The UK's largest specialist children's publisher, publishing books from babies to teens, inspiring children to read. Publishes award-winning books, magazines, ebooks and apps. Egmont has a growing portfolio of digital publishing which includes: the first Flips books for Nintendo DS, apps for iPhone and iPad, ebooks and enhanced ebooks and online virtual worlds. Egmont UK is part of the Egmont Group and owned by the Egmont Foundation, a charitable trust dedicated to supporting children and young people. It is Scandinavia's leading media group and Europe's largest children's publisher telling stories through books, magazines, film, TV, music, games and mobile in 30 countries throughout the world. Founded 1878.

Egmont Press

email childrensreader@euk.egmont.com
Picture book and gift (ages 0+), fiction (ages 5+). Authors include Michael Morpurgo, Enid Blyton, Andy Stanton, Michael Grant, Lemony Snicket, Kristina Stephenson, Giles Andreae, Jan Fearnley and Lydia Monks. Submission details: visit website to see current policy.

Egmont Publishing Group

email charcterpr@euk.egmont.com
Egmont Publishing Group is the UK's leading licensed character publisher of books and magazines for children from birth to teen. Books portfolio includes Thomas the Tank Engine, Mr Men, Fireman Sam, Ben 10, Bob the Builder, Baby Jake and Everything's Rosie and covers a wide range of formats from storybooks, annuals and novelty books to colouring, activity and sticker books. Magazines portfolio includes *Thomas & Friends*, *Disney Princess*, *Toy Story*, *Barbie*, *Ben 10*, *Tinker Bell*, *Fireman Sam*, *We Love Pop* and girls' pre-teen magazine *Go Girl* and boys' lifestyle title *Toxic*.

Faber and Faber Ltd*

Bloomsbury House, 74–77 Great Russell Street, London WC1B 3DA
tel 020-7927 3800
website www.faber.co.uk
Publisher & Chief Executive Stephen Page, *Publishing Director, Children's Books* Leah Thaxton, *Communications Director* Rachel Alexander, *Sales & Services Director* Charlotte Robertson, *Consumer Marketing Director* Matt Haslum, *Production Director* Nigel Marsh, *Rights Director* Lisa Baker

High-quality picture books, general fiction and non-fiction, drama, film, music, poetry. For children: fiction for 5–8 and 9–12 years, teenage fiction, poetry and some non-fiction. Authors include T. S. Eliot, Ted Hughes, Philip Ardagh, Justin Fletcher, Harry Hill, Betty G. Birney, Francesca Simon, Karen McCombie, Jennifer Gray, Mackenzie Crook, Natasha Frarrant.
Only accepts submissions through an agent; no unsolicited MSS.

CJ Fallon

Ground Floor, Block B, Liffey Valley Office Campus, Dublin 22, Republic of Ireland

tel +353 (0)1 6166400
email editorial@cjfallon.ie
website www.cjfallon.ie
Executive Directors Brian Gilsenan (managing), John Bodley (financial)

Educational textbooks. Founded 1927.

Featherstone Education – see Bloomsbury Publishing Plc

David Fickling Books

31 Beaumont Street, Oxford OX1 2NP
tel (01865) 339000
website www.davidficklingbooks.co.uk
Publisher David Fickling

Picture books, fiction for 5–8 and 9–12 years, young adult fiction and poetry. Will consider unsolicited MSS (first 3 chapters only); include covering letter and sae and allow 3 months for response. If possible, find an agent first. Founded 2000.

Fidra Books

27 Bell Place, Edinburgh EH3 5HT
tel 0131 343 3118
email info@fidrabooks.com
website www.fidrabooks.com
Contact Vanessa Robertson (*managing director*)

Specialises in reprinting children's books ranging from 1930s adventure stories to iconic 1960s fantasy novels and from pony books to school stories. No unsolicited MSS. Founded 2005.

First and Best in Education

Earlstrees Court, Earlstrees Road, Corby, Northants NN17 4HH
tel (01536) 399011
email sales@firstandbest.co.uk
website www.shop.firstandbest.co.uk
Contact Anne Cockburn (editor)

Education-related books (no fiction, no primary). Currently actively looking for new ideas for educational books. Email submissions to anne@firstandbest.co.uk. Founded 1992.

Fisherton Press

150 South Birkbeck Road, London E11 4JH
email general@fishertonpress.co.uk
website www.fishertonpress.co.uk
Director Ellie Levenson

A small independent publisher producing picture books for children under 7 that adults also like reading. Interested in receiving ideas and MSS from authors and portfolios and book ideas from illustrators.

Flame Tree Publishing

6 Melbray Mews, Fulham, London SW6 3NS
tel 020-7751 9650
email info@flametreepublishing.com
website www.flametreepublishing.com

Ceo/Publisher Nick Wells, *Managing Director* Francis Bodiam

Occasional children's novelty books and early learning. Part of Flame Tree Publishing Ltd. Founded 1992.

Floris Books*

15 Harrison Gardens, Edinburgh EH11 1SH
tel 0131 337 2372
email floris@florisbooks.co.uk
website www.florisbooks.co.uk
Commissioning Editors Sally Polson, Eleanor Collins

Children's activity books, novels, board and picture books. Also for adults: religion, science, philosophy, holistic health, organics, Mind, Body & Spirit, crafts, parenting. Approx. 70 titles each year. Founded 1978.

Kelpies (imprint)

Contemporary Scottish fiction – picture books (for 3–6 years), young readers series (for 6–8 years) and novels (for 8–15 years). Recent successes include *The Accidental Time Traveller* by Janis MacKay and *There Was a Wee Lassie Who Swallowed a Midgie* by Rebecca Colby, see website. Children's fiction submissions must fit into the Kelpies imprint.

Will consider unsolicited MSS. For novels send synopsis and sample chapters. For picture books send text and illustrations, text only or illustrations only. Include author/illustrator biography and sae for return of work. Must be Scottish in theme.

Folens Publishers

Hibernian Industrial Estate, off Greenhills Road, Tallaght, Dublin 24, Republic of Ireland
tel +353 (0)1 4137200
website www.folens.ie
Chairman Dirk Folens, *Managing Director* John O'Connor, *Primary Managing & Commissioning Editor* Deirdre Whelan, *Secondary Managing Editor* Margaret Burns

Educational (primary, secondary, comprehensive, technical, in English and Irish). Founded 1956.

Blackwater Press (imprint)

Senior Editor Sarah Deegan

Picture books and *Brainstorm* series of activity books. Recent successes include *Bin Bling* by Aoileann Garavaglia (activity book). Founded 1993.

Will consider unsolicited MSS. Send synopsis and first chapter. Allow 6 weeks for response.

Galore Park Publishing Ltd*

338 Euston Road, London NW1 3BH
tel 020-7873 6412
website www.galorepark.co.uk

Educational textbooks and revision guides for students studying at independent schools. *So You Really Want To Learn* range of textbooks for children 11+ years and *Junior* range for children 8–10 years.

Books

Courses include Latin, French, English, Spanish, maths and science. Founded 1999.

Gardner Education Ltd

Unit 2, Aston Way, Middlewich, Cheshire CW10 0HS
tel 0845 230 0775
email education@gardnereducation.com
website www.gardnereducation.com
Managing Director Stuart Withers

A specialist supplier of primary and secondary literacy books to schools and parents. Range includes book banded publications, dyslexia friendly texts, Accelerated Reader and Catch Up Literacy approved titles, books tailored for struggling and reluctant readers, and a massive selection of titles to cater for all primary and secondary reading preferences. Founded 1999.

Ginn – see Pearson UK

GL Assessment*

9th Floor East, 389 Chiswick High Road, London W4 4AL
tel 020-8996 3333
email information@gl-assessment.co.uk
website www.gl-assessment.co.uk
Chairman Philip Walters

Independent provider of tests, assessments and assessment services for education. Its aim is to help educational professionals to understand and maximise the potential of their pupils and students. Publishes assessments for the 0–19 age group, though the majority of its assessments are aimed at children 5–14 years. Testing and assessment services include literacy, numeracy, thinking skills, ability, learning support and online testing. Founded 1981.

Gomer Press

Llandysul, Ceredigion SA44 4JL
tel (01559) 363090
email gwasg@gomer.co.uk
website www.gomer.co.uk
website www.pontbooks.co.uk
Managing Director Jonathan Lewis, *Editors* Sioned Lleinau, Rhian Evans

Picture books, novels, stories, poetry and teaching resources in the Welsh language. Prelimary enquiry essential. Founded 1892.

Pont Books – the imprint for Gomer's English books for children

email Cathryn@gomer.co.uk
website www.pontbooks.co.uk
Editor Cathryn Gwynn

Picture books, novels, stories, poetry for children and teaching resources with a Welsh dimension. No unsolicited MSS; preliminary enquiry essential.

W.F. Graham

2 Pondwood Close, Moulton Park, Northampton NN3 6RT
tel (01604) 645537
email books@wfgraham.co.uk
website www.wfgraham.co.uk

Activity books including colouring, dot-to-dot, magic painting, puzzle, word search and sticker books.

Granada Learning*

9th Floor East, 389 Chiswick High Road, London W4 4AL
tel 020-8996-3333
website www.gl-education.com

Educational multimedia company publishing innovative assessment and curriculum-based resources for the UK and abroad. It has a catalogue of over 200 products for preschool children, primary and secondary, through to A level. Products are developed by teachers and educationalists. The Granada Learning Group includes Granada Learning Professional Development, GL Assessment and schoolcentre.net.

Hachette Children's Group*

Carmelite House, 50 Victoria Embankment, London EC4Y 0DZ
website www.hachettechildrens.co.uk
Ceo Hilary Murray Hill

Hodder Children's Books (imprint)
Publishing Director Anne McNeil

Fiction, picture books, novelty, general non-fiction and audiobooks.

Orchard Books (imprint)
Publishing Director Megan Larkin

Fiction, picture and novelty books.

Little, Brown Books for Young Readers (imprint)
Publishing Director Karen Ball

Fiction, novelty, general non-fiction and audiobooks.

Franklin Watts (imprint)
Publishing Director Rachel Cooke

Non-fiction and information books.

Wayland (imprint)
Editorial Director Debbie Foy

Non-fiction and information books.

Orion Children's Books (imprint)
Publishing Director Fiona Kennedy

Fiction, picture books, novelty, general non-fiction and audiobooks.

Hachette UK*

Carmelite House, 50 Victoria Embankment, London EC4Y 0DZ
tel 020-7873 6000
website www.hachette.co.uk
Chief Executive Tim Hely Hutchinson, *Directors* Jamie Hodder Williams (Ceo, Hodder & Stoughton, Headline, John Murray Press, Quercus), Chris

Emerson (Coo), Jane Morpeth (managing, Headline), Marlene Johnson (managing, Hachette Children's), David Young (Deputy Ceo, Hachette UK/Ceo, Orion), Malcolm Edwards (managing, Orion), Alison Goff (Ceo, Octopus), Ursula Mackenzie (Chairman, Little, Brown Book Group), Pierre de Cacqueray (finance), Richard Kitson (commercial/Chairman, Hachette Australia and Hachette New Zealand), Dominic Mahony (group HR), Michael Pietsch (Ceo, Hachette Book Group USA), Clare Harington (group communications), Diane Spivey (group contracts), Hilary Murray Hill (Ceo, Hachette Children's Group), David Shelley (Ceo, Little, Brown Book Group), Lis Tribe (managing, Hodder Education)

Part of Hachette Livre SA since 2004. Hachette UK group companies: Hachette Children's Books (page 46), Headline Book Publishing, Hodder Education Group, Hodder & Stoughton, Hodder Faith, John Murray, Little, Brown Book Group, Orion Group (page 50), Octopus Group, Hachette Ireland, Hachette Australia (page 60), Hachette New Zealand.

Haldane Mason Ltd

PO Box 34196, London NW10 3YB
tel 020-8459 2131
email info@haldanemason.com
website www.haldanemason.com
Directors Sydney Francis, Ron Samuel

Illustrated non-fiction books and box sets, mainly for children. No unsolicited material. Imprints: Haldane Mason (adult), Red Kite Books (children's). Founded 1995.

Interested in non-fiction only; email first to check interest.

HarperCollins Publishers*

1 London Bridge Street, London SE1 9GF
tel 020-8741 7070
also at Westerhill Road, Bishopbriggs, Glasgow G64 2QT
tel 0141 772 3200
website www.harpercollins.co.uk
Ceo Charlie Redmayne

For adults: fiction (commercial and literary) and non-fiction. Subjects include history, celebrity memoirs, biographies, popular science, Mind, Body & Spirit, dictionaries, maps and reference. All fiction and trade non-fiction must be submitted through an agent, or unsolicited MSS may be submitted to www.authonomy.com (an online community that connects readers, writers and publishing professionals managed by editors at HarperCollins). Owned by News Corporation. Founded 1819.

HarperCollins Audio (imprint)
Director of Audio Jo Forshaw
See page 87.

HarperCollins Children's Books
website www.harpercollinschildrensbooks.co.uk
Publisher Ann-Janine Murtagh

Annuals, activity books, novelty books, picture books, painting and colouring books, pop-up books and book and CD sets. Fiction for 5–8 and 9–12 years, young adult fiction and series fiction; poetry; film/TV tie-ins. Publishes approx. 265 titles each year. Picture book authors include Oliver Jeffers, Judith Kerr and Emma Chichester Clark, and fiction by David Walliams, Michael Morpurgo, Louise Rennison and Lauren Child. Books published under licence include *Noddy*, *Dr Seuss*, *Hello Kitty* and *Paddington Bear*.

No unsolicited MSS: only accepts submissions via agents.

Collins Education (imprint)
Managing Director Colin Hughes
Books, CD-Roms and online material for UK primary and secondary schools and colleges.

Hawthorn Press

1 Lansdown Lane, Stroud, Glos. GL5 1BJ
tel (01453) 757040
email info@hawthornpress.com
website www.hawthornpress.com
Directors Martin Large

Publishes books for a creative, peaceful and sustainable world. Series include Early Years, Steiner/Waldorf Education, Crafts, Personal Development, Art and Science, Storytelling. Founded 1981.

Heinemann – see Pearson UK

Hippo – see Scholastic Ltd

Hodder Children's Books – see Hachette Children's Group

Hodder Headline Ltd – see Hachette UK

Hogs Back Books Ltd

The Stables, Down Place, Hogs Back, Guildford GU3 1DE
tel (01483) 506030
email enquiries@hogsbackbooks.com
website www.hogsbackbooks.com
Director/Commissioning Editor Karen Stevens

Children's picture books and teenage fiction. Founded 2009.

Welcomes texts and submissions from illustrators but cannot return material without prior arrangement.

Hopscotch

(a division of MA Education)
St Jude's Church, Dulwich Road, London SE24 0PB
tel 020-7501 6736
email sales@hopscotchbooks.com
website www.hopscotchbooks.com
Associate Publisher Angela Morano-Shaw

Teaching resources for primary school teachers. Founded 1997.

Books

Practical Pre-School Books
Early years teacher resources.

Hutchinson Children's Books – see
Penguin Random House UK

Igloo Books Ltd
Cottage Farm, Mears Ashby Road, Sywell,
Northants NN6 0BJ
tel (01604) 741116
email editorial@igloobooks.com
website www.igloobooks.com

Adult and children's: cookery, lifestyle, gift, trivia,
fiction, non-fiction (adult), licensed books, novelty,
board, picture, activity books, audio (children's),
education, ebooks and apps. Not currently accepting
submissions. Founded 2005.

IWM (Imperial War Museums)
Lambeth Road, London SE1 6HZ
tel 020-7416 5000
email publishing@iwm.org.uk
website www.iwm.org.uk

IWM tells the stories of people who have lived,
fought and died in conflicts involving Britain and the
Commonwealth since 1914. Drawing on the IWM's
unique collections, a large range of books linked to
exhibitions and archives is published. Books are
produced both in-house and in partnership with
other publishers.

Jolly Learning Ltd
Tailours House, High Road, Chigwell, Essex IG7 6DL
tel 020-8501 0405
email info@jollylearning.co.uk
website www.jollylearning.co.uk
Director Christopher Jolly

Educational: primary and English as a Bilingual
Language. The company is committed to enabling
high standards in the teaching of reading and writing.
Publishes approx. 25 titles each year and has 300 in
print. Recent successes include *Jolly Phonics Extra*,
My Jolly Phonics and *Jolly Dictionary*. Imprint: Jolly
Phonics. Founded 1987.
    Unsolicited MSS are only considered for add-ons
to existing products.

Miles Kelly Publishing
Harding's Barn, Bardfield End Green, Thaxted,
Essex CM6 3PX
tel (01371) 832440
email hello@mileskelly.net
website www.mileskelly.net
Director Gerard Kelly

High-quality illustrated non-fiction and fiction titles
for children and family: activity books, board books,
story books, poetry, reference, posters and wallcharts.
Age groups: preschool, 5–10, 10–15, 15+. See also
entry in *Book packagers* (page 91). Founded 1996.

Kelpies – see Floris Books

Kingfisher – see Pan Macmillan

The King's England Press
111 Meltham Road, Lockwood, Huddersfield,
West Yorkshire HD4 7BG
tel (01484) 663790
email sales@kingsengland.com
website www.kingsengland.com

Poetry collections for both adults and children plus
history books. Successes include *The Spot on My
Bum: Horrible Poems for Horrible Children* by Gez
Walsh, *Revudeville* and *Turned Out Nice Again* by
Deborah Tyler-Bennett, and *Jordan's Guide to British
Steam Locomotives*, by Owen Jordan. Founded 1989.
    Also publishes reprints of Arthur Mee's *The King's
England* series of 1930s guidebooks and books on
folklore, and local and ecclesiastical history, plus
children's and adult fiction.
    See website for guidelines. Currently not accepting
new unsolicited proposals.

Jessica Kingsley Publishers*
73 Collier Street, London N1 9BE
tel 020-7833 2307
email hello@jkp.com
website www.jkp.com
Managing Director Jessica Kingsley

Psychology, psychiatry, arts therapies, social work,
special needs (especially autism spectrum), education,
law, practical theology and a small children's list
focusing on books for children with special needs.
Founded 1987.

Kube Publishing Ltd
(formerly the Islamic Foundation)
Markfield Conference Centre, Ratby Lane,
Markfield, Leics. LE67 9SY
tel (01530) 249230
email info@kubepublishing.com
website www.kubepublishing.com
Managing Director Haris Ahmad

Books on Islam for adults and children.

Ladybird Books
80 Strand, London WC2R 0RL
tel 020-7010 3000
email ladybird@uk.penguingroup.com
website www.ladybird.co.uk

Ladybird publishes books across a wide range of
formats for children aged from birth to 7 years. They
include tactile books for babies, nursery rhymes,
classic fairy tales and reading schemes, alongside
licensed character publishing.

Leckie & Leckie*
Dipford House, Queens Square Business Park,
Huddersfield Road, Honley, Holmfirth HD9 6QZ

tel 0141 772 3200
email info@leckieandleckie.co.uk
website www.leckieandleckie.co.uk

Educational resources. Dedicated to the ongoing development of materials specifically for education in Scotland, from Standard Grade Foundation to Advanced Higher Level and including new resources for the Curriculum for Excellence. Over 220 titles are currently available in the study guide range. Subsidiary of HarperCollins Publishers.

Frances Lincoln Children's Books (Quarto Publishing Group UK)

(The Aurum Publishing Group)
74–77 White Lion Street, London N1 9PF
tel 020-7284 9300
email reception@frances-lincoln.com
website www.frances-lincoln.com
Director David Inman (managing), *Publisher* Rachel Williams

Novelty books, picture books, art, science, religion, poetry, culture, diversity.

Submit material either through an agent or direct. The focus should be on cultural diversity.

Frances Lincoln Ltd

4 Torriano Mews, Torriano Avenue, London NW5 2RZ
tel 020-7284 4009
email reception@frances-lincoln.com
website www.frances-lincoln.com
Directors John Nicoll (managing), Maurice Lyon (editorial, children's books)

Illustrated, international co-editions: gardening, architecture, environment, interiors, photography, art, walking and climbing, design and landscape, gift, children's books. Founded 1977.

Lion Hudson plc

Wilkinson House, Jordan Hill Road, Oxford OX2 8DR
tel (01865) 302750
email info@lionhudson.com
website www.lionhudson.com
Managing Director Nick Jones

Books for children and adults. Children's books published under Lion Children's Books and Candle Books imprints include picture stories, illustrated non-fiction and information books on the Christian faith. Also specialises in children's Bibles and prayer collections. Submissions: hardcopy with return postage if return required. Founded 1971 as Lion Publishing; merged with Angus Hudson Ltd in 2003.

Little Tiger Group

1 The Coda Centre, 189 Munster Road, London SW6 6AW
tel 020-7385 6333
website www.littletiger.co.uk
website www.littletiger.co.uk/imprint/caterpillar-books

website www.littletiger.co.uk/imprint/stripes-publishing
Ceo Monty Bhatia

Little Tiger Press (imprint)

email contact@littletiger.co.uk
website www.littletiger.co.uk
Publisher Jude Evans, *Editorial Directors* Amelia Hepworth, Barry Timms

Children's picture books, board books and activity books for preschool–7 years. See website for submissions guidelines. Founded 1987.

Caterpillar Books (imprint)

email contact@littletiger.co.uk
website www.littletiger.co.uk/imprint/caterpillar-books
Publisher Thomas Truong, *Editorial Director* Pat Hegarty

Books for preschool children, including pop-ups, board books, cloth books and activity books. Founded 2003.

Stripes (imprint)

email contact@littletiger.co.uk
website www.littletiger.co.uk/imprint/stripes-publishing
Publisher Jane Harris, *Commissioning Editor* Katie Jennings

Fiction for children aged 6–12 years. Mainly series publishing. Will consider new material from authors and illustrators; see website for guidelines. Founded 2005.

Longman – see Pearson UK

McGraw-Hill School Education*

McGraw-Hill House, Shoppenhangers Road, Maidenhead, Berks. SL6 2QL
tel (01628) 502730
email ukschools@mcgraw-hill.com
website www.mcgraw-hill.co.uk/schools
Schools Manager Katie Donnison

Educational publisher for primary and secondary education in English, maths, science, humanities and other subject areas, including intervention and learning support.

Macmillan Publishers Ltd – see Pan Macmillan

Mantra Lingua Ltd

Global House, 303 Ballards Lane, London N12 8NP
tel 020-8445 5123
email info@mantralingua.com
website www.mantralingua.com
website www.discoverypen.co.uk
Managing Directors R. Dutta, M. Chatterji

Publishes picture books and educational resources. The unique talking pen technology enables any book to be sound activated. All resources are or can be narrated in multiple languages and educational posters for schools and museums have audio visual features to compact information. The company is looking for illustrators, authors, translators and audio narrators who are keen on the communications space. Founded in 2002. Divisions other than Education: Museums and Heritage, www.discoverypen.co.uk. The talking pen technology is being used by many museums of various sizes. The company is looking for illustrators and trail writers, tel: 0845 600 1361. Birding: www.birdvoice.net. The talking pen technology is used to help bird watchers double their bird recognition skills. The company is looking for specialist audio recordings of birds, frogs and other animals from around the world, tel: 0845 600 1361.

Kevin Mayhew Ltd
Buxhall, Stowmarket, Suffolk IP14 3BW
tel (01449) 737978
email info@kevinmayhew.com
website www.kevinmayhew.com
Directors Kevin Mayhew, Barbara Mayhew

Christianity: prayer and spirituality, pastoral care, preaching, liturgy worship, children's, youth work, drama, instant art, educational. Music: hymns, organ and choral, contemporary worship, piano and instrumental, tutors. Greetings cards: images, spiritual texts, birthdays, Christian events, musicians, general occasions. Contact Manuscript Submissions Dept before sending MSS/synopses. Founded 1976.

The Mercier Press†
Unit 3, Oak House, Riverview Business Park, Blackrock, Cork, Republic of Ireland
tel +353 (0)21 4614700
email info@mercierpress.ie
website www.mercierpress.ie
Directors J.F. Spillane (chairman), M.P. Feehan (managing), D. Crowley

Books for adults and children. Subjects include Irish literature, folklore, history, politics, humour, current affairs, health, Mind, Body & Spirit and general non-fiction. Founded 1944.

National Association for the Teaching of English (NATE)
50 Broadfield Road, Sheffield S8 0XJ
tel 0114 255 5419
email info@nate.org.uk
website www.nate.org.uk
Chair Bethan Marshall, *Co-Directors* Mick Connell & Joe Walsh, *Editor & Publications Manager* Gary Snapper

Educational (primary, secondary and tertiary): teaching English, drama and media. Subscription magazine: *Teaching English*. Imprint: NATE. Founded 1963.

Nosy Crow
The Crow's Nest, 10A Lant Street, London SE1 1QR
tel 020-7089 7575
email hello@nosycrow.com
website www.nosycrow.com
Managing Director Kate Wilson, *Editorial Director* Camilla Reid

Award-winning children's books and apps. IPG Children's Publisher of the Year 2012 and 2013. Founded 2010.
Submissions by email to adrian@nosycrow.com.

Oberon Books
521 Caledonian Road, London N7 9RH
tel 020-7607 3637
email info@oberonbooks.com
website www.oberonbooks.com
Managing Director Charles Glanville, *Publisher* James Hogan, *Associate Publisher & Senior Editor* Andrew Walby

New and classic play texts, programme texts and general theatre and performing arts books. Founded 1986.

The O'Brien Press Ltd†
12 Terenure Road East, Rathgar, Dublin 6, Republic of Ireland
tel +353 (0)1 4923333
email books@obrien.ie
website www.obrien.ie
Directors Michael O'Brien, Ide ní Laoghaire, Ivan O'Brien, Mary Webb

For children: fiction for all ages; illustrated fiction for 3+, 5+, 6+, 8+ years, novels (10+ and young adult) – contemporary, historical, fantasy. Also for adults: biography, politics, history, true crime, sport, humour, reference, fiction, crime fiction. No poetry or academic. Founded 1974.
Unsolicited MSS (sample chapters only), synopses and ideas for books welcome – submissions will not be returned.

Orchard Books – see Hachette Children's Group

The Orion Publishing Group Ltd
Orion House, 5 Upper St Martin's Lane, London WC2H 9EA
tel 020-7240 3444
website www.orionbooks.co.uk
Directors Arnaud Nourry (chairman), Peter Roche (chief executive), Malcolm Edwards (deputy chief executive)

For adults: fiction and non-fiction and audio. Imprints include Everyman, Gollancz, Orion, Phoenix and Weidenfeld & Nicolson. Part of Hachette UK (see page 46). Founded 1992.

Orion Children's Books (division)
Publisher Fiona Kennedy, *Editorial Manager* Jane Hughes

Picture books, fiction for ages 5–8 and 9–12, teenage fiction, series fiction and audio. Publishes approx. 50 titles each year and has about 350 in print. Recent successes include books by Francesca Simon, Michelle Paver and Sally Gardner. Imprint: Orion Children's Books.

Will consider unsolicited MSS. Allow 2 months for response. Submissions via agents take priority.

Oxford University Press*

Great Clarendon Street, Oxford OX2 6DP
tel (01865) 556767
email enquiry@oup.com
website www.oup.com
Ceo Nigel Portwood, *Group Finance Director* Giles Spackman, *Global Academic Business Managing Director* Tim Barton, *Managing Director, Oxford Education* Kate Harris, *ELT Division Managing Director* Peter Marshall, *Human Resources Director* Paul Lomas, *Academic Sales Director* Alastair Lewis

Archaeology, architecture, art, belles lettres, bibles, bibliography, children's books (fiction, non-fiction, picture), commerce, current affairs, dictionaries, drama, economics, educational (foundation, primary, secondary, technical, university), encyclopedias, ELT, electronic publishing, essays, foreign language learning, general history, hymn and service books, journals, law, medical, music, oriental, philosophy, political economy, prayer books, reference, science, sociology, theology and religion; educational software; *Grove Dictionaries of Music & Art.* Trade paperbacks published under the imprint of Oxford Paperbacks. Founded 1478.

Children's and Educational Division

Managing Director, Oxford Education Kate Harris, *Sales, Marketing & Operations Director* Richard Hodson, *Content & Strategy Director* Rod Theodorou, *Children's Publisher* Liz Cross, *Dictionaries Publisher* Vineeta Gupta, *Director Digital & Home/School Services* Simon Tanner-Tremaine, *Director, Secondary* Clare Varlet-Baker, *Sector Director, International* Elspeth Boardley, *Director Primary* Jane Harley, *Managing Director of Asia Education* Adrian Mellor
Picture books, fiction, poetry and dictionaries. Authors include Tim Bowler, Gillian Cross, Julie Hearne and Geraldine McCaughrean.

Pan Macmillan*

20 New Wharf Road, London N1 9RR
tel 020-7014 6000
website www.panmacmillan.com
Managing Director Anthony Forbes Watson, *Creative Director* Geoff Duffield, *Publishers* Jeremy Trevathan (adult), Robin Harvie (non-fiction), Paul Baggaley (Picador), Carole Tonkinson (Bluebird)

Novels, literary, crime, thrillers, romance, sci-fi, fantasy and horror. Autobiography, biography, business, gift books, health and beauty, history, humour, natural history, travel, philosophy, politics, world affairs, theatre, film, gardening, cookery, popular reference. Publishes under Macmillan, Tor, Pan, Picador, Sidgwick & Jackson, Boxtree, Bluebird, Macmillan Audio, Macmillan New Writing. No unsolicited MSS except through Macmillan New Writing. Founded 1843.

Campbell Books (preschool imprint)

Editorial Director Stephanie Barton
Early learning, pop-up, novelty, board books for the preschool market. 0–6: picture books, activity and novelty (*publishers* Stephanie Barton & Suzanne Carnell), 6+ : fiction, non fiction, poetry (*publisher* Venetia Gosling).

Kingfisher (imprint)

tel 020-7014 6000
Publisher Belinda Rasmussen
Non-fiction: activity books, encyclopedias, general history, religion, art, music, philosophy, folklore, language, mathematics, nature, science and technology, novelty books, graded readers. Publishes approx. 50 new non-fiction titles and has about 500 in print. Imprint of Macmillan Children's Books.

Macmillan Science and Education

The Macmillan Campus, 4 Crinan Street, London N1 9XW
tel 020-7833 4000
website http://se.macmillan.com
Ceo, Science & Education Annette Thomas, *Ceo, Education* S.J. Allen, *Ceo, Science & Scholarly* S.C. Inchcoombe, *Director* D.J.G. Knight

Parragon Books Ltd

Chartist House, 15–17 Trim Street, Bath BA11HA
tel (01225) 478888
email uk_info@parragon.com
website www.parragon.com
Global Publishing Director April Sankey, *Children's Publisher* Rachel Lawrence

Activity books, novelty books, picture books, fiction for 5–8 years, reference and home learning, book and CD sets. Licensed character list. No unsolicited material.

Pavilion Children's Books

1 Gower Street, London WC1E 6HD
tel 020-7462 1500
website www.pavilionbooks.com
Commissioning Editor Katie Deane

Children's books: from baby and picture books to illustrated classics and fiction. Part of Pavilion Books Company Ltd. Submissions via an agent only.

Recent successes include *The Story of the Little Mole* by Werner Holzwarth, *The Journey Home* by Fran Preston-Gannon, *War Game* by Michael Foreman and *Bug Detective* by Maggie Li.

Pearson UK*

Edinburgh Gate, Harlow, Essex CM20 2JE
tel 0845 313 6666

email schools@longman.co.uk
website www.pearsoned.co.uk
President Rod Bristow

Harcourt (imprint)

Educational resources for teachers and learners at primary, secondary and vocational level. Provides a range of published resources, teachers' support, and pupil and student material in all core subjects for all ages. Imprints: Ginn, Heinemann, Payne-Gallway, Raintree, Rigby.

Longman (imprint)

tel (0800) 579579
email schools@longman.co.uk
website www.longman.co.uk

Educational: primary and secondary. Primary: literacy and numeracy. Secondary: English, maths, science, history, geography, modern languages, design and technology, business and economics, psychology and sociology.

Penguin Longman (imprint)

ELT.

York Notes (imprint)

Literature guides for students.

Penguin Longman – see Pearson UK

Penguin Random House UK*

20 Vauxhall Bridge Road, London SW1V 2SA
tel 020-7840 8400
website www.penguin.co.uk
Ceo, Penguin Random House UK Tom Weldon, *Deputy Ceo* Ian Hudson, *Chairman* Gail Rebuck, *Directors* Mark Gardiner (finance), Graham Sim (creative), Brian Davies (overseas operations), Richard Cable (managing, Vintage Publishing), Rebecca Smart (managing, Ebury Publishing), Susan Sandon (managing, Cornerstone), Garry Prior (deputy group sales), Mark Williams (managing, distribution)

Penguin Random House UK comprises of 8 publishing companies and more than 45 imprints. The company is part of the global Penguin Random House company which was formed in 2013 following the merger of Penguin and Random House.

80 Strand, London WC2R 0RL
tel 020-7010 3000
Managing Director, PRH Children's Francesca Dow, *Managing Director, Michael Joseph* Lousie Moore, *Managing Director, Penguin General* Joanna Prior, *Managing Director, Penguin Press* Stefan McGrath, *Group Sales Director* Mike Symons

61–63 Uxbridge Road, London, W5 5SA
tel 020-8579 2652
Mananing Director, Transworld Publishers Larry Finlay

Penguin Digital

tel 020-7840 8400 (Dan Franklin)
email Dfranklin2@penguinrandomhouse.co.uk
tel 020-7840 8400 (Videl Bar-Kar)
email vbar-kar@penguinrandomhouse.co.uk
Digital Publisher Dan Franklin, *Audio Publisher* Videl Bar-Kar

DK (division)

website www.dk.com
Ceo John Duhigg

Illustrated non-fiction for adults and children: gardening, health, medical, travel, food and drink, history, natural history, photography, reference, pregnancy and childcare, film and TV.

Ebury Press (imprint)

tel 020-7840 8400
Deputy Publisher Andrew Goodfellow

General commercial non-fiction, autobiography, memoir, popular history, sport, travel writing, popular science, humour, film/TV tie-ins, music, popular reference, cookery, lifestyle.

Ebury Enterprises

tel 020-7840 8400
Publishing Director Carey Smith

Gift books, branded and bespoke books.

Penguin Random House Children's Division UK (company)

80 Strand, London WC2R 0RL
tel 020-7010 3000
61–63 Uxbridge Road, London W5 5SA
tel 020-8231 6800
website www.penguin.co.uk
website www.kidsatrandomhouse.co.uk
Managing Director Francesca Dow, *Publisher* Annie Eaton (fiction), *Publisher* Amanda Punter (fiction), *Publisher* Juliet Matthews (media & entertainment), *Editorial Director* Alice Blacker (picture books), *Commissioning Editor* Andrea MacDonald (picture books), *Head of Licensing & Consumer Products* Susan Bolsover, *New Business Manager* Rich Haines (licensing & consumer products), *Art Director* Anna Bilson.

Children's paperback and hardback books: wide range of picture books, board books, gift books and novelties; fiction; non-fiction, popular culture, digital and audio. Pre-school illustrated developmental books for 0–6 years; licensed brands; children's classic publishing and merchandising properties. No unsolicited MSS or original artwork or text. Imprints: Ladybird, Puffin, Penguin, Bantam Press, Bodley Head Children's Books, Jonathan Cape Children's Books, Corgi Children's Books, Doubleday Children's Books, Hutchinson Children's Books, Red Fox Children's Books.

Tamarind Books (imprint)

tel 020-8231 6800
email info@tamarindbooks.co.uk
website www.tamarindbooks.co.uk

Olympia
Publishers

Olympia Publishers are one of the fastest growing independant publishing companies located in the heart of London.

We strive to make publishing an enjoyable and rewarding experience for authors, enabling them to gain the success that they deserve.

Our dedicated Editorial, Production and Maketing teams make this a reality.

Authors Welcome

You may submit a synopsis and three sample chapters **online** by visiting our website: **www.olympiapublishers.com** or submit by post:

Submissions
Olympia Publishers
60 Cannon Street
London
EC4N 6NP

T: 0203 755 3166
E: editors@olympiapublishers.com

 @OLYMPIAPUB    /OLYMPIAPUBLISHERS

Elliot Mackenzie Publishers Ltd

Pegasus Elliot Mackenzie Publishers Ltd has been publishing high quality books for more than fifteen years. We use a combination of traditional publishing methods as well as the latest in technology to maximise the potential of each book.

Our dedicated and knowledgeable team support the author throughout all stages: editorial, graphics and marketing and promotion, working with them to produce a first-rate book that is attractive and marketable.

We have a wide range of contacts worldwide and welcome submissions from both new and previously published authors from the UK and overseas.

Our separate imprints ensure that we can include a wide variety of genres, including fiction, non-fiction, children's books, poetry and erotica.

Vanguard Press   Nightingale Books   Pegasus   Chimera

Authors are invited to submit sample chapters and a synopsis.

Visit our website and submit online at:
www.pegasuspublishers.com

Sheraton House, Castle Park, Cambridge, CB3 0AX
Telephone 01223 370012 Fax 01223 370040

Deputy Publisher Sue Buswell

Multicultural children's books. Fiction: picture books (4–8 years), board books for babies (0–3 years), board books for toddlers (2–5 years). Non-fiction: biography (8–12 years). Books feature on National Curriculum. Founded 1987.

Will consider unsolicited MSS with sae. Allow one month for response. Looking for books which give black children a high positive profile.

Razorbill (imprint)
Publisher Amanda Punter
Commercial teen fiction. Launched 2010.

BBC, Ladybird, Warne
Category Publisher, Warne Nicole Pearson, *Editorial Director, Ladybird* Heather Crossley, *Publisher, Media & Entertainment* Juliet Matthews, *Publishing Director, Media & Entertainment* Eric Huang, *Art Director, Media & Entertainment* Kirstie Billingham, *Creative Director* Ronnie Fairweather

Specialises in preschool illustrated developmental books for 0–6 years, non-fiction 0–8 years; licensed brands; children's classic publishing and merchandising properties. No unsolicited MSS.

Phaidon Press Ltd
Regent's Wharf, All Saints Street, London N1 9PA
tel 020-7843 1000
email enquiries@phaidon.com
website www.phaidon.com
Managing Director James Booth-Clibborn, *Publishers* Emilia Terragni, Deborah Aaronson

Visual arts, lifestyle and culture.

Phoenix Yard Books
Phoenix Yard, 65 King's Cross Road,
London WC1X 9LW
tel 020-7239 4968
email hello@phoenixyardbooks.com
website www.phoenixyardbooks.com

Picture books, poetry and fiction for 3–13 age group. Particularly seeking young fiction (6–9 years). Please read the detailed submissions guidelines on website before submitting.

Piccadilly Press
5 Castle Road, London NW1 8PR
tel 020-7267 4492
email books@piccadillypress.co.uk
website www.piccadillypress.co.uk
Managing Director & Publisher Brenda Gardner

Picture books, children's fiction, young adult fiction, series fiction, parental advice trade paperbacks. Publishes approx. 25–30 titles each year and has over 200 in print. Successes include *Letters from an Alien Schoolboy* by Ros Asquith, *Downtown Dinosaurs: Dinosaur Olympics* by Jeanne Willis, *Don't Panic, Annika!* by Juliet Clare Bell and Jennifer E. Morris

and *My Humongous Hamster* by Lorna Freytag. Founded 1983.

Will consider unsolicited MSS. Send synopsis and 3 sample chapters plus sae. Allow 6 weeks for response. Interested in publishing young adult books that deal with contemporary issues.

Picthall & Gunzi Ltd
21A Widmore Road, Bromley, Kent BR1 1RW
tel 020-8460 4032
email chez@picthallandgunzi.demon.co.uk
email chris@picthallandgunzi.demon.co.uk
website www.picthallandgunzi.com
Managing Director Chez Picthall, *Publisher & Editorial Director* Christiane Gunzi

High-quality, photographically illustrated non-fiction for children: activity books, board books, novelty books, early learning. Age groups: preschool and KS1. Acquired by Award Publications Ltd (page 40).

Point – see Scholastic Ltd

Pont Books – see Gomer Press

Poolbeg Press Ltd†
123 Grange Hill, Baldoyle, Dublin 13,
Republic of Ireland
tel +353 (0)1 8063825
email info@poolbeg.com
website www.poolbeg.com
Directors Kieran Devlin (managing), Paula Campbell (publisher)

Children's and teenage fiction. Also adult popular fiction, non-fiction, current affairs. Imprints: Poolbeg, Ina Nut Shell. Founded 1976.

Portland Press Ltd*
Charles Darwin House, 12 Roger Street,
London WC1N 2JL
tel 020-7685 2410
email editorial@portlandpress.com
website www.portlandpress.com
Head of Publishing Niamh O'Connor

Biochemistry and molecular life science books for graduate, postgraduate and research students. Illustrated science books for children: *Making Sense of Science* series. Founded 1990.

Priddy Books
Chancery House, 53–64 Chancery Lane,
London WC2A 1QT
tel 020-7418 5515
website www.priddybooks.com
Publisher Roger Priddy, *Operations Director* Sally Poulson

Specialises in baby/toddler and preschool books: activity books, board books, novelty books, picture books.

Prim-Ed Publishing
Bosheen, New Ross, Co. Wexford,
Republic of Ireland

tel 0870 876 0151
email sales@prim-ed.com
website www.prim-ed.com
Managing Director Seamus McGuinness

Educational publisher specialising in copymasters (photocopiable teaching resources) for primary school and special needs lower second level students. Books written by practising classroom teachers.

Puffin – see Penguin Random House UK

Pure Indigo Ltd
Publishing Department, 17 The Herons, Cottenham, Cambridge CB24 8XX
tel 07714 201555
email ashley.martin@pureindigo.co.uk
website www.pureindigo.co.uk/publishing
Commissioning Editor Ashley Martin

Pure Indigo Publishing develops innovative junior series fiction. All titles are available in both print and digital formats and are distributed internationally with select partners. The company also develops software products that complement the product range. The junior series fiction titles are developed in-house and on occassion authors and illustrators are commissioned to complete project-based work. For consideration for commissions visit the website. Not currently accepting submissions.

QED Publishing
6 Blundell Street, London N7 9BH
tel 020-7812 8600
email qedpublishing@quarto.com
website www.qed-publishing.co.uk
website www.quarto.com
Publisher Zeta Jones, *Editorial Director* Victoria Garrard

Edutainment is the key focus of QED's approach – aims to both educate and entertain. Humour, fresh design and great illustrations combine to make learning engaging and fun for children 4–11 years. QED's diverse range of titles covers innovative non-fiction to clever and original picture books.

The Quarto Group, Inc.
The Old Brewery, 6 Blundell Street, London N7 9BH
tel 020-7700 9000
email info@quarto.com
website www.quarto.com
Chairman Timothy Chadwick, *Ceo* Marcus Leaver, *Chief Financial Officer* Mick Mousley, *Director, Quarto International Co-editions Group* David Breuer, *President & Ceo, Quarto Publishing Group USA* Ken Fund, *Managing Director, Quarto Publishing Group UK* David Inman

The Quarto Group is a leading global illustrated book publisher and distribution group. It is composed of three publishing divisions; Quarto International Co-editions Group; Quarto Publishing Group USA; and

Quarto Publishing Group UK; plus Books & Gifts Direct (a direct seller of books and gifts in Australia and New Zealand) and Regent Publishing Services, a specialist print services company based in Hong Kong. Quarto has nine children's imprints across its three publishing divisions; these are: Quarto International Co-editions Group (Quarto Children's Books, QED Publishing, Ivy Kids, small world creations, words & pictures, Marshall Children's Books); Quarto Publishing Group UK (Wide Eyed Editions, Frances Lincoln Children's Books); Quarto Publishing Group US (Walter Foster Jr.).

Quest – see Top That! Publishing plc

Ragged Bears Ltd
79 Acreman St., Sherborne, Dorset DT9 3PH
tel (01935) 816933
email books@ragged-bears.co.uk
website www.ragged-bears.co.uk
Managing Director Pamela Shirley

Preschool picture and novelty books, first chapter books to young teen fiction. Emailed submissions preferred but if posted send sae. Do not send original artwork. Imprint: Ragged Bears. Founded 1994.

Raintree – see Pearson UK

Ransom Publishing Ltd
Unit 7, Brocklands Farm, West Meon GU32 1JN
tel (01730) 829091
email ransom@ransom.co.uk
website www.ransom.co.uk
Directors Jenny Ertle (managing), Steve Rickard (creative)

Teen fiction, reading programmes and books for children and adults who are reluctant and struggling readers. Range covers high interest age/low reading age titles, quick reads, reading schemes and titles for young able readers. Series include *Reading Stars*, *The Outer Reaches*, *Shades 2.0*, *Boffin Boy*, *PIG* and *Dark Man*. Email for submission guidelines. Founded 1995.

Red Bird Publishing
Kiln Farm, East End Green, Brightlingsea, Colchester, Essex CO7 0SX
tel (01206) 303525
email info@red-bird.co.uk
website www.red-bird.co.uk
Publisher Martin Rhodes-Schofield

Innovative children's activity packs and books produced with a mix of techniques and materials such as Glow in the Dark, Mirrors, Stereoscopic 3D, Moiré and other optical illusions. Authors are specialists in their fields. Activity books, novelty books, picture books, painting and colouring books, teaching books, posters: hobbies, nature and the environment, science. Age groups: preschool, 5–10, 10–15. No unsolicited MSS.

Red Kite Books – see Haldane Mason Ltd

Rigby – see Pearson UK

Rising Stars*
PO Box 105, Rochester, Kent ME2 4BE
tel 0800 091 1602
email info@risingstars-uk.com
website www.risingstars-uk.com
Managing Director Andrea Carr

Educational publisher of books and software for primary school age children. Titles are linked to the National Curriculum Key Stages, QCA Schemes of Work, National Numeracy Framework or National Literacy Strategy. Approach by email with ideas for publishing. Acquired by Hodder Education in January 2015.

Rockpool Children's Books Ltd
6 Kitchener Terrace, Ferryhill,
Co. Durham DL17 8AX
tel 07711 351691
email stuart@rockpoolchildrensbooks.com
website www.rockpoolchildrensbooks.com
Publisher & Creative Director Stuart Trotter

Picture and board books, apps and ebooks. Blog: www.rockpoolchildrensbooks.blogspot.com. Founded 2006.

SAGE Publications Ltd*
1 Oliver's Yard, 55 City Road, London EC1Y 1SP
tel 020-7324 8500
email info@sagepub.co.uk
website www.uk.sagepub.com

Founded over 50 years ago, SAGE is an independent publisher of books and resources for education professionals. Primary/elementary education and children's development.

Salariya Book Company Ltd
Book House, 25 Marlborough Place,
Brighton BN1 1UB
tel (01273) 603306
email salariya@salariya.com
website www.salariya.com
Managing Director David Salariya

Children's art, picture books, fiction and non-fiction. Imprints: Book House, Scribblers, Scribo. Founded 1989.

Schofield & Sims Ltd
Dogley Mill, Fenay Bridge, Huddersfield HD8 0NQ
tel (01484) 607080
email post@schofieldandsims.co.uk
website www.schofieldandsims.co.uk
Chairman C.N. Platts

Educational: nursery, infants, primary; posters. Founded 1901.

Scholastic Ltd*
Euston House, 24 Eversholt Street,
London NW1 1DB
tel 020-7756 7756
website www.scholastic.co.uk
Chairman M.R. Robinson, *Co-Group Managing Directors* Catherine Bell, Steve Thompson

Children's fiction, non-fiction and picture books, education resources for primary schools. Owned by Scholastic Inc. Founded 1964.

Scholastic Children's Books (division)
Euston House, 24 Eversholt Street, London NW1 1DB
tel 020-7756 7761
email submissions@scholastic.co.uk
website www.scholastic.co.uk
UK Publisher Miriam Farbey, *Editorial Director (non-fiction)* Elizabeth Scoggins, *Publisher (fiction & picture books)* Samantha Smith, *Editorial Director (picture, novelty, gift books)* Pauliina Malinen-Teodoro, i Antonia Pelari

Activity books, novelty books, picture books, fiction for 5–12 years, teenage fiction, series fiction and film/TV tie-ins. Recent successes include *Horrible Histories* by Terry Deary and Martin Brown, *His Dark Materials* trilogy by Philip Pullman, *The Hunger Games* by Suzanne Collins, and *Tabby McTat, Stick Man, Zog, Tiddler*, and *The Highway Rat* by Julia Donaldson and Axel Scheffler. Imprints: Scholastic, Alison Green Books, Marion Lloyd Books, Klutz.

No unsolicited manuscripts. Unsolicited illustrations are accepted, but do not send any original artwork as it will not be returned.

The Chicken House
See page 42.

Scholastic Educational Resources (division)
Book End, Range Road, Witney, Oxon OX29 0YD
tel (01993) 893456
Managing Director Gordon Knowles

Professional books, classroom materials and online resources for primary teachers.

Scholastic Book Fairs (division)
See page 93.

Scripture Union
207–209 Queensway, Bletchley, Milton Keynes, Bucks. MK2 2EB
tel (01908) 856000
email info@scriptureunion.org.uk
website www.scriptureunion.org.uk
Director of Ministry Development (Publishing) Terry Clutterham

Christian books and bible reading materials for people of all ages; educational and worship resources for churches; adult fiction and non-fiction; children's fiction and non-fiction (age groups: under 5, 5–8

Books

years, 8–10 years and youth). Publishes approx. 40 titles each year for children/young people and has 200–250 in print. Recent successes include The *Bible Storybook* range and *Essential 100* by Whitney Kuniholm. Scripture Union works as a charity in over 120 countries and publishes in approx. 20. Founded 1867.

Will not consider unsolicited MSS.

SEN Press Ltd
41 Station Road, Smallford, St Albans, Herts AL4 0HB
tel (01727) 825761
email info@senpress.co.uk
website www.senpress.co.uk
Publisher Janie Nicholas

Literacy and Life Skills resources for 14–19 years with special needs. Founded 2003.

Simon & Schuster UK Ltd*
222 Gray's Inn Road, London WC1X 8HB
tel 020-7316 1900
email enquiries@simonandschuster.co.uk
website www.simonandschuster.co.uk
Directors Ian Chapman (Ceo), Lara Hancock (children's picture books), Meg Wang (licensed character list)

Adult non-fiction (history, biography, current affairs, science, political, popular culture, sports books and memoirs). Adult fiction (mass-market, literary fiction, historical fiction, commercial women's fiction, general fiction). Bespoke and illustrated titles. Children's and young adult fiction, picture books, novelty, pop-up and licensed character. Founded 1986.

Simon & Schuster Audioworks
Fiction, non-fiction and business.

Smart Learning
PO Box 321, Cambridge CB1 2XU
tel (01223) 477550
email admin@smart-learning.co.uk
website www.smart-learning.co.uk

High-quality teaching and learning resources for both teachers and children – from Foundation Stage through to KS3. Publishes software and books to enhance the teaching and learning of ICT, phonics, literacy, PSHE and citizenship and English.

Stacey International
19 Catherine Place, LondonSW1E 6DX
tel 020-7221 7166
email info@stacey-international.co.uk
website www.stacey-international.co.uk
Founder Tom Stacey

Illustrated books for children 3–12 years. Publishers of the *Musgrove* series.

Storysack Ltd
Grange House, 2 Geddings Road, Hoddesdon Herts EN11 0NT
tel (01992) 454636
email enquiries@storysack.com
website www.storysack.com

Storysacks for children 3+ years. Storysacks are cloth bags of resources to encourage children and parents to enjoy reading together. Each sack is based around a picture story book with a supporting fact book on a similar theme, a parent guide, characters and a game. Founded 1999.

Strawberry Jam Books
1 Sugworth Lane, Radley, Abingdon OX14 2HZ
email strawberryjambooks@live.co.uk
website www.hilaryhawkes.co.uk/strawberryjambooks
Key contacts Hilary Hawkes (general & editorial), David Hawkes (website)

Childrens' books and resources for preschool–12 years. A non-profit social enterprise producing children's stories and resources that promote kindness, friendship, understanding of differences, feelings and emotions and disabilities and inclusion. Website provides free downloadable stories and resources. Also purchasable print book versions and teaching resources for primary schools or children's groups. Donates story and gift packs to qualifying beneficiary groups. All works are written or created in-house. No unsolicited MSS. Founded 2012.

Strident Publishing Ltd
22 Strathwhillan Drive, Hairmyres, Glasgow G75 8GT
tel (01355) 220588
email info@stridentpublishing.co.uk
website www.stridentpublishing.co.uk
Executive Director Keith Charters, *Commissioning Editor* Alison Stroak

Fiction for children 7–18 years, including young adult/adult crossover, 7+ years: 'timeless classic' feel, 9+ years: general, teen: general, but especially contemporary social realism, young adult/adult crossover: high quality accessible (often edgy) literature. Publishes approx. 15 books a year. Renowned for taking provocative young adult titles and for the energetic marketing of all of its titles. Works closely with authors who present in schools/at festivals. Authors include: young adult/adult: Gillian Philip (*Firebrand*) and Janne Teller (*Nothing*); teen: Linda Strachan (*Spider* – winner of the Catalyst Award); 9+ years D.A. Nelson (*DarkIsle* – winner of the Scottish Children's Book Awards), Catherine MacPhail (*Granny Nothing*), Matt Cartney (*The Sons of Rissouli*), Nick Green (*The Cat Kin*) and Hazel Allan (*Bree McCready*); 7+ years: Emma Barnes (*Jessica Haggerthwaite* – Branford Boase shortlisted) and Paul Biegel (*The King of the Copper Mountains*).

Email proposed blurb together with the first 3 chapters and covering letter stating why book is likely to appeal to readers. Founded 2005.

Stripes – see Little Tiger Group

Studio Fun International Ltd

The Ice House, 124–126 Walcot Street,
Bath BA1 5BG
tel (01225) 463401
email jennifer.fifield@studiofun.com
website www.studiofun.com
International Director Jennifer Fifield

Innovative, high-quality books designed to encourage children to use their creativity and imagination. Board, novelty, film/TV tie-ins. Licensed characters and brands. Also a wide range of children's religious titles. Fully owned subsidiary of Reader's Digest Association Inc. Founded 1981.

Sweet Cherry Publishing*

Unit E, Vulcan Business Complex, Vulcan Road,
Leicester LE5 3EB
tel 0116 212 9780
email info@sweetcherrypublishing.com
website www.sweetcherrypublishing.com
Director Mr A. Thadha

Children's series fiction specialist. Children's picture books, novelty books, gift books, board books, educational books and series fiction for all ages. Also welcomes young adult novels especially trilogies or series fiction. Likes to publish a set of books as a box set or in a slipcase. See website for submission guidelines. Founded 2011.

Tamarind Books – see Penguin Random House UK

Tango Books Ltd

PO Box 32595, London W4 5YD
tel 020-8996 9970
email sheri@tangobooks.co.uk
email edith@tangobooks.co.uk
website www.tangobooks.co.uk
Directors Sheri Safran, David Fielder, Submissions Edith Fricker (tel 020-8996 9973)

Creates and produces international co-productions of children's novelty books only (touch-and-feel, flaps, pop-ups, foils, etc). Publishes in UK under Tango Books imprint. No flat picture books. Produces mainly for 0–6 years but some for up to 12 years. Books are highly visual with lots of illustrations and minimal text, except for non-fiction where there is scope for longer texts. Big multicultural novelty book list. Founded 1983.

The max. word count for 0–6 years is 500 words. Text should be for novelty format (repetition works well). No particularly British themes or characters. No poetry. Artwork: modern style, fresh and fun. Likes collage, bright and bold styles, pen and ink coloured in; less keen on watercolour unless very special. Send submissions with sae for their return or preferably by email. Allow one month for reply.

Tarquin Publications

Suite 74, 17 Holywell Hill, St Albans AL1 1DT
tel (01727) 833866

email info@tarquinbooks.com
website www.tarquinbooks.com
Director Andrew Griffin

Mathematical models, puzzles, codes and logic and paper engineering books for intelligent children. Publishes 7–8 titles each year and has 103 in print. Recent successes include Magic Moving Images and Mini Mathematical Murder Mysteries. Founded 1970.
Do not send unsolicited MSS. Send a one-page proposal of idea.

Taylor & Francis Group*

2 and 4 Park Square, Milton Park, Abingdon,
Oxon OX14 4RN
tel 020-7017 6000
email info@tandf.co.uk
website www.tandf.co.uk
website www.informa.com
Managing Director, Taylor & Francis Books Ian Bannerman

Academic and reference books, including education. Imprints include CRC Press, Europa, Garland Science, Psychology Press, Routledge, Spon and Taylor & Francis.

Tech-it-Forward

email forward@press-alt.com
website www.press-alt.com

Tech-it-Forward is an independent publishing house researching publishing in the field of tech-education. The company aims to publish distinctive, innovative and original titles beyond the curriculum. Imprint: Tif. Members of JISC TechDis and Load 2 Learn. Founded 2014.

The Templar Company Ltd

The Granary, North Street, Dorking,
Surrey RH4 1DN
tel (01306) 876361
email info@templarco.co.uk
email submissions@templarco.co.uk (submissions)
website www.templarco.co.uk
Directors Mike McGrath (managing), Amanda Wood (creative), Helen Bowe (sales & marketing)

Publisher and packager of high-quality illustrated children's books, including novelty books, picture books, pop-up books, board books, fiction, non-fiction and gift titles. Send submissions via email.

Three Hares Publishing

4 Winton Avenue, London N11 2AT
tel 020-8245 2606
email hello@threeharespress.com
website www.threeharespublishing.com
Publisher Yasmin Standen

Looking for submissions and will consider fiction/non-fiction, novels, children's books, short stories. No picture books. Published a number of established authors and first-time authors. Interested in

Books

discovering new talent. Visit website for submission guidelines, online submissions only via website. Founded 2014.

TickTock Books Ltd

Carmelite House, 50 Victoria Embankment, London EC4Y 0DZ
tel 023-122 6400
email info@octopus-publishing.co.uk
website www.ticktockbooks.com

Imprint of Octopus Books. A growing children's imprint, publishing fun non-fiction and activity books. Publishes from popular science for older kids to hands-on novelty for preschool.

Tide Mill Press – see Top That! Publishing plc

Titan Books

144 Southwark Street, London SE1 0UP
tel 020-7620 0200
website www.titanbooks.com
Publisher & Managing Director Nick Landau

Graphic novels, including *Simpsons* and *Batman*, featuring comic-strip material; film/TV tie-ins and cinema reference books. No fiction or children's proposals, no email submissions and no unsolicited material without preliminary letter. Email or send large sae for current author guidelines. Division of Titan Publishing Group Ltd. Founded 1981.

Top That! Publishing plc

Marine House, Tide Mill Way, Woodbridge, Suffolk IP12 1AP
tel (01394) 386651
email customerservice@topthatpublishing.com
website www.topthatpublishing.com
Chairman Barrie Henderson, Directors David Henderson (managing), Simon Couchman (creative), Stuart Buck (production), Ian Peacock (financial), Daniel Graham (editorial), Steve Munnings (sales)

Children's activity books, novelty books, picture books, reference, character, gift books, early learning books, apps and digital animations. Imprint: Top That Publishing. Founded 1999.

Trentham Books

(imprint of the Institute of Education Press)
20 Bedford Way, London WC1H 0AL
tel 020-7911 5383 (production), or 020-7911-5563 (editorial)
email trenthambooks@ioe.ac.uk

Education (including specialist fields – multi-ethnic issues, equal opportunities, bullying, design and technology, early years), social policy, sociology of education, European education, women's studies. Does not publish books for use by parents or children, or fiction, biography, reminiscences and poetry.

Troika Books

Well House, Green Lane, Ardleigh, Colchester, Essex CO7 7PD

tel (01206) 233333
email martin-west@btconnect.com
website www.troikabooks.com
Publisher Martin West, Rights Petula Chaplin, Publicity & Marketing Andrea Reece, Editor Jess West

Publishes children's books from picture books through to young adult. Including early readers, fiction for 7–9 years, poetry. Founded 2012.

Usborne Publishing Ltd

Usborne House, 83–85 Saffron Hill, London EC1N 8RT
tel 020-7430 2800
email mail@usborne.co.uk
website www.usborne.com
Publishing Director Jenny Tyler, Editorial Director, Fiction Rebecca Hill, General Manager Robert Jones

Baby books, novelty books, activity books, picture books, fiction for children 6–8 and 9–12 years, young adult fiction, series fiction, ebooks, reference, poetry and audio. Reference subjects include practical, craft, natural history, science, languages, history, art, activities, geography. Publishes 300 titles each year and has about 2,500 in print. Founded 1973.

Looking for high-quality imaginative children's fiction. No unsolicited MSS.

Wacky Bee Books

Shakespeare House, 168 Lavender Hill, London SW11 5TG
020-7801 6300
email hello@wackybeebooks.com
website www.wackbeebooks.com
Director Louise Jordan

Publishing books with a buzz for children 5–12 years. No picture books or young adult fiction. First title *Geronimo, the Dog Who Thinks He's a Cat* by Jessie Wall. IPG member. Submission enquires by email to submissions@wackybeebooks.com. Founded 2014.

Walker Books Ltd*

87 Vauxhall Walk, London SE11 5HJ
tel 020-7793 0909
website www.walker.co.uk
Directors Roger Alexander (chairman, non-executive), Karen Lotz (group managing), Ian Mablin (non-executive), James Cunningham (group finance), Jane Winterbotham (publishing), Ed Ripley (sales & marketing), Alan Lee (production), Helen McAleer (development), Annette Watson (business affairs), Sharon Kelly (HR), Alan Mitchell (UK finance), Publishers Deirdre McDermott, Caroline Royds, Denise Johnstone-Burt, Gill Evans, Donna Cassanova

Activity books, novelty books, picture books, fiction for 5–8 and 9–12 years, young adult fiction, series fiction, film/TV tie-ins, plays, poetry, digital and audio. Publishes approx. 300 titles each year and has 1,700 in print. Recent successes include the *Alex Rider* series by Anthony Horowitz, *Chaos Walking* by Patrick Ness, *Maisy* by Lucy Cousins, *Where's Wally?* by Martin Handford, the *Mortal Instruments* series by Cassandra Clare, *I Want My Hat Back* by Jon Klassen, *A Bit Lost* by Chris Haughton and *Pop-up London* by Jennie Maizels. Imprint: Walker Books and Walker Entertainment. Founded 1980. Write to the Editor. Allow 3 months for response. Founded 1980.

Ward Lock Educational Co. Ltd

BIC Ling Kee House, 1 Christopher Road, East Grinstead, West Sussex RH19 3BT
tel (01342) 318980
email wle@lingkee.com
website www.wardlockeducational.com
Director Wai Kwok Allen Au

Primary and secondary pupil materials, Kent Mathematics Project: *KMP BASIC* and *KMP Main* series covering Reception to GCSE, *Reading Workshops*, *Take Part* series and *Take Part* starters, teachers' books, music books, *Target* series for the National Curriculum: *Target Science* and *Target Geography*, religious education. Founded 1952.

Warne – see Penguin Random House UK

Franklin Watts – see Hachette Children's Group

The Watts Publishing Group Ltd – see Hachette Children's Group

Wayland – see Hachette Children's Group

Wildgoose Education Ltd

(Pictorial Charts Educational Trust)
Unit 3, Coalville Business Park, Jackson Street, Coalville, Leics. LE67 3NR
tel (01530) 518568
email enquires@wildgoose.ac
website www.wildgoose.ac

Developers and distributors of educational resources for primary and secondary teachers. Resource packs, photopacks and posters.

WingedChariot Press

7 Court Royal, Eridge Road, Tunbridge Wells, Kent TN4 8HT
email apps@wingedchariot.com
website www.wingedchariot.com
Director Neal Hoskins

Children's books in translation. Founded 2005.

Wordsworth Editions Ltd

8B East Street, Ware, Herts. SG12 9HJ
tel (01920) 465167
email enquiries@wordsworth-editions.com
website www.wordsworth-editions.com
Managing Director Helen Trayler

Reprints of classic books: literary; children's classics; poetry; reference; Special Editions; mystery and supernatural. Because the company specialises in out-of-copyright titles, it is not able to consider new material for publication. Founded 1987.

Y Lolfa Cyf

Talybont, Ceredigion SY24 5HE
tel (01970) 832304
email ylolfa@ylolfa.com
website www.ylolfa.com
Director Garmon Gruffudd, *Editor* Lefi Gruffudd

Welsh-language books; Welsh-language tutors; Welsh- and Celtic-interest books in English. Popular biographies and sports books in English. Founded 1967.

York Notes – see Pearson UK

ZigZag Education

Unit 3, Greenway Business Centre, Doncaster Road, Bristol BS10 5PY
tel 0117 950 3199
email submissions@publishmenow.co.uk
website www.zigzageducation.co.uk
website www.publishmenow.co.uk
Development Director John-Lloyd Hagger, *Strategy Director* Mike Stephens

Teaching resources for UK secondary schools: English, maths, ICT, geography, history, science, business studies, politics. Founded 1998.

ZooBooKoo International Ltd

4 Gurdon Road, Grundisburgh, Woodbridge, Suffolk IP13 6XA
tel (01473) 735346
email karen@zoobookoo.com
website www.zoobookoo.com
Sales Director Karen Wattleworth

Designer/manufacturer of ZooBooKoo Original Cube Books, multi-level educational folding cube books. Recent successes include *World Football, Human Body, Kings and Queens, French Phrases* and *United Kingdom*.

Books

Children's book publishers overseas

Listings are given for children's book publishers in Australia (below), Canada (page 62), France (page 64), Germany (page 65), Italy (page 66), the Netherlands (page 66), New Zealand (page 66), South Africa (page 67), Spain (page 69) and the USA (page 69).

AUSTRALIA

Member of the Australian Publishers Association

ACER Press

19 Prospect Hill Road, Private Bag 55, Camberwell, Victoria 3124
tel +61 (0)3 9277 5555
email info@acer.edu.au
website www.acer.edu.au
General Manager/Publisher Ben Dawe

Publisher of the Australian Council for Educational Research. Produces a range of books and assessments including professional resources for teachers, psychologists and special needs professionals.

Allen & Unwin Pty Ltd*

83 Alexander Street, Crows Nest, NSW 2065
postal address PO Box 8500, St Leonards, NSW 1590
tel +61 (0)2 8425 0100
email info@allenandunwin.com
website www.allenandunwin.com
Chairman Patrick Gallagher, *Exectuive Director* Paul Donovan, *Ceo* Robert Gorman, *Finance Director* David Martin, *Group Publishing Director* Sue Hines, *Publishing Director* Tom Gilliatt, *Publishing Director – Books for Children & Young Adults* Eva Mills

Picture books, fiction for children 5–8 and 9–12 years, teenage fiction, series fiction, narrative non-fiction and poetry. Also adult/general trade books, including fiction, academic, especially social science and history. Imprint: Allen & Unwin. Founded 1990.
Will consider unsolicited MSS (but not picture book texts). Prefers to receive full MSS by post, with a brief synopsis and biography. Allow 3 months for response. Seeking junior fiction, quirky non-fiction by wise, funny, inventive authors with a distinctive voice.

Bloomsbury Publishing PTY Limited

(Sydney office of Bloomsbury Publishing)
Level 4, 387 George St, Sydney, NSW 2000
tel +61 (0)2 8820 4900
email au@bloomsbury.com
website www.bloomsbury.com
Managing Director Kate Cubitt

Supports the worldwide publishing activities of Bloomsbury Publishing: caters for the Australia and New Zealand territories. See Bloomsbury Children's & Educational Division on page 40.

Cengage Learning Australia*

Level 7, 80 Dorcas Street, South Melbourne, Victoria 3205
tel +61 (0)3 9685 4111
website www.cengage.com.au
Educational books.

Hachette Australia Pty Ltd*

Level 17, 207 Kent Street, Sydney, NSW 2000
tel +61 (0)2 8248 0800
email auspub@hachette.com.au
website www.hachette.com.au
Directors Richard Kitson (Ceo), Louise Sherwin-Stark, David Cocking, Fiona Hazard, Justin Ractliffe, Phill Knight (ADS)

General, children's: picture books, fiction for children 5–8 and 9–12 years, teenage fiction and series fiction. Accepts MSS via website: www.hachette.com.au/manuscriptsubmissions

HarperCollins Publishers (Australia) Pty Ltd Group*

postal address PO Box A565, Sydney South, NSW 1235
tel +61 (0)2 9952 5000
website www.harpercollins.com.au
Publishing Director Shona Martyn, *Head of Children's* Cristina Cappelutto

Literary fiction and non-fiction, popular fiction, children's, reference, biography, autobiography, current affairs, sport, lifestyle, health/self-help, humour, true crime, travel, Australiana, history, business, gift, religion. Now accepting unsolicited submissions online through *The Wednesday Post*. Visit www.wednesdaypost.com.au for more details.

Little Hare Books*

Level 4, 50 Yeo Street, Neutral Bay, NSW 2089
tel +61 (0)2 9908 8222
email info@hardiegrantegmont.com.au
website http://hardiegrant.com.au/egmont/little-hare-books

Publishes high-quality children's books in Australia, New Zealand and the UK: early childhood, picture books, fiction and puzzle/activity books.
Check website for details of when submissions are accepted. In January 2010, Little Hare became an imprint of Hardie Grant Egmont.

McGraw-Hill Education*

Level 2, The Everglade Building, 82 Waterloo Road, North Ryde NSW 2113

Books

postal address Private Bag 2233, Business Centre, North Ryde, NSW 1670
tel +61 (0)2 9900 1800
website www.mcgraw-hill.com.au/
Publishing Director Nicole Meehan, *Managing Director* Cindy Jones

Educational publisher: higher education, primary education and professional (including medical, general and reference). Division of the McGraw-Hill Companies. Founded 1964.

Always looking for potential authors. Has a rapidly expanding publishing programme. See website for author's guide.

New Frontier Publishing*

Suite 3 Level 2, 18 Aquatic Drive, Frenchs Forest, NSW 2086
tel +61 (0)2 9453 1525
email info@newfrontier.com.au
website www.newfrontier.com.au
Director Peter Whitfield

Aims to uplift, educate and inspire through its range of children's books. Activity books, picture books, fiction, dictionaries, textbooks. Caters for 5–10 year-olds.

Unsolicited MSS accepted. Understanding of existing list crucial. Downloadable submissions pack available via website.

Pan Macmillan Australia Pty Ltd*

Level 25, 1 Market Street, Sydney, NSW 2000
tel +61 (0)2 9285 9100
email pansyd@macmillan.com.au
website www.panmacmillan.com.au
Directors Cate Paterson (publishing), Katie Crawford (sales), Tracey Cheetham (publicity & marketing)

Commercial and literary fiction; children's fiction, non-fiction and character products; non-fiction; sport.

Penguin Australia Pty Ltd*

707 Collins Street, Melbourne, Victoria 3008
tel +61 (0)3 9811 2400
postal address PO Box 23360, Melbourne, VIC 8012
website www.penguin.com.au
Managing Director Gabrielle Coyne, *Publishing Director – Books for Children & Young Adults* Laura Harris, *Associate – Books for Children & Young Adults* Jane Godwin, *Executive Editor* Lisa Riley

Picture books, fiction for children 5–8 and 9–12 years, teenage fiction, series fiction and film/TV tie-ins. Also for adults: fiction and general non-fiction. Publishes approx. 85 titles each year and has about 500 in print. Recent successes include *Cuthbert's Babies* by Pamela Allen (picture book), *Rascal* books by Paul Jennings (younger readers) and *Saving Francesca* by Melina Marchetta (young adult). Children's imprints: Puffin (paperback). Part of Penguin Random House. Founded 1935.

Will consider unsolicited MSS but submit only one MS at a time. Send proposals to The Editor, Books for Children and Young Adults, at the postal address (above). Enclose a sae for return of material. Does not accept proposals by email or fax.

Penguin Random House Australia Pty Ltd*

Level 3, 100 Pacific Highway, North Sydney, NSW 2060
tel +61 (0)2 9954 9966
email random@randomhouse.com.au
website www.randomhouse.com.au
Ceo Gabrielle Coyne, *Publishing Director* Nikki Christer, *Director of Marketing, Publicity & Digital ANZ* Sally Bateman, *Head of Publicity & Marketing* Karen Reid

General fiction and non-fiction; children's, illustrated. Imprints: Arrow, Avon, Ballantine, Bantam, Black Swan, Broadway, Century, Chatto & Windus, Corgi, Crown, Dell, Doubleday, Ebury, Fodor, Heinemann, Hutchinson, Jonathan Cape, Knopf, Mammoth UK, Minerva, Pantheon, Pavilion, Pimlico, Random House, Red Fox, Rider, Vermilion, Vintage, Virgin. Subsidiary of Bertelsmann AG. Part of Penguin Random House.

For Random House and Transworld Publishing, unsolicited non-fiction accepted, unbound in hard copy addressed to Submissions Editor. Fiction submissions are only accepted from previously published authors, or authors represented by an agent or accompanied by a report from an accredited assessment service.

Prim-Ed Publishing Pty Ltd

5 Bendsten Place, Balcatta, WA 6021
tel +61 (0)8 9240 9888
website www.prim-ed.com

Educational publisher specialising in blackline master or copymasters and student workbooks for schools and homeschoolers.

Puffin – see Penguin Australia Pty Ltd

University of Queensland Press*

PO Box 6042, St Lucia, Queensland 4067
tel +61 (0)7 3365 7244
email uqp@uqp.uq.edu.au
website www.uqp.com.au
Ceo Greg Bain

Australian children's and young adult fiction. Submissions via agents only. Founded 1948.

Scholastic Australia Pty Ltd*

76–80 Railway Crescent, Lisarow, Gostord, NSW 2250
tel +61 (0)2 4328 3555
website www.scholastic.com.au
Publisher Andrew Berkhut

Children's fiction and non-fiction. Founded 1968.

CANADA

*Member of the Canadian Publishers' Council

†*Member of the Association of Canadian Publishers*

Annick Press Ltd†

15 Patricia Avenue, Toronto, Ontario M2M 1H9
tel +1 416-221-4802
email annickpress@annickpress.com
website www.annickpress.com
Owner/Director Rick Wilks, *Associate Publisher*
Colleen MacMillan, *Creative Director* Sheryl Shapiro,
Office Manager Elaine Burns

Preschool to young adult fiction and non-fiction.
Publishes approx. 24 titles each year. Recent successes
include: (fiction) *Blue Gold* and *War Brothers* (novel
and graphic novel); (non-fiction) *Before the World
Was Ready, Bones Never Lie* and *The Bite of the
Mango*; (picture books) *The Man With the Violin*. To
send MS or illustration submission, please visit the
website www.annickpress.com and view submission
guidelines. Founded 1975.

Approx. 25% of books are by first-time authors.
No unsolicited MSS. For illustrations, query with
samples and sase to Creative Director. Responds in 6
months.

Dundurn Press†

3 Church Street, Suite 500, Toronto,
Ontario M5E 1M2
tel +1 416-214-5544
email kmcmullin@dundurn.com
website www.dundurn.com
Publisher Kirk Howard

Young adult fiction and non-fiction. Founded 1972.

Fitzhenry & Whiteside Ltd

195 Allstate Parkway, Markham, Ontario L3R 4T8
tel +1 800-387-9776
email godwit@fitzhenry.ca
website www.fitzhenry.ca
Publisher Sharon Fitzhenry

Fiction and non-fiction (social studies, visual arts,
biography, environment). Publishes 10 picture books,
5 early readers/chapter books, 6 middle novels and
7 young adult books each year. Founded 1966.

Approx. 10% of books are by first-time authors.
Emphasis is on Canadian authors and illustrators,
subject or perspective. Will review MS/illustration
packages from artists. Submit outline and copy of
sample illustration. For illustrations only, send
samples and promotional sheet. Responds in
3 months. Samples returned with sase.

HarperCollins Publishers Ltd*

2 Bloor Street East, 20th Floor, Toronto,
Ontario M4W 1A8
tel +1 416-975-9334
email hccanada@harpercollins.com
website www.harpercollins.ca
President David Kent

Literary fiction and non-fiction, history, politics,
biography, spiritual and children's books. Founded
1989.

Kids Can Press Ltd†

25 Dockside Drive, Toronto, Ontario M54 0B5
tel +1 416-479-7000
email customerservice@kidscan.com
website www.kidscanpress.com/canada
Editorial Director Yvette Ghione

Juvenile/young adult fiction and non-fiction.
Publishes 16–22 picture books, 8–12 young readers,
10–18 middle readers and 2–3 young adult titles each
year. Recent successes include *Virginia Wolf* by Kyo
Maclear and Isabelle Arsenault, Melanie Watt's
award-winning *Scaredy Squirrel* series, *If the World
Were a Village* by David J. Smith – part of the
CitizenKid series – and the *Binky the Space Cat*
books. Publishers of *Franklin the Turtle* and *Elliot
Moose* characters. Founded 1973.

Approx. 10–15% of books are by first-time
authors. Submit outline/synopsis and 2–3 sample
chapters. For picture books, submit complete MS.
Responds in 6 months. Only accepts MSS from
Canadian authors. Fiction length: picture books –
1,000–2,000 words; young readers – 750–1,500 words;
middle readers – 10,000–15,000 words; young adult –
over 15,000 words. Non-fiction length: picture books –
500–1,250 words; young readers – 750–2,000 words;
middle readers – 5,000–15,000 words.

McGraw-Hill Ryerson Ltd*

300 Water Street, Whitby, Ontario L1N 9B6
tel +1 905-430-5000
website www.mheducation.ca/
President & Ceo David Swail

Educational and trade books.

Madison Press Books

155 Edward Street, Aurora, Ontario L4G 1W5
tel +1 416-923-5027
website www.madisonpressbooks.com
Publisher Oliver Salzmann

Illustrated non-fiction for children 8–12 years.

Nelson Education*

1120 Birchmount Road, Scarborough,
Ontario M1K 5G4
tel +1 416-752-9448
website www.nelson.com
President Greg Nordal, *Senior Vice President & Market
Director, School Division* Chris Besse, *Senior Vice
President, Media & Production Services* Susan Cline,
Senior Vice President, People & Engagement Marlene
Nyilassy

Educational publishing: school (K–12), college and university, career education, measurement and guidance, professional and reference, ESL titles. Division of Thomson Canada Ltd. Founded 1914.

Oberon Press
205–145 Spruce Street, Ottawa, Ontario K1R 6P1
tel +1 613-238-3275
email oberon@sympatico.ca
website www.oberonpress.ca

General fiction, short stories, poetry, some biographies, art and children's. Only publishes Canadian writers.

Orca Book Publishers†
Box 5626, Station B, Victoria, BC, V8R 6S4
tel +1 800-210-5277
email orca@orcabook.com
website www.orcabook.com

Books for children and young adults. Will consider MSS from Canadian writers only. No submissions by fax or email. See website for submission guidelines. No poetry. *Orca Echoes* (for 7–8 years), *Young Readers* (for 8–11 years), juvenile novels (for 9–13 years), *Orca Currents* (intermediate novels aimed at reluctant readers with simple language and short, high-interest chapters), young adult fiction, *Orca Soundings* (high-interest teen novels aimed at reluctant readers). Founded 1984.

Orca Echoes, Orca Young Readers (also called chapter books) and juvenile fiction: Contemporary stories or fantasy with a universal theme, a compelling, unified plot and a strong, sympathetic child protagonist who grows through the course of the story and solves the central problem him/herself. Well-researched stories dealing with, or taking their inspiration from, historical subjects, but not thinly disguised history lessons. Length: *Orca Echoes* 5,500–6,000 words; *Young Readers* 14,000–18,000 words; juvenile fiction 25,000–35,000 words. Send query with sample chapter FAO Children's Book Editor.

Stories for *Orca Currents* should have appropriate storylines for middle school (family issues, humour, sports, adventure, mystery/suspense and fantasy) with strong plots, credible characters/situations. Awkward moralising should be avoided. Protagonists are between 12–14 years old and should be appealing and believable. Length: 14,000–16,000 words; 12–16 short chapters. Send a chapter-by-chapter outline and one sample chapter FAO Melanie Jeffs, Editor.

Teen or young adult fiction: Issue-oriented contemporary stories exploring a universal theme, with a compelling, unified plot and strong, sympathetic protagonist(s). Well-researched stories dealing with, or taking their inspiration from, historical subjects, but not thinly disguised history lessons. Length: up to 50,000 words. Send queries to Teen Fiction Editor.

Orca Soundings: Stories should reflect the universal struggles that young people face. They need not be limited to 'gritty' urban tales but can include adventures, mystery/suspense and fantasy. Interested in humorous stories that will appeal to teens of both sexes. 'Disease-of-the-week' potboilers or awkward moralising should be avoided. Protagonists are between 14–17 years old and should be appealing and believable. Length: 14,000–16,000 words, 12–16 short chapters. Send a chapter-by-chapter outline and one sample chapter FAO Andrew Wooldridge, Editor.

Currently seeking picture book MSS of up to 1,500 words. Submit complete MS FAO Children's Book Editor. No queries.

Pearson Canada*
(formerly Prentice Hall Canada and Addison-Wesley Canada)
26 Prince Andrew Place, Toronto, Ontario M3C 2T8
tel +1 416-447-5101
website www.pearsoned.ca
President Dan Lee

Academic, technical, educational, children's and adult, trade.

Penguin Random House Canada Ltd*
320 Front Street, Suite 1400, Toronto, Ontario M5V 3B6
tel +1 416-364-4449
website www.penguinrandomhouse.ca
Ceo R. Bradley Martin

Literary fiction, commercial fiction, memoir, non-fiction (history, business, current events, sports), adult and children's. No unsolicited MSS; submissions via an agent only. Imprints: Anchor Canada, Allen Lane Canada, Appetite by Random House, Bond Street Books, Doubleday Canada, Emblem, Fenn, Hamish Hamilton Canada, Knopf Canada, McClelland & Stewart, Penguin Canada, Portfolio Canada, Puffin Canada, Random House Canada, Razorbill Canada, Seal Books, Signal, Tundra Books, Viking Canada, Vintage Canada. Subsidiary of Penguin Random House. Formed on I July 2013 as part of the worldwide merger of Penguin and Random House.

Pippin Publishing Corporation
PO Box 242, Don Mills, Ontario M3C 2S2
tel +1 416-510-2918
email jld@pippinpub.com
website www.pippinpub.com
President/Editorial Director Jonathan Lovat Dickson

ESL/EFL, teacher reference, adult basic education, school texts (all subjects), general trade (non-fiction).

Raincoast Books†
2440 Viking Way, Richmond, BC V6V 1N2
tel +1 604-448-7100
email info@raincoast.com
website www.raincoast.com
Ceo John Sawyer

Books

Non-fiction for adults. Fiction and non-fiction for children. Imprints: Polestar, Press Gang.

Will not accept unsolicited MSS. Send a query letter via regular mail for the attention of the Editorial Department. For young adult fiction, submit query letter with a list of publication credits plus one-page outline of the plot. No queries via email. Allow up to 9 months for reply. Only accepts material from Canadian residents.

Red Deer Press

195 Allstate Pky, Markham, Ontario L3R 4T8
tel +1 905-477-9700
email rdp@reddeerpress.com
website www.reddeerpress.com
Publisher Richard Dionne, *Children's Editor* Peter Carver

Literary fiction, sci-fi, non-fiction, children's illustrated books, young adult fiction, teen fiction. Publishes books that are written or illustrated by Canadians and that are about or of interest to Canadians. Imprints: RJS (Robert J. Sawyer) Books (sci-fi). Publishes 14–18 new books per year. Founded 1975.

Children's picture books MSS from established authors with a demonstrable record of publishing success are preferred. Not currently accepting new MSS.

Ronsdale Press†

3350 West 21st Avenue, Vancouver, BC V6S 1G7
tel +1 604-738-4688
email ronsdale@shaw.ca
website www.ronsdalepress.com
Director Ronald B. Hatch

Ronsdale is a Canadian publisher based in Vancouver, BC, with some 250 books in print. Founded 1988.

Scholastic Canada Ltd*

175 Hillmount Road, Markham, Ontario L6C 1Z7
tel +1 905-887-7323
email custserv@scholastic.ca
website www.scholastic.ca
Art Director Andrea Casault

Serves children, parents and teachers through a variety of businesses including Scholastic Book Clubs and Book Fairs, Scholastic Education, Classroom Magazines, Trade and Éditions Scholastic. Publishes recreational reading for children and young people from kindergarten to Grade 8 and educational materials in both official languages. Its publishing focus is on books by Canadians. Wholly owned subsidiary of Scholastic Inc.

No unsolicited MSS. Artists may submit electronic samples of their work along with their website/contact information to the art director. Never send originals. Please visit www.scholastic.ca for information.

Tundra Books

(a division of Random House of Canada Ltd, a Penguin Random House company)
320 Front Street West, Toronto, ON
tel +1 416-364-4449
email tundra@mcclelland.com
website www.penuinrandomhouse.ca
Editorial Director Tara Walker

Publisher of high-quality children's picture books and novels, renowned for its innovations. Publishes books for children to teens. Imprints: Jordan Fenn, Publisher of Fenn/Tundra (sport-themed children's books). Founded 1967.

Whitecap Books Ltd†

210–314 West Cordova Street, Vancouver, BC V6B 1E8
tel +1 604-681-6181
website www.whitecap.ca
President Sharon Fitzhenry, *Publisher* Nick Rundall, *Associate-Publisher* Jesse Marchand

Diverse list features books on food, wine, gardening, health and well-being, regional history and regional guidebooks. Publishes books for children and youth under Walrus Books imprint. Successes include Diane Swanson's *Safari Beneath the Sea* which won the Orbis Pictus Award and Joan Marie Galat's *Dot to Dot in the Sky* series. Market expanded into the United States through Midpoint Books. Founded 1977.

Submissions must be sent by mail. Full details can be found on our website at http://www.whitecap.ca/submissions.

FRANCE

l'écoles des loisirs

11 Rue de Sevres, 75006, Paris
tel +33 (0)1 4222 9410
email edl@ecoledesloisirs.com
website www.ecoledesloisirs.com
Managing Director Louis Delas

Specialises in children's literature from picture books to young adult fiction.

Flammarion

87 quai Panhard et Levassor, 75647 Paris Cedex 13
tel +33 (0)1 4051 3100
website www.flammarion.com
Ceo Teresa Cremisi

Leading French publisher. Children's imprints include: Albums du Père Castor, Castor Poche, Tribal, Etonnants Classiques, GF – Flammarion, Chan – OK. Founded 1875.

Père Castor (imprint)

Children's Publisher Hélène Wadowski
Children's picture books, junior fiction, activity

books, board books, how-to books, comics, gift books, fairy tales, dictionaries and records and tapes. Covers 0–16 years.

Gallimard Jeunesse

5 rue Gaston Gallimard, 75328 Paris
tel +33 (0)1 4954 4200
website www.gallimard-jeunesse.fr
Children's Publisher Hedwige Pasquet

Publisher of high-quality children's fiction and non-fiction including board books, novelty books, picture books, pop-up books. Founded 1911.

Hachette Livre/Gautier-Languereau

43 quai de Grenelle, 75905 Paris Cedex 15
tel +33 (0)1 4392 3000
website www.hachette.com
Director Arnaud Nourry

Picture books and poetry. Publishes approx. 55 titles each year. Recent successes include *Cyrano* by Tai Marc Le Thanh and Rébecca Dautremer and *Princesses* by Philippe Lechermeier and Rébecca Dautremer. Founded 1992.

Will consider unsolicited MSS. Allow 2 months for response.

Kaléidoscope

11 Rue de Sèvres, F–75006 Paris
tel +33 (0)1 4544 0708
email infos@editions-kaleidoscope.com
website www.editions-kaleidoscope.com
Children's Publisher Isabel Finkenstaedt

Specialises in up-market picture books for children 0–6 years. Founded 1988.

Editions Sarbacane

35 Rue d'Hauteville, 75010 Paris
tel +33 (0)1 4246 2400
email e.beulque@sarbacane.net
website www.editions-sarbacane.com
Editorial Director (picture books) Emmanuelle Beulque, *Publisher & Editorial Director (comics & graphic novels)* Frédéric Lavabre, *Foreign Rights (comics & graphic novels)* Sylvain Coissard, *Foreign, TV & Film Rights (picture books & fiction)* Phi-Anh Nguyen

High-quality activity books, board books, picture books and young adult fiction, fiction for children from preschool age to adult.

Le Sorbier

7 rue de Savoie, 75006 Paris
tel +33 (0)1 4046 4320
website www.editionsdelamartiniere.fr
Publisher Françoise Mateu

High-quality picture books for children up to 10 years and illustrated reference books for 9–12 years. Imprint of Editions de la Martiniere.

GERMANY

Carlsen Verlag

Völckersstrasse 14–20, D 22765 Hamburg
tel +49 (0)40 398040
email info@carlsen.de
website www.carlsen.de
Publisher Renate Herre

Children's picture books, board books and novelty books. Illustrated fiction and non-fiction. Teenage fiction and non-fiction. Publishes both German and international authors including Stephenie Meyer, J.K. Rowling and Philip Pullman. Publisher of the *Harry Potter* series. Imprint: Chicken House Deutschland. Age groups: preschool, 5–10, 10–15, 15+. Founded 1953.

Unsolicited MSS welcome but must include a sae for its return. Do not follow up by phone or post. For illustrations, submit no more than 3 colour photocopies and unlimited b&w copies.

Deutscher Taschenbuch Verlag GmbH & Co. KG (dtv junior)

Tumblingerstraße 21, D–80337 Munich
tel +49 (0)89 381672810
email verlag@dtv.de
website www.dtvjunior.de
Children's Publishing Director Susanne Stark

Fiction and non-fiction for children, teenagers and young adults. Authors include Kate Di Camillo, Kevin Brooks, Colleen Hoover, Libba Bray, Eva Ibbotson, Sarah Dessen. Founded 1971.

Carl Hanser Verlag

Vilshofener Strasse 10, 81679 München
tel +49 (0)89 998300
email info@hanser.de
website www.hanser-literaturverlage.de
Children's Publisher Saskia Heintz

High-quality hardback books for all ages from preschool to young adults. Board books, picture books, fiction and non-fiction. Age groups: 3–10, 10–15, 15+. Founded 1993.

Ravensburger Buchverlag

Robert-Bosch-Straße 1, 88214 Ravensburg
tel +49 (0)751 860
email buchverlag@ravensburger.de
website www.ravensburger.de
Ceo Johannes Hauenstein

Activity books, novelty books, picture books, fiction for children 5–8 and 9–12 years, teenage fiction, series fiction and educational games and puzzles. Publishes approx. 450 titles each year and has 1,500 in print. Founded 1883.

Will consider unsolicited MSS for fiction only. Allow 2 months for response.

ITALY

Edizoni Arka srl
Via Raffaello Sanzio, 7–20149, Milan
tel +39 02-4818230
email arka@arkaedizioni.it
website www.arkaedizioni.it
Publisher Ginevra Viscardi

Picture books and some general fiction for preschool children and children up to 10 years.

De Agostini Editore
Via Giovanni da Verrazano, 15, 28100 Novara
tel +39 03-214241
website www.deagostini.it
Publisher Annachiara Tassan

Illustrated and children's books.

Edizioni El/Einaudi Ragazzi/Emme Edizioni
Via J. Ressel 5, 34018 San Dorligo della Valle TS
tel +39 040-3880311
email edizioniel@edizioniel.it
website www.edizioniel.com
Children's Publisher Orietta Fatucci

Activity books, board books, picture books, pop-up books, non-fiction, novels, poetry, fairy tales, fiction. Age groups: preschool, 5–10, 10–15, 15+. Publishes over 270 new titles a year.

Giunti Editore S.p.A.
Via Bolognese, 165–50139, Florence
tel +39 055-50621
email info@giunti.it
website www.giunti.it
President Sergio Giunti

Activity books, board books, novelty books, picture books, colouring books, pop-up books and some educational textbooks.

Arnoldo Mondadori Editore S.p.A. (Mondadori)
Via private Mondadori 1, 20090 Segrate, Milan
tel +39 02-75421
email infolibri@mondadori.it
website www.mondadori.it
Ceo Ernesto Mauri

Activity books, board books, novelty books, picture books, painting and colouring books, pop-up books, how-to books, hobbies, leisure, pets, sport, comics, poetry, fairy tales, education, fiction and non-fiction. Age groups: preschool, 5–10, 10–15, 15+. Founded 1907.

Adriano Salani Editore S.p.A.
Via Gherardini 10, 20145 Milano
tel +39 02-34597624
email info@salani.it
website www.salani.it
Publisher Luigi Spagnol

Picture books, how-to books, comics, gift books, fiction, novels, poetry, fairy tales. Age groups: preschool, 5–10, 10–15, 15+.

THE NETHERLANDS

Lemniscaat BV
Posbus 4066, 3006 AB, Rotterdam
tel +31 10-2062929
email info@lemniscaat.nl
website www.lemniscaat.nl
Publisher Jean Christophe Boele van Hensbroek

Well-known independent children's book publishers based in the Netherlands, publishing picture books, juvenile novels and young adult literature. Lemniscaat has its own list of titles in the Netherlands, China, Italy and the US. Founded 1963.

Rubinstein Publishing
Prinseneiland, 43-1013 LL, Amsterdam
tel +31 20-4200772
email info@rubinstein.nl
website www.rubinstein.nl
Publisher Dik Broekman

Independent publisher specialising in audiobooks for children. Also produces novelty books.

Van Goor
PO Box 97, 3990 DB Houten
tel +31 30-7998300
website www.unieboekspectrum.nl

High-quality picture books, middle-grade and literary fiction for age groups 8 years and older, young adult.

Zirkoon Uitgevers/Baekens Books
Schilpdel II, 2202 VA Noordwijk
tel +31 86-577566
email info@baeckensbooks.nl
Children's Publisher Iris de Roy van Zuydewijn

High-quality picture books, activity books, board books, novelty books, pop-up books, poetry, fiction and some non-fiction.

NEW ZEALAND

*Member of the New Zealand Book Publishers' Association

Cengage Learning New Zealand*
Unit 4ʙ, Rosedale Office Park, 331 Rosedale Road, Albany, North Shore 0632
postal address PO Box 33376, Takapuna, North Shore 0740
tel +64 (0)9 415 6850
General Manager, Higher Education Alex Chamoun

Educational books.

Edify Ltd*
PO Box 36502, Northcote, Auckland 0748
tel +64 (0)9 972 9428

email gethelp@edify.co.nz
website www.edify.co.nz
Ceo Adrian Keane

Edify is a publishing, sales and marketing business providing its partners with opportunities for their products and solutions in the New Zealand educational market. Exclusive representatives of Pearson and the New Zealand based educational publisher, Sunshine Books.

Gecko Press*

PO Box 9335, Marion Square, Wellington 6141
tel +64 (0)4 801 9333
email info@geckopress.com
website www.geckopress.com
Publisher Julia Marshall

Children's books: picture books, junior fiction and non-fiction. Translates and publishes award-winning children's books from around the world. Selects books strong in story, illustration and design, with a strong 'heart factor'. Established 2005.
See website for guidelines.

HarperCollins Publishers (New Zealand) Ltd*

Unit D, 63 Apollo Drive, Rosedale, Auckland 0632
tel +64 (0)9 443 9400
email publicity@harpercollins.co.nz
postal address PO Box 1, Shortland Street, Auckland
website www.harpercollins.co.nz

General literature, non-fiction, reference, children's. HarperCollins New Zealand does not accept proposals or MSS for consideration for publishing, except via the Wednesday Post portal on its website.

McGraw-Hill Book Company New Zealand Ltd*

Level 8, 56–60 Cawley Street, Ellerslie, Auckland
postal address Private Bag 11904, Ellerslie, Auckland 1005
tel +64 (0)9 526 6200
website www.mcgraw-hill.com.au

Educational publisher: higher education, primary and secondary education (grades K–12) and professional (including medical, general and reference). Division of the McGraw-Hill Companies. Founded 1974.
Always looking for potential authors. Has a rapidly expanding publishing programme. See website for author's guide.

New Zealand Council for Educational Research

Box 3237, Education House, 178–182 Willis Street, Wellington 6011
tel +64 (0)4 384 7939
email info@nzcer.org.nz
website www.nzcer.org.nz
Director Robyn Baker, *Publisher* David Ellis

Education, including educational policy and institutions, early childhood education, educational achievement tests, Maori education, curriculum and assessment. Founded 1934.

Penguin Random House New Zealand Ltd*

Private Bag 102902, Rosedale, North Shore, Auckland 0745
tel +64 (0)9 442 7400
email publishing@penguinrandomhouse.co.nz
website www.penguinrandomhouse.co.nz
Publishing Director Debra Millar, *Managing Director* Margaret Thompson

Adult and children's fiction and non-fiction. Imprints: Penguin, Vintage, Black Swan, Godwit, Viking, Puffin Books. Part of Penguin Random House. Founded 1973.

RSVP Publishing Company*

PO Box 47166, Ponsonby, Auckland 1144
tel/fax +64 (0)9 372 8480
email rsvppub@iconz.co.nz
website www.rsvp-publishing.co.nz
Managing Director/Publisher Stephen Ron Picard, *Sales & Marketing Director* Chris Palmer

Fiction, metaphysical, children's. Founded 1990.

SOUTH AFRICA

*Member of the Publishers' Association of South Africa

Cambridge University Press*

(African Branch)
Lower Ground Floor, Nautica Building, The Water Club, Beach Road, Granger Bay, Cape Town 8005
tel +27 (0)21) 412 7800
email capetown@cambridge.org
website www.cambridge.org/africa
Publishing Director Johan Traut

Distance learning materials and textbooks for sub-Sahara African countries, as well as primary reading materials in 28 local African languages.

Educat Publishers Pty Ltd

396 Lansdowne Road, Lansdowne, Cape Town, Western Cape 7780
tel +27 (0)21 697 3669
email educatorders@mgh.co.za
website www.educat.co.za
Ceo Keith Blair

Educational products including science and maths, product designs for schools and retail, as well as mass markets. Age groups: preschool, 5–10, 10–15, 15+.

Heinemann Publishers (South Africa)

Heinemann House, Building No 5, Grayston Office Park, 128 Peter Road, Sandton

postal address PO Box 781940, Sandton 2146
tel +27 (0)11 322 8600
email customerliaison@heinemann.co.za
website www.heinemann.co.za
Managing Director Naëtt Atkinson

Educational publisher: school textbooks, library books, e-learning and professional development materials for all schools in South Africa.

Human & Rousseau

12th Floor, Naspers, 40 Heerengracht, Roggebaai 8012
tel +27 (0)21 406 3033
email nb@nb.co.za
website www.humanrousseau.co.za

General Afrikaans and English titles. Quality Afrikaans literature, popular literature, general children's and youth literature, cookery, self-help. Founded 1959.

Best Books (imprint)
Education.

Jacklin Enterprises (Pty) Ltd

PO Box 521, Parklands 2121
tel +27 (0)11 265 4200
Managing Director M.A.C. Jacklin

Children's fiction and non-fiction; Afrikaans large print books. Subjects include aviation, natural history, romance, general science, technology and transportation. Imprints: Mike Jacklin, Kennis Onbeperk, Daan Retief.

Macmillan Education South Africa

2nd Floor, The Piazza, 34 Whiteley Road, Melrose Arch 2116
tel +27 (0)11 731 3300
postal Private Bag X19, Northlands 2116
website www.macmillan.co.za
Managing Director Mandla Balisa

Educational titles for the RSA market.

NB Publishers (Pty) Ltd*

PO Box 879, Cape Town 8000
tel +27 (0)21 406 3033
email nb@nb.co.za
website www.nb.co.za
Director Eloise Wessels, *Director* Musa Shezi

General: Afrikaans fiction, politics, children's and youth literature in all the country's languages, non-fiction. Imprints: Tafelberg, Human & Rousseau, Queillerie, Pharos, Kwela, Best Books and Lux Verbi. Founded 1950.

New Africa Books (Pty) Ltd

1st Floor, 6 Spin Street, Cape Town 7700
tel +27 (0) 21 467 5860
email info@newafricabooks.co.za
postal address PO Box 46962, Glosderry 7702
website www.newafricabooks.co.za

General books, textbooks, literary works, contemporary issues, children and young adult. Formed as a result of the merger of David Philip Publishers (founded 1971), Spearhead Press (founded 2000) and New Africa Educational Publishing.

Oxford University Press, Southern Africa*

Vasco Boulevard, N1 City, Goodwood, Cape Town 7460
tel +27 (0)21 596 2300
email steve.cilliers@oup.com
email oxford.za@oup.com
postal address PO Box 12119, N1 City, Cape Town 7463
website www.oxford.co.za
Managing Director Steve Cilliers

Reference books for children and school books: preschool and foundation, intermediate and senior phases; dictionaries, thesauruses, atlases and teaching English as a main and as a second language.

Pearson Marang (Pty) Ltd*

PO Box 396, Cnr Forest Drive and Logan Way, Pinelands, 7405, Cape Town 8000
tel +27 (0)21 532 6000
email pearsonza.enquiries@pearson.com
website www.pearson.co.za
Learning Resources Director Preschool–Grade 7 Karen Simpson

Educational and general publishers. Heinemann and Maskew Miller Longman are part of Pearson.

Shuter and Shooter Publishers (Pty) Ltd*

110 CB Downes Road, Pietermaritzburg, KwaZulu-Natal 3201
tel +27 (0)33 846 8700
email sales@shuters.com
postal address PO Box 61, Mkondeni, KwaZulu-Natal 3212
website www.shuters.com
Chief Execute Officer P.B. Chetty

Core curriculum-based textbooks for use at foundation, intermediate, senior and further education phases. Supplementary readers in various languages; dictionaries; reading development kits, charts. Literature titles in English, isiXhosa, Sesotho, Sepedi, Setswana, Tshivenda, Xitsonga, Ndebele, isiZulu and Siswati. Founded 1925.

Via Afrika Publishers

PO Box 5197, Cape Town 8000
11th Floor, 40 Heerengracht, Naspers Building, Cape Town 8001
tel +27 (0)21 406 3528
email customerservices@viaafrika.com
website www.viaafrika.com
Ceo Christina Watson

Educational materials for South African schools and FET colleges, for all learning areas and subjects at all grades/levels: languages materials, literature and other materials in all official languages of South Africa. Imprints: Acacia, Action, Afritech, Afro, Atlas, Bateleur Books, Collegium, Idem, Juta/Gariep, KZN Books, Nasou; Stimela, Van Schaik (literature), Via Afrika.

SPAIN

Grupo Anaya
C/ Juan Ignacio Luca de Tena, 15–28027 Madrid
tel +34 913 938 800
website www.anaya.es
Managing Director Carlos Lamadrid

Non-fiction: education textbooks for preschool–15+.

Editorial Cruilla
C/ Balmes 245, 4th, 08066 Barcelona
tel +34 902 123 336
email editorial@cruilla.com
website www.cruilla.com
Publishing Director Enric Masllorens i Escubós

Activity books, novelty books, fiction for children 5–8 and 9–12 years, teenage fiction and poetry. Publishes approx. 120–130 titles each year. Recent successes include El Vaixell de Vapor (series), Vull Llegir! and Molly Moon Stops the World/Molly Moon's Incredible Book of Hypnotism. Subsidiary of Ediciones SM. Founded 1984.

Destino Infantil & Juvenil
Edificio Planeta, Diagonal 662–664, 08034 Barcelona
tel +34 93 496 7001
email infoinfantilyjuvenil@planetao.es
website www.edestino.es
Children's & Young Adult Director Marta Bueno Miró

Fiction for children 6–16 years. Picture books, pop-up books, fiction and some unusual illustrated books. Age groups: preschool, 5–10, 10–15, 15+.

Libros del Zorro Rojo
Sant Joan de Malta, 39, 202A, 08018 Barcelona
tel/fax +34 933 076 850
email editorial@librosdelzorrorojo.com
website www.librosdelzorrorojo.com
Editorial Director Fernando Diego García

Small independent publisher specialising in children's and young adult books. Main focus is picture books for young children and classics with high-quality illustrations for young readers.

Editorial Libsa
San Rafael 4, Poligono Industrail,
28108 Alcobendas/Madrid
tel +34 916 572 580
email libsa@libsa.es
website www.libsa.es

President Amado Sanchez, Children's Books Editor Maria Dolores Maeso

Publisher and packager of highly illustrated mass market books: activity books, board books, picture books, colouring books, how-to books, fairy tales.

Penguin Random House Grupo Editorial
Travessera de Gracia 47–49, 08021 Barcelona
tel +34 933 660 300
website www.randomhousemondadori.es

Preschool activity, novelty and picture books through to young adult fiction. Also a packager and printer. Part of Penguin Random House.

Beascoa (division)
Character publishing, including Disney and Fisher-Price.

Nube de Tinta (division)
Provides novels to a broad range of readers from young adult to adult who share a love of reading.

Montena (division)
Contemporary literary fiction including fantasy.

Vicens Vives SA
Avenida Sarriá 130–132, 08017 Barcelona
tel +34 93 252 3700
email e@vicensvives.es
website www.vicensvives.es
Managing Director Roser Espona de Rahola

Activity and novelty books, fiction, art, encyclopedias, dictionaries, education, geography, history, music, science, textbooks, posters. Age groups: preschool, 5–10, 10–15, 15+.

USA

*Member of the Association of American Publishers Inc.

Abingdon Press
2222 Rosa L. Parks Blvd., PO Box 280988,
Nashville TN 37228
tel +1 800-251-3320
website www.abingdonpress.com
President & Publisher Neil Alexander, Chief Content Officer & Book Editor Brian K. Milford, Chief Ministry Officer Justin Coleman

General interest, professional, academic and reference, non-fiction and fiction, youth and children's non-fiction and VBS; primarily directed to the religious market. Imprint of United Methodist Publishing House with tradition of crossing denominational boundaries.

Harry N. Abrams Inc.
115 West 18th Street, New York, NY 10011
tel +1 212-206-7715
email abrams@abramsbooks.com
website www.abramsbooks.com
Ceo/President Michael Jacobs

Books

Art and architecture, photography, natural sciences, performing arts, children's books. No fiction. Founded 1949.

Harry N. Abrams Books for Young Readers
tel +1 212-519-1200
website www.abramsyoungreaders.com
Director, Children's Books Howard W. Reeves
Fiction and non-fiction: picture books, young readers, middle readers, young adult.
   For picture books submit covering letter and complete MS, for longer works and non-fiction send query and sample chapter with sase.

Aladdin Paperbacks – see Simon & Schuster Children's Publishing Division

All About Kids Publishing
PO Box 159, Gilroy, CA 95021
tel +1 408-337-1152
email lguevara@aakp.com
website www.aakp.com
Publisher Mike G. Guevara, *Editor* Linda L. Guevara
Fiction and non-fiction picture books and chapter books. Recent successes include *A, My Name is Andrew* by Mary McManus-Burke (picture book) and *The Titanic Game* by Mike Warner (chapter book). Founded 2000.
   See website for guidelines. Not currently taking submissions.

Alyson Books, Inc.
245 West 17th Street, 12th Floor, New York, NY 10011
email publisher@alyson.com
website www.alyson.com
Editor Angela Brown
Publishes ebooks that deal with gay or lesbian issues. Successes include *Daddy's Wedding* by Michael Willhoite.
   For young adult books submit synopsis and sample chapters with sase. See website for submission guidelines.

Amistad Press – see HarperCollins Publishers

The Julie Andrews Collection – see HarperCollins Publishers

Atheneum Books for Young Readers – see Simon & Schuster Children's Publishing Division

Avisson Press, Inc.
3007 Taliaferro Road, Greensboro, NC 27408
tel +1 336-288-6989
email avisson4@aol.com
Publisher Martin Hester
Biography for young adults. Successes include *I Can Do Anything* by William Schoell and *The Girl He Left Behind* by Suzanne Middendorf. Founded 1995.
   Submit synopsis and 2 sample chapters.

Avon Books – see HarperCollins Publishers

Bantam Books – see Penguin Random House

Barefoot Books
2067 Massachusetts Avenue, Cambridge, MA 02140
tel +1 617-576-0660
email publicity@barefootbooks.com
website www.barefootbooks.co.uk
Currently not accepting MS submissions or queries. Accepts illustrator samples via mail only. Please mail samples (no original artwork) for the attention of the Acquisitions Editor. Recent successes include *The Boy Who Grew Flowers* by Jen Wojtowicz, illustrated by Steve Adams (4–9 years, picture book). Founded 1993 (UK); 1998 (USA).
   Length: 500–1,000 words (picture books), 2,000–3,000 words (young readers).

Barron's Educational Series Inc.
250 Wireless Boulevard, Hauppauge, NY 11788
tel +1 800-645-3476
email barrons@barronseduc.com
website www.barronseduc.com
Chairman/Ceo Manuel H. Barron, *President/Publisher* Ellen Sibley
Series books for children 0 to young adult. Publishes picture books, activity kits, sticker books and young adult fiction and non-fiction, including young adult fan books. Successes include *Ella Bella Ballerina* series by James Mayhew, *5 Seconds of Summer: The Ultimate Fan* Book, by Malcom Croft and *Ballet Spectacular* by Lisa Miles. Also for adults: cookbooks, Mind, Body & Spirit, crafts, business, pets, gardening, family and health, art. Founded 1941.
   Reviews MS/illustration packages from artists: send query letter with 3 chapters of MS with one piece of final art, remainder roughs. For illustrations only send tearsheets plus résumé. Send to Bill Kuchler, Art Director.
   Approx. 15% of books are by first-time authors. Submit outline/synopsis and sample chapters with sase for response. Responds to MSS in 3 months. Send to Acquisitions Manager. See website for full details.

Bick Publishing House
16 Marion Road, Branford, CT 06405
tel +1 203-208-5253
email bickpubhse@aol.com
website www.bickpubhouse.com
Adults: health and recovery, living with disabilities, wildlife rehabilitation. Non-fiction for young adults: philosophy, psychology, self-help, social issues, science. Recent successes include *What Are You Doing with Your Life? Books on Living for Teenagers* by J. Krishnamurti; *The Teen Brain Book: Who and What Are You?*, *Talk: Teen Art of Communication* and *Cosmic Calendar: The Big Bang to Your Consciousness* by Dale Carlson. Founded 1993.

Big Idea Productions (Veggie Tales)
Building 2A, 230 Franklin Road, Franklin, TN 37064
tel +1 615-224-2200
email customerservice@bigidea.com
website www.veggietales.com

Children's/juvenile fiction and non-fiction, picture books for ages 3+. Also books on child guidance/parenting, reference and gift books. Successes include *Lord of the Beans* by Phil Vischer (picture book) and *Mess Detectives* by Doug Peterson (storybook).

Material must be highly innovative and creative, and must conform to the Big Idea style. Send query with sase.

Bloomsbury Publishing USA
(New York office of Bloomsbury Publishing)
1385 Broadway, New York, NY 10018
tel +1 212-419-5300
email ChildrensPublicityUSA@bloomsbury.com
website www.bloomsburyusa.com
Publishing Director George Gibson, *Other Contacts* Cindy Loh (children's), Kevin Ohe (academic), Priscilla McGeehon (Fairchild), Bill Sarr (chief financial officer)

Supports the worldwide publishing activities of Bloomsbury Publishing Plc: caters for the US market. See Bloomsbury Children's & Educational Division on page 40.

Blue Sky Press – see Scholastic Inc.

Boyds Mills Press
815 Church Street, Honesdale, PA 18431
website www.boydsmillspress.com

Activity books, picture books, fiction, non-fiction, and poetry for 18 years and under. Successes include *Drive* by Nathan Clement, *One Whole and Perfect Day* by Judith Clarke and *I'm Being Stalked by a Moonshadow* by Doug MacLeod. Publishes approx. 80 titles each year. Founded 1991.

Will consider both unsolicited MSS and queries. Send to above address and label package 'Manuscript Submission'. Looking for middle-grade fiction with fresh ideas and subject matter, and young adult novels of real literary merit. Non-fiction should be fun and entertaining as well as informative, and non-fiction MSS should be accompanied by a detailed bibliography. Interested in imaginative picture books and welcomes submissions from both writers and illustrators. Submit samples as b&w and/or colour copies or transparencies; submissions will not be returned. Include sase with all submissions. Send art samples to above address and label package 'Art Sample Submission'.

Calkins Creek Books (imprint)
US history and historical fiction.

Front Street (imprint)
See page 75.

Wordsong (imprint)
Poetry.

Calkins Creek Books – see Boyds Mills Press

Candlewick Press
99 Dover Street, Somerville, MA 02144
tel +1 617-661-3330
email bigbear@candlewick.com
website www.candlewick.com
President/Publisher Karen Lotz, *Creative Director/Associate Publisher* Chris Paul, *Executive Editorial Director/Associate Publisher* Liz Bicknell, *Editorial Director* Mary Lee Donovan

Books for babies through teens: board books, picture books, early readers, first chapter books, novels, non-fiction, novelty books, poetry, graphic novels. Publishes 100 picture books, 30 middle readers and 20 young adult titles each year. Recent successes include *Sam and Dave Dig a Hole* by Mac Barnett and illustrated by Jon Klassen (picture book); *Flora and Ulysses* by Kate DiCamillo (middle-grade fiction); and *The Kingdom of Little Wounds* by Susann Cokal (young adult fiction). Subsidiary of Walker Books Ltd, UK.

Approx. 5% of books are by first-time authors. Submit MS via a literary agent. No unsolicited MSS accepted. For illustrations, send résumé and portfolio for the attention of Art Resource Coordinator. Responds in 6 weeks. Samples returned with sase. Founded 1991.

Candlewick Entertainment
Group Editorial Director Joan Powers, *Group Art Director* Kristen Nobles
Media-related children's books, including film/TV tie-ins.

Carolrhoda Books – see Lerner Publishing Group

Cartwheel Books – see Scholastic Inc.

Charlesbridge Publishing
85 Main Street, Watertown, MA 02472
tel +1 617-926-0329
email tradeeditorial@charlesbridge.com
website www.charlesbridge.com
President & Publisher Brent Farmer

Fiction and non-fiction picture books and transitional books for preschool–14 years. Lively, plot-driven story books plus nursery rhymes and humorous stories for the very young. Non-fiction list specialises in nature, concept and multicultural books. Publishes 60% non-fiction, 40% fiction picture books and transitional books. Recent successes include *Pig Pig Returns* by David McPhail, *The Cazuela That the Farm Maiden Stirred* by Samantha Vamos, *Music Was It* by Susan Goldman Rubin, *The Ink Garden of Brother Theophane* by C.M.

Books

Millen and *Digging for Troy* by Jill Rubalcaba and Eric H. Cline. Founded 1980.

Send full MSS; no queries. Responds to MSS of interest. Length: 1,000–10,000 words. For illustrations, send query with samples, tearsheets and résumé.

Chicago Review Press
814 North Franklin Street, Chicago, IL 60610
tel +1 312-337-0747
email frontdesk@jpg.com
website www.chicagoreviewpress.com
Publisher Cynthia Sherry

General publisher. Non-fiction activity books for children. Imprint Zephyr publishes professional development titles for teachers. Founded 1973.

Interested in hands-on educational books. See website for submission guidelines.

Chronicle Books*
680 Second Street, San Francisco, CA 94107
tel +1 415-537-4200
email frontdesk@chroniclebooks.com
website www.chroniclebooks.com
website www.chroniclekids.com
Chairman & Ceo Nion McEvoy, *Publisher* Christine Carswell

Traditional and innovative children's books. Looking for projects that have a unique bent – in subject matter, writing style or illustrative technique – that will add a distinctive flair. Interested in fiction and non-fiction for children of all ages as well as board books, decks, activity kits and other unusual or 'novelty' formats. Publishes 60–100 books each year. Also for adults: cooking, how-to books, nature, art, biographies, fiction, gift. Founded 1967.

For picture books submit MS. For older readers, submit outline/synopsis and 3 sample chapters. No submitted materials will be returned. Response approx. 3 months.

Clarion Books – see Houghton Mifflin Harcourt

Clear Light Books
823 Don Diego, Santa Fe, NM 87505
tel +1 505-989-9590
website www.clearlightbooks.com
Publisher Harmon Houghton

For adults: art and photography, cookbooks, ecology/environment, health, gift books, history, Native America, Tibet, Western Americana. Non-fiction for children and young adults: multicultural, American Indian, Hispanic.

Looking for authentic American Indian art and folklore. Send complete MS with sase.

CMX – see DC Comics

David C Cook
4050 Lee Vance View, Colorado Springs, CO 80918
tel +1 719-536-0100

website www.davidccook.com

Christian education resources for preschool to teenagers.

Cooper Square Publishing
4501 Forbes Boulevard, Suite 200, Lanham, Maryland 20706
tel +1 301-459-3366
website www.nbnbooks.com

Part of the Rowman & Littlefield Publishing Group. Founded 1949.

NorthWord Books for Young Readers (imprint)
11571 K–Tel Drive, Minnetonka, MN 55343
tel +1 800-462-6420
email rrinehart@rowman.com
website www.nbnbooks.com

Picture books and non-fiction nature and wildlife books in interactive and fun-to-read formats. Not accepting MSS at present. Founded 1989.

Rising Moon (imprint)
email editorial@northlandbooks.com
website www.northlandbooks.com

Illustrated, entertaining and thought-provoking picture books for children, including Spanish–English bilingual titles. Founded 1998.

Seeking fresh picture book MSS about contemporary everyday life of children: edgy, innovative, spirited (e.g. *Do Princesses Wear Hiking Boots?* and *It's a Bad Day*). Also seeking exceptional Latino-themed picture books about multicultural living, contemporary issues, Latino role models (e.g. *My Name is Celia* and *Lupe Vargas and Her Super Best Friend*). Additionally seeking picture books that relate to western and southwestern USA, original stories with a Southwest flavour, fractured fairy tales (e.g. *The Treasure of Ghostwood Gully* and *The Three Little Javelinas*).

Two-Can Publishing (imprint)
website www.northlandbooks.com

Non-fiction books and multimedia products for children 2–12 years to entertain and educate. Not accepting MSS at present.

Joanna Cotler Books – see HarperCollins Publishers

Cricket Books
Carus Publishing Company,
Cricket Magazine Group, 30 Grove Street, Suite C, Peterborough, NH 03458
email customerservice@caruspub.com
website www.cricketmag.com

Picture books, chapter books, poetry, non-fiction and novels for children and young adults. Recent successes include *Breakout* by Paul Fleischman and *Robert and the Weird & Wacky Facts* by Barbara Seuling, illustrated by Paul Brewer. Also publishes

Cricket, the award-winning magazine of outstanding stories and art for 9–14 year-olds, and other magazines for young readers. Founded 1973. Division of Carus Publishing.

Not accepting MSS submissions at this time.

Crown Books – see Penguin Random House

Darby Creek Publishing – see Lerner Publishing Group

Dawn Publications
12402 Bitney Springs Road, Nevada City, CA 95959
tel +1 800-545-7475
email chris@deep-books.co.uk
website www.dawnpub.com
Editor & Co-Publisher Glenn Hovemann, *Art Director & Co-Publisher* Muffy Weaver

Dedicated to inspiring in children a deeper understanding and appreciation for all life on Earth. The aim is to help parents and teachers encourage children to bond with the Earth in a relationship of love, respect and intelligent cooperation, through the books published and the educational materials offered online. Recent successes include *The Mouse and the Meadow, On Kiki's Reef, The Swamp Where Gator Hides, Over In A River, Noisy Frog Sing-Along* and *Jo MacDonald Hiked in the Woods*. UK Distributor: Deep Books Ltd, www.deep-books.co.uk or 0208-693 0234.

See website for guidelines.

DC Comics
1700 Broadway, New York, NY 10019
tel +1 212-636-5400
website www.dccomics.com

Activity books, board books, novelty books, picture books, painting and colouring books, pop-up books, fiction, fairy tales, art, hobbies, how-to books, leisure, entertainment, film/TV tie-ins, calendars, comics, gift books, periodicals, picture cards, posters, CD-Roms, CD-I, internet for preschool age to 15+ years.

DC Comics has published and licensed comic books for over 60 years in all genres for all ages, including super heroes, fantasy, horror, mystery and high-quality graphic stories for mature readers. Imprints: WildStorm, Vertigo. A Warner Bros. Company.

CMX (imprint)
Translated manga from Japan in its original format.

MINX (imprint)
Original graphic novels for teenage girls.

Delacorte Press Books for Young Readers – see Penguin Random House

Dial Books for Young Readers – see Penguin Random House

Disney Books for Young Readers – see Penguin Random House

Tom Doherty Associates, LLC
175 5th Avenue, New York, NY 10010
tel +1 212-388-0100
email enquiries@tor.com
website www.tor.com/

Fiction and non-fiction for middle readers and young adults. Publishes 5–10 middle readers and 5–10 young adult books each year. Successes include *Hidden Talents, Flip* by David Lubar (fantasy, 10+ years), *Briar Rose* by Jane Yolen (fiction, 12+ years), *Strange Unsolved Mysteries* by Phyllis Rabin Amert (non-fiction). For adults: fiction – general, historical, western, suspense, mystery, horror, sci-fin, fantasy, humour, juvenile, classics (English language); non-fiction. Imprints: Tor Books, Forge Books, Orb Books, Starscope, Tor Teen. Founded 1980.

For both fiction and non-fiction, submit outline/synopsis and complete MS. Responds to queries in one month; MSS in 6 months for unsolicited work. Fiction length: middle readers – 30,000 words; young adult – 60,000–100,000 words. Non-fiction length: middle readers – 25,000–35,000 words; young adult – 70,000 words. For illustrations, query with samples to Irene Gallo, Art Director. Responds only if interested.

Tor (imprint)
Science fiction and fantasy.

StarScape (imprint)
Science fiction and fantasy for 10–12 years.

Tor Teen (imprint)
Science fiction and fantasy for 12+ years.

Doubleday Books for Young Readers – see Penguin Random House

Dover Publications Inc.
31 East 2nd Street, Mineola, NY 11501
tel +1 516-294-7000
website www.doverpublications.com

Activity books, novelty books, picture books, fiction for children 5–8 and 9–12 years, teenage fiction, series fiction, reference, plays, religion, poetry, audio and CD-Roms. Also adult non-fiction. Publishes approx. 150 children's titles and has over 2,500 in print. Successes include *Easy Noah's Ark Sticker Picture, How to Draw a Funny Monster* and *Pretty Ballerina Sticker Paper Doll*. Founded 1941.

Will consider unsolicited MSS but write for guidelines.

Dragon Books – see Pacific View Press

Dragonfly Books – see Penguin Random House

Dutton Children's Books – see Penguin Random House

EDCON Publishing Group

30 Montauk Boulevard, Oakdale, NY 11769–1399
tel +1 631-567-7227
email info@edconpublishing.com
website www.edconpublishing.com

Supplemental instructional materials for use by education professionals to improve reading and maths skills. Includes early reading, *Classics* series, *Easy Shakespeare*, fiction and non-fiction, reading diagnosis and vocabulary books. Founded 1970.

Edupress

401 S. Wright Road, Janesville, WI 53547
tel +1 800-694-5827
email edupress@highsmith.com
website www.edupress.com/edupress

Educational materials. Founded 1979.
See website for guidelines.

Eerdmans Publishing Company

2140 Oak Industrial Drive NE, Grand Rapids, MI 49505
tel +1 616-459-4591
website www.eerdmans.com
President Anita Eerdmans

Independent publisher of a wide range of religious books, from academic works in theology, biblical studies, religious history and reference to popular titles in spirituality, social and cultural criticism and literature. Founded 1911.

Eerdmans Books for Young Readers (imprint)
website www.eerdmans.com/youngreaders
Acquisitions Editor Kathleen Merz, *Art Director* Gayle Brown

Picture books, biographies, middle reader and young adult fiction and non-fiction. Publishes 12–18 books a year. Seeks MSS that are honest, wise and hopeful but also publishes stories that delight with their storyline, characters or good humour. Stories that celebrate diversity, stories of historical significance, and stories that relate to current issues are of special interest.

Accepts unsolicited submissions. Send to Acquisitions Editor; responds in 4 months only to submissions of interest. For illustrations, send photocopies or printed media and include a list of previous illustrated publications. Send to Gayle Brown. Samples will be kept on file; they will not be returned.

Encyclopaedia Britannica Inc.

331 North La Salle Street, Chicago, IL 60610
tel +1 312-347-7159
email international@eb.com
website www.britannica.com

Encyclopedias, reference books, almanacs, videos and CD-Roms for adults and children 5–15+ years.

Enslow Publishers, Inc.

Box 398, 40 Industrial Road, Berkeley Heights, NJ 07922–0398
tel +1 908-771-9400
email customerservice@enslow.com
website www.enslow.com
President Mark Enslow, *Vice President/Publisher* Brian Enslow

Non-fiction library books for children and young adults. Founded 1976.

Eos – see HarperCollins Publishers

Evan-Moor Educational Publishers

18 Lower Ragsdale Drive, Monterey, CA 93940
tel +1 800-714-0971
email marketing@evan-moor.com
website www.evan-moor.com
Founder & Ceo William E. Evans

Educational materials for parents and teachers of children (3–12 years): activity books, textbooks, how-to books, CD-Roms. Subjects include maths, geography, history, science, reading, writing, social studies, art and craft. Publishes approx. 50 titles each year and has over 500 in print. Founded 1979.

Less than 10% of books are by first-time authors. Query or submit outline, table of contents and sample pages. Responds to queries in 2 months; MSS in 4 months. See website for submission guidelines. For illustrations, send résumé, samples and tearsheets to the Art Director. Primarily uses b&w material.

Farrar Straus Giroux Books for Young Readers

175 Fifth Avenue, New York, NY 10010
website http://us.macmillan.com/publishers/farrar-straus-giroux#FYR

An imprint of Macmillan Children's Publishing Group. Books for toddlers through to young adults: picture books, fiction and non-fiction for all ages, and poetry (occasionally). Publishes 70 hardcover originals plus 10 paperback reprints each year and has approx. 500 titles in print.

Submission details: Approx. 10% of books are by first-time authors. No unsolicited MSS.

Flux Books, a division of Llewellyn Worldwide

2143 Wooddale Drive, Woodbury, MN 55125–2989
tel +1 800-843-666
email publicity@fluxnow.com
email submissions@fluxnow.com
website www.fluxnow.com
Editor Brian Farrey-Latz (acquiring editor)
Publisher Bill Krause

From their very first teen novels in 2006, Flux set out to be different. Consistently provocative, independently alternative and striving to find unique voices that unsettle, surprise, inform and ignite. See website at www.fluxnow.com, or via social media.

Walter Foster Publishing Jr.
3 Wrigley, Suite A, Irvine, CA 92618
tel +1 800-426-0099
email info@walterfoster.com
website www.walterfoster.com
Director Ann Landa

Instructional art books for children and adults. Also art and activity kits for children. A division of Quarto Publishing Group US.

Free Spirit Publishing
217 Fifth Avenue North, Suite 200, Minneapolis, MN 55401–1299
tel +1 612-338-2068
email help4kids@freespirit.com
website www.freespirit.com
President Judy Galbraith

Award-winning publisher of non-fiction materials for children and teens, parents, educators and counsellors. Specialises in SELF-HELP FOR KIDS® and SELF-HELP FOR TEENS® materials which empower young people and promote positive self-esteem through improved social and emotional health. Topics include self-esteem and self-awareness, stress management, school success, creativity, friends and family, peacemaking, social action and special needs (i.e. gifted and talented, children with learning differences). Publishes approx. 18–22 new products each year, adding to a backlist of over 200 books and posters. Free Spirit authors are expert educators and mental health professionals who have been honoured nationally for their contributions on behalf of children. Founded 1983.

Front Street
815 Church Street, Honesdale, PA 18431
tel +1 570-253-1164
email contact@boydsmillpress.com
website www.frontstreetbooks.com
Editorial Director Larry Rosler, *Art Director* Tim Gillner

Imprint of Boyds Mill Press. Books for children and young adults: picture books, fiction (5–8, 9–12, teenage). Recent successes include *The Adventurous Deeds of Deadwood Jones* by Helen Hemphill, *Child of Dandelions* by Shenaaz Nanji and *Piggy* by Mireille Geus. Imprint of Boyds Mills Press. Founded 1994.

For fiction, submit the first 3 chapters and a plot summary. For picture books, submit the entire MSS. Include an sase if return required. Allow 3–4 months for response.

Fulcrum Resources
4690 Table Mountain Drive, Suite 100, Golden, CO 80403
tel +1 303-277-1623
website www.fulcrum-books.com

Books and support materials for teachers, librarians, parents and elementary through middle school children in the subjects of science and nature, literature and storytelling, history, multicultural studies, and Native American and Hispanic cultures. Imprint of Fulcrum Publishing.

Gale Cengage Learning*
27500 Drake Road, Farmington Hills, MI 48331–3535
tel +1 248-699-4253
website www.gale.cengage.com

Education publishing for libraries, schools and businesses. Serves the K–12 market with the following imprints: Blackbirch Press, Greenhaven Press, KidHaven Press, Lucent Books, Sleeping Bear Press, UXL.

Greenhaven Press (imprint)
High-quality non-fiction resources for the education community. Publishes 220 young adult academic reference titles each year. Successes include the *Opposing Viewpoints* series. Founded 1970.

Approx. 35% of books are by first-time authors. No unsolicited MSS. All writing is done on a work-to-hire basis. Send query, résumé and list of published works.

KidHaven Press (imprint)
Non-fiction references for younger researchers.

Lucent Books (imprint)
Non-fiction resources for upper-elementary to high school students. Successes include *Women in the American Revolution* and *Civil Liberties and the War on Terrorism*.

No unsolicited MSS. Query with résumé.

Sleeping Bear Press (imprint)
email sleepingbearpress@cengage.com
website www.sleepingbearpress.com
High-quality picture books.

Laura Geringer Books – see HarperCollins Publishers

Golden Books for Young Readers – see Penguin Random House

Greenhaven Press – see Gale Cengage Learning

Greenwillow Books – see HarperCollins Publishers

Grosset & Dunlap – see Penguin Random House

Gryphon House, Inc.
PO Box 10, 6848 Leon's Way, Lewisville, NC 27023
+1 800-636-092

website www.gryphonhouse.com
Early childhood (0–8 years) books for teachers and parents.

Looking for books that are developmentally appropriate for the intended age group, are well researched and based on current trends in the field, and include creative, participatory learning experiences with a common conceptual theme to tie them together. Send query and/or a proposal.

Hachai Publishing

527 Empire Boulevard, Brooklyn, New York, NY 11225
tel +1 718-633-0100
email info@hachai.com
website www.hachai.com

Jewish books for children 0–8+ years.

Welcomes unsolicited MSS. Specialises in books for children 2–4 years and 3–6 years. Looking for stories that convey the traditional Jewish experience in modern times or long ago, traditional Jewish observance, and positive character traits.

Hachette Book Group USA*

1290 Avenue of the Americas, New York, NY 10019
tel +1 212-364-1100
website www.hachettebookgroup.com

Divisions: Center Street, Grand Central Publishing; Hachette Audio; Hachette Nashville; Hyperion; Little, Brown and Company; Little, Brown and Company Books for Young Readers; Orbit. Imprints: Grand Central: Business Plus, Forever, Forever Yours, Grand Central Life & Style, Twelve, Vision. Hachette Nashville: Center Street, FaithWords, Jericho Books. Little, Brown and Company: Back Bay Books, Mulholland Books. Little, Brown Books for Young Readers: LB Kids, Poppy Orbit: Orbit, Redhook, Yen Press (see page 86).

Handprint Books

413 Sixth Avenue, Brooklyn, New York, NY 11215–3310
tel +1 718-768-3696
email info@handprintbooks.com
website www.handprintbooks.com
Publisher Christopher Franceschelli, *Executive Editor* Ann Tobias

A range of children's books: picture and story books through to young adult fiction. Imprints: Handprint Books, Ragged Bears, Blue Apple.

Welcomes submissions of MSS of quality for works ranging from board books to young adult novels. For novels, first query interest on the subject and submit a 7,500-word max. sample. Accepts MSS on an e-submission basis only, sent as attachments in a word processing format readily readable on a PC. Artwork should be sent as small jpgs; artists' website addresses may also be submitted. No series fiction, licensed character (or characters whose primary avatar is

meant to be as licences), 'I-Can-Read'-type books, or titles intended primarily for mass merchandise outlets.

Harcourt Trade Publishers

215 Park Avenue South, New York, NY 10003
tel +1 212-592-1034
website www.hmhbooks.com
President/Publisher Dan Farley, *Editorial Director* Liz Van Doren

Fiction and non-fiction (history and biography) for readers of all ages. Part of the Houghton Mifflin Harcourt Book Group.

Harcourt Children's Books

Publisher Lori Benton, *Editorial Director, Harcourt Children's Books* Allyn Johnston

Quality picture books, contemporary and historical fiction for teen readers, board and novelty books, gift items, and non-fiction for children of all ages. Also reading and teacher guides for teachers of children 8–14+ years. The original publisher of such classics as *The Little Prince, Mary Poppins, The Borrowers, Half Magic, Ginger Pye* and *The Moffats*. Recent successes include *Where Did That Baby Come From?* by Debi Gliori and *Juliet Dove, Queen of Love* by Bruce Coville (fiction, 8–12 years). Imprints: Gulliver Books, Silver Whistle, Red Wagon Books, Harcourt Young Classics, Green Light Readers, Voyager Books/Libros Viajeros, Harcourt Paperbacks, Odyssey Classics, Magic Carpet Books.

Does not accept unsolicited query letters or emails, MSS and illustrations. Only accepts material via literary agents.

HarperCollins Publishers*

10 East 53rd Street, New York, NY 10022
tel +1 212-207-7000
website www.harpercollins.com
President/Ceo Brian Murray

Adult fiction (commercial and literary) and non-fiction. Subjects include biography, business, cookbooks, educational, history, juvenile, poetry, religious, science, technical and travel. Imprints: Amistad, Avon, Avon A, Avon Inspire, Avon Red, Caedmon, Collins, Collins Design, Ecco, Eos, HarperAudio, Harper Mass Market, Harper Paperbacks, Harper Perennial, Harper Perennial Modern Classics, HarperCollins, HarperEntertainment, HarperLuxe, HarperOne, William Morrow, Morrow Cookbooks, Rayo. No unsolicited material; all submissions must come through a literary agent. Founded 1817.

HarperCollins Children's Books (division)

1350 Avenue of the Americas, New York, NY 10019
tel +1 212-261-6500
website www.harperchildrens.com
President/Publisher Susan Katz

Children's classic literature. Imprints: Amistad Press,

Julie Andrews Collection, Joanna Cotler Books, Eos, Laura Geringer Books, Greenwillow Books, HarperChildren's Audio, HarperCollins Children's Books, HarperEntertainment, HarperTeen, HarperTrophy, Rayo, Katherine Tegen Books.
Successes include *Goodnight Moon*, *Where the Wild Things Are*, *The Giving Tree* and *Charlotte's Web*. Does not accept unsolicited or unagented MSS.

Amistad Press (imprint)
Books by and about people of African descent on subjects and themes that have significant influence on the intellectual, cultural and historical perspectives of a world audience.

The Julie Andrews Collection (imprint)
website www.julieandrewscollection.com
Books for young readers that nurture the imagination and celebrate a sense of wonder. Includes new works by established and emerging authors, out-of-print books and books by Ms Andrews herself.

Avon Books (imprint)
Series and popular fiction for young readers: romance, mystery, adventure, fantasy. Series include *Making Out*, *Animal Emergency*, *Get Real* and *Enchanted Hearts*, and authors include Bruce Coville, Beatrice Sparks and Dave Duncan.

Collins (imprint)
Non-fiction for toddlers to teens, including books published in conjunction with the Smithsonian Institution, the Emily Post Institute and TIME for Kids, as well as Seymour Simon's award-winning titles and the classic *Let's-Read-and-Find-Out Science* series.

Joanna Cotler Books (imprint)
Literary and commercial picture books and fiction for all ages. Authors and illustrators include Clive Barker, Francesca Lia Block, Sharon Creech, Jamie Lee Curtis, Laura Cornell, Patricia MacLachlan, Barbara Robinson, Art Spiegelman, Jerry Spinelli and William Steig.

Eos (imprint)
Science fiction and fantasy.

Laura Geringer Books (imprint)
Publisher Laura Geringer
Fiction. Publishes 6 picture books, 2 young readers, 4 middle readers and one young adult title each year. Recent successes include *If You Take a Mouse to School* by Laura Numeroff, illustrated by Felicia Band (3–7 years) and *The Dulcimer Boy* by Tor Seidler, illustrated by Brian Selznick (8+ years). Authors and artists include William Joyce, Laura Numeroff, Felicia Bond, Bruce Brooks, Richard Egielski and Sarah Weeks.
Submissions via a literary agent only. Length: picture books – 500 words; young readers – 1,000

words; middle readers – 25,000 words; young adult – 40,000 words.

Greenwillow Books (imprint)
Books for children of all ages. Publishes 40 picture books, 5 middle readers and 5 young adult books each year. Recent successes include *Olive's Ocean* by Kevin Henkes.
No unsolicited MSS or queries. Unsolicited mail will not be opened or returned.

HarperChildren's Audio (imprint)
Offers bestselling children's books and young adult favourites in CD and other audio formats.

HarperCollins e-Books (imprint)
Middle-grade and young adult fiction. Many titles contain ebook features not found in print editions.

HarperEntertainment (imprint)
Film/TV tie-ins, from pre-school through to teens. Recent titles include *The Chronicles of Narnia*, *Ice Age 2*, *X-Men*, *Charlotte's Web*, *Spider-Man* and *Shrek*.

HarperFestival (imprint)
Books, novelties and merchandise for children 0–6 years. Classic board books include *Goodnight Moon* and *Runaway Bunny*.

HarperTeen (imprint)
Books that reflect teen readers' own lives: their everyday realities and aspirations, struggles and triumphs. From topical contemporary novels to lighthearted series books, to literary tales. Authors include Meg Cabot, Walter Dean Myers, Louise Rennison, Chris Crutcher and Joyce Carol Oates.

HarperTrophy (imprint)
Children's books. Authors and illustrators include picture books by Maurice Sendak, *I Can Read* books by Arnold Lobel, novels by Laura Ingalls Wilder, E.B. White, Katherine Paterson and Beverly Cleary.

Rayo (imprint)
Culturally inspired Spanish, English and bilingual books, as well as translations of award-winning and highly popular English titles. The list celebrates the rich Latino heritage.

Katherine Tegen Books (imprint)
Story books that entertain, inform and capture the excitement, the joys and the longings of life.

TOKYOPOP (imprint)
Manga titles based on existing HarperCollins works, as well as original manga titles conceived by HarperCollins authors.

History Compass LLC
25 Leslie Road, Auburndale, MA 02466
tel +1 617-332-2202
email info@historycompass.com
website www.historycompass.com

Books

The history of the USA presented through the study of primary source documents. Successes include *Get a Clue!* (grades 2–8) and *Adventures in History* series (grades 4–8). Other series include *Perspectives on History* (grades 5–12+) and *Researching American History* (8–15 year-olds and ESL students). Also historical fiction for younger readers. Founded 1990.

Holiday House Inc.

425 Madison Avenue, New York, NY 10017
tel +1 212-688-0085
email info@holidayhouse.com
website www.holidayhouse.com
Vice President/Editor-in-Chief Mary Cash

General. Publishes 35 picture books, 10 young reader, 15 middle reader and 8 young adult titles each year. Recent successes include *Lafayette and the American Revolution* by Russell Freedman. Approx. 20% of books are by first-time authors.

Send entire MS. Only responds to projects of interest. Will review MS/illustration packages from artists: send MS with dummy and colour photocopies.

Henry Holt Books for Young Readers

(an imprint of Macmillan Children's Publishing Group)
175 Fifth Avenue, New York, NY 10010
website www.mackids.com, www.macteenbooks.com
Vice President & Publisher Laura Godwin

Publishes picture books, chapter books, middle-grade titles, and young adult titles.

Houghton Mifflin Harcourt*

222 Berkeley Street, Boston, MA 02116
tel +1 617-351-5000
website www.hmhco.com

Reference, fiction and non-fiction for adults and young readers. Also educational content and solutions for K-12 teachers and students. Founded 1832.

Houghton Mifflin Harcourt Books for Young Readers (imprint)

222 Berkeley Street, Boston, MA 02116-3764
tel +1 617-351-5000
215 Park Avenue South, New York, NY 10003
tel +1 215-420-5800
website www.hmhbooks.com
Editorial Assistant Christine Krones, *Associate Editor* Adah Nuchi, *Creative Director* Sheila Smallwood
Picture books, fiction, poetry and non-fiction for children, preschool through high school. Recent successes include *The Testing* by Joelle Charbonneau and *Sleep Like a Tiger* by Mary Logue and illustrated by Pamela Zagarenski. Imprint: Clarion Books.

For fiction, submit complete MS. For non-fiction, submit outline/synopsis and sample chapters. Responds only if interested. For illustrations, query with samples (colour photocopies and tearsheets). Responds in 4 months.

Houghton Mifflin Harcourt/Clarion Books (imprint)

215 Park Avenue South, New York, NY 10003
tel +1 212-420-5800
Vice-President & Publisher, Clarion Books Dinah Stevenson, *Creative Director* Christine Kettner
Picture books, fiction, poetry and non-fiction for children preschool through high school. Recent successes include *Mr. Wuffles!* by David Wiesner. Founded 1965.

For fiction and picture books, send complete MS. For non-fiction, send query with up to 3 sample chapters.

Hunter House Publishers

(an imprint of Turner Publishing Company)
424 Church Street, Suite 2240, Nashville, TN 37219
tel +1 615-255-2665
email submissions@turnerpublishing.com
website www.hunterhouse.com

Non-fiction books on children's physical, mental and emotional health, including books for tweens, and children's life skills and activity books (games, classroom and fitness activites) for use by parents, teachers, youth leaders, camp counselors, coaches. Recent successes include *Horse Mandalas/Mandala Horses* and *Writing from Within Workbook* and *Writing from Deeper Within*. Writers should look at the *SmartFun* books series. Founded 1978.

Hyperion Books for Children

114 Fifth Avenue, New York, NY 10010–5690
tel +1 212-633-4400
website www.hyperionbooks.com

Board and novelty books, picture books, young readers, middle grade, young adult, non-fiction (all subjects at all levels). Recent successes include *Don't Let the Pigeon Drive the Bus*, written and ilustrated by Mo Willems, *Dumpy The Dump Truck* series by Julie Andrews Edwards and Emma Walton Hamilton (3–7 years) and *Artemis Fowl* by Eoin Colfer (young adult novel, *New York Times* bestseller). Imprints include Michael di Capua Books, Jump at the Sun, Volo. Founded 1991.

Approx. 10% of books are by first-time authors. Only interested in submissions via literary agents. For illustrations, send résumé, business card, promotional literature or tearsheets to be kept on file to Anne Diebel, Art Director.

Ideals Publications

(a division of Worthy Publishing Inc)
2630 Elm Hill Pike, Suite 100, Nashville, TN 37214
website www.idealsbooks.com

Picture books and board books for young children (2–8 years). See website for submission guidelines. Digital submissions not accepted.

Illumination Arts Publishing

PO Box 1865, Bellevue, WA 98009
tel +1 425-968-5097

email liteinfo@illumin.com
website www.illumin.com
Editorial Director John Thompson

Picture books. Publishes books to inspire the mind, touch the heart and uplift the spirit. Successes include *The Right Touch*. Founded 1987.
Length: 300–1,500 words.

Impact Publishers Inc.

PO Box 6016, Atascadero, CA 93423–6016
tel +1 805-466-5917
email submissions@impactpublishers.com
website www.impactpublishers.com

Psychology and self-improvement books and audio tapes for adults, children, families, organisations and communities. Recent successes include *The Divorce Helpbook for Kids*, *The Divorce Helpbook for Teens* and *Jigsaw Puzzle Family* by Cynthia MacGregor and *Teen Esteem: A Self-Direction Manual for Young Adults* by Pat Palmer and Melissa Alberti Froehner. Founded 1970.

Only publishes non-fiction books which serve human development and are written by highly respected psychologists and other human service professionals. Rarely publishes authors outside of the US. See website for guidelines.

Incentive Publications by World Book

2400 Crestmoor Road, Suite 211, Nashville, TN 37215
tel +1 615-385-2967
website www.incentivepublications.com
President of World Books Don Keller

Acquired by World Books in 2013. Produces supplemental resources for student use and instruction and classroom management improvement materials for teachers. Specializes in supplemental resources for middle grades students and teaching strategies for grades K–12. More than 400 titles are available. Founded 1969.

Send a letter of introduction, table of contents, a sample chapter and sase for return of material.

innovativeKids

18 Ann Street, Norwalk, CT 06854
tel +1 203-838-6400
email info@innovativekids.com
website www.innovativekids.com

Beginning reader books, activity books, infant/toddler books, preschool books and games, and science learning tools in a wide range of themes and subjects. Recent successes include *A Kid's Guide to Giving*, *Phonics Comics* series, *Groovy Tube* series and *iBaby* series. Founded 1999.

Just Us Books, Inc.

356 Glenwood Avenue East Orange, NJ 07017
tel +1 973-672-7701
email info@justusbooks.com
website www.justusbooks.com
Publishers Cheryl Hudson, Wade Hudson

Publishers of Black-interest books for young people, including preschool materials, picture books, biographies, chapter books and young adult fiction. Focuses on Black history, Black culture and Black experiences. Imprint: Sankofa Books. Founded 1988.

Currently accepting queries for young adult titles, targeted to 13–16 year-old readers. Work should contain realistic, contemporary characters, compelling plot lines that introduce conflict and resolution, and cultural authenticity. Also considers MSS for picture books and middle reader chapter books. Send a query letter, 1–2pp synopsis, a brief author biog that includes any previously published work, plus a sase.

Kaeden Books

PO Box 16190, Rocky River, OH 44116
tel +1 800-890-7323
email info@kaeden.com
website www.kaeden.com

Educational publisher specialising in early literacy books and beginning chapter books. Founded 1986.

Accepts samples of all styles of illustration but is primarily looking for samples that match the often humorous style appropriate for juvenile literature. Send samples, no larger than 8.5 x 11ins to keep on file.

Seeking beginning chapter books and unique non-fiction MSS (25–3,000 words). Vocabulary and sentence structure must be appropriate for young readers. No sentence fragments. See website for complete guidelines.

Kar-Ben Publishing – see Lerner Publishing Group

KidHave Press – see Gale Cengage Learning

Kingfisher – see Houghton Mifflin Harcourt

Klutz – see Scholastic Inc.

Alfred A. Knopf Books for Young Readers – see Penguin Random House

Knopf Trade – see Penguin Random House

Wendy Lamb Books – see Penguin Random House

Laurel-Leaf Books – see Penguin Random House

LB Kids – see Little, Brown & Company

Lee & Low Books, Inc.

95 Madison Avenue, Suite 1205, New York, NY 10016
tel +1 212-779-4400
email general@leeandlow.com
website www.leeandlow.com

Vice President/Editorial Director Louise May, *Associate Editor* Jessica Echeverria

Children's book publisher specialising in multicultural literature that is relevant to young readers. The company's goal is to meet the need for stories that children of colour can identify with and that all children can enjoy and which promote a greater understanding of one another.

Focuses on fiction and non-fiction for children 5–12 years which feature children/people of colour. Of special interest are realistic fiction, historical fiction, and non-fiction with a distinct voice or unique approach. Does not consider folktales or animal stories.

MS should be no longer 1,500 words for fiction and 3,000 words for non-fiction. Send MS with a covering letter that includes a brief biography of the author, including publishing history, and stating if the MS is a simultaneous or an exclusive submission. No submissions via email. Writer will be contacted within 6 months if publisher is interested. Makes a special effort to work with artists of colour. Founded 1991.

Lerner Publishing Group

241 First Avenue North, Minneapolis, MN 55401–1607
tel +1 612-332-3344
email info@lernerbooks.com
website www.lernerbooks.com
Publisher Adam Lerner

Independent publisher of high-quality children's books for K–12 schools and libraries: picture books, fiction for children 5–8 and 9–12 years, teenage fiction, series fiction and non-fiction. Subjects include biography, social studies, science, sports and curriculum. Publishes approx. 300 titles each year and has about 1,500 in print. Founded 1959.

No unsolicited submissions for any imprint.

Carolrhoda Books (imprint)
website www.carolrhodabooks.com
Picture books aimed at children 5–8 years; longer fiction for 7+ years, including chapter books and middle-grade and young adult novels; biographies. Authors and illustrators include Nancy Carlson and Chris Monroe.

Darby Creek Publishing (imprint)
High-interest, creative series fiction titles for grades K–8.

Kar-Ben Publishing (imprint)
website www.karben.com
Books on Jewish themes for children and families. Subjects include the High Holidays, Passover, Sukkot and Simchat Torah, Hanukkah, Purim, Selichot, Tu B'Shevat, crafts, cooking, folk tales, and contemporary stories, Jewish calendars, music and activity books. Founded 1974.

Lerner Publications Company (imprint)
Non-fiction books for grades K–8 in social studies, science, reading/literacy and mathematics.

Millbrook Press (imprint)
Maths, science, American history, social studies and biography for a younger age bracket.

Twenty-First Century Books (imprint)
Maths, science, American history, social studies and biography for secondary school age bracket.

Arthur A. Levine Books – see Scholastic Inc.

Little, Brown & Company
1271 Avenue of the Americas, New York, NY 10020
tel +1 212-522-8700
email publicity@littlebrown.com
website www.hachettebookgroup.com

General literature, fiction, non-fiction, biography, history, trade paperbacks, children's. Founded 1837.

Little, Brown Books for Young Readers
website www.lb-kids.com
website www.lb-teens.com
Publisher Megan Tingley, *Creative Director* Gail Doobinin

Picture books, board books, chapter books, novelty books and general non-fiction and novels for middle-grade and young adult readers.

Successes include *The Gulps* by Rosemary Wells, illustrated by Marc Brown, *The Gift of Nothing* by Patrick McDonnell; *Chowder* by Peter Brown, *How to Train Your Dragon* by Cressida Cowell, *Atherton* by Patrick Carman, *Nothing But the Truth (and a Few White Lies)* by Justina Chen Headley, *Story of a Girl* by Sara Zarr, *Eclipse* by Stephenie Meyer, *America Dreaming* by Laban Carrick Hill and *Exploratopia* by The Exploratorium. Publishes approx. 1,135 books a year.

Only interested in solicited agented material. Does not accept unsolicited MSS or unagented material. For illustrations, query Art Director with b&w and colour samples; provide résumé, promotional sheet or tearsheets to be kept on file. Does not respond to art samples. Do not send originals; copies only.

LB Kids (imprint)
Novelty and brand/licensed books focusing on interactive formats, licensed properties, media tie-ins, and baby and toddler-focused projects. Authors/artists include Sandra Magsamen, Rachel Hale and Ed Emberley.

Poppy (imprint)
Series for teenage girls, including *Gossip Girl* and *The It Girl*, *The Clique* and *The A-List*.

Llewellyn Worldwide – see Flux Books, a division of Llewellyn Worldwide

Lucent Books – see Gale Cengage Learning

Margaret K. McElderry Books – see Simon & Schuster Children's Publishing Division

McGraw-Hill Professional*
2 Penn Plaza, 12th Floor, New York, NY 10121
tel +1 212-904-2000
website www.mhprofessional.com
website www.mgeducation.com

Macmillan Publishers Inc.
175 Fifth Avenue, New York, NY 10010
tel +1 646-307-5151
email press.inquiries@macmillanusa.com
website http://us.macmillan.com

Imprints: Bedford/St Martins; Farrar, Straus & Giroux; Farrar, Straus & Giroux BYR; Feiwel & Friends; 01 First Second; Henry Holt and Company; Henry Holt BYR; Macmillan Audio; Picador; Square Fish; St Martin's Press; Tor/Forge (see Tom Doherty Associates, LLC on page 73); W.H. Freeman; and Worth.

Marshall Cavendish Benchmark
Marshall Cavendish Corporation,
99 White Plains Road, Tarrytown, NY 10591
tel +1 914-332-8888
email customerservice@marshallcavendish.com
website www.marshallcavendish.us

Non-fiction books for young, middle and young adult readers. Subjects include: American studies, the arts, biographies, health, mathematics, science, social studies, history, world cultures. Imprint of Marshall Cavendish Corporation.

Non-fiction subjects should be curriculum-related and are published in series form. Length: 1,500–25,000 words. Send synopsis with one or more sample chapters and sample table of contents.

Marshall Cavendish Children's Books
Marshall Cavendish Corporation,
99 White Plains Road, Tarrytown, NY 10591
tel +1 914-332-8888
email customerservice@marshallcavendish.com
website www.mceducation.us

Picture books and novels for middle grade and teens. Send manuscripts to Margery Cuyler. Does not accept submissions via email. Imprint of Marshall Cavendish Corporation.

Milet Publishing, LLC
814 North Franklin Street, Chicago, IL 60610
email info@milet.com
website www.milet.com

Picture books in English; bilingual picture books; adventurous and international young fiction; language learning books.
Not currently accepting new submissions.

Milkweed Editions
1011 Washington Avenue South, Suite 300,
Minneapolis, MN 55415

tel +1 612-332-3192
email editor@milkweed.org
website www.milkweed.org
Publisher Daniel Slager

Children's novels (8–13 years). Recent successes include Perfect (contemporary) and Trudy (contemporary). For adults: literary fiction, non-fiction, books about the natural world, poetry. Founded 1979.
Full length novels of 90–200pp. No picture books or poetry collections for young readers. Submit complete MS. Responds in 6 months. Will consider simultaneous submissions.

Millbrook Press – see Lerner Publishing Group

MINX – see DC Comics

Mitchell Lane Publishers, Inc.
PO Box 196, Hockessin, DE 19707
tel +1 302-234-9426
email customerservice@mitchelllane.com
website www.mitchelllane.com
President Barbara Mitchell

Non-fiction for young readers, middle readers and young adults. Recent successes include Vote America and The Railroad in American History.

Mondo Publishing*
980 Avenue of the Americas, New York, NY 10018
tel +1 888-886-6636
email info@mondopub.com
website www.mondopub.com

Classroom materials and professional development for K–5 educators.

Morgan Reynolds Publishing
620 South Elm Street, Suite 223, Greensboro, NC 27406
tel +1 800-535-1504
email editorial@morganreynolds.com
website www.morganreynolds.com

Biographies for juveniles and young adults. Successes include Elizabeth I of England in the European Queens series and Ulysses S. Grant: Defender of the Union in the Civil War Generals series. Founded 1993.
MSS of 25,000–30,000 words, with 8–10 chapters of 2,500–3,000 words each. See website for submission guidelines.

Thomas Nelson Publisher
PO Box 141000, Nashville, TN 37214
tel +1 800-251-4000
email publicity@thomasnelson.com
website www.thomasnelson.com
Ceo Mark Schoenwald

Acquired by HarperCollins in 2012. Bibles, religious, non-fiction and fiction general trade books for adults and children. Founded 1798.

Books

North–South Books

600 Third Avenue, 2nd Floor, New York, NY 10016
tel +1 917-210-5868
website www.northsouth.com

Successes include *The Rainbow Fish* by Marcus Pfister and *Little Polar* by Hans de Beer. Publishes 100 titles a year. Imprint: Night Sky.

Publishes fresh, original, fiction with universal themes that could appeal to children 3–8 years. Accepting picture book submissions from US authors and illustrators.

NorthWord Books for Young

Readers – see Cooper Square Publishing

Orchard Books – see Scholastic Inc.

The Overlook Press

141 Wooster Street #4B, New York, NY 10012
tel +1 212-673-2210
website www.overlookpress.com
President & Publisher Peter Mayer

Non-fiction, fiction, children's books (*Freddy the Pig* series). Imprints: Ardis Publishing, Duckworth. Founded 1971.

Richard C. Owen Publishers, Inc.

PO Box 585, Katonah, NY 10536
tel +1 914-232-3903
website www.rcowen.com
Contact Phyllis Greenspan

Books for grades K–6.

All work must be submitted as hard copy. Books for young learners: Seeks high-interest stories with charm and appeal that children 5–7 years can read by themselves. Interested in original, realistic, contemporary stories, as well as folktales, legends, and myths of all cultures. Non-fiction content must be supported with accurate facts. Length: 45–1,000 words. Also beginning chapter books up to 3,000 words.

Pacific View Press

PO Box 406, Navarro, CA 95463
tel +1 415-285-8538
email nancy@pacificviewpress.com
website www.pacificviewpress.com

Multicultural children's books, Traditional Chinese Medicine, Asia and Asian–American affairs.

Dragon Books (imprint)

Multicultural non-fiction and literature for children focusing on the culture and history of China, Japan, the Philippines, Mexico and other countries on the Pacific Rim. Books are intended to encourage pride in and respect for the shared history that makes a people unique, as well as an awareness of universal human experiences. Successes include *Cloud Weavers: Ancient Chinese Legends* by Rena Krasno and Yeng-

Fong Chiang and *Exploring Chinatown: A Children's Guide to Chinese Culture* by Carol Stepanchuk, illustrated by Leland Wong. Founded 1992.

Parragon Publishing

440 Park Avenue South, 13th Floor, New York, NY 10016
tel +1 212-629-9773
email info_northamerica@parragon.com
website http://www.parragon.com/us/home/

Children's non-fiction books of all kinds, from activity to reference. Adult titles include cookbooks, lifestyle, gardening, history.

Pearson Education*

One Lake Street, Upper Saddle River, NJ 07458
tel +1 201-236-7000
email communications@pearsoned.com
website www.phschool.com, www.pearsoned.com

Educational secondary publisher of scientifically researched and standards-based instruction materials for today's Grade 6–12 classrooms with a mission to create exceptional educational tools that ensure student and teacher success in language arts, mathematics, modern and classical languages, science, social studies, careers and technology, and advanced placements, electives and honors. Part of the Curriculum Division of Pearson Education, Inc.

Pearson Scott Foresman

One Lake Street, Upper Saddle River, NJ 07458
tel +1 201-236-7000
website www.pearsonschool.com

Elementary educational publisher. Teacher and student materials: reading, science, mathematics, language arts, social studies, music, technology, religion. Its educational resources and services include textbook-based instructional programmes, curriculum websites, digital media, assessment materials and professional development. Part of the Curriculum Division of Pearson Education Inc. Founded 1896.

Pelican Publishing Company

1000 Burmaster Street, Gretna, LA 70053
tel +1 504-368-1175
email editorial@pelicanpub.com
website www.pelicanpub.com
Publisher/President Kathleen Calhoun Nettleton

Children's books. Also art and architecture books, biographies, holiday books, local and international cookbooks, motivational works, political science, social commentary, history, business.

Send a query letter, outline if chapter book, résumé and sase. No queries or submissions by email. No unsolicited MSS for chapter books. Most young children's books are 32 illustrated pages when published; their MSS cover about 4pp when typed continuously (1,100 words maximum). Proposed books for middle readers (8+ years) should be at least 90pp. Brief books for readers under 9 years may be submitted in their entirety. Founded 1926.

Penguin Random House*

1745 Broadway New York, NY 10019
tel +1 212-782-9000
website http://global.penguinrandomhouse.com
Ceo Markus Dohle

With nearly 250 independent imprints and brands on 5 continents, more than 15,000 new titles and close to 800 million print, audio and ebooks sold annually, Penguin Random House is the world's leading trade book publisher. The company, which employs about 12,500 people globally, was formed on July 1, 2013 by Bertelsmann and Pearson, who own 53 percent and 47 percent, respectively. Like its predecessor companies, Penguin Random House is committed to publishing adult and children's fiction and non-fiction print editions, and is a pioneer in digital publishing. Its book brands include storied imprints such as Doubleday, Viking and Alfred A. Knopf (US); Ebury, Hamish Hamilton and Jonathan Cape (UK); Plaza & Janés and Alfaguara (Spain); and Sudamericana (Argentina); as well as the international imprint DK. Its publishing lists include more than 70 Nobel Prize laureates and hundreds of the world's most widely read authors. Penguin Random House champions the creative and entrepreneurial independence of its publishers, who work to maximize readership for its authors and to protect their intellectual property.

Penguin Young Readers
345 Hudson Street, New York, NY 10014
tel +1 212-366-2000
website www.penguin.com/children
President Don Weisberg
Penguin Young Readers Group is a leader in children's publishing with imprints that are home to many authors and artists including Laurie Halse Anderson, Jay Asher, Judy Blume, Jan Brett, Eric Carle, Harlan Coben, Ally Condie, Andrea Cremer, Roald Dahl, Tomie dePaola, Sarah Dessen, Anna Dewdney, Gayle Forman, Adam Gidwitz, John Green, John Grisham, Anthony Horowitz, Oliver Jeffers, Marie Lu, Mike Lupica, Richelle Mead, Brad Meltzer, Judy Schachner, Ruta Sepetys, Rick Yancey, as well as other popular authors and artists. Penguin Young Readers Group also incorporates perennial favorites such as *The Little Engine That Could*, *Madeline*, *Encyclopedia Brown*, *The Outsiders* and the *Nancy Drew and Hardy Boys* series. Imprints: Dial Books, Dutton, Grosset & Dunlap, Kathy Dawson Books, Nancy Paulsen Books, Philomel, Puffin, G. P. Putnam's Sons, Razorbill, Viking and Frederick Warne.

Random House Children's Books
1745 Broadway, New York, NY 10019
tel +1 212-782-9000

website www.randomhousekids.com
President & Publisher Barbara Marcus
Random House Children's Books is the world's largest English-language children's trade book publisher. Creating books for preschool children through young adult readers, in all formats from board books to activity books to picture books and novels, Random House Children's Books brings together award-winning authors and illustrators, world-famous franchise characters and multimillion-copy series. Random House Children's Books publishes many of the world's bestselling and highly acclaimed authors and illustrators for young people today including Dr. Seuss, Marc Brown, Roald Dahl, Carl Hiaasen, Lauren Kate, Christopher Paolini, Philip Pullman, Leo Lionni, James Dashner, Brandon Sanderson, Louis Sachar, Richard Scarry and Markus Zusak. The company is home to many series licenses and characters such as Babar, Barbie, the Berenstain Bears, Disney, Little Golden Books, Nickelodeon, Pat the Bunny, Sesame Workshop, Junie B. Jones and the Magic Tree House. Imprints: Alfred A. Knopf Books for Young Readers, Delacorte Press, Random House Books for Young Readers, Little Golden Books, Schwartz and Wade, Wendy Lamb Books, Ember, Bluefire, Dragonfly, Yearling Books, Laurel-Leaf, Princeton Review and Sylvan Learning.

Philomel – see Penguin Random House

Poppy – see Little, Brown & Company

Puffin Books – see Penguin Random House

Simon Pulse Paperback Books – see Simon & Schuster Children's Publishing Division

Rayo – see HarperCollins Publishers

Razorbill – see Penguin Random House

Rising Moon – see Cooper Square Publishing

Roaring Brook Press

175 Fifth Avenue, New York, NY 10010
tel +1 646-307-5151
website http://us.macmillan.com/RoaringBrook.aspx
Publisher Simon Boughton, *Editorial Director, Neal Porter Books* Neal Porter, *Executive Editor* Nancy Mercado

Picture books, fiction (including graphic novels) and non-fiction for young readers, from toddler to teen. Publishes about 40 titles a year. Successes include *My Friend Rabbit* by Eric Rohmann (2003 Caldecott Medal winner), *The Man Who Walked Between the Towers* by Mordicai Gerstein (2004 Caldecott Medal winner) and *A Sick Day for Amos* illustrated by Erin Stead (2011 Caldecott Medal winner). Imprint: First Second Books. Division of Holtzbrink Publishers. Does not accept unsolicited MSS or submissions.

Books

Running Press Book Publishers

2300 Chestnut Street, Suite 200, Philadelphia, PA 19103
tel +1 215-567-5080
email perseus.promos@perseusbooks.com
website www.perseusbooksgroup.com/runningpress
Publisher Chris Navratil, Directors Francis Soo Ping Chow (design), Lisa Cheng (editorial, kids), Marlo Scrimizzi (assistant editor, kids), Allison Devlin (marketing)

General non-fiction, science, history, children's fiction and non-fiction, cookbooks, pop culture, lifestyle, illustrated gift books, Miniature Editions™. Imprints: Running Press, Running Press Miniature Editions, Running Press Kids, Courage Books. Member of the Perseus Books Group. Founded 1972.

Running Press Kids (imprint)

Picture books, activity books, young adult fiction. Recent successes include the Doodles series.

Scholastic Education*

557 Broadway, New York, NY 10012
tel +1 212-343-6100
website www.scholastic.com/home

Educational publisher of research-based core and supplementary instructional materials. A leading provider in reading improvement and professional development products, as well as learning services that address the needs of the developing reader – from grades pre-K to high school.

Publishes 32 curriculum-based classroom magazines used by teachers in grades pre-K–12 as supplementary educational materials to raise awareness about current events in an age-appropriate manner and to help children develop reading skills. Magazines include Scholastic News®, Junior Scholastic®, The New York Times Upfront®, Science World®, Scope® and others, covering subjects such as English, maths, science, social studies, current events and foreign languages. The magazine's online companion, Scholastic News Online is the leading news source for students and teachers on the internet.

Scholastic Education has also developed technology-based reading assessment and management products to help administrators and educators quickly and accurately assess student reading levels, match students to the appropriate books, predict how well they will do on district and state standardised tests, and inform instruction to improve reading skills.

Its wholly owned operations in Australia, Canada, New Zealand and the UK have original trade and educational publishing programmes. Division of Scholastic Inc.

Scholastic Library Publishing (division)

90 Sherman Turnpike, Danbury, CT 06816
tel +1 203-797-3500
website www.scholastic.com
Editor-in-Chief Kate Nunn

Online and print publisher of reference products. Major reference sets include Encyclopedia Americana®, The New Book of Knowledge®, Nueva Enciclopedia Cumbre®, Lands and Peoples and The New Book of Popular Science.

Scholastic Inc.*

557 Broadway, New York, NY 10012
tel +1 212-343-6100
email news@scholastic.com
website www.scholastic.com

Scholastic is the world's largest publisher and distributor of children's books and a leader in education technology and children's media. Founded: 1920. Divisions: Scholastic Trade Publishing, Scholastic Reading Club, Scholastic Book Fairs, Scholastic Education, Scholastic International, Media, Licensing and Advertising. Imprints include: Arthur A. Levine Books, Cartwheel Books, Chicken House, David Fickling Books, Graphix™, Orchard Books, Point™, PUSH, Scholastic en español, Scholastic Licensed Publishing, Scholastic Nonfiction, Scholastic Paperbacks, Scholastic Press, Scholastic Reference™ and The Blue Sky Press® are imprints of the Scholastic Trade Book Publishing division. In addition, Scholastic Trade Books includes Klutz®, a highly innovative publisher and creator of "books plus" for children.

Scholastic Trade Books, Children's Book Publishing

Award-winning publisher of original children's books. Publishes over 500 new titles a year including the branding publishing properties Harry Potter® and Captain Underpants®, the series Clifford The Big Red Dog®, I Spy™, and Scholastic's The Magic School Bus®, as well as licensed properties such as Star Wars® and Scooby Doo™. Imprints: Blue Sky Press®, Michael di Capua Books, Cartwheel Books®, The Chicken House™, Graffix, Arthur A. Levine Books, Little Shepherd, Orchard Books®, Point, PUSH, Scholastic Paperbacks, Scholastic Press and Scholastic Reference™.

Schwartz & Wade Books – see Penguin Random House

Silver Moon Press

400 East 85th Street, New York, NY 10028
tel +1 800-874-3320
email mail@silvermoonpress.com
website www.silvermoonpress.com

Children's book publisher: test preparation, science, multiculture, biographies, historical fiction. Successes include Stories of the States, Mysteries in Time and Adventures in America series.

Simon & Schuster Children's Publishing Division*

1230 Avenue of the Americas, New York, NY 10020
tel +1 212-698-7200

website www.simonsayskids.com
President & Publisher Jon Anderson, *Vice-President & Publishers* Valerie Garfield, Justin Chanda, Mara Anastas

Preschool to young adult, fiction and non-fiction, trade, library and mass market. Imprints: Aladdin Paperbacks, Atheneum Books for Young Readers, Libros para niños, Little Simon, Margaret K. McElderry Books, Simon & Schuster Books for Young Readers, Simon Pulse, Simon Spotlight. Division of Simon & Schuster, Inc. Founded 1924.

Aladdin Paperbacks (imprint)
Editorial Director Fiona Simpson
Reprints successful hardbacks from other Simon & Schuster imprints (primarily). Recent successes include the *Dork Diaries* series and the *Goddess Girls* series.

Accepts query letters with proposals for middle-grade series and single-title fiction, beginning readers, middle-grade and commercial non-fiction. Send MS for the attention of the Submissions Editor. Send artwork submissions to Debra Sfetsios.

Atheneum Books for Young Readers (imprint)
Vice-President & Publisher Justin Chanda, *Editorial Director* Caitlyn Dlouhy
Picture books, chapter books, mysteries, biography, science fiction, fantasy, graphic novels, middle-grade and young adult fiction and non-fiction. Covers preschool–young adult. Publishes 20–30 picture books, 4–5 young readers, 20–25 middle readers and 10–15 young adult books each year. Successes include *Out of My Mind* by Sharon Draper, *The Fantastic Flying Books of Mr. Morris Lessmore* by William Joyce, *Click Clack Boo* by Doreen Cronin and Betsy Lewin and *The Thng About Luck* by Cynthia Kadohata.

Approx. 10% of books are by first-time authors. No unsolicited MSS. Send query letter only. Responds in one month. For illustrations, send résumé, samples and tearsheets to Ann Bobco.

Margaret K. McElderry Books (imprint)
Vice-President & Publisher Justin Chanda, *Editorial Director* Karen Wojtyla
Picture books, easy-to-read books, fiction (8–12 years, young adult), poetry, fantasy. Covers preschool to young adult. Publishes 10–12 picture books, 2–4 young reader titles, 8–10 middle reader titles and 5–7 young adult books each year. Recent successes include *Bear Stays Up for Christmas* by Karma Wilson and Jane Chapman, *Rumble* by Ellen Hopkins, *The Mortal Instruments* and *The Infernal Devices* series by Cassandra Clare, *The Goblin Secrets* by William Alexander and *Doll Bones* by Holly Black.

Approx. 10% of books are by first-time authors. No unsolicited MSS. Fiction length: picture books – 500 words; young readers – 2,000; middle readers – 10,000–20,000; young adult – 45,000–50,000. Non-fiction length: picture books – 500–1,000 words; young readers – 1,500–3,000 words; middle readers – 10,000–20,000 words; young adult – 30,000–45,000 words. For illustrations, query with samples to Ann Bobco, Executive Art Director. Responds in 3 months. Samples returned with sase.

Simon Pulse Books (imprint)
Editorial Director Liesa Abrams
Young adult series and fiction. Recent successes include the *Uglies* and *Leviathan* series by Scott Westerfield and the *Sea Breeze* series by Abbi Glines.

Accepts query letters. Send MS for the attention of the Submission Editor. Send artwork submissions to Russel Gordon.

Simon & Schuster Books for Young Readers (imprint)
Publisher Justin Chandu, *Editorial Director* David Gale
Fiction and non-fiction, all ages. Recent successes include the *Rot & Ruin* series by Jonathan Maybery, the *Hush Hush Saga* by Becca Fitzpatrick, the *UnWind* series by Neal Shusterman, *The Arcana Chronicles* by Kresley Cole and *Creepy Carrots* by Aaron Reynolds and Peter Brown.

No unsolicited MSS. Send query letter only. Responds in 2 months. Seeking challenging and psychologically complex young adult novels ; also imaginative and humorous middle-grade fiction.

Paula Wiseman (imprint)
email paulawiseman@simonandschuster.com
Vice-President & Publisher Paula Wiseman
Picture books, fiction and non-fiction. Publishes 10 picture books, 2 middle readers and 2 young adult titles each year. Recent successes include *Sniff, Lick and Munch* by Matthew Van Fleet and the *Amelia Notebook* series by Marissa Moss.

Approx. 10% of books are by first-time authors. Submit complete MS. Length: picture books – 500 words; others standard length. Considers all categories of fiction. Will review MS/illustration packages from artists. Send MS with dummy.

Sleeping Bear Press – see Gale Cengage Learning

StarScape – see Tom Doherty Associates, LLC

Sterling Publishing Co., Inc.
1166 Avenue of the Americas, 17th Floor, New York, NY 10036
tel +1 212-532-7160
email editorial@sterlingpublishing.com
website www.sterlingpublishing.com
Executive Vice-President Theresa Thompson

Adult non-fiction and children's board books, picture books and non-fiction. Subsidiary of Barnes & Noble. Founded in 1949.

Sterling Children's (imprint)
Non-fiction: crafts, hobbies, games, activities, origami, optical illusions, mazes, dot-to-dots, science

experiments, puzzles (maths/word/picture/logic), chess, card games and tricks, sports, magic.

Non-fiction: Write explaining the idea and enclose an outline and a sample chapter. Include information and a résumé with regard to the subject area and publishing history, and sase for return of material. No email submissions. Send submissions FAO Children's Book Editor.

Sandy Creek (imprint)

Fiction and non-fiction for children 0–14 years including activity books, picture books, encyclopedias.

Flashkids (imprint)

Workbooks and flash cards for preschool, elementary and middle school students.

Katherine Tegen Books – see HarperCollins Publishers

TOKYOPOP – see HarperCollins Publishers

Tor Books – see Tom Doherty Associates, LLC

Twenty-first Century Books – see Lerner Publishing Group (Millbrook Press imprint)

Two-Can – see Cooper Square Publishing

Viking Children's Books – see Penguin Random House

Walker & Co.

175 Fifth Avenue, New York, NY 10010
tel +1 212-674-5151
website www.walkerbooks.com
website www.bloomsburykids.com
Publishers Emily Easton (children's), George Gibson (adult)

Picture books, non-fiction and fiction (middle grade and young adult). Publishes 20 picture books, 5–8 middle readers and 5–8 young adult books each year. Walker Books and Walker Books for Young Readers are imprints of Bloomsbury Publishing Plc (page 40).

Approx. 5% of books are by first-time authors. Approx. 65% of books are acquired via literary agents. Particularly interested in picture books, illustrated non-fiction, middle-grade and young adult fiction. No series ideas. Send 50–75pp and synopsis for longer works; send the entire MS for picture books. Include sase for response only.

Weigl Publishers Inc.

350 5th Avenue, 59th Floor, New York, NY 10118
tel +1 866-649-3445
email linda@weigl.com
website www.weigl.com

Educational publisher: children's non-fiction titles. Successes include *The Backyard Animals* and *Learning to Write* series.

Albert Whitman & Company

250 South Northwest Highway, Suite 320, Park Ridge, Illinois, IL 60068
tel +1 847-581-0033
email mail@awhitmanco.com
website www.albertwhitman.com

Books that respond to cultural diversity and the special needs and concerns of children and their families (e.g. divorce, bullying). Also novels for middle-grade readers, picture books and non-fiction for children 2–12 years. Founded 1919.

Send to submissions@awhitmanco.com. For submissions guidelines see website.

Paula Wiseman – see Simon & Schuster Children's Publishing Division

Wordsong – see Boyds Mills Press

Workman Publishing Company*

225 Varick Street, New York, NY 10014
tel +1 212-254-5900
email info@workman.com
website www.workman.com
Editor-in-Chief Susan Bolotin

Non-fiction including parenting. Founded 1968.

World Book, Inc.

233 North Michigan Avenue, Suite 2000, Chicago, IL 60601
tel +1 800-975-3250
email service@worldbook.com
website www.worldbook.com

EA leading publisher of authoritative, age-appropriate and reliable print and digital educational and reference materials for children and adults. Committed to creating educational products that meet highest standards aiming to inspire a lifelong love of learning. Trade companies include children's book publisher Bright Connections Media (www.brightconnectionsmedia.com) and Incentive Publications (www.incentivepublications.com) which specializes in supplemental resources for children and teachers. Founded 1917.

Yearling Books – see Penguin Random House

Yen Press

Hachette Book Group, 237 Park Avenue, New York, NY 10017
email yenpress@hbgusa.com
website www.yenpress.com

Graphic novels and manga in all formats for all ages. Currently not seeking original project pitches from writers who are not already working with an illustrator. For submission guidelines see under Contact on website. Division of Hachette Book Group. Founded 2006.

Children's audio publishers

Many of the audio publishers listed below are also publishers of print and electronic books.

Abbey Home Media Group Ltd
435–437 Edgware Road, London W2 1TH
tel 020-7563 3910
email info@abbeyhomemedia.com
website www.abbeyhomemedia.com
Chairman Ian Miles, *Directors* Anne Miles, Dan Harriss, Emma Evans

Activity books, board books, novelty books, picture books, non-fiction, reference books and CDs. Advocates learning through interactive play. Age groups: preschool, 5 to 10 years.

Barefoot Books Ltd
294 Banbury Road, Oxford OX2 7ED
tel (01865) 311100
email help@barefootbooks.co.uk
website www.barefootbooks.co.uk
Owner, Co-founder and Ceo Nancy Traversy, *Co-founder and Editor-in-Chief* Tessa Strickland

Narrative unabridged audiobooks, spoken and sung. Founded 1993.

Barrington Stoke – see page 40

Canongate Audio Books
Eardley House, 4 Uxbridge Street, London W8 7SY
tel 020-7467 0840
website www.canongate.tv

CDs of classic children's literature such as *Just William*, *Billy Bunter* and *Black Beauty*; also adult, classic and current literary authors. Founded 1991.

Cló Iar-Chonnachta Teo
Indreabhán, Conamara, Co. Galway,
Republic of Ireland
tel +353 (0)91 593307
email eolas@cic.ie
website www.cic.ie
Ceo Micheál Ó Conghaile, *General Manager* Deirdre O'Toole

Predominantly Irish-language children's books with accompanying CD/cassette of stories/folklore/poetry. Established 1985.

Dref Wen
28 Church Road, Whitchurch, Cardiff CF14 2EA
tel 029-2061 7860
website www.drefwren.com
Directors Roger Boore, Anne Boore, Gwilym Boore, Alun Boore, Rhys Boore

Welsh-language and dual-language children's books. Founded 1970.

The Educational Company of Ireland
Ballymount Road, Walkinstown, Dublin 12,
Republic of Ireland
tel +353 (0)1 4500611
email info@edco.ie
website www.edco.ie
Chief Executive Martina Harford

Irish language CDs. Trading unit of Smurfit Kappa Group – Ireland. Founded 1910.

Hachette Children's
338 Euston Road, London NW1 3BH
tel 020-7873 6000
website www.hodder.co.uk
Managing Director Marlene Johnson

Publishes outstanding authors from within the Hodder group as well as commissioning independent titles. The list includes fiction and non-fiction. Children's titles include *Winnie the Pooh*, *Wallace & Gromit* and the *Magic Roundabout Adventures*. Founded 1994.

HarperAudio
77–85 Fulham Palace Road, London W6 8JB
tel 020-8741 7070
website www.harpercollins.co.uk
Director of Audio Jo Forshaw

Publishers of a wide range of genres including fiction, non-fiction, biography and crime and thriller. An imprint of HarperCollins. Founded 1990.

Macmillan Digital Audio
20 New Wharf Road, London N1 9RR
tel 020-7014 6000
email audiobooks@macmillan.co.uk
website www.panmacmillan.com
Digital & Communications Director Sara Lloyd, *Audio Publishing Manager* Rebecca Lloyd

Children's titles include *The Gruffalo* by Julia Donaldson and Axel Scheffler. Also adult fiction, non-fiction and autobiography. Founded 1995.

Naxos AudioBooks
5 Wyllyotts Place, Potters Bar, Herts. EN6 2JD
tel (01707) 653326
email info@naxosaudiobooks.com
website www.naxosaudiobooks.com
Managing Director Anthony Anderson

Classic literature, modern fiction, non-fiction, drama and poetry on CD. Also junior classics and classical music. Founded 1994.

Penguin Audiobooks
20 Vauxhall Bridge Road, London SW1V 2SA
tel 020-7840 8400

email vbar-kar@penguinrandomhouse.co.uk
website www.penguin.co.uk/shop/audio
Audio Publisher, Penguin Digital Videl Bar-Kar

Contemporary and classic literature for younger listeners. Authors include Cathy Cassidy, Charlie Higson, Lauren Child, Roald Dahl and Eoin Colfer. Now part of Penguin Random House UK. Founded 1993.

Puffin Audiobooks – see Penguin Audiobooks

SmartPass Ltd

15 Park Road, Rottingdean, Brighton BN2 7HL
tel (01273) 306203
email info@smartpass.co.uk
website www.smartpass.co.uk
website www.spaudiobooks.com
website www.shakespeareappreciated.com
Managing Director Phil Viner, *Creative Director* Jools Viner

Unabridged plays, poetry and dramatisations of novels as guided full-cast dramas for individual study

and classroom use. Student editions present the text with an explanatory commentary and teacher editions offer audio commentary options and CD-Rom classroom materials. Titles include *Macbeth, Romeo and Juliet, Twelfth Night, Henry V, Othello, King Lear, Hamlet, Julius Caesar, The Works of Shakespeare, A Kestrel for a Knave, Animal Farm, An Inspector Calls, Great Expectations, The Mayor of Casterbridge, Pride and Prejudice, Pre-Twentieth Century Poetry* and *War Poetry.*

Usborne Publishing Ltd

Usborne House, 83–85 Saffron Hill,
London EC1N 8RT
tel 020-7430 2800
email mail@usborne.co.uk
website www.usborne.com
Publishing Director Jenny Tyler, *General Manager* Robert Jones

Founded 1973.

Children's book packagers

Many illustrated books are created by book packagers, whose particular skills are in the areas of book design and graphic content. In-house editors match up the expertise of specialist writers, artists and photographers who usually work on a freelance basis.

Aladdin Books Ltd
2–3 Fitzroy Mews, London W1T 6DF
tel 020-7383 2084
email sales@aladdinbooks.co.uk
website www.aladdinbooks.co.uk
Directors Charles Nicholas, Bibby Whittaker

Full design and book packaging facility specialising in children's non-fiction and reference. Founded 1980.

Nicola Baxter Ltd
16 Cathedral Street, Norwich NR1 1LX
tel (01508) 766585, 07778 285555
email nb@nicolabaxter.co.uk
website www.nicolabaxter.co.uk
Director Nicola Baxter

Full packaging service for children's books in both traditional and digital formats. Happy to take projects from concept to finished work or supply bespoke authorial, editorial, design, project management, or commissioning services. Produces both fiction and non-fiction titles in a wide range of formats, for babies to young adults and experienced in novelty books and licensed publishing. Founded 1990.

Bender Richardson White
PO Box 266, Uxbridge, Middlesex UB9 5NX
tel (01895) 832444
email brw@brw.co.uk
website www.brw.co.uk
Directors Lionel Bender (editorial), Kim Richardson (sales & production), Ben White (design)

Design, editorial and production of activity books, non-fiction and reference books. Specialises in non-fiction: natural history, science, history and educational. Founded 1990.
   Writers should send a letter and synopsis of their proposal. Opportunities for freelancers.

The Book Guild Ltd
The Werks, 45 Church Road, Hove BN3 2BE
tel (01273) 720900
email info@bookguild.co.uk
website www.bookguild.co.uk
Directors Carol Biss (managing), Janet Wrench (production)

Fiction for children 5–8, 9–12 years and young adult. Produces approx. 10–15 children's titles each year. Offers a range of publishing options: a comprehensive package for authors incorporating editorial, design, production, marketing, publicity,

distribution and sales; editorial and production only for authors requiring private editions; or a complete service for companies and organisations requiring books for internal or promotional purposes – from brief to finished book. Write for submission guidelines. Founded 1982.

Bookmart Ltd
Blaby Road, Wigston, Leicester LE18 4SE
tel 0116 275 9060
email books@bookmart.co.uk
website www.bookmart.co.uk
Publishing Director Linda Williams

Colour illustrated titles: children's fiction and non-fiction, poetry, novelty books, pop-up books, activity books. Age groups: preschool, 5–10, 10–15.

Brown Bear Books Ltd
1st Floor, 9–17 St Albans Place, London N1 0NX
tel 020-7424 5640
Children's Publisher Anne O'Daly

Specialises in high-quality illustrated reference books and multi-volume sets for trade and educational markets. Opportunities for freelancers. Imprint of Windmill Books.

John Brown Group – Children's Division
136–142 Bramley Road, London W10 6SR
tel 020-7565 3000
email andrew.hirsch@johnbrownmedia.com
website www.johnbrownmedia.com
Ceo Andrew Hirsch (operations), Sara Lynn (creative)

Creative development and packaging of children's products including books, magazines, teachers' resource packs, partworks, CDs and websites.

Cambridge Publishing Management Ltd
Burr Elm Court, Main Street, Caldecote, Cambs. CB23 7NU
tel (01954) 214000
email j.dobbyne@cambridgepm.co.uk
website www.cambridgepm.co.uk
Managing Director Jackie Dobbyne, *Editorial Manager* Ed Robinson

Independent publishing services company that specialises in the complete project management of both printed and digitally published content. Works with publishers, non-publishers (corporate clients, public sector organisations and charities) and self-publishers. Subject expertise includes education,

English as a Foreign language, English Language Teaching, Modern Foreign Language, academic, professional and illustrated reference. Can handle high-volume series and multi-component courses for major publishers. Also offers a personal service to independent companies and individuals. Provides all elements of the editorial, design and production process from developing content to providing print-ready files to printers. Offers a cost-effective route to publication. All core activities are conducted in-house. Founded 1999.

Creations for Children International

Steenweg op Deinze 150, 9810 Nazareth, Belgium
tel +32 9-2446090
email info@c4ci.com
email jan.meeuws@c4ci.com
email marc.jongbloet@c4ci.com
website www.c4ci.com, www.inkypress.com

Packagers of high-quality mass market children's illustrated books, including one of the largest catalogues of illustrated fairy tales illustrated by Van Gool.

Also: story books, activity books, board books, colouring books, pop-up books, novelty books, picture books and non-fiction books.

Creative Plus Publishing Ltd

2nd Floor, 151 High Street, Billericay, Essex CM12 9AB
tel (01277) 633005
email enquiries@creative-plus.co.uk
website www.creative-plus.co.uk
Managing Director Beth Johnson

Provides all editorial and design from concept to finished pages for books, partworks and magazines along with cost-effective instructional videos. Specialises in licensed characters, make-and-do, illustrated non-fiction. Opportunities for freelancers. Founded 1989.

Design Eye Ltd

226 City Road, London EC1V 2TT
tel 020-7812 8601
website www.quarto.com/co_ed_designeye_uk.htm
Publisher Sue Grabham

Co-edition publisher of innovative Books-Plus for children. Highly illustrated, paper-engineered, novelty and component-based titles for all ages, but primarily children's preschool (3+), 5–8 and 8+ years. Mainly non-fiction, early concepts and curriculum-based topics for the trade in all international markets. Opportunities for freelance paper engineers, artists, authors, editors and designers. Unsolicited MSS not accepted. Founded 1988.

Graham-Cameron Publishing & Illustration

59 Hertford Road, Brighton BN1 7GG
tel (01273) 385890

email enquiry@gciforillustration.com
and Helen Graham-Cameron, Graham-Cameron Illustration, The Art House, Uplands Park, Sheringham, Norfolk NR26 8NE
tel (01263) 821333
website www.gciforillustration.com
Partners Helen Graham-Cameron, Duncan Graham-Cameron

Offers illustration and editorial services for picture books, information books, educational materials, activity books, non-fiction and reference books. Illustration agency with 37 artists. Do not send unsolicited MSS. Founded 1985.

Hart McLeod Ltd

14a Greenside, Waterbeach, Cambridge CB25 9HP
tel (01223) 861495
email jo@hartmcleod.co.uk
website www.hartmcleod.co.uk
Director Joanne Barker

Primarily educational and general non-fiction with particular expertise in reading books, school texts, English Language Teaching and electronic and audio content. Opportunities for freelancers and work experience. Founded 1985.

Hawcock Books

2 The Firs, Combe Down, Bath BA1 5ED
tel (07976) 708720
website www.hawcockbooks.co.uk

Designs and produces highly creative and original pop-up art and 3D paper-engineered concepts. Most experience is in developing, providing editorial assistance, printing and manufacturing pop-up books and novelty items for the publishing industry. Also undertakes demanding commissions from the advertising world for model-making, point-of-sale and all printed 3D aspects of major campaigns.

HL Studios Ltd

Riverside House, Two Rivers, Station Lane, Witney, Oxon OX28 4BH
tel (01993) 706273
email info@hlstudios.eu.com
website www.hlstudios.eu.com

Primary, secondary academic education (geography, science, modern languages) and co-editions (travel guides, gardening, cookery). Multimedia (CD-Rom programming and animations). Opportunities for freelancers. Founded 1985.

Hothouse Fiction Ltd

The Old Truman Brewery, 91 Brick Lane, London E1 6QL
tel 020-3384 2609
email ben.horslen@hothousefiction.com
website www.hothousefiction.com
Directors Reg Wright, Richard Maskell

Creative packager producing commercial series fiction for children 5 years to teen. Genres include fantasy, horror, romance, magical, historical, animals, comedy and adventure. No unsolicited MSS. Supplies a full brief for all its projects. Selects writers for projects on the basis of unpaid writing samples, but successful writers paid an advance and royalty for published books. Welcomes new writers; visit website to register.

Miles Kelly Packaging
The Bardfield Centre, Great Bardfield,
Essex CM7 4SL
tel (01371) 811309
email info@mileskelly.net
website www.mileskelly.net
Directors Gerard Kelly, Jim Miles, Richard Curry

Publishers of high-quality illustrated non-fiction titles for children and family. See also page 48. Founded 1996.

Little People Books
The Home of BookBod, Knighton,
Radnorshire LD7 1UP
tel (01547) 520925
email littlepeoplebooks@thehobb.tv
website www.littlepeoplebooks.co.uk
Directors Grant Jessé (production & managing),
Helen Wallis (rights & finance)

Packager of audio, children's educational and textbooks, digital publications. Parent company: Grant Jessé UK.

Orpheus Books Ltd
6 Church Green, Witney, Oxon OX28 4AW
tel (01993) 774949
email info@orpheusbooks.com
website www.orpheusbooks.com
website www.Q-files.com
Executive Directors Nicholas Harris, Sarah Hartley

Produces children's books and ebooks for the international co-editions market: non-fiction and reference. Orpheus Books are the creators of Q-files.com, the free online children's encyclopedia. Founded 1993.

Picthall & Gunzi Ltd
21A Widmore Road, Bromley BR1 1RW
tel 020-8460 4032
email chez@picthallandgunzi.demon.co.uk
email chris@picthallandgunzi.demon.co.uk
website www.picthallandgunzi.com
Managing Director Chez Picthall, *Editorial Director & Publisher* Christiane Gunzi

Offers a complete package, from initial concept to publication, producing high-quality, illustrated non-fiction for children of all ages: early learning, novelty, activity, board books, non-fiction. Acquired by Award Publications Ltd (page 40).

The Puzzle House
Ivy Cottage, Battlesea Green, Stradbroke,
Suffolk IP21 5NE

tel (01379) 384656
email puzzlehouse@btinternet.com
website www.the-puzzle-house.co.uk
Partners Roy Preston & Sue Preston

Editorial service creating crossword, quiz, puzzle and activity material for all ages. Founded 1988.

The Quarto Group, Inc.
The Old Brewery, 6 Blundell Street, London N7 9BH
tel 020-7700 9000
email info@quarto.com
website www.quarto.com
Chairman Timothy Chadwick, *Ceo* Marcus Leaver,
Chief Financial Officer Mick Mousley, *Director,*
Quarto International Co-editions Group David Breuer,
President & Ceo, Quarto Publishing Group USA Ken
Fund, *Managing Director, Quarto Publishing Group*
UK David Inman

The Quarto Group is a leading global illustrated book publisher and distribution group. It is composed of three publishing divisions: Quarto International Co-editions Group; Quarto Publishing Group USA; and Quarto Publishing Group UK; plus Books & Gifts Direct (a direct seller of books and gifts in Australia and New Zealand) and Regent Publishing Services, a specialist print services company based in Hong Kong. Quarto has nine children's imprints across its three publishing divisions; these are: Quarto International Co-editions Group (Quarto Children's Books, QED Publishing, Ivy Kids, small world creations, words & pictures, Marshall Children's Books); Quarto Publishing Group UK (Wide Eyed Editions, Frances Lincoln Children's Books); Quarto Publishing Group US (Walter Foster Jr.).

Small World Design
72A Pope Lane, Penwortham, Preston,
Lancs. PR1 9DA
tel (01772) 750885
email sue.chadwick@smallworlddesign.co.uk
website www.smallworlddesign.co.uk
Partners Sue Chadwick, David Peet

Bespoke illustration, design and creation of preschool to early teens material for children, including novelty, sticker and activity books, games, jigsaw puzzles and licensed products. Founded 1995.

Tangerine Designs Ltd*
5th Floor, The Old Malthouse, Clarence Street,
Bath BA1 5NS
website www.tangerinedesigns.co.uk

Packagers and international co-edition publishers of children's books. Brands include: *The Little Dreamers,*
Jolly Maties, Baby Eco, Little Eco. Specialising in novelty books, book-plus and innovations. Submissions accepted from UK only; must enclose sae if return required. See website for submissions procedure. Founded 2000.

The Templar Company Ltd
The Granary, North Street, Dorking,
Surrey RH4 1DN

tel (01306) 876361
email info@templarco.co.uk
email submissions@templarco.co.uk (submissions)
website www.templarco.co.uk
Directors Mike McGrath (managing), Amanda Wood (creative), Helen Bowe (sales & marketing)

Publisher and packager of high-quality illustrated children's books, including novelty books, picture books, pop-up books, board books, fiction, non-fiction and gift titles. Send submissions via email.

Tiptoe Books

Bradley's Close, 74–77 White Lion Street, London N1 9PF
tel 020-7520 7600
email enquiries@amberbooks.co.uk
website www.tiptoebooks.co.uk
Managing Director Stasz Gnych, *Deputy Managing Director* Sara Ballard, *Publishing Manager* Charles Catton, *Head of Production* Peter Thompson, *Design Manager* Mark Batley, *Picture Manager* Terry Forshaw

Illustrated non-fiction, multi-volume sets, calendars and sticker books for children of all ages. Subjects include history, ancient civilizations, the natural world, fantasy and general reference. Opportunities for freelancers. Children's books imprint of Amber Books Ltd.

Toucan Books Ltd

The Old Fire Station, 140 Tabernacle St, London EC2A 4SD
tel 020-7250 3388
website www.toucanbooks.co.uk
Directors Robert Sackville West, Ellen Dupont

International co-editions; editorial, design and production services. Founded 1985.

Umbrella Books

mobile (07971) 111256
email gary@allied-artists.net
website www.umbrella-childrensbooks.com
Contact Gary Mills

Packager of colourful and clever children's preschool novelty formats for generic and licensed books.

David West Children's Books

6 Princeton Court, 55 Felsham Road, London SW15 1AZ
tel 020-8780 3836
email dww@btinternet.com
website www.davidwestchildrensbooks.com
Proprietor David West, *Partner* Lynn Lockett

Packagers of children's illustrated reference books. Specialises in science, art, geography, history, sport and flight. Produces 50 titles each year. Opportunities for freelancers. Founded 1986.

Windmill Books Ltd

1st Floor, 9–17 St Albans Place, London N1 0NX
tel 020-7424 5640
Children's Publisher Anne O'Daly

Specialises in high-quality illustrated reference books and multi-volume sets for trade and educational markets. Opportunities for freelancers.

Working Partners Ltd

9 Kingsway, London WC2B 6XF
tel 020-7841 3939
email enquiries@workingpartnersltd.co.uk
website www.workingpartnersltd.co.uk
Managing Director Chris Snowdon, *Operations Director* Charles Nettleton

Children's and young adult fiction series: animal fiction, fantasy, horror, historical fiction, detective, magical, adventure. Recent successes include *Rainbow Magic*, *Beast Quest* and *Warriors*. Founded 1995.
Unable to accept any MSS or illustration submissions. Pays advance and royalty; retains copyright on all work created. Selects writers from unpaid writing samples based on specific brief provided. Always looking to add writers to database: to register details visit www.workingpartnersltd.co.uk/apply/.

Children's book clubs

Not all the companies listed here are 'clubs' in the true sense: some are mail order operations and others sell their books via book fairs.

Baker Books

Manfield Park, Cranleigh, Surrey GU6 8NU
tel (01483) 267888
email enquiries@bakerbooks.co.uk
website www.bakerbooks.co.uk

International school book club for children aged 3–16. Operates in international and English-medium schools.

Bibliophile

5 Datapoint, South Crescent, London E16 4TL
tel 020-7474 2474
email orders@bibliophilebooks.com
website www.bibliophilebooks.com
Secretary Annie Quigley

Promotes value-for-money reading. Upmarket literature and classical music on CD available from mail order catalogue (10 p.a.). Over 3,000 titles covering art and fiction as well as travel, history and children's books. Founded 1978.

The Book People Ltd

Park Menai, Bangor LL57 4FB
tel 0845 602 4040
email sales@thebookpeople.co.uk
website www.thebookpeople.co.uk

Popular general fiction and non-fiction, including children's and travel. Monthly.

Letterbox Library

Unit 151 Stratford Workshops, Burford Road, London E15 2SP
tel 020-8534 7502
email info@letterboxlibrary.com
website www.letterboxlibrary.com

Specialises in children's books that celebrate equality and diversity, including multicultural and disability titles. Also provides pre-selected packs for early years settings and schools. Mail order catalogues and website. Well-established, not-for-profit, workers' co-operative and social enterprise. Orders taken online, by fax or by post.

Red House

PO Box 142, Bangor LL57 4FBZ
tel 0845 606 4280
email enquiries@redhouse.co.uk
website www.redhouse.co.uk

A member of The Book People family. Aims to help parents to select the right books for their children at affordable prices. Founded 1979.

Scholastic Book Fairs

Westfield Road, Southam, Warks. CV47 0RA
tel 0845 603 9091 (freephone)
website www.scholastic.co.uk/bookfairs
Managing Director Steven Thompson

Sells directly to children, parents and teachers through 25,000 week-long events held in schools throughout the UK.

Children's bookshops

The bookshops in the first part of this list specialise in selling new children's books and are good places for writers and illustrators to check out the marketplace. Most of them are members of the Booksellers Association and are well known to publishers. A list of second-hand and antiquarian children's bookshops follows. Independent Booksellers Week takes place each year in late June/early July, and March 2015 saw the first Indie Book Day in the UK.

Badger Books
email info@badgerbooks.co.uk
website www.badgerbooks.co.uk
Proprietors Nic and Janet Tall

Online business specialising in selling modern reprints of sought-after children's books.

Bags-of-Books
1 South Street, Lewes BN7 2BT
tel (01273) 479320
email bagsofbooks@bags-of-books.co.uk
website www.bagsofbooks.co.uk
Proprietors Anna Morgan and Gavin Teasedale

Independent children's bookshop situated within a 15th-century building and filled with a wide range of titles. Hosts author visits.

Barefoot Books Studio
294 Banbury Road, Summertown, Oxford OX2 7ED
tel (01865) 311100
email oxford-events@barefootbooks.co.uk
website www.barefootbooks.com

Bookshop, studio and café which aims to be a hub in the local community for families. Regularly staged events include story time, arts and crafts, music and yoga.

Blackwell's Children's Bookshop
Blackwell's Bookshop, 50 Broad Street,
Oxford OX1 3BQ
tel (01865) 333694
email childrens@blackwell.co.uk
website www.blackwell.co.uk

Stocks over 10,000 titles for children of all ages and holds a regular events programme including author visits to schools. The children's department is at the back of the ground floor of Blackwell's flagship bookshop in central Oxford.

The Book Burrow @ Aardvark Books & Café
The Bookery, Manor Farm, Brampton Bryan,
Bucknell SY7 0DH
email aardvaark@btconnect.com
website www.aardvark-books.com
Proprietors Sheridan and Sarah Swinson

Book and play space with a castle, enchanted forest, pirate cabin and princess seat. Extensive range of books, mostly new but with some second-hand and rare.

Children's events throughout the year. BA member.

The Book House, Summertown
267 Banbury Road, Summertown, Oxford OX2 7HT
tel (01865) 510887
email anybook@thebookhousesummertown.co.uk
website www.thebookhousesummertown.co.uk
Co-Managers Renée Holler, Kate Kay, David Whittaker

Sister establishment to The Book House, Thame. Stocks titles for adults and children; half of the shop is dedicated to young readers.

The Book House, Thame
93 High Street, Thame, Oxon OX9 3HJ
tel (01844) 213032
email anybook@thebookhousethame.co.uk
website www.thebookhousethame.co.uk
Proprietor Brian Pattinson

Specialises in children's books alongside a wide range of titles for all ages. Established in the community for over 40 years, the Book House holds its own literary festival every October.

The Book Nook
First Avenue, Hove BN3 2FJ
tel (01273) 911988
email info@booknookuk.com
website www.booknookuk.com
Proprietors Vanessa Lewis and Julie Ward

Specialist children's bookshop set in a child-friendly environment with author events, daily story time, café and pirate ship. Named Children's Bookseller of the Year at *The Bookseller* Industry Awards 2015.

Booka Bookshop and Café
26–28 Church Street, Oswestry, Shrops. SY11 2SP
tel (01691) 662244
email mail@bookabookshop.co.uk
website www.bookabookshop.co.uk
Proprietors Carrie and Tim Morris

Independent bookshop and café offering a wide range of books, cards and gifts. Hosts a regular programme of author talks and signings, organises themed events, runs bookclubs and works with schools and the local library. Named Independent Bookshop of the Year 2015 at *The Bookseller* Industry Awards.

Bookworm Ltd
1177 Finchley Road, London NW11 0AA
tel 020-8201 9811
email bookworm1@btconnect.com
website www.thebookworm.uk.com

Independent children's bookshop catering for all ages, from babies to young adults. Also supplies books to schools. Hosts author visits and holds regular story time sessions.

The Broadway Bookshop
6 Broadway Market, London E8 4QJ
tel 020-7241 1626
email books@broadwaybookshophackney.com
website www.broadwaybookshophackney.com
Proprietor Jane Howe

General independent bookshop specialising in literary fiction with a strong selection of children's books for all ages.

Browns Books For Students
22–28 George Street, Hull HU1 3AP
tel (01482) 325413
email enquiries@brownsbfs.co.uk
website www.brownsbfs.co.uk

Supplies any book in print to schools, colleges and international schools. Full school servicing of books on request.

Chapter One Bookshop
136 Crockhamwell Road, Woodley, Reading RG5 3JH
tel/fax 0118 944 8883
email chapteronewoodley@gmail.com
website www.chapteronewoodley.co.uk
Proprietors John and Mary Baker

General bookshop with a specialisation in children's titles.

The Children's Bookshop – Hay-on-Wye
Toll Cottage, Pontvaen, Hay-on-Wye,
Herefordshire HR3 5EW
tel (01497) 821083
email sales@childrensbookshop.com
website www.childrensbookshop.com
Proprietors Judith Gardner, Colin Gardner

Second-hand and antiquarian children's books.

Children's Bookshop (Huddersfield)
37–39 Lidget Street, Lindley, Huddersfield,
West Yorkshire HD3 3JF
tel (01484) 658013
email barry@hudbooks.demon.co.uk
website http://childrensbookshuddersfield.co.uk

Children's Bookshop (Muswell Hill)
29 Fortis Green Road, London N10 3HP
tel 020-8444 5500
email admin@childrensbookshoplondon.co.uk
website www.childrensbookshoplondon.com

Family-owned specialist children's bookshop. Stocks approximately 12,000 titles and 25,000 books for children from babies to teenagers. Also offers services for schools and individuals. Founded 1974.

The Edinburgh Bookshop
219 Bruntsfield Place, Edinburgh EH10 4DH
tel 0131 447 1917
email mail@edinburghbookshop.com
website www.edinburghbookshop.com
Proprietor Marie Moser

Named UK Children's Bookseller of the Year at *The Bookseller* Industry Awards 2014. Events programme includes author visits, writers' workshops and a twice-weekly story time for the under 5s. Founded 2007.

Far from the Madding Crowd
20 High Street, Linlithgow EH49 7AE
tel (01506) 845509
email jill@maddingcrowdlinlithgow.co.uk
website www.maddingcrowdlinlithgow.co.uk

Independent bookshop with eclectic range of titles, including children's and preschool with a brand-new dedicated story-telling hub.
 Strong influence from Scottish publishers.

Glowworm Books & Gifts Ltd
Unit 2, 5 Youngs Road, East Mains Industrial Estate, Broxburn, West Lothian EH52 5LY
tel (01506) 857570
website www.glowwormbooks.co.uk

Specialises in supplying books for children, especially those who find reading difficult due to physical or special educational challenges.

Heath Educational Books
Willow House, Willow Walk, Whittaker Road,
Sutton, Surrey SM3 9QQ
tel 020-8644 7788
email orders@heathbooks.co.uk
website www.heathbooks.co.uk
Proprietor Richard Heath

Supplies books to schools and teachers throughout Europe. Large showroom.

Hunting Raven Books
10 Cheap Street, Frome, Somerset BA11 1BN
tel (01373) 473111
website www.huntingravenbooks.co.uk
Proprietors John and Caroline Birkett-Smith

Long-established independent bookship with extensive range of books and gifts for all ages and a strong children's section. Holds events, signings and children's competitions regularly, including the annual ABC (Authors & Books for Children) Day.

Jubileebooks.co.uk Ltd

31A Vanburgh Park, Blackheath, London SE3 7AE
tel 020-8293 6060
email enquiries@jubileebooks.co.uk
website www.jubileebooks.co.uk

Offers a wide range of children's books and resources to schools. Organises literacy and book-related events in the UK and worldwide. Service includes consultancy, new library set-up, book fairs, author visits, reading and writing projects, literacy INSET and training conferences. Founded 1996.

Madeleine Lindley Ltd

Book Centre, Broadgate, Broadway Business Park, Oldham OL9 9XA
tel 0161 683 4400
email enquiries@madeleinelindley.com
website www.madeleinelindley.com

Supplies books to schools and nurseries, provides information services and runs open days and training courses for teachers. Hosts author/publisher events for teachers and children.

The Mainstreet Trading Company

Main Street, St Boswells, Scottish Borders, TD6 0AT
tel (01835) 824087
email info@mainstreetbooks.co.uk
website www.mainstreetbooks.co.uk
Proprietors Rosamund and Bill de la Hay

General bookshop with a particular focus on children's books. Named Independent Bookseller of the Year at the The Bookseller Industry Awards 2012.

Nickel Books

9 Merlin Close, Sittingbourne ME10 4TY
tel 07462 778570
email enquiries@nickelbooks.co.uk
website www.nickelbooks.co.uk
Proprietor Andrea Don

Mail-order only. Specialises in children's books, from birth to teenage; also books for parents.

Norfolk Children's Book Centre

Alby, Norwich NR11 7HB
tel (01263) 761402
email marilyn@ncbc.co.uk
website www.ncbc.co.uk

Specialist children's bookshop for readers of all ages. Offers services to schools in East Anglia including storytelling, talks to children and parents, approval services and INSET for teachers. School library assessment and rejuvenation nationwide.

Octavia's Bookshop

24 Black Jack Street, Cirencester GL7 2AA
tel (01285) 650677

email info@octaviasbookshop.co.uk
website www.octaviasbookshop.co.uk
Proprietor Octavia Karavla

Independent bookshop in which more than half the stock is dedicated to children's titles, from buggy books to teen fiction and classics. Book groups are available for children aged six upwards. Named Children's Independent Bookseller of the Year at the The Bookseller Industry Awards 2013.

The Oundle Bookshop

13 Market Place, Oundle, Peterborough PE8 4BA
tel (01832) 273523
website www.colemans-online.co.uk/oundle-bookshop.html

Peters Books & Furniture

120 Bromsgrove Street, Birmingham B5 6RJ
tel 0121 666 6646
website www.peters-books.co.uk

Specialist supplier of children's books and library furniture to schools and public authorities, with a book and furniture showroom and online ordering facilities and ten specialist children's librarians. Also provides a library design and installation service, an e-book lending platform for schools and public library authorities and book-related promotional material and information including WRDmag, a reader development magazine for 8–12 year-olds. Peters also holds its own annual book awards, Peters Book of the Year, as well as regular professional development events for teachers and librarians, featuring expert speakers, authors and illustrators.

Pickled Pepper Books

10 Middle Lane, Crouch End, London N8 8PL
tel 020-3632 0823
email info@pickledpepperbooks.co.uk
website www.pickledpepperbooks.co.uk
Proprietors Urmi Merchant and Steven Pryse

Family-run specialist children's bookshop with a café and weekly programme of events for under 5s including story times, art and craft, music groups, Spanish and French sing-alongs and NCT coffee mornings. After-school events include book groups for 9–12 year olds and teens' creative writing and illustration clubs. The bookshop also hosts regular interactive author events, as well as innovative theatre and puppet shows.

Rhyme & Reason

681 Ecclesall Road, Sheffield S11 8TG
tel 0114 266 1950
email enquiries@rhyme-reason.co.uk
website www.rhyme-reason.co.uk

Stocks new books for adults and children of all ages. The shop works with local schools, libraries and festival organisers to promote author events. Special interests include poetry, fiction and natural history. As a member of the Booksellers' Association, the shop sells and redeems National Book Tokens. Advice and recommendations are available. Customer orders for any book in print are supplied promptly.

Seven Stories – see page 385

Storytellers, Inc.
7 The Crescent, St Anne's on Sea, Lytham St Anne's, Lancs. FY8 1SN
tel (01253) 781690
email info@storytellersinc.co.uk
website www.storytellersinc.co.uk
Proprietors Carolyn Clapham and Katie Clapham

Independent bookshop with dedicated children's section and junior book clubs for readers aged 8–9, 10–12 and 13–15 respectively. Also supplies books to local schools, offers a literary consultancy service and its own book introduction project (Cool Books in School). Regional winner (North) in the Independent Bookshop of the Year category at *The Bookseller* Industry Awards 2015.

Tales On Moon Lane
25 Half Moon Lane, London SE24 9JU
tel/fax 020-7274 5759
email info@talesonmoonlane.co.uk
website www.talesonmoonlane.co.uk
Proprietor Tamara Macfarlane

Specialist children's bookshop which runs yearly children's literature festivals in February and October, as well as weekly storytelling sessions for preschool children.

Victoria Park Books
174 Victoria Park Road, London E9 7HD
tel 020-8986 1124
email info@victoriaparkbooks.co.uk
website www.victoriaparkbooks.co.uk
Proprietors Jo and Cris De Guia

Specialist children's bookshop including dual-language books. Reading groups for toddlers.

West End Lane Books
277 West End Lane, London NW6 1QS
tel 020-7431 3770
email info@welbooks.co.uk
website www.welbooks.co.uk

Independent family-owned bookshop, carrying fiction and non-fiction books and stationery. Offers twice-weekly (Monday and Thursday, 4pm) story-time sessions for preschool children. Hosts regular author talks and book groups, and also offers a children's personal shopper and a party bag and gift list service. The Review Crew is a school holiday club offering free advance editions of books in return for free short reviews on the shop's website.

BOOKSELLERS FOR COLLECTORS

Blackwell's Rare Books
48–51 Broad Street, Oxford OX1 3BQ
tel (01865) 333555
email rarebooks@blackwell.co.uk
website www.rarebooks.blackwell.co.uk

Deals in early and modern first editions of children's books, among other subjects. Catalogues are issued periodically, which include modern and antiquarian children's books.

Bookmark Children's Books
Fortnight, Broad Hinton, Swindon, Wilts. SN4 9NR
tel (07788) 841305
email leonora-excell@btconnect.com
Contact Anne Excell, Leonora Smith

Mail-order bookseller, specialising in books for collectors, ranging from antiquarian to modern. A wide range of first editions, novelty and picture books, chap-books, ABCs, annuals, etc. Also a selection of vintage toys, games, greetings cards and illustrated postcards, dolls and nursery china. Catalogues of children's books and related juvenilia issued. Book search service available within this specialist area. Member of PBFA, exhibiting at PBFA book fairs in London, Oxford and Bath. Send sae. Established 1973.

Paul Embleton
12 Greenfields, Stansted Mountfitchet, Essex CM24 8AH
tel (01279) 812627
email paulembleton@btconnect.com
website www.abebooks.com

Sells by post via the Internet and sends subject lists to regular customers. Receives visitors by appointment. Specialises in books and ephemera for the picture postcard collector and maintains a good stock of children's books and ephemera, mostly Victorian and Edwardian chromolithographic by such publishers as Nister and Raphael Tuck, and items of any age by collectable illustrators.

Ian Hodgkins & Co Ltd
47 Lansdown, Stroud, Glos. GL5 1BN
tel (01453) 755233
email enquiries@ianhodgkins.com
website www.ianhodgkins.com
Contact Simon Weager

Dealer in rare and out-of-print books and related material. Specialist in Beatrix Potter and fairy tales and 19th-century British art and literature. Free catalogues in all specialist areas published regularly.

Marchpane Children's Books
16 Cecil Court, Charing Cross Road, London WC2N 4HE

Books

tel 020-7836 8661
email enquiries@marchpane.com
website www.marchpane.com

Antiquarian children's books only. Open Mon–Sat 10.30am–6.00pm.

Plurabelle Books

Unit 8, Restwell House, Coldhams Road,
Cambridge CB1 3EW
tel (01223) 415671
email books@plurabelle.co.uk
website www.plurabellebooks.co.uk
Contact Michael Cahn

Second-hand bookseller specialising in academic books on literature, reading, history of education and children's literature. Free book search for out-of-print books. Catalogue published three times a year. Visitors welcome by appointment.

Ripping Yarns Bookshop

355 Archway Road, London N6 4EJ
tel 020-8341 6111
email yarns@rippingyarns.co.uk
website www.rippingyarns.co.uk

Vintage bookshop, opposite Highgate Tube station, with a large general stock, including poetry, politics, plays and ephemera. Has an especially large collection of 19th and 20th century children's books.

Rose's Books

14 Broad Street, Hay-on-Wye,
Herefordshire HR3 5DB
tel (01497) 820013
email enquiry@rosesbooks.com
website www.rosesbooks.com
Contact Maria Goddard

Specialises solely in rare, out-of-print children's books and located in the international book town of Hay-on-Wye. Stock available via website. Catalogues and specialist lists issued regularly. Open 10.00am–5.30pm Monday to Friday, 9.30am–5.30pm Saturday and Sunday. Children's books purchased – single items or collections. Established 1986.

Henry Sotheran Ltd

2–5 Sackville Street, Piccadilly, London W1S 3DP
tel 020-7439 6151
email rh@sotherans.co.uk
Contact Rosie Hodge

Large showroom with hundreds of important children's books spanning two centuries, specialising in first editions and illustrated works by pivotal artists. Issues two specialist catalogues free, on request.

Resources about children's books

Caroline Horn selects some of the best print and online resources about children's books for readers, writers and illustrators.

There are many books written about children's books, offering practical advice on selecting books or invaluable research material for those pursuing degrees and diplomas in children's literature. For those who want to keep up to date with news and trends in picture books, middle grade fiction and YA novels, there is also a host of blogs and websites sharing news and updates on a daily basis.

Books

BOOKS

Book Trust Best Book Guide
Published annually by Book Trust
website www.booktrust.org.uk/books/children/best-book-guide

Book Trust's independent annual 'pick of the best' in children's paperback fiction published in the previous calendar year. It is designed to help parents and those interested in children's reading to select books for children, from babies to teenagers. Printed in full colour, each book featured has a short review, colour coding to indicate reading age and interest level, and bibliographic information.

The Cambridge Guide to Children's Books in English
Edited by Victor Watson
Published by Cambridge University Press (2001)
ISBN 978–0–5215–50642

Reference work providing a critical overview of children's books written in English across the world. It includes the history of children's books from pre-Norman times to the present, taking on board current developments in publishing practices and in children's own reading. Entries on TV, comics, annuals and the growing range of media texts are included.

The Oxford Companion to Children's Literature
Edited by Daniel Hahn
Published by Oxford University Press (2015)
ISBN 978–0–19969514-0

An indispensable reference book for anyone interested in children's books. Over 900 biographical entries deal with authors, illustrators, printers, publishers, educationalists and others who have influenced the development of children's literature. Genres covered include myths and legends, fairy tales, adventure stories, school stories, fantasy, science fiction, crime and romance. This book is of particular interest to librarians, teachers, students, parents and collectors.

The Reading Bug – and how you can help your child to catch it
by Paul Jennings
Published by Penguin Books (2004)
ISBN 978–0–1413–18400

Paul Jennings is a well-known children's author. This book explains, in his unique humorous style, how readers can open up the world through a love of books. He cuts through the jargon and the controversies to reveal the simple truths, which should enable adults to infect children with the reading bug.

Sticks and Stones: The Troublesome Success of Children's Literature from Slovenly Peter to Harry Potter
by Jack Zipes
Published by Routledge (2002)
ISBN 978–0–4159–38808

Jack Zipes – translator of the Grimm tales, teacher, storyteller and scholar – questions whether children ever really had a literature of their own. He sees children's literature in many ways as being the 'grown-ups' version' – a story about childhood that adults tell kids. He discusses children's literature from the 19th century moralism of Slovenly Peter (whose fingers get cut off) to the wildly successful *Harry Potter* books. Children's literature is a booming market but its success, this author says, is disguising its limitations. *Sticks and Stones* is a forthright and engaging book by someone who clearly cares deeply about what and how children read.

1001 Children's Books You Must Read Before You Grow Up
Edited by Julia Eccleshare
Published by Cassell Illustrated (2009)
ISBN 978–1–8440–36714

This aims to provide an introduction to the best of children's literature, ranging from international classics to contemporary writers. Reviews of each book are accompanied by line drawings and artwork from the books themselves. A number of authors including Michael Morpurgo and Jacqueline Wilson also write about their favourite books. The reviews are ordered according to the book's publication date, from past to present, and age range of the reader.

The Ultimate Book Guide

Edited by Daniel Hahn, Leonie Flynn and Susan Reuben
Published by A&C Black (2009)
ISBN 978–1–4081–04385

Over 600 entries covering the best books for children aged 8–12, from classics to more recently published titles. Funny, friendly and frank recommendations written for children by their favourite and best-known authors including Anthony Horowitz, Jacqueline Wilson, Celia Rees, Darren Shan, David Almond and Dick King-Smith. Plus features on the most popular genres.

The Ultimate First Book Guide

by Leonie Flynn and Daniel Hahn
Published by A&C Black (2008)
ISBN 978–0–7136–73319

Comprehensive reference to help children aged 0–7 with their first steps into the world of books. Covers board books and novelty books, through to classic and contemporary picture books, chapter books and more challenging reads. It includes recommendations and features from top authors and experts in the field of children's books, including former Children's Laureate Michael Rosen, Tony Bradman, Malachy Doyle and Wendy Cooling. There are also special features on a variety of topics and themed lists, and a selection of cross-references to other titles children may enjoy.

The Ultimate Teen Book Guide

Edited by Daniel Hahn and Leonie Flynn
Published by A&C Black (2010, 2nd edn)
ISBN 978–1–4081–04378

Listings of over 700 books that might interest teenage readers, recommended and reviewed by authors such as Melvin Burgess, Anthony Horowitz, Meg Cabot, Eoin Colfer and Philip Pullman. Reviews cover the classics to cult fiction, and graphic novels to bestsellers, and each is cross-referenced to other titles as suggestions of what to read next. The book also contains essays on areas of teenage writing including *Race in Young Adult Fiction* by Bali Rai and *Off the Rails* by Kevin Brooks. There are also the results of a national teen readers' poll, plus reviews from teen readers.

ONLINE

ACHUKA Children's Books UK

website www.achuka.co.uk

An online guide to children's and adults' books

focusing on new books and titles published by Achuka. With author interviews and news.

Amazon

website www.amazon.co.uk, www.amazon.com

UK and US online bookstore with millions of books available on their websites at discounted prices, plus a personal notification service of new releases, reader reviews, bestsellers and book information.

Armadillo

website https://sites.google.com/site/armadillomagazinenew

An online magazine about children's books, including reviews, interviews, features and profiles. New issues are posted at the end of March, June, September and December. It was founded in 1999 by author Mary Hoffman as a review publication for children's books.

BBC Education

website www.bbc.co.uk/schools

Information about UK schools' curriculum. Useful for those wishing to write for educational publishers but also for keeping abreast of curricular topics.

The Bookbag

website www.thebookbag.co.uk

A UK-based website focused on great reviews about children's books, there are also booklists and information about book awards, as well as articles and author interviews.

Books for Keeps

website booksforkeeps.co.uk

Featuring a quarterly online magazine for children's books including book reviews and features.

Book Trust

website www.booktrust.org.uk/books/children

Dedicated children's division of Book Trust and a useful site for professionals working with young readers. Information on events, prizes, books, authors, etc.

Branford Boase Award

website http://www.branfordboaseaward.org.uk

The website for the annual children's book award dedicated to debut children's writers and their editor and includes a writing competition for young people.

Children's BBC

website www.bbc.co.uk/cbbc

Website of the CBBC channel with games, activities and news for children.

The Children's Book Council

website www.cbcbooks.org

The Children's Book Council in the USA is dedicated

to encouraging literacy and the enjoyment of children's books. The website includes reviews of children's books published in the USA, forthcoming publications and author profiles. A good site for checking out the US marketplace.

Children's Laureate
website www.childrenslaureate.org.uk

Official website of the Children's Laureate with resources and activities for children.

Children's Literature
website www.childrenslit.com

US website of the Children's Literature Comprehensive Database (CLCD), a subscription database with over 400,000 reviews of children's books. Plus links to US author and illustrator websites.

Cilip Carnegie & Kate Greenaway Medals
website http://www.carnegiegreenaway.org.uk/home

This website follows the only UK children's book award where the winners are selected by specialist children's librarians. The website includes a 'shadowing' area for schools to leave their comments about the books, plus interviews with shortlisted authors.

Girls Heart Books
website http://girlsheartbooks.com

A blog written by a group of authors who focus on the 8–12 years age range offering daily blogs, competitions, inspiration and guidance.

Good Reads for Children
website www.goodreads.com/genres/childrens

The Amazon-owned website supports consumer reviews about books for children that can be researched by categories including Middle Grade and Picture Books, etc.

The Guardian
website www.guardian.com/childrens-books-site

Children's books website including news, reviews and author interviews. Children can contribute their own reviews and comments.

Guy's Read
website www.guysread.com

US web-based resource aimed at helping boys find material they like to read.

The History Girls
website http://the-history-girls.blogspot.co.uk

A regular blog whose contributors are 'a group of bestselling, award-winning writers of historical fiction', with interviews, news and information about new books.

The Horn Book
website www.hbook.com

US website hosting *The Horn Book Guide Online*, a comprehensive, fully searchable database of over 80,000 book titles for children and young adults, and a monthly e-newsletter for parents, *Notes from the Horn Book*. Plus much more.

House of Illustration
website www.houseofillustration.org.uk

The brainchild of author and illustrator Quentin Blake, the House of Illustration celebrates all forms of illustration, run regular talks and events and supports schools-based activities.

US website with information, reviews, author links and features on children's books. Part of The Book Report Network.

National Literacy Trust
website www.literacytrust.org.uk

The organisation is focused on developing literacy among adults and children and its website documents its activities.

Picture Book Den
website http://picturebookden.blogspot.co.uk

An independent website created by professional children's authors based in the UK and Ireland where they share their passion for picture books, with blogs on getting published, writing picture books, etc but not reviews.

ReadingZone.com
website www.readingzone.com

A magazine-style website, created with Arts Council support, dedicated to children's books including monthly book reviews by teachers and librarians as well as children, chapters to download, author interviews, news, activities and a regular newsletter. There are distinct areas for teachers, librarians, families, children and teenagers.

Scottish Book Trust
website www.scottishbooktrust.com

Information on books for children of all ages in Scotland plus a national programme of events with children's writers: author tours, festivals, writing competitions and exciting activities.

Seven Stories
website www.sevenstories.org.uk

The Seven Stories National Centre for Children's Books, based in Newcastle, provides regular events and exhibitions dedicated to children's literature which are highlighted on its website.

Books

Stories from the Web
website www.storiesfromtheweb.org

A members-only website developed by Leeds, Bristol and Birmingham Library Services that provides information on library clubs, stories, reviews and a chance to email authors.

The Story Museum
website www.storymuseum.org.uk/1001stories

1001 inspirational stories from around the world to watch, hear, read and tell.

Teen Reads
website www.teenreads.com

US website with information, reviews, author links and features on teenage books. Part of The Book Report Network.

UK Children's Books
website www.ukchildrensbooks.co.uk

Directory of authors, illustrators and publishers involved in children's books and reading promotion.

UKYA
website UKYA.co.uk

Dedicated to teen fiction by UK authors, the website includes booklists by genre, special features and interviews. It is run by a group of UK YA authors.

Who Next ... ?
website www.whonextguide.com

Writers of children's fiction are listed with suggestions of other authors who write in a similar way, together with key book and series titles. There is a small annual subscription fee for accessing the information.

Write4Kids
website www.write4kids.com

US site with articles and information about the art of writing children's books. Also *Children's Book Insider* newsletter.

YALC
website www.childrenslaureate.org.uk/yalc

The annual UK YA Literature Convention, inspired by former Children's Laureate Malorie Blackman, enables YA fans to meet a range of authors during a programme dedicated to all things YA.

Caroline Horn is editor of www.ReadingZone.com.

Notes from a Children's Laureate

Anthony Browne was the Children's Laureate 2009–11. Here he shares his passion for picture books and explains the importance of the Shape Game to develop the act of looking.

It was a long road to becoming the Children's Laureate but I believe it all started with the Shape Game, a simple drawing game that my brother and I thought we'd invented when we were young. I have spoken of this game to children all over the world, and they've made me realise that its prevalence in my own childhood was by no means unique. Children everywhere have invented their own versions of the Shape Game. It has certainly been a very important part of my career, for I have played it in every book I've made.

The rules are very simple: the first person draws an abstract shape; the second person, ideally using a different coloured pen, transforms it into something. It seems that all children love this game and are very good at it – far better than adults are. It is an unfortunate part of growing up that we lose a great deal of contact with our visual imagination. The wonder with which we look at the world diminishes, and this inhibits both our inclination to draw (most adults give up entirely) and also our ability to draw with any real creative value.

Even though the Shape Game is great fun to play, I believe it also has a serious aspect. Essentially, the game is about creativity itself. Every time we draw a picture, or write a story, or compose a piece of music, we are playing the Shape Game. When children ask me (and they always do) where I get my inspiration from, I tell them it's from the same place that they get theirs – from things that happened to me when I was a boy, or things that happened to my own children, from other people's stories, from films, from paintings, or from dreams. There are so many sources of inspiration. Everything comes from somewhere else, and when we create something we're transforming our own experience into a picture, a book, or perhaps a piece of music. We are playing our own Shape Game.

In my early years my father was the landlord of a pub near Bradford and apparently I used to stand on a table in the bar and tell stories to customers about a character called Big Dumb Tackle (whoever he was). I spent much of my childhood playing sport, fighting and drawing with my older brother and then studied graphic design in Leeds. While I was at art college my father died suddenly and horrifically in front of me, and this affected me hugely. I went through a rather dark period which didn't sit very happily with the world of graphic design. After leaving college I dabbled rather unsuccessfully in the advertising world then heard about a job as a medical artist and thought that it sounded interesting – it was. I worked at Manchester Royal Infirmary for three years painting delicate watercolours of grotesque operations. It taught me a lot more about drawing than I ever learned at art college, and I believe it taught me how to tell stories in pictures. I thought that it was probably time to move on when strange little figures started appearing in these paintings – and so began a career designing greetings cards. I continued to do this for many years working for the Gordon Fraser Gallery.

Gordon Fraser became a close friend and taught me a lot about card design which was to prove very useful when I started doing children's books. I experimented with many styles and many subjects, from snowmen to dogs with big eyes to gorillas. I sent some of my designs to various children's book publishers and it was through one of these that I met Julia MacRae who was to become my editor for the next 20 years. She taught me much of what I know about writing and illustrating children's books.

In 1976 I produced *Through the Magic Mirror*, a strange kind of book in which I painted many of the pictures before I wrote the story. I followed this with *A Walk in the Park*, a story I was to revisit 20 years later with *Voices in the Park*. Probably my most successful book is *Gorilla*, and it was around the time it was published in 1983 that I was badly bitten by a gorilla whilst being filmed for television at my local zoo.

I have published 45 books and been very lucky to win awards for some of these – the Kate Greenaway Medal twice (page 411) and the Kurt Maschler 'Emil' three times. In 2000 I was awarded the Hans Christian Andersen Medal (page 409), which is an international award and the highest honour a children's writer or illustrator can win, and I was the first British illustrator to receive it. My books have been translated into 28 languages. My illustrations have been exhibited in many countries – USA, Mexico, Venezuela, Colombia, France, Korea, Italy, Germany, Holland, Japan and Taiwan – and I've had the pleasure of visiting these places and working with local children and meeting other illustrators.

In 2001–2 I worked at Tate Britain with children using art as a stimulus to inspire visual literacy and creative writing activities. It was during this time that I conceived and produced *The Shape Game*.

In 2009 I was appointed Children's Laureate. In this capacity, my aim was to encourage more children to discover and love reading, focusing particularly on the appreciation of picture books, and the reading of both pictures *and* words. I strongly believe that picture books are special – they're not like anything else.

Sometimes I hear parents encouraging their children to read what they call 'proper' books (that's books without pictures) at an earlier and earlier age. This makes me sad, as picture books are perfect for sharing, and not just with the youngest children. As a father, I understand the importance of the bond that develops through reading and talking about picture books with your child. I believe the best picture books leave a tantalising gap between the pictures and the words, a gap that's filled by the reader's imagination, adding so much to the excitement of the book. Picture books are for everybody at any age, not books to be left behind as we grow older.

I also try to encourage the act of looking. Research has shown that visitors to art galleries spend an average of 30 seconds looking at each painting, and considerably more time reading the captions. It's an unfortunate element of growing up that we can lose a great deal of contact with our visual imagination, and by encouraging children – and adults – to play the Shape Game I hope this will change.

In the best picture books the pictures contain clues; they tell you what characters are thinking or how they're feeling. By reading these clues we get a far deeper understanding of the story. In the UK we have some of the best picture book makers in the world, and I want to see their books appreciated for what they are – works of art.

In spite of my concerns about the state of the market for picture books, I am optimistic about the future. I realise now more than ever that I am incredibly lucky to love what I do. Straight after finishing art college I was disheartened because it seemed inevitable that in order to make a living from art I would have to make massive compromises. The experience of doing those advertising jobs made any dreams I once had seem futile. I was getting paid, but the fun of drawing had been taken away. I retrieved some of the fun when

I was a medical illustrator, and I enjoyed making many of the card designs, but it wasn't until I discovered picture books that I learned it was possible to have as much fun with a paintbrush as I had done as a child *and* get paid for it. This is what I love most about my job. What I do now is exactly what I did then: tell stories and draw pictures. Nothing much has changed, not even my approach. Drawing was always my favourite thing to do, and you could say that my career is comparable to other little boys growing up and being paid to play with Lego or dress up as cowboys.

I am also extremely lucky that I have been able to continue 'playing' for a living for so long. I could never stop drawing. Even if I was to give up doing it for a living I would carry on drawing for pleasure. But doing it for a living *is* doing it for pleasure, so there really is no reason to stop!

Anthony Browne was the Children's Laureate 2009–11. His first book, *Through the Magic Mirror*, was published in 1976 and the classic, *Gorilla*, in 1983 won many awards, including the Kate Greenaway Medal and the Kurt Maschler Award. He has published a number of titles featuring the character Willy, the chimp. His other books include *Zoo, Alice's Adventures in Wonderland, Voices in the Park, Bear's Magic Pencil* and *Me and You*. In 2000 he was the first British illustrator to win the the Hans Christian Andersen Award, for his services to children's literature. *The Shape Game* was based on his experiences as Illustrator in Residence at Tate Britain in London 2001–2. His most recent book is *Willy's Stories* (Walker Books 2014).

See also...
- *Notes from Jacqueline Wilson*, page 106
- *Who do children's authors write for?*, page 119
- *Writing books to read aloud*, page 131
- *Notes from the first Children's Laureate*, page 265

Books

Notes from Jacqueline Wilson

Jacqueline Wilson shares her first experience of becoming a writing success.

I knew I wanted to be a writer ever since I was six years old. I thought it would be the most magical job in the world. You could stay at home by yourself and write stories all day long.

I loved making up stories. I had a serial story permanently playing in my head. I used to mutter the words, acting each imaginary character in turn, but I soon learnt that this made people stare or giggle. I mastered the art of saying the words silently, experiencing all sorts of extraordinary adventures internally, while I sat staring seemingly blankly into space. No wonder I was nicknamed Jacky Daydream at school. My Mum thought I wasn't all there, and was forever giving me a shake and telling me not to look so gormless. She laughed at me when I confided that I wanted to be a writer. 'Don't be so daft Jac! Who on earth would want to read a book written by *you?*' she said.

She had a point. I was a totally unexceptional little girl, shy and anxious, barely able to say boo to a goose. My Mum wanted a daughter like Shirley Temple. She even permed my wispy hair to try to turn it into a cloud of golden ringlets. I ended up looking as if I'd been plugged into a light socket. I couldn't sing like Shirley, I couldn't tap dance like Shirley, and although I could recite long poems with dutiful expression I got so nervous performing I once wet myself on stage.

I didn't *want* to perform, well, certainly not in public. I would act out my stories enthusiastically whenever I was by myself, but I was a total shrinking violet in front of other people. I wasn't the life and soul of the party at school. I didn't clamour to have my friends round to play. I preferred playing elaborate imaginary games all by myself.

I saw a writing career as a wonderful grown-up version of these games. I suppose in a way it *is* – but I had no idea what it's *really* like to be a children's author. I don't think I've had a quiet day at home writing my book for weeks!

I suppose it used to be like that long ago. I've been writing children's books for over 40 years. For the first 20 years very few people had ever heard of me. I wrote several books a year for a whole variety of publishers. They were published, and if I hunted high and low I occasionally saw one title in a bookshop down at the end of the Ws. I got a few pleasant reviews, and I was stocked in libraries, but that was about it. I've got copies of my first 40 books and they're all first editions – because they didn't go into any other editions. Publishing was so different in those days. You were kept on lists even if your books barely covered their advances – although eventually my first publisher told me they didn't see the point in buying any more of my books because they were never ever going to be popular.

I was upset, of course, but I felt their remarks were justified. I wrote about lonely imaginative children, all of them odd ones out. I thought that only odd children themselves would want to read them. I was worried that I'd never find another publisher but very luckily for me I was taken on by Transworld (now Random House Children's Books). I had the idea of writing a story about a fierce little kid in a children's home desperate to be fostered. I decided to tell it as if this child herself was writing her own life story. I wanted her to have a contemporary quirky kind of name. Something like … Tracy Beaker.

I knew I wanted the book to have lots of black and white illustrations as if Tracy herself had drawn them. I wanted several to a page, even in the margins. David Fickling was my editor then and he's always been very open to suggestions. 'Brilliant!' he said, rubbing his hands. 'I think I know just the chap too. He's done some wonderful illustrations for poetry books. His name's Nick Sharratt. Let's all meet.'

So Nick and I met in the publishing offices. We were both very shy at first. Nick seemed lovely and very talented but I wasn't quite sure he was wacky enough for Tracy-type illustrations. Then I needed to bend down to get a pen out of my handbag on the floor. I saw Nick's socks peeping out from his trouser hem – astonishingly bright canary yellow socks. I knew everything was going to be fine the moment I saw those amazing socks. In fact it became a running joke between us and I'd buy him ever more zany spotty stripy socks all colours of the rainbow.

We've worked on nearly 45 books together now and it's been just as magical as I'd hoped – but not at all as I'd imagined. I don't stay home all by myself and write my books. I have a beautiful book-lined study but I'm hardly ever in it. Most days I do my writing on trains or in the back of cars, scribbling frantically in my notebook on my way to endless meetings and events. I'm lucky enough to be able to write happily in these rather distracting conditions, though it's sometimes embarrassing if the train is crowded. I write in the first person, and my lovely Italian notebooks look like private journals. If a business man glances from his *Daily Telegraph* to my notebook, God knows what he thinks if he reads my fictional teenage girl musing; *I so fancy the boy I saw on the bus. How will I ever get to go out with him?*

People often ask me why I think my books have been so successful. I think there are several reasons, apart from sheer luck. They look great, with Nick's fantastic covers, and his lively black and white illustrations inside break up the text and make it less forbidding for inexperienced readers. I care passionately about language and play little word games with my readers, though I try to write in an immediate colloquial style through my child narrators. My publishers promote my books with energy and commitment. Nowadays they cosset me wonderfully when I embark on my three-week book tours, putting me up in luxurious hotels and giving me a delightfully cheery driver with a very comfortable car. But obviously you don't get this five-star treatment until your books sell in their millions. I believe the *real* secret of my success is the fact that I started doing many school and library visits early on, talking about my books. In fact I don't think there's a single county in the UK where I haven't given a talk.

I vividly remember my very first talk to a small docile group of Year 7s in a secondary school. I was so nervous I could barely eat breakfast beforehand. I hoped I acted like a reasonably competent sociable adult but inside I was still that shy little girl, terrified of performing. However, I could see the whole point of giving talks to children. It was a wonderful way of introducing them to the delights of reading in general, and to my own books in particular! That was why I was willing to put myself through this torture.

I didn't really know what to talk *about*. It seemed like terrible showing off simply talking about myself and my own work. I ended up reading an extract from Daisy Ashford's *The Young Visiters* to show that children could very occasionally have their work published, and then reading an extract from *Jane Eyre*, which had been my favourite book when I was 12. I realised soon enough that this was completely the wrong approach. The children thought the Daisy Ashford bizarre and *Jane Eyre* boring. They only livened up when I changed tack and talked about what I'd been like when I was young. I started to relate to them properly, and found I could tell them funny stories about myself as an earnest teenager, my experiences as a very junior journalist, and then chat to them about my latest book and how it came to be written.

I learnt how to give a talk – but it was a long time before I actually *enjoyed* doing it. I still got very fussed and anxious about it, and I hated it if I couldn't win every child over. After a while you learn that there will be an occasional kid who will give everyone a hard time. You just have to do your best and try to interest all the others. I slogged round several schools and libraries up and down the country every single week – and I learnt so much. This is where children's authors are so lucky. We can meet so many of our readers and find out what they like – and what they don't.

I only go to individual schools and libraries now as special favours to friends, but I still do many talks at festivals. Once you do something enough times you get so used to it you simply can't find it scary. I never get the slightest bit nervous now, even if I've got an audience of hundreds. I had to perform in the garden of Buckingham Palace in front of the Queen and 3,000 children and even that wasn't too worrying. It's just part of my job and I find it great fun.

But I got it right when I was six years old. The *most* magical part of being a writer is staying at home by myself and writing stories all day long.

Jacqueline Wilson has sold over 35 million books in the UK, and has won many major awards. She was the Children's Laureate 2005–7. *Jacky Daydream* (Random House 2007) is an account of her own childhood. Her most recent children's book is *The Butterfly Club*, illustrated by Nick Sharratt (Doubleday Children's Books 2015), and her website is www.jacquelinewilson.co.uk.

See also...

- *Getting started*, page 1
- *What makes a children's classic?*, page 8
- *How it all began*, page 112
- *Getting published*, page 114
- *Who do children's authors write for?*, page 119
- *Teenage fiction*, page 174

A word from J.K. Rowling

J.K. Rowling shares her first experience of becoming a writing success.

Books

I can remember writing *Harry Potter and the Philosopher's Stone* in a café in Oporto. I was employed as a teacher at the language institute three doors along the road at the time, and this café was a kind of unofficial staffroom. My friend and colleague joined me at my table. When I realised I was no longer alone I hastily shuffled worksheets over my notebook, but not before Paul had seen exactly what I was doing. 'Writing a novel, eh?' he asked wearily, as though he had seen this sort of behaviour in foolish young teachers only too often before. '*Writers' & Artists' Yearbook*, that's what you need,' he said. 'Lists all the publishers and … stuff', he advised before ordering a lager and starting to talk about the previous night's episode of *The Simpsons*.

I had almost no knowledge of the practical aspects of getting published; I knew nobody in the publishing world, I didn't even know anybody who knew anybody. It had never occurred to me that assistance might be available in book form.

Nearly three years later and a long way from Oporto, I had almost finished *Harry Potter and the Philosopher's Stone*. I felt oddly as though I was setting out on a blind date as I took a copy of the *Writers' & Artists' Yearbook* from the shelf in Edinburgh's Central Library. Paul had been right and the *Yearbook* answered my every question, and after I had read and reread the invaluable advice on preparing a manuscript, and noted the time-lapse between sending said manuscript and trying to get information back from the publisher, I made two lists: one of publishers, the other of agents.

The first agent on my list sent my sample three chapters and synopsis back by return of post. The first two publishers took slightly longer to return them, but the 'no' was just as firm. Oddly, these rejections didn't upset me much. I was braced to be turned down by the entire list, and in any case, these were real rejection letters – even real writers had got them. And then the second agent, who was high on the list purely because I liked his name, wrote back with the most magical words I have ever read: 'We would be pleased to read the balance of your manuscript on an exclusive basis … '.

J.K. Rowling is the bestselling author of the *Harry Potter* series (Bloomsbury), published between 1997 and 2007, which have sold over 450 million copies worldwide, are distributed in more than 200 territories, translated into 78 languages and have been turned into eight blockbuster films. The first in the series, *Harry Potter and the Philosopher's Stone*, was the winner of the 1997 Nestlé Smarties Gold Prize and *Harry Potter and the Goblet of Fire* (2000) broke all records for the number of books sold on the first day of publication. She has also written two small volumes that appear as the titles of Harry's schoolbooks within the novels: *Fantastic Beasts and Where to Find Them* and *Quidditch Through the Ages* (Bloomsbury 2011) which were published in aid of Comic Relief. *The Tales of Beedle the Bard* was published in 2008 in aid of J.K. Rowling's children's charity Lumos and in 2015 her Harvard Commencement Speech was published as a book, *Very Good Lives*, also in aid of Lumos. In 2012 J.K. Rowling's digital company Pottermore was launched, where fans can enjoy her new writing and immerse themselves deeper in the wizarding world, and purchase the ebooks of the *Harry Potter* series. J.K. Rowling has written a novel for adults: *The Casual Vacancy* (Little, Brown 2012) and crime novels under the pseudonym Robert Galbraith: *The Cuckoo's Calling* (Little, Brown 2013) and *The Silkworm* (Little, Brown 2014).

See also...
- *Spotting talent*, page 5
- *Teenage fiction*, page 174

Books

Writing the unexpected

David Almond describes how he became a children's writer.

I never expected to be a children's writer. I was a sensible grown-up adult so I'd write books for sensible grown-up adults. Which I did, or tried to do, for nearly 20 years. I worked as a part-time teacher, so I had a salary, and time to write. (Important: take care of yourself; poverty is not a creative force.) I wrote stories for tiny magazines. I spent five years writing a novel. It was taken on by my first agent, the angelic Maggie Noach.

'This is it!' I thought.

We sent it to every single UK publisher. Every publisher sent it back.

'Five years to write a book!' people said. 'And nobody wants to publish it! You going to do something sensible now?'

'Yes. I'm writing the next book.'

'You must be daft!'

'I know. I must. So what?'

There was nothing I could do. I was driven to write. I worked hard, aimed high, felt daft. Maggie stood by me. I got halfway through the new novel, somehow knew it was going wrong, but wasn't sure why. I ditched it and started a series of stories based on my childhood. When these were done (two years later!) I was taking a break, walking empty-headedly along the street when a new story started telling itself in my brain. As soon as I started to write it, I knew that it was the best thing I'd ever written, that it was somehow the culmination of everything I'd done before, and to my astonishment I knew that it was a book for the young. I had a sense of liberation, of new possibilities opening up. The book was called *Skellig* and at times it weirdly seemed to write itself. It took me six months to finish, was immediately accepted by Hodder, and it changed everything.

I suppose it shows that, just as in writing a story, you can make lots of plans, but you have to be prepared for the totally unexpected. And you shouldn't try to define yourself too closely. Allow yourself to experiment, to play, to be surprised by what appears on the page and in your artistic life. Talent matters, but hard work, doggedness, thick skin, as-piration, and the courage to feel daft, matter just as much.

And agents and publishers matter. They can seem to be distant elusive creatures, and the thought of reaching them can induce much paranoia. But they truly are looking for new books, new talent. Otherwise, why allow themselves to be listed in this *Yearbook*? And most of them are really very nice, and they do understand the trials and joys and tribulations of being a writer or an artist.

Take the great advice that's in this *Yearbook*. Research the publishing possibilities that are in it. Read widely and allow yourself to be profoundly influenced by the writers and artists you love. But remember there's only one you. Your work at its best will have the individual stamp of you. So be brave. Write or illustrate your best work in your best possible way then when you feel it's ready, send it out. And while you're waiting for a response? Have a little celebration, then crack on with the next work.

David Almond is the author of *Skellig, The Savage, My Name is Mina, The Boy Who Swam With Piranhas, Half a Creature From the Sea, A Song for Ella Grey* and many other novels, stories and plays. His books have been translated into 40 languages and are widely adapted for stage and screen. His awards include the Carnegie

Medal, Eleanor Farjeon Award, and the Hans Christian Andersen Award. He is Professor of Creative Writing at Bath Spa University.

See also...

- *Getting started*, page 1
- *What makes a children's classic?*, page 8
- *Who do children's authors write for?*, page 119
- *Writing for different genres*, page 134

How it all began

Eoin Colfer shares his first experience of becoming a writing success.

I have in my time purchased several copies of the *Writers' & Artists' Yearbook*, yet there is only one copy on my bookshelf. This, I suspect, is a common complaint. When other writers visit my bat-cave – sorry, office – they don't bother asking for a signed first edition of my book, instead they make off with my *Yearbook* secreted up their jumpers. This inevitably happens shortly after I have completed the laborious task of attaching colour-coded paperclips to pages of interest. I know what you're thinking. Colour-coded paper-clips. That explains a lot.

My obsession with the *Yearbook* began in the dark era of glitter eye shadow and ozone-puncturing hairdos known as the Eighties. I had recently finished college, and like all males in their twenties, knew all there was to know about the world. The population in general, I decided with humble altruism, deserved the benefit of my wisdom. And the best way to reach my prospective public was through literature.

So I wrote a book. Not content with that, I designed the cover, multi-tasking even before the phrase was coined. This book qualified as a book because it had many words and quite a few pages. Secure in my sublime self-delusion, I got hold of an industrial stapler, bound the whole lot together and crammed a copy into the nearest postbox. One copy would be sufficient, sent to the country's foremost publishers. I settled back on the family *chaise longue* and waited for the publisher's helicopter to land in the garden.

Seasons passed and the helicopter never materialised. Not so much as a postcard from the honoured house. Sighing mightily I widened my net, sending copies of my book to several other publishers. I got some replies this time. Would that I had not. Most were civil enough. We regret to inform you, etc … the opening phrase that haunts every writer's dreams. Still, at least they were polite. But a few less generic replies dropped onto my doormat. There was one note in which the handwriting deteriorated in spots, as the editor suffered from sporadic fits of laughter. A pattern was beginning to emerge. Could it be possible that my manuscript was flawed? Was there a chance that my presentation was not all that it could be? Did genius have to be packaged?

Help arrived in the form of an editor's response. 'We regret to inform you …' it began. Nothing new there. I was becoming inured. But there was an addendum pencilled below the type. Get the *Writers' & Artists' Yearbook*. It's worth the investment.

Reluctant as any Irish man in his twenties is to take advice from anyone besides his mother, I decided to act on this particular recommendation. The *Yearbook* paid for itself almost immediately. The mere act of purchasing the fat volume made me feel like a legitimate writer. I left the shop, making certain that my grip did not obscure the book title.

At home, I was amazed to discover that the *Yearbook* was not just a list of publishers. Every possible scrap of information needed by the upcoming or established writer was included (for more details buy the book … and if there are paperclips attached, it is mine: please return it!) but what I needed to know was detailed under the heading 'Submitting material'. Next time, I vowed. Next time.

Next time turned out to be nearly a decade later. My self-esteem had recovered sufficiently to brave the sae trail once more. So I wrote an introductory letter and an interesting summary of the book, and included the first 50 pages – double-spaced.

It worked. Two weeks later I had a publisher. Now I can't put the entire thing down to the *Yearbook*, but it certainly played its part. In public of course, I take all the credit myself. I am a writer after all. But packaging and presentation in my opinion made the difference between desktop and trash, to use a computer analogy.

A few years later my brothers advised me that I needed an agent, as they were running short on beer money. Once again the *Yearbook* was consulted. Not only were the agents listed but they were categorised. These *Yearbook* people were cut from the same cloth as myself. I could almost imagine their desks stacked with coloured paperclips.

My research paid off, and within weeks I was sitting in a top-class Soho hotel treating my new agent to a flute of champagne. Although she insists it was a glass of Guinness in a Dublin pub and she paid.

Since then, I haven't looked back. Things are going well enough for me to be invited to write this article. If you are published and reading this book, hide it away and beware those with baggy jumpers. If you are as yet unpublished, then keep the faith and make sure that all around you can see the title.

Eoin Colfer has written several bestselling children's novels, including the *Artemis Fowl* books which have won awards including British Children's Book of the Year, WHSmith Children's Book of the Year, Bisto Merit Awards and the South African Book Club Book of the Year. The eighth and final book in the series was published in 2012 and the first *Artemis Fowl* film is currently in production. Eoin's book *Half Moon Investigations* was turned into a hit TV series by the BBC. His two crime novels for adults, *Plugged* (2011) and *Screwed* (2013), are both published by Headline. The first two books in his *W.A.R.P.* series are *Reluctant Assassin* (2013) and *The Hangman's Revolution* (2014), and the third, *The Forever Man*, will be published in September 2015. He was made Ireland's Children's Laureate in May 2014.

See also...

Getting published

Andy Stanton describes how he found his agent and his first publishing deal.

Good evening. You are holding in your hands one of two things. You are either holding one of the most powerful little books on the planet, a book which has the potential to CHANGE YOUR LIFE FOR EVER; or you are holding a cool little lifestyle accessory, a book which you can keep on your shelf to announce to yourself and others: 'Oh, I'm a writer-sort of person, I'm sure I'll use this book one day. But in the meantime, doesn't it look *professional*.' If you're holding the second version of the book, I'm not knocking you. For years before I got published I would frequently buy the latest copy of the *Writers' & Artists' Yearbook*, with the vague and magical idea that simply owning it was enough to effect an alchemical reaction in my life and turn me into a *writer*, with all the bunting, parades and adoring women that I imagined would naturally accompany such a position.

Well, the years wore on and I discovered something quite annoying: The *Writers' & Artists' Yearbook*, and indeed the *Children's Writers' & Artists' Yearbook*, won't actually turn you into a writer. Take another look at the book you are holding right now and know the dreadful truth. However much you stroke this book; however prominently you display it on your shelves; however much you pray to it at night – there is one component you have to bring along yourself. And (double-annoyingly, because I am very lazy and hate working) that extra component is this: You must write something. You must do some work. And only then will this book become something that could CHANGE YOUR LIFE FOR EVER. It certainly changed mine.

In 2002, I sat down and finally did the one thing I'd never done in all those years of wishing and longing and imagining all those adoring women. I wrote a story from start to finish. It was called *The Story of Mr Gum* and I wrote it partly to make my little cousins laugh, but mostly to see if I could actually finish a piece of work. Having written it, I promptly forgot about it for two years. When I rediscovered it, it was 2004 and I finally had a real and practical reason to buy the *Writers' & Artists' Yearbook*. But I found that fate had other, better plans for me, in the shape of the brand spanking new, first ever edition of the *Children's Writers'& Artists' Yearbook*. Just like its big brother, but so much easier! Now I wouldn't have to trawl through endless agents' listings, figuring out which ones accepted children's writers – no, every page of this publication was just for me. All the work had already been done. (Well, nearly all the work. I've already mentioned that one pesky component you'll have to provide yourself.)

Within a month, the book had found me an agent. She's great, by the way, and she's in this latest edition too. But no plugs, Eve White, no plugs. A month or so after I found [unnamed agent] I had a publishing deal. And in 2006, Egmont published my little story as *You're a Bad Man, Mr Gum!*. Well, folks, it's been a pretty amazing ride since then. There are now nine *Mr Gum* titles, which have sold over a million copies in this country alone. Additionally, I've written two books for Barrington Stoke and published a truly revolting picture book with Puffin. And it all started here, in these pages.

It's a shame it took me all that time to figure out how amazingly powerful this type of book can be. I hope it doesn't take you quite so long. See, it's a hard equation but it's fair. You get out what you put in. And if you put in something good, there's no book better qualified to help you reap your rewards (though a word of warning – the adoring women thing never really materialised). Well, that's enough from me. It's your turn now. You have here all the tools you need to CHANGE YOUR LIFE FOR EVER. So go to it! And the very best of luck.

Andy Stanton has been a medical secretary, a film script reader and a cartoonist, amongst other things. His favourite expression is 'good evening' and his favourite word is 'captain'. *You're a Bad Man, Mr Gum!* was his first book, published in 2006, and is the first in the *Mr Gum* series (Egmont), for which he has won the Roald Dahl Funny Prize, the Red House Children's Book Award and the Blue Peter Book Award for the Most Fun Story with Pictures. His other books are *Here Comes the Poo Bus!* (Puffin), *The Story of Matthew Buzzington* (Barrington Stoke) and *Sterling and the Canary.* His most recent book is *Mr Gum in 'The Hound of Lamonic Bibber': Bumper Book*, illustrated by David Tazzyman (Egmont Books 2011).

See also...

Notes from a successful children's author and illustrator

Lauren Child describes how *Clarice Bean, That's Me* came to be published and shares her experiences of taking advice from publishers and editors.

My first attempt at writing a children's book was when I was 18 – my friend Bridget and I had an idea. Everything seemed simple – we were going to write a book, get it published and get on with something else. Almost immediately, and by sheer fluke, we had an interested publisher. We were invited along for a 'working lunch' to discuss the story development. The editor made some suggestions for improvement which we were quite happy about – we really had no objection to rewriting; we were happier still with the business lunch and were fuelled by the confidence of youth that life would always be this easy. We did nothing, of course, and the whole thing fell through which, with hindsight, was a relief – I think we would both be squirming now. It was a number of years later before I even thought to write anything else.

Please yourself

The next time I learnt the hard way, by trekking around uninterested publishers with my portfolio – something it would be almost impossible to do now, as no one wants to see unsolicited work. I used any contacts I had, however distant. I forced myself to phone complete strangers in order to get appointments and advice, which I hated doing. When I met with publishers they seemed to have very set views on what a children's book should be. I listened to their advice and always tried to write the book they wanted me to write. But, whenever I went back to them with my work, there was always something missing – I could never write the book they had in mind.

So, unable to interest publishers, no matter how hard I tried to give them what they said they wanted, I forgot about the whole project and got on with other things. One day, having reached a rather low point in my life, and having looked at every possible career path, a friend suggested that I leave my portfolio of designs, drawings and ideas with her so she could show it to her business manager who had created and managed various successful companies. When I met with this woman, I mentioned I had an interest in film and animation and also designing products for children. Although I had no relevant training, she suggested that I try to write a children's book because, hopefully, it would prove I could create characters and invent a world for them. I think that I was just at a point where I was ready to listen – perhaps because she was very successful, perhaps because it made sense, perhaps because she was a complete stranger.

I started to write the odd sentence, then draw a character, then write a bit more ... there was no order to it, no plot structure. I wasn't even sure what I was writing, all I knew was that I was interested when I hadn't been before. I think it helped enormously that I wasn't fixated on creating the perfect children's book – it was merely a means to an end, a way to get into something else. I stopped being self-conscious about what I was doing and stopped trying to please everyone else. When I took this book – *Clarice Bean, That's Me* – to publishers, the difference was very obvious – they were all interested! However, no one was willing to take it on – they all thought it was unpublishable and told me so. But I had written something that had at least got their attention.

Listening to publishers

Nearly every publisher made suggestions of what I should change in order for this book to be published, some of them quite fundamental. I was told to drop the illustrations and simplify the text. I was told that varying fonts and integrating text and pictures was too complicated, that it would confuse young readers. I listened to them all; I considered what they had to say, but I knew they were all wrong – I knew they were wrong because I knew I wouldn't be happy with the end result. Because I had written something which felt right to me, it seemed better not to be published at all than to publish a book that wasn't really mine. After four or so long years, I eventually found a publisher who was willing to take the book on pretty much as it was.

And I think this is one of the most important things to know – how far will you go, how far *should* you go to be published? When it comes to this you have to follow your gut instinct. Despite my experience, I do think it is important to listen to what publishers have to say – it is always wise to listen, but it is not always right to take it on board. In the end, they can give you the benefit of their experience, but they cannot write the book for you, and you cannot write the book for them. As the writer, the book has to come from you. Of course, if more than one or two people pick up on the same thing then it may be worth following that advice, but for me it is never worth making a change when, after much consideration, it still feels wrong.

Know who you are writing for

When it comes to the question of writing for the 6–9 year-old market, I would say there is no formula. I don't write for 6–9 year-olds, I write for myself. My books are for anyone who wants to read them. For me, writing young fiction is less about writing for a particular audience or age group and more about telling a story that interests me. I have never thought 'Is this a book for 6–9 year-olds?' or 'Is this a book for 8–12 year-olds?'. I feel the same when writing picture books; they are there to be enjoyed by both adults *and* children because while the child looks at the pictures, it is the adult who usually reads the story.

How does a writer come up with the interesting ideas in the first place? As an adult writing a children's book, is it helpful – even necessary – to have children of your own? My own view is that it is simply irrelevant. First, we have all been children and anyone who wants to write for children must have strong feelings from his or her own childhood to draw upon. But more importantly, good fiction writing is not about imitation – it is about imagination. Just as having children does not mean you have anything to say to them in book form, so not having children is no bar to writing in a manner to which they will respond. Writing for anyone is about having something to say – a point of view. Writing for children is no different. When it comes to writing fiction, I think that any good writer will see children as people first, and as children second. Of course the context of childhood experiences is different from those of adults, but there is no emotion experienced as a child which is not felt equally in adult life.

At the more practical level, I do not believe that there are any fixed rules. I know that many writers plot a book out before they start, and I had always been told that I needed to plot my books and understand where they were going if I was to write successfully. But

I never begin writing a book knowing how it is going to end. I never normally know how it is going to start either. I generally just begin with a sentence taken at random. For me, it is all about an idea taking hold, and the writing tends to be more about a feeling than anything. *Clarice Bean, Don't Look Now* began as a book about love and ended up being a book more about loss than anything else. I wrote a few sentences about Clarice's inability to sleep and from that the whole mood of the book was determined. I started to write about insomnia and then wondered why Clarice might experience this, which led to thinking about her worries, which in turn led to the idea that she might be feeling very insecure and start questioning things around her. So, in a way, a few sentences shaped the whole plot because they reflected something that I felt personally at the time. I didn't try to force a story that I wasn't interested in writing; instead it became a book about Clarice's anxieties, her inability to explain the world to herself, and some recognition on her part that not only is life something which cannot be controlled, but it's also something which can only be imperfectly understood.

I write a lot of material and read it over and over, until I see what themes are emerging and then I look for a way to hang it all together. Once it has a solid plot, I start to cut. Writing picture books is a very good discipline for writing novels because with just 800 or so words to play with, you have to decide what is important and what isn't: what exactly is this book *about*? Writing picture books makes you much less frightened of editing out the bits that you love. You really can't be indulgent, and have to pare your writing down to the essence of what that story is about. Although of course a novel gives you much more freedom – *Don't Look Now* was 42,000 words – I still consciously try to make sure that every chapter is pushing the story forward and has something to say.

A good editor

That brings me on to another important part – your editor. I really have to trust who I am working with. I rely so much on my editor because of the patchwork way I work. A good editor will let you debate back and forth until you've finally reached a point where you know that you can't make something any better. You do have to trust them because it is so easy to lose your perspective about your own work. You may think it's great and not listen to criticism, but more often than not you will get doubtful and think it's all rubbish, and that's where an editor can keep you believing in your work.

If there's a single piece of advice I could offer for writing fiction, it would be to write from the heart. When I wrote *Clarice Bean, That's Me*, I became passionate about what I was writing and found it exciting. If you're bored when you're writing, you will write a boring book. And no matter how hard you find the early stages, keep going. You just need to write and write until you've written the imitation stuff out of you. It is hard but it is very rewarding too. Writing is one of the best things in the world – a licence to discuss ideas – even if it's just with yourself.

Lauren Child's picture books have won many awards, including the Kate Greenaway Medal in 2000 for *I Will Not Ever Never Eat a Tomato* (2000); the Smarties Gold Award in 2002 for *That Pesky Rat* (2002); and the Smarties Bronze Award for *Clarice Bean, That's Me* (1999); *Beware of the Storybook Wolves* (2000); and *What Planet Are You From, Clarice Bean?* (2001). In 2002 she published *Utterly Me, Clarice Bean*, the first of three Clarice Bean novels. In 2007 she illustrated a new edition of Astrid Lindgren's *Pippi Longstocking*. Her fourth Charlie and Lola book, *Slightly Invisible*, was published in 2010. Three animated TV series of *Charlie & Lola* have been shown on CBBC and on channels around the world, and the series has won four BAFTAs. *Feel the Fear*, featuring Ruby Redfort, and *The New Small Person* were both published in September 2014. Lauren has written and/or illustrated approximately 40 books. Her website is www.milkmonitor.com.

Who do children's authors write for?

When writing a children's book, who is an author really writing for? Michael Rosen shares his thoughts on this question and suggests what an author needs to take into account when writing.

People who can write for children don't come with a same format personality or a made-to-measure range of skills. We aren't people who can be easily categorised or lumped together. In part, this is because the world of children's books is constantly changing, starting out from a very diverse base in the first place. This derives from the fact that the world children inhabit is changing and indeed that there is a recognition within the children's books milieu that books are for everyone, not just one small section of the population.

In a way, this means that this is a great time to be writing or illustrating children's books. But that comes with a warning: diverse and changing – yes – but within a set of conventions (I won't say 'rules') and formats. Quite often, people who have written some stories or poems for children ask if I would take a look at them. Sometimes, the first problem that I can see with what they've written is that it doesn't 'fit in'. Or, another way of putting it, the writer hasn't taken a look at what's out there in the bookshops and schools and thought: how can I write something that could go alongside that book, or fit the same niche that that particular book occupies?

But what about artistic freedom? What about the rights of the writer to write about anything? Two things in response to that: nothing can stop you writing about anything you want to, however you want to. But there's no point in kidding ourselves that writing is really 'free'. We all write with our 'reading heads' on. That's to say, we write with the words, sentences, pages, chapters, plots, characters, scenes of the books we've read. If you say to yourself, 'I want to write a novel' or 'I want to write a picture book text', you're only doing so because your mind is full of novels or picture book texts. They are the 'already written' or the 'already read' material we write with. This affects everything we write, right down to the shape and structure of what we write, the tone we hit in the passages we write, the kinds of dialogue and thoughts we put into the writing. A crude analogy here is cooking. We cook with the ingredients that we are given. But more: if we say, we are going to make a cake, there is an understood outcome of what that will be (the cake), and an agreed set of ingredients that can arrive at that understood outcome. So, in a way, we not only cook with appropriate and given ingredients, we also cook with an understood outcome in mind. It has a shape, a smell and a taste that we expect the moment someone says, 'Here is a cake'. Our memory of past cakes prepares our mind and taste for what is to come. This set of memories of past writing and reading is what is in our mind as we write and indeed in the minds of the child readers as they sit down to something they can see is a book. These are what are known as the 'intertexts' we read and write with – memories of past texts.

Secondly, I would say that if you're interested in being published, then you have to look very, very closely at what publishers publish. This means looking at books not only from the point of view of what they say and how they say it. It also means looking at what kind of book it is and inquiring whether there are other books like it. How would you categorise it? This line of questioning puts into your mind a sense of format, of shape, of outcome to guide you as you write. Another analogy: an architect who is asked to design a house knows that he or she has to create rooms that are high enough and large enough for people to live in, that there is a basic minimum of kitchen and bathroom, there is a door to get in and out of, and so on. If it fulfils these conditions, we will call it a house – and not a factory, or a warehouse, say. It's a great help sometimes to look at books from an architect's point of view: what is particular to a book that makes it work? Ask yourself, how did the writer reveal what was coming next? Or, how did the writer hold back and conceal what was coming next? (Writing is a matter of revealing and concealing!) How did the writer arouse your interest? Was it an invitation to care about the people or creatures in the story? Or was it more to do with events or happenings? Or both? Did the book announce itself as being of a particular genre: thriller, historical fiction, comedy, etc? How did it do that? What are the requirements of that genre? Or is it a hybrid?

If all this sounds too technical let me introduce you to someone: the child. If you say to yourself, I'm going to write for children, then even as you say this, you're putting an imagined child (or children) into your mind. This is what literary theorists call 'the implied reader'. We do this in several ways. There might be a real child we know. Robert Louis Stevenson wrote *Treasure Island* largely as part of his relationship with his stepson, Lloyd. But even though we might say, 'RLS wrote it for Lloyd', this doesn't really explain things. What Stevenson was doing, possibly without knowing it, was keeping a mental map of Lloyd's speech and personality in his mind, so as he wrote, he had his version of Lloyd in his head monitoring, guiding and censoring what he was writing.

There is no single way of importing the implied child reader into your head. Some writers do it from memory, connecting with the child they once were and using that version of themselves to guide them in what they write and how they write it. They use memories of what they liked to read, how they themselves spoke and thought and perhaps wrote, when they were a child. Others immerse themselves in the company of children – their own, their grandchildren, nephews and nieces or children in playgroups, nurseries or schools. And some do it by immersing themselves so thoroughly in children's books that they pick up the implied child reader from the actual books. And of course, it's possible to work a combination of all of these ways. What I don't think you can do is ignore them all.

In fact, what you write can't avoid an implied reader. That may seem odd, because you might say that you had no one in mind when you wrote this or that. The reason you can't avoid it is because the language we use comes already loaded up with its audience. So, if I write, 'Capitalism is in crisis', this is a phrase that implies an audience that first of all understands English, then understands the words 'capitalism', 'crisis' and the phrase 'in crisis'. But more than that, it's an audience that wants to read something like that and is, in a sense, hungry or prepared and sufficiently 'read' to want to read such a sentence – or, more importantly, to go on wanting to read what comes next. If I write, 'My Dad was attacked by a banana …' then I'm already positioning the reader to think about someone who is a child and that child is telling something a bit absurd or possibly funny, perhaps the beginning of a family anecdote or family saga. It's also a 'tease', in that a reader who 'gets it', will know that bananas don't attack anyone. It implies a reader who knows that. In other words, the 'implied reader' is 'inscribed' into what we write. In a way, these implied readers are stuck to the words, phrases, sentences, plots and characters we write.

This means that as we write – and when we go back over what we've written – we need to think about the implied reader we've put there. Who is the child who is going to 'get it'? Who is the child who won't? What kind of children are we talking to? What aspects of those implied children's minds and childhoods are we talking to? The fearful person in the child? The envious one? The yearning one? The lonely one? The greedy one? And so on.

A last thought: we talk of 'writing for children'. To tell the truth, I don't think we do just write for children. I think we write as a way for adults to join the conversations that adults have with adults, adults have with children, children have with children – on the subject of what it means to be a child and live your life as a child. Because it's literature, this conversation often comes in code, with ideas and feelings embodied in symbols (teddy bears, giants, etc), it arouses expectations and hopes (what's coming next?) and because it's literature that children can and will read, it often comes along according to predictable outcomes (getting home, getting redeemed, being saved) that remove the obstacles to unhappiness and imperfection that the story began with, and so on. Nevertheless, children's literature has a magnificent history of saying important things to many people, often in a context where adults are caring for children. I think that's a good thing to attempt.

Michael Rosen has been writing since he was 16 and published his first book in 1969. As an author and by selecting other writers' works for anthologies he has been involved with over 140 books. His most recent books are *Send for a Superhero!* (Walker 2013), *Don't Forget Tiggs* (Andersen Press 2014), *The Bus is for Us* (Walker 2015) and *Uncle Gobb and the Dread Shed* (Bloomsbury 2015). He was the Children's Laureate 2007–9 and has an MA and a PhD in Children's Literature. He is Professor of Children's Literature at Goldsmiths, University of London, where he co-devised and co-teaches the MA in Children's Literature. His website is www.michaelrosen.co.uk.

See also...
- *Spotting talent*, page 5
- *What makes a children's classic?*, page 8
- *A writer's ten commandments*, page 122
- *My writing rules!*, page 124

A writer's ten commandments

Michael Morpurgo offers a list of suggestions to help writers get the best out of their writing.

A *writer's ten commandments* … 'suggestions' may be a better word. Many of these I have not kept but know should be kept.

1 **Read widely and often.** It's how writers take exercise. Every book is a voyage of someone else's discovery. It is how you learn good and bad technique (useful to know both). It is how you explore the minds of other writers who have faced the blank page, stiffened their sinews, and done it. You can wonder at their achievement, at their mastery, and discover how it is done. Every book you read informs, builds confidence. With every book you read you are subconsciously finding your own voice. The more you read the more the music in words, the rhythm and cadence of a sentence becomes second nature. So read aloud sometimes – listen to literature, don't just read it.

2 **Get the habit.** Have a notebook handy, a writer's sketchbook – and jot down thoughts and ideas, memories, snatches of overheard conversations, moments of high drama, of quiet reflection. Frequency is important. The more you do it the less inhibited you become; the less you worry about words, the easier the flow comes. The habit takes the fear out of it. Writing becomes as natural a form of communication as speech. From these jottings will emerge the ideas for your stories and poems.

3 **Live as full a life as possible, outside writing.** Get out there, go places, meet people, experiment, take risks, move outside your comfort zone. Drink in the world around you, fill the well constantly, or else it will run dry. If that happens, then as a writer you are up a gumtree without a paddle – so to speak.

4 **Take time, whacks of it, before you settle on the subject of the story you want to write.** Read around it, dream around it, research around it, convince yourself you really want to spend months, possibly years of your life roaming around in this idea, developing it, loving it. Don't be in a hurry to decide. But once you've decided don't look back. Your story could turn to stone. And you could too.

5 **Live in dreamtime for as long as it takes before you ever set pen to paper.** Don't confront the blank page or screen till you've dreamed up the set design, till your players are walking live on your stage, strutting and fretting, till you can see them and hear them, till you know them intimately and the world they live in. You don't have to have decided where they will take you, what the denouement might be – remember that when it comes as a surprise to you, it'll be a surprise to the reader too.

6 **Be comfortable when you write.** You will be tense, and excited and anxious. So arrange yourself so that you don't hurt yourself. Wrists, shoulders, neck, the lower back bear the brunt of writing. Don't hunch over. Don't stay sitting too long. Get up and walk about every half hour. If you dry up, don't sit over it. Go for a walk, put it out of your mind and come back fresh. Do what I do, what Robert Louis Stevenson did, write on your bed, pillows piled up behind you, relaxed, at ease with yourself. Then you can go to sleep easily too – a very useful writing technique I find.

7 **Once you begin, finish it.** Go through with it to the final full stop. Every abandoned manuscript is a knockback, a huge dent in a writer's confidence. And confidence is the

key to a writer's morale. Writers' block is simply a lack of confidence engendered by a lack of sufficient dreamtime.

8 **Mean every word you write.** What we are asking of a reader is to suspend disbelief. Our technique as writers, our writing voice, can help here. But most important is that we have to believe in the story we're writing. We mustn't pretend, we must mean it. Mean it and they'll read as you meant it and they'll listen. Mean it and they'll be moved to laughter and tears.

9 **Rewrite, cut – if in doubt, cut it out!** Edit yourself before anyone else does. You are your own best editor. Which is not to say that we don't need a good editor, we absolutely do. But never send it off half done, not right, not truly imagined and thought through. Read it out loud to yourself – feel the rhythm, listen to the music. It's fun and the best fault-finder I know.

10 **Forget all about getting published, being famous, being rich.** Abandon those dreams if you have them. Excise all such aspirations and ambitions. This is a prerequisite to becoming a writer of truth and integrity – I'm not sure if any other kind of writing is worth bothering about.

And one for luck: Don't sit around waiting for a publisher's or an agent's response to your book. You've done it, done your best. Simply get on with dreaming up your next one. If the reject letter comes, don't be downhearted. We've all been there. You pick yourself up, dust yourself down, and on you go …

This article first appeared in *Writing Children's Fiction: A Writers' & Artists' Companion* © Yvonne Coppard and Linda Newbery 2013.

Michael Morpurgo is the author of more than 100 books and was the Children's Laureate 2003–5. One of his best-loved titles, *War Horse,* reached wide audiences as a stage play at London's National Theatre and as a film, directed by Stephen Spielberg. Michael's many awards include the Blue Peter Book of the Year, the Whitbread Children's Book Award, the Nestlé Smarties Book Prize, the Red House Children's Book Award and (three times) the Prix Sorcières. With his wife, Clare, he set up Farms for City Children, a charity which enables urban children to experience country life and animal husbandry; there are now three working farms which have been visited by thousands of children.

See also...
● *My writing rules!,* page 124
● *Editing your work,* page 307

My writing rules!

When he says 'My writing rules!' Jon Mayhew isn't being big-headed but is instead offering some tips for writing books for children.

I'm always fascinated by articles that give writing tips. It may be because I'm curious about other writers and how they work or it may be because I realise that you never stop learning. The one thing I've realised as I delve into these articles is that established writers always break the 'rules'.

My writing rules or tips or suggestions in this article are things I've picked up as my writing has progressed, and they work for me. Some will seem really obvious; others may be new to you. None of them are 'rules' really.

A sympathetic character

I always want my main character to be one that children will like. That isn't to say that the main character is always a paragon of virtue or even particularly pleasant. In *Mortlock*, Josie is a fairly 'aspirational' character, she has abilities and is bright and brave, but my other main protagonists are far from perfect. Necessity Bonehill is a nasty piece of work to begin with; she fights with people, steals from younger pupils in her school and shows no respect for the adults who are responsible for her. And yet, the reader is given an insight into why she is such an abrasive character. Some children might enjoy a little vicarious rule-breaking too.

Edgy Taylor from the *The Demon Collector* is another spiky character. A street child who collects prime (dog poo to you and I), he isn't well-disposed towards other people. Poor Edgy's plight would probably be enough to have you sympathise with him but I chose to give him a pet too. I was worried that readers would just feel sorry for Edgy, rather than like him. Making him a boy who cares for a dog signals to the reader that he has a soft side. A footnote on writing about animals: beware, they wander off and linger behind just like the real thing. You'll be romping off into adventure in chapter eight and suddenly realise that the dog is still sniffing at a tree root in chapter three!

In short, I try to make my characters have appeal, a few flaws and some skills.

A single point of view

I stick to this one for my own sanity and I think it makes life easier for children reading if the story is relayed through one point of view. Some children aged between eight and 12 will cheerfully make sense of multiple narratives but many will be confused. I also think that the reader is able to get closer to a character if they are in that character's head at all times. Obviously, this creates problems if you have supporting characters who come and go or a party that is split up, but sometimes the surprise and drama of reunion can have more impact when working through one viewpoint.

Killing the word 'was'

I have a pathological hatred of the word 'was'. It's the first word I go for when I start editing a book. For me, 'was' deadens the action and makes things passive. It's part of showing rather than telling, so rather than say, 'It was raining', I would rather think about what the rain was *doing*. Rattling on a tin roof, perhaps, or bouncing off the pavements or maybe soaking into the hood of the character's flimsy coat.

Description: hiding the vegetables in the food

Children are notorious skimmer and skippers: if they come to a boring bit, they'll skip it, gloss over it or, in the worst cases, abandon the book. Sometimes, I imagine myself as some kind of Ancient Mariner, gripping the child's sleeve and imploring them to listen to one more episode rather than ditching my book for the Xbox. A huge, long description or explanation will kill the pace of a story.

The answer is to include snippets of description as you go along, rather like hiding those nasty green vegetables in the rich gravy everyone loves! In this example, we learn something about the build of the two characters:

> 'Pleased to meet you,' Oginski said, wrapping the man's slight hand in his own giant fist.

Information can thus be gradually leaked to the reader without the need for long paragraphs of description.

Exposition

Huge explanations of back story or events that have happened without the main character's knowledge need to be handled very carefully for the same reason as heavy description. You'll lose your readers. I get around this by releasing details a bit at a time in the form of letters or diary entries. By giving out information piecemeal, the sense of mystery increases and children love trying to second-guess a puzzle!

Sometimes, my characters tell a tale that holds a nugget of back story. *The Demon Collector* has a whole string of legends supporting it and I found that if a character tells them as stories in their own right, this ingredient doesn't slow the main story down. Rather than wrapping the story in speech, it is laid out as a tale and given its own chapter.

Make things worse

This is something of a watchword with me and it has got me into no end of trouble! Is your character trapped in a room? Put a tiger in there with him. There's nothing more frustrating than reading about how a character easily overcomes every obstacle. There has to be a struggle. Even worse, if a threat is mentioned but never materialises, think how annoyed the reader will be. If there are crocodiles on the river bank, you don't creep past them and say 'Phew! So glad they didn't wake up!' They should wake up and at least nearly take a chunk out of someone.

Obviously you have to be careful, as having your hero eaten in chapter one tends to shorten the book. But as a general rule, making things worse doesn't let the character or the reader off the hook. In Mortlock, I had a situation in which my characters found themselves locked in a room. 'Easy,' I thought, 'They can pick the lock.' So, following my own rules, I put bolts on the doors. They were locked in those rooms for weeks while I tried to figure out how they could escape. So question each scene and ask yourself if it can be any worse. Making things worse can cause headaches but the end result is pure excitement.

Short, punchy chapters with a hook at the end

Being 8–12 years old, your audience has less control over their waking hours and social time than a teenager. Parents may still dictate when an eight year-old goes to bed, has their dinner, and does their homework. This means that time is at a premium. This age group does a lot of its reading just before bedtime. With that in mind, I try to make my chapters about 1,500–1,800 words long and no longer than 2,000 words. This is a readable chunk and I have been told by readers that they fly through the books as a result. I think 1,500 words is the lower limit as shorter chapters influence the flow and pace of the story and it becomes 'choppy'.

I also like to end each chapter on a cliff-hanger, for obvious reasons. This can be tricky, especially if the chapter has been more of a reflective and information-gathering nature.

Pace

An unfortunate by-product of making things worse is that your story rocks along at an exhausting pace and nobody gets a chance to sleep or eat or discover things. It's important to slow things down every now and then. Children don't mind the slowing of pace if characters are finding things out and discovering clues. Children will quickly spot if your characters haven't eaten for days. Detail such as food builds a sense of place or person – children are always interested in food!

Never trust a child...

I'm often asked if I 'try my work out on real children'. The honest answer is that I don't. My own children do read my work. My daughter doesn't think much of it (not her cup of tea) although she is proud of her dad, and my teenage sons are often torn between wanting to say they enjoy my books and the unwritten rule that stipulates that anything parents do is rubbish!

Children will often tell you what they think you want to hear. They will be flattered that you have given them an exclusive preview and so their opinions should be gauged with extreme caution!

I tend to write for my 'inner 11-year-old'. I think about what thrilled me as a child and test my work on my younger self. I've found it useful to indulge in a little introspection in the past. I go on a nostalgia trip, listening to music, thinking of smells and sights of my youth. Somehow, for me it opens up a link to the past and that 'inner 11-year-old'. Then I can dream up worlds that excite me, heroes that inspire and adventures that thrill. The great thing is, nobody can send me to bed anymore!

Jon Mayhew is the author of *Mortlock*, which was shortlisted for the 2011 Waterstone's Children's Book Prize and longlisted for the 2011 Branford Boase Award, *The Demon Collector* and *The Bonehill Curse*. Jon hails from the misty marshes of Wirral, described as a haunt of 'godless people' even in the days of Sir Gawain and the Green Knight! He spent most of his childhood playing in the ruins of a Victorian zoo and when he wasn't doing that, he was writing or telling stories. He loves traditional music and running too ... which you'd realise is a useful combination if you'd heard him play the mandolin. Jon's new series, *Monster Odyssey*, is published by Bloomsbury.

See also...

• *A writer's ten commandments*, page 122

Playing with other people's toys: adventures in licensed publishing

Steve Cole owes his writing career to TV and film tie-ins. Here he explores the value, benefits and rewards, as well as the challenges, constraints and practicalities for a writer in this important area of the publishing world today.

Books

In any creative media, populism and commercialism come with certain stigmas attached, and children's fiction is no different. While literary titles sit loftily at one end of the artistic scale, film, TV, online and multimedia tie-ins are typically less celebrated. Ask any publishing director if they were drawn to the business because they longed to put out, say, *Tree Fu Tom* or *Assassin's Creed* titles, I'm fairly sure what the response would be. But if you ask a reluctant child reader to choose between a book they've never heard of and one with characters they've seen and loved on a screen someplace, chances are they'll sneer at the former and grab the latter.

Such media tie-ins are a mainstay of the book world. Publishers pay for the rights to exploit a TV show or film or brand, then devise a publishing programme intended to earn them back the money they've spent and generate a whole lot more. If the range is planned with care, well promoted and well received, it can generate excellent profit for the publisher. And that guaranteed income allows them to take gambles with riskier literary propositions.

You can see what's in it for the publisher. What's in it for the writer?

Popular perceptions

Tie-in work may involve you compromising your own style to a greater or lesser extent – and that may lead to a little soul-searching. After all, you're pandering to someone else's creations, aiming to appeal to someone else's fans. Are you selling your soul? Depending on the sort of tie-in, literary snobs may think that you're just 'churning it out' for the money. Accusations of 'hack', real or imagined, may ring fearfully in your ears. What's the matter – aren't you good enough to make up your own characters?

That can be the perception. From my own experience, I can assure you that this sort of writing seldom comes more quickly than any other form, if you're giving of your best. It depends what you want from your writing – and how commercial you want to get.

Starting off

When tie-ins are done well, they can truly inspire. Certainly they featured heavily in my personal journey into reading and writing.

At primary school I was a good reader with a good vocabulary, so my teachers sought to stretch me with books I was too young to properly appreciate. While I was polite about the likes of *I Am David* and *The Iron Man*, I secretly felt that *Doctor Who* and the *Planet of the Daleks* blew them all away! As a child I read for pleasure, not advancement, and my collection of *Doctor Who* books was my greatest treasure. Teachers never guessed that here was the source of my 'wow words', and my reason for wanting to invent stories.

How to get in?

Some authors manage to make a little niche for themselves in tie-in publishing and happily stay there, writing their way into the latest in pop culture. Others, myself included, start off there and diversify into other areas.

I certainly owe my own writing career to tie-ins. When I worked for BBC pre-school magazines, budgets were tight so I would sometimes write humorous poems in-house for nothing. I sent off some examples to a publisher to show what I could do – as luck would have it – just as they were looking for writers for some poem pop-up books. My book-writing career was suddenly under way.

If you have no experience, writing samples for fiction packagers can be a way to get noticed (see 'Fiction packagers' below). Or if you can do work experience at children's magazines, that is a great way to get to know the licensed market – and a good opportunity to leave your work on the editor's desk for their opinion! If you then write to a publisher with on-spec samples for a range they publish and can mention an existing association with a magazine, you will be taken more seriously – as long as your work is up to scratch, of course.

Suddenly, you've got a foot on the rung of the ladder.

Where will it lead?

Experience of one licensed property helps you to get more work elsewhere; if you do a good job on one, chances are you'll be asked back for another. Some shows will have more appeal to you than others, of course, but the more you do, the more experience you'll get. And even the humblest of jobs can bring unexpected opportunities. When I wrote the *Charlie's Angels Action File* for Puffin (under the name Samantha Cole – girl power!), I worked with the publishing director. Later she founded a children's list at a literary agency and asked if I'd like to join up. Thirteen years later, I'm still with her and very happily so.

Just for money?

Although a professional writer obviously has to consider income when allocating time to projects, enthusiasm for and enjoyment of the work is essential; otherwise you might as well be doing something else all together.

Writing for other characters can be fun, as well as a means of income, particularly if those characters have a personal appeal. Did you know that Kingsley Amis wrote the first James Bond continuation novel after Ian Fleming's death (under a pseudonym)? And these days, all kinds of authors – from Patrick Ness to Jenny Colgan, Marcus Sedgwick to A.L. Kennedy – have written *Doctor Who* tie-in fiction.

Sure, it can be frustrating having to fit into an existing style, but I see it as a good exercise for an author; all experience is useful. Writing to order and to a particular style helps you define your *own* style. I worked hard on developing mine as a reaction to playing literary chameleon, and as my own books took off I didn't get as much time for the tie-ins that launched my career (save the odd adventure for *Doctor Who*). So when I was approached to write *Young James Bond*, working with the Ian Fleming estate on a character I'd loved all my life, I really couldn't resist.

But whether it's Mr Bond or *Mr Bean*, there are various factors that set tie-in publishing apart from a book you've dreamed up yourself.

Tone and branding

This is perhaps the most important thing to consider: a tie-in should always reflect the work that spawned it. It should aim to capture something of the TV/film experience in book form, embodying the same tone and appeal. At the same time, it needs to be suitable for the age group.

In the case of *Young Bond*, this presents challenges in that it's a young adult spin-off from the Ian Fleming books, which were aimed squarely at adults, rather than the more child-friendly movies. So while the book is aimed at teens, there's a strong adult crossover, and the writer walks the line between it.

Doctor Who, with its family audience, is a less prescriptive example; fiction and non-fiction are offered in various forms, from shorter, simpler books and annuals aimed at younger readers to full-cast audio plays to more challenging novels and short stories aimed at teens and adults. Because the style of the TV series shifts from episode to episode, so the books can accommodate a diverse range of voices without a 'house style'.

Working from advance materials

It's important you get a feel for the characters you're working for. If you're writing a movie tie-in, the book will be timed to be published near the film's release date, so you will only have a script and some advance visual material to work with. (I once had to write an 'Essential Guide' to a Dreamworks movie before the ending to the script had been finalized – which was interesting!)

With TV shows you may be allowed to view rough-cuts of episodes as well as scripts, to give you a feel. The scripts usually come watermarked with your name on them, so if they escape into the wild or end up on Ebay, your guilt will be known and you'll be blacklisted forever more … For bigger shows that fear leaking of any materials, you may well have to travel to production company headquarters for meetings with the brand manager and to view episodes. It's not unreasonable to wrangle expenses from the publisher for this.

Interference

When it's your own book you're writing, you have to deal with your editor. That's fine, and can be fun – after all, you have an ongoing interaction with your editor. If you're writing for someone else's characters, you have to deal with your editor and the rights-holders. This will result in an additional level of editorial interference that may be constructive or may be maddening – often both.

Larger companies, particularly film studios, may have dedicated staff to coordinate publishing programmes and formally approve the text. If it's someone with a creative/authorial background, this can be the most efficient arrangement. If it's an administrative role only, it can result in cold-blooded 'box-ticking' approach to the check-edit that becomes a sort of corporate vandalism. I've had carefully compiled manuscripts, designed to be read aloud, reduced to little more than story synopses with a line of speech on every spread – but at the end of the day, you're in no position to argue! All you can do is suck up the edits and complete the job like the professional you are …

Taking credit and fee

You won't always get your name on the front of a tie-in book. If you've experienced the corporate vandalism effect I described earlier, this may be a relief. Either way, you will normally be identified as the author on the title page or prelim pages, which means you can still register them for PLR (Public Lending Right; see page 297). Tie-in books can perform very well, so this may mean bonus money down the line.

Fiction packagers

Related to tie-in publishing – though generally a little more relaxed – is the world of the fiction packager. Many successful fiction series are brought to publishers not by a single

Books

author but by a 'fiction factory' such as Working Partners (*Beast Quest, Rainbow Magic*) or Hothouse (*Secret Kingdom*). A (usually) pseudonymous author fronts the series, though dozens of writers may contribute different books to the range (the trick to telling who is to read the 'Special thanks to …' credit at the front).

Unpublished and un-agented writers are accepted if their prose samples are up to scratch (Working Partners state: 'What we're interested in is finding the best voices to bring our stories to life.') The author is given a detailed character brief and synopsis and invited to pitch sample chapters on spec for a project. If accepted – and if the book then finds a publisher – that author will get to write the complete book.

Some of my earliest fiction was for Working Partners and working with the creative editors there taught me a lot. Writing fiction for them that was outside my comfort zone was a good, stretching experience!

In conclusion

It's not only newbies who come to write for other people's characters. Experienced writers who wish to fit more writing and income into their schedule get involved. Even if you're not the biggest fan of what you're writing about, the work can tide you over while you work on that bestseller you know is inside you …

The important thing to remember is that when you write a tie-in, you are not simply pleasing yourself, hoping readers will buy into your agenda. You're not writing for reviewers, or librarians, or award panels. You're writing just for your readers. You're writing for children.

Kids don't comprehend literary snobbery. But they know what they like. And you're helping them get it, while stimulating them into reading at the same time. Isn't that cool?

Steve Cole is a bestselling children's author and lifelong fan of Ian Fleming's James Bond. His book series include the *Doctor Who, Astrosaurs, Cows-in-Action, Secret Agent Mummy, Z-REX, Slime Squad* and *Tripwire* books, plus his new *Young Bond* series. His latest children's novel is *Stop Those Monsters!* (Simon & Schuster 2015). *Secret Agent Mummy: The Hieroglyphs of Horror* (Red Fox) will be published in January 2016. In other careers Steve has worked as an editor of books and magazines for readers of all ages. See more at www.stevecolebooks.co.uk and follow him on Twitter @SteveColeBooks.

See also...
- *Getting started, page 1*
- *Marketing, publicising and selling children's books, page 24*
- *Public Lending Right*, page 297
- *Writing to a brief*, page 352

Writing books to read aloud

Bestselling author Anne Fine looks at why and how books are read aloud to children.

The first thing to say about writing books to read aloud is that they should be as much of a pleasure to read alone silently as any other story. Indeed, at first it's difficult to see where any differences might lie. Certainly when it comes to stories for the very young we tend to have a picture in our heads of the exhausted parent inviting the child to 'clean your teeth, hop into bed, and I'll read you a story'. And since all days are long for a parent, nobody wants their offspring to be worked into a frenzy all over again. So, in the classic bedtime stories for the younger child, there's very often a softer humour and a gentler tone, and a satisfactory and fulfilling ending.

And for the older child, there often isn't.

So, same old story really. No rules (or having to face the fact that rules appear to be there only for some other writer to irritate you intensely by making a fortune breaking them). But there are always the basic guidelines.

Keep things as simple as they can be for your particular story. With picture books you can of course assume that the child is propped up beside the reader, sharing each illustration as it comes along. But by the time the child is six, maybe they would prefer to snuggle down and shut their eyes to listen. So do you really have to take half a dozen sentences to describe the rigging, and the number and nature of the sails, and exactly how the ship was armed? Couldn't you just refer to it as 'the most magnificent galleon that ever sailed the seas' and leave it at that? After all, if those cannon ever come to be fired, we'll hear about it later.

Listeners are easily distracted. One minute they're all ears; the next, they're actually more interested in tracking the progress of a fly across the ceiling. Of course they're not going to admit they've lost the thread of the story, in case the parent snatches the opportunity to suggest they're too tired to listen and makes for the door, or the teacher decides it's time to move on to the workbooks. But their attention does stray. So it is best to try (as ever) to order your tale so you can start at the beginning and move on in sequence, steering clear of flashbacks.

On this matter of keeping things simple, does it sound mad to say that plots can be overrated? And never more so than in books designed to be read aloud to the young. In my own very short chapter book, *It Moved!*, Lily takes a stone in for Show and Tell and claims it sometimes moves, and we just get to see who in the class believes her and who doesn't, and how they all react over a day of watching it. In the *Stories of Jamie and Angus*, Jamie is an amiable child of about four in a perfectly normal household. His favourite soft toy is a little Aberdeen Angus bull. In the first story, Angus ends up in the washing machine when he's supposed to be 'dry clean only'. In another, the pair sort out the books in their bedroom according to their own rather strange shelving preferences. In yet another, they do little more than draw 'angry eggs'. The stories almost couldn't be more plain and domestic, and yet we still run through joy and misery, jealousy, anxiety, distress, fear, empathy, generosity, self-sacrifice, fury, resentment – the entire mercurial gamut of pre-school emotions. So do be confident that, especially for the very young, a tremendous amount can be forged from what seems, at first sight, not very much at all. With writing –

just as with practically everything else in life – it's not what you do but the way that you do it.

Children, like adults, have to *care* about what's being read. We adults tend to ask the 'Can I be *bothered* with these people?' question before returning a book, half-read, to the library. It's a test even harder to pass when you're writing for young ones. Remember Robert Browning:

> *If you want your songs to last*
> *Base them on the human heart*

because children love to identify with someone or something in the story – it doesn't really matter what. It could be another child, or a puppy, or even a lost pebble. But they do have to care. So perhaps it's best to make sure that, all the way through, your listener knows what your character (or puppy, or pebble) is feeling. And make sure that these are thoughts and emotions they will recognise. A child of six isn't 'disappointed that the weather is unpleasant'. It's all far more immediate. He feels the tears pricking because his socks are wet and his woolly hat is itching and his coat's too tight under his armpits. Ever heard them moan?

Joan Aiken once remarked that anyone who writes for the young 'should, ideally, be a dedicated semi-lunatic'. But you can go too far. The problem is one of differing – and shifting – levels of sophistication. What makes one child hoot with laughter will cause another to sneer, and there is in any case an entirely undefinable line between cashing in on a child's acceptance of the unlikely or the magical, and offering them something they think of as simply being 'stupid'. You might, for example, get away with the idea that the horse the child rescued from its cruel owner is being secretly kept in the garage, only to find your young readers baulking at the suggestion that Mum could walk in to fetch a screwdriver and not even notice it.

Avoid being arch. Of course there are differing levels at which many shared books can be read. The older reader often gets a sly chuckle out of things that sail right over the head of somebody smaller. But the joke does usually have to be at least potentially inclusive, so that, the tenth time around, out comes the thumb, down comes the chubby hand to stop you turning the page, and out comes the question: 'Daddy was just teasing them, really, wasn't he?' 'Mum *really* wanted to get back to reading the paper, didn't she?' In the benighted language of the National Curriculum, the child's already 'drawing inferences from text' (or, as we used to call it back in the good old days, 'reading').

Does it help to read your work aloud to children to see how it goes down? Not really, no. For one thing most children are notoriously polite and gentle with people they love, or strangers who come into class. And the sheer joy of having their opinions canvassed can send them haywire. One says, 'I liked this bit!' You beam, and all the other hands shoot up. 'I liked that bit!' 'And I liked that bit!' Everyone wants to have a go at the pleasure of shouting out to the visitor.

So trust your own judgement. You are the writer, after all. Try reading it aloud to an imaginary son or daughter or class. You'll soon notice which bits you're rushing through because they're tiresome, and which of the sentences you're tripping over because they're too clumsy or long. You'll realise that, yes, you *can* put that rather ambitious word into a story for four year-olds because the very context and the way in which it will be read out will make its meaning transparent.

Are there some subjects best avoided in books to be shared between adults and children? Again, it's hard to say. Some parents will read anything the child demands. Others, like teachers, will beach up on things like 'pottymouth' poetry ('Well, *you* just said bogey! And you just said poo *twice!*'). Or books that appear to encourage the child to relish – or, worse, be amused by – cruelty and the infliction of pain. I watched as at least 30 parents with small children trooped out of a book fair when one enthusiastic author read out a passage from one of his history books about red hot pokers being driven up people's bottoms. (I wondered, frankly, why the others stayed.) He may justifiably argue that he's sold hundreds of thousands of copies, but I would guess that few of them have been read aloud by squeamish parents to imaginative children before the lights go out. So use your sense.

What about *how* a book is read aloud? Should that make a difference to how you write it? I don't see how it can. After all, some readers treat the words in the old-fashioned way, and simply speak them with intelligence and inflections sympathetic to the meaning. They read, in short, as if it were a *book*. Others go half-mad, acting out every sentence, doing all the voices in different accents, shouting the yells and whispering the quiet bits. They treat the pages in front of them pretty well as a script for a stage performance. Like every other author whose work has been professionally recorded, I've shuddered through one actor's butchering of my work with his frantic showing off, and also been startled to find tears pricking as another has used her skills to mine a poignancy I had forgotten about or never even realised was there. It's their own voice that most writers hear in their head as they put down the words, so go along with that.

And that's the root of all writing, when it comes down to it. Your own voice. Children are strange. Ralph Waldo Emerson defined them as 'curly dimpled lunatics'. They assume that they're immortal. (Why else do adults have to step in so smartly and often, simply to keep them alive?) And children are at one with eternity. (When did you last see a nine year-old glance at a clock and say, 'My God! It's three already! And I've got nothing done!') Their lives may change immeasurably. See how the language of their stories has moved so seamlessly over the centuries from tumbledown cottages in dark forests, through secret gardens and kind governesses, to the babysitter and the stepbrother. But in their essential nature – however individual and various those natures may be – children have barely changed at all.

So the successful children's authors will always be those who can best make their work chime in with the child's capacity to understand and enjoy it. And since, like Walt Whitman, all children 'contain multitudes', that gives the writer enormous scope to get it very, very wrong or very, very right.

Anne Fine OBE, FRSL is one of the best known and most popular writers for children of all ages and was Children's Laureate 2001–3. She has twice won both the Carnegie Medal and the Whitbread Children's Book of the Year Award and at the Galaxy British Book Awards has twice been voted Children's Author of the Year. She has also won the *Guardian* Children's Fiction Prize and dozens of other awards in the UK and abroad. Her work is translated into more than 45 languages. Her latest book for children is *Blue Moon Day*. Anne also writes for adults. Her website is www.annefine.co.uk.

Writing for different genres

Malorie Blackman looks at the different genres of children's books with a view to helping writers decide what kind of story they could write.

Take a trip to your local library or bookshop and peruse the children's section. (Also check out the books for young adults.) The books will probably be sorted into age ranges, for example books for babies and toddlers, books for the 5+ age range, books for 7+, 9+, 11+ and books for young adults or 14+. Take a closer look. There will probably be a separate poetry section (but not always) and a separate non-fiction or reference section. Take an even closer look. Are the books in the fiction section divided by genre? Probably not. There are so many different genres (and sub-genres) and so many books which span more than one genre that it would be a thankless task to sort books in this way. But we all have views on the types of stories we like to read – and write.

For the purposes of this article (and my sanity), I shall only be looking at the main fiction genres for children. My genre list is by no means definitive or exhaustive, but what I want to do is present some guidelines for some of the genres and some examples of books for further reading. Let me say straight away that a number of the books I've listed below quite happily overlap other genres as well. Take my own book for young adults, *Noughts and Crosses*, as an example. The story is about the friendship of two teenagers, Callum and Sephy, which eventually turns into a deep, undying love. Does that make it a romance/ love story? The story takes place in an alternative version of contemporary Britain. So it's a fantasy story – right? Callum is a 'Nought' (white) and Sephy is a 'Cross' (black) and their society has strict demarcation lines where the two groups are not encouraged to integrate. Noughts are the minority and historically the ex-slaves of the Crosses. As the book takes an angled look at modern-day racism, does that make it a real-life/contemporary story? Genre can be a hard one to pin down.

One of the first pieces of advice I received when I started writing was 'write about what you know'. Even though this advice is a useful starting point, I don't necessarily agree with it. After all, that's why we have imaginations, to take us outside of our own limited realm of experience. My advice would be to write what you *care* about rather than what you know. If you care about it, but don't know too much about it, then you'll take the trouble to find out, to do proper research. And if you care about it, then you'll write with a passion and a heart that will shine through.

Beware of choosing to write in a genre simply because it appears to be 'currently fashionable'. You may feel that you'll have more chance of being published or making money that way, but it's unlikely to be true. If you don't truly believe and feel every word you write, it will show. And what is 'currently fashionable' may not be so in one or two years' time. For a while in the mid to late 1990s, horror stories were the thing. Over the last few years, fantasy has been even bigger. But that also means there is more competition as every writer hoping to make some fast money jumps on that bandwagon. What makes your story more original, inventive and readable than the next one? If you can't answer that question, think long and hard about the type of story you are writing – and why.

Thrillers

Under this heading, I include the sub-genres of crime, ghost and horror stories. The key to thrillers is the battle between the protagonist or central character in your story and the antagonist or opponent. Your protagonist must have someone or something to battle against. Weak antagonists make for a weak story. Look at the *Harry Potter* series, for example (though they are not strictly speaking thrillers). Harry has to battle against the formidable Voldemort. Now if Voldemort was a weak enemy and easily vanquished, it would've made Harry's fight against him far less interesting. An antagonist doesn't have to be a person. It can be an organisation, the *status quo*, an object, but whatever it is, the reader should empathise with the protagonist's struggle against it.

Good examples: *I Am the Cheese* by Robert Cormier, *Cirque du Freak* series by Darren Shan, various by Sophie McKenzie.

Action

Always a favourite, action books are packed with incident. The most successful books in this genre certainly possess that page-turning quality which makes them incredibly hard to put down. Crime-busting spy thrillers are particularly popular. The protagonists are usually teenagers who invariably have to use their intelligence to get themselves out of myriad tricky situations.

Good examples: *Alex Rider* series by Anthony Horowitz, *Cherub* series by Robert Muchamore.

Mystery and adventure

These kinds of books catapult their readers into rip-roaring adventures. Most children love a puzzle element in a story and love the challenge of solving it. The puzzle element also provides that essential page-turning quality required for a successful book. The reader should not just want but *need* to know what is going to happen next. These types of stories, as well as thrillers, need endings which provide some resolution and a sense of closure. The puzzle presented in the story needs to be solved to be truly satisfying.

When I'm writing a mystery or an adventure story, I always make sure that the protagonist's troubles get worse in the middle of the story. Much worse. For example, in chapter one of my novel, *Hacker*, one of the protagonists, Vicky, is accused of cheating in a Maths test by hacking into her teacher's computer to get the answers. But there's worse to come. When she gets home, she and her brother Gib find out that their dad has been arrested for siphoning off millions from the bank where he works. Worse is to come! Vicky and her brother have a huge bust-up when Gib tells Vicky that her real parents drowned to get away from her and that she's not his sister and she never will be (Vicky is adopted). So not only does poor Vicky have her own school problems to deal with, she has to find a way to prove her dad innocent and find her own place within her family.

Good examples: *Wolf* by Gillian Cross, *Creepers* by Keith Gray, the *Wells and Wong* mystery series by Robin Stevens.

Survival

Survival stories include stories where the protagonist is alone, with limited resources and having to rely on his/her wits to survive. These types of stories tend to involve a lot of interior monologue so that the reader can really get inside the head of the main character(s). The danger with this type of story is that the protagonist's plight can become a bit monotonous, so new, *believable* challenges have to be employed throughout the story and there has to be a real sense of jeopardy should the protagonist fail. These are great stories for having the protagonist learn a lot about themselves in the process. Characters in these books have to make a real emotional journey for the reader to care about them.

Good examples: *Wolf Brother* by Michelle Paver, *Kensuke's Kingdom* by Michael Morpurgo.

Animals and nature

There are two basic types of animal story – where real animals act in a 'realistic' way and anthropomorphosised animals, i.e. animals who are in fact humans. The latter allows children to identify with the main character(s) and to share in their adventures. Animals can be used to portray complex emotions in a way that is instantly identifiable to children but also one step removed. In this way, animals can be used to write stories about a number of difficult topics for younger children, such as bereavement or loneliness.

Good examples: *Watership Down* by Richard Adams, *The Sheep Pig* by Dick King Smith, *Fire, Bed and Bone* by Henrietta Branford.

Real life/contemporary

This is a vast genre which covers any kind of contemporary circumstance. These books – which are more than thrillers or mysteries – live or die by the central character(s). The protagonists don't necessarily need to be sympathetic, but we must empathise with them at least, otherwise readers won't bother to finish the book. This genre includes school and family stories, stories that deal with disfigurement or disability – the list is endless. When I write one of these stories, I always write a short five-page biography of each of my major characters: their favourite foods, their favourite types of music, their likes and dislikes, loves and hates, what their friends love about them, what their friends find annoying, etc. I will never start writing any novel until I know my main characters inside out. That way I'll know how they'll react in any given situation. And my characters become real people to me, and sometimes when I'm writing they'll behave in ways that surprise me. I take that as a good sign. It means my characters have really taken on a life of their own.

Good examples: *Holes* by Louis Sacher, *The Illustrated Mum* by Jacqueline Wilson, *Stone Cold* by Robert Swindells, *(Un)arranged Marriage* by Bali Rai, *Junk* by Melvin Burgess, *Speak* by Laurie Halse Anderson, *The Art of Being Normal* by Lisa Williamson.

War

Unfortunately a genre which is always relevant. This genre allows the writer to examine the best and the worst of human nature.

Good examples: *Private Peaceful* by Michael Morpurgo, *I Am David* by Anne Holm, *Goodnight Mister Tom* by Michelle Magorian.

Romance and love stories

This is a popular genre for exploring relationships, and stories tend to be aimed at young adults. Romances may encompass any of the other genres mentioned in this article, including the paranormal and dystopian fiction.

Good examples: *Saskia's Journey* by Theresa Breslin, *Forever* by Judy Blume, *No Shame, No Fear* by Ann Turnbull.

Sports

This genre uses sport to illustrate and illuminate the major character(s) or society as a whole.

Good examples: *Keeper* by Mal Peet, *McB* by Neil Arksey, various by Tom Palmer.

Fantasy

Hugely popular, this genre seems to have taken over from traditional myths and legends. It appeals to the sense that there is something inside or outside of us which we may or may not be able to control, and stories often contain a magical element.

Good examples: *Harry Potter* series by J.K. Rowling, *Artemis Fowl* by Eoin Colfer, *His Dark Materials* series by Philip Pullman, *A Monster Calls* by Patrick Ness.

Historical

Research, research, research. Do your research. For me, the best historical stories shine a light on the way we live now. This genre of course includes war, which is listed separately.

Good examples: *Sawbones* by Catherine Johnson, *Coram Boy* by Jamila Gavin.

Humour

Humour is always popular. It's easy and engaging to read but hard to do well. Anthony Horowitz's *Diamond Brothers* series are fantastically funny crime novels and a particularly successful example of a fusion of genres. I've put them in this category though because for me, the antagonist in each of the *Diamond Brother* stories is almost incidental. I don't mean the books have weak antagonists; they don't. But it is the humour rather than the crimes in these stories that I more easily remember.

Good examples: *Geek Girl* by Holly Smale, *The Hundred Mile-an-Hour Dog* by Jeremy Strong, *I Know What You Did Last Wednesday* by Anthony Horowitz, *The Astounding Broccoli Boy* by Frank Cottrell-Boyce.

Science fiction

Science fiction is a vast genre. It can take you to other worlds, other times, other spaces and places, other minds. The writer who first turned me on to science fiction as a child was John Wyndham. I found his book *Chocky* totally mind-blowing. And it woke me up to the possibilities of science fiction. Science fiction isn't only spaceships and aliens from other planets – though there's nothing wrong with that. This genre allows for new technology and methodologies to be explored as in *Unique* by Alison Allen Grey, which explores the idea of cloning, or my own book, *Pig-Heart Boy*, which uses as its starting point the whole notion of xenotransplantation (the transplantation of organs from one species into another). The title of my book gives away the species of the donor and the recipient.

Good examples: *Mortal Engines* by Philip Reeve, *Unique* by Alison Allen Grey, *Hex* by Rhiannon Lassiter, various by Malcolm Rose, *Phoenix* by S.F. Said.

Poetry/narrative verse

Over the last few years, there has been a welcome increase in the number of stories told in narrative verse. This genre is particularly useful for those children for whom unrelenting pages of prose can be quite daunting, but who still want to be told a story as opposed to reading a series of different poems on unrelated subject matter. Narrative verse stories contain all the drama and heart of prose stories but are an interesting form to use when telling the story. As a writer, you need to be very clear as to why you want to tell your story in this way. And bear in mind that narrative verse is very hard to translate, thus limiting foreign edition options – but don't let that stop you. If your story needs to be told in narrative verse – then go for it. Stories told this way should vary in rhyme, rhythm and cadence or they quickly become boring.

Good examples: *Love That Dog* by Sharon Creech, *Cloud Busting* by Malorie Blackman, *Locomotion* by Jacqueline Woodson.

Short stories

The sad fact is, short stories are a very hard sell. Random short stories across many different genres are an even harder sell. Short stories which focus on a particular genre may be easier to get published but not compared to writing a novel.

Good examples: *A Thief in the Village and other stories* by James Berry, various anthologies edited by Tony Bradman.

Graphic novels

A number of well-known children's books have also had graphic novel editions published. These include *Stormbreaker* by Anthony Horowitz and *Artemis Fowl* by Eoin Colfer. Graphic novels are expensive to produce so it is rare for an unknown author to be published in this form by a children's publisher. Manga novels are becoming increasingly popular so this may change in the near future.

Fairy stories, myths and legends

These types of stories appear to have fallen out of fashion somewhat, which is a great shame. As a child I loved fairy stories and books of myths and legends from around the world. There was something very comforting in knowing that a true heart and a courageous spirit would eventually triumph over adversity. However, as Rick Riordan shows, there's plenty of material in fairy stories and legends which can still be used and given a completely modern twist.

Good example: *Percy Jackson* series by Rick Riordan.

Malorie Blackman OBE was the Waterstones Children's Laureate 2013–15. She has written more than 60 books for children, including picture books and novels for all ages and reading abilities, and also writes television scripts. Her novels for older children include: *Hacker* (1992), *Thief!* (1995) and *Pig-Heart Boy* (1997), which she subsequently adapted as a series for television which won several awards, including a BAFTA for best children's drama in 2000. Her multi award-winning *Noughts & Crosses* series includes *Noughts & Crosses* (2001), *Knife Edge* (2004), *Checkmate* (2005) and *Double Cross* (2008). In 2005 she was honoured with the Eleanor Farjeon Award in recognition of her contribution to children's books, and in 2008 she received an OBE for her services to children's literature. Her most recent novels are *Boys Don't Cry* (2010) and *Noble Conflict* (2013). Her website is www.malorieblackman.co.uk.

See also...

Writing for a variety of ages

Geraldine McCaughrean has written for both babies and adults – and all ages in between. In this article she looks at the variety of writing forms she has been published in.

Books

I spent my teenage years writing adult novels about things I knew nothing of, and (not surprisingly) having publishers turn them down. When I became an adult, I was published as an author of children's books, because at least I knew the world from a child's perspective: everyone has been a child. I was hugely prolific back then and, since each publication day felt like a fluke, constantly on the lookout for the chance to write more before my luck broke. It did not occur to me to specialise – in novels, in picture books, in educational or mainstream. Did you know that a baby's bath toy, if it has 25 words or more printed on it, becomes a book and exempt of VAT? I have reason to know this. I'm not proud, me.

Once my children's books started to win prizes, I was able to get adult novels published, too. Once, just once, I got paid the same for a 32-page picture book text that took a day to write as I got for a 600-page novel that had taken me two years. So which would I rather do? The answer is 'both', plus a few more titles for the ages in between, and a sprinkling of retellings for the fun of it. I have tried my hand at writing for almost every age, from toddler to adult. Three words are not enough to cover the many variants of Writing for Children. Each age range brings its own pleasures; each is as different from the others as crossword-puzzling is from writing a shopping list.

I confess that, when my daughter was small, I got very interested in writing picture books. As she grew older, my interest rose up in parallel with the pencil marks on the doorframe. Young children aren't much functional use though, beyond their inspirational qualities. Horribly partisan, they love everything a parent or grandparent reads to them, regardless of merit. They only become really useful guinea-pigs later.

Picture books

At the core of a successful picture book is a good visual idea that hasn't already been done. Unfortunately, such ideas don't come along to order. And a nice little story won't cut it as a picture book text. Since the text is not there to describe the pictures, it has to do something else. You have, essentially, to lay $14\frac{1}{2}$ visual opportunities in the lap of an artist, one for each spread plus the last verso.

The words mustn't vie with the pictures for room. The younger the age-pitch, the fewer the words – not just because the font size will be bigger, but because the child's concentration is shorter between page turns. A very young child's world does not extend far beyond home, parents, pets, toys and playschool, it's true. But within an astonishingly short time, nonsense, adventure, humour, delicious big words, sadness, bravery, magic, and wonder have all entered the child's ken. But whichever end of the scale you are writing for, there is always a third party to consider: the poor benighted soul who may be obliged to read this book over and over and over.

I once submitted a text, sure it would fail on grounds of conceptual sophistication. The young brain is slow to acquire the concept of Time, and this text was about a grandmother telling her granddaughter why she doesn't need a clock to tell her the time. It is my bestselling picture book, because grandparents love it. Children seem to, too, but then they haven't read Piaget's work on conceptual development so they don't know any better.

I embark on a picture book as I would poetry rather than prose, pouring on the word play and euphonious vocabulary, making the most of the aural splendour of words. It's almost sure to be read aloud, and small children love big language. After all, they have been acquiring new words every day without the aid of a dictionary, and are very good at it … which is why writing for the next age bracket is more depressing.

School readers

Gone is the invitation to roll in glistening language like a lamb in dew. Grim school gates have clanged behind us and there is literacy fodder on the lunch menu. Over and above the big, famous reading schemes, *a lot* of books are published for use with learner-readers; it's nice work if you can get it. Well, it's work.

Here, it is all simple vocabulary, simple syntax and a list of prohibitions: no pigs, knives, alcohol, guns, occult … From the fairy-tale world of stepsisters hacking off their heels, and pigs boiling water in readiness for the salivating wolf on the roof, the child moves forward into a bald landscape where female tractor drivers commute between capital and full stop, avoiding unpleasantness and pork products on the way. I'm generalising, of course, but it feels 'cabin'd, cribb'd and confin'd'. The design is functional, the illustration generally cheap – and the editors rewrite your words, leaving you wondering why they didn't just write it themselves in the first place.

Younger fiction for independent readers

So the next, independent-reading phase – for, say, 7–9 year-olds – ought to offer a merciful relief. The sector is horribly dominated by collectible series, of course, and since you won't beat them, you may want to join them in Pink-Pong land: pink prettiness for girls and naughty nasties for boys. Heigh-ho. Surely there must be a Middle Way between the female tractor driver and the pink sequin fairy? There is, of course. There are some wonderful books out there that reward close reading – just not enough.

I began writing for this age group after sitting on a few judging panels, where oddly few attractive entries had been submitted for the 7–9 year-old category. I still think it is a neglected age group – and it's such fun to write for too, especially if your publisher can match you with a good sparky illustrator. Surely this is just the age when books should be covetable, tempting objects in themselves – miraculous little wedges of wonder with which to prop open new doors.

The best thing about writing for the primary age is that the school visits are more fun. Adult authors can be recluses if they want, so long as they are interesting recluses who can hint at a dark and sensational past during their 'rare and long-awaited' interviews. But if you're a children's author you do school visits. It's useful, informative, punctures any illusion of achievement, and, for many authors, is a way of making ends meet. In primary and middle schools the audience is largely on your side and ready to join in (even those who hate books). Some authors can win over Year 8s, 9s and 10s as well. It's just that I've been trying for 30 years, and coming away exhausted from willing them to like me, speak to me, forgive my crime of polluting the world with books they don't want to read. With forethought – think! – I *could* have confined myself to writing for Years 1–7 and saved myself a lot of tears.

Myth, legend and retellings

The National Curriculum – little as I care for it – has its advantages for a children's author. For instance, there are two 'Myth' slots (Years 5 and 7), which have brought the ancient gods out of their dingy library alcove and made them popular again. I keep going back to myth and legend, because they are an encounter with the Big Stuff: terror, love, creation, war, fate, heroism, atonement, death, Fate and God … It feels good to roam among the 'ageless' stories, where all narrative has its roots. And its juggernaut splendour crushes petty political correctness under its wheels without anyone even noticing.

I like to alternate original fiction with retellings of existing stories. After all, why incessantly create new beasts when there are magnificent old ones who have roamed the earth for centuries and should never be allowed to become extinct?

Teenage and young adult fiction

When history looks back on the last decade's fiction, will Black-and-Red look like the Plague sweeping Europe, killing the weaklings, leaving behind it empty fields and full graveyards? Some days it feels like it. I love writing for teenagers – just not the same teenagers who read Black-and-Red, since I have no insight into them whatsoever. I'm not going to attempt to 'get down wiv the undead' because I would be rubbish at it. I shall confine myself to writing for those who are experiencing adolescence much as I experienced mine. There may not be many of them but at least I'll get it right. There is nothing messier or more painful than a failed jump on to a bandwagon.

Even if the plague of vampires, angels and werewolves passes, it may leave one permanent scar. Bookshelves at Foyles bookshop in London are now divided into 'teen fiction' and 'young adult' (other shops have other labels). I admit I needed the distinction explained to me. Apparently, Teen Fiction covers gore, sex, horror, S&M soft porn, vampires, the Undead, occult, necro-fantasy and anything your mother would rather you didn't read. Young Adult covers … well, anything else (apart from Fantasy which has a bookcase of its own). Choose your destination now, you writers for teenagers, because your book will only be shelved in one of these places. It will be similarly categorised online.

Incidentally, Remedial Literacy books, for older readers with younger reading ages are *the* boom sector of the industry just now. (Sad but true.)

Older fiction

I have left my favourite category till last. And it's one marked for extinction. Research shows that the complex, linguistically challenging 12+ novel will be the first to go. The *latest* research indicates that children's average reading age regresses in secondary school relative to their actual age: they favour simpler books than top juniors – or else don't read at all. So keep away. Those of us already aboard will go on bailing with increasing frenzy, but why join a sinking ship? Why would you?

Perhaps because it is the most pleasurable, diverse, gratifying field of all. These readers have the skill and stamina to tackle a long book, can appreciate character, style and satire, tackle politics, philosophy, morality, and are open to new departures. They're still reading at age 12 because they like books! They have worked out that, inside a book, they are free from the oppression of either teacher or parent. No need yet to fan their libido or steer a path through their bleak angsty fantasies. The author is free to revel in language and character, to experiment, to cultivate fertile plots.

Consequently, the field is hugely overcrowded and is the area where contracts are being cancelled, projects abandoned, authors turned out of the circus to fend for themselves in the wild. Morale is understandably low.

Annoyingly, books decide for themselves what they want to be, and there is no point in cutting them off at the knees to pretend they are younger, or standing them on a chair to pretend they are older. However selfish it sounds, a book gains most from an author at ease with the story and writing for the joy of it. A book is only as old as it feels.

Children's books span such a variety of forms – far more than for adults. When you consider the distance between babyhood and teenage years, it is hard not to relish the number of possibilities strewn along the way.

Geraldine McCaughrean has been a full-time writer for 35 years and has produced over 160 books and plays. Seven times shortlisted for the Carnegie Medal (which she won in 1989), her novels do not fit readily into any one category, but tend towards adventure. She won the chance to write a sequel to J.M. Barrie's *Peter Pan and Wendy* for Great Ormond Street Hospital; and *Peter Pan in Scarlet* was published in 2006 and has been translated into 50 languages. Her most recent novel is *The Middle of Nowhere* (Usborne 2013).

See also...
• *Children's books: genres and categorisation,* page 35
• *Writing for different genres,* page 134
• *Fiction for 6–9 year-olds,* page 143

Fiction for 6–9 year-olds

Alison Stanley worked for many years as a commissioning editor of young fiction. She gives here what she regards as essential components of a good fiction book for younger readers.

When teaching six-year-olds in the mid-1970s, 'reading' was something that involved a queue of children at my desk, waiting to be heard struggling through their less-than-stimulating reading scheme books. There had to be a better way of developing reading skills, especially as the delight of sharing real books with the children during 'storytime' at the end of the day, was such a marked contrast. I had no idea in those days about the business of publishing, and I certainly never imagined that many years later I would be commissioning books for that very same age group to read and enjoy. But without that classroom experience, I doubt that I would have begun to appreciate the needs of the young beginner reader. Nor would I have experienced that magical moment when a child just breaks through the reading skills barrier and begins to read unaided for the very first time. The anticipation in excitedly turning over the page to find out what happens next; the thrill of a guessed word being right; and the beginning of reading for pleasure are all magical moments to witness.

Books for younger readers

Here are some of my favourite books for younger readers that have stood the test of time. Read them and you'll know what I mean!

Happy Families series by Janet and Allan Ahlberg (Puffin)

Horrid Henry series by Francesca Simon (Orion)

The Littlest Dragon by Margaret Ryan (Collins)

Mr Majeika series by Humphrey Carpenter (Puffin)

The Worst Witch by Jill Murphy (Puffin)

Spider McDrew by Alan Durant (Collins)

The Black Queen by Michael Morpurgo (Random House)

Morris the Mouse Hunter by Vivian French (Collins)

Clarice Bean by Lauren Child (Orchard Books)

Lizzie Zipmouth by Jacqueline Wilson (Random House)

There's a Viking in My Bed by Jeremy Strong (Puffin)

Beginner readers

What makes a good book for children just beginning to read on their own – one that will stimulate and motivate them, and let them know that reading is an enjoyable and rewarding activity? Firstly and simply – beginner readers need good stories. Strong plots that are easy to follow, so that when faced with an unrecognisable word, the child can predict what is going to happen and be able to have a go at reading that 'difficult' word. Lively and appealing characters are essential too, especially if featured in more than one book.

Beginner readers like stories that reflect their experiences of the world but also ones that will stretch their imaginations. Stories with a fantasy element rooted in the real world where something ordinary becomes extraordinary in a familiar world, are always popular. The language of the stories should be rhythmic with plenty of repetition and alliteration. Sentences need to be short enough so they don't get split by a page turn, but long enough so that the story doesn't read in a stilted fashion.

Books for beginner readers require a generous typeface and good clear layout with plenty of illustrations giving clues to the text. This will help make the transition from shared picture books to reading alone a smooth one.

Last, but definitely not least, there is one vital thing to remember when writing stories for the beginner reader … beginner readers read *slowly*. Wacky, fast-paced humour within the text does not work when read word for word, very slowly. Humour in the text needs to be obvious, relate to the child's world and work when read at a snail's pace (see *Writing humour for young children* on page 154 for inspirational advice on writing funny fiction).

Ten questions

To summarise, ten questions commissioning editors and literary agents may ask themselves when assessing manuscripts for younger readers are:

Plot
• Is it a good story?
• Will it make sense when read slowly?
• Will it keep the reader wanting to turn over the pages?
• Is the story strong enough to stand up to the competition?

Setting
• Is the story set in a world that children will be familiar with?
• Are there events in the story that children will relate to?

Characters
• Are the characters appealing and original?
• Are the characters rounded enough for the beginner reader to want further books about them?

Language
• Is the vocabulary suitable for the young beginner reader?
• Is there plenty of repetition, alliteration and rhythmic writing?

I would also want to know about the author. I'd want to know if the manuscript was written by a published author, and if so, do his or her books sell? (Never forget that publishing is a commercial venture.) If it is a new author, I'd like to know if he or she is seen to be a major new talent who will progress to write further books.

The editorial process can help with many of these points, but the originality and uniqueness of a story belong to the author. Because there are so many books written for this age group, it takes a special author to create something new and appealing, something that will stand the test of time.

Confident readers

Once children become fluent readers, there's usually no stopping them in their quest to read more, and soon move on to longer novels. It's at this stage that they are exploring the different genres – humour, horror, adventure, or themes such as school stories, animal stories and football stories, amongst others. They're also finding out which authors they like to read and will be actively seeking out new books by that author. Confident readers come in all shapes, sizes, ages and with different backgrounds and personalities and it is essential that this is reflected in a broad range of reading matter.

Alison Stanley was a commissioning editor at Puffin Books and at HarperCollins Children's Books, where she was responsible for developing the younger end of the fiction list. She also commissioned more than 40 titles for the Collins Education *Big Cat* series and many articles for the first *Children's Writers' & Artists' Yearbook*.

See also...
• *Children's books: genres and categorisation*, page 35
• *Who do children's authors write for?*, page 119
• *Writing books to read aloud*, page 131

From rags to riches: becoming a first-time novelist

Having a debut novel published within a year of finding an agent is a swift journey indeed. But it took Jenny McLachlan years of writing and rewriting to craft *Flirty Dancing* into its final form.

In *Flirty Dancing*, my debut novel for teens, 15-year-old Bea Hogg experiences a rags-to-riches transformation from shy schoolgirl to dazzling swing-dancer. When Bea enjoys her moment of ultimate triumph, she turns to her friend and asks, 'Really?'. She can't believe what is happening to her. Similarly, my journey from amateur writer to published author could read like a fairy tale.

In July 2013, I sent the opening three chapters of my finished manuscript to Julia Churchill, children's agent at A.M. Heath (see page 243), and less than a year later *Flirty Dancing* was published. Having heard Julia speak at the Winchester Writers' Festival (see page 423), I was thrilled when she agreed to represent me and soon I was enjoying a day out with Julia in London, visiting publishers who all wanted to publish *Flirty Dancing*. After a brief bidding skirmish, I accepted a four-book deal with Bloomsbury that allowed me to leave my teaching job and write full time – the ultimate fairy tale ending for an unpublished writer.

The thing is, Sleeping Beauty had to do 100 years sleeping before she was kissed and Snow White had to keep house for seven, admittedly small, men prior to the arrival of her prince. Similarly, my journey to publication involved a long, less glamorous back story.

I finished writing my first draft of *Flirty Dancing* seven years before it was published. Having attempted to write for different audiences and within a range of genres, Bea's story came alive in my head and then alive on the page. Previous attempts at writing seemed flat and self-conscious by comparison, but when I wrote about Bea and her friends, I knew I had found my voice.

I sent three chapters of that first version to a handful of publishers (chosen carefully from the *Children's Writers' & Artists' Yearbook*, of course). I remember waddling to the post box – I was nine months pregnant – and posting the A4 envelopes and thinking, *watch out J.K. Rowling!* Well, clearly I was heading for a fall. I got a couple of rejections and, mortified, stuffed *Flirty Dancing* to the back of a drawer and got on with my real life.

However, Bea's story refused to go away and I had a niggling sense that I'd given up on her too quickly. Plus, my mum kept asking when I was going to do something with my 'jive book' – and she's a persistent lady. After several years of changing nappies and mashing bananas, I reread *Flirty Dancing*. Immediately – and rather painfully – I recognised that although it had a gripping plot, it wasn't that well written.

Like most writers, I pored over every article and book that offered advice on how to get published – my *Children's Writers' & Artists' Yearbook* was well thumbed. Somewhere, I had read that if a book was well written, and if it could be marketed, then it would be published. I found this hugely reassuring: admittedly, my book wasn't good enough, but it was within my control to make it better.

First, I needed to find out exactly what was wrong with it. With a baby in the sling and a toddler in the pushchair, I headed straight down to my local library and took out a pile of teen romcoms. Back home, I soon discovered that I was competing against books that were snappy, hilarious and basically more exciting than my book. The world of children's fiction moves quickly and I had fallen behind. Having compared *Flirty Dancing* with the competition, I rewrote the entire manuscript. I changed the narrative to the present tense, threw the reader straight into the action, made my jokes funnier and edited out half-hearted phrases. Gradually, the quality of my book started to resemble the published ones I was reading. Then, one magical day, I realised that my book might actually be a bit *better* than them.

The book I was reading at the time was part of a series. Suddenly it seemed obvious that publishers would be far more interested if they knew I had several books to offer rather than a one-off novel. Night after night, I lay awake thinking about my fictitious characters and working on their back stories. Then I had a sitting-bolt-upright-in-bed-moment when I realised that I already had the series: there were four main characters in *Flirty Dancing*, and each character had a story that was waiting to be told. Working quickly, I planned out each book. This led to a further revision of my manuscript as my newly developed characters now had voices that needed to be heard more clearly.

I knew that *Flirty Dancing* was getting there, but I wasn't sure how to take the plunge and send it to potential agents and publishers. At a wedding, I got chatting to H.L. Dennis, author of the *Secret Breakers* series, and she told me about the Winchester Writers' Festival where she had met her publisher. She explained that at the festival writers could have one-to-one meetings with agents, publishers and authors. The opportunity to get honest feedback from the people I needed to impress sounded like an excellent, if absolutely terrifying, idea. I booked a place at the festival, reserved my one-to-one appointments and then obsessively revised my opening chapters before sending them off to the editors and agents I had chosen to meet.

On the day of the festival, I was filled with nervous energy. I knew that my book was as good as I could make it, and that the feedback I received would tell me if I had any chance of getting it published. I wore special bright red shoes, my lucky pants and I shaved my legs: nothing could be left to chance. I love the Yeats' line, 'I have spread my dreams under your feet; Tread softly because you tread on my dreams.' For me, the vulnerability he is describing perfectly sums up how I felt as I sat down for my first one-to-one appointment with a commissioning editor.

'Well,' she said, smiling. I smiled back. There was a long pause. 'Can I just say how much I loved your book? I particularly liked the ninny joke.'

'Really?' I said.

'Really.'

With a spring in my step, I went to my next event. I had circled a talk being given by Julia Churchill and I didn't want to miss it …

I don't want to understate the utter thrill of the past year or the excitement of seeing my book published. It is just as brilliant as my overly fertile imagination envisaged. But when you are wondering if it is worth the investment in time and effort of changing the tense of your entire manuscript, or seemingly endlessly searching for the perfect word to describe a starlit sky, or taking the risk of introducing a character who you want readers to fall in love with, the answer is, yes, of course it is. This is what writers do, and *you* are a writer. Remember, Cinderella had to do a hell of a lot of housework before her dream came true.

Jenny McLachlan is the author of *Flirty Dancing* (Bloomsbury Childrens 2014), the first in a series of four romantic comedies for teenage girls. *Love Bomb* was published in March 2015 and is followed by *Sunkissed* in August 2015. Until the publication of *Flirty Dancing*, she was the head of English at a secondary school. Jenny taught for 14 years before she secured her book deal.

See also...

- *Overnight success*, page 148
- *How to sell your book to an agent*, page 230

Books

Overnight success

Lauren St John describes how she became an overnight success after 20 years of writing and being published.

I was ten when I first decided to become a novelist. At the time we were living on a farm in what was then Rhodesia and books were in short supply. When I did get a new *Famous Five*, Nancy Drew or Black Stallion novel, I'd devour it so quickly and feel so bereft when I reached the end that quite often I'd simply turn it over and start again.

One day, a visitor presented me with a box of secondhand books, among which was a novel written by a 13-year-old. The idea that a teenager could become a published author blew me away. I set to work at once writing a book about a sheep and a snake in a woodpile. I'd heard that it was important to write what you know and I had a string of adopted lambs. Added to which, the woodpile in our garden practically writhed with snakes – most of them poisonous.

The other thing I'd heard about publishers was that your manuscript needed to be typed. To this end, I had my mum take me to the nearest farm we could find that had a typewriter. There, I spent a busy afternoon working my way through a bottle of Tipp-Ex and filling a wastepaper basket with crumpled balls of paper. I never managed to type a single perfect page and that was the thing that defeated me. Publishers, I'd heard, were only interested in perfection.

By the time I turned 11, my principle goals were fame and saving animals. I didn't really care how I became famous and I didn't see lack of talent as a bar of any kind, especially if I achieved my number one ambition: becoming a pop star like Olivia Newton-John. Depending on the day of the week, I also wanted to become an Academy award-winning actress, an artist, an Olympic gold medal-winning eventer or a vet. English was my best subject but I didn't want to become a journalist like the career guidance counsellor advised because I thought journalists were quite horrible.

The funny thing was, I had a brief foray into most of these careers. Having left school at 16 (school, I'd decided, was interfering with my success) and had a couple of months at an art school in Cape Town, I announced to my parents that I wanted to move to the UK to become a pop singer. Until this point I'd led a fairly sheltered life on our farm and at a girl's boarding school (government, not private) and most sane adults would have fallen about laughing before saying a categorical: 'Are you out of your mind? Absolutely not!' End of story.

Fortunately, my parents are just the right side of crazy. My dad is a farmer and ex-soldier who's survived ambushes, snake bites, and being gored by a bull and attacked by a crocodile, so very little fazes him. He essentially shrugged and said it was fine if that's what I wanted to do. His main concern was that I didn't starve. My mum is a big believer in the following of dreams, so her response was: 'Here's an air ticket and a little pocket money. Bon voyage!'

By the age of 18 I'd spent a year working as a veterinary nurse in Maidenhead, Berkshire, waitressed and had a fleeting stint teaching horse-riding in Sussex. I'd also tried writing another novel. Having decided that songwriting was the way forward, I was back on the farm in Zimbabwe, riding my horse and working on my singing when my mum called (my parents were now divorced). 'There's a journalism course starting at Harare Polytechnic tomorrow,' she said, 'and you're going to be on it.'

My protests were in vain. When I was accepted onto the course, I grudgingly agreed to try it for two weeks. 'If I don't like it,' I told her, 'I'm quitting.'

In fact, I loved it. Few of our lecturers ever showed up, subjects such as sociology were started then aborted without explanation (I left college able to type only 25 words a minute because our typing teacher quit after two weeks and was never replaced), and our photography studies took place without cameras.

Once, we were taken on a rural reporting assignment where the only food available was goat curry. We slept on mud floors and the communal showers had no curtains. And yet I've never laughed more or learned more than I did that year. It remains one of the best experiences of my life. My diploma is not (in my opinion) worth the paper it's printed on, and yet my time at Harare Polytechnic taught me two things that I believe are critical for any writer:

• **Discipline.** You can write like Dostoevsky but if you can't deliver the goods when you're meant to deliver them, you're going to make a lot of people cross and mess up many production schedules.

• **The danger of preconceptions.** The ability to read people is a critical skill in a writer, as is psychological insight, but more important still is the capacity to have an open mind and the curiosity to look beneath the surface. The flashy, showy people, the beautiful ones, are rarely as interesting as the quiet ones sitting in the corner. As the *Desiderata* says, 'Listen to others, even the dull and the ignorant, for they too have their story.' The same applies to places and to stories.

It was while I was at college that I became obsessed with golf. By the time I graduated, three months later, I was so in love with it that I refused to get a real job. I spent the best part of a year working part-time for a shady promotions company. The director and I spent every available hour playing golf. The following March, with my 20-year-old brain turning slowly to mush, I decided that if I did have to work for a living I'd become a golf journalist. So I hopped on a plane with enough money for one month's rent and moved to London.

A white giraffe out of the blue

How I got from there to becoming a children's author is a long story. Suffice to say that it's taught me that no experience is ever wasted. Veterinary nursing, midnight feasts at boarding school, spending a decade on the PGA men's tour seeing the world and talking to Tiger, hanging out with musicians in Nashville, or childhood dreams of becoming a pop singer or winning the Badminton Horse Trials – it all comes in handy if you're an author, especially if you write for children.

People often ask me where I get my ideas, but the truth is that until I wrote *The White Giraffe* I'd never had a single decent plot idea for a novel in my life. Not one. And I'd been trying to dream one up since I was ten.

The White Giraffe itself came out of the blue. At the time I was struggling to find work. I'd spent eight years working as golf correspondent to *The Sunday Times*, as well as writing music features for other newspapers and eight well-received non-fiction books. Yet most of those books were out of print and when it came to convincing editors to take my stories, I couldn't get arrested. I knew I'd hit rock bottom when, desperate for money and fresh out of confidence, I wrote a piece on spec for *Your Cat* magazine and they turned it down. I call it my 'Your Cat' moment. I was forced to sell my flat because I couldn't pay the mortgage. I was fast coming to the conclusion that I'd have to give up writing and find a real job.

In 2005, I was on my way to do some Christmas shopping when, out of nowhere, an image of a girl riding a giraffe popped into my head. When I was a teenager we lived for six years on a farm and game reserve where we actually had a pet giraffe (along with warthogs, a goat, eight horses, eight cats, six dogs and the occasional python) and I thought, 'Wouldn't it be the coolest thing on earth if you could actually ride a giraffe?' And right there on the street the whole story came into my head, including the girl's name, Martine.

I envisioned *The White Giraffe* as a picture book and decided that one day, when I retired, I'd have a tinker with it. But I found I couldn't stop thinking about it. In January, I attempted the first chapter. To my astonishment, it was effortless. The images that poured into my mind were so vivid it was like watching a movie.

After that, I couldn't stop writing. The best part was that, throughout the whole process, I couldn't shake the feeling that the story was being gifted to me. Each day when I sat down to write, I had the strongest sensation that all I had to do was listen for the words. As a consequence, if a name or a plot twist came to me, I used it, no matter how bizarre.

I had the first draft completed in a month. It was 20,000 words long and, as numerous rejections testified, it needed more work done on it. I was prepared to accept that it was probably quite bad, but because of the way the story had come to me I was convinced that it had something special about it. I had a policy. If I disagreed with an editor's criticism of it, I ignored it. If I thought they had a valid point, I did my best to make the suggested changes. If more than two or more people disliked something in the book, I would concede that they might be right. Yet nothing I did seemed to make a difference. When my agent at the time told me the book was unpublishable, I was devastated.

Eighteen months, 20,000 more words and a change of agent later, four publishers wanted the book. In the meanwhile, I'd written a synopsis for my memoir, *Rainbow's End*, which was bid for by five publishers in the UK, three in the USA and two in the Netherlands. Hamish Hamilton in the UK and Simon & Schuster in the USA bought *Rainbow's End* and Orion gave me a four-book deal for the *White Giraffe* series. After nearly 20 years of trying, I was an 'overnight' success!

Ten children's books on, I'm still pinching myself. Every day I do the short distance commute from my bed to my computer and moments later I'm having an adventure. I might be escaping a volcano with Laura Marlin, saving the Amazon jungle with an ant named Anthony or riding at Badminton, but whatever it is it'll be fun.

I've learned to trust my imagination and the strange process by which stories come to me, out of nowhere and fully formed. *Dead Man's Cove*, the first Laura Marlin mystery, for instance, came to me after I read an article on the singer Laura Marling and thought that Laura Marlin would be a good name for a girl detective. At the time I was reading a book on modern day slavery and the two things coalesced in my imagination. The conservation themes in my *White Giraffe* series were inspired by my African childhood and my work rescuing leopards and dolphins with the wildlife charity, Born Free.

After decades without a solitary book idea, I now find enormous joy in thinking up plots. If you're stuck for ideas, remember that life is infinitely stranger than fiction. There is a wealth of potential bestsellers in every newspaper. A news story about a stowaway could be turned into a novel about a girl whose father works at the airport who rescues a boy. A story about a jungle plane crash could be turned into a girl's own adventure story about the lone survivor of a crash who has to cross the Amazon with a mongrel dog to make it to safety.

Finding *your* 'overnight' success

My number one piece of advice to would-be children's authors is to put the finding of an agent or publisher at the bottom of your priority list. I meet a staggering number of people who've barely written a chapter and yet are utterly obsessed with how to write a query letter and marketing strategies for their books. Trust me when I tell you that none of those things matter if you can't tell a good story.

Concentrate on writing the best book you can. Write from the heart, write for the love of it and write with passion. Contrary to popular belief, publishers and agents are desperate to find great novels. If you follow the advice above, there's no reason at all that yours can't be one of them. Remember that practice makes perfect. Write, write, write. If you value quality of plot and prose over marketing strategies and have faith and perseverance, chances are you will find your book a home.

Then, like me, you'll be an 'overnight' success!

Lauren St John is the author of the multi award-winning children's series that includes *The White Giraffe*, *Dolphin Song*, *The Last Leopard* and *The Elephant's Tale*. *Dead Man's Cove*, the first book in her Laura Marlin Mysteries series, won the 2011 Blue Peter Book of the Year Award and was shortlisted for the Children's Book of the Year at the Galaxy National Book Awards. Her bestselling *The One Dollar Horse* series (Orion), has been followed by *The Glory* (Orion 2015), now optioned by Canyon Creek Films. She has also written eight non-fiction adult books, including *Rainbow's End*, a memoir or her childhood in Zimbabwe. Her first adult novel, *The Obituary Writer*, was published by Orion in 2013.

See also...
- *Spotting talent*, page 5
- *What makes a children's classic?*, page 8
- *From rags to riches: becoming a first-time novelist*, page 145

Being an illustrator *and* a writer

Writer and illustrator of children's books, Liz Pichon, tells how persistence, hard work – and following the urge to create the kind of books *you* would have enjoyed as a child – can bring successful and very enjoyable results.

I always loved drawing and writing stories, but it wasn't something I ever thought I could do for a living. I was a bit hopeless at spelling (and still am). My route to becoming an author came through being asked to work on other people's stories as an illustrator. I found it too stressful sitting around waiting for someone else to give me a job, so I had a go at writing my own picture book ideas to illustrate as well. I already had an agent for my illustration work in books (Caroline Walsh at David Higham Associates), who was very encouraging (and has stuck by me for over 16 years).

My first picture book, *Square Eyed Pat*, was published in 2004. This was followed by *My Big Brother, Boris*, which won the Smarties Book Prize Silver Award (0–5 Years) and gave me more confidence to keep writing and drawing.

The *Tom Gates* series started life as a picture book idea. Publishers said they liked the format but didn't think there was sufficient story. So eventually, after rewriting it in different formats, I sat down and wrote afresh the first pages in a school exercise book. I imagined Tom writing about a rotten camping holiday he'd had with his family which included his teacher's comments as well as lots of drawings and doodles.

This was about the third (or fourth) go I'd had at it. But when Caroline sent out this version we got seven offers from seven different publishers within two weeks – which of course had NEVER happened to me before.

Here's my advice to anyone who wants to write or illustrate children's books:
• Be persistent. I know lots of people who have had their first efforts turned down or ideas rejected. But if the comments from publishers are positive, keep going and don't give up. Take feedback on board, especially if you're being told the same thing from different publishers. (However, some of my best ideas have lingered around for a while.)
• Think about what kind of books YOU really enjoyed reading when you were a child. I was crazy about a series about a bear called Mary Plain. Looking at them now, I realise that the quality of those books wasn't amazing, but Mary used to write letters with lots of drawings and doodles as part of them. I loved these bits so much that I would skip through the whole book to devour her letters. This is exactly why the *Tom Gates* books have so many doodles and drawings in them: I wanted to write a book that I would have enjoyed as a child.

The *Children's Writers' & Artists' Yearbook* is a fantastic source of information, STUFFED full of useful FACTS to help you get writing (and drawing). So be sure to make good use of it. And if you're lucky enough to get a book published – ENJOY it! Put together an event and do anything you can to help it along the way. I love going to schools and doing events now, although I found it tricky at first. It's really fantastic to be invited to talk about your books and meet the children and other people who are reading them. I often get ideas from going out and about.

The *Tom Gates* series is now published in 33 different languages and I've recently completed book nine. And I can honestly say I've never worked so hard on anything or enjoyed myself so much. So keep going and don't give up!

Here's my feet ═══ ═══ not touching the ground

– because that's what has happened to me since *The Brilliant World of Tom Gates* was published in April 2011.

Liz Pichon is a writer and illustrator of children's books, including *A Tale of Two Kitties, Bored Bill, My Big Brother, Boris* (winner of the Smarties Book Prize Silver Award in 2004), *The Very Ugly Bug, Spinderella, Square Eyed Pat, Penguins, My Little Sister, Doris* and *The Three Horrid Pigs and the Big Friendly Wolf*. The ninth book in her *Tom Gates* series, *Yes! No (Maybe...)* was published in May 2015 by Scholastic. *The Brilliant World of Tom Gates* won the 2011 Roald Dahl Funny Prize (7–14 Years), the 2012 Red House Children's Book Award (Younger Readers) and the 2012 Waterstones Children's Book Prize (Best Fiction for 5–12s); and *Tom Gates – Genius Ideas (Mostly)* won the 2013 Blue Peter Book Awards (Best Story). Find out more on her website http://lizpichon.com/ and follow her on Twitter @LizPichon.

See also...

Writing humour for young children

Like most adults, children love humour. But in both cases the joke will fall flat unless it is aimed at the right audience. Jeremy Strong has ten rules for writing humour for young children.

The snappy bit: some simple rules
1 Never allow your bum to become gratuitous.
2 Write wrong.
3 Self mutilation is highly recommended.
4 Words are essential.
5 Pulchritude? No way.
6 Inside every 20-plus there's an eight year-old trying to get out.
7 You calling me a wozzer? Mankynora!
8 Just who do you think you're talking to?
9 Surprise!
10 Ha! I laugh at death.

The expansive bit. We begin at the beginning.

Rule Nine: Surprise!
Ha ha! That's pretty much self explanatory.

Rule Six: Inside every 20-plus there's an eight year-old trying to get out.
Years ago, when I first began writing for children, I was often asked (by adults) why it was that the stories I wrote seemed to appeal to children. You have to imagine an adult asking this question, in a tone of voice that mixes one part admiration to nine parts complete bewilderment. I used to answer, fairly truthfully, that only my exterior had aged along with my chronological age, and that I was still aged about eight inside. The adult would usually laugh and would go away as bewildered as they were before they'd asked the question. The point here is, I think, that it isn't possible to really understand except from a child's viewpoint. If you have forgotten what it was like to be a child then you're unlikely to understand. No matter what you write you must keep your audience firmly in mind. You are writing specifically for them.

Rule One: Never allow your bum to become gratuitous.
To make matters worse, adults often think the things that make children laugh are puerile. To some extent this is true and it is easy to make a child laugh by playing 'lowest common denominator' jokes – jokes that refer to farts, snot, bums, knickers, etc. But whilst employing these guaranteed tickle-sticks it is easy to forget that children also like quite sophisticated jokes.

As for the bums and farts, it's okay to pop them in here and there but, for the sake of at least some self respect, keep them to a minimum and shun the gratuitous bum.

Rule Four: Words are essential.
Children love word play, and they love 'knowing' jokes – for example, jokes that are aware of how bad they are, or referential jokes that make use of things familiar to them, the things that mark out their lives, such as school, parents, family.

Then there is the matter of what children can read and understand. Obviously, this is going to vary not only with age but with ability. There are children of six who can read like 11-year-olds, and *vice versa*, with all shades in between and quite frequently further beyond. Nevertheless, as a writer, you need to aim towards the centre. In this article I am going to concentrate on 6–11 year-olds because those are the ages I taught for 17 years.

Let's look at language. Things need to be fairly simple. Shorter, rather than longer sentences work best. But like all rules this one can be deliberately misused. For example, at some appropriate point in a story you might wish to hurl yourself into some ever-increasing sentence that just seems to plunge on and on at a relentless pace and with reckless abandon like a runaway car because that happens to be one of the best ways your writing can capture the manic activity that is going on in your story at that particular point. Maybe it is a description of a runaway car. You get the point. Children respond to this positively because, anchored as it is in a normally short and simple style of writing, the over-long sentence becomes not only a writing device, but also a source of humour.

Rule Ten: Ha! I laugh at death.

As with comedy for other age groups, nothing is held sacred. You will, however, have to obey the obvious rules that generally apply to writing for children, and also steer clear of the PC police. You can be smutty, but not dirty. You can be unkind to animals, but they mustn't be in a circus, unless you're a signed up freedom fighter for 'Say no! to performing dumb creatures'.

You can laugh about death. (It's an emotional release. Honest.) You can even have stereotypes and clichés – but in this instance don't expect to get published.

Rule Two: Write wrong.

Children love to recognise things that are wrong, and this is where word play often has great effect. Characters that get their words or spellings wrong are a good source of humour, not only because it is funny in its own right, but because children love the empowerment of recognising what's wrong. (You will, incidentally, lose brownie points for using words like 'empowerment'.)

Rule Seven: You calling me a wozzer? Mankynora!

Invented words can also be a terrific source of enjoyment for both writer and reader, especially when they are used as expletives – sort of coded (and therefore safe) swear words. Mankynora! Wozzer yourself! Let's also take a look at sophistication. You have to ask yourself, am I writing a joke for an adult or a child? I know for a fact that I am guilty of putting jokes for adults in some stories – jokes I know only an adult will understand. (Or sometimes a joke that a child will get on one level, but where the adult will see a second 'hidden' joke or implication.) The reason I do this is because I can't resist the temptation if it's a good one. Besides, many children's books are read to them by adults, and so I am putting in something to make it more enjoyable for them. Nevertheless, you need to make sure that the vast majority is firmly in the child's grasp.

Rule Five: Pulchritude? No way.

Whilst on the subject of sophistication it is worth thinking about the words you use. With each word you need to ask yourself: can a child of 'x' years read and understand this word? Apply a bit of common sense. There are some words a child might not understand but it

Books

might be worthwhile introducing such a word to them, allowing the context to help reveal its meaning.

The word 'sophistication' itself is a reasonable example. Many junior children would not understand it but, although it's long, it's not too difficult to work out what it says and you could argue that it's a good word for a child to know. On the other hand, the word 'pulchritudinous' is not only very hard for a child to work out but it is extremely unlikely you would need to use such a word when writing for junior children.

Rule Three: Self mutilation is highly recommended.

You have to be rigorously self disciplined about this. No matter how good a joke is, you have to cut it out if it's not actually funny to your audience. The humour also needs to arrive and leave quickly. Anything that takes pages to set up is not worth it and the longer it takes the more likely it is that your writing will become increasingly false and unnatural as you struggle with all the scaffolding you require to hold up the joke.

Rule Eight: Just who do you think you're talking to?

It is a mistake to think that the things adults laugh at in children make good material for children's books. They don't, for the simple reason that it's funny to the adult watching the child, and not the other way round. All of this points to one of the cardinal rules for writing anything: be aware of your audience. Keep that firmly in mind and you can't go far wrong. I was going to finish by writing: May the fart be with you. Then I realised that it would not only be out of place, but one fart too many.

Jeremy Strong writes humorous fiction for 8–11 year-olds. His books include *There's a Viking in My Bed*, which was made into a popular BBC television series; *The Hundred-Mile-an-Hour Dog*, for which he won the Federation of Children's Book Groups Children's Book Award; *Stuff*, which won the 2006 Manchester Book Award; and *Beware! Killer Tomatoes*, which won four book awards, including the Sheffield Children's Book Award. His most recent books are *Kidnapped! The Hundred-Mile-an-Hour Dog's Sizzling Summer* and titles in the *Cartoon Kid* series, all published by Puffin Books. His website is www.jeremystrong.co.uk.

See also...
● *Who do children's authors write for?*, page 119
● *Writing for different genres*, page 134

Writing ghostly stories for children

Cornelia Funke describes the adventure of writing ghost stories for children. She highlights the questions writers can ask themselves when creating in this genre and considers how scary the stories can be for children.

I am not sure whether I liked ghost stories as a child. I know that at some point I loved Oscar Wilde's *Ghost of Canterville* (and now think it is the most touching ghost story ever told). But the first one I remember was written by a German, Otfried Preussler, whose *Satanic Mill* is an unforgettable tale: Preussler's ghosts were bowling with their own heads, as far as I recall.

Different types of ghosts

The funny ghosts who try to be scary and are not scary at all. We meet them in fairy tales, myths and Hollywood movies. They are slimy and loud, easily frightened by human heroes and of course are the most obvious choice for a ghost story written for children.

The first ghost I wrote about was that kind of ghost: Hugo, an ASG (Averagely Spooky Ghost), to be precise. I created him when an editor friend asked me many years ago to write a ghost story for 8–12 year-olds (don't we love it when publishers put our audience in cleanly separated boxes?). The story became a series of books, *Ghosthunters*, about a boy who is very afraid of ghosts but becomes a famous ghost hunter, with the assistance of the ASG. I had immense fun writing about COHAGs (Completely Harmless Ghosts), FOFIFOs (Foggy Fug Ghosts) and GHADAPs (Ghosts with a Dark Past). Interestingly, with every book my ghosts became darker and scarier.

My young readers became quite obsessed with the series and sent me lots of suggestions for ghost types. I heard from teachers that boys who despised reading had stolen *Ghosthunters* books from their tables to secretly devour them. My stories invited readers to play with fear – to make fun of it, hunt it, destroy it.

Ghosts are perfect for that. They are the impersonation of our greatest fears – the fear of the night, of death and what may await us on the other side. Not only that – they impersonate guilt, redemption, sadness that can't even be cured by death, they can bear witness to unspeakable crimes and of the inescapable heritage of the past.

Heavy themes.

Nothing suitable for children?

Oh yes, they are. All of them.

Children take life very seriously. Life, death, pain, loss … they still face the big questions, because they haven't learned to look away. We can develop quite a skill in that as grown-ups. Children want to look at the dark because they know that what they fear becomes even more frightening when they turn their back on it or lock it away.

Young readers often don't have emotional memories attached to the themes of death, loss and guilt, which makes them much tougher when they play with them. But they've heard about them, the great monsters waiting … and they love to encounter them on the safe grounds of a printed page. As for the children who do know – we so easily forget that many know quite a lot about death and loss, even guilt – they long for stories that help them to cope with the dark by asking questions about it or maybe even give meaning to it. For them, stories can be both shelter and comfort, without looking away, and ghosts can be the perfect travel companions into realms that know about pain and fear.

Books

It was a long journey through life for me between *Ghosthunters* and *Ghost Knight*. During that period, I learned some things about death and loss, about human nature, good and evil – all this apart from the fact that I had always been completely obsessed with knights. (*The Once and Future King* by T.H. White is still my favourite book).

Serious ghosts

The ghosts I found for *Ghost Knight* were not funny. If you intend to write a ghost story that walks on the darker side of this genre I recommend that you find your heroes in real places. Children love the enchantment of fiction that makes them discover reality. The ghosts I found in Salisbury, Lacock and Kilmington were human, and shadows of ourselves. They take my young readers on a journey into their own future as grown ups, but they also tempt them to travel into the past, to Salisbury Cathedral, Lacock Abbey and Kilmington Graveyard. These are all places where they can touch and breathe times gone and lost and follow in the steps of those who have lived before them.

I will never forget the reading I did at Salisbury Cathedral late at night, surrounded by children and parents. It took place, of course, next to the tomb of William Longespee, the man who had inspired my ghostly hero and incarnated my dreams about knights, and who at the same time allowed me to bow to what Oscar Wilde taught me about the sadness of ghosts.

Writing a ghost story

So, as you see, a ghost story is not just a ghost story. Maybe that is especially true for one written for children. There are so many paths to take. A good story always starts with the right questions. Ghost stories like to hide from us, dress themselves in a dozen veils. In readings I always try to explain this by comparing them to a labyrinth. Each one is full of traps and surprises, full of characters that hide between the hedges and love to jump at the poor writer who is trying to find his way through. There are whispers. A story likes to keep its secrets, but it also likes to be chased, found out, hunted and tamed. So it teases you by giving you hints and wrong tracks. And there you are, a pen in your hand (well, as in my case, you may write using a computer), a Moleskine notebook under my arm (well, once again, you may just carry your laptop … be careful though, there's nowhere to plug in in the labyrinth). You are stumbling down the narrow paths, looking for the one that is exactly right – the one that won't be so long and windy that it bores your readers to death; the one that shows all the secrets, all the characters hiding and whispering … It is the greatest adventure to find the heart of a story. And it's true storyline. Of course this endeavour is especially scary when you are looking for a ghost story! You may only find out after turning several corners that you are dealing with a scary ghost. Did I give you the impression that you choose whether it will be funny or scary? I apologise. The story chooses, once you enter its labyrinth. So make sure you ask the right questions before you decide on the one you enter. What do you want the labyrinth to grow for you?

Do you want your readers to love the ghost whose story you'll tell? Do you want them to pity it? Or fear it? Once again – you may answer all these questions and then find that a completely different story emerges. It has happened to me. Many times.

What age group do you intend to tell your story for? Once again, this is a good question and it needs to be asked. But be ready to change your answer if the story demands it.

The setting. Once you've decided on where the story will be set it will be hard to change it, especially if you choose an existing location. With an imagined one you leave most decisions to the labyrinth (which can be interesting!). With a real place, you walk in with a map, with your research and knowledge guiding you. A real place, with all its history, can be like a bag of provisions for your writer's journey. It can be your main character, all the food you need. It will tell you about landscapes, weather, buildings – even characters – and your readers will be able to follow your tracks in their own world, making a wonderful adventure. I still receive photos showing children in Venice who have followed the tracks of my book, *The Thief Lord*. And I heard about a boy who knelt in front of Longespee's tomb in Salisbury Cathedral after meeting him in *Ghost Knight*.

Oh – one more question: who will you be? The hero? Somebody who watches him/her and all the others, a narrator who knows everything? The god of the story? (Well, ghosts don't accept these gods but try, if you want to.) Most likely, you will be all of them. That's the joy of being a writer. You can live a thousand lives and take a thousand shapes.

Yes, go and write ghost stories! And write them for children! Even the dark ones, soaked in tragedy and the shadows of death – maybe those especially. Children are the most magical audience. They slip into a story like a fish into water. Without hesitating. Without asking how deep it is and where you got it from. They will travel the past on their printed wings. They will face their fear of gravestones and shadows moving in the dark. They will consider the possibility that life may not end in death and wonder why it scares them to see proof of it. They'll remember those who came before them and may even get a glimpse at the never-ending circle of life. And if all that gets too scary, just let them chase the ghosts – to save the good ones and send the bad ones to hell.

Hurrah for ghost stories!

Cornelia Funke (pronounced Foon-kuh) is a multiple award-winning author of children's fiction and has sold over 20 million copies of her books worldwide. She was brought to the attention of Barry Cunningham at the Chicken House (see page 42) when a young German girl living in England asked him why her favourite author's books were not available in English. The Chicken House published her latest title at that time in English translation, *The Thief Lord*, in 2006 and it stayed at No 2 of the *New York Times* bestseller list for 25 weeks. It was followed by *Dragon Rider*, the *Inkheart* trilogy and the *Ghosthunter* series, and *Ghost Knight* (Orion Children's Books 2012). Her most recent books are *Young Werewolf* and *The Moonshine Dragon*, both published by Barrington Stoke. She was born in Germany and lives in Los Angeles.

See also...
- *Spotting talent*, page 5
- *Who do children's authors write for?*, page 119
- *Writing horror for children*, page 160

Writing horror for children

'Nine stories you'll wish you'd never read', it warns on the cover of *Horowitz Horror*. Anthony Horowitz writes about writing horror for children and, aware of children's thirst for blood and intestines, airs the question of just how far an author can go.

As much as it's fun to be asked to write about writing, I hope anyone reading this will take it all with a medium-sized pinch of salt. The only incontrovertible law of writing I ever came upon was set down by my great hero, the American screenwriter William Goldman in *Adventures in the Screen Trade*. NOBODY KNOWS ANYTHING. It deserves the capital letters. If you're setting out to write a horror story for children, what follows may be useful. But your own instincts are probably better. Anyway, here is my experience for what it's worth.

Children love horror. You need look no further than the worldwide success of writers like Darren Shan to see it. Years ago, the *Goosebumps* series had covers that promised far more than the contents ever delivered but for a time they were littered across every school yard and made their author, R.L. Stine, a millionaire. Even the *Harry Potter* films have become progressively darker with one character cutting off his own hand, the death of a teenager and the truly hideous appearance of 'he who must not be named'.

And yet, the first – indeed the most crucial – question you have to ask yourself is: how far can you go? This is something of which I'm always painfully aware. Go into a classroom and talk to the children and you will discover that far enough is never enough. They want the blood, the intestines, the knife cutting through the flesh ... the full monty. The problem, of course, is that if you give it to them you risk alienating the school librarians, bookshop buyers and the parents, and your book may never actually reach its intended audience.

When I visit schools, I always advise children to keep their own writing blood-free. Teachers don't like it, I tell them. I remind them that the scariest moment in any horror film is when the hand reaches for the door handle in the dark. That's when the music jangles and your imagination runs riot. What happens after the door is open is almost incidental. It seems to me that what you imagine will always be scarier than what you see – and this is a rule I apply to my own writing. For my money, the most effective passage in *Raven's Gate* comes when Matt gets lost, cycling through a wood in the dark. Every road brings him back to the same point. Slowly he begins to realise that he is never going to escape. There's no blood. No monsters. But it seems to work.

But at the same time – if you don't actually deliver, you're going to disappoint and so lose your audience. In my view, this is what went wrong with *Goosebumps* and it's the reason why they're no longer so popular. There has to be blood. How much of it and how far you go is up to you. Like I say, there are no rules. Take a look at the opening of Darren Shan's *Lord Loss*. The death of the parents leaves nothing to the imagination but teachers still love him. I don't know how he gets away with it.

Perhaps it's a question of context. A random act of violence or mutilation might seem very horrible in a book by, say, Jacqueline Wilson. But that's because her characters are so real, her world so recognisable. But when you write a horror story, you have a different departure point. Even before your readers buy the book, they know what to expect and they open it in exactly the same way as they might get on a ghost train at a fairground.

They expect a certain number of skeletons and monsters and read the book in the knowledge that (a) it's only a ride, and (b) it will eventually deliver them back into the daylight.

The daylight, though, I think is important. I was genuinely shocked by the death of the teenager – Cedric Diggory – in *Harry Potter and the Goblet of Fire*. Not that J.K. Rowling needs to worry about the rules. But I've always thought that although it's reasonable to slap around your heroes, to frighten them and to hurt them, it's somehow irresponsible and wrong to kill them. No children have ever died in any of my books. Actually, none of them have ever felt real pain – again, because of the context. A child being chased by devil dogs through the swamps of Yorkshire may seem to be having a tough time. But that's nothing compared to a child in a London supermarket being slapped and screamed at by his mother. That, to me, is real horror.

Enough of these generalities. If you're thinking of writing something dark and scary for a young audience, here are just a few thoughts that might help.

• **You need an original story**. It may seem obvious but the realm of horror is stuffed with haunted castles, wicked stepmothers, evil magicians and all the rest of it. I know because I've used plenty of them myself. But a strong, simple idea will set you apart from the pack. Look at Justin Somper's success with *Vampirates*, a clever collision of swashbuckling and the supernatural. Or Garth Nix (*Mister Monday*) who time and time again comes up with hugely imaginative universes, completely new ideas.

• **Think about your central characters**. If they're likeable enough and idiosyncratic enough, you can – and will – get away with murder. There are some quite horrible things in Philip Pullman's *Northern Lights* with children kidnapped, stripped of their souls and turned into zombies. But we never doubt that Will and Lyra will win through.

• **Don't lose your sense of humour**. Mixing a few laughs in with the general mayhem doesn't lessen the horror. It helps the reader to deal with it. Paul Jennings, the Australian author, has produced some wonderfully twisted stories that would be far nastier if he didn't write with a smile.

• **Forget that you're writing for children**. This advice may seem incompatible with what I've already written but for me it's always been vital. If you sit at your desk with children in mind, it's all too easy for your work to become patronising and flabby. Of course it's important to consider levels of violence, what sort of language is applicable, how far you can go – but these should all be at the back of your mind. When I write horror, I try to scare myself. Darkness, solitude, the sense of being lost, the figure glimpsed out of the corner of your eye. I'm pretty sure that what scares children scares adults too. There's no need to cherry-pick, or to filter the frissons!

• **Think visually**. The awful truth is that children are seeing more and more horror films with a 15 certificate, and they're also playing computer games with an incredible amount of electronic gore. Both films and games have a language which, I think, translates well to books. My generation was literary. Today's generation is visual. That's my theory, anyway, and I hope my audience will 'see' as much as read my work.

My intention has always been to entertain children – by which I mean neither educating them, improving them nor terrorising them. As to the last of these, I only ever got it wrong once. I wrote a short horror story (it's in *Horowitz Horror 2*) where the first letter of each sentence spelled out a message to the reader. That message went something along the lines of: 'As soon as you have read this, I'm coming to your house to kill you.'

About a year later, I received a note from a very angry and distressed mother who told me that she now had a traumatised daughter. My story, she said, was wilfully irresponsible and she suggested that I write a letter to her daughter, apologising.

I totally agreed. The next day I wrote a nice letter to the girl, explaining that I had intended to be mischievous rather than malevolent, that it was only a story, that she shouldn't have taken it so seriously.

Unfortunately, the first letter of every sentence in my letter spelled out: 'I am going to kill you too.'

Anthony Horowitz OBE juggles writing books, films, television series, plays and journalism. He has written over 40 books including the bestselling teen spy series, *Alex Rider*, which is estimated to have sold 19 million copies worldwide and which he adapted into a movie that was released in 2006. Anthony is also an acclaimed writer for adults and was commissioned by the Conan Doyle Estate and Orion Books to write two new Sherlock Holmes novels. *The House of Silk* was published in 2011 and was internationally lauded as the top title of the autumn. He followed this with a sequel, *Moriarty*, which was published in October 2014. In 2014 it was announced that Anthony had been commissioned by Ian Fleming Publications and The Ian Fleming Estate to write a new James Bond book incorporating original, unpublished material by Ian Fleming. This is due to be published by Orion in the UK and HarperCollins in the USA on 8 September 2015. Anthony's television series include the BAFTA award-winning drama *Foyle's War*, *Injustice*, *Collision*, *Poirot* and *Midsomer Murders*. Anthony was awarded an OBE for services to literature in 2014.

See also...

- *Who do children's authors write for?*, page 119
- *Writing for different genres*, page 134
- *Writing ghostly stories for children*, page 157
- *Writing crime fiction for teenagers*, page 167

Writing historical novels for children

Michelle Paver shares her thoughts on how to approach writing historical novels for children and the importance of focusing on the story.

Books

Books about how to get published sometimes advise new writers to research the market thoroughly. Read the competition, see what sells – that sort of thing. If that appeals to you, fine, but I've never liked the idea and have never done it. In my view it isn't necessary, or even a good thing. You might just find it confusing and intimidating, and it could put you off what you really want to write.

I think it's better to concentrate on the story *you* want to write. The characters. The premise. The historical setting. You may not even know *why* you want to write it. But you do, and that's the main thing.

The period

Before you make a start, though, it's worth asking yourself why you want to set the story in your chosen historical period. Are you especially attracted to it? Did you daydream about it as a child; maybe you still do? Or does it simply have a vague appeal, perhaps based on having seen a few films or read some novels set in that time?

There's no harm in being drawn to a particular period for tenuous reasons. But if that is the case, I'd suggest that you become a little more familiar with it before deciding whether to use that time for your story. You'll need to know your chosen period pretty thoroughly; and if you decide halfway through writing your novel that it isn't quite as fascinating as you'd thought, then the chances are that the reader will think so too, and your story probably won't work. In short, you must be prepared to live and breathe it for months or even years.

The story is king

This would seem to be the logical point to talk about research, but I'm going to leave that for later because I don't think it's the most important thing. The most important thing is the story. Always. And particularly for children. In general, children don't read a book because it got a great review in *The Times*, or because they want to look impressive reading it on the train. They read it because they want to know what's going to happen next.

That might seem trite, but it's amazing how easy it is to forget, especially when you've done a ton of research on a particular period, and there are so many terrific things about it that you just can't wait to share with everybody else.

So it's worth reminding yourself that the basics of any good story need to be firmly in place: characters about whom you care passionately; a protagonist who wants or needs something desperately; perhaps a powerful villain or opposing force which poses a significant threat. Big emotions: anger, envy, pride, hate, loyalty, love, grief. And just because the book will be read by children, don't shy away from the bad stuff (although obviously, you'll need to handle it responsibly). Death, violence, neglect, loneliness. Children want to know. They're curious about everything.

The beginning

Everyone knows that the first page of a story is critical, but this is especially so for children. In fact, the first paragraph is even more critical. And the first sentence is the most critical of all.

This poses a special challenge if you're writing a historical novel. How do you root the story in the past without getting bogged down in clunky exposition?

There's no magic formula, but the idea of 'show, don't tell' is a good place to start. Perhaps you could begin with a situation that's specifically of that period, like a witch-burning. Or, as part of the story, weave in an object of the period, like a flint knife.

You might be tempted to write a 'prologue', like the ones they used to have at the beginning of old movies ('London, England. The Cavaliers and Roundheads are at War ...'). By all means write one of these. I did, for the first draft of *Wolf Brother*. But you may well ditch it before you finish the final draft. You may find that by then it has done its work by helping to anchor you, the writer, in the period. If you leave it in, it might have a distancing effect for the reader, diminishing the immediacy of the story.

Telling the story

What I said about the beginning of the story goes for the rest of it, too. The challenge for the writer of historical novels is to make the reader 'live' the story along with the characters. Somehow you've got to make them see, feel, touch, taste that period – without resorting to wodges of boring description that might slow things down, or overdone 'period' dialogue which is tiring to read and may distance the reader.

Again, there's no formula, but a good guiding principle is to make the essential exposition an integral part of the story. Make this a story that couldn't really have happened at any other time in history – even though the emotions involved are universals with which the reader can readily identify.

If you do this, then it'll become fairly clear what needs to stay in and what should come out. And there will probably be a lot of cutting. Pare down the exposition to what's essential. For instance, you may not need to explain the background to the entire war; just the particular skirmish in which your heroine has been caught up.

And for the essential exposition, it can help to introduce it in a highly charged emotional way: perhaps an argument or a fight. 'Exposition as ammunition' was a favourite motto of the film-maker Ingmar Bergman and it's one that can serve you well. But don't get so hung up on explaining things that you lose sight of the emotional focus of the scene.

The same goes for 'period atmosphere'. I would think long and hard before including anything for this reason alone. Try to make your period details part of the story. Then cut them back, then cut them back some more. What you need is a swift, vivid, unforgettable image with *just* enough detail to bring it alive – but no more.

Research

Which brings me (finally) to research. Some novelists don't do any. If that works for them, that's great. But if you're setting your story in the past, I don't think you can get by without doing at least some. And probably rather a lot. You need to know, intimately, what it was like to live back then. It's the little everyday details which interest readers, particularly children. What did people eat, wear, live in? How did they fight, travel, work, entertain themselves? What did they *think*? How were they similar to us? How were they different? And the more you can actually experience some of this for yourself the better – for example, by location research, trying out the food of the period – because it will give you all sorts of intriguing ideas and insights that you couldn't have got in a library.

Bear in mind, too, that research isn't just a matter of getting the details right. It'll probably spark ideas for the story itself: incidents, twists, particular scenes. These are gold dust. Use them. (Provided, of course, that they work in the context of the story as a whole.)

Perhaps the hardest thing about research is that the vast bulk of what you've lovingly unearthed isn't going to make it into the final draft. Be ruthless about keeping *only* those details that you really need: either to move the story along, or to develop character, or to set the scene. And shun any whiff of teaching; this is a story, not a history lesson.

This means that you'll probably go through a rather painful process of cutting over the course of your first, second, and successive drafts. But don't grieve too deeply for your lost treasures. *You* know all that background, and your in-depth knowledge will give your writing an assurance that it wouldn't otherwise have.

Language and style

This can be especially tricky: a kind of balancing act between keeping the story and the characters accessible, while leaving the language with just enough special vocabulary or dialogue to remind us that we're in another time. All this without distancing us too much, or (just as bad) without obvious anachronisms.

I'm often asked if I write differently when I'm writing for children, as opposed to when I'm writing for adults. The answer is, no, not at all. For me, it's the nature of the story that dictates the language and the style. If you're writing a story set in a middle-class Victorian home, your vocabulary and style will be utterly different from that which you'd use if you were writing about a forest of the Stone Age.

Having said that, if children are going to be among your readers, one important thing to bear in mind is that lengthy flashbacks can weaken the force of a story by reducing its immediacy. Because children read to know what's going to happen next, it helps too, to have unexpected twists, surprises, action, high emotion, flashes of humour, and lots of dialogue, as well as the odd cliff-hanger chapter ending. You've got to give them a reason to turn the page; and to keep turning the pages, all the way to the end.

Who are you writing for?

'What age group are you "aiming" at?' is a frequently asked question. For myself, the answer is: none. Apart from a general idea that I'm not writing a picture book for six-year-olds, I prefer to leave age groups to editors and publishers, and concentrate on the story.

Besides, once you start thinking in terms of 'aiming' a story at a particular group of people, where does it end? For instance, say you're 'aiming' a story at 9–12 year-olds. Well, what kind of 9–12 year-olds? They're not a homogeneous mass. Boys or girls, or both? And what kind? Middle-class or underprivileged? Immigrant or home-grown? Gifted, average, or special needs? If you start thinking like that, you run the risk of killing your story.

The same thing goes for the publisher's Holy Grail of the 'crossover' novel that's read by both adults and children. If you have this at the forefront of your mind when you're writing, it's unlikely that you'll do justice to the story. It may well end up being a mess which *nobody* will want to read.

Although this may sound a bit uncompromising, I have the same view when it comes to trying out your story on your own children – if you have them – or on others. In my view, this is risky and I prefer not to do it. (Well, in my case, I couldn't, because I don't have children, and don't know any very well.) In fact, quite a few children's writers don't have children of their own, but what many do have is a strong memory of what it was like to be a child and an ability to write from a child's perspective. That's what you need. Not market research.

Being true to your story, knowing your chosen period inside out but only including the most telling of details ... Of course, none of this is going to guarantee success. But with luck, it'll improve your chances on the slush pile. *And* you'll have a lot more fun than if you'd been slavishly studying the market!

Michelle Paver is the author of the bestselling *Chronicles of Ancient Darkness* series, which has been published in 37 languages and film rights were sold to Sir Ridley Scott. *Ghost Hunter*, the final book in the series, won the 2010 Guardian Children's Fiction Prize. The series has also been recorded as audiobooks read by Sir Ian McKellen. Her ghost story for adults, *Dark Matter*, was published in 2010 to critical acclaim. Her new ghost story *Thin Line* will be published in autumn 2016 by Orion. Her website is www.michellepaver.com.

See also...

Writing crime fiction for teenagers

Anne Cassidy is the author of more than 30 novels for teenagers and she explains here why she thinks the crime genre is perfect for teenage fiction.

I love crime fiction and that's why I write it for teenagers. In my first book, *Big Girls' Shoes* (1990), two teenage girls overhear a murder during a phone call. In *Dead Time*, a teenage girl sees a boy she hates get stabbed to death on a bridge over a railway line. The deaths are brutal and the books are dark. I make no apology for this. Crime fiction has to move the reader. The crimes have to be horrible so that the reader cares about the victim. I've locked up a victim in a container and left him to die. I've pushed a girl off a 16-storey block of flats, I've drowned several hapless teens and I've even poisoned one with arsenic pasta. I have no mercy.

I've written 30-plus novels for teenagers, all concerned with crime of one sort or another. I wrote a series in the 1990s called *The East End Murders* and three books in the *The Murder Notebooks* series. In between I've written a line of standalone thrillers, most of which have a murder at their core.

Characters and narrative

Writing for teenagers is not different in kind to writing for adults. You have a particular audience and you have a story to tell. In my case the audience is teenagers and the stories I tell fall into the crime genre.

In general terms, books for teenagers have two main features. Firstly, the main character is usually a teenager and the story centres round them. This teenager has to be completely and utterly believable. This is a writer's first challenge. What you don't do is focus on the external features of today's teenagers; the music, the fashions, the mobile phones and the 'teen' speak patois are ephemeral. What you're really looking for is the emotional core of your teenage protagonist and for that you have to go back and find your own teenage self again. When I wrote my first teen novel I dredged up as many memories as I could. I listened to lots of the music I'd liked at the time (much of it still among my favourites). I looked at family photographs. I spoke to family members and thought back to my own schooldays, writing down a rough journal of anything and everything that I remembered; names, places, books, lessons, clothes, shops. I revisited my own past and what I found, when I got there, was a teenager who'd spent her teen years feeling hard done by, where the tantalising promises of near adulthood had become mired in the day-to-day life of being a schoolgirl/daughter/sister. There I found the emotional core of my teenager: the struggle to move forward into adulthood while everything seemed to pull her back. I realised that contemporary teenagers are no different. The fashions, the temperament and the reliance on electronic gadgets are all modern but at heart today's teens are the same as I was 40 years ago. They have within them that essential contradiction of adolescence; negotiating the passage to adulthood, shrugging off the child they once were. So my teenage characters embody this struggle in one form or another.

The second feature of a teen book is that the story drives the novel. Novels for teenagers must have a strong narrative and this story has to move forward in every chapter. In general you cannot have pages and pages of musings about the meaning of life or overindulge in

Books

descriptive passages. But this doesn't mean that your story can't explore universal and important themes or that it cannot establish a sense of place. In my book *Looking for JJ*, a ten-year-old girl kills her friend and we meet her six years later when she is released from prison. The narrative follows her trying to live with a new identity. The theme of the book is forgiveness. Has she the right to expect a second chance in life after what she did?

The story of a crime teen novel should start when something dramatic is happening. *The Dead House* starts when the main character, Lauren, revisits the house in which her family were murdered ten years before. She alone survived. In *Forget Me Not* a child is abducted. In *Just Jealous* a girl is staring at the body of a boy who has been shot. The main character and others emerge through this early action and take shape quickly. By the end of the first chapter the reader should have a strong sense of story and character and an inkling of which direction the book is heading.

This is why I think the crime genre is so perfect for teenage fiction and why I have enjoyed writing it for so many years. A crime novel naturally starts with a dramatic event, often a murder. The main character is often involved in some aspect of the discovery of that murder. In a teen novel the main character will perhaps discover the body or be a friend of the victim, or perhaps he or she may be a murder suspect. The story will be told through his or her eyes whether it is in third- or first-person narrative. The rest of the novel will mirror an adult crime thriller in that there will be clues and red herrings, and secrets and lies will be exposed. There will be police involvement in some way and the tools of detection will be used – surveillance, research, interrogation. These things will happen whether the main character is a school student or a boy on the run. At the end of the book the killer will be exposed and the secrets revealed.

Language and savvy teenagers

Don't underestimate the teenage reader. Teenagers watch a lot of crime on television. When I visit schools I often ask them about it and they list anything from *CSI* to *Jonathan Creek* to *Morse* and *Poirot*. They are used to the complex narrative that a crime story necessarily needs. They like the twists and turns and the cliff-hangers and the secrets that emerge from the story. When teenagers are gripped by a story they will hold on to the various strands and read with gusto until they find out 'whodunnit'.

One of the main questions when writing for teenagers is 'How explicit can the content be?'. The writer is always writing with one eye on the reader and another on the 'gatekeeper': the librarian, teacher or parent. This is not just a matter of censorship. Teenagers as a group are not natural readers. They do not scour the review pages for new books and they do not haunt the shelves of Waterstones. They often find their books through librarians, teachers and parents and then from word of mouth via friends. So these 'gatekeepers' are not to be feared but rather to be seen as your most demanding reader. They will not 'promote' your book unless they think it is really good. I think how explicit the content can be is a matter of taste and style rather than censorship. In crime fiction the question is particularly relevant. Modern crime fiction encompasses some truly stomach-turning gore but, again, the question for me is whether its plot delivers the shocks and surprises needed to make a good crime novel. If it does, then the gore is window dressing for a particular audience. I do not have serial killer/torture violence in my books but this is an artistic decision rather than because of a fear of censorship. I think the taking of a small child or the murder of a mother and her baby or a teenage boy dying from a single punch is 'gore' enough. Who? Why? and How? are the questions that interest me.

My books are read by 12–14 year-olds onwards. The content is grown up and for this reason my characters are usually over 16. This is not a problem for the readers as teenagers like reading about older characters. It means, though, that my characters can do more grown-up stuff. A 17-year-old staying out all night or having a relationship is acceptable, whereas if the character was aged 14 it might cause added problems for the plot. My characters don't swear and I originally made this decision in part to avoid having my books kept out of school libraries just because of a couple of four-letter words. As time went on though and these four-letter words started to appear in other teen books it became a matter of choice. Conversation in novels is never realistic, it simply approximates to the way we think people speak; in sentences, cogently, without interruption. In reality speech is all over the place, fragmented and often incomprehensible. Likewise with swearing. If you stand near any group of teens you will be shocked at the range and frequency of swear words. If I were to try and replicate their speech the page would be peppered with four-letter words so I decided to leave them out altogether and let the reader supply them.

Series fiction and standalone novels

Crime fiction takes a number of forms but the most obvious two are series fiction and standalone novels. I have written both. The joy of a series is that it allows you to follow through on a group of characters and build a 'soap'-type plot from book to book. However, each book must stand up by itself and be a self-contained crime mystery. If a teenager picks book three of a series to read first they must have a satisfying plot and be informed of all the salient 'soap' developments without spoiling the enjoyment of reading books one or two. This is particularly relevant to me with my *Murder Notebook* series. These books are standalone murder mysteries but they all involve stepbrother Joshua and stepsister Rose who are both on a quest to find out about their parents' disappearance five years before. This disappearance is the continuing story of this series and each standalone murder mystery must in some way add to their knowledge of what happened to their parents. It's complicated but huge fun to do.

Standalone novels don't usually involve a 'detective' as such. They usually start with a teenager being drawn into some tricky situation and seeing how that teenager copes. In my book *Heart Burn*, Ashley owes a boy a favour. The favour he asks of her is illegal and dangerous. She agrees to help him and ends up fearing for her life. Standalone novels are often viewed as more 'literary' than series fiction. I think this is rubbish as series fiction has been written by many great writers. Patrick Ness has had his *Chaos Walking* series shortlisted for major awards and Kate Atkinson has given the adult crime novel a 'literary' feel with her *Case History* books.

What should you write – series or standalone novels? You should write the story that you want to write. If you have a good crime story to tell then decide which format it needs and write it. Don't underestimate your teenage audience. They are savvy and love a good murder mystery. Enough said!

Anne Cassidy is a full-time writer and has written more than 30 novels. *Butterfly Grave* (Bloomsbury 2013) is the most recent in her *Murder Notebooks* series and the sequel to *Looking for JJ* is *Finding Jennifer Jones* (Hot Key Books 2014).

See also...
- *Writing thrillers for teenagers*, page 170
- *Teenage fiction*, page 174

Books

Writing thrillers for teenagers

Sophie McKenzie considers the ingredients for writing a successful thriller for teenagers.

When people ask me what sort of books I write, I tend to reply that I write thrillers for teenagers and, more recently, for adults as well. But actually, I do no such thing – at least not deliberately … I just write the kind of stories I like to read, involving characters I care passionately about. And I write to please myself – not for a specific audience. So here's the only rule I'm going to suggest you stick to – always write what matters to you … not what you think other people want, need or expect. Everything else (i.e. the rest of this article) is just my opinion – a few thoughts and suggestions that helped me and might be useful to you.

A strong story

This is definitely my number one requirement in a top thriller – whatever the age of the audience. Remember that a story is *not* simply an interesting situation, though it may start with one. In a story, stuff happens. A good way to check if you have a really interesting story is to look at whether the scenario you've created gives your main character something they really want or need – *and* a big fat problem that gets in the way of that ambition. In my book, *Girl, Missing*, for instance, Lauren *really* wants to find out who her birth mother is and whether she was stolen from her original home as a toddler. Her main problem, at the start of the story, is that her parents refuse to talk about her adoption. This also means that Lauren can't look to her parents to sort out her problem, thus ensuring the story follows one of the basic principles of children's fiction and gets the adults out of the way as fast as possible! It also deepens the problem, as Lauren starts to suspect that her adoptive parents may have been the ones who stole her from her birth mother.

High stakes

Your character's needs and problems must be important to them. If they care and you care, chances are you'll get your reader to care too.

There are millions of things your character might want or need to find fulfilment and/ or salvation. And a top story will certainly need an original twist. But there are a few fundamental ambitions that almost everyone relates to. Most thrillers and adventure stories revolve around one or more of the following, though there are others:

• Coming home. This is a common desire, especially in children's stories – I'm talking here about characters who are trying to find their way back home – like Dorothy in *The Wizard of Oz* – and about characters trying to find a new home – like Harry in Robert Westall's marvellous *The Kingdom by the Sea*.

• Working out who you really are and/or finding your place in the world. This is another huge need shared by characters in identity/rites of passage stories as varied as *Being* by Kevin Brooks and the *Pretties* series by Scott Westerfeld. This 'goal' is particularly common in teenage fiction – identity issues seem to resonate strongly with adolescents aware they are no longer children but not yet sure how to be adults.

• Then there's love. Will the boy get the girl; will the child be reunited with the parents?

• And, of course, there's survival. Whether your character's goal is to save his own life, the lives of those he loves or the entire planet, survival stories usually involve plenty of action and interesting villains. In fact, baddies often provide stories with the best problems: imagine the Harry Potter books without Voldemort or *101 Dalmatians* without Cruella de Vil.

Not worrying about taboo subjects

Personally I don't think there's any subject that can't be tackled. What counts is how you treat the material. Teenagers, like the rest of us, want to read about subjects that matter to them. Families, friendships, loss, guilt, identity, ambitions in work and in love – are all relevant. Sometimes I think teens get a raw deal. Just because young people are aware of difficult topics doesn't necessarily mean they want to read about them in a heavy duty way. Beware of turning your thriller into an 'issues' book in which the main character only 'angsts' and 'never acts'. If you want to write a thriller around a challenging topic, that's great. Just make sure there's a strong story holding the whole thing together. In *Blood Ties,* I wanted to write about how it might feel to discover, aged 15, you'd been cloned as a replacement for your dead sister. That could easily have been the starting point for a much less pacy book than the one I ended up writing, which attempts to weave its thought-provoking subject material in and out of a fast-moving action story.

A central character to care about and identify with

A good story *has* to involve individuals we care about. And a teenage novel will usually feature one or more teenage protagonists. If memory (I was a teen), personality (I act like a teen) and research (I talk to teens) don't help you imagine yourself into the head of an adolescent, then you may struggle to write teenage books.

The stories I like best often incorporate a relationship drama that bubbles under the main action. From a writing point of view, focusing on the development of a romantic relationship – as well as a high-octane thriller plot – helps make your characters more interesting and your story more meaningful. *The Set-Up* is the first book in my *Medusa Project* series about a group of teens with psychic abilities. It begins with Nico, who narrates the story, discovering he has the gift of telekinesis. He uses this developing power on missions as well as trying to impress the girl he likes, Ketty. By the second book of the series, *The Hostage*, Nico and the other teens have been brought together to form a crime-fighting force. Much action and danger ensues from this, yet the story – this time narrated by Ketty herself – also focuses on what she really thinks about Nico.

Will boys read stories that contain an element of romance? Well, many won't, but I'm also certain that it's a complete myth to say that boys don't care about romantic relationships at all – they just don't want you to spend pages analysing them!

A clear sense of the point of view you're writing from

Whose story are you telling? Make sure you know, right from the start. Then try and keep that character at the centre of the action, moving the story along. In his commentary on the film adaptation of *The Lord of the Rings*, director Peter Jackson talks about the importance of turning the camera on the film's heroes at least every third shot. A useful tip – which translates in novel terms as follows: don't stray too far from what your main character can think, feel, see, touch, smell and hear. Writing from an omnipotent, narrator perspective is a perfectly valid choice but it does tend to distance the reader from the main character's mind. Almost all children love to identify with their heroes. And thrillers definitely benefit from the immediacy of a strong viewpoint. I wrote each book in the *Medusa Project* series from a different character's point of view to explore each character's particular psychic power and personality.

Planning and plotting before you write

Some writers plan. Some don't. Personally, I like to plan the foundations – the outline of the story showing where the characters are going – before I start. But I save the fun stuff – showing how the characters are going to get there – for while I'm writing.

I came to the conclusion that planning was helpful after starting no fewer than 17 books in my first year of serious writing. Some of these had some merit – an interesting character here, an exciting scene there – but almost all of them fell apart by chapter five or so because the plots simply didn't pan out. Planning can feel like an overwhelming task. But unless you try and work through your story in advance, it's all too easy for the whole thing to crumble in your hands. This is, of course, particularly true for thrillers, which require suspenseful twists and turns in order to deliver their thrills.

Managing a plot is a bit like driving a chariot pulled by several huge, powerful horses. You have to concentrate on what you're doing – and be as fit and strong as possible – in order to hold together the reins and make sure that the various strands of the story you're weaving don't career down separate paths and send your chariot tumbling to the ground.

If you want to write thrillers, study thriller writers

I spent a lot of time studying other peoples' plots, working out how various authors whose plotting skills I admire handled that aspect of their writing. For instance, I read the first three books in Anthony Horowitz's *Alex Rider* series and wrote down everything that happened (literally, just the actions) that moved the story on.

That experience taught me many things – not least the value of breaking my plots into manageable amounts. When planning *The Set-Up*, I knew halfway through the story that Nico, the main character, would discover the man he had trusted up to that point was actually plotting to betray him. This enabled me to break the story down into two halves, making it less daunting to plan each one.

Have a laugh along the way

Just because you're writing a thriller doesn't mean your story can't have its lighter moments. An ironic narrative voice, a character with a great sense of humour or a funny situation do more than make the reader laugh – they provide a release for tension, allowing the next plunge into suspense to be even more powerful.

Creating suspense – hooks and hangers

The most important chapter is the first – get that right, drawing your reader in with a dramatic 'inciting incident' (as Robert McKee puts it in *Story*) and you will, hopefully, have set up your story in an interesting way and hooked the reader in. Some sort of conflict is usually necessary here, as exemplified by one of the best kids' thriller first chapters I've ever read – *Thief* by Malorie Blackman. And never forget the power of D.R.A.T. – that's the Desperate Race Against Time, guaranteed to inject a shot of excitement into any story!

Cliffhangers are great too – whenever I'm coming to the end of a scene, I try and work out what I need to write to give the reader a pay-off for sitting through that chapter – and what I can leave unexplained, as a hook to make them want to turn the next page.

And finally...

Here are my top three tips for producing a thrilling story: (1) Get into the story as fast as possible; (2) Make sure that every plot twist is unexpected but convincing; (3) Don't be indulgent ... if what you've written doesn't move the story on, cut it.

In the end, if all else fails, remember that so long as you're trying to write the best book you're capable of writing, nothing else really matters. So don't give up.

Sophie McKenzie is the award-winning author of *Girl, Missing* and *Blood Ties*, which won the Red House Children's Book Award. She has worked as a journalist, editor and creative writing teacher but now writes full time. Her thrillers include sequels *Sister, Missing* and *Missing Me*, plus *Blood Ransom* and *Every Second Counts* – as well as the six-book *Medusa Project* series. Sophie has also written two romance series: the *Luke & Eve* stories and the *Flynn* books, comprising *Falling Fast, Burning Bright, Casting Shadows* and *Defy the Stars*. Her latest teen novel is the suspense mystery *All My Secrets*. Sophie has also written three thrillers for adults, *Close My Eyes* (2013), *Trust in Me* (2014) and *Here We Lie* (September 2015). All these novels are published by Simon & Schuster UK. Sophie's website is www.sophiemckenziebooks.com and she can also be found on Facebook (sophiemckenzieauthor) and Twitter @sophiemckenzie_.

See also...
- *Writing crime fiction for teenagers*, page 167
- *Teenage fiction*, page 174
- *Writing for the teenage market*, page 327

Books

Books

Teenage fiction

Gillie Russell writes about teenage fiction from an agent's perspective.

Perhaps now is the most exciting time to be writing for teenagers and young adults. There have been such notable successes that the thirst for new authors writing for this age group seems to have grown enormously. That said, we have to remember that the sales of successful writers including Stephenie Meyer with her *Twilight* series and Suzanne Collins with *The Hunger Games*, have added huge numbers of adults into the mix, too.

I am often asked what the difference is between writing for teenagers and writing for adults. For me, the significant difference is that teenagers come to books without life experience. They are on the brink of self-discovery, before being plunged into the everyday grind of earning a living – if indeed they can even find a job. They are open, honest and questioning as an audience and this, I believe, is why so many terrific writers want to write for this age group. As an audience, young adults are a challenge to write for, but satisfyingly able to digest complex ideas. Most book fairs will offer new writing for teenagers on incest, bullying, sibling rivalry, relationships, parental separation and drugs. These powerful themes can make inspiring and life-changing books, covering life as teenagers live it – and often their only way of confronting and understanding issues is through books that reflect their own lives and dilemmas.

But of course teenagers, like adults, need well-crafted stories in many different genres – they like humour and history, fantasy and adventure, just as much as they like books which reflect their own worlds. They need inspirational and aspirational books where they can identify with the protagonists in a real and engaging way.

In the last few years, with the growth of the internet, the market for young adult (YA) books, alongside the trending 'new adult' market, has increased the interest in the kinds of genres that spawn television and feature films with great success. These books have traditionally been published on children's lists, which has meant that there has been greater investment in authors who are writing for the YA market. Genre fiction, largely fantasy and science fiction, has always had a strong following, but with easy access to the internet and the ability to share information and passions, these areas of fiction particularly have increased. Fan fiction, something new to traditional publishers and agents, has become something that we all track and follow and has produced global bestselling authors. No one could have predicted quite how important this area, with its worldwide sales, has been in changing the face of teen and YA publishing.

Of course the very stuff of series like *Twilight* echo classic stories such as *Jane Eyre*, *Wuthering Heights* and Mary Shelley's *Frankenstein*; they chronicle forbidden love under extreme circumstances, and are atmospheric and scary. In the case of Suzanne Collins' *The Hunger Games*, it is also about the destruction of our planet, the corruption of our governments and our ethics, and how we fight to maintain some sense of the individual in a seemingly powerless state. All of which have a resonance with today's teen audience.

We may worry that this new generation of readers spends too much time on the internet, but it is still about reading and content – and now it's about where that content is available. It's an exciting time for teenagers because they feel empowered to write themselves, as well as being avid followers of other writers. Global brands like *Twilight* and *The Hunger Games* spring out of a need, perhaps, to experience 'other worlds' at a time when our own is changing so fast, and we're worried about what humankind is doing to our planet.

Getting teenagers to read

Of course, not all teenagers and young adults will want to read these kinds of books, and a variety of genres and narrative styles is key. We know that fighting for their attention in a world where there is increased pressure on passing exams, all kinds of distraction on the internet with social networks and fan sites, favourite television programmes that can be watched at any time of day or night, is a huge challenge. Finding the right 'voice' is probably the most essential part of making a teen book successful – something we as agents are always talking about: that manuscript that takes your breath away when you read the first page and stays with you for days. But clearly to attract teen readers, it is vital for children to develop the reading habit, and reading stamina, early in their lives, and to discover that losing themselves in a book can be as exciting as their other distractions. Key to this of course is retaining our libraries.

Variety is key

Significantly, it is more than a decade since when we talked about books for teenagers we thought of those authors who wrote the gritty, the realistic, the edgy books, still popular, of course: Melvyn Burgess, Malorie Blackman, Anne Fine, for example. Since that time, Anthony Horowtiz's *Alex Rider* series, with its thrilling adventures, and Robert Muchamore's *CHERUB* books, full of edgy adventure and teen romance, have almost taken the place of the more gritty issue-based fiction. Meg Rosoff's *How I Live Now* was one of the first contemporary prize-winning books which hinted at a threatening, contemporary dystopian world, but also included teen sex and a sense of how young people could survive on their own in an alien adult environment; survival and empowerment being key and attractive to the target audience. And that book had a 'crossover' audience.

The 'crossover'/YA/teen transition

There was a great deal of talk a few years ago about the 'crossover' book, where an adult market had been identified for a children's book, a phenomenon which was probably kick-started with the first *Harry Potter* book. Publishers became aware that they could attract a bigger section of the market for their authors. Perhaps the first truly major YA/crossover book was Mark Haddon's *The Curious Incident of the Dog in the Night-Time*, which appealed to both markets, and was successful in two editions. Not only is this now one of the most successful books ever published globally, but it has been adapted into an award-winning play, as has Michael Morpurgo's *War Horse*, which is also a feature film. Significantly, not all 'teen' books will be as successful as YA books if they're writing about 'issues' from a teen perspective. True teen books dealing with teen-centred stories about real life, growing up, friends and family are often the best written and the hardest to sell as those who would read them are also drawn towards adult books. So there is no real certainty that the explosive growth of YA books will make these areas as successful as the wide variety of fantasy. Research shows that the average age of readers of the *Twilight* series, for example, was 26; it was the film that brought vast numbers of teens to the books.

Is reading still cool? Perhaps it is, where it's largely associated with new technology – television, film, iPads, e-readers, iPhones, etc that will make it cool – and no one can see what you're reading.

Where do we go from here?

How do we enable wonderful writers to reach their target audience? We are constantly on the lookout for new and talented authors – those who will make a difference. We are always seeking writers who can combine the culturally important with the commercially successful in an increasingly competitive and difficult marketplace. This is a challenge. We need to try not to let the global brands dominate our thinking and our publishing strategy. There is new talent emerging all the time for teens: Moira Young's Costa-winning *Blood Red Road*, for example, Sophie McKenzie's books, and authors such as Patrick Ness, Sarah Dessen and Neil Gaiman – all inspiring and engaging in their different ways. Children's authors are now dominating the market in a way that was unheard of a few years ago, and this can only be a thrilling time for teenage fiction.

Gillie Russell is the agent for children's and YA fiction at Aitken Alexander Associates (see page 239) and was formerly Fiction Publishing Director at HarperCollins Children's Books.

See also...

Writing series fiction for girls

Karen McCombie outlines the challenges and offers tips on successfully writing series fiction.

'How many books have you written?' I'm typically asked at book talks.

'Umm …' I uselessly answer, always vowing to tot up my titles so I don't umm uselessly ever again. (At *that* question at least. I did umm a lot when a girl in the audience once asked me which of my books was the worst. Ahem.)

Well, I've just counted, and there are 80 of them lining my office shelves (with several more commissions in the pipeline), written over 17 years. It's a bit of a fearsome number, but that's due to the fact that (a) I come from a background of writing for teenage magazines where you have to crank out a feature by lunchtime or you're slacking, and (b) in the early days, I got paid £2.50 per book (near enough) and *had* to write speedily to make any money.

(I'm not so speedy these days, because I get paid a bit more money, *and* because my optimum writing time used to be 3–7pm, which doesn't work now that I have a daughter. At 3.30pm, instead of knocking out an unstoppable word rate, I'm frantically scouring the kitchen to figure out what snacks I can give my pre-teen eating machine.)

Glancing along my slightly bowed shelves, it dawned on me that very many of my books are one of a series, which I suppose does qualify me to write a feature-ette on the subject. And how did series suddenly become my thing? It wasn't deliberate. While I was still freelancing for magazines, I wrote a couple of standalone teen novels for Scholastic, which didn't exactly sprint up the Nielsen BookScan charts. Luckily for me, my friend Marina Gask, then editor of the now-defunct *Sugar* magazine, came up with the idea of doing a younger '*Hollyoaks*'-style series of books in conjunction with HarperCollins, with the *Sugar* branding. There were to be 20 books, written by three authors (Marina, myself and Sue Dando, former editor of the also defunct *Just Seventeen* magazine) all under one pseudonym (the jaunty 'Mel Sparke').

It wasn't an easy ride – the style and storylines were decided and endlessly amended by a disjointed committee of editors (fine) and magazine bigwigs (not so fine). The pay was terrible (both book and magazine publishers had to get a cut, leaving a whole lot of not much for the writers). It got slightly complicated when – with only a few titles under their belts – Marina was lured off to edit another magazine, and Sue announced she was pregnant, leaving me as the one and only Mel (Mc)Sparke.

But a frantic 12 out of the 20 books later, I'd come to like the pace of a series, of getting to know and develop characters. In fact, my next teen standalone novel for Scholastic accidentally became a mini-series, when I developed two more books (*Bliss…* and *Wonderland*) using characters from a first (*My Funny Valentine*).

Scholastic then asked me to have a go at a slightly younger series. They wanted the ten to earlier teen mix; they wanted family and friends; they wanted funny. I wanted to be writing books full time, so I said yes please, very fast. The series turned into *Ally's World*, which took me pleasantly by surprise when it became a bestseller. (Yay!)

Since then, there's been *Stella Etc, Sadie Rocks* (both Scholastic), the slightly younger *Indie Kidd* series (Walker), *You, Me and Thing* (Faber) and *The Angels Next Door* (Puffin), interspersed with a bundle of novels.

So, what words of wisdom can I impart about series writing? Well, none, probably, so you'll have to accept these random noodlings instead …

Have ideas that aren't going to bore you

Mull over strong/quirky/endearing characteristics for your, er, characters; you could be writing about them for a long time, if you're lucky, and you don't want to end up running out of empathy with them quickly. In fact, you want them to almost become embedded as virtual buddies in your brain. I was with a friend at London Zoo, melting at the sight of a Short-Eared Elephant Shrew (think mutant mouse/sparrow/mini-kangaroo crossover) and sighed, 'Tor would love that!'. 'Who's Tor?' asked my friend. 'The kid brother of Ally, from *Ally's World* …' I muttered in reply, wondering if I seemed deranged. (Not as deranged as a mutant mouse/sparrow/mini-kangaroo, to be fair.)

Also, choose a setting that has lots of possibilities. The town in the *Sugar*-branded series was made up and based on nowhere in particular, and I found it monstrously hard to get a handle on how big/small it was and geographically where things were/weren't.

When it came to *Ally's World*, I set it on my doorstep (Crouch End, North London), and happily referenced every park, pet shop, travelling fair and local caff with confidence.

Think of a story arc

I held my breath when Scholastic commissioned the first three *Ally's World*s, not sure how many it might run to. Ooh, now they want six? Wonderful. I got my story arc in place, based on the mystery of where Ally's missing mum might be. Oh, they want to stretch it to ten books? Wheee! Right, time to make that arc stretch without going wobbly. Oh, 14 you say? I think I did it – *know* I did it; I made that story arc extend without visible signs of bolted-on wiffle.

On the flip side, as a writer, your series might not run as long as you'd love it to, so be ready to reign in your arc and tie up all the loose ends without appearing to rush it. (Hey, it's a tricky one, but if writing's your job, it's just another technical problem you've got to solve without the reader noticing the slightest bump in the reading road.)

Make each book in the series a standalone novel

Just because the whole of a series is in print, it doesn't guarantee that every book in that series is going to be on every bookshop shelf. So while the story arc arcs away, each book *must* be a standalone read. The girl who picks up *Angels Like Me* – No 3 in my Puffin *Angels Next Door* trilogy – has to love it for itself. She mustn't feel frustrated by the Great Unknown of what's gone before, even though she'll (hopefully) want to seek out the earlier instalments asap.

Which brings me on to the fact that you have to learn to recap on old storylines in a non-drab way. The first three chapters in a series book are torture. They take infinitely longer than the rest of the book, where the story can meander and unravel itself, unhindered by the problem of having to re-introduce characters and plots without (a) smacking your readers in the face with obviousness, and (b) boring them.

So what's the answer? A lot of thinking and rewriting, quite a bit of mucking around with the different techniques you can use to reiterate. In other words, the answer is that it's not easy, and you've just got to factor it in as something important to get right, and don't stress over the extra time it might take to fix.

Do what your readers love but don't repeat yourself

OK, so I know my readers like 'Funny, Family and Friends'. But coming off the back of *Ally's World*, it took a long time to figure out what I should do next. With *Stella Etc*, as well as the 3Fs, I added a touch of magic realism, a dollop of history and mystery, and sparked a heated debate amongst fans about the identity of a mental old lady in a meringue hat with a penchant for feeding fairycakes to overweight seagulls.

Sadie Rocks was a shorter, four-part series, in which I entertained myself with adding in splashes of black humour which included a character who was a 17-year-old trainee funeral director with a sideline in stand-up comedy.

I gave the mum in *Indie Kidd* my second-favourite dream job – running an animal rescue centre – leaving the way open for many strange and wonky pets to inhabit Indie's world (and living room).

As for my latest series (plural), *You, Me and Thing* stars a strange, small, otherworldly creature discovered by two feuding nine-year-old neighbours, while *Angels Next Door* is a tale of everyday girls who just, er, happen to be twelve-year-old trainee celestial beings.

All a little different for me to write, but all with my trademark voice, I guess.

Scribble yourself a who's who as you go

Stunningly important advice, all to do with continuity, which I regularly don't do, and regret. But if you keep a notepad to hand with the sole purpose of jotting down names, eye colours, favourite foods, individual tics, family members, pets and predilections, you'll save yourself much angst and finger fatigue from flicking back through previous books while cursing yourself. (Yeah, says the author who gave the gran in the first *Ally's World* two different names, and has been alerted to the fact by endless eagle-eyed readers ever since, despite it being corrected in later print runs.)

Never bleed a good idea dry

At the time, I think Scholastic would have been happy if I'd extended the *Ally's World* series to 20, but I might have lost the will to live, despite adoring that family as if it was my own (well, the character of Ally was loosely based on my worrisome 13-year-old self, and Colin the three-legged cat was my neighbour's). There was no way I wanted to drag out the series with potentially shoehorned-in plots; not when I was pleased with the books as they were and didn't feel any of the 14 were weaker than others (though the 11-year-old critic at my recent book talk might beg to differ).

But never say never to going back to something that's fun!

They kept emailing. They kept pleading for more. I resisted for a long, long time, till one *Ally's World* fan said, 'I'd *love* to read a whole book about Ally's ditzy older sister, Rowan!' And that one remark embedded itself in a dusty corner of my mind, eventually erupting as *The Raspberry Rules*, a linked-to-the-series novel about Ally's older, nuttier fairy lights-obsessed sister. It was a blast to write – like bumping into an old (slightly mad) friend.

Well, those are my noodlings; advice that I revisited myself, when I was immersed in the world of angels with my last series. Though my 'Who's who' continuity notes for *Angels Next Door* read rather strangely – i.e. 'Bee: The angels' pet dog. Snow-white fluffy fur. Like a poodle mash-up; part poodle/part golden retriever/part cloud.' And yes, you're right; authors' notes would indeed seem very strange, if read out of context …

Karen McCombie lives in 'Ally's World' (i.e. Crouch End, North London) with her husband, daughter and one beautiful-but-bitey cat. She has written more than 80 books and sold over a million copies. Her most recent series is the *Angels Next Door* trilogy (Puffin 2014) and her latest novel is *Catching Falling Stars* (Scholastic 2015). Her website is www.karenmccombie.com.

Notes from a series author

Francesca Simon shares her early experiences of success in writing for children.

I started writing stories when I was eight. Because I adored Andrew Lang's fairy tale collections, I wrote my own prince and princess stories. Unfortunately, like many would-be writers I was great at starting stories but terrible at finishing them. So I put my notebook away and thought maybe I'd be a lawyer. That is, until I was a Yale undergraduate and opened a law book. I read half a page, my eyes glazed, and I abandoned all thoughts of the legal profession.

After Oxford, where I read 'Old and Middle English' (very useful for all the alliteration in *Horrid Henry*), I fell into freelance journalism which I enjoyed. Then in 1989 my son Joshua was born and everything changed.

I love to read and we started looking at board books together from the time he was four months old. And I was suddenly overwhelmed with ideas for picture books. This surprised me, as I'd never had any interest in writing for children. When I fantasised about being a writer, I just assumed I would write for adults.

One publisher (who shall remain nameless) quickly returned my first story, 'Wriggling Fingers'. The editor not only hated the story, but obviously thought I was of unsound mind to think something so scary would appeal to babies. This rejection letter detailing my failings went on and on and on … Not a good start. I was clearly one f those deluded new mums who thought she could write for children.

But the ideas kept coming. And I kept writing stories and sending them off. An agent eventually took me on (thank you, *Writers' & Artists' Yearbook*). I got a lot of rejections but a few encouraging comments, for example 'This story isn't right for us, but please send us more of your work.' Then finally, about a year after I started writing, one absolutely amazing day, Julia MacRae Books accepted *Papa Forgot*, about a grandfather looking after his grandson, who forgets every single instruction the anxious parents have given him, but somehow they have a wonderful evening. I will always remember the moment when my agent rang to tell me that my first book was going to be published. For me, that's the day I became a writer. Soon after, Macmillan accepted *But What Does the Hippopotamus Say?*, an animal noise book featuring noisy kangaroos, camels, and yaks, as well as cows, horses and sheep. And then Hodder accepted *What's That Noise?*, which was based on one particular evening when my son, then a toddler, called me repeatedly up to his room because he kept hearing things that go bump. After that I started writing for children full time.

A year later, the brilliant Judith Elliott, who had just joined Orion to create a brand new children's list, turned down a story but asked to meet me. Would I consider writing a first-time reader?

Of course! So in 1993 I wrote a one-off comic story about two brothers, one horrid, one perfect, and their parents who favour the latter. As the eldest of four, I know something about sibling rivalry, and I have a very strong memory of those childhood battles. Plus, there is something irresistibly comic about families. Who hasn't been on the car journey from hell, or fought to the death for control of the TV remote?

Unfortunately, this was not what I'd been asked for. Judith pointed out that the language was much too difficult for a first reader (I foolishly never thought to read one) but she liked the story. Could I write three more, and then she'd publish *Horrid Henry* as a book for newly confident readers instead? (Hurrah for the creative editor!) I was terrified, as I'd never written to order before, but thought I could just about dream up three more stories about Horrid Henry and Perfect Peter. *Horrid Henry* wasn't an instant success: in fact it wasn't until the fourth book, *Horrid Henry's Nits*, that the series took off.

Looking back, much of my writing career seems accidental. If I hadn't had a child, I'd never have written for children. If Judith hadn't asked me to write a few more Horrid Henry stories, I would probably have filed *Horrid Henry's Perfect Day* with all my other rejects and my life now would be very different.

Francesca Simon has had over 50 books published. Her *Horrid Henry* series has sold over 20 million copies and is published in 27 countries. The final book in the series, *Horrid Henry's Cannibal Curse*, was published in July 2015. She won the Children's Book of the Year in 2008 at the British Book Awards for *Horrid Henry and the Abominable Snowman* and *Horrid Henry and the Football Fiend* was the most borrowed children's library book in 2009. The sequel to *The Sleeping Army* is *The Lost Gods* (Profile Books 2013). Her latest picture book *Hello, Moon!* is published by Orchard Press (2014).

See also...
- *Who do children's authors write for?* page 119
- *Fiction for 6–9 year-olds,* page 143
- *Writing series fiction for girls,* page 177
- *Writing to a brief,* page 352

Who am I today? Writing under multiple pseudonyms

A prolific author who prefers not to be pigeonholed, Julia Golding (or is that Joss Stirling, or Eve Edwards?) explains the creative, practical and commercial advantages of writing under different names.

Time for a rethink

Here are some things I believed before I started on the writer's career path.

1 Getting published was the finish line.
2 Having, say, six books published in my lifetime would constitute a career.
3 Somehow points 1 + 2 would add up to an income.

I can now tell you, a decade after my first book was published, that all three are way off target. I aimed at my future career with no Robin Hood accuracy; I was pretty much firing my arrows straight up into the air and was just lucky they didn't hit me on the way down. So to help you think through the realities of what it's like to make a living as a writer and what strategies you might use, here are a few arrows more precisely directed.

Once you get your work onto the bookshelf, the challenge then becomes *staying* published. You are at the beginning rather than at the end of a very long march. How can you achieve more than a brief passage across the literary stage? It is really difficult to do, so don't let anyone tell you otherwise. We all have to find our own way and mine recently has been simply to multiply myself.

One for all, and all for one

In an essay from 2011 in the *New York Times*, Carmela Ciuraru, author of *Nom de Plume: A (Secret) History of Pseudonyms* (HarperCollins 2011), lists the three traditional reasons for adopting a name: 'Women writing as men. Writers with dirty secrets to hide. Highbrow writers slumming it in trashy genres.' She then goes on to suggest some others which include: a sign of mental disorder; to adopt a name that sounds like a great author rather than ordinary Joe Bloggs; to be freed up to imagine yourself as someone else; to cope with the modern day online world where multiple identities are normal – a practice she calls 'self promotion under the pretense of hiding'. Oddly, for someone who has written a book on the subject, she has missed in her essay *all* the reasons I do it – and these are the very ones that might come in useful for an aspiring writer. This is best explained by telling my own story.

Looking back, I now see that I was incredibly fortunate with my debut year. I won a couple of major prizes with *The Diamond of Drury Lane* (Egmont Books 2006) and had three other books published with two publishers. This meant that my publishers, my agent and I already knew I had the ability to be prolific. Ten years on, I have had 30 novels published. When people ask me how I can possibly 'write so much!' (and it is always said with an implied exclamation mark) I find it very hard to answer. It is just what I do. I suppose I am something of a dynamo, powered by the desire to tell stories, so the novel ideas do not stop. Like Dory in *Finding Nemo*, I just keep swimming. I am greatly helped by the fact that writing is my idea of fun. It isn't my intention to terrorize my editors with my fiendish efficiency, honest – though it is amusing to reverse the usual expectation and have the publishers apologizing for missing deadlines. If you do not already know, this is not industry standard.

My creative productivity was definitely a plus at the beginning of my career but, a few years in, it did start to become a problem. Reviews began to discuss the amount I was writing rather than the actual book in question and I had a vague sense that I was breaking some kind of rule within the author world. I wasn't supposed to do this – though no one quite said it to my face. The second hitch was more practical: I was competing against

Famous noms de plume

Author name	Pen name
Eric Blair	George Orwell
Anne Brontë	Acton Bell
Charlotte Brontë	Currer Bell
Agatha Christie	Mary Westmacott
David Cornwell	John le Carré
Charles Dodgson	Lewis Carroll
Mary Ann Evans	George Eliot
Daniel Handler	Lemony Snicket
Ruth Rendell	Barbara Vine
J.K. Rowling	Robert Galbraith

myself on my own bookshelf. There is only so much room and attention that the trade will give a writer and it was being spread too thin.

So what was my solution? I decided to learn from writers such as Nora Roberts/J.D. Robb, Jayne Ann Krentz/Amanda Quick/Jane Castle and Iain Banks/Iain M. Banks. These internationally successful authors handle their books in different genres by publishing them under different names. The variation is minor for Banks – the middle initial goes on his science fiction. American romance writer, Nora Roberts, adopts J.D. Robb as a name more suited to her futuristic detective stories and is incredibly prolific under both. Krentz uses her three different names for books set in the past, present and future. That gave me the idea of splitting my middle grade fiction (age 9–12) from my teen books, and so Joss Stirling came into being.

And just like buses, after waiting a while, the offers started coming along in twos and threes. At the same time as I was writing my first Joss, I was approached by Puffin to write a historical YA book. How to handle? OK, why not spin off another name?, I thought. Rather than launch Joss as doing two different things for teens, I decided to keep the brands straight and have contemporary romance as Joss and historical YA as (… scratches head …) Eve Edwards!

The advantages

I soon saw that the multiple names brought advantages. Creatively I found it fed something in me, rather like an actor landing a variety of good roles. It was greatly liberating. My family ask me 'Who have you been today?' when we gather at supper. Have I been darkly romantic as Joss, or grappling with the serious issues of World War I as Eve, or running with monsters and mythical creatures as Julia? No one can pigeonhole me as a writer.

There are commercial advantages too. I get three spots in most bookshops, hopefully increasing the chance someone will pick one up while browsing. Writing as Julia Golding, I have in mind a mixed audience up to the age of about 13 and I cover a wide range of genres from fantasy to thriller. Both Joss and Eve write romances, something only a few boys will read or admit to reading. By keeping the hearts-and-flowers out of Golding books, I have not alienated a swathe of readers. The flipside of this is that Eve and Joss both write with teens as their target audience, so the situations, dilemmas and language suit that older group. There does not have to be an age warning on the jacket, which might be the case if, known for writing for the pre-teens, I suddenly branch off into more mature material.

And the final advantage is that, in a difficult book market, I can easily keep on reinventing myself so I always have something to offer that a publisher wants (at least I hope so). If one genre is flagging and publishers have stopped contracting in that area, I can put it aside and return to it when the market is ready for that kind of book again.

And the disadvantages? So far I've not come across any serious ones but I suppose there is a dilution of identity. I am happy with that because my motivation for writing is to entertain and inspire readers while making enough money to live on. If I get fan mail to Joss, Eve or Julia saying how much a particular book was enjoyed, I'm content. It is not about seeing my name up in lights but whether my books are in stock.

Three names are also more work for the author. I run three online identities and answer three lots of fan mail. I toyed with the idea of amalgamating everything under one roof but decided that diminished the value of branding for difference, which was my aim in the first place, so I have had to knuckle down and put in the hours for the necessary administration and web managing to make a success of the pen names.

When is it time to change hats?

So when might you want to consider doing a quick swap in the literary equivalent of Mr Benn's changing room? Is your old hat looking a bit tired and do you need a new one? Should you put aside the beret for a Stetson, or a spaceman's helmet for a wizard's hat? Here are some times in your career when that might be a good idea:

Scenario 1

Publishers love debut authors but they no longer (or very rarely) stay around to help you make your reputation if you do not do reasonably well as a first timer. This is not because they are cruel and callous, even if it feels that way; it is because they are commercial entities. If your debut does not win the prizes and only sells a few thousand copies, what can you do next? I have heard some new writers speak as if it is the end of the road, but it really does not have to be. If you think you will not get a hearing as you have already shot your bolt, why not submit a new book under a different name? The book should be the only thing by which you are judged. You do not need to drag around a sense of unfulfilled promise like the ghost of Jacob Marley and his cash boxes.

Scenario 2

Do you have too many stories for one name to bear? For example, maybe you have a high fantasy series in mind and a contemporary real life story to offer to publishers. Thinking commercially, a chocolate bar manufacturer does not put Mars and Twix out under the same name, so why should you put your different 'tastes' out together? Remember Iain M. Banks and Roberts/Robb. You do not have to go the whole way to a new identity but you could differentiate with two versions of your pen name.

Scenario 3

So you have made a name for yourself writing mermaid and animal stories for the younger end of the market and now want to deal with some challenging YA subjects, such as suicide, drugs, bullying, sex and violence. You probably do not want to bring your readers with you – not for a few years anyway. Being known as a writer for the littlest readers might also stand in your way for getting the new departure taken seriously. To keep your audiences straight, a pseudonym removes the need for book jacket explanations and keeps publishers happy.

Final thought

When I started out on the pseudonym route, I kept it quiet. It wasn't a secret but neither did I want too many people to know. Like J.K. Rowling (but without the millions), I didn't want my Robert Galbraith equivalent to be reviewed through the lens of my existing reputation.

Yet since the books took off in their own right, I have become extremely relaxed and open about the fact that I write under three names. I have links on all my websites and a YouTube video explaining why I do it (*One Author, Three Names!* www.youtube.com/watch?v=Fl4OMud5594). Really keen readers feed across to the other names. It works best with Julia Golding readers growing up because they will find teen books waiting for them when they are ready, but there is plenty of cross-fertilization all three ways. This benefits me, of course, but it also means that a child or young person who would never dream of reading a different genre might just have their horizons expanded by taking that small step into the world of a different pseudonym. And I find that a very pleasing thought.

Julia Golding is an award-winning writer for children and young adults, who also writes under the pen names of Joss Stirling and Eve Edwards. She has now published over 30 books in genres ranging from historical adventure to fantasy. Her latest book, a fantasy historical adventure, *Mel Foster and the Demon Butler* will be published in August 2015. Her websites are: www.juliagolding.co.uk; http://eve-edwards.co.uk; www.jossstirling.co.uk.

See also...

- *Children's books: genres and categorisation*, page 35
- *Writing and the children's book market*, page 12
- *Marketing, publicising and selling children's books*, page 24
- *Writing thrillers for teenagers*, page 170
- *Teenage fiction*, page 174

Books

Ghostwriting children's books

Di Redmond outlines the challenges and rewards for ghostwriters when working with celebrities.

Publishers know that celebs sell. You've only got to run down the bestseller list to see that celebs' books are selling well – very well. But you can't help but wonder, did that footballer, pop star, fashion model or diva really write that children's book? It has to be said, sometimes not. Instead, publishers use professional ghostwriters, mainly because they can rely on them to deliver the manuscript on time and in the right publishable form and know it won't have wandered too far from the synopsis they approved at the beginning of the writing process. So, in our age of celeb writers, there are opportunities to be had for good ghostwriters.

How to become a ghostwriter

If you're interested in ghostwriting you'll need to put the word about by contacting agents and publishers. It's a genre that had never crossed my mind until I was approached by a publishing house. They were on a very tight schedule – they needed six books, 10,000 words each in three months and a synopsis by yesterday! I've written well over 100 books and I know from experience that there's nothing more reassuring to a publisher than a well-developed synopsis that lays down the bones of the story, outlines the chapters and describes the location. I usually write a synopsis for free: it helps to get the project moving and it also necessitates feedback from the editor and the celeb in question. I've always found this exchange really useful as it means the ghostwriter, the editor and the celeb are in agreement at the start of the writing process.

The publishers like the 'ghost' to meet the celeb before the contract is signed. A working chemistry is important (if you can't stand the sight of each other the book will never get written). Another reason to meet the celeb is to establish the 'tone' of the book you'll be writing for them. The subject matter chosen by the celeb will be based on their interests or expertise. It might be about ballet dancing, show jumping, football or becoming a pop idol. If the tone isn't forthcoming, the ghostwriter should make some suggestions. For example, if the book is about show jumping, is it a posh show-jumping circuit or is it about kids at a local riding school? Whatever the choice of subject, the ghostwriter must be interested in it too otherwise the project will become unbearable. I was recently asked to ghostwrite a book but the subject matter was so alien to me I had to turn it down. It's best to be realistic right from the start otherwise you'll waste everybody's time, including your own.

The celeb may furnish you with lots of material, or may not give you much more than his or her famous name. Each of my encounters has been different. I had a long meeting with one celeb who I never saw again; she was happy to jump-start the project and leave it to me and the editorial team to get on with the job. Other celebs really want to get involved in the writing process. They might read every draft, make notes, add comments, or even change the plot line. In terms of writing, especially if you're working to a tight deadline, waiting for feedback can be a time-consuming process if the celeb is, for example, filming abroad or playing in a World Cup match.

What does a ghostwriter do?

A large part of a ghost's job is to listen to and make sense of the story they're being told. Other people's stories (even famous celebs) can become rambling anecdotes that don't have much of a plot line, hold little tension and may not have a satisfactory conclusion. The ghost needs to keep the celeb on track, clear up inconsistencies in the story, establish the target age group and clarify any publishing issues which may not be obvious to the celeb. For example, if the book in question is a picture book the celeb needn't go into great detail about the colour of the clothes the characters are wearing as the illustrations will do that for her. Similarly, the celeb may present you with material that is not suitable for the age range, for example if you're writing for 7–10 year-olds you won't want excessive kissing and cuddling. The editor may have discussed publishing issues with the celeb but it doesn't necessarily mean that he or she will have fully understood the differences between a 32-page picture book and a 10,000-word story with some black-and-white illustrations.

As a ghost you need to be able to write quickly because celebs are usually on a tight deadline. When they decide to publish a book they want it instantly or certainly before they leave for their next big commitment. Take as many notes as you can on that first meeting just in case you never see your celeb again and use a tape recorder if possible. Once your celeb is swept away you'll be lucky if you get an email or a phone call from them. Basically, you're on your own with a deadline looming. As far as the celeb and her agent are concerned, you've been paid to do the job, so do it! That said, if you're a good ghost you'll always have the backing of your editor and hopefully the celeb's agent, so most problems will be amicably sorted out.

What rights does a ghostwriter have?

The celeb might be generous and share the writing credit with the ghost or he or she might choose to ignore the ghost altogether. Make sure you know this kind of detail at the contract stage; there's no point in complaining later if you've signed your name away. Books are not big earners compared to the millions a celeb might net for a lead part in a major film. Be aware from the outset that the celeb's agent and the publishing house which commissioned you will both take a cut. You'll undoubtedly be expected to sign a contract with a 'total buy-out clause' so don't automatically expect to get a royalty fee (some ghosts do but I never have). At best, there's a chance your name might appear on the inside back cover and if it does, this will guarantee you an annual Public Lending Right (see page 297) payment. You will also have to sign a confidentiality clause which means you can't go blabbing to the press or even chat to your mates about the contents of the book. People ask me over and over again, 'Isn't it frustrating not being able to say, I wrote that book?' The answer is no. In signing the contract you're giving the book away, you know from the word go that the celeb's glamorous picture will be on the front cover, her introduction will be on the first page, she'll be doing the book launch and the autograph signing and if the book's a huge success she'll be at the televised book award. I actually enjoy the reflected glory I get from being a ghostwriter and smile to myself when I see my celebs being interviewed about their books and how they personally enjoyed the new challenges that writing presented.

Whatever happens, don't be walked over. Fight for the best deal and stay focused on the fact that the book won't get written without you.

Lastly, don't expect a thank you crate of champagne or huge bouquet on publication because once that book is in print it really does belong to the celeb who never wrote it!

Di Redmond is a prolific writer for stage, radio and television. She has published over 100 books and is an established celebrity ghostwriter.

Writing non-fiction for children

Jen Green introduces the world of writing non-fiction to commission.

When I tell people I write for children, I almost always qualify it instantly, to counter any impression I am aiming to be the next J.K. Rowling. 'I write factual books, not fiction.' I add, to looks of bemusement: 'I write information books for schools and libraries ... the sort of books parents buy for their children. I write about things like countries – evolution – Nelson Mandela – the human body... ancient Egypt – volcanoes – sharks – dinosaurs.' Predictably, it's these last few subjects that finally bring a glimmer of recognition – oh, those kind of books. My responses to further enquiries include: 'Yes, all my books are published, or about to be. They're done to commission. No, I don't know exactly how many – hundreds.' At this point I add, to forestall incredulity: 'Most of the books I write don't take long. I work for a flat fee – no royalties.' This at last seems to reassure people I'm neither someone they should have heard of, nor am I making a mint.

Such is the world of children's non-fiction (CNF for short) – the Cinderella of the children's publishing world. Unlike our flashy, high-profile sister, fiction, CNF is an unsung heroine that gets precious little recognition any time, anywhere. We who write it rarely win awards and are hardly ever even invited to the ball. Far from the glamorous world of launches, lunches and advances, CNF falls within the prosaic world of work for hire. Not that I'm complaining. For 20 years, writing non-fiction for adults and children has provided me with creative work that's always interesting and absorbing. Each project is genuinely a fresh challenge, a blank canvas I'm always eager to start work on. Writing CNF allows me to earn enough to keep the bank manager at bay while working in a sphere I feel passionate about, educational publishing. It gives me the opportunity to work from home rather than join the daily grind of commuting, and the freedom to organise my work schedule as I choose. It continues to provide me with a living in these straitened times of cuts and downturns – just.

I got into freelance writing 20 years ago after working for as many years as a commissioning editor first of adult and then children's books. And I got into that via a brief academic career, writing a doctorate and teaching literature at university and adult evening classes. Having helped with the gestation of many books and rewritten a great many to a greater or lesser extent as part of my publishing job, I decided it would be just as easy to write my own. And it was. My career in publishing gave me not only the expertise to know what to write and the confidence to do it, but also quite a lot of contacts that proved useful as a freelancer. However, networking is something you never stop working at, particularly because the high turnover of editors within children's publishing means you continually need to make new contacts. Looking back, I was probably lucky to get into freelance writing the way I did, when I did. Back in the 1990s it was pretty hard to break into non-fiction; it's even harder today.

Touting for work

So how do you go about becoming a CNF writer? How do you attract the commissions I mentioned above? The choice is simple: you can either sit around waiting for that elusive email or phone call, or get the ball rolling and approach the publishers yourself. If you are starting out, your only option is the proactive one.

Begin by tracking down the publishers and packagers who produce the sort of books you want to write (a packager is a company that puts books together for a publisher, who then sells and markets them). You can do this either online, in bookshops or libraries, or using the invaluable *Children's Writers' & Artists' Yearbook*. You'll need the editors' names and emails – again, find these online or in the *Yearbook*. Ring the publisher to confirm the editor's email and check the drill for sending unsolicited emails – will an attachment be automatically deleted by anti-spam software? If possible, ask to be put through to the editor to introduce yourself before you follow up by email.

Hone your CV and hopefully your list of published titles, and send them with a carefully worded covering email, targeted at the company you are approaching. Your email should list the areas you specialise in or hope to write about. Nine times out of ten, you won't get a response – many editors receive scores of such speculative emails every day, and don't have time to respond to them. However, the tenth time you may strike lucky, sometimes from a quarter you least expect. Keep trying and don't lose heart.

You may also approach a publisher with a proposal for a one-off book or series. To do this you will need to have researched what is already published, and found a gap in the market that will suit the publisher in question. Include details of the intended readership and an idea of the treatment and illustrations you think will be appropriate. A short outline and perhaps a text sample could be helpful, but never send the whole thing. I've heard tell of writers who have carefully worked up a proposal to be turned down (or worse, receive no response at all), only to come across their idea in print with another author's name on it a few years later. It happens rarely but it does happen, and there's little to do but chalk it up to experience.

Your aim is to build a client base of a dozen or so publishers who regularly give you work. Clients range from publishers of books, ebooks and online information – the field is wide and getting wider. But it has to be said, the going is also getting tougher, with cuts to government spending on libraries and education, and the proliferation of free online information producing a decline in factual book publishing, and reduced print-runs keeping fees low. Most writers I know also do editing and project management work, and some undertake school visits or teach as well as write. It pays to be versatile. You may also attract work and develop new contacts by producing your own website, writing a blog, attending book fairs and/or joining an online writer's group.

The commission

In CNF the commission from the publisher is usually brief initially. It may be very brief indeed if the book is in a series, consisting of the book title – 'Can you write a book about killer beetles in a series about deadly animals/a book about germs in a series about hygiene/about Viking battles in our new series about ancient wars?'. (In the old days, CNF writers were often offered a whole series, but one or two titles is more common nowadays.) You should be told the total word count, the age range/reading level and treatment, for example humorous or child-friendly. You will need to know the deadline for synopsis and manuscript (the time is almost always short!) and of course, the fee. You may be able to negotiate a little on the fee, but rest assured, if you won't write it for that money, someone else will. Don't start work until you have a contract, unless you know and trust the publisher, and can take their commissioning email in lieu of contract.

Check the contract carefully before signing, to see it is acceptable and conforms to what you've agreed in terms of the fee split, deadline, etc. You agree to give up copyright in return for the fee. The contract will almost certainly contain an indemnity clause. In this you warrant that your work is original, not libellous and will not harm or injure any reader following your instructions or advice. You agree to indemnify (compensate) the publisher in case they are sued for libel, breach of copyright, etc; you usually undertake to pay any legal costs. Since the sums involved could potentially be huge, lawyers' fees being what they are, compared to the small sum you are being offered to write the thing, this clause will invariably concentrate your mind on the need to avoid plagiarism at all costs. (This includes self-plagiarism, repeating what you've written in other books in which you don't own the copyright.) Cases of writers having to pay out in this context are very, very rare, but they do happen.

Research and outline

The first stage is to write a synopsis (a.k.a. book plan or outline), complete with a picture list, i.e. the illustrations you envisage will be needed to put the subject across. You may be required to write a sample spread. Before beginning work you will need a detailed brief from the publisher with full details of age range, reading level, or key stage in the National Curriculum if the book is for the educational market. A sample spread design for the series from the publisher will be very useful even if it only has 'dummy' text (gobbledygook), as it will show you the design, word count, look, boxes if any, and details of how the text works with the illustrations – captions, labels, etc. In writing the synopsis, you will need to gather research materials from a variety of sources, unless you have the subject so thoroughly at your fingertips you can write it off the top of your head. If you are writing for an educational publisher, you need to familiarise yourself with the requirements of the National Curriculum. Having digested your research, you then devise a structure that will allow you to explain and explore your subject following a logical order. Some authors write incredibly detailed outlines. Others, like myself, write just a few sentences explaining the content of each double-page spread or the thrust of the chapter.

Following comments from the publisher, you may need to revise the synopsis. Once it has been approved you are clear to start writing, unless you are writing to designed spreads, in which case you will have to wait for them to be created.

Writing and rewriting

Good non-fiction writing for both adults and children needs to be accurate, informative, and user-friendly. It must be comprehensive within the word count. You will need to explain your subject in clear and graphic language that is tailored to the age range and otherwise fulfils the publisher's brief. In CNF the trick is to cover the basics and, for older readers, air the issues while keeping the reader on board. Your tone should be light and easy-going, the style seemingly effortless. Use simple examples to grab and retain the reader's attention. You need to entertain and not put the reader off by including too many facts. As one publisher said to me recently, our aim is to 'inform with an informal touch'. All this, and you also need to develop your own voice. It's a tall order especially at first, but it does get easier with practice.

To my mind, the key is to understand your subject thoroughly so you can retell it in your own words. Every writer's method is different. My method is to write in the morning, then research the next day's writing towards the end of the day and again in the early morning. Personally, I compose longhand and then edit onscreen to avoid spending more time at the computer than I have to, but I do understand this is a dinosaur-like method of proceeding. Only when I have composed and edited my work onscreen do I go back and check facts and dates as necessary. Having printed out my day's work, I start the research for the next day and plan a structure for what I'm going to say. I may make notes as I read, but in my own words so there's no danger of plagiarism, and this helps to fix the subject in my head, so it becomes inward.

In the early morning I review my notes and reread my research. Then I put my sources away and allow time for the information to percolate. In my case this involves going for an hour's walk. When I return, I write usually without referring to my notes and certainly not my sources. In this way I explore the topic from memory, and the story I'm telling comes out in my own voice, following an order that makes sense to me. Yes, it is a bit like taking an exam every day, but it works for me. Once I've finished writing the manuscript, I go back over it and do a final edit, also supplying any endmatter, such as glossary, timeline, and/or bibliography, that is required.

Once the document has been emailed to the publisher, the bulk of your work is over. However, you still have to answer queries, do any rewriting necessary, write captions and check layouts and proofs to ensure that the text and illustrations work together on the page. One day the finished book appears, which is a nice surprise and satisfying, but by then your mind is on new projects. Grumbles? I've got a few, who hasn't? I think the skilled job I do is worth a lot more than I get paid, and a bit more recognition wouldn't go amiss, either. But to go back to telling people what I do: someone once responded that they'd never met anyone who enjoyed their job before. And it's true, I still enjoy it and find it engaging. I still get a kick out of learning and writing about new subjects. And after 15 years, that can't be bad.

Dr Jen Green worked as an editor for 20 years and is now a full-time writer and editor. She has written over 300 books for children and adults, mainly on geography, nature, environment, history and the arts. She lives in Sussex.

See also...
- *Copyright questions*, page 315
- *The Society of Authors*, page 375

Children's writing in the digital age

New technology is changing the face of publishing and the digital impact on the children's market is becoming increasingly evident. New creative opportunities for writers are arising to meet digital possibilities and writers today can self-publish their work more easily than ever before. Alongside this, as Linda Strachan points out, the power of a great story continues to be in demand.

As a children's writer I find it both exciting and terrifying, the way technology is changing so fast. Children of the next generation will take for granted things we could hardly have imagined just ten years ago. In a world full of new technology, which sometimes appears to be taking over our lives, established concepts are constantly being challenged and the possibilities are endless.

In this ever-changing world one constant is the power of a great story, regardless of the marvels of technology and the many varied ways it can be delivered. From the darkest reaches of time humans have told stories, cave paintings depict tales of bravery and prowess, and folk tales through the ages have created and passed on myths and legends in every culture. It doesn't matter whether a story is accessed in the form of a paper book, ebook, film, stage play, game or spoken word; we look for the excitement, the reassurance and often the discovery that we are not alone or as different as we might feel. Stories are the way we make sense of the world, discover more about it and writers, particularly children's writers, have often used story to challenge perceptions and social mores. Whether fiction or non-fiction, as writers it is our job to communicate in a way that grabs our readers of whatever age and in whatever format they want and need. Instead of hiding under the covers at the thought of change, it is worth remembering that technology is just a tool. It is the quality of the writing that really matters, whether using pen and paper, computer or any other format.

Social media

Ours is a solitary business as most writers work alone. The internet allows us to do much of our research from our desks at the click of a mouse, but we can also connect with the outside world by joining communities of writers from all over the globe. Although it is a great way to network, social media can be a mixed blessing; uplifting and depressing in equal measures. Everyone likes to share success, so it can seem as if everyone else is having a wonderful time and becoming more and more successful, but in reality few want to admit so publicly to any failure. The other side is the support and encouragement from other children's writers, which can be heart-warming on this emotional rollercoaster as we navigate the challenging world of publishing.

Often the biggest problem with social networking and blogging for a writer is lost writing time; the hours when you could be writing, that just disappear. If you like and enjoy it, social networking can work well for you and your books. Having a platform in the form of a website or blog and creating a rapport with your readers, or their parents, can build you a following which publishers will happily take into account when assessing the commercial potential of a book, although it is not likely to be a determining factor in any decision. Some writers spend a lot of time on social media communicating with friends and family or other writers, which though pleasant is not necessarily building an audience and might be time better used writing their next book.

The importance of libraries

Libraries are important places as far as children's writers and our readers are concerned. Librarians organise projects and reading challenges, as well as the school and library visits that often form a large part of a children's writer's income. Public Lending Right (PLR; see page 297) is another source of income for a writer, based on book loans, and with libraries now buying fewer and fewer books this impacts on both writers and publishers. Particularly under fire in the current climate, libraries are often undervalued by the powers that be, with many being closed completely and others becoming filled with computers at the expense of bookshelves. Budgets are being cut and librarians, both in public libraries and school libraries, often find themselves either job-sharing or lost in a cost-cutting exercise. For families, public libraries are a wonderful resource and the advent of ebooks is part of the change in technology that libraries are adapting to, but it may be a while before there is any hard evidence about how many 7–11 year-olds actually read on electronic devices rather than paperbacks, and how many young people want to borrow ebooks from public libraries. In schools a professionally trained librarian is a huge benefit as their often encyclopedic knowledge can put the right book in the hands of a particular child, sometimes the one book that will open the door and create a reader for life. Librarians also help writers keep in touch with our young audience. They organise events where children can meet writers and understand the passion that goes into creating the characters they enjoy reading about, and discover that we (writers), are real people. Technology may do many things but it cannot replace a dedicated, knowledgeable and enthusiastic librarian.

Apps

The emergence of apps, particularly story apps for very young children, has been an exciting development but although the stories they tell might be similar to picture books, apps are quite different creatures. They allow children to physically interact with the story, but is that better than accessing stories in book form? I think it is just a different use of stories for play and learning. A book, when shared with very young children, can create a sense of calm and a way to understand the world; to have fun discussing and discovering the secrets hidden in the text and the illustrations. For the very youngest children board books reveal that there is something exciting inside this hard object, but even babies are discovering that a screen can be a game and it can tell a story, too. It has been suggested that children engage more with the story when they are not looking for the next image to move around on a screen, or trying to make it interactive. I have seen a young child move their hand across a picture book page to see if it made anything move or change. But this is not necessarily a bad thing as it shows how children adapt and learn to use different media in different ways, even at a very young age. By the time babies today grow up, technology is likely to play an even greater part in their lives than it already does in ours.

Apps and ebooks are available on various devices, phones, tablets and e-readers. Research shows that 28% of 3–4 year-olds use a tablet computer at home (*Children and Parents: Media Use and Attitudes Report*, Ofcom, October 2013) and, as with other digital technology, I think apps for children will find a comfortable way to coexist with books, rather than replace them. For a long time yet I suspect parents will still want to snuggle down to read a book with a young child at bedtime. Children are growing up amongst this technology and, as with anything else in their lives, parents will decide how much screen time is right for their child, just as they decide when it is time to switch off the light after reading a book.

Apps can also be designed to assist struggling and reluctant readers. Mairi Kidd, Managing Director of dyslexia-specialist publisher Barrington Stoke (see page 40) is excited and concerned by the technology: 'We wanted to wait until we were confident that our app would allow us to replicate the books exactly – and actually enhance accessibility.' Their new multi-folio app will also include the facility to change background colours and access virtual reading aids.

Working with technology and understanding it is key to producing great apps and that is where writers come in. On the Picture Bbook Den blog, author Moira Butterfield said, 'I want publishers to call on us authors for ideas, not just on computer whizzes. I think we should get into the mix and offer our creativity.'

But is an app the same as a book? Kate Wilson, Managing Director of Nosy Crow (see page 50), which publishes books and apps, insists that it is important to design different content for screen and says '… there's no point in squashing a picture book onto a phone.' The company is looking for writers to provide '… excellent, thought-through concepts, with your vision of the multimedia and interactive elements that could be added to your brilliant text.' Now there's a challenge.

Ebooks

In 2013, a new phenomenon began: a dedicated ebook-only imprint, from a major publisher, aimed at Young Adult and 'New Adult' readers. Bloomsbury Spark ebooks publish 15–20 ebook titles a year. Although their website does suggest that 'after sales reach a certain level of success' they would consider a print run, one can imagine that this might only be for those few titles that become runaway successes.

There are positives but also negatives with ebooks. One successful ebook author noted that books which are only available in digital format are rarely eligible for book awards and there are few, if any, book festivals or schools that would invite an author who did not have a physical book available. It might be because publishers have little or no marketing spend for ebooks and the discounts available to retailers on ebooks is minuscule. This has an impact as book sales are often an important revenue strand for festivals. Possibly this is something that will change as the model of bookselling and book buying evolves.

Self-publishing ebooks

More writers than ever, particularly for slightly older readers, are taking self-publishing as a route to publication, for a variety of reasons. Some prefer to have the control it gives them over everything from design to marketing, and for books that have earned little in the way of royalties with a publisher, it can sometimes provide a slow but steady income. Established writers with a book that has gone out of print, or a further book in a series that has been dropped by the original publisher, often turn to self-publishing, particularly if they already have an existing fan-base. As one children's author told me, 'I'm thinking of e-publishing an 8–12 novel I've got stashed away – and I wouldn't have contemplated it a year ago. The trouble is, I've even less idea about marketing ebooks to kids than ordinary books.'

Without proper editing and layout any self-published book can turn out to be unreadable. These professional skills are well worth paying for. Writers looking to self-publish as a paper book or ebook should be wary of trying to save money by skimping on professional help. For ebook publishing you need to make sure it works technically for all formats, and be informed when thinking about pricing, etc. Marketing is incredibly important. Letting people know your book is out there and making it stand out in the huge crowd of other ebooks available requires a level of hard work, dedication and enthusiasm for self-promotion which should not be underestimated. It takes determination and a lot of time and energy. This is time that could be spent writing if your book is taken up by a traditional publisher, but if it is something you enjoy and are prepared for, the self-publishing route can be successful.

Authors Electric (http://authorselectric.blogspot.co.uk) is one of many blogs offering lots of good advice to those considering self-publishing ebooks. It is a group of independent and independently published writers who blog about their books and their experiences in ebook publishing.

Multiple platform publishing

Publishers are looking for great ideas as well as excellent writing. According to Philippa Dickinson (former Managing Director of Random House Children's Publishers UK and until recently Consultant Children's Publisher at Penguin Random House UK Children's, see page 52), 'If you can think of a way of doing something new and original in the way of storytelling which will appeal to a very big audience, then work it up well and take it to a publisher. They might find that interesting, especially if it can be delivered inexpensively and across multiple platforms – but the concept and story still has to be very, very good.'

Traditional publishers are aware of the changing face of the industry. Books are now available in so many formats: hardback, paperback, board book, mini, book plus toy/gift, and digital. These are included as a matter of course when considering whether or not they will make an offer for a book.

For publishers, ebooks also offer the chance to issue books in short series of novellas or chapters that test the market and can grow the readership, with very little expense.

But it is easy, with all the hype, to assume that digital is the only thing that matters. Books are here to stay, for the foreseeable future anyway, although possibly they will not always be the most dominant part of the market. But some publishers are thinking in terms of bringing back classics in new printed formats and print on demand, also creating beautiful books that will become objects of desire. Dickinson said, 'There are some big changes coming which are already challenging the traditional publishing and bookselling models both in the domestic markets and internationally. PRH UK Children's is already developing its vision for a new kind of children's publisher.'

Without a crystal ball it is difficult to know what will happen in the future with new technology emerging and new ways to use it. As always, we are limited only by our imagination and willingness to experiment, but that's what writers do best.

Linda Strachan is the author of over 60 books. She writes for a wide range of ages from picture books to edgy Young Adult novels – including the bestselling *Hamish McHaggis* series and award-winning *Spider* (Strident 2008), *Dead Boy Talking* (Strident 2010) and *Don't Judge Me* (Strident 2012). Her educational books are used in schools worldwide. She has also written a writing handbook for adults, *Writing for Children* (A&C Black 2008). Linda lives in Scotland and is the current chair of the Society of Authors in Scotland. She is an inspirational creative writing tutor and speaker, travelling widely at home and abroad presenting in schools, libraries, universities, conferences and festivals. Her website is www.lindastrachan.com.

See also...
• *What do self-publishing providers offer?*, page 203

From self-publishing to contract

Janey Louise Jones shares her tale of how she successfully self-published her first *Princess Poppy* book, which led to a contract with Random House and huge sales.

My journey to self-publishing

For some children, a bookshop has more delicious flavours than a sweetshop. I was one of those children. When I was a little girl, I wanted to be a writer *and* a princess. So, with my *Princess Poppy* books now selling in their millions around the world, I find myself reflecting on the life experiences which have led to me realising my childhood dreams.

People often say that the story of Princess Poppy, going from a childhood notion, to kitchen table, to self-published success, then on to a Random House contract, is a fairy tale in itself. Perhaps so, but even fairy tales are laced with problems and trials, and self-publishing has been a very challenging experience. I highly recommend starting alone as a way of presenting a vision, proving strong sales and learning the full craft of producing a book – but it is not an easy process.

As a child, I saw witches at my window, and fairies in the moonlight. I loved ballet and the flower fairies, and made petal perfume. I was idealistic and romantic and although I was very loved, I never felt special enough. So I developed a perfectionist streak – always driven to do my very best. I began to express my feelings and identity through words. Like so many book lovers, I loved the physical look and texture of a book as much as what it said to me.

Growing up in the 1970s, it wasn't fashionable to be gender specific for children. Being ultra-feminine was frowned upon as frothy in a way that it isn't now. Did any other girls of the 1970s have a dark brown, checked, floor-length party dress, or was I especially unlucky? I felt a conflict between wanting to be educated, well read and serious on the one hand, and wanting to be a pretty fairy princess, on the other. Could I possibly be 'Fairy Blue Stocking'?

My favourite childhood books included *The Secret Garden*, *Little House on the Prairie*, *Little Women*, *The Children of the New Forest* and *The Diary of Anne Frank*. Later on, at Edinburgh University in the late 1980s, I became intrigued with the concept of 'the novel' and through my love of Victorian and early twentieth century authors, I was asked to contribute to *Chambers Dictionary of Literary Characters*. This was my first formal writing experience, which taught me the valuable lesson that when it comes to writing, effort and remuneration are not always commensurate.

Somehow, during my degree course, the wistful child within me resurfaced and I produced a storyboard for a magical, mythical character – Princess Poppy. People often ask me: 'Is she your child, your daughter?' (I have three boys). But no, she isn't my child, she is *me* as a child. I found it difficult to enter adulthood and Poppy beckoned me back to my childish dreams. So, the cliché that one's first and best work is autobiographical is certainly true for me.

Back at this early stage, I lacked confidence and direction, my ideas blowing in the wind – all too easily blown away. (It is so important to hold with your vision at this stage.) In fact, I was convinced by someone that there was no chance of such a character coming to life and so I actually put Poppy to one side for many years. I also heard the well-rehearsed adages that you can't write well until you're at an age when you've experienced life, and also that if you're a proper writer, it will just happen. There might be a bit of truth in these notions.

I became an English teacher, in an Edinburgh girls' school akin to that of Miss Jean Brodie. Then like any self-respecting princess in an ivory tower, I needed to be rescued by a dashing knight. Or, to put it another way, teaching wasn't much fun, and domesticity seemed more appealing. Conveniently, I fell in love with a Royal Marine Commando. This fitted neatly into my script. After a fairy tale wedding, I settled into the real 'grown-up' world of motherhood.

My main writing outlet in this period was a mother's answer to *Bridget Jones's Diary* – Jane Jones's Dairy – a kitchen sink drama of the daily intrigues of the 'stay-at-home-mum' with three infants under four years of age. My years of 'extreme mothering' definitely prepared me for the world of publishing and made my writing much more real and touching.

Curiously, Poppy re-emerged with great vibrancy when my grandmother died in 2000. I wrote about my wonderful granny, Emma Brown, in a eulogy entitled *Pale Pink, Lace and Pearls*. This piece of writing was so well received in my family, that I felt a burst of confidence, which is very elusive when little children take over your world. I finally left behind my own childishness and began to write as an adult, looking into childhood.

I found that Poppy was becoming an 'every girl' princess, instead of a traditional or mythical princess as she had been before. The theme of my Poppy stories is that through family love, every girl is a true princess. I don't like the idea of so-called 'alpha females' – lucky girls who are richer, prettier or smarter – every child has a right to feel equally special. Poppy is innocent, but not old-fashioned. Although I am nostalgic in some ways in my writing, I often think there is something rather brutal about girl stories of the 1950s, as if children were somehow less cherished then, so my books do not hark back. I prefer to reach the children who are growing up, right now, in the twenty-first century. Childhood is so precious and I want to prolong it, as most mothers do, so I attempt to evoke a world which is both contemporary and yet aspires towards a sweeter way of life.

Self-publishing Princess Poppy

As the Poppy book idea gathered energy, the story became quite focused. The decision to focus on one clear plot was a breakthrough after months of endless bright ideas. I plumped for a birthday party to introduce the heroine, her world and the cast of additional characters. The biggest challenge was with the visual, illustration side of my first book. I collected a roomful of reference materials: wild flowers, books, cards, magazines, fairies, photographs, butterflies, bridesmaids, princesses, tiaras and ballerinas. Slowly and almost imperceptibly, my own sketches became good enough for the trial book. Asking artists to sketch Poppy was potentially tricky. What if the publisher liked the pictures, but not the words, or *vice versa*? Arrangements between authors and illustrators at pitching stage have to be very clear cut.

I decided to self-publish when I became frustrated with the slow ways of the publishing world. I had sent off a few versions of Poppy, as well as some other ideas, and I'd had one helpful phone call from a publisher and some other words of encouragement – but no deal was in sight. I was in the Lake District when I realised that Beatrix Potter had self-published, along with many other stars such as Virginia Woolf, John Grisham and James Joyce. I decided there and then to speed up my career by producing the book as I imagined it. I had every confidence of it selling well. I dismissed the idea of using a firm specialising in self-publishing, even though some are perfectly respectable because I believed, and still do, that you can project manage it yourself and use your budget on strong production values instead of a middle-person.

There is something about making the financial investment which proves one's serious intentions: you can produce your book with plenty of trial copies for the cost of a holiday. I broke the self-publishing process down into the following ten-point battle plan:

1 Write a good, fast-paced story of the right length for your audience. (Ask for a few objective opinions. If there is not one common criticism, ignore all negative comments.) Remember: theme, character, plot and dialogue are the building blocks of any story.
2 Edit it objectively. (Ask a friend if necessary.) Know when to let go of words. Ask yourself if it is truly original. Innovate, don't imitate.
3 Illustrate it if it's a picture book. (Ask an artist to do this, either for a fee or as part of the pitch.)
4 Think of a wonderful jacket design, explore fonts, imagery and message.
5 Design and lay out the pages. (Use a professional designer who will also advise on a printer.)
6 Have it printed in sensible quantities. Use a printer who has produced 'perfect bound' books before, i.e. *not* those stapled down the spine, which would look amateurish. Test the market with a few hundred copies.
7 Hand-sell it to bookshops, both chains and independents.
8 Have it distributed. Ensure that the distributor has relationships with all the national chains.
9 Promote it to get it noticed (radio, television, articles).
10 Offer to do events and festivals to ensure ongoing sales.

After self-publishing: getting the deal and beyond

The first Princess Poppy book sold 40,000 copies in six months, which meant that the concept was noticed in the trade. All the main bookseller chains, as well as independents, were incredibly supportive. I was invited to visit headquarters of booksellers and soon the chains were distributing the book to their branches. All of this relied on good distribution, which is hard to find with only one title, but persistence is the key.

I paid for professional public relations which helped a lot, but is not essential. I began to be invited to book parties across Edinburgh and found that the publishing reps from large publishing houses were very willing to help. They took news of my book to London offices and soon I was being invited to these for meetings. At this point, I produced a second book, and a doll, which showed the series potential of the Princess Poppy concept. But it was all getting too much for one person. I was running a business now, with printers to liaise with as well as the press, the distributors and events co-ordinators. When two offers for Poppy came in on my newly set up email, I didn't have to think twice about accepting.

I have been lucky enough to have a great relationship with my editor and publisher. Working with a major publisher requires the right amount of compromise, without losing personal direction and control. I believe in professional standards and feel that being part of an arts-based work cycle is no excuse for being chaotic. I always deliver texts on time and try not to be needlessly awkward or diva-ish. The author is simply a bit-part player in the successful production of a book. If you are incredibly hung up on ownership of rights, trademarks and the like, then self-publishing really might be best for you. Ironically, once you are published by a traditional publisher, you have to let all of that go.

I wouldn't change the way I did it, as I understand the whole world of publishing much more than I would have done otherwise. And I may never have got the deal at all, without self-publishing first. For those who say it is vain to self-publish, I would say, yes it is, as is the whole idea of wanting others to pay for your written words. But when one's main pleasure in life is reading, it makes perfect sense to create stories for others to enjoy. I can think of no better career, and when fan letters drop through the door, the whole process is complete.

Janey Louise Jones continues to write the *Princess Poppy* series for Random House. Her ballet school series, *Cloudberry Castle*, is published by Floris Books and her angel series, *Angel Academy*, is published by Usborne. She is also working on a series for younger girls, *Tiger Lily*. Janey has recently signed a nine-book deal with Capstone Books for the *Superfairies* series and also for *Lady Lily*, a historical drama.

See also...

An indie's journey to award-winning success

Setting aside the idea of her novel being published traditionally, Griselda Heppel found the high standards and professionalism of a self-publishing company gave her the best of both worlds.

It used to be so simple. Aspiring writers had two options: to land a contract with a traditional publishing house or, failing that, pay for publication themselves, thus earning the undying scorn of the literary world for anyone resorting to the so-called 'vanity press'. A book not published in the usual way must, the argument went, by definition be badly written, poorly edited and have no appeal to anyone but the writer and their own loyal family.

Well, if that was true once it isn't anymore. In today's competitive publishing world it is extremely hard for unknown authors to be taken on by traditional firms. Where once an editor might have had time to nurture a new talent, now financial realities demand strong projected sales that makes such slow-burn methods increasingly unlikely. The new book and the new author have to be winners from the word go and that is a big ask, especially if your book does something no one has ever tried before.

Like creating a children's version of *Dante's Inferno*, for instance.

I've always loved stories that draw on great myths and epics: *The Iliad* and *The Odyssey*, Greek and Roman legends, Norse sagas, King Arthur and Robin Hood. Classical works provide rich narrative material and form the basis for many of the best books ever written for children. Yet the *Inferno*, in which Dante imagines himself descending into ever darker circles of Hades, having to deal with Cerberus, Harpies, Minotaur, Furies – a gold-mine of fantasy and adventure if ever there was one – seems to have been neglected in this respect, and I was determined to put that right. Dante became 12-year-old Ante (Antonia) who finds herself plunged on this hellish journey, accompanied by her arch enemy, Florence, and a mysterious 13-year-old boy called Gil (Virgil – a reference to the Roman poet who is Dante's guide).

When I sent the completed manuscript to publishers and agents, it attracted some interest but ultimately no offers. Some of the rejection letters contained useful feedback, for which I was grateful. Others told me my story was too complicated for children; they'd be confused by the combined themes of Hell, mythical creatures and the First World War (an important element in *Ante's Inferno*). I knew they were wrong about this. My book had already been read by 40 or so children, aged 9–16 years, not one of whom had any difficulty in understanding it, and the fact that young people's abilities can still be so underestimated frankly puzzled me.

It struck me that however much I rewrote *Ante's Inferno*, as an unknown author I'd never get past this conservative view from mainstream publishing companies. I realised that if I wanted to see my book in print, I'd have to get on with it myself. I knew it would be hard but there were advantages: how and when the book was published would be up to me, I could commission my own cover illustration and I'd have the final say on design, print and production. I'd be in control.

The rapid growth in recent years of ways in which to self-publish has opened up a number of choices to authors. I was determined that *Ante's Inferno* should be a top-quality book, well-designed with high production values. There'd be an ebook version, of course, but for children the act of holding, feeling, smelling a book is a vital part of their enjoyment (actually, it is for me too); *Ante's Inferno* should be a pleasure to pick up in bookshops, where it wouldn't look out of place among all the traditionally published titles, and retailers should be able to order it from their wholesalers in the usual way. In short, what I needed was an established publishing company that would do a professional job.

Google 'self-publishing' and you'll come up with a bewildering array of companies offering services. Some of these are very basic and very cheap and, not surprisingly, their books look it. But there are others whose high standards mean their products can compete with the best of any published books. I settled on Matador, which, as an imprint of trade publishing company Troubador, offers partnership services to authors supported by professional expertise in copy-editing, design, production, marketing and distribution fields. 'For authors whose work we are happy to publish,' says Matador on its home page, 'we will undertake as much or as little of the publishing process as required.'

And there you have it: the gulf between self-publishing and the low quality control associated with the vanity press. Submitting your manuscript to Matador does not guarantee publication. Matador may offer partnerships in which authors take on financial risk, but they will only do so if they consider the books to be of a high enough standard. If not, an author will be advised to rework the manuscript, perhaps after undergoing a critical assessment from a literary consultancy or a professional editor. A significant proportion of all books offered to Matador are rejected in this way.

This brings me to the heart of getting your book published by whatever method, traditional or independent: the quality of the book itself. I rewrote *Ante's Inferno* many times, responding to feedback from literary agents, editors and writing mentors, before sending it to Cornerstones Literary Consultancy for a critique. Their editorial report was tough and hard-hitting. It was difficult criticism to take on board but it proved invaluable, enabling me to resolve structural issues and tighten up the writing. By the time I submitted *Ante's Inferno* to Matador, it had already gone through a rigorous editorial process and was a much better book as a result.

Once taken on by Matador, I could have left it all to them but I didn't want to. For the cover, I commissioned Hilary Paynter, a top wood engraver, to create a dark and menacing image of the path down to Hell, reminiscent of the atmospheric illustrations of *Dante's Inferno* by Gustave Doré. I had input on jacket and page design but was glad for my publisher to take charge of production, printing, distribution and marketing. I had no illusions that bookshops throughout the UK would instantly stock *Ante's Inferno* – the thousands of new children's titles that appear every year are all fighting for the same space, after all – but Matador would present them with every opportunity to do so.

Next came the hard bit: promotion. Unless you have the full weight – and budget – of a large firm's publicity department, it is extremely difficult to get your book noticed by the media. Even authors signed by traditional publishing companies can be disappointed to find the funds allocated to publicising their book are relatively small. Increasingly they are expected to promote themselves, in a way not demanded before (and often contrary to their nature – not all authors are confident extroverts!). It's not enough just to write books, it seems; you need to establish an online presence by blogging, tweeting and updating Facebook and website pages with amusing snippets (not just sales pitches) to charm and entertain potential readers. All this can be fun, but it's also time-consuming, not to mention stressful (am I tweeting/blogging/facebooking enough?).

I entered this world of social media with some trepidation but found it a great way of connecting with other writers, readers, agents and editors and making new friends, as well as spreading the word about *Ante's Inferno* and garnering a good number of reviews. In addition, my publishers ran a publicity campaign which achieved a decent amount of press coverage – local, mainly, but also some on a national level – on radio programmes, in newspapers and magazines. Eager to share my interest in Dante with children, I put together an illustrated talk about the themes that inspired *Ante's Inferno*. This goes down extremely well in schools (Years 5–8) and I fit in a few school visits every term.

It was a wonderful feeling when *Ante's Inferno* won a Silver in the Wishing Shelf Awards (www.thewsa.co.uk), swiftly followed by – even more exciting – the Children's category of the People's Book Prize (www.peoplesbookprize.com). Both competitions are judged exclusively by readers: the Wishing Shelf Awards by schoolchildren alone, and the People's Book Prize by any member of the public, either online or through their local library. For me it was a solid endorsement, not just of *Ante's Inferno*, but of the independent publishing method I'd gone for.

There are downsides, however. Partnership publishing has been a terrific experience but there's no disguising the amount of time and effort it takes up, arguably leaving less of both for the writing itself. A well-known, mainstream firm can inevitably give a book wider exposure than *Ante's Inferno* has achieved (though selling out its first 1,000 copy print run in eight months isn't bad).

Still, I have a tried and trusted model that works and a growing fan base keen to read my next book, *The Tragickall History of Henry Fowst*, due out in August 2015. For this tale of an ordinary 13-year-old boy who, somewhat unwisely, calls up a demon to help him with his problems, Hilary Paynter and Pete Lawrence have created another brilliantly spooky cover. While the design process – both for the jacket and pages inside – has taken longer this time, leading to some panicky moments over deadlines (something familiar to all publishers!), the thrill of seeing my vision for the book translated into reality remains as strong as ever. So strong in fact that, while as a writer I'll always be open to the possibility of mainstream publishing, it would take a very good offer to tempt me.

Perhaps even a Faustian pact.

Hm, now there's an idea …

Griselda Heppel read English at Cambridge and worked in publishing before moving to Oxford with her husband to bring up their four children. *Ante's Inferno* was published in 2012 by Matador (see page 208) and you can find out more at www.griseldaheppel.com. Her next novel, *The Tragickall History of Henry Fowst*, will be published on 28 August 2015.

See also...
- *From self-publishing to contract,* page 196
- *What do self-publishing providers offer?,* page 203
- *Self-publishing providers,* page 206

What do self-publishing providers offer?

Jeremy Thompson presents the options for engaging an author services company.

Books

Now that self-publishing is widely accepted and it is easier to do it than ever before, authors are presented with a broader range of opportunities to deliver their book or ebook to readers. This brings with it a greater responsibility to you, the author and publisher, to make the right choices for your publishing project. The various options for self-publishing may seem bewildering at first, and each has their pros and cons. But some relatively simple research will prove invaluable in ensuring you make the right choices for your book.

Motivation influences method

There are many reasons why authors choose to self-publish, and contrary to popular belief, the decision to do so is not usually motivated by the aspiration to be a bestselling novelist! That is only one reason; others include the wish to impart knowledge to a wider audience; the desire to publish a specialist book with a relatively small target audience; the fulfilment of a hobby; publishing as part of a business or charity; and yes, vanity (a wish to see one's name on a book cover is fine, as long as you have realistic expectations of your work).

Understanding why you are self-publishing is important, as the reasons for doing so can help point to the best way in which to go about it. For example, if you are publishing simply for pleasure, and have few expectations that your book will 'set the world alight', then you'd be wise not to invest in a large number of copies; using 'print on demand' (POD) or producing an ebook could be the way forward. If you have a book that you're publishing to give away or sell as part of your business to a relatively captive audience, then a short print run of, say, 300 copies might be wise, as the more copies you print, the greater the economies of scale. If you want your novel to reach as many readers as possible and to sell it widely, you'll need to have physical copies to get into the supply chain and in front of potential readers, so opt for a longer print run of perhaps 500 or more copies.

Decisions on how to self-publish are often influenced by the money you are prepared to invest in (and risk on) your project. Making a decision on what self-publishing route to take based on financial grounds alone is fine, as long as you understand the implications of that decision. For example, as the name implies, print-on-demand (POD) books are only printed when someone actually places an order for a copy; there are no physical copies available to sell. As POD books are largely sold on a 'firm sale' basis, bookshops will rarely stock them, so most POD sales will be made through online retailers. In addition, as the POD unit cost is higher than if a quantity of books are printed in one go, the retail price of a book is likely to be fairly high in order to cover the print cost and retailer's discount, and make you, the publisher, some profit. Authors often assume that POD is some miracle form of low-cost book publishing but, if that were so, why aren't all the major commercial publishers distributing all of their books in this way? The disadvantages of POD include limited distribution and high print cost; these can work for many types of book, like specialist non-fiction titles or academic books that command high cover prices, but it can be difficult to make it cost-effective for mass market books.

At the other end of the scale, printing 3,000 copies of a novel will only pay off if you can get that book onto the retailers' shelves and in front of potential readers, or if you have some other form of 'captive' readership that you can reach with your marketing. Distribution to retailers works largely on the 'sale or return' model, using distribution companies and sales teams to sell new books to bookshops (and whatever you may have heard to the contrary, bookshops are still the largest sellers of books in the UK). If you can't get your book into that distribution chain, you are limiting the prospect of selling your 3,000 copies, and money tied up in unsaleable stock is wasted.

Publishing an ebook is also an increasingly popular method of self-publishing, but it too has its pros and cons. On the up side, it can be done very cheaply and quickly; the flip side is that, as hundreds of new ebooks are published each day, how do you get yours noticed? Making your ebook available through one retailer (e.g. Kobo) effectively limits your potential readership … what about readers with a Kindle, a Sony Reader or a Nook? How and where should you market your ebook?

As a self-publisher, you need to make sure you understand the limitations of each form of publishing method before you decide on the best route for your book(s). It can make the difference between success or failure for your book.

Choosing an author services company

In its truest sense, self-publishing means that you as author undertake all the processes undertaken by a commercial publisher to bring a book to market: editing, design, production, marketing, promotion and distribution. If you're multi-talented and have a lot of spare time, then you may want to do all of these things yourself, but for most authors it's a question of contracting an author services company to carry out some or all of the tasks required. It should be noted that most author services companies make their money by selling their services to you as the author; very few have a lot of market knowledge and even fewer offer any real form of active marketing or have a retail distribution set-up. Choosing the right company to work with is crucial in ensuring that your self-publishing expectations stand a chance of being met. Author services companies come in various guises, but they can broadly be broken into three categories:

• **DIY POD services.** You upload your manuscript and cover design, and your book (or ebook) is simply published 'as is'. It's relatively cheap, and great if you are not too concerned about the design quality of your book and POD or electronic distribution is what you want.

• **Assisted services companies.** These companies offer typesetting and cover design, and perhaps some limited distribution and marketing options. If you're looking for a better product and some basic help in selling your book then this could be right for you.

• **Full service companies.** These suppliers tend to work at the higher quality end of the self-publishing market, offering authoritative advice, bespoke design, active trade and media marketing and, in a couple of cases, real bookshop distribution options.

In addition, there is a plethora of companies and individuals offering component parts of the book production and marketing process, such as copy-editing, proofreading, cover design, public relations, etc.

The key for any self-publisher in choosing a company to work with is research. Having decided why you are self-publishing and set your expectations from doing so, the next step is to see who offers what, and at what cost, and to match the right company with what you are seeking. A search on the internet for 'self-publishing' will present you with many choices, so explore the company websites, compare what is being offered, and generally get a feel for what each says they do. Are they just selling services to authors, or are they selling their authors' books? Do they offer active marketing or just 'marketing advice'? Don't take their word for it, though: seek independent advice from other authors or independent industry commentators – there are plenty out there. Which companies are widely recommended by authors and experts alike, and which are not?

Having identified some services that look as if they will help you meet your publishing expectations, you need to establish how much it will cost. Get detailed quotations from companies and compare like-for-like. Ask questions of those companies if anything is in doubt: ask to see a contract; ask for a sample of their product (many companies still produce appalling quality books!). Talk to someone at each of the companies you are considering, and ask to speak to one of their current authors. Time spent at this stage will ensure that you get a good feel for the company you're considering working with, and that can be the difference between a happy self-publishing experience and a disastrous one.

Marketing and distribution

Authors often concentrate on producing a book or ebook and ignore the part of the equation that actually sells the book. Examine carefully what author services companies offer in this respect. Distribution includes all the processes involved in getting a book or ebook in front of potential readers, but many companies offer only a limited, online-only service. Marketing is the process of alerting both the media (whether in print, on air or online) and potential readers that a book is available. Similarly, very few companies spend much effort to actively market their authors' work. The right choice of marketing and distribution service can make or break a book even before production has started.

As the author and self-publisher, you must decide how the world will find out about your book, and how to get it into the hands of readers. You will need to make decisions on whether POD distribution or wider retail distribution is required; whether the marketing services offered by an author services company are enough for your book; or if a public relations company might be the way forward. And, of course, all of this has a cost implication.

A brave new world

Self-publishing offers authors a host of opportunities to get their projects published and available to readers. Making the right decisions to meet your expectations for your book or ebook in the early stages of the publishing process will pay dividends in ensuring both an enjoyable self-publishing experience, and one that successfully meets your goals.

Understand your motivations for self-publishing; set realistic expectations for your book or ebook; research the production options well; understand distribution choices; give marketing the importance it requires; and above all, enjoy your self-publishing experience!

Jeremy Thompson founded Troubador Publishing (www.troubador.co.uk) in 1996 and started the Matador (www.troubador.co.uk/matador) self-publishing imprint in 1999, which has since helped over 5,000 authors to self-publish. Troubador also publishes the *Self-Publishing Magazine* (quarterly, print and online), runs the annual Self-Publishing Conference and holds a 'Self-Publishing Experience' (in its third year in 2015). Troubador also runs Indie-Go (www.indie-go.co.uk), offering component author services, and Matador Distribution & Marketing, offering distribution and marketing to books published independently or using another self-publishing company.

Self-publishing providers

This is a selection of the ever-expanding list of companies that offer editorial, production, marketing and distribution support for authors who want to self-publish. As with all the organisations mentioned in the *Yearbook*, we recommend that you check carefully what companies offer and what they charge.

Acorn Independent Press Ltd

82 Southwark Bridge Road, London SE1 0AS
tel 020-3488 0820
email info@acornselfpublishing.com
website www.acornselfpublishing.com
Editorial Director Leila Dewji, *Sales & Marketing Director* Ali Dewji

Self-publishing service provider for authors at all stages of their careers. Offers three main packages, ranging from £1,100–£3,900, all of which come with personal service and the option to meet face-to-face prior and throughout the process.

Albury Books

Albury Court, Albury, Thame, Oxon OX9 2LP
tel (01844) 337000
email hannah@alburybooks.com
website www.alburybooks.com

International publishing house that collaborates with writers and illustrators to self-publish and/or re-publish their work through the Albury Bookshelf platform. Offers services for each stage of the publishing process including editing, illustration, layout and art direction. Provides ISBNs and print-on-demand or short print runs and co-edition deals. Also organises marketing campaigns and submissions for awards. Each book published is listed for sale in the Albury online store and made available to major booksellers. Founded 2013.

Amolibros

Loundshay Manor Cottage, Preston Bowyer, Milverton, Somerset TA4 1QF
tel (01823) 401527
email amolibros@aol.com
website www.amolibros.com
Director Jane Tatam

Offers print and ebook design, production, copy-editing, and distribution through online retailers. Sales and marketing services include design and production of adverts, leaflets, author websites, distribution of press releases, and direct mail campaigns.

Author House UK

1663 Liberty Drive, Bloomington, IN 47403, USA
tel 0800 197 4150
website www.authorhouse.co.uk

Offers editorial services, interior and cover design, illustration, marketing and publicity advice and distribution for hardcover and paperback print-on-demand books, as well as ebook conversion and distribution services. Colour and b&w publishing packages start at £499, speciality packages at £949 and ebook-only packages at £299.

Author Solutions

1663 Liberty Drive, Bloomington, IN 47403, USA
website www.authorsolutions.com

Owns several self-publishing imprints, including iUniverse, Author House, Author House UK, Palibrio, Xlibris, and Trafford Publishing. US-based. A Penguin Random House company.

authorization!

Well House, Green Lane, Ardleigh, Essex CO7 7PD
tel (01206) 233333
email martin-west@btconnect.com
website www.authorizationuk.com
Contact Martin West

Publishing services company specialising in children's picture books and fiction for ages 5–7, 7–9 and young adults.

The Better Book Company

5 Lime Close, Chichester, West Sussex PO19 6SW
tel 0800 907 0018
email betterbook@mac.com
website http://thebetterbookcompany.com

Offers interior and cover design, editing, proofreading and printing services. Two sets of proofs are sent to the author for approval prior to printing.

Blurb

website www.blurb.co.uk
Founder, President & Ceo Eileen Gittins

Provides downloadable book-making software, templates and customisable layouts for creating print books or ebooks with audio and video for iPad. Publications can be sold online through the Blurb bookshop and the iBookstore. Photobooks and trade books, novels or poetry can be printed in hardcover or softcover and in a variety of sizes. Prices are based on extent. Authors may retain 100% of the mark-up for a print book, or 80% of the retail price they set for an ebook sold through the Blurb bookstore; monies received from other retailers may vary. Discounts are available for volume orders on print books. For pricing details, see www.blurb.co.uk/pricing-calculator.

BookBaby
tel +1 503-961-6878
email books@bookbaby.com
website www.bookbaby.com

US-based provider offering ebook creation and distribution services as well as cover design and customisable author websites. BookBaby partners with Firstediting.com to provide editorial services. Its print operations offer printing services across a range of formats. A variety of products is available but pricing and commission levels vary; see website for full details.

BookPrinting UK
Remus House, Coltsfoot Drive, Woodston, Peterborough PE2 9BF
tel (01733) 898102
email info@bookprintinguk.com
website www.bookprintinguk.com

Offers colour and b&w printing and print-on-demand books in a range of bindings. Can provide custom illustration and interior layout options, as well as typesetting. Supplies templates for formatting manuscript files before sending. Can also distribute print books direct to customers. Prints bookmarks, posters and flyers.

CompletelyNovel
website http://completelynovel.com

Provides online publishing tools for authors to upload their manuscripts to create and distribute print-on-demand books and ebooks. A number of sales and distribution options are available. Website also offers a cover-creator option, as well as self-publishing advice on topics including editing, cover design and social media marketing.

CreateSpace
website www.createspace.com

Publishing engine of Amazon. Allows writers and users to self-publish and distribute books, DVDs, CDs and video downloads on demand.

ebook Versions
27 Old Gloucester Street, London WC1N 3AX
website www.ebookversions.com

Offers ebook self-publishing and distribution through online retailers including Kindle, Apple iBookstore, Kobo, Nook and WH Smith. Packages begin at £95 and are based on conversion of a manuscript of up to 100,000 words. Print-on-demand and distribution options are also available. Can convert different types of books including comics, scientific and technical to ebooks, and creates illustrated and reference ebooks for large screen tablets incorporating audio, video and interactivity.

Fast Print Publishing
9 Culley Court, Bakewell Road, Orton Southgate, Peterborough PE2 6XD
tel (01733) 404828
email info@fast-print.net
website www.fast-print.net

Print-on-demand and ebook self-publishing and distribution packages. Also proofreading (£11 per 1,000 words), page layout (£1.50 per 100 words), cover design and marketing services. Retail and distribution packages are also available to retailers including Waterstones, Amazon and Foyles.

Grosvenor House Publishing
Crossweys, 28–30 High Street, Guildford GU1 3EL
tel (01483) 243450
website www.grosvenorhousepublishing.co.uk
Co-founders Kim Cross, Jason Kosbab

Publishes for a range of genres including children's and non-fiction in colour, b&w, print-on-demand, paperback, hardback and ebook formats. Offers a £795 publishing package which includes typesetting and five free print copies as well as an ISBN and print and ebook distribution via online retailers. Authors can design covers online. Marketing services include producing posters and postcards, and website set-up from template with two years' hosting. Ebook publishing costs £195 if the print edition of the book has been produced by the company and £495 otherwise. Print costs and royalties depend on book specification. A proofreading service is offered at a rate of £5 per 1,000 words. See website for full list of costs.

The Hilary Johnson Authors' Advisory Service
3 Maple Drive, South Wootton, King's Lynn, Norfolk PE30 3JL
tel (01553) 676611
email enquiries@hilaryjohnson.com
email hilary@hilaryjohnson.demon.co.uk
website www.hilaryjohnson.demon.co.uk
Contact Hilary Johnson

Provides a manuscript reading and critique service for fiction, short-story, children's and non-fiction authors. Specialist advice for genres including science fiction, romance, crime, thrillers, film/TV/radio scripts and poetry. Additionally offers copy-editing and proofreading. Assessment of covering letter and synopsis before submitting to literary agents is also available. Advises on manuscript presentation.

I_AM Self-Publishing
82 Southwark Bridge Road, London SE1 0AS
tel 020-3488 0565
email hello@iamselfpublishing.com
website www.iamselfpublishing.com

Produces print books and ebooks for self-publishing authors. Services include: design, typesetting, editing, proofreading, print-on-demand and short-run printing in b&w and full colour, ebook conversion, author branding and backlist re-publication. Also

Books

offers an authors' marketing course. Authors can opt for either a global, managed distribution service to the major ebook retailers for an 80% royalty, or an Amazon-only option to retain 100% of royalties. Packages range from £400–£1,900. Works with large media organisations, literary agencies and individual authors alike.

iUniverse

1663 Liberty Drive, Bloomington, IN 47403, USA
tel +1 812-330-2909
website www.iuniverse.com

Offers editorial (proofreading/copy-editing), cover and interior design, production and marketing services. (Services are available on an individual basis.) Also offers assistance with publicity campaigns, including press release, video and social media, as well as print-on-demand and ebook self-publishing and distribution services through online retailers. Packages range from $899 (Select) to $4,299 (Book Launch).

Kindle Direct Publishing

website https://kdp.amazon.com

Ebook self-publishing and distribution platform for Kindle and Kindle Apps. Its business model offers up to a 70% royalty (on certain retail prices between $2.99–$9.99) in many countries and availability in Amazon stores worldwide. POD options are available through CreateSpace, an Amazon company (see www.createspace.com). Note that KDP Select makes books exclusive to Amazon (which means they cannot be sold through an author's personal website, for example), but authors can share in the Global Fund amount every time the book is borrowed from the Kindle Owners' Lending Library.

Kobo Writing Life

website www.kobo.com/writinglife

Ebook self-publishing platform where authors can upload manuscripts and cover images, and Kobo then coverts the files into ebooks before distributing them through the Kobo ebookstore. Authors are able to set pricing and DRM territories, as well as track sales. Royalty rates of either 70% or 45% are offered, depending on price or territory (see user guide for details). Free to join.

Lightning Source UK

Chapter House, Pitfield, Kiln Farm,
Milton Keynes MK11 3LW
tel 0845 121 4567
email enquiries@lightningsource.co.uk
website www.lightningsource.com

Established supplier and distributor of print-on-demand books and ebooks. No prices given on the website, but an exhaustive list of FAQs is provided.

Lulu

website www.lulu.com/gb

Self-publishing platform and distributor for ebooks and print-on-demand books through online retailers

including Amazon and iBooks. Authors can upload a file and design their own cover for free. Optional paid-for services include cover design, editorial, publicity services and associated materials. See website for full breakdown of costs and royalty information.

Matador

Troubador Publishing Ltd, 9 Priory Business Park, Wistow Road, Kibworth Beauchamp,
Leicester LE8 0RX
tel 0116 279 2299
email enquiries@troubador.co.uk
website www.troubador.co.uk/matador
Managing Director Jeremy Thompson

Offers print-on-demand, short-run digital- and litho-printed books and ebook production, with distribution through high-street bookshops and online retailers, plus worldwide ebook distribution. Author services include all book and ebook production, trade and retail marketing, plus bookshop distribution via Orca Book Services. Founded 1999.

Peppermint Books

Unit 2b, Church View Business Park,
Coney Green Road, Clay Cross, Chesterfield S45 9HA
tel (01246) 866165
email sales@peppermintbooks.co.uk
website www.peppermintbooks.co.uk

Produces short-run digitally printed perfect-bound paperback and hardback books in a variety of sizes, with a choice of different types of paper. Images can be included and ISBNs provided. A final proof copy is sent to the author before the complete order is printed. Cover design using stock or author-supplied images is also available for £225. See the website for a price calculator for paperback book production.

PublishNation

Suite 544, Kemp House, 152 City Road,
London EC1V 2NX
email david@publishnation.co.uk
website www.publishnation.co.uk
Publisher David Morrison

Offers print-on-demand paperback and Kindle format ebooks, available through Amazon. Publication in both print and digital formats costs £195 or £125 for Kindle format. Images may be included from £2.95 each. A range of book sizes is available, as are free template book covers. Enhanced cover design costs £40. Marketing services include creation of a press release, social media accounts and author website. Standard proofreading is £7 per 1,000 words, while an 'express' option from £125 focuses on the beginning of the manuscript. Editorial critique reports range in price from £99 for manuscripts of up to 15,000 words to £219 for manuscripts of up to 120,000 words.

SilverWood Books
14 Small Street, Bristol BS1 1DE
tel 0117 910 5829
email info@silverwoodbooks.co.uk
website www.silverwoodbooks.co.uk
Publishing Director Helen Hart

Offers bespoke author services tailored to an individual project, as well as three publishing packages, with prices dependent on specification. Services offered include cover and page design, typesetting, ebook hand-formatting and conversion, print-on-demand, short-run and lithographic printing, one-to-one support and coaching. Distributes to bookshops via wholesalers and to online retailers including Amazon. Also provides the Amazon Look Inside feature, and lists books in its own SilverWood online bookstore. UK wholesale distribution via Central Books. Nielsen Enhanced Data Listing. Marketing services include creating a press release, media target list, social media set-up, online book trailer campaign and virtual blog tours. Editorial services include an initial assessment and manuscript appraisal. Copy-editing from £7.30 per 1,000 words; proofreading from £6.75 per 1,000 words.

Wise Words Editorial
email info@wisewordseditorial.com
website www.wisewordseditorial.com

Provides proofreading services for fiction and non-fiction manuscripts and ebooks. Rate is £5/$8.50 per 1,000 words for proofreading documents over 50,000 words. Authors are sent a file showing edits as well as the final proofread file.

WRITERSWORLD
2 Bear Close Flats, Bear Close, Woodstock, Oxon OX20 1JX
tel (01993) 812500
email enquiries@writersworld.co.uk
website www.writersworld.co.uk
Founder & Owner Graham Cook

Book publisher specialising in self-publishing, print-on-demand books and book reprints. Also issues the ISBN on behalf of authors, pays them 100% of the royalties and supplies them with copies of their books at print cost. Established 2000.

Xlibris
Victory Way, Admirals Park, Crossways, Dartford, Kent DA2 6QD
tel 0800 056 3182
email info@xlibrispublishing.co.uk
website www.xlibrispublishing.co.uk

Established POD publisher, offering b&w, colour and speciality publishing packages, with prices starting at £599 (Basic). Speciality packages include poetry and children's. Services include design, editorial, ebook creation and distribution with online booksellers, website creation and marketing materials including a press release and book video. Royalties: 10% to author if sold via retail partner, and 25% if sold via Xlibris directly.

York Publishing Services
64 Hallfield Road, Layerthorpe, York YO1 7ZQ
tel (01904) 431213
email enqs@yps-publishing.co.uk
website www.yps-publishing.co.uk

Offers print and ebook publishing options, as well as distribution to bookshops and online retailers including Amazon. Services include copy-editing, proofreading, page and cover design, and printing. Provides page proofs and sample bound copy before main print run. Marketing services include compiling a press pack with press release sent to media; social media set-up (£250 plus VAT), posters and direct mail campaigns. Book is also listed on the YPS online bookstore. Printing and editing price dependent on specification. Ebook production costs £120 plus VAT; upload and account set-up with retailers £150 plus VAT.

Poetry
Flying the poetry flag

Poet and anthologist John Foster explains the difficulties faced by aspiring children's poets and offers practical advice on writing poetry for children.

Once upon a time, there was a teacher who enjoyed sharing poems with the children she taught. As well as reading them poems from books in the class library, she read some of the poems she had written herself. She was encouraged by their response and decided to see if she could get the poems published. She looked in publishers' catalogues and found that there were numerous anthologies of poetry for children, as well as a number of single author collections.

She chose a publisher and sent them her poems. The publisher liked the poems. But as she was unknown they did not think they could risk a single author collection. However, they thought her poems showed promise, so they forwarded them to one of their anthologists. Although the anthologist liked the poems too, they did not fit into the anthology that he was currently working on. But he added her to the list of contacts to whom he sent details of new anthologies, specifying the subject of the collection and the types of poem he was looking for. When he next did an anthology, she submitted a number of poems for consideration and the anthologist chose three of them to be included.

She managed to track down other anthologists and they sent her details of the anthologies they were compiling. She became a regular contributor to anthologies and an established name in the children's poetry world, and gave up full-time teaching so that she could accept invitations to visit schools to read her poems and run poetry workshops. She struggled to find a publisher to do a single author collection. But eventually she managed to get a collection published and it sold well on her school visits. She didn't make a fortune from writing children's poetry, but her success and the obvious enjoyment children got from her poems was gratifying.

That was how it was in the late 1980s, throughout the 1990s and in the early 2000s, when children's poetry was in fine fettle. How lucky she and the rest of us children's poets were then and how times have changed. Whereas in those days there were plenty of poetry books for children published annually, now there are only a few and new anthologies are a rarity.

Briefly, in 2010/11 it looked as if children's poetry might be making a comeback. Writing in the summer 2011 *Carousel* magazine (see page 337), Brian Moses heralded what he hoped was a new spring for children's poetry, spearheaded by the launch of a new poetry list by Salt Publishing and a new imprint from Frances Lincoln. However, the Salt Children's Poetry Library has failed to make an impact and, despite the best efforts of Macmillan, A&C Black and Frances Lincoln, children's poetry publishing remains in the doldrums.

What explains the dearth of new children's poetry books? There are a number of factors involved. But it has nothing to do with children's attitudes towards poetry. Children enjoy reading poetry as much as they did in the boom years of the 1990s. Children's poets are as much in demand at Book Weeks in schools as they have always been. They perform their poems to rapt audiences, who go on to get their parents to buy whatever poetry books they have managed to get publishers to publish or, in desperation, have self-published.

So why has children's poetry publishing declined? It is partly due to the attitude of booksellers. They argue that poetry books don't sell. Of course they don't, if they don't stock them. Walk into the children's section of a bookshop today and you'll find a handful of poetry books, often hidden away on the bottom shelf, alongside the joke books. In the past, you'd find a shelf full of poetry books at eye-level.

In the eyes of the book buyers, who control what is stocked in bookshops, children's poetry isn't fashionable at present. This has a knock-on effect. The publisher's sales team report back that poetry books don't sell, despite the evidence to the contrary from the travelling poets, who sell hundreds of pounds' worth of their books during their school visits. So the publishers only publish a fraction of the poetry books that they used to. It's a vicious circle.

And the economic climate doesn't help. A full-colour poetry book aimed at younger children is like a picture book in terms of how much it costs to produce. But poetry doesn't translate in the way that stories do, so it isn't possible to sell foreign rights as a way of recouping the costs of production. It can be hard for a commissioning editor to convince the publishing committee to back a poetry project that will not make much money on the first printing.

The aspiring children's poet faces a daunting task. There aren't the anthologies that it was possible to contribute to in the past and it is even harder these days to get a single author collection accepted. But if you are determined to write children's poetry, here are a few tips.

Get inspired by children

Starting with the most obvious, get to know children's language. If you are writing about an experience from a child's point of view, you must get the language right. It is, perhaps, not surprising that many of the most successful children's poets are from a teaching background – for example, Tony Mitton, Wes Magee, Judith Nicholls, Paul Cookson and Brian Moses. Teachers not only know what children's interests are, but they also know how children think and how they express themselves. Steep yourself in children's language, not just the language of your children and those of your friends, but of children from all sorts of backgrounds and cultures.

Try to arrange to visit schools in different areas. But always go through the correct channels with a letter to the literacy co-ordinator, copied to the headteacher, explaining the reasons you would like to visit. Schools these days are, quite rightly, very security-conscious.

If you are visiting a school, you can offer to run a writing workshop. You have the opportunity to try out your poems too. There's nothing like a deafening wall of silence greeting that punchline which you thought they would find so amusing to let you know that, in fact, the poem doesn't work!

Visiting schools is also worthwhile because you can bring yourself up to date with how poetry is being used in the classroom. For example, the new curriculum requires that pupils learn poems by heart. Literacy co-ordinators will therefore be on the lookout for new performance poems. There is an educational as well as a trade market for children's poems and it is worth knowing what the educational publishers might be looking for.

Schools are also a good source of ideas. Many a poem comes from a child's tale or a teacher's comment. In one school, I met a girl called Alison, who told me what had happened when she tried to pull a loose tooth out with a piece of string. So I went home and wrote this poem, 'When Allie Had a Loose Tooth':

When Allie had a loose tooth
She did as her dad said.
She went into the kitchen
And found a piece of thread.
She tied it round the tooth.
She tied it to the door.
But when she slammed the door shut,
The knob fell on the floor.

Appealing to the reader

Visiting schools will also give you an idea of what interests children have and what subjects to write about. Then it's up to you to think of something that will appeal to them. But a word of warning: be careful of being risqué just to appeal to the reader. Avoid being rude for the sake of it, and especially don't be crude. Besides, you could easily get yourself labelled! During a performance in Glasgow, I included two poems which made references to 'bottoms' and 'knickers', getting the usual delighted response from the audience. However, I was taken aback when I asked them to suggest why publishers won't allow me to illustrate my poetry books. Instead of giving me the expected – and correct – answer that my drawings are no good, the first boy that I asked said: 'Because your poems are dirty!'

You want your poems to stand out for some reason, so try to come up with something that is different. One way of making your poem stand out is to write it in a more unusual form. For example, say you are going to write a poem about St George and the dragon, instead of writing it in couplets, you could write it in the form of an encyclopedia entry, as a series of entries in St George's diary or even as a text message. Try experimenting with forms, not just haiku and cinquains but triolets, villanelles and univolics. You can find examples in *The Works 8 – Every shape, style and form of poem that you could ever need for the Literacy Hour* (Macmillan 2009).

Children enjoy the ridiculous and the bizarre, but getting an idea can be hard. If you are stuck for a humorous idea, one way of trying to find one is to look through a book of jokes. I was racking my brains to think of an idea for a new poem to include in a book of magic poems, when I came across this joke: Why are the ghosts of magicians no good at conjuring? Because you can see right through their tricks! This led to:

The ghost of the magician said:
'I'm really in a fix.
The trouble is the audience
Sees right through all my tricks!'

I learned a great deal about how to write children's poetry by being an anthologist. So study the work of established children's poets and learn, for example, about how to play

Poetry

with words by reading Roger McGough's poems and about how to write storypoems as dramatic monologues by reading Michael Rosen's poems. You can get ideas, too, from researching what established poets have written. Two of my nonsense poems, both of which are well received in schools, 'The Land of the Flibbertigibbets' and 'On the Clip, Clop Clap' were inspired by Spike Milligan poems – 'The Land of the Bumbly Boo' and 'On the Ning Nang Nong'.

If you get the opportunity, go along to a school, library or festival at which a children's poet is performing. In addition to listening to what they have to say, you may be able to talk to them afterwards. But don't expect them necessarily to be prepared to look at your poems and to give you a free tutorial on how to write children's poetry.

It's also worth looking at the websites of established writers. One particularly useful website is The Poetry Zone (www.poetryzone.co.uk), set up by the poet Roger Stevens. It consists of articles about writing children's poetry, as well as reviews and interviews with children's poets. The children's section of the Poetry Archive (www.poetryarchive.org) is worth visiting too.

Getting into print

So how does the aspiring children's poet get published? As I've explained, it's far harder now than it used to be, in the days when there were lots of anthologies being published. One way is to do it yourself. Self-publishing is not as expensive as it used to be. You can get 500 copies of an A5 booklet printed for around £500 and, if you get onto the school circuit, you can sell them directly yourself and more than cover your costs.

Then, there's the internet. You can post your poems on a website. You won't, of course, make any money from doing so and once the poems are out there, then there's the danger that someone else will copy them and claim to have written them. But at least they'll be there for people to read.

You can also consider publishing your poems as an ebook. But there are so many other books available as ebooks that you probably won't sell many copies.

It's not easy for the aspiring children's poet to get recognised at present and you certainly won't make a fortune. But children's poetry is far from dead, as the enthusiastic audiences that greet visiting poets in schools show. So good luck! Keep writing. Visit schools and fly the poetry flag. Join the campaign for a national poetry month, such as exists in the USA. Children's poetry may not be as fashionable as it once was, but it's far from finished!

John Foster's collection of his own poems *The Poetry Chest* is published by Oxford University Press. His latest books include *How Do You Make a Skeleton Laugh?* (OUP 2012) and *What Do You Call a One-eyed Dinosaur?* (OUP 2013). He has collaborated with Korky Paul on the forthcoming *A Rocketful of Space Poems* (Frances Lincoln). His website is www.johnfosterchildrenspoet.co.uk.

See also...

- *An interview with my shadow,* page 215
- *Poetry organisations,* page 217

Poetry

An interview with my shadow
Brian Patten talks about writing poetry.

Who are you?
I'm your shadow.

What's that you're eating?
It's the shadow of an apple.

Surely shadows can't detach themselves from walls and eat shadow-apples?
They can if they are writers' and poets' shadows.

Why do you write for children as well as for adults?
I don't know, it just happened that way. But I really do believe that writing for one is no easier than writing for the other. If somebody tries to write for adults and finds they aren't any good at it, then they will very likely be even worse at writing for children.

Can you really appreciate poetry at seven or even 11 years old?
Of course you can! Adults have no monopoly on feelings. I suspect that many adults never feel as intensely about things as they did when they were younger.

What are the best kinds of things to write about?
You can write about anything you want. Sometimes the weirder the better. At ten you will probably write very different poems than when you're 14 and when you are 40 you'll write different poems again.

How about telling stories through poems?
Very short stories, yes. But not long stories. For long stories children prefer prose, and quite rightly I think. Part of poetry is to do with condensing, not expanding. It is different if you are writing a series of poems about the same character or about a particular situation or unusual creatures, or seeing certain themes from different angles. Then snapshots can build up into a story. But there have been very few successful long story-poems written for children.

I thought poets were supposed to be daydreamers. Some people think poetry is a bit soft.
Modern poetry for children is usually anarchic – anything but soft. Having said this, there is an awful lot of bad so-called 'children's poetry' about. Almost as much as bad 'adult poetry'.

How so?
Well, there is more rhyme and word play in contemporary children's poetry than in contemporary adult poetry. People can make things rhyme, but they either don't or can't work on the scansion, and then the whole metrical structure falls apart. People who think they can get away with writing sloppy verse simply because it's for children are deluding themselves. No matter how good an idea, it is the execution of the work that brings it to life.

Did you intend that last sentence to be ironic?
Yes. And it is true. Would-be writers forget it at their peril! Children won't be fobbed off with lazy work.

Poetry

Why did you begin writing poetry? Did anyone teach you?

No, one day I just started writing things down. You see, as a child I lived in this tiny house with three adults. They were all unhappy people. My mother was young and couldn't afford a place of her own, so we lived with my grandmother. My grandmother wore callipers and she dragged herself round the house by her hands. I remember thinking they were like talons.

What has this got to do with poetry and beginning to write it?

Everybody in that little house was miserable and they didn't talk to each other, and although they knew they were miserable and why they were miserable, they couldn't explain why.

You mean they could not express themselves?

Yes, and because they could not express themselves they kept everything walled up inside them, where it hurt and festered for want of light.

Were you like this as well?

To begin with. I don't know how it happened, or why, but I realised the only way I could express my feelings was by writing them down. I think that is how I started to become a poet. I began writing down what I felt. So really, I began writing poetry before I even began reading it. I needed to express my feelings and writing poetry was like writing a very intense diary.

Would you say you were a 'real' poet at that age? I mean, when you began writing did you think that you would ever become a professional poet?

No. That happened when I began changing words and moving lines around. When you begin to *make* something out of the words is when the professional element comes into play. A good poem is something that carries your feelings and ideas inside it. People remember a good poem because of the way it is written, just as much as because of what it says.

Would you like a bit of my apple?

I'm not sure. What does a shadow-apple taste like?

Brian Patten was born in Liverpool and writes poetry for adults and children. His recent books for adults are *Collected Love Poems* (Harper Perennial 2007) and *Selected Poems* (Penguin 2007), and for children, *The Big Snuggle-Up* (2011) and *Can I Come Too?* (2013), both illustrated by Nicola Bayley and published by Andersen Press. His website is www.brianpatten.co.uk.

See also...
• *Flying the poetry flag*, page 211
• *Poetry organisations*, page 217

Poetry organisations

Poetry is one of the easiest writing art forms to begin with, though the hardest to excel at or earn any money from. Below are some organisations which can help poets take their poetry further.

WHERE TO GET INVOLVED

The British Haiku Society

Flat 4, 2 Clifton Lawn, Ramsgate, Kent, CT11 9PB
email membership@britishhaikusociety.org.uk
website www.britishhaikusociety.org.uk

The Society runs the prestigious annual James W. Hackett International Haiku Award and the annual British Haiku awards in two categories – haiku and haibun. It is active in promoting the teaching of haiku in schools and colleges, and is able to provide readers, course/workshop leaders and speakers for poetry groups, etc. Founded 1990.

Literature Wales

(formerly Academi)
Cambrian Buildings, Mount Stuart Square,
Cardiff Bay, Cardiff CF10 5FL
tel 029-2047 2266
email post@literaturewales.org
website www.literaturewales.org

The Welsh National Literature Promotion Agency, which has a huge resource available for poets and poetry. It organises events and tours, promotes poets and poetry, offers poetry advice, locates poetry publishers, offers financial help to poets and to organisers wishing to book poets, and much more. To take advantage of its services you have to live or be in Wales, which has the largest number of poets per 1,000 population anywhere in the western world.

The Poetry Book Society

The Dutch House, 307–308 High Holborn,
London WC1V 7LL
tel 020-7831 7468
email info@poetrybooks.co.uk
website www.poetrybooks.co.uk
website www.poetrybookshoponline.com
website www.childrenspoetrybookshelf.co.uk

This unique book club for readers of poetry was founded in 1953 by T.S. Eliot, and is funded by the Arts Council England. Every quarter, selectors choose one outstanding publication (the PBS Choice), and recommend 4 other titles; these are sent to members, who are also offered substantial discounts on other poetry books. The Poetry Book Society also administers the T.S. Eliot Prize, produces the quarterly membership magazine, the *Bulletin*, and has an education service providing teaching materials for primary and secondary schools.

The Poetry Business

Bank Street Arts, 32–40 Bank Street, Sheffield S1 2DS
tel 0114 346 3037

email office@poetrybusiness.co.uk
website www.poetrybusiness.co.uk

Dedicated to helping writers reach their full potential by running supportive workshops.

Poetry Can

12 Great George Street, Bristol BS1 5RH
tel 0117 933 0900
email admin@poetrycan.co.uk
website www.poetrycan.co.uk

Literature organisation specialising in poetry. It organises events such as the Bristol Poetry Festival, runs a lifelong learning programme and offers information and advice in all aspects of poetry.

Poetry Ireland

32 Kildare Street, Dublin 2, Republic of Ireland
tel +353 (0)1 6789815
email info@poetryireland.ie
website www.poetryireland.ie

Poetry Ireland is the national organisation dedicated to developing, supporting and promoting poetry throughout Ireland. It is the only professional and dedicated national organisation for literature in Ireland. For over 35 years the organisation has supported poets and writers at all stages of their careers through both performance and publication opportunities, creating meaningful encounters between writers and the public. The organisation delivers through four core strands: Publication, Readings, the provision of an Information & Resource Service, and Education & Outreach. Through its Education & Outreach remit, Poetry Ireland offers a broad spectrum of services within the literary arts – from poetry to children's fiction, storytelling and drama.

The Poetry Society

22 Betterton Street, London WC2H 9BX
tel 020-7420 9880
email info@poetrysociety.org.uk
website www.poetrysociety.org.uk

The Poetry Society is Britain's leading voice for poets and poetry. Founded in 1909 to promote a more general recognition and appreciation of poetry, the Society has nearly 4,000 members. With innovative education, commissioning and publishing programmes, and a packed calendar of performances, readings and competitions, the Society champions poetry in its many forms.

The Society also publishes education resources for teachers and educators; organises high-profile events including an Annual Lecture and National Poetry Day celebrations; runs Poetry Prescription, a critical appraisal service; and provides an education advisory service, INSET packages for schools and networks of schools, a poets in schools service, school membership, youth membership and a website.

A diverse range of events and readings take place at the Poetry Café beneath the Society's headquarters in London's Covent Garden. The Society also programmes events and readings throughout the UK.

Competitions run by the Society include the annual National Poetry Competition, with a first prize of £5,000; the biennial Corneliu M. Popescu Prize for Poetry Translated from a European Language into English; the Ted Hughes Award for New Work in Poetry; SLAMbassadors UK; and the Foyle Young Poets of the Year Award.

Tower Poetry

Christ Church, Oxford OX1 1DP
tel (01865) 286591
email info@towerpoetry.org.uk
website www.towerpoetry.org.uk

Tower Poetry exists to encourage and challenge everyone who reads or writes poetry. Funded by a generous bequest to Christ Church, Oxford, by the late Christopher Tower, the aims of Tower Poetry are to stimulate an enjoyment and critical appreciation of poetry, particularly among young people in education, and to challenge people to write their own poetry.

WHERE TO GET INFORMATION

Your local library is a good first port of call, and should have information about the poetry scene in the area. Many libraries are actively involved in speading the word about poetry as well as having modern poetry available for loan. Local librarians promote writing activities with, for example, projects like Poetry on Loan and Poetry Places information points in West Midlands Libraries.

Alliance of Literary Societies (ALS)

email ljc1049@gmail.com
website www.allianceofliterarysocieties.org.uk
President Jenny Uglow

The ALS is the umbrella organisation for literary societies and groups in the UK. Formed in 1973, it provides support and advice on a variety of literary subjects, as well as promoting cooperation between member societies. Its journal, *ALSo…*, appears annually. Founded 1973.

Arts Council England

Head Office 21 Bloomsbury Street,
London WC1B 3HF
tel 0845 300 6200
email enquiries@artscouncil.org.uk
website www.artscouncil.org.uk

Arts Council England has 9 regional offices and local literature officers can provide information on local poetry groups, workshops and societies (see page 391). Some give grant aid to local publishers and magazines and help fund festivals, literature projects and readings, and some run critical services.

Arts Council of Wales

Bute Place, Cardiff CF10 5AL
tel 0845 8734 900
email info@artswales.org.uk
website www.artswales.org.uk

The Arts Council of Wales is an independent charity, established by Royal Charter in 1994. It has three regional offices and its principal sponsor is the Welsh Government. It is the country's funding and development agency for the arts, supporting and developing high-quality arts activities. Its funding schemes offer opportunities for arts organisations and individuals in Wales to apply, through a competitive process, for funding towards a clearly defined arts-related project.

National Association of Writers' Groups (NAWG)

65 Riverside Mead, Peterborough PE2 8JN
email chris.huck@ymail.com
website www.nawg.co.uk

NAWG aims to bring cohesion and fellowship to isolated writers' groups and individuals, promoting the study and art of writing in all its aspects. There are many affiliated groups and associate (individual) members across the UK.

The Northern Poetry Library

Morpeth Library, Gas House Lane, Morpeth, Northumberland NE61 1TA
tel (01670) 620390
email morpethlibrary@northumberland.gov.uk
website www.northumberland.gov.uk

The Northern Poetry Library is the largest collection of contemporary poetry outside London and houses over 15,000 titles and magazines covering poetry published since 1945. Founded 1968.

The Poetry Trust

9 New Cut, Halesworth, Suffolk IP19 8BY
tel (01986) 835950
email info@thepoetrytrust.org
www.thepoetrytrust.org

The Poetry Trust is one of the UK's flagship poetry organisations, delivering a year-round live and digital programme, creative education opportunities, courses, prizes and publications. Over the last decade the Poetry Trust has been running creative workshops for teachers, and this extensive experience has been condensed into a free user-friendly handbook (pdf download), *The Poetry Toolkit*. The Trust also produces *The Poetry Paper*, featuring exclusive interviews and poems.

The Scottish Poetry Library

5 Crichton's Close, Canongate, Edinburgh EH8 8DT
tel 0131 557 2876
email reception@spl.org.uk
website www.scottishpoetrylibrary.org.uk

The Scottish Poetry Library is the place for poetry in Scotland for the regular reader, the serious student or the casual browser. It houses over 40,000 items: books, magazines, pamphlets, recordings and the Edwin Morgan Archive of his published works. The core of the collection is contemporary poetry written in Scotland, in Scots, Gaelic and English, but historic Scottish poetry as well as contemporary works from almost every part of the world are also available. All resources, advice and information are readily accessible, free of charge. The SPL holds regular poetry events, including reading and writing groups, details of which are available on the library website. Closed Saturday, Sunday and Monday. Founded 1984.

ONLINE RESOURCES

There is a wealth of information available for poets at the click of a mouse: the suggestions below are a good starting point.

British-Irish Poets

website www.jiscmail.ac.uk/cgi-bin/
webadmin?A0=BRITISH-IRISH-POETS

Email discussion list (innovative poetry).

The Children's Poetry Archive

website http://childrenspoetryarchive.org

World's premier online collection of recordings of poets reading their work. Visitors to the website may listen, free of charge, to the voices of contemporary English-language poets and of poets from the past. Featured poets include Allan Ahlberg, Roald Dahl and Jackie Kay, but the Archive is added to regularly.

LoveReading4Kids

website www.lovereading4kids.co.uk

Recommendation site for children's literature from toddlers to teens.

The Poetry Kit

website www.poetrykit.org

Collates a wide variety of poetry-related information, including events, competitions, courses and more, for an international readership.

Poetry Space

website www.poetryspace.co.uk

Specialist publisher of poetry and short stories, as well as news and features, edited by Susan Jane Sims. Operates as a social enterprise with all profits being used to publish online and in print, and to hold events to widen participation in poetry. Submissions of poems, stories novel extracts, photographs and artwork accepted all year for Young Writers' and Artists' Space – online (18s and under). Please e-mail Eleanor Bennett (eleanor@poetryspace.co.uk). Founded 2010.

The Poetry Toolkit

website www.thepoetrytrust.org

The Poetry Trust has been running creative workshops for teachers for over a decade, and this extensive experience has been condensed into a free user-friendly handbook (pdf download), *The Poetry Toolkit*.

Seven Stories – National Centre for Children's Books

website www.sevenstories.org.uk

Seven Stories is the only place in the United Kingdom dedicated to the art of children's books. Its website features a blog and online catalogue that may be of use for researchers and authors.

Teachit: English Teaching Resources

website www.teachit.co.uk

Free online library for English, media and drama teachers, offering teaching packs, worksheets, lesson plans, online lessons and useful links. Covers Key Stages 3, 4 and 5. Online bookshop also.

Write Out Loud

website www.writeoutloud.net/directory

Directory listing publications, festivals, competitions and other poetry resources.

WHERE TO CELEBRATE POETRY

Festival information should be available from Arts Council England offices (see page 391). See also *Children's literature festivals and trade fairs* on page 419.

The British Council

10 Spring Gardens, London SW1A 2BN
tel 020-7389 3194
email general.enquiries@britishcouncil.org
website http://literature.britishcouncil.org

Visit the website for a list of forthcoming festivals.

StAnza: Scotland's International Poetry Festival

email info@stanzapoetry.org
website www.stanzapoetry.org

StAnza is international in outlook. It is held each March in St Andrews, Scotland's oldest university town. The festival is an opportunity to engage with a wide variety of poetry, to hear world-class poets reading in exciting and atmospheric venues, to experience a range of performances where music, film, dance and poetry work in harmony, to view exhibitions linking poetry with visual art and to discover the part poetry has played in the lives of a diverse range of writers, musicians and media personalities. The simple intention of StAnza is to celebrate poetry in all its forms. Founded 1988.

COMPETITIONS

There are now hundreds of competitions to enter and as the prizes increase, so does the prestige associated with winning such competitions as the National Poetry Competition.

To decide which competitions are worth entering, make sure you know who the judges are and think twice before paying large sums for an anthology of 'winning' poems which will only be read by entrants wanting to see their own work in print. The Poetry Library publishes a list of competitions each month (available free on receipt of a large sae).

Literary prizes are given annually to published poets and as such are non-competitive. An A–Z guide to literary prizes can be found on the Book Trust website (www.booktrust.org.uk/prizes).

WHERE TO WRITE POETRY

Apples and Snakes
The Albany, Douglas Way, London SE8 4AG
tel 0845 521 3460
email info@applesandsnakes.org
website www.applesandsnakes.org

Organisation for performance poetry in England, with a reputation for producing innovative work that raises the profile of spoken word and pushes the boundaries of the artform for artists, audiences and participants. Runs a variety of programmes for poets, including participatory workshops. Founded 1982.

Arvon
Lumb Bank – The Ted Hughes Arvon Centre,
Heptonstall, Hebden Bridge,
West Yorkshire HX7 6DF
tel (01422) 843714
email lumbbank@arvon.org
Totleigh Barton, Sheepwash, Beaworthy, Devon EX21 5NS
tel (01409) 231338
email totleighbarton@arvon.org
The Hurst – The John Osborne Arvon Centre,
Clunton, Craven Arms, Shrops. SY7 0JA
tel (01588) 640658
email thehurst@arvon.org
website www.arvon.org

Arvon's three centres run five-day residential courses throughout the year for anyone over the age of 16, providing the opportunity to live and work with professional writers. Writing genres explored include poetry, narrative, drama, writing for children, song-writing and the performing arts. Bursaries are available to those receiving benefits. Founded 1968.

Cannon Poets
22 Margaret Grove, Harborne, Birmingham B17 9JH
Meets at The Moseley Exchange, The Post Office Building, 149–153 Alcester Road, Moseley, Birmingham B13 8JP usually on the first Sunday of each month (except August) at 2pm
website www.cannonpoets.org.uk

Cannon Poets have met monthly since 1983. The group encourages poetry writing through:

• workshops run by members or visitors
• break-out groups where poems are subjected to scrutiny by supportive peer groups
• 10-minute slots where members read a selection of their poems to the whole group
• publication of its journal, The Cannon's Mouth (quarterly).

Members are encouraged to participate in poetry events and competitions.

City Lit
Keeley Street, London WC2B 4BA
tel 020-7492 2600
email infoline@citylit.ac.uk
website www.citylit.ac.uk

Offers classes on poetry appreciation as well as practical workshops.

Kent & Sussex Poetry Society
Camden Centre, Market Square, Tunbridge Wells, Kent TN1 2SW
email info@kentandsussexpoetrysociety.org
website www.kentandsussexpoetry.com
Secretary Mary Gurr

A local group with a national reputation. Organises monthly poetry readings (third Tuesday of each month), workshops and an annual poetry competition.

The Poetry School
81 Lambeth Walk, London SE11 6DX
tel 020-7582 1679
website www.poetryschool.com

Teaches the art and craft of writing poetry (to adults, with very occasional focus on children's poetry). Offers courses, small groups and one-to-one tutorials, from one-day workshops to year-long courses, in London and in other city locations across England. Activities for beginners to advanced writers, both unpublished and published. Face-to-face, downloadable and online activities. Three new programmes a year plus social network for poets at www.campus.poetryschool.com.

Shortlands Poetry Circle

Ripley Arts Centre, 24 Sundridge Avenue, Bromley
tel (01689) 811394
email shortlands@poetrypf.co.uk
website www.poetrypf.co.uk/shortlands.html, https://
shortlandspoetrycircle.wordpress.com (blog)

Tŷ Newydd

Llanystumdwy, Cricieth, Gwynedd LL52 0LW
tel (01766) 522811
email tynewydd@literaturewales.org
website www.tynewydd.org

Tŷ Newydd runs residential writing courses
encompassing a wide variety of genres, including
poetry, and caters for all levels, from beginners to
published poets. All the courses are tutored by
published writers. Writing retreats are also available.

HELP FOR YOUNG POETS AND TEACHERS

National Association of Writers in Education (NAWE)

PO Box 1, Sheriff Hutton, York YO60 7YU
tel/fax (01653) 618429
email pjohnston@nawe.co.uk
website www.nawe.co.uk
Deputy Director Anne Caldwell

National organisation which aims to widen the scope
of writing in education, and coordinate activities
between writers, teachers and funding bodies. It
publishes the magazine *Writing in Education* and has
created a writers' database that can identify writers
who fit the given criteria (e.g. speaks several
languages, works well with special needs, etc.) for
schools, colleges and the community. Publishes
*Reading the Applause: Reflections on Performance
Poetry by Various Artists*. Write for membership
details. NAWE's mission is to further knowledge,
understanding and enjoyment of creative writing and
to support good practice in its teaching and learning
at all levels. NAWE promotes creative writing as both
a distinct discipline and an essential element in
education generally. Its membership includes those
working in Higher Education, the many freelance
writers working in schools and community contexts,
and the teachers and other professionals who work
with them. NAWE incorporates The Writer's
Compass (formerly literaturetraining), providing
information and advice on professional development
for writers and other literature professionals. It runs a
national database of writers, publishes two journals –
Writing in Education and *Writing in Practice* – and
holds a national conference.

Poetry Society Education

The Poetry Society, 22 Betterton Street,
London WC2H 9BX
tel 020-7420 9880
email education@poetrysociety.org.uk
website www.poetrysociety.org.uk/education

The Poetry Society has an outstanding reputation for
its exciting and innovative education work. For over
30 years it has been introducing poets into
classrooms, providing comprehensive teachers'
resources and producing lively, accessible
publications for pupils. It develops projects and
schemes to keep poetry flourishing in schools,
libraries and workplaces, giving work to hundreds of
poets and allowing thousands of children and adults
to experience poetry for themselves.

Through projects such as the SLAMbassadors UK,
the Foyle Young Poets of the Year Award and Young
Poets Network, the Poetry Society gives valuable
encouragement and exposure to young writers and
performers.

Schools membership offers Poetry Society
publications, books and posters, a subscription to
Poems on the Underground and free access to a
consultancy service giving advice on working with
poets in the classroom. Youth membership is
available (for age 11–18; £15 p.a.) and offers
discounts, publications, poetry books and posters.

The Poetry Trust – see The Poetry Trust on page 218

The Saison Poetry Library (Children's Collection)

Level 5, Royal Festival Hall, London SE1 8XX
tel 020-7921 0664
email info@poetrylibrary.org.uk
website www.poetrylibrary.org.uk

The Children's Collection comprises c. 20,000 items
for young poets of all ages, including poetry on CD
and DVD. The library has an education service for
teachers and writing groups, with a separate
collection of books and materials for teachers and
poets who work with children in schools. Group
visits can be organised inviting children to interact
with the collection in various ways, from taking a
Poetry Word Trail across Southbank Centre, to
exploring how the worlds of science and poetry
interact, and from engaging with war poetry via the
Letters Home booklet to becoming a Poetry Library
Poetry Explorer. Nursery schools can also book a Rug
Rhymes session for under-5s. Children of all ages can
join for free and borrow books and other materials. A
special membership scheme is available for teachers
to borrow books for the classroom. Contact the
library for membership details and opening hours.

Young Poets Network

website www.youngpoetsnetwork.org.uk

Online resource from The Poetry Society comprising
features about reading, writing and performing
poetry, plus new work by young poets and regular
writing challenges. Aimed at young people up to 25.

YOUNG POETRY COMPETITIONS

Children's competitions are included in the
competition list provided by the Poetry Library (free
on receipt of a large sae).

Poetry

Foyle Young Poets of the Year Award

The Poetry Society, 22 Betterton Street,
London WC2H 9BX
tel 020-7420 9880
email education@poetrysociety.org.uk
website www.poetrysociety.org.uk/content/
competitions/fyp

Free entry for children aged 11–17 years with unique prizes. Annual competition. Poems must be written in English. Opens March and closes for entries on the 31st July each year. Founded 2001.

SLAMbassadors UK

The Poetry Society, 22 Betterton Street,
London WC2H 9BX
tel 020-7429 9894, 020-7420 4818, 07847 378892,
07847 372 892
email jtaylor@poetrysociety.org.uk
website http://slam.poetrysociety.org.uk
Contact Joelle Taylor

An annual poetry slam championship for 12–18-year-olds. Young people across the UK are invited to enter by filming themselves performing a spoken word piece or rap and submitting it online for consideration by judges. Prizes include the opportunity to perfom at a showcase event, workshops with respected spoken word artists and further professional development opportunities. Established 2002.

Christopher Tower Poetry Prize

Christ Church, Oxford OX1 1DP
tel (01865) 286591
email info@towerpoetry.org.uk
website www.towerpoetry.org.uk/prize/

An annual poetry competition (open from November to March) from Christ Church, Oxford, open to 16–18 year-olds in UK schools and colleges. The poems should be no longer than 48 lines, on a different chosen theme each year. Prizes: £3,000 (1st), £1,000 (2nd), £500 (3rd). Every winner also receives a prize for his or her school.

FURTHER READING

Chisholm, Alison, *The Craft of Writing Poetry*, Allison & Busby, 1997, repr. 2001

Chisholm, Alison, *A Practical Poetry Course*, Allison & Busby, 1994, o.p.

Corti, Doris, *Writing Poetry*, Writers News Library of Writing/Thomas & Lochar, 1994

Fairfax, John, and John Moat, *The Way to Write*, Penguin Books, 2nd edn revised, 1998

Greene, Roland, *et al.*, *Princeton Encyclopedia of Poetry and Poetics*, Princeton University Press, 4th edn, 2012

Hamilton, Ian, *The Oxford Companion to Twentieth-century Poetry*, Clarendon Press, 1994

Livingstone, Dinah, *Poetry Handbook for Readers and Writers*, Macmillan, 1993, o.p.

Maxwell, Glyn, *On Poetry*, Oberon Books, 2012

Padel, Ruth, *52 Ways of Looking at a Poem: A Poem for Every Week of the Year*, Vintage, 2004

Padel, Ruth, *The Poem and the Journey: 60 Poems for the Journey of Life*, Vintage, 2008

Reading the Applause: Reflections on Performance Poetry by Various Artists, Talking Shop, 1999

Riggs, Thomas (ed.), *Contemporary Poets*, St James Press, 7th edn, 2003

Roberts, Philip Davies, *How Poetry Works*, Penguin Books, 2nd edn, 2000

Sampson, Fiona, *Writing Poetry: The Expert Guide*, Robert Hale, 2009

Sansom, Peter, *Writing Poems*, Bloodaxe, 1993, reprinted 1997

Sweeney, Matthew and John Hartley Williams, *Write Poetry and Get It Published*, Hodder and Stoughton, 2010

Whitworth, John, *Writing Poetry*, A&C Black, 2nd edn, 2006

See also...

• *Flying the poetry flag*, page 211
• *Interview with my shadow*, page 215

Literary agents
How to get an agent

Because children's publishing is highly competitive and the market is crowded, in this article Philippa Milnes-Smith explains that finding an agent isn't child's play.

If you have ambitions to be a children's writer or illustrator, do not think that the process of getting published will be any easier than for the adult market. It's just as tough, if not tougher, partly because a lot of writers and would-be writers see writing for children as an easy option. It can't be that difficult to write a kid's book, can it? After all, it is just for kids …

Nowadays, too, there is extra competition in the children's field: the high profile of successes since J.K. Rowling's *Harry Potter* series and Philip Pullman's *His Dark Materials* have drawn the attention of many professional writers who have previously only written for the adult market and who see it as a new and lucrative area for their talents. Celebrities from all parts of the globe and from every field, from soap to sport to YouTube sensations, have also entered the fray. The children's market is both crowded and highly competitive.

So, what is a literary agent and why would I want one?

If you can answer a confident 'yes' to all the questions below, and have the time, resources and inclination to devote to the business side of being an author, you possibly don't need an agent.

• Do you have a thorough understanding of the publishing market and its dynamics?
• Do you know who are the best publishers for your book and why? Can you evaluate the pros and cons of each? Do you know the best editors within these publishers?
• Are you up to navigating the fast-changing world of digital publishing?
• Are you financially numerate and confident of being able to negotiate the best commercial deal available in current market conditions?
• Are you confident of being able to understand fully and negotiate a publishing or other media contract?
• Do you know the other opportunities for your work beyond publishing and how these might be exploited? Could you deal with the complexities of a franchise?
• Do you enjoy the process of selling yourself and your work?

An agent's job is to deal with all of the above on your behalf. A good agent will do all of these well – and let you get on with the important creative work of being an author. And they should be able to see the long-term strategy and opportunities.

Is that all an agent does?

Some agents will provide more editorial and creative support; some will help on longer-term career planning; some will be subject specialists; some will involve themselves more on marketing and promotion; all should work in the best interests of their clients.

If I am writing and/or illustrating for children's books, do I need a specialist children's agent?

Most specialist children's agents would probably say you definitely need a specialist; many general agents will say you don't really need a specialist. In the end you will have to make up your own mind about whether an individual agent is right for your work and right for you as an individual. Knowledge, experience and excellent industry contacts (in the right companies and the right categories) are essential qualities in an agent who is going to represent you. If you are writing younger fiction, an agent whose expertise is in adult books with a few forays into young adult fiction probably won't have a full grasp of its potential. If your project is something specifically for the schools and education market it may well require different representation than for the consumer market: projects for educational publishers usually need to be tailored to the education syllabus in a very particular way. If your work has dimensions beyond traditional publishing, again you will need an agent who can deal with this.

If you are interested only in illustrating work by other people rather than developing your own projects and would like to try illustration work across a broad range of genres and formats, you may be best served by an artists' agent rather than a literary agent (see *Illustrators' agents* on page 284).

I am writing a text for an illustrated book – do I need to send some illustrations for an agent to consider it?

No, not unless you are an accomplished illustrator or intend to do the illustrations yourself. The wrong illustrations will put off an agent as they will a publisher. A good text should speak for itself. And never, in any case, send in original artwork, only send copies.

What if I have a brilliant novelty proposal, like a pop-up book? Do I need to show how it is going to look in its finished state?

If you can do it competently and it helps demonstrate how different and exciting your project is, you can certainly do this. But be prepared for the fact that you may need to make more than one, as the original runs the risk of getting damaged through handling or, when the worst comes to the worst, getting lost.

I definitely do want an agent. Where do I begin?

Firstly, using this *Yearbook* (see page 239) and the internet, identify the agents to whom your work will appeal. Then think about who will buy your book and why. An agent will only take someone on if they can see how and why they are going to make money for the client and themselves (and, of course, a client who is making no money tends quickly to become an unhappy client). Then do some further research online about both the agent and agency.

So the agent just thinks about money?

Well, some agents may just think about money. And it is certainly what some authors and artists think about a lot. *But* good agents do also care about the quality of work and the clients they take on. They are professional people who commit themselves to doing the best job they can. They also know that good personal relationships count. This means that, if and when you get as far as talking to a prospective agent, you should ask yourself the questions: 'Do I have a good rapport with this person? Do I think we will get along? Do I understand and trust what they are saying?' Follow your instinct – more often than not it will be right.

So how do I convince them that I'm worth taking on?

Start with the basics. Make your approach professional. Make sure you only approach an appropriate agent who deals with the category of book you are writing/illustrating. Check to whom you should send your work and whether there are any specific ways your submission should be made. In hard copy, only submit neat typed work on single-sided A4 paper and good quality copies of any artwork. Only send an electronic submission if the agency in question states this is acceptable. Send a short covering letter with your project explaining what it is, what the intended audience is and providing any other *relevant* context. Always say if and why you are uniquely placed and qualified to write a particular book. Provide a brief, relevant autobiographical paragraph, something that gives a sense of who you are. Think of the whole thing in the same way as you would a job application, for which you would expect to prepare thoroughly in advance. But also remember to make your approach personal and interesting: you want it to encourage the agent to read your work. You might only get one go at making your big sales pitch to an agent. Don't mess it up by being anything less than thorough.

And if I get to meet them?

Treat it like a job interview (although hopefully it will be more relaxed than this). Be prepared to talk about your work and yourself. An agent knows that a prepossessing personality in an author is a great asset for a publisher in terms of publicity and marketing – they will be looking to see how good your interpersonal skills are. Do also take the chance to find out, if you are discussing children's projects in particular, how and where they submit their clients' work and how well they understand the children's market themselves. Also check that they have good relationships with the sort of publishers/media companies with whom you think your work belongs. Don't be afraid to question them on their credentials and track record. If you have personal recommendations and referrals from other writers, publishers and other industry contacts, do follow these up. Ask, too, about representation in digital and other media, as well as overseas. Is this agent going to get their clients' work noticed by the right people in the right places and win them the best deals?

Will they expect me to be an expert on children and the children's market?

Not as such, but they might reasonably expect you to have an interest in what children like and enjoy and show an understanding of a child's eye view of the world. Basically, an agent will be looking for a writer/illustrator who is in sympathy with the target audience. However, it won't do any harm if you spend time at your local bookshop and/or library and befriend your local librarian or specialist children's bookseller to find out what books and authors are working well and if anyone is doing exactly what you plan to do. It's good, basic market research, as is browsing what else is available through internet retailers and reading other good children's books. For example, if you are planning a series of picture books about a ballet-dancing mouse, you need to be aware that *Angelina Ballerina* has already been out there for many years.

And if they turn my work down? Should I ask them to look again? People say you should not accept rejection.

No means no. Don't pester. It won't make an agent change his or her mind. Instead, move on to the next agency who might feel more positive towards your work. The agents who reject you may be wrong. But the loss is theirs.

Even if they turn my work down, isn't it worth asking for help with my creative direction?

No. Agents will often provide editorial advice for clients (some go as far as running their own creative groups) but are under no obligation to do so for non-clients. Submissions are usually sorted into two piles of 'yes, worth seeing more' and 'rejections'. To get teaching and advice, creative writing courses (see page 425) and writers' and artists' groups are better options to pursue. And, however you do it, it is vital to practise and develop your creative skills. You wouldn't expect to be able to play football without working at your ball skills. If you are looking to get your work published, you will be competing with professional writers and artists – and those who have spent years working daily at their craft.

There are also particular considerations that need to be given to the craft of creating children's books. In a picture book, the text needs to work specifically with the illustrations: the fewer words there are, the more they matter. In writing fiction for a young age group, where language and sentence construction have to be simple enough for a seven-year-old child, the writer often has to work much harder to generate emotion and excitement and give the story personality. When illustrating children's poetry, the artist has to be able to develop and enhance the meaning of the words to just the right level. However you look at it, children's books are a demanding business – and not child's play.

Philippa Milnes-Smith is a literary agent and children's and YA specialist at the agency LAW (Lucas Alexander Whitley; see page 244). She was previously Managing Director of Puffin Books and is a past president of the Association of Authors' Agents.

See also...

What do agents *do* for their commission?

Generally, literary agents take 15% of their clients' earnings as their commission. Julia Churchill explains what she does in her role of literary agent in return for that percentage.

My role as a literary agent is to help my authors have successful careers. I endeavour to make money in as many rights streams as possible (with an eye on the long term), and enable an easier professional life for my clients so that they can focus on writing. My job involves spotting talent, helping to develop it and selling it.

Some of my clients came to me as established authors wanting to take their careers up a gear, but most have come via my slush pile, as debut writers. I get well over 100 submissions a week, and I may take on a new writer every few months (if I'm lucky). Spotting talent is often where my job starts. I think I have good taste, and I know that my taste isn't unique. If I love a book, it is likely that there are others who will love it too.

I tend not to follow trends, but I am aware of them. There are two markets to consider, and a good agent will have a clear understanding of both. The first is what I focus on when I sell books to publishers. The editor is the buyer and I need to think about their enthusiasms and needs for their list. Then there's the real market, which is reflected in what people are buying from booksellers right now. Both these markets change constantly and part of my job is to keep up to date with trends, and the preferences of individual editors. This knowledge feeds into my decision-making when considering new authors and guidance for my existing clients, although there are also many opportunities outside of obvious trends. To some extent I'm looking for what's fashionable, but more than anything I'm looking for what may be evergreen.

What I am looking for

When I read a manuscript, I'm looking to connect with a voice, a concept, a character and a story, a book with something to say. I'm looking for clarity and intent in the storytelling, and to be taken somewhere new.

Most debut manuscripts that arrive in my office are not yet ready to sell to a publisher, and I may work with the author to focus on what's best about the character(s) and story. Every edit is different. We may sit down together with a cup of tea and talk through the book, exploring such questions as: What does the writer do best? Where does the story lose focus? How can we keep raising the stakes? Why does this section not work? Is it needed? Is the story pulling in too many directions? What is the book about, in the small ways and the big ways?

Before I offer to represent an author, I'll talk them through the work that I think their manuscript needs. I want to be sure, for the author's sake as well as my own, that we're pointed in the same direction and in sync with our ambitions. It's my job to help the author bring out what is best in the manuscript. Sometimes these conversations are about the architecture of the book, and at other times just the interior design. I don't always work on my clients' books. I simply do what's necessary to maximise the chance of achieving a book deal and the value of that deal.

Literary agents

When I'm satisfied that the book is ready, I submit it to editors. On occasion, I may approach just one editor, and one publishing house, if there is a very specific reason why this would be the best possible outcome for the author. This is matchmaking. More often, I send out the manuscript widely in order to find the publisher with the most passion for the book and the best plan for it.

Selling the book

My favourite aspect of being a literary agent is seeing talent before the rest of the world does. The publishing business relies on having champions for books and an agent is the first professional champion. The agent shares their passion about a book with editors, who in turn pass it on to sales and marketing experts, publicists, reviewers, bloggers, librarians, booksellers, and then finally readers.

Sometimes it takes just a few days to sell a book and for other books it can take months – on occasion it has taken years. An auction is lively, but more than anything it's a logistical challenge and requires being organised and systematic. Auctions provide an opportunity for the agent and author to see each publisher's vision, and they give maximum leverage for the best possible deal. Although the idea of an auction may sound exciting, I probably get as much professional satisfaction from humbly selling a book that's been very tough to place as I do from an eight-publisher auction that takes days to tie up.

Looking at contracts

Being a literary agent is not all about passionate pitches, editorial chats over cups of tea, and champagne celebrations. There is some glamour to our business, but in many ways an agent's job is quite mundane and is taken up with working on contracts between publishers and authors. A contract has a long life and it requires rigour and experience to convert a publisher-friendly contract into one that is author friendly. Negotiating contracts is not confined to increasing the advance and pushing for the best royalty and high discount rates, although that is where an agent is likely to show the most immediate value. It's also about ensuring that the author gets their rights back if the book stops selling above a certain level, that the pay-out is staggered in a way that favours the author, that certain sub-rights revert if they are unexploited, that the delivery and acceptance terms are favourable, that in a multi-book deal the books are accounted separately, that the split of sub-rights are as good as they possibly can be, that there is total clarity on what electronic rights the publisher has and that they don't cut across the author's reserved rights. The list of considerations is long: there is a lot to cover in a contract.

An agency will often sell translation rights, and television and film rights. Some of my clients make more money in Brazil or Norway than they do in the USA or UK. And while some markets shrink, others thrive, so for books with reach, it's important to have a strong international team and relationships with film scouts and production companies.

As in any career, a writer is faced with opportunities and decisions to make. Some are small and possibly of little consequence, and some are big and important to get right. Every now and then, there are huge forks in the road which require bravery, clear-minded counsel and an ally. The role of an agent is to be informed and to guide each of their authors to make the best decisions. On behalf of the author an agent is responsible for talking through grievances, ensuring that publishers deliver what has been promised, feeding into conversations about strategy regarding their work, saying 'no' when it's appropriate, finding work, and pushing back.

While everyone concerned in the publishing process wants a book to succeed, my interests as an agent are the same as those of my client. Publishers' interests obviously dovetail with those of the author, but they aren't identical. This is why we generally find ourselves harmonious and in accord with the process, but occasionally in conflict with it. It's my job to have the necessary conversations to look after my authors, to do everything I can to ensure they have the career they want. We are in it together.

Julia Churchill is the Children's Agent at A.M. Heath Ltd (see page 243). She is always on the lookout for new writing talent and considers the slush pile to be the greatest place on earth. She is looking for debut and established authors with storytelling magic, from picture book texts through to young adult fiction.

See also...

How to sell your book to an agent

Literary agents wade through slush piles to find a manuscript that shines out and entices them to read more. Madeleine Milburn offers some helpful tips on how to get your submission noticed.

Submission packages for agencies are usually of a similar format. Most require you to send a covering letter, synopsis and the all-important first three chapters. When you feel that your manuscript is as good as it can be and you are ready to submit to an agent, here are some key tips to consider.

The title

Use a strong and compelling title that grabs an agent's attention. Bestselling titles resonate with a reader before they open a book, for instance *The Hunger Games, Diary of a Wimpy Kid, Twilight, Gangsta Granny, The Fault in Our Stars* or *The Book Thief*. Don't use a title that only makes sense to a reader once they have read the story. Think of how you, as a reader, approach books in bookshops. What grabs your attention?

The covering letter

A covering letter should include a brief introduction, for example, 'I am currently seeking representation for my debut novel …', followed by an intriguing sentence that will draw the reader into your story; a slightly longer, enticing blurb; a reason why you have chosen the agent you are submitting to; a short profile; and a brief sentence or two about what you are/will be working on next.

Pitch your book in your letter, *not* in your synopsis. The letter is the place to get an agent excited about your opening chapters and where you need to 'sell' your book. Read the back cover blurb of books in the genre you are writing in, and study why they rouse your attention and interest. Practise pitching your book in a single sentence to get to the core of your story. You need to position your book straight away and make it evident to the agent what genre you are writing in.

Imagine your book on the shelves of a bookshop. Where would it sit? Next to Suzanne Collins or John Green? I want to see that a writer has researched the market and knows that there is a readership for their work. An editor who loves your book will need to persuade the rest of the publishing team that there is a market for it. But when comparing yourself to another author, please don't say you are 'the next' J.K. Rowling; instead express the hope that your work will appeal to 'readers of' J.K. Rowling.

Only mention your achievements that are relevant to the book you are submitting. I applaud Duke of Edinburgh adventurers, dirt road bikers, members of Save the Whale foundations and other wonderfully colourful hobbyists, but unless the activity is specifically relevant to your book, for now, please keep the information short and sweet. Use the covering letter to sell the story, not yourself. I'd love to hear everything about you later, over a coffee, if I ask you to meet up.

Pitch just one book in your letter. If you have written more than one book, choose the one you'd like to launch your writing career with. If an agent loves the book you are submitting, he or she will be interested in all of your work. If you write both adult and children's stories, pick one (for now). A prospective editor will want your next book to appeal to the same readers as your first book – and I like to do two- or even three-book deals with publishers to ensure that they are committed to developing an author's career.

The synopsis

A synopsis is a straightforward chronological account of the *most important* things that happen in a story. A lot of agents read this last, or only read it if they want to see more chapters. Don't include every single detail; try to stick to one A4 page. If there are any twists or plot revelations, don't keep them hidden. The agent needs to see how original your plotting is compared to what is currently on the market, so this aspect can be crucial to deciding whether your manuscript is requested.

The opening chapters

Your first three chapters are extremely important as, together with your covering letter, they are what an agent judges your work by. They need to be strong, enticing and compelling. There must be a strong sense of atmosphere, empathy or intrigue. Be wary of including irrelevant background information or context at this stage: it never grips readers' attention when they are not yet familiar with the characters. At worst, it can also slow the pace and be boring.

Strong characters are so important. Everyone remembers characters rather than the intricate details of a plot – just think James Bond, Sherlock Holmes and Harry Potter. Let your readers do the work. Create suspense and hook us in with a central character so that we are desperate to know more about them and read on.

Don't make your chapters too long to get around the three-chapter limit. I sometimes get asked whether I'd like to see more than three chapters because theirs are relatively short and the answer is 'no thank you'. I don't count a Prologue as a chapter though.

I personally read everything that comes into my 'slush pile'. I represent a wide range of adult, young adult and children's fiction, and would be delighted to look at your work.

Madeleine Milburn is a literary agent (see page 245) and in 2011 was chosen as one of the book trade's Rising Stars in the *Bookseller*. Madeleine Milburn's agency blog provides an insight into her literary agency and the book trade as a whole (www.mmla.co.uk). She is always on the lookout for new writers, self-published authors, or authors who are mid-career. Her Twitter handle is @agentmilburn.

Checklist for submitting to an agent

- Make sure your book has a strong title.
- Research the market and check that the length of your novel is appropriate for the genre you are writing in.
- Print out the manuscript and check that all spelling is correct. You will be surprised at how many errors you find.
- Take care to follow the instructions that are specific to each agency. For instance, I like to see 1.5 line spacing for the opening chapters and a one-page synopsis.
- Create a strong and attention-grabbing one-line hook that captures the heart of your story and will entice people to buy and read your book.
- Write a compelling back cover blurb.
- Consider all the selling points for your book. Write a summary of the book's appeal: be clear who the audience is and confident that they will identify with the book. Know the strengths of your manuscript and why it is unique. Think about what previous experience you have that could help promote your book.
- Tailor your profile to be relevant to your writing career. State if you are on a creative writing course, are a member of any writing clubs or societies and if you have won any writing competitions.
- If you have been published before, it is important to be upfront about it. Provide any writing history and say whether you have had an agent in the past.
- Write a synopsis that summarises your book's plot in chronological order with the ending included.

See also...

- *How to get an agent*, page 223
- *What do agents do for their commission?*, page 227
- *Meet the parents: agent, author and the birth of a book*, page 232

Literary agents

Meet the parents: agent, author and the birth of a book

Stephanie Thwaites describes the agent's role in the route to a happy marriage between author and publisher.

Before I started work experience at Curtis Brown I had no idea what a literary agent did. Within my first year as an assistant I had tackled mountains of filing, collected dry cleaning, responded to fan mail, received a gift from Penhaligons, and drawn up my first audio rights contract. While my daily duties have certainly changed since then, the variety and excitement of the job still keeps my pulse racing and I never know what exactly will await me each morning.

As a children's agent, it amazes me that we haven't yet quashed the idea that writing for children is easy, or somehow easier than writing for adults. Shorter doesn't mean simpler. In fact, writing for children can be more difficult than writing for adults because of the very specific demands of the market. Quality writing alone won't work – a strong idea and engaging plot is vital. Then there's the challenge of finding the right voice, avoiding being patronising and keeping an energetic pace throughout. Thanks to a couple of high-profile success stories, new writers can start with inflated and unrealistic expectations. Part of our job as agents is to explain the business to new clients and to encourage them to have reasonable and achievable goals. While it is crucial to be positive and aim high, it is also worth remembering that there's really no such thing as an overnight success and children's authors often work incredibly hard for years before seeing the fruits of their labour. Young readers' taste evolves rapidly and writers and their representatives cannot afford to rely too heavily on 'author loyalty' when it comes to building a career and body of work. This is a readership with an ever-changing face as new child readers discover new authors, and existing readers are continually moving on too. A lot of children's authors and illustrators have other jobs and don't rely solely on writing for their income. Many work tirelessly visiting schools, speaking to children, teachers and librarians, appearing at literary festivals and running workshops. More recently, writers have been encouraged to develop new skills – to create their own websites, use social networking, join Twitter, try blogging and even make Skype appearances. It's not enough for authors just to write and deliver their books – they are expected to promote them ever more energetically too.

The role of the agent

An agent is involved throughout the life of a book, and aims to support an author by acting as a sounding board for ideas, giving feedback on material before it reaches an editor, liaising with editors at different publishing houses, guiding the author, providing specialist industry knowledge and enabling them to find the right home for their book and to strike the best deal. An agent negotiates the terms, and often sells the translation, US, audio and film rights (collectively known as subsidiary rights), which can sometimes be as important as the original publishing deal. Agencies manage the accounting side – invoicing, chasing payments and checking royalty statements – together with handling miscellaneous requests.

Enormous changes are currently taking place in the publishing world and it is an agent's responsibility to keep abreast of new developments and to consider how their clients will be affected by these changes. A good agent will ensure their authors are in a position to seize new opportunities; and where a 'traditional' approach is not effective, the agent should be able to try other approaches and work with their authors to devise new strategies. Ideally, the relationship will be career-long for both agent and author. When the road is bumpy, the agent feels keenly the successes and disappointments of their authors. The unfortunate reality is that most authors will not become instant bestsellers and it can take years and a great deal of patience and determination for an author to build a strong foundation.

Manuscript submissions

It is natural to assume that agents spend all of their working day reading manuscripts but in fact the majority of reading takes place outside of office hours. With limited time to focus on new submissions, we have to be very selective about the material we read in full and unfortunately we often have to make decisions based on just three chapters. However, even before we reach the opening page, we will already have formed a first impression from the covering letter. A letter which is poorly executed, sloppy, riddled with spelling mistakes or addressed to 'Mr Curtis Brown' or 'Dear Editor' will not pique our interest. The letter should be arresting but not gimmicky; informative but brief. Writing the perfect letter is an art in itself. I prefer to receive just one page with an overview of the story, the age range of the target readership, an idea of where it could be positioned and a line or two about the author. It is important to remember that this may be your only opportunity to communicate with an agent and it's worth bearing in mind how many times a book will be pitched beyond this initial letter – to editors (in the UK, USA and translation markets), to their teams in-house, to buyers and to customers. Asserting that your own children have enjoyed it probably isn't the most persuasive argument to advance.

To give you the best chance at securing an agent it is worth starting your research well before submitting your manuscript. If you're reading this, no doubt you are already doing just that. Check that you are approaching the right agents – look at their interests and consider the writers and genres they represent. Make sure you follow submission guidelines and try to resist chasing up your manuscript too soon. It is not unheard of now for approaches to be made via Twitter. Writing is, to an extent, a job like any other job. Just as you would research a company or industry before an interview, so you should do your homework before writing a covering letter. Reading other titles and reviewing what else is being published successfully will help give you a sense of the area you are writing in and of what might appeal to your target readership. If there's a gap in the market, sometimes there's a reason for that – it could be due to a lack of demand or just that it's the wrong moment for the subject. The style of books we might have enjoyed as children may not make it through an acquisitions meeting where publishers have to assess costs and sales potential. However, while awareness of what is commercially viable is important, a great story will always be irresistible. Writers should follow their instincts and inspiration and write what comes naturally.

The most satisfying success stories are the small, unlikely, unexpected ones. There's no substitute for a book that wins your heart. We've all heard reports of 22 publishers turning down a manuscript before one publisher takes a chance with it, offering a tiny advance and subsequently retiring on the profits as it becomes a blockbuster. The subjectivity and unpredictability of publishing is simultaneously frustrating and thrilling and there's no feeling quite like reading a manuscript then witnessing it go on to make waves and inspire young readers.

As a new writer, sharing your work with others can be a terrifying experience, but inviting feedback is a good form of preparation. An editor I know came up with a brilliantly simple but useful phrase: 'The end is not the end' – you might think you've finished a manuscript but usually this is just the beginning. Publishing is a collaborative process and compromise is often necessary if you are to succeed. Publishing a book involves many different parties and while you won't agree with all of them at all times it is important to be able to work as part of a team – albeit with the author as the star player.

Arranging a happy marriage

Just as an author might need to develop different skills and wear a number of hats, not just that of writer, so the agent will adopt a range of roles. Our strategies and activities might differ from client to client, project to project and day to day. To sum this up it might help to adopt a matrimonial analogy for the role of the agent in relation to author, and editor and publishing house. The agent can be seen as a bizarre hybrid of marriage broker, ceremony officiator, marriage counsellor and sometimes mother of the bride! How exactly? Well, we're responsible for helping the author to choose their publishing partner, introducing them to the right match – an editor who they will really connect with and a publishing house where they can thrive. Sometimes we might find there are several suitors and the agent will help the author weigh up the options and select the most suitable partner. So the agent acts as matchmaker for the 'author-bride', the principal player on the wedding day. Next we conduct the negotiations and handle the contractual side of the arrangement, outlining each side's obligations. The agent, at this juncture, is a cross between cleric and the pre-nup lawyer. Combining two families is never easy, and the extended publishing family can include marketing and publicity departments, production, sales and accounting and rights teams. Ensuring good relations can sometimes be a challenge. The agent will keep a close eye on these areas and promote good communication and, hopefully, marital bliss. Ultimately, however, like the proud and loving mother of the bride we remain firmly on the side of the bride, representing her best interests and advising and guiding her, sharing her disappointments and rejoicing in her triumphs.

Stephanie Thwaites is a literary agent at Curtis Brown (see page 241) and her blog is at http://childrensliteraryagent.co.uk.

See also...

Do you *have* to have an agent to succeed?

Bestselling children's author Philip Ardagh has over 100 titles to his credit but chooses not to have a literary agent to represent him. In this article he tells us why.

There are a lot of people out there who think that they're children's writers ('I was a child myself once, you know') and who send unsolicited manuscripts directly to publishers in their hundreds – possibly thousands – every year. These manuscripts usually end up on what is called the 'slush pile'. Some publishers won't even read them. Some do but, usually, only after a very long time. Many manuscripts are very badly written or very badly presented. Some are perfectly good but a little too much like something already out there in the bookshops, or they lack that indefinable something that makes them stand out from the crowd. Others are perfectly good but are sent to completely the wrong publisher. The best children's fantasy novel ever isn't going to appeal to a publisher specialising in adult DIY manuals, is it? Getting an agent cuts through this process.

Having an agent

Firstly, if an agent submits a manuscript it will go to the publisher they think that it's best suited to, and probably to the most suitable editor within that company – more often than not someone they know or have had dealings with in the past. So your manuscript is being seen by the right people at the right place. It's also neatly bypassed the slush pile. It will actually get read. Hurrah! The agent has acted as a filter. The publisher knows that, if you've been taken on by a reputable agent, your words are probably *worth* reading. You're ahead of the game.

An agent knows the ins and outs of advances, royalties, escalators, foreign rights, and a million and one other things that make the humble writer's head spin. Agents know the 'going rates' and will get you the very best deal they can if a publisher wants to publish your work. And, should there be problems further down the line, your agent can play the bad guy on your behalf – renegotiating contracts and doing the number crunching – whilst you only deal with the nice fluffy creative side with your editor.

That's the theory, of course, and much of it is true. They take their 10–15% share but they're not a charity and, if they're on a percentage of your earnings, it's generally in their interest to make you as much money as possible, isn't it?

The question is: is it possible to be a successful children's author without an agent? Of course it is. Anything's possible. I'm an agentless author and I'm doing fine, but not without help, advice, common sense, good luck and, as time has passed, experience.

So what are the disadvantages of having an agent? If you've got the right agent, the answer is probably very few, if any. Sure, you're not earning the full advance or royalty because you're giving them a percentage but your manuscript may never have become a book (or the advance and royalty may have been much lower) if they didn't represent you in the first place. If you have an agent you don't get directly involved in every aspect of negotiation and discussion with your publisher because you've handed that role over. And if you like the on-hands approach (for that read 'are a control freak'), you may miss out on that but, overall, the pros seem to outweigh the cons.

If you're *not* happy with your agent, though, it can be a very different story. You're not your agent's only client and you may feel – rightly or wrongly – that they're not giving you enough attention. Many is the writer and illustrator I know who has said, 'I find more work for myself than my agent does', or who isn't happy with the advance they've received and said, 'I'm not sure why my agent was so keen for me to agree to this deal.' Another familiar lament is, 'She seemed so enthusiastic when I first signed up, but now she's gone really quiet.' Your filter has become a barrier.

There may also be jobs which your agent is reluctant for you to take. In children's non-fiction, many authors are still paid flat fees, and small ones at that. Many agents will tell you not to touch them with a barge pole but – if you are at the beginning of your career – who knows what that little job might lead to? I once wrote the text to a book that owed its subsequent international success not to the beauty of my prose but to the illustrations and brilliant paper engineering. My fee was peanuts and, in immediate financial terms, it made no difference if the book sold three copies or 300,000. But it did my writing career the power of good. My name was associated with a successful title, I got known by various people within that particular publishing house, I went on to write many more books for them *with* royalties, and added to my reputation, generating interest from other publishers.

Going it alone

I enjoy that getting-to-know aspect of developing a relationship with publishers and, when it comes to contracts, I have a very useful not-so-secret secret weapon. I may not have an agent but I can call on the contracts experts at the Society of Authors (see page 375). As a member of the Society, they'll go through a contract line by line for me, free and for nothing, offering comments, suggestions and advice. They also publish excellent easy-to-understand pamphlets on various aspects of publishing. If you're not already a member, rush out and join immediately! If you don't understand something, don't be afraid to ask.

Remember, whatever impression a publisher might give, there is very rarely such a thing as a standard contract, written in stone, that can't be altered; sometimes significantly. Be prepared to concede some minor points, maybe, in return for sticking to your guns over a point which may really matter to you. (Different things matter to different writers.)

My big break came by luck, but luck borne out of developing contacts and making real friendships in the course of my agentless foray into the children's publishing world. The bulk of my 100 or so titles are non-fiction, but the bulk of my income and 95% of my recognition comes from my fiction, but one grew from the other. Because I was involved and enthusiastic, I was invited to promote one of my non-fiction titles at a sales conference. As a result of how I ad-libbed at the conference, following a mighty cock-up, I was asked if I wrote fiction. *Awful End* (my first Eddie Dickens book) was pulled out of the drawer and a deal was done. One thing had, indeed, led to another. Eddie's adventures are in over 30 languages and read around the world, and have picked up a few literary awards along the way.

Your rights

Publishers love to have world rights to books. Agents love to sell the rights separately. You can see why. An agent will argue that they can get more for you (and therefore more for them) by selling foreign rights separately to foreign publishers – perhaps creating a US auction for your fabulous book, for example – rather than your signing everything over to your UK publisher in one fell swoop. If, however, you sell the world rights to the publisher, and you have a good relationship with them, they're in effect acting as your agent on foreign deals and can still negotiate some excellent ones *in consultation with you*. And, having your world rights, they can share in your international success when it comes, so may be more keen to nurture you (and your money-generating, recognition-building world rights) in the future than, possibly, another writer whom they only publish in the UK.

And remember, an advance is an advance of royalties. If the advance is small and the book is a success, it simply means that the advance is earned out sooner and the cheques start rolling in. My advance for *Awful End* was just a four figure sum, but the money I've earned from additional royalties has been very-nice-thank-you-very-much. And my advances for the later Eddie Dickens books and other fiction were significantly larger.

Making the right decision

I know from friends and colleagues that, when you're starting out, you can find it as hard to get an agent as a publisher, which is why some people choose to go straight for the publishing houses. My advice – and this may surprise some of you – is to stick at trying to get an agent. If I was starting out now, I'd do that. Having an agent from the beginning makes sense.

If you're dead against the idea, feeling convinced that you can do a great job (see Philippa Milnes-Smith's checklist on page 223) or are exhausted trying, there are a few obvious things you can do. Even now, I sometimes ask myself 'Am I getting the very best deal?' and 'Could an agent do better for me?' Financially, the answers to these are probably 'Maybe not' and 'Yes', but are these the right questions? Surely what I need to ask is: 'Am I happy with this deal?' and 'Is it a reasonable sum reflecting what I think I'm worth and showing the commitment and understanding of the publisher?' And the answer to that is, more often than not, 'Yes'. And remember, money ain't the be-all and end-all. A good working relationship with an editor and publisher who understand you, consult with you, nurture you and your writing, promote and market you in a way you're happy with is beyond price.

Approaching a publisher

But let's not get ahead of ourselves. One of the most important, important, *important* – it's important, get it? – things you need to be sure of before sending a manuscript to an agent *or* a publisher is that it's ready to be seen. Some unpublished writers are so keen to show their work to others in the hope of getting it published as soon as possible that it's still in a very raw state. They're not doing themselves any favours. In fact, they could be ruining their chances. Sure, there is such a thing as overworking a piece, but you really need to be confident that it's about as good as it's going to get, especially if you're bypassing the agent route and going direct to the publisher. With no agent 'filter', you've got to be sure that you're representing yourself, through your work, in the very best possible light.

Look in bookshops to find out who publishes what. Once you've chosen a publisher, look them up in this *Yearbook*, find out their submissions procedure and ring them up. Ask the receptionist the name of the person you should send your manuscript or sample chapters to. This way you can address and write a letter to a particular person, rather than taking the 'Dear Sir/Madam' approach.

The covering letter you should write to the publisher is almost identical to the one for writing to a prospective agent (see *How to get an agent* on page 223 and *How to sell your book to an agent* on page 230) except, of course, that you should also include the reason why you think they'd be the right people to publish your work.

Finally, do treat the business side of selling yourself as a business. It's not simply that 'the writing's the important bit' and that it'll 'sell itself'. Network, send in invoices on time, get in touch when you say you'll get in touch and be contactable (there's no excuse for dropping off the radar in this age of emails and mobile phones). If you're shy or don't like parties, still go to the ones you're invited to by your publisher. You never know what that chance meeting with that rather scruffy bloke by the chilli dips might lead to. He could end up turning your book into a 24-part television series.

Oh, and one last thing: never admit that, secretly, you enjoy writing so much that you'd happily be published for nothing. Oops. Me and my big mouth!

Agented or agentless, good luck.

Philip Ardagh won the Roald Dahl Funny Prize in 2009 and was the first prizewinner to be shortlisted again (in 2013). He is probably best known for his award-winning *Eddie Dickens* adventures, which have been translated into over 30 languages, but he also writes children's non-fiction. He is currently working on his series *The Grunts*, illustrated by Axel Scheffler, and collaborating with illustrator Elissa Elwick on an up-coming picture book series. Philip's radio credits include having written and edited the BBC's first truly interactive radio drama series, *Arthur Storey and the Department of Historical Correction*. He has collaborated with Sir Paul McCartney and is an 'irregular regular reviewer' of children's fiction for the *Guardian*.

See also...
- *How to get an agent*, page 223
- *What do agents do for their commission?*, page 227
- *How to sell your book to an agent*, page 230
- *Meet the parents: agent, author and the birth of a book*, page 232
- *Publishing agreements*, page 287
- *The Society of Authors*, page 375

Children's literary agents UK and Ireland

The *Children's Writers' & Artists' Yearbook*, along with the Association of Authors' Agents and the Society of Authors, takes a dim view of any literary agent who asks potential clients for a fee prior to a manuscript being placed with a publisher. We advise you to treat any such request with caution and to let us know if that agent appears in the listings below. However, agents may charge additional costs later in the process but these should only arise once a book has been accepted by a publisher and the author is earning an income. We urge authors to make the distinction between upfront and additional charges. Authors should also check agents' websites before making an enquiry and should familiarise themselves with submission guidelines.

*Member of the Association of Authors' Agents

The Agency (London) Ltd*
24 Pottery Lane, London W11 4LZ
tel 020-7727 1346
email hd-office@theagency.co.uk
website www.theagency.co.uk
Children's Book Agent Hilary Delamere

Represents picture books, including novelty books, fiction for all ages including teenage fiction and series fiction (home 15%, overseas 20%). Works in conjunction with overseas agents. Submission guidelines on website. No reading fee. The Agency also represents screenwriters, directors, playwrights and composers; for more information email info@theagency.co.uk. Founded 1995.

Aitken Alexander Associates Ltd*
18–21 Cavaye Place, London SW10 9PT
tel 020-7373 8672
email reception@aitkenalexander.co.uk
website www.aitkenalexander.co.uk
Agent Gillie Russell

Children's and young adult fiction (home 15%, overseas 20%). Handles fiction for the 9+ age group and teenage/YA fiction. No picture books. Email preliminary letter with half-page synopsis and first 30pp of sample material via agency website or to submissions@aitkenalexander.co.uk. No reading fee.
    Children's authors include Matthew Brown, Sue Durrant, Jane Hardstaff, Tom Hoyle, Mark Lowery, Debbie McCune, Louise Rennison, Benjamin Scott and Moira Young. Founded 1977.

Darley Anderson Children's Book Agency Ltd*
Estelle House, 11 Eustace Road, London SW6 1JB
tel 020-7386 2674
email childrens@darleyanderson.com
website www.darleyandersonchildrens.com
website www.darleyanderson.com
Darley Anderson (Managing Director), Clare Wallace

(Agent), Camilla Wray (Agent), Peter Colegrove (Financial Director)

Children's fiction (for all ages from picture book to middle grade through to young adult and crossover), non-fiction and illustrators (home 15%, USA/ translation 20%, film/TV/radio 20%). No scripts or screenplays. Send covering letter, short synopsis and first three chapters/illustration samples. If posting, return postage/sae essential for return of work.
    Clients include Cathy Cassidy, Laura Cassidy, John Connolly, Caroline Crowe, Jonathan Eyers, Martyn Ford, Helen Grant, Polly Ho-Yen, Clare Mackie, Adam Perrott, Beth Reekles, Jennifer Ridyard, Dave Rudden, Loretta Schauer, Lorna Scobie, Kim Slater, Ying Sy, Amie Wallace.

ANDLYN
tel 020-3290 5638
email submissions@andlyn.co.uk
website www.andlyn.co.uk
Founder and Agent Davinia Andrew-Lynch

Specialises in children's fiction and content. Represents authors of picture books, middle grade and YA fiction. This also includes graphic novels for these age groups. Particularly looking for storytellers whose material has cross-media/platform potential. Commission: 15% home and audio, 20% USA, foreign/translation, film/TV, multi-platform and online media rights. No reading fee. See website for submission guidelines. Founded 2015.

Bath Literary Agency
5 Gloucester Road, Bath BA1 7BH
tel (01225) 314676
email gill.mclay@bathliteraryagency.com
website www.bathliteraryagency.com
Contact Gill McLay

Specialist in fiction for children and young adults. Also accepts submissions in non-fiction and picture books. For full submission details, refer to the website. No reading fee. Founded 2011.

The Bell Lomax Moreton Agency*

Suite C, 131 Queensway, Petts Wood, Kent BR5 1DG
tel 020-7930 4447
email info@bell-lomax.co.uk
website www.bell-lomax.co.uk
Executives Eddie Bell, Pat Lomax, Paul Moreton,
June Bell, Josephine Hayes, Helen Mackenzie-Smith,
Lauren Clarke, Sarah McDonnell

Quality fiction and non-fiction, biography, children's, business and sport. No unsolicited MSS without preliminary letter. No poetry, screenplays or scripts. No reading fee. Founded 2000.

The Bent Agency*

21 Melliss Avenue, Richmond TW9 4BQ
email info@thebentagency.com
website www.thebentagency.com
Agents Gemma Cooper, Molly Ker Hawn (UK);
Jenny Bent, Heather Flaherty, Louise Fury, Susan
Hawk, Victoria Lowes, Beth Phelan, Brooks Sherman
(USA)

Represents authors of fiction for adults, children and teenagers, and selected non-fiction with commercial appeal. Offices in the UK and US. Unsolicited submissions welcome by email only: query and first ten pages pasted into body of email. See complete guidelines at www.thebentagency.com/submission.php. Founded 2009.

The Blair Partnership*

Middlesex House, Fourth Floor,
34–42 Cleveland Street, London W1T 4JE
tel 020-7504 2520
email info@theblairpartnership.com
email submissions@theblairpartnership.com
website www.theblairpartnership.com
Founding Partner Neil Blair, Managing Partner Dan
Marks, Agents Zoe King, Liz Bonsor

Considers all genres of fiction and non-fiction for adults, young readers and children. Will consider unsolicited MSS. Email a covering letter, a one-page synopsis and the first ten pages to: submissions@theblairpartnership.com.

A multi-platform rights management agency, works in partnership with some of the best creative talent in the world to build their brands by effective management of their IP throughout the world and across books, film, TV, digital and all other media and platforms.

Clients include the Class of 92/Salford FC, the Alexander Wilson estate, Frank Lampard, Maajid Nawaz, J.K. Rowling, Pete Townshend and a select number of talented debut writers including Claire Barker, Michael Byrne, Simon David Eden, Tatum Flynn, Dan Freedman, the Freeman Brothers, Keaton Henson, Inbali Iserles, Karl James, Jennifer Kincheloe, Kieran Larwood, Sophie Nicholls, Justine Pattison and Zoom Rockman.

Bright Literary Agency

Studio 102, 250 York Road, London SW11 3SJ
email mail@thebrightgroupinternational.com
website www.brightgroupinternational.com
Contact Vicki Willden-Lebrecht

A boutique children's literary agency born out of the success of The Bright Agency, a leading children's illustration agency with a global client list. Works across all genres of children's publishing including novelty, picture books and fiction. Email submissions in pdf or Word format only to literarysubmissions@brightgroupinternational.com. See website for full submission guidelines. Founded 2009.

Jenny Brown Associates*

33 Argyle Place, Edinburgh EH9 1JT
tel 0131 229 5334
email lucy@jennybrownassociates.com
website www.jennybrownassociates.com
Contact Lucy Juckes

Represents children's writers and illustrators. Also adult fiction and general non-fiction. No reading fee. See website for submission guidelines.

Clients include Sam Angus, Keith Gray, Jonathan Meres, Alison Murray. Founded 2002.

Felicity Bryan Associates*

2A North Parade, Banbury Road, Oxford OX2 6LX
tel (01865) 513816
email agency@felicitybryan.com
website www.felicitybryan.com

Fiction for children aged 8–14 and young adult, and adult fiction and general non-fiction (home 15%, overseas 20%). Translation rights handled by Andrew Nurnberg Associates; works in conjunction with US agents.

Children's authors include David Almond, Jenny Downham, Sally Gardner, Natasha Farrant, Chelsey Flood, Pauline Francis, Clare Furniss, Julie Hearn, Esme Kerr, Liz Kessler, Katherine Langrish, Linda Newbery, Annabel Pitcher, Meg Rosoff, Lauren St John, Matthew Skelton, Lydia Syson, Eleanor Updale, Lisa Williamson, Jeanne Willis.

The Catchpole Agency

53 Cranham Street, Oxford OX2 6DD
tel 07789 588070
email james@thecatchpoleagency.co.uk
email celia@thecatchpoleagency.co.uk
website www.thecatchpoleagency.co.uk
Proprietors James Catchpole, Celia Catchpole

Agents for authors and illustrators of children's books from picture books through to young adult novels. Commission from 10% to 15%. See website for contact and submissions details. Founded 1996.

Anne Clark Literary Agency

PO Box 1221, Harlton, Cambridge CB23 1WW
tel (01223) 262160
email submissions@anneclarkliteraryagency.co.uk
website www.anneclarkliteraryagency.co.uk
Contact Anne Clark

Specialist in fiction for children and young adults, also picture book texts (home 15%, overseas 20%).

Submissions by email only. See website for submission guidelines. No reading fee. Founded 2012.

Conville & Walsh Ltd*

Haymarket House, 28–29 Haymarket, London SW1Y 4SP
tel 020-7393 4200
website www.convilleandwalsh.com

Fiction for 5–8 and 9–12 year-olds, teenage fiction, series fiction and film/TV tie-ins (home 15%, overseas 20%). Not taking on picture books. Also handles adult literary and commercial fiction and non-fiction. Submissions welcome: first three chapters, cover letter, synopsis by email or post with sae. No reading fee. Part of the Curtis Brown Group of Companies; simultaneous submission accepted.

Children's authors include John Burningham, Kate Cann, Katie Davies, Rebecca James, Astrid Lindgren estate, P.J. Lynch, Joshua Mowll, Peadar O'Guilin, Paula Rawsthorne, Niamh Sharkey, Nicky Singer, Piers Torday, Steve Voake. Founded 2000.

Coombs Moylett Maclean Literary Agency

120 New Kings Road, London SW6 4LZ
tel 020-8740 0454
email lisa@cmm.agency
website www.cmm.agency
Contacts Lisa Moylett, Jamie Maclean

Specialises in well-written commercial fiction, particularly in the genres of historical fiction, crime/mystery/suspense and thrillers, women's fiction across a spectrum ranging from chick-lit sagas to contemporary and literary fiction. Also looking to build a children's list concentrating on YA fiction. Considers most non-fiction particularly history, biography, current affairs and cookery. Works with foreign agents. Commission: home 15%, overseas 20%, film/TV 20%. No reading fee. Does not handle poetry, plays or scripts for film and TV.

Creative Authors Ltd

11a Woodlawn Street, Whitstable, Kent CT5 1HQ
email write@creativeauthors.co.uk
website www.creativeauthors.co.uk
Director Isabel Atherton

Fiction, women's fiction, literary fiction, non-fiction, humour, history, science, autobiography, biography, business, memoir, mind, body & spirit, health, cookery, arts and crafts, crime, children's fiction, picture books, young adult, graphic novels and illustrators (home 15%, overseas 20%). Only accepts email submissions.

Authors and illustrators include Fiona McDonald, Rose Mannering, Stephanie Rohr, Keith Souter, Bethany Straker, Ben Joel Price, Jing Guo, Jules Miller, Ged Adamson, Kate Louise, Grace Sandford, Kate Ormand. Founded 2008.

Rupert Crew Ltd*

6 Windsor Road, London N3 3SS
tel 020-8346 3000
email info@rupertcrew.co.uk
website www.rupertcrew.co.uk
Directors Doreen Montgomery, Caroline Montgomery

International representation, handling accessible literary and commercial fiction and non-fiction for the adult and children's (8+) markets. Home 15%; overseas, TV/film and radio 20%. No picture books, plays, screenplays, poetry, journalism, science fiction, fantasy or short stories. No reading fee. No unsolicited MSS: see website for current submission guidelines. Founded 1927 by F. Rupert Crew.

Curtis Brown Group Ltd*

Haymarket House, 28–29 Haymarket, London SW1Y 4SP
tel 020-7393 4400
email cb@curtisbrown.co.uk
website www.curtisbrown.co.uk
website www.curtisbrowncreative.co.uk
website www.curtisbrownbookgroup.wordpress.com
Chairman Jonathan Lloyd, *Joint Ceos* Ben Hall and Jonny Geller, *Directors* Jacquie Drewe, Nick Marston, Sarah Spear *Books* Jonny Geller (Managing Director), Felicity Blunt, Sheila Crowley, Anna Davis, Jonathan Lloyd, Lauren Pearson (Children's & Young Adult), Norah Perkins (Estates), Vivienne Schuster, Karolina Sutton, Stephanie Thwaites (Children's & Young Adult), Gordon Wise

Represents prominent writers and estates, including classic children's stories, debut authors, international bestsellers and formats ranging from print and audio to digital and merchandise. Children's fiction ranges from picture books to young adult novels across many genres. Looking for books for 8–12 year olds and young adult titles with strong voices, original concepts and outstanding storytelling. Curtis Brown manages the international careers of authors with strong relationships in translation and US markets.

Stephanie Thwaites and Lauren Pearson work on the children's and young adult list and are actively seeking new clients. While no longer accepting submissions by post, for more information on submissions, as well as the children's writing courses offered from time to time as part of Curtis Brown Creative, consult www.curtisbrowncreative.co.uk. Founded 1899.

DHH Literary Agency

23–25 Cecil Court, London WC2N 4EZ
tel 020-7836 7376
email submission@dhhliteraryagency.com
website www.dhhliteraryagency.com

Children's fiction and non-fiction. Also adult fiction, women's commercial fiction, crime and literary fiction; and non-fiction including history, science, cookery and humour. No plays or scripts, poetry or short stories. Send informative preliminary email with first three chapters and synopsis. No reading fee. Will suggest editorial revisions where appropriate. New authors welcome. Founded 2008.

Diamond Kahn & Woods Literary Agency

Top Floor, 66 Onslow Gardens, London N10 3JX
tel 020-3514 6544
email info@dkwlitagency.co.uk
email submissions.ella@dkwlitagency.co.uk
email submissions.bryony@dkwlitagency.co.uk
website www.dkwlitagency.co.uk
Directors Ella Diamond Kahn, Bryony Woods

Accessible literary and commercial fiction (including all major genres) and non-fiction for adults; and children's, young adult and crossover fiction (home 15%, USA/translation 20%). Interested in new writers. No reading fee, email submissions only. Send three chapters and synopsis to one agent only. See website for further details on agents, their areas of interest and submission guidelines.

Eddison Pearson Ltd*

West Hill House, 6 Swains Lane, London N6 6QS
tel 020-7700 7763
email info@eddisonpearson.com
website www.eddisonpearson.com
Contact Clare Pearson

Children's and young adult books, fiction and non-fiction, poetry (home 10%, overseas 15–20%). Small, personally run agency. Enquiries and submissions by email only; email for up-to-date submission guidelines by return. No reading fee. May suggest revision where appropriate.

Authors include Valerie Bloom, Sue Heap, Caroline Lawrence, Robert Muchamore.

Frank Fahy

129 Delwood Close, Castleknock, Dublin 15, Republic of Ireland
tel +353 (0)86 2269330
email frank.fahy0@gmail.com
website www.frank-fahy.com
Agent Frank Fahy

Adult and children's fiction and non-fiction (home 15%, overseas 20%). *Authors* include Sheila Agnew, Dr Frances Fahy, Amy Lynch, Barnaby Newbolt, Dr Henrike Rau, Susan Weir.

Fraser Ross Associates

6 Wellington Place, Edinburgh EH6 7EQ
tel 0131 553 2759, 0131 657 4412
email lindsey.fraser@tiscali.co.uk
email kjross@tiscali.co.uk
website www.fraserross.co.uk
Partners Lindsey Fraser, Kathryn Ross

Writing and illustration for children's books, fiction and non-fiction for adults. See website for client list

and submission guidelines. Submissions can be emailed to fraserrossassociates@gmail.com. Founded 2002.

Annette Green Authors' Agency

5 Henwoods Mount, Pembury,
Tunbridge Wells TN2 4BH
tel (01892) 263252
website www.annettegreenagency.co.uk
Partners Annette Green, David Smith

Full-length MSS (home 15%, overseas 20%). Literary and general fiction and non-fiction, popular culture, history, science, teenage fiction. No dramatic scripts, poetry, science fiction or fantasy. No reading fee. Preliminary letter, synopsis, sample chapter and sae essential.

Greene & Heaton Ltd*

37 Goldhawk Road, London W12 8QQ
tel 020-8749 0315
email submissions@greeneheaton.co.uk
email info@greeneheaton.co.uk
website www.greeneheaton.co.uk
Contact Nicola Barr

Children's fiction and non-fiction. Handles fiction for 5–8 and 9–12 year-olds, teenage fiction, series fiction, poetry and non-fiction. No picture books. Also handles adult fiction and non-fiction. Send a covering letter, synopsis and the first 50pp (or fewer) with a sae and return postage. Email submissions welcome but no reply guaranteed; type 'Children's' in subject line.

Children's authors include Helen Craig, Andy Cutbill, Josh Lacey, Lucy Christopher, Viviane Schwarz. Founded 1963.

The Greenhouse Literary Agency

4th Floor, 9 Kingsway, London WC2B 6XF
tel 020-7841 3959
email submissions@greenhouseliterary.com
website www.greenhouseliterary.com
Director Sarah Davies, *UK Agent* Polly Nolan, *US Agent* John Cusick

Specialist children's book agency with a reputation for impressive transatlantic deals. Represents fiction from picture books through to teen/young adult (USA/UK 15%, elsewhere 25%). Represents both UK and Commonwealth (Polly Nolan) and North American (Sarah Davies and John Cusick) authors. No non-fiction. No reading fee. Queries by email only, see website for details.

Authors include Jennifer Bell, Julie Bertagna, Romily Bernard, Caroline Carlson, Sarwat Chadda, Donna Cooner, Harriet Goodwin, Swapna Haddow, Jill Hathaway, Dawn Kurtagich, Lindsey Leavitt, Jon Mayhew, Wendy Mills, Megan Miranda, Sinéad O'Hart, C.J. Omololu, Gavin Puckett, Jeyn Roberts, Erica L. Scheidt, Tess Sharpe, Tricia Springstubb, Julie Sykes, Blythe Woolston, Brenna Yovanoff. Founded 2008.

Marianne Gunn O'Connor Literary Agency

Morrison Chambers, Suite 17, 32 Nassau Street, Dublin 2, Republic of Ireland
email mgoclitagency@eircom.net
Contact Marianne Gunn O'Connor

Commercial and literary fiction, non-fiction, biography, children's fiction (home 15%, overseas 20%, film/TV 20%). Email enquiry with a half-page outline. Translation rights handled by Vicki Satlow Literary Agency, Milan.

Hardman & Swainson

4 Kelmscott Road, London SW11 6QY
tel 020-7223 5176
email caroline@hardmanswainson.com
email joanna@hardmanswainson.com
email hannah@hardmanswainson.com
website www.hardmanswainson.com
Directors Caroline Hardman, Joanna Swainson

Literary and commercial fiction, crime and thiller, women's, accessible literary, YA and older children's fiction. Non-fiction, including memoir, biography, popular science, history, philosophy. No poetry or screenplays (home 15%, US/translation/film/TV 20%). No reading fee. Will work editorially with the author where appropriate. Submissions by email only to submissions@hardmanswainson.com.

Clients include Rebecca Wait, Dinah Jefferies, Abby Clements, Liz Trenow, Vanessa Greene, Michele Gorman, Alastair Gunn, Cathy Bramley, Ali McNamara, Giovanna Fletcher, Sara Crowe, Eleanor Wood, Stuart David, Nick Russell-Pavier, Ann Morgan and Prof. Daniel M. Davis. Founded 2012.

Antony Harwood Ltd

103 Walton Street, Oxford OX2 6EB
tel (01865) 559615
email mail@antonyharwood.com
website www.antonyharwood.com
Contacts Antony Harwood, James Macdonald Lockhart, Jo Williamson (children's)

General and genre fiction; general non-fiction (home 15%, overseas 20%). Will suggest revision. No reading fee.

Children's authors include James Dawson, Tamsyn Murray, Jennifer Gray, Garth Nix, Sean Williams. Founded 2000.

A.M. Heath & Co. Ltd*

6 Warwick Court, London WC1R 5DJ
tel 020-7242 2811
website www.amheath.com
Contact Julia Churchill

Children's fiction and non-fiction from picture books to young adult (home 15%, USA/translation 20%). Also handles adult literary and commercial fiction and non-fiction. Digital submission via website.

Submit synopsis and sample chapters. No reading fee. Will suggest revision.

Children's authors include Nicholas Allan, Cat Clarke, Anne-Marie Conway, Sarah Crossan, Stephen Davies, John Dougherty, Pip Jones, Michelle Harrison, Sarah Lean, Joanna Nadin, Amy Sparkes, Holly Webb, Rebecca Westcott and the estates of Noel Streatfield, Helen Cresswell, Joan Aiken and Christianna Brand. Founded 1919.

Sophie Hicks Agency

email info@sophiehicksagency.com
website www.sophiehicksagency.com
Agents Sophie Hicks, Sarah Williams

Fiction for 9+ (UK/US 15%, translation 20%). Also handles adult fiction and non-fiction. No poetry or scripts. Email submissions only, see website for guidelines.

Children's authors include: Herbie Brennan, Jamie Buxton, Anne Cassidy, Lucy Coats, Eoin Colfer, Andrew Donkin, Sarah Dyer, Emerald Fennell, Padraig Kenny, Paul Kidby, Paula Leyden, Oisin McGann, Sarah Mussi, Siobhan Parkinson, Alexander Gordon Smith, David Lee Stone, Kate Thompson and Mark Walden.

David Higham Associates Ltd*

7th Floor, Waverley House, 7–12 Noel Street, London W1F 8GQ
tel 020-7434 5900
email dha@davidhigham.co.uk
website www.davidhigham.co.uk
Managing Director Anthony Goff, Books Veronique Baxter, Anthony Goff, Caroline Walsh, Alice Williams Foreign Rights Alice Howe, Film/TV/Theatre Nicky Lund, Georgina Ruffhead

Children's fiction, picture books and non-fiction (home 15%, USA/translation 20%, scripts 10%). Handles novelty books, picture books, fiction for 5–8 and 9–12 year-olds, teenage fiction, series fiction, poetry, plays, film/TV tie-ins, non-fiction and audio. Also handles adult fiction, general non-fiction, plays, film and TV scripts; 35% of list is for the children's market. See website for submissions policy. No reading fee. Represented in all foreign markets.
Also represents illustrators for children's book publishing (home 15%). Submit colour copies of artwork by post or via email. Include samples that show children 'in action' and animals.

Clients (children's market) include Jenny Alexander, R.J. Anderson, Antonia Barber, Julia Bell, Joe Berger, Tim Bowler, Alan Brown, Mike Brownlow, Charles Causley, Kathryn Cave, Jason Chapman, Lauren Child, Peter Collington, Trish Cooke, Anne Cottringer, Cressida Cowell, Roald Dahl, Nicola Davies, Susie Day, Kady Macdonald Denton, Jane Devlin, Matt Dickinson, Berlie Doherty, Ruth Eastham, Eve Edwards, Jonathan Emmett, Kat Falls, Anne Fine, Corina Fletcher, Susan Gates, Jamila Gavin, Maggi Gibson, Julia Golding, Sally Grindley,

Ann Halam, Candida Harper, Carol Hedges, Leigh Hodgkinson, Edward Hogan, Belinda Hollyer, Meredith Hooper, William Hussey, Julia Jarman, Sherryl Jordan, Anna Kemp, Clive King, Bert Kitchen, Rebecca Lisle, Saci Lloyd, Jo Lodge, Tim Lott, Geraldine McCaughrean, Kirsty McKay, Tom McLaughlin, Jackie Marchant, Hazel Marshall, Simon Mason, David Miller, Gwen Millward, Pratima Mitchell, Tony Mitton, Nicola Moon, Michael Morpurgo, Sarah Mlynowski, Jenny Nimmo, Martine Oborne, Claire O'Brien, Kate O'Hearn, Liz Pichon, Tamora Pierce, Chris Powling, Charlie Price, Lucy Daniel Raby, Gwyneth Rees, Adrian Reynolds, Jasmine Richards, Fiona Roberton, Rachel Rooney, Veronica Rossi, J.O. Sharpe, Nick Sharratt, Emily Smith, Alexander McCall Smith, Keris Stainton, Paul Stickland, Joss Stirling, Jeremy Strong, Frances Thomas, Theresa Tomlinson, Ann Turnbull, Jenny Valentine, Martin Waddell, Philip Webb, Alex Williams, Gina Wilson, Jacqueline Wilson and David Wojtowycz. Founded 1935.

Shelley Instone Literary Agency

56 Queens Road, London SW14 8PJ
tel 020-8876 8209
email info@shelleyinstoneliteraryagency.co.uk
website www.shelleyinstoneliteraryagency.co.uk
Director Shelley Instone

Represents the voices of established and debut authors in adult fiction, children's fiction and non-fiction. Works in conjunction with rights specialist Louisa Pritchard and the Knight Hall Agency for TV and film. Specialist area is in children's from junior fiction (5–9) to middle grade (9–12). Also YA and NA (13+). Commission: home 15%, overseas 20%. See website for submission guidelines.
    Authors include Ciara Hegarty and Sally Poyton.

Johnson & Alcock Ltd*

Clerkenwell House, 45–47 Clerkenwell Green, London EC1R 0HT
tel 020-7251 0125
website www.johnsonandalcock.co.uk
Contact Anna Power, Ed Wilson

All types of children's fiction and non-fiction (ages 9+), young adult and teenage fiction, (home 15%, US/translation/film 20%). No short stories, poetry or board/picture books.
    Send first three chapters (or 50pp), full synopsis, and brief covering letter with details or writing experience. For submission guidelines see website. No reading fee but return postage essential. Founded 1956.

LAW (Lucas Alexander Whitley Ltd)*

14 Vernon Street, London W14 0RJ
tel 020-7471 7900
website www.lawagency.co.uk
Contacts Philippa Milnes-Smith, Elizabeth Briggs

Children's books (home 15%, overseas 20%). Novelty books, picture books, fiction for 5–8 and 9–12 year-

olds, including series, young adult, film/TV and non-fiction. Unsolicited and debut work considered. See website for further information about the clients and genres represented and essential information on submissions. Represented in all markets. No reading fee. Founded 1996.

Lindsay Literary Agency

East Worldham House, Alton, Hants GU34 3AT
tel (01420) 83143
email info@lindsayliteraryagency.co.uk
website www.lindsayliteraryagency.co.uk
Directors Becky Bagnell, Kate Holroyd Smith

Children's books, middle grade, teen/YA, picture books. No reading fee. Will suggest revision.
    Authors include Pamela Butchart, Sam Gayton, Ruth Hatfield, Peter Jones, Mike Lancaster, Rachel Valentine. Founded 2008.

Christopher Little Literary Agency LLP*

(in association with Curtis Brown Group Ltd))
48 Walham Grove, London SW6 1QR
tel 020-7736 4455
email info@christopherlittle.net
website www.christopherlittle.net
Contact Christopher Little

Fiction for 9–12 year-olds and teenage fiction (home 15%, overseas 20%, digital 20%); no illustrated children's or short stories. Also handles adult fiction and non-fiction. No unsolicited submissions.
    Children's authors include Cathy Hopkins and Darren Shan. Founded 1979.

London Independent Books

26 Chalcot Crescent, London NW1 8YD
tel 020-7722 7160
Proprietor Carolyn Whitaker

Specialises in teenage fiction (home 15%, overseas 20%). Handles fiction for 9–12 year-olds, teenage fiction and young adult fiction. Also handles adult fiction; approx. one-third of list is for the children's market. Submit two chapters and a synopsis with return postage. No reading fee. Will suggest revision of promising MSS.
    Authors include Simon Chapman, Joseph Delaney, Elizabeth Kay, Derek Kielty, Chris Wooding. Founded 1971.

Luithlen Agency

88 Holmfield Road, Leicester LE2 1SB
tel 0116 273 8863
website www.luithlenagency.com
Agents Jennifer Luithlen, Penny Luithlen

Children's fiction, all ages to YA (home 15%, overseas 20%), performance rights (15%). See website for submission information. Founded 1986.

Eunice McMullen Ltd

Low Ibbotsholme Cottage, Off Bridge Lane, Troutbeck Bridge, Windermere, Cumbria LA23 1HU

tel (01539) 448551
email eunicemcmullen@totalise.co.uk
website www.eunicemcmullen.co.uk
Director Eunice McMullen

Specialises exclusively in children's books, especially picture books and older fiction (home 15%, overseas 15%). Handles novelty books, picture books, fiction for all ages including teenage, series fiction and audio. No unsolicited scripts. Telephone or email enquiries only. No reading fee.

Authors include Margaret Chamberlain, Sam Childs, Caroline Jayne Church, Ross Collins, Emma Dodd, Charles Fuge, Cally Johnson Isaacs, Sarah Massini, David Melling, Angela McAllister, Angie Sage, Gillian Shields. Founded 1992.

Andrew Mann Ltd*

United House, North Road, London N7 9DP
email info@andrewmann.co.uk
website www.andrewmann.co.uk
Contacts Tina Betts, Louise Burns

Children's fiction and non-fiction (home 15%, overseas 20%). Handles picture books, fiction from 5+ up to YA (teenage fiction), series fiction, film/TV tie-ins and non-fiction. Also handles adult fiction; 25% of list is for children's market. Submit synopsis and first 30pp. Email submissions only. No reading fee. See submission guidelines on website before submitting work. Founded 1968.

Marjacq Scripts*

Box 412, 19–21 Crawford Street, London W1H 1PJ
tel 020-7935 9499
email enquiries@marjacq.com
website www.marjacq.com
Contact Philip Patterson (books), Sandra Sawicka (foreign rights), Luke Speed (film/TV)

All full-length MSS (direct 15%, sub-agented 20%), including commercial and literary fiction and non-fiction, crime, thrillers, commercial, women's fiction, graphic novels, children's, science fiction, history, biography, sport, travel, health. No poetry. No musicals. Send first three chapters with synopsis, preferably by email. May suggest revision. Film and TV rights, screenplays, documentaries: send full script with 1–2pp synopsis/outline. Interested in documentary concepts and will accept proposals from writer/directors: send show reel with script. Sae essential for return of submissions.

MBA Literary and Script Agents Ltd*

62 Grafton Way, London W1T 5DW
tel 020-7387 2076
website www.mbalit.co.uk
Children's book agents Diana Tyler, Sophie Gorell Barnes, Laura Longrigg, *Film & TV agent* Jean Kitson

Fiction and non-fiction, children's books (home 15%, overseas 20%) and TV, film, radio and theatre scripts (TV/theatre/radio 10%, films 15%). See

website for submission guidelines. Works in conjunction with agents in most countries. UK representative for Harlequin.

Clients include Sita Brahmachari, Christopher William Hill, Suzi Moore, Christopher and Christine Russell. Founded 1971.

Madeleine Milburn Ltd Literary, TV & Film Agency*

10 Shepherd Market, Mayfair, London W1J 7QF
tel 020-7499 7550
email submissions@madeleinemilburn.com
website www.mmla.co.uk
Director Madeleine Milburn, *Assistant* Cara Lee Simpson, *Rights Executive* Rachael Sharples

Represents a dynamic and prize-winning range of children's and young adult fiction. Specialist areas include 6–8 years, 9–12 years, 12+, teen, YA, new adult and books appealing to both children and adults. Award-winning and popular fiction including fantasy, real life/contemporary, psychological suspense, crime, thrillers, mystery, action, survival, historical, fairies, myths and legends, animals and nature, war, science fiction, sports, comedy, romance, love stories, coming of age, tear-jerkers, American, Irish, Australian and film/TV tie-ins.

Represents British, American and international authors. Handles all rights in the UK, US and foreign markets including fim/TV/theatre/radio and digital (home 15%, USA/translation/film 20%).

International associates worldwide including Creative Artists Agency (CAA) in LA for film. Enhances author careers in print and digital format. Also manages sucessful self-published authors.

No longer accepts submissions by post. See submission guidelines and agency news on website. No reading fee. Works editorially with all clients.

Authors and illustrators include Holly Bourne, Jenna Burtenshaw, Anne Cameron, Simon Cherry, C.J. Daugherty, Carina Rozenfeld, S.B. Hayes, L.A. Jones, Caleb Krisp, Dave Lowe, Geoffrey Malone, Holly Martin, Matt Ralphs, Radhika Sanghani, Caireann Shannon, Rupert Wallis, Eliza West, Lara Williamson. Founded 2012.

Miles Stott Literary Agency Ltd*

East Hook Farm, Lower Quay Road, Hook, Haverfordwest, Pembrokeshire SA62 4LR
tel (01437) 890570
email nancy@milesstottagency.co.uk
website www.milesstottagency.co.uk
Director Nancy Miles, *Associate Agents* Victoria Birkett, Mandy Suhr

Specialist in children's novelty books, picture books, fiction for 6–9 and 10–12 year-olds, young adult fiction and series fiction (home 15%, overseas 20%).

Email submissions only to submissions@milesstottagency.co.uk including covering letter, brief synopsis and three sample

chapters. For picture books email complete text and/
or pdfs of sample artwork. No reading fee.

Authors include Rachel Bright, Frances Hardinge,
Gill Lewis, Mark Sperring, Zoe Marriott. Founded
2003.

Catherine Pellegrino & Associates
148 Russell Court, Woburn Place,
London WC1H 0LR
email catherine@catherinepellegrino.co.uk
website www.catherinepellegrino.com
Director Catherine Pellegrino

Provides a full agenting service for children's writers,
from picture books through to new adult. Founded
2011.

Pollinger Limited*
(formerly Laurence Pollinger Ltd, successor of Pearn,
Pollinger and Higham)
Drury House, 34–43 Russell Street,
London WC2B 5HA
tel 020-7404 0342
email info@pollingerltd.com
website www.pollingerltd.com

Managing Director Lesley Pollinger, *Agent* Katy
Loffman

All types of fiction for children of all ages, from
picture books to young adult novels. For submission
guidelines see website.

Children's clients Hayley Long, Saviour Pirotta,
Michael Coleman, Catherine Fisher, Philip Gross,
Frances Hendry. Founded 1935.

Redhammer Management Ltd
186 Bickenhall Mansions, Bickenhall Street,
London W1U 6BX
tel 020-7486 3465
email admin@redhammer.info
website www.redhammer.info
Vice President Peter Cox

Specialises in works with international potential
(home 17.5%, overseas 20%). Unpublished authors
must have major international potential, ideally book,
film and/or TV. Submissions must follow the
guidelines given on the website. Do not send
unsolicited MSS by post. No radio or theatre scripts.
No reading fee.

Children's clients include Peggy Brusseau, Michelle
Paver, Mal Peet, David Yelland. Founded 1993.

Rogers, Coleridge & White Ltd*
20 Powis Mews, London W11 1JN
tel 020-7221 3717
email info@rcwlitagency.com
website www.rcwlitagency.com
Chairman Gill Coleridge, *Managing Director* Peter
Straus, *Finance Director* Nelka Bell, *Directors* Stephen
Edwards, Georgia Garrett, Laurence Laluyaux, David
Miller, Peter Robinson, Zoe Waldie, Claire Wilson,

Agents Sam Copeland, Jennifer Hewson, Cara Jones,
Rebecca Jones (foreign).

Children's fiction (home 15%, USA 20%). Handles
picture books, fiction for 5–8 and 9–12 year-olds and
teenage fiction. See website for submissions
information. No reading fee. Will suggest revision.

Founded in 1967 by Deborah Rogers (1938–2014),
who received the highest honour in the trade, the
London Book Fair Lifetime Achievement Award, in
2014.

Elizabeth Roy Literary Agency
White Cottage, Greatford, Nr Stamford,
Lincs. PE9 4PR
tel (01778) 560672
website www.elizabethroy.co.uk

Children's fiction and non-fiction – writers and
illustrators (home 15%, overseas 20%). Send
preliminary letter, synopsis and sample chapters with
names of publishers and agents previously contacted.
Return postage essential. No reading fee. Founded
1990.

Uli Rushby-Smith Literary Agency
72 Plimsoll Road, London N4 2EE
tel 020-7354 2718
email uli.rushby-smith@btconnect.com
Director Uli Rushby-Smith

Fiction and non-fiction, literary and commercial
(home 15%, USA/foreign 20%). No poetry, picture
books, plays or film scripts. Send outline, sample
chapters (no disks) and return postage. No reading
fee. Founded 1993.

Caroline Sheldon Literary Agency Ltd*
71 Hillgate Place, London W8 7SS
tel 020-7727 9102
email carolinesheldon@carolinesheldon.co.uk
email felicitytrew@carolinesheldon.co.uk
website www.carolinesheldon.co.uk
website www.carolinesheldonillustrators.co.uk
Contacts Caroline Sheldon, Felicity Trew

All types of children's books plus adult fiction and
non-fiction (home 15%, USA/translation 20%, film/
TV 15%). All writing for children from picture books
up through 7–9 year-olds, 9–12 year-olds to young
adult. All major genres including contemporary,
comic, fantasy, historical fiction and humour. Also
non-fiction. Illustrators also represented. Also
specialises in the sale of books to TV/film.

Authors – send submissions by email only with
Submissions/Title of work/Name of author in subject
line. Include full introductory information about
yourself and your writing and the first three chapters
only or equivalent length of work.

Illustrators – send introductory information about
yourself with samples. If submitting by email type
Artist's Submission in subject line and attach samples
of your work and/or link to your website. Prefer not

to view images via a download link from file delivery services. If submitting by post include printed samples together with a large sae. If available, include texts or book dummies. Founded 1985.

Dorie Simmonds Agency Ltd*

Riverbank House, One Putney Bridge Approach, London SW6 3JD
tel 020-7736 0002
email info@doriesimmonds.com
Contact Dorie Simmonds

Children's fiction (UK/USA 15%; translation 20%). No reading fee but sae required. Send a short synopsis, two to three sample chapters and a cv with writing/publishing background.
Clients include award-winning children's authors. Founded 1997.

The Standen Literary Agency

4 Winton Avenue, London N11 2AT
tel 020-8245 2606
website www.standenliteraryagency.com
Director Yasmin Standen
Children's fiction – middle grade and up, all YA, no picture books (home 15%, overseas 20%). Interested in discovering new writers and launching the careers of first-time writers. Send submissions by email only; no submissions by post. Send first three chapters and synopsis (one side of A4) with a covering letter, all double-line spaced. No reading fee. Also handles literary and commercial fiction for adults. See website for further information.
Authors include Zara Kane, Christina Banach, Andrew Murray. Founded 2004.

Abner Stein*

10 Roland Gardens, London SW7 3PH
tel 020-7373 0456
website www.abnerstein.co.uk
Contacts Caspian Dennis, Sandy Violette

Fiction, general non-fiction and children's (home 15%, overseas 20%). Not taking on any new clients at present.

Rochelle Stevens & Co

2 Terretts Place, Upper Street, London N1 1QZ
tel 020-7359 3900
email info@rochellestevens.com
website www.rochellestevens.com
Directors Rochelle Stevens, Frances Arnold

Children's drama scripts for film, TV and theatre (10%). Also adult drama scripts for film, TV, theatre and radio. Send preliminary letter, cv, short synopsis and opening ten pages of a drama script by post (sae essential for return of material). See website for full submission guidelines. No reading fee. Founded 1984.

Sarah Such Literary Agency

81 Arabella Drive, London SW15 5LL
tel 020-8876 4228

email info@sarahsuch.com
website sarahsuchliteraryagency.tumblr.com
Director Sarah Such

High-quality literary and commercial non-fiction and fiction for adults and children (home 15%, TV/film 20%, overseas 20%), including debut young adult novels, picture books and graphic novels. No reading fee. Will suggest revision. Submit synopsis and a sample chapter (as a Word attachment by email) plus author biography. No postal submissions unless requested. No unsolicited MSS or telephone enquiries. TV/film scripts for established clients only. No radio or theatre scripts, poetry, fantasy, self-help or short stories. Translation representation: The Buckman Agency, The English Agency (Japan) Ltd. Film/TV representation: Lesley Thorne, Aitken Alexander Associates Ltd. Always looking for original children's and YA writers and projects.
Authors include: Matthew De Abaitua, Nick Barlay, Salem Brownstone, Ali Catterall, Rob Chapman, Ian Critchley, John Harris Dunning, Rob Harris, John Hartley, Marisa Heath, Wayne Holloway-Smith, Vina Jackson, Maxim Jakubowski, Antony Johnston, Louisa Leaman, Mathew Lyons, Sam Manning, Vesna Maric, David May, Kit McCall, Benjamin Myers QC, Ben Osborne, Marian Pashley, Greg Rowland, John Rowley, Caroline Sanderson, Tony De Saulles, Nikhil Singh, Sara Starbuck, Michael Wendling. Founded 2006.

United Agents LLP*

(incorporating AP Watt)
12–26 Lexington Street, London W1F 0LE
tel 020-3214 0800
email info@unitedagents.co.uk
website www.unitedagents.co.uk
Agent Jodie Hodges (children's/young adult writers and illustrators). Other agents also represent children's writers. See website for individual lists.

Fiction and non-fiction (home 15%, USA/translation 20%). No reading fee. See website for submission details. Founded 2008 and 1875.

Jo Unwin Literary Agency

c/o Rogers, Coleridge & White, 20 Powis Mews, London W11 1JN
email jo@rcwlitagency.com
website www.jounwin.co.uk
Contact Jo Unwin

Represents authors of literary fiction, commercial women's fiction, YA fiction and fiction for children aged 9+ (picture books only accepted if written by established clients). Also represents comic writing and narrative non-fiction.

Ed Victor Ltd*

6 Bayley Street, Bedford Square, London WC1B 3HE
tel 020-7304 4100
website www.edvictor.com

Fiction, non-fiction, children's and film/TV (home 15%, USA 15%, film/TV 15%, translation 20%).

Watson, Little Ltd*

Suite 315, ScreenWorks, Highbury Grove,
London N5 2ER
tel 020-7388 7529
email office@watsonlittle.com
website www.watsonlittle.com
Contact James Wills (Managing Director), Donald Winchester (Agent), Laetitia Rutherford (Agent)

Fiction: literary, commercial women's, crime and thriller. Non-fiction: history, science, popular psychology, memoir, humour, cookery, self-help. Children's fiction and non-fiction. No poetry, TV, play or film scripts (home 15%, USA/Translation 20%). Send informative preliminary letter, synopsis and sample chapters. *Overseas associates* The Marsh Agency Ltd; *Film and TV associates* Ki Agency and The Sharland Agency; *US associates* Howard Morhaim Literary Agency and The Gersh Agency.

Whispering Buffalo Literary Agency Ltd

97 Chesson Road, London W14 9QS
tel 020-7565 4737
email info@whisperingbuffalo.com
website www.whisperingbuffalo.com
Director Mariam Keen

Commercial/literary fiction and non-fiction, children's and young adult fiction (home 15%, overseas 20%). Special interest in book-to-screen adaptations; TV and film rights in novels and non-

fiction handled in-house. No reading fee. Will suggest revision. Founded 2008.

Eve White*

54 Gloucester Street, London SW1V 4EG
tel 020-7630 1155
email eve@evewhite.co.uk
website www.evewhite.co.uk
Contact Eve White, Jack Ramm

Young, middle grade, teenage and young adult fiction and film/TV tie-ins (home 15%, overseas 20%). Also handles adult commercial and literary fiction and non-fiction; 50% of list is for the children's market. No reading fee. Will suggest revision where appropriate. See website for up-to-date submission requirements. No submissions by mail.

Children's clients include Andy Stanton, Rae Earl, Tracey Corderoy, Kate Maryon, Ruth Warburton, Sarah Naughton, Michaela Morgan, Simon Nicholson, Ivan Brett, Susanna Corbett, Kara Lebihan, Abie Longstaff, Rachael Mortimer, Ciaran Murtagh, Adam Britten, Kate Scott, Elli Woollard. Founded 2003.

Susan Yearwood Literary Agency

2 Knebworth House, Londesborough Road,
London N16 8RL
tel 020-7503 0954
email childrens@susanyearwood.com
website www.susanyearwood.com
Contact Susan Yearwood

Children's fiction, 9–12 years and young adult (home 15%, overseas 20%). Send first 30pp and a synopsis via email. No reading fee. Founded 2007.

Children's literary agents overseas

Before submitting material, writers are advised to visit agents' websites for detailed submission guidelines and to ascertain terms.

AUSTRALIA

Australian Literary Management
2–A Booth Street, Balmain, NSW 2041
tel +61 (0)9 818 8557
email alpha@austlit.com
website www.austlit.com

For full details of genres represented and submission guidelines, see website. Does not consider scripts of any kind or books for children by unpublished authors. Does not accept self-published work or writing by non-Australian authors.

The Author's Agent
PO Box 577 Terrigal, NSW 2260
email brian.cook@theauthorsagent.com.au
website www.theauthorsagent.com.au

Specialises in adult fiction, narrative non-fiction and children's books. Does not accept submissions by email. For detailed guidelines, see website.

Golvan Arts Management
PO Box 766, Kew, Victoria 3101, Australia
email golvan@ozemail.com.au
website www.golvanarts.com.au

Represents a wide range of writers including writers of both adult and children's fiction and non-fiction, poetry, screenwriters and writers of plays. Also represents visual artists and composers. See the General Information section on the website before making contact.

CANADA

The Cooke Agency
email agents@cookeagency.ca
website www.cookeagency.ca
Agents Dean Cooke, Sally Harding, Suzanne Brandreth, Ron Eckel, Rachel Letofsky

Literary fiction, commercial fiction (including science fiction, fantasy, crime and horror), women's commercial fiction, non-fiction (specifically narrative-driven works in the areas of popular culture, practical non-fiction in the areas of health and wellness, science, history, politics and natural history), and middle-grade and young adult books. No children's picture books, poetry or screenplays. Accepts only electronic queries, no attachments. See website for submission guidelines. Founded 1992.

Pamela Paul Agency
12 Westrose Avenue, Toronto, Ontario M8X 2A1
tel +1 416-410-4395
email agency@interlog.com
Contact Pamela Paul

Children's fiction only. Not accepting queries at this time. Founded 1989.

Carolyn Swayze Literary Agency Ltd
7360-137th Street, Suite 319, Surrey, BC V3W 1A3
email reception@swayzeagency.com
website www.swayzeagency.com
Proprietor Carolyn Swayze

Fiction and non-fiction for teens and middle-grade readers. No science fiction, poetry, screenplays or children's picture books. Eager to discover strong voices writing contemporary or supernatural stories if the metaphor reflects relevant themes. No telephone calls: make contact by email or post. Send query including synopsis and short sample. Provide résumé, publication credits, writing awards, education and experience relevant to the book project. If querying by post include email or sase for return of materials. No original artwork or photographs. Allow six weeks for a reply. Founded 1994.

Transatlantic Agency
2 Bloor Street East, Suite 3500, Toronto, Ontario M4W 1A8
tel +1 416-488-9214
website www.transatlanticagency.com
Contacts Marie Campbell, Fiona Kenshole, Amy Tompkins

Specialises in children's and young adult fiction. Refer to the website for submission guidelines. Founded 1993.

NEW ZEALAND

Glenys Bean Writer's Agent
PO Box 639, Warkworth 0941, New Zealand
email info@glenysbean.com
Directors Fay Weldon, Glenys Bean

Adult and children's fiction, educational, non-fiction, film, TV, radio (10–20%). Send preliminary letter, synopsis and sae. No reading fee. Founded 1989.

Total Fiction Services
PO Box 46–031, Park Avenue, Lower Hutt 5044
tel +64 (0)4 565 4429
email tfs@elseware.co.nz
website www.elseware.co.nz

General fiction, non-fiction, children's books. No poetry, or individual short stories or articles.

Literary agents

Enquiries from New Zealand authors only. Email queries but no attachments. Hard copy preferred. No reading fee. Also offers assessment reports, mentoring and courses.

USA

Member of the Association of Authors' Representatives

Adams Literary*

7845 Colony Road, C4 Suite 215, Charlotte, NC 28226
tel +1 704-542-1440
email info@adamsliterary.com
website www.adamsliterary.com
Agents Tracey Adams, Josh Adams

Exclusively children's: from picture books to teenage novels (home 15%, overseas 20%). Submissions through website. See website for guidelines. Founded 2004.

Bradford Literary Agency

5694 Mission Center Road, Suite 347, San Diego, CA 92108
email queries@bradfordlit.com
website www.bradfordlit.com

Currently looking for fiction (romance, urban fantasy, women's, mystery, thrillers, children's and YA) and non-fiction (business, relationships, biography, memoir, self-help, parenting, narrative humour). Not currently looking for poetry, screenplays, short stories, westerns, horror, new age, religion, crafts, cookbooks or gift books. Query by email only. For detailed submission guidelines, see website. No reading fee.

Andrea Brown Literary Agency

email andrea@andreabrownlit.com
website www.andreabrownlit.com
President Andrea Brown, Senior Agent Laura Rennert
Agents Kelly Sonnack, Caryn Wiseman, Jennifer Rofe, Jennifer Laughran, Jamie Weiss Chilton, Jennifer Mattson, Lara Perkins

Exclusively all kinds of children's books. Represents both authors and illustrators. Email submissions only. See website for guidelines. Founded 1981.

Browne & Miller Literary Associates*

410 South Michigan Avenue, Suite 460, Chicago, IL 60605
tel +1 312-922-3063
email mail@browneandmiller.com
website www.browneandmiller.com
Contact Danielle Egan-Miller

General fiction and non-fiction (home 15%, overseas 20%). Select young adult projects. Works in conjunction with foreign agents. Will suggest revision; no reading fee. Founded 1971.

Maria Carvainis Agency Inc.*

Rockefeller Center, 1270 Avenue of the Americas, Suite 2320, New York, NY 10020

tel +1 212-245-6365
email mca@mariacarvainis.com
President & Literary Agent Maria Carvainis

Young adult fiction (home 15%, overseas 20%). Also handles adult fiction and non-fiction. No reading fee. Query first; no unsolicited MSS. No queries by email. Works in conjunction with foreign, TV and movie agents.

The Chudney Agency

72 North State Road, Suite 501, Briarcliff Manor, NY 10510
tel +1 201-758-8739
email steven@thechudneyagency.com
website www.thechudneyagency.com
Contact Steven Chudney

Children's books (and some adult). See website for full guidelines for queries and submissions, and for details of genres represented. Founded 2002.

Curtis Brown Ltd*

10 Astor Place, New York, NY 10003
tel +1 212-473-5400
website www.curtisbrown.com
Ceo Timothy Knowlton, President Peter Ginsberg, Contacts Elizabeth Harding (Vice President), Ginger Knowlton (Executive Vice President), Ginger Clark, Jonathan Lyons

Fiction and non-fiction, juvenile, film and TV rights. No unsolicited MSS. See individual agent's entry on the Agents page of the website for specific query and submission information. No reading fee; no handling fees. Founded 1914.

Liza Dawson Associates

350 Seventh Avenue, Suite 2003, New York, NY 10001
website www.lizadawsonassociates.com
Ceo Liza Dawson, Cfo, Foreign Rights Manager Havis Dawson; Caitlin Blasdell, Hannah Bowman, Monica Odom, Caitie Flum. (To query agents by email, the address style is queryfirstname, e.g. queryliza@lizadawsonassociates.com)

A full-service agency which draws on expertise as former publishers. Young adult, middle grade: literary, thrillers, mysteries, romance, historical fiction, sci-fi and fantasy, contemporary. See website for submission guidelines and email contacts.
Authors include Annie Barrows, Sage Blackwood, Pierce Brown, Angela Cerrito, Greg van Eekhout, Lindsey Eyre, Merrie Haskell, Rosamund Hodge, Shallee McArthur, Rachel Neumeier, Lisa Ann O'Kane, Sarah Prineas, Joel Ross.

Sandra Dijkstra & Associates*

PMB 515, 1155 Camino Del Mar, Del Mar, CA 92014
tel +1 858-755-3115
website www.dijkstraagency.com
Contacts Sandra Dijkstra, Elise Capron, Jill Marr, Roz Foster, Thao Le, Andrea Cavallaro, Jessica Watterson

Young adult science fiction and fantasy only (home 15%, overseas 20%). Works in conjunction with foreign and film agents. Email submissions only. Please see website for the most up-to-date guidelines. No reading fee. Founded 1981.

Dunham Literary, Inc.*
110 William Street, Suite 2202, New York, NY 10038–3901
email dunhamlit@gmail.com
website www.dunhamlit.com
Contact Jennie Dunham, Bridget Smith

Children's books (home 15%, overseas 20%). Handles picture books, fiction for 5–8 and 9–12 year-olds and teenage fiction. Also handles adult literary fiction and non-fiction; 50% of list is for the children's market. Send query by post or to query@dunhamlit.com. Do not send full MS. No reading fee. Founded 2000.

Dystel & Goderich Literary Management*
1 Union Square West, New York, NY 10003
tel +1 212-627-9100
website www.dystel.com
Contacts Michael Bourret, Jim McCarthy, Stacey Glick, John Rudolph

Children's fiction (home 15%, overseas 19%). Handles picture books, fiction for 5–8 and 9–12 year-olds, teenage fiction and series fiction. Looking for quality young adult fiction. Also handles adult fiction and non-fiction. Send a query letter with a synopsis and up to 50pp of sample MS. Will accept email queries. No reading fee. Will suggest revision.
Children's authors include James Dashner, Richelle Mead, Sara Zarr, Morgan Rhodes, Lisa McCann, Geoff Herbach, A.S. King, Amy Plum. Founded 1994.

Educational Design Services LLC
5750 Bou Avenue, Suite 1508, N. Bethesda, MD 20852
tel +1 301-881-8611
email blinder@educationaldesignservices.com
website www.educationaldesignservices.com
Contact B. Linder

Specialises in educational texts for K–12 market (home 15%, overseas 25%). No picture books or fiction. Send query by email or with sase, or send outline and one sample chapter by email or with sase for return of material. Founded 1981.

The Ethan Ellenberg Literary Agency*
548 Broadway, Suite 5E, New York, NY 10012
tel +1 212-431-4554
email agent@ethanellenberg.com
website www.ethanellenberg.com
President & Agent Ethan Ellenberg

Fiction and non-fiction (home 15%, overseas 20%). Interested in all types of children's fiction: new adult,

young adult, middle grade, chapter books, picture books. Will consider all genres: literary, mystery, romance, fantasy, sci-fi, humorous. No scholarly works, poetry, short stories or screenplays.
    Will accept unsolicited MSS and seriously consider all submissions, including first-time writers. For fiction submit synopsis and first three chapters. For shorter children's works send complete MS. Illustrators should send a representative selection of colour copies (no original artwork). Unable to return any material from overseas. See website for full submission guidelines. Founded 1983.

Flannery Literary
1140 Wickfield Court, Naperville, IL 60563
tel +1 630-428-2682
email jennifer@flanneryliterary.com
website www.flanneryliterary.com
Contact Jennifer Flannery

Specialises in children's and young adult, juvenile fiction and non-fiction (home 15%, overseas 20%). Send query letter by post or email. Founded 1992.

Folio Literary Management*
The Film Center Building, 630 9th Avenue, Suite 1101, New York, NY 10036
website www.foliolit.com

Represents both first-time and established authors. Seeks upmarket adult fiction, literary fiction, commercial fiction that features fresh voices and/or memorable characters, narrative non-fiction. Folio Jr is devoted exclusively to representing children's book authors and artists. Consult agents' submission guidelines on the website before making contact.

Barry Goldblatt Literary LLC*
320 Seventh Avenue, #266, Brooklyn, New York, NY 11215
tel +1 718-832-8787
email query@bgliterary.com
website www.bgliterary.com
Contact Barry Goldblatt

Represents young adult and middle-grade fiction, as well as adult science fiction and fantasy. No non-fiction. Has a preference for quirky, offbeat work. Query only.

The Greenhouse Literary Agency
4035 Ridge Top Road, Suite 550, Fairfax, VA 22030
tel +1 571-758-5615
email submissions@greenhouseliterary.com
website www.greenhouseliterary.com
Director Sarah Davies, *US Agent* John Cusick, *UK Agent* Polly Nolan

Children's fiction from picture books through to teen/young adult (USA/UK 15%, elsewhere 25%). Represents both US and UK authors. No non-fiction or poetry. No material for adults. No reading fee. Will suggest revision. Queries by email only, see website for details.

Literary agents

Authors include Courtney Alameda, Jennifer Bell, Martha Brockenbrough, Caroline Carlson, Sarwat Chadda, Donna Cooner, Elle Cosimano, Ashley Elston, Jessie Humphries, Dawn Kurtagich, Lindsey Leavitt, Catherine Linka, Cori McCarthy, Dawn Metcalf, Wendy Mills, Megan Miranda, Hannah Moskowitz, C.J. Omololu, Jeyn Roberts, Tess Sharpe, Michelle Schusterman, Tricia Springstubb, Vin Vogel, Tommy Wallach, Sharon Biggs Waller, Blythe Woolston, Kat Yeh, Brenna Yovanoff. Founded 2008.

John Hawkins & Associates Inc.*

80 Maiden Lane, Suite 1503, New York, NY10038
tel +1 212-807-7040
email jha@jhalit.com
website www.jhalit.com
Agents Moses Cardona (President), Warren Frazier, Anne Hawkins

Fiction, non-fiction, young adult. No reading fee. Founded 1893.

kt literary*

9249 S. Broadway 200–543, Highlands Ranch, CO 80129
tel +1 720-344-4728
email contact@ktliterary.com
website www.ktliterary.com
Contact Kate Schafer Testerman, Sara Megibow, Renee Nyen

Primarily middle-grade and young adult fiction. No picture books. In adult, also seeking romance, science fiction, fantasy and erotica (Sara Megibow only). Email a query letter and the first three pages of manuscript in the body of the email (no attachments) as per website instructions. No snail mail.

Clients include Maureen Johnson, Stephanie Perkins, Matthew Cody, Ellen Booraem, Trish Doller, Amy Spalding, Jaleigh Johnson, Miranda Kenneally, Stefan Bachmann.

Gina Maccoby Literary Agency*

PO Box 60, Chappaqua, NY 10514
tel +1 914-238-5630
email query@maccobylit.com
Contact Gina Maccoby

Specialises in children's books: fiction, non-fiction, picture books, MS/illustration packages for middle grade and young adult (home 15%, overseas 20–25%). All queries by email. No unsolicited submissions. Founded 1986.

McIntosh & Otis Inc.*

353 Lexington Avenue, New York, NY 10016
tel +1 212-687-7400
email info@mcintoshandotis.com
website www.mcintoshandotis.com
Head of Children's Dept Christa Heschke

Fiction for 5–8 and 9–12 year-olds, teenage fiction, series fiction, poetry and non-fiction for children.

Also handles adult fiction and non-fiction. No unsolicited MSS for novels; query first via email, see website for instructions. No reading fee. Will suggest revision. Founded 1928.

William Morris Agency Inc.

1325 Avenue of the Americas, New York, NY 10019
tel +1 212-586-5100
website www.wma.com

Erin Murphy Literary Agency

2700 Woodlands Village, Suite 300–458, Flagstaff, AZ 86001–7127
tel +1 928-525-2056
website http://emliterary.com
President Erin Murphy, *Senior Agent* Ammi-Joan Paquette, *Associate Agent* Tricia Lawrence

Children's books: fiction, non-fiction, picture books, middle grade, young adult (home 15%, overseas 20–30%). No unsolicited queries or submissions; considers material only by referral or through personal contact such as at conferences. Founded 1999.

Olswanger Literary LLC

1660 Chandler Drive, Fair Lawn, NJ 07410-2715
email anna@olswangerliterary.com
website www.olswanger.com
Contact Anna Olswanger

Specialises in children's illustrated books, middle-grade fiction and adult non-fiction. Email enquiries only. Include the first five pages of MS in the body of the email.

Alison Picard, Literary Agent

PO Box 2000, Cotuit, MA 02635
tel +1 508-477-7192
email ajpicard@aol.com

Adult fiction and non-fiction, children's and young adult (15%). No short stories, poetry, plays, screenplays or sci-fi/fantasy. Please send query via email (no attachments). No reading fee. Founded 1985.

Pippin Properties Inc.

110 West 40th Street, Suite 1704, New York, NY 10018
tel +1 212-338-9310
email info@pippinproperties.com
website www.pippinproperties.com
Contact Holly McGhee, Elena Giovinazzo, Heather Alexander

Exclusively children's book authors and artists (home 15%, overseas 25%), from picture books to middle-grade and young adult novels. Query by email. Founded 1998.

Susan Schulman, A Literary Agency LLC*

454 West 44th Street, New York, NY 10036
tel +1 212-713-1633

email susan@schulmanagency.com
website www.schulmanagency.com

Agents for negotiation in all markets (with co-agents) of fiction, general non-fiction, for the picture book, middle grade and young adult markets, and associated subsidiary rights including plays, television adaptation and film (home 15%, UK 7.5%, overseas 20%). No reading fee. Return postage required.

Stimola Literary Studio, Inc.*
308 Livingston Court, Edgewater, NJ 07020
tel +1 201-945-9353
email info@stimolaliterarystudio.com
website www.stimolaliterarystudio.com
Contact Rosemary B. Stimola

Children's fiction and non-fiction, from preschool to young adult (home 15%, overseas 20%). Most clients come via referral. Founded 1997.

S©ott Treimel NY*
434 Lafayette Street, New York, NY 10003
tel +1 212-505-8353
email general@scotttreimelny.com
website www.scotttreimelny.com
Founder Scott Treimel

Exclusively children's books: middle grade, young adult novels and MS/illustration packages by artist/illustrator only. No picture book MSS (home 15%, overseas 25%). Interested in seeing first chapter books, series, middle-grade and teenage fiction, commercial non-fiction for middle grade. No religious books. Periodicially open to submissions: presently closed. Blog: ScottTreimelNY.blogspot.com. Founded 1995.

Waverly Place Literary Agency
189 Waverly Place, Suite 4, New York, NY 10014–3135
email waverlyplaceliterary@aol.com
website www.waverlyplaceliterary.com
Agent Deborah Carter

Children's and adult fiction and non-fiction (home 15%, overseas 20%). Looking for picture books, middle grade and young adult novels that bring something new to their bookselling category. Actively pursuing new writers with formal training and published authors who want to try something new.

Prospective authors should be receptive to editorial feedback and willing to revise. Interested in intelligent books: no vulgar subject matter or copycats. Children's and teen multicultural fiction, mysteries and thrillers, historical fiction, animal stories, fantasy grounded in reality, narrative and serious non-fiction and anything not mentioned here that authors feel would be of interest to the agent. Note to picture book writers: will only consider those who have at least three complete manuscripts and have taken workshops in writing for young children. Prefers queries by email with no attachments. If no response within two weeks, query again.

Writers House LLC*
21 West 26th Street, New York, NY 10010
tel +1 212-685-2400
website www.writershouse.com

Fiction and non-fiction, including all rights; film and TV rights. See website for submission guidelines and contact details for agents. Founded 1974.

Illustrating for children
Picture books for children: the writer's story

Winnie the Witch has been waving her magic wand for 28 years. More than 5 million books have been sold, in over 25 languages. Author Valerie Thomas describes how, working together, writer, illustrator and publisher made Winnie into a star.

Beginnings

Many more than 28 years ago I was working in the Curriculum Department of an Australian Education Department, writing teaching materials and academic articles. I had written a few articles for newspapers and magazines, and a couple of children's stories for the school magazine. But I had never really considered myself to be a writer.

I wrote a few stories for a reading scheme. A friend working for an educational publisher gave me a list of words, I sent her some stories, and she accepted them all. *Winnie the Witch* was one of them. But the publisher folded, my friend lost her job and the stories were returned to me. I put them in the bottom drawer and forgot about them.

Some years later Oxford University Press sent some samples of their new reading scheme to our department. One of the stories was *Greta the Green Cow*, a lovely story about a cow that gave green milk. I thought of *Winnie the Witch*, took it out of the bottom drawer and sent it off to OUP. They accepted it for their scheme and I assumed it would be a modest production.

A year went by, and I wondered. Finally I wrote to OUP and enquired. Yes, it was still being considered and had been given to a new illustrator, Korky Paul, who had taken it to a Greek island for the summer. I waited.

One day a parcel arrived – the proofs of *Winnie the Witch*. They were amazing. Instead of the line illustrations I had imagined, every page was a wonder, a delight. Winnie's house was a mansion, and the detail on each page demanded close scrutiny. If you have never seen a Winnie book, have a look at one and you will see what I mean.

Working with the illustrator

The process for the first Winnie book was simple. I wrote the story and the editor gave it to Korky, who took it away and illustrated it. He illustrated it exactly as it was – no discussion, no changes. *Winnie the Witch* was not part of a reading scheme. She came out in a beautiful shiny book and won the Children's Book Award. Success seemed assured. But it took time.

For nine years I wrote more Winnie stories and Korky rejected them all. I came over to England with more stories and Korky rejected them. Then one day we went out to lunch and I spilt a glass of red wine over the pile of stories. Korky selected one, dripping with red wine, and agreed to illustrate it. That was *Winnie in Winter*.

Now we are creating a new Winnie story every year, but progress was slow in the early years. The first book came out in 1987, the second in 1996 and subsequent titles in 1999 and 2002. There were discussions, arguments and plenty of tears – from me (I don't think Korky cried …).

The Winnie experience is the usual process for a picture story book: a writer sends a story to a publisher, who finds an artist. But there are other ways. I was working with an artist and showed him some of my other (non-Winnie) stories. He liked one of them, so together we took the proposal to a publisher, who accepted it. I was able to see the illustrations in progress and be consulted, and I replaced one episode that the artist felt didn't work. The illustrations were almost finished when the publisher decided to leave the children's book market, and sold the children's list to another publisher where the new editor had little interest in our book – though it did get published.

Working with the editor

There are three people in the picture book relationship. The editor is of prime importance. For my first Winnie book, as an unknown and untested writer, I worked with a junior editor. She suggested that Winnie shouted 'Abracadabra!' before each spell. A good idea, I thought, and wrote it in. It turned out to have been an inspired suggestion. All over the world, children now shout 'Abracadabra!' as Winnie waves her wand. My editor made no other suggestions and there were no changes to the text. That has never happened since; my more recent editors tend to make many more suggestions and we work together on perfecting every word on every page.

I have worked with three editors each with different methods. For the first few books the three of us would meet: editor, illustrator and writer. I was very much the junior partner. But gradually I learned to stand up for myself, and we settled into a reasonably harmonious working relationship. I still live in Australia, so we could only meet in person if I was in England. In the days before email communication, sometimes I would only see amendments to my original manuscript when page proofs arrived in the mail.

Nowadays, being on the other side of the world is not a big problem. Together my editor and I decide on a theme for the year's book, and I write a story, or several stories. The editor accepts or rejects, suggests changes; there are compromises, sometimes arguments, but finally we have a story. Only then is it presented to Korky. As Korky illustrates it, some text changes are made, to accommodate page divisions or some feature of the illustration. I am consulted on each change and for the most part all goes smoothly. I am often surprised when I see the illustrations. I picture as I write, and sometimes Korky's pictures are quite different from my mental images. Often they are vastly superior and a lovely surprise, like Winnie's house. Sometimes they are not. But I accepted early in the relationship that, as long as my words were not changed, I had no say over the illustrations.

Themes and ideas

For the first few books I would think of a theme and write a story. Sometimes I wrote several, and Korky and the editor chose one. Korky has suggested a few themes: he wanted a pirate story because he liked drawing pirates, and I was happy with that. The editor has suggested some: *Winnie's Haunted House* came about because the publishers wanted a book they could feature for Halloween. The marketing department is consulted before a theme is agreed upon. I enjoyed doing a dinosaur story when dinosaurs were popular a few years ago. Then robots were the next big thing – hence *Winnie's Big Bad Robot*.

One story, *Winnie at the Seaside*, was unexpectedly traumatic. It was a hot summer, and Winnie wanted a swim, so she and Wilbur (her cat) flew off to the seaside, where Winnie's broomstick was washed away by the sea. Luckily she still had her magic wand, so she magicked up an enormous wave which crashed onto the beach as it brought back her broomstick, drenching the angry sunbathers. The illustrations were finished and the proofs were ready when the 2004 Boxing Day tsunami struck off the Indonesian coast, with massive loss of life. A big wave crashing onto a beach would never again be funny. So our story suddenly had a new ending: a whale spouts the broomstick onto the beach, and Winnie goes home and magics up a swimming pool.

Working without an agent

I have never had an agent, which was probably a mistake, in hindsight. The *Winnie the Witch* contract was my first, and I signed it with barely a glance. They were publishing my book! And giving me a £400 advance! Oh joy! By the time *Winnie in Winter* was published in 1996 I had learned a little more about contracts and negotiated a higher royalty. But the first book – with the smallest royalty – has been by far the biggest seller. Since then I have had an expert check my contracts if I have had any doubts.

Perseverence

So what have I learned in the 28 years? First and most importantly, never give up. Through-out the nine years between the first and second Winnie books I kept on writing. After each rejection I would pick myself up and try again. Of course, I was lucky. If the Australian reading scheme had gone ahead, Winnie would have faded away many years ago. I was lucky that the wonderful Korky Paul arrived just as Winnie was looking for an illustrator. I was lucky that Oxford University Press is the publisher. The marketing and editorial staff have worked hard to promote Winnie. There are now board books, activity books, stories for older readers, even a doll.

Apart from luck and perseverance, a little talent is useful. But there have been many very talented writers who have never had a word published. I once worked with a man who told me he had written more words than Harold Robbins and had never had one of those words published. But he kept on writing. I do hope he finally made it into print.

Valerie Thomas is the author of *Winnie the Witch* (Oxford University Press 1987) and has written a further 16 stories in the bestselling *Winnie the Witch* series, illustrated by Korky Paul. The most recent book in the series is *Winnie's Haunted House* (Oxford University Press 2015). She was born in Australia and has lived there most of her life, working as a teacher before becoming a writer.

See also...

- *On being a storyteller: the illustrator's story*, page 258
- *Notes from a series author*, page 180
- *Notes from a successful children's author and illustrator*, page 116
- *Being an illustrator* and *a writer*, page 152

Illustrating for children

On being a storyteller: the illustrator's story

Korky Paul describes his craft and role as an illustrator, what inspires and unlocks his visual concept of the writer's story, and the steps involved in creating the final artwork.

I am an illustrator. I am not a writer. I seldom meet the authors of the books I illustrate. For me a picture book always begins with someone else's manuscript. I prefer not to have a brief, giving me descriptions of place or character. A good writer should include these in the manuscript, and that is where I glean inspiration – finding stimulation on how to tell the story visually.

A good writer entrusts the illustrator, the image-maker, to interpret their work. But both writer and illustrator are equally important to the success of a picture book.

The early years

I studied Fine Arts at Durban Art School, South Africa and landed a job as a junior visualiser at a glitzy advertising agency De Villiers & Schonveldt in Cape Town. They called me 'the new drawer'. No personal statement required – no showing of qualifications, no listing of hobbies, just a presentation of me and my portfolio … and a vague introduction from an old school friend.

It was the best thing that happened to me and definitely helped my future as an illustrator. I learnt to take ideas and concepts to pencil rough stage. I learnt layout, design, composition, typography and the importance of promotion and advertising. But most of all, I learnt that craft and skill are essential to any creative endeavour.

'Drawer' is a fair job description of what I did then but, I realize, not an accurate description of what I do now. Now I am a drawer *and* a storyteller – not verbally, but through my illustrations.

Becoming an illustrator

In the '70s I fled apartheid South Africa for Europe and continued to work in advertising while trying to crack the children's book world as an illustrator. My brother, Donald, worked for Oxford University Press. He wrangled a meeting for me with the then Children's Books editor, Ron Heapy, who was wary. You can imagine – some bloke working at OUP Africa Sales Division has an older brother who draws …

He looked at my portfolio, then photocopied a few illustrations. 'We'll put these on file', he intoned, followed by the usual 'Don't phone us, we'll phone …'.

Then, as I slunk out feeling depressed, Ron handed me a manuscript: 'Do me three drawings. It's an A4 format, paperback, double staple bound and part of an Oxford reading programme. It's about a witch who lives in a black house with a black cat. Written by an Australian, Valerie Thomas.'

A few weeks later, I returned with three full-colour illustrations in a large picture book format.

'That's not what I asked for,' he muttered.

'I know. But it's a great story', I replied. 'Pity to publish it as an A4 staple bound …'

Winnie the Witch has since appeared in 16 picture books, has been translated into 30 languages and sold nearly 6 million copies. I am amazed and delighted.

Working from the manuscript

I liken illustrating picture books to making a movie. As the drawer, you are the cinematographer, director, casting agent, costume designer, set designer *and* are responsible for locations, camera, lighting, props and continuity! The text is the soundtrack and that special combination between words and pictures makes for good storytelling. As in a movie, neither text nor illustration can exist comfortably on its own.

What do I look for in a story? The subject matter is unimportant; I will draw anything. What appeals to me are stories with an unexpected ending or a neat, clever twist. If on the first reading the story inspires me, filling my head with images, I feel confident I can do it justice.

I may discuss themes or ideas with a writer, but I choose not to be involved in the writing of drafts or final manuscripts. I leave this to the author and editor. I prefer to work from an A4 clean-typed, double-spaced text of a final manuscript approved by author and editor.

Creating the flatplan

The next stage is to divide the manuscript into 12 double-page spreads. This is known as 'doing the flatplan' and this all-important process should always be assigned to the illustrator. It is the key factor in determining the pace and rhythm of the story. I always urge writers to concentrate on writing the story and not to concern themselves with the flatplan. At this stage, it distracts the illustrator.

The majority of picture books contain 32 pages:
- Page 01 glues to the inside front cover
- Page 32 glues to the inside back
- Pages 02+03 are the front end papers
- Page 30+31 are the back end papers
- Page 04 is the copyright details + dedication page
- Page 05 is the title page
- Pages 06+07 are Spread 1
- Pages 08+09 are Spread 2, etc
- Pages 28+29 are Spread 12

This makes a total of 8 pages allocating 24 pages, or 12 'double-page spreads' for the text and the illustrations.

Now you begin the process of visual storytelling while decoding someone else's written imagination. I read the finished manuscript several times, scribbling scenes or characters that drift into my mind's eye. I look for key words or phrases to prompt an image. Returning to the movie analogy, the flatplan is the shooting script. There are no fixed rules, but a good tip is to treat each spread as a chapter.

Generally the first task I do is to pencil in the following:
- Spreads 1+2 — the beginning
- Spreads 6+7 — the middle
- Spreads 11+12 — the surprise ending
- Spreads 3, 4, 5 — for build-up to the middle part

• Spreads 8, 9, 10 — for build-up to the 'neat twist'.

Then I look for cues for the remaining spreads:

• An introduction of a new character (or new characters)

• Passage of time, i.e. day/night scenes

• Change of scene

• A 'cliffhanger' sequence needing a page-turn to discover the outcome.

I have to be aware of the pace, rhythm and drama of the story, and the writing style when breaking down the text.

Preparatory sketches and ideas

In most of the picture books I've illustrated the writer offers little or no description of the characters' appearance or the environment they inhabit. In a picture book this is redundant as I will imagine and draw these aspects, unless the writer offers significant keys to the action or plot.

Some characters require hours of doodling before I feel they're right. It's difficult to articulate how you decide on a look or a face, as it's something that develops within you. For each spread, I select incidents I feel will visually expand the story, the drawing adding imaginative layers as the tale unfolds. This process requires endless scribbles, preparatory sketches and oodles of time – but it's such fun!

In *Winnie the Witch*, the writer Valerie Thomas used only one adjective to describe our heroine's home: 'black'. My initial sketches showed a picturesque cottage with thatched roof and timber beams. The results were dull and commonplace.

'What's the opposite of cottage?' I asked myself. Answer: 'stately home'. This opened the story for me. The rooms and paraphernalia of a stately home would serve as a dramatic backdrop for Winnie's antics with her cat, Wilbur. The real challenge lay in illustrating it all in black! This is where my training as a fine artist mattered. Our classical art training taught us that, when painting black, add reds for warm and blues for cold black.

The grid template

This is the skeleton of the book. The roughs and the finished art are done 25% larger than the printed size. Using InDesign or Quark I prepare the grid template for the left-hand page (verso) and the right-hand page (recto) on A3 photocopy paper at 125% showing:

• *Trim* (page edge)

• *Bleed* (extra 5mm on all outside edges)

• *Spine* (the centre of the spread using a dotted line)

• *Live picture area* (by showing the margins on the verso and recto pages using a dotted line)

• *20mm margin* top and left and right sides of the pages

• *25mm margin* on the bottom of both pages.

• Any other layout info, which is common to all pages

• 15 copies at least of verso and recto are printed.

The pencil roughs

Each A3 verso and recto page are glued together to make a single spread, thus becoming A2 size. On a separate piece of paper I print out the text for that spread with typesetting at 125%. With a pencil I sketch in my ideas, moving the text around to fit with the illustration. It is very important that text and pictures work together.

Many of my spreads are dense with detail, enticing reluctant readers to have fun, to explore the illustrations, talk about them, even stimulate their own stories. The backgrounds or environments contain layer upon layer of detail, tales within tales connected to the story or elaborating on its themes. I try to create a world with many imaginary creatures, inhabiting a world festooned with stuff.

When I am satisfied with the pencil sketch and position of the typesetting, I redraw over the pencil lines using a dip-pen and black Kandahar ink, making alterations and improvements to the pencil where necessary. Often, the roughs cover many pieces of paper; I arrange and glue these into 'collage' drawings. Sometimes a preparatory drawing is exactly what I want but is the wrong size; I'll enlarge or reduce it on a photocopier, then collage it into position on the rough.

The finished art

The finished artwork is done on a 190gm^2 Saunders's Waterford CP/NOT Surface watercolour paper. I tape the completed rough onto a light box (a drawing board with a glass worktop and strip lights beneath the glass; an essential drawing aid).

Over the rough I tape down the watercolour paper, flick on the lights so the rough sketch underneath shows through. With a very sharp HB pencil I lightly trace in the illustration, again altering and improving. The primary reason for tracing the rough onto the watercolour paper is to position the illustration exactly where I want it. Also, it helps avoid drawing too close to the edge of the page, or into areas reserved for text, or drawing crucial details over the spine or gutter.

How to present your idea for a picture book

Below are four items you need to include in your presentation:

1 **Story** (written by you or someone else). Divide the manuscript into a flatplan of 12 spreads. Text should be clean typed, double-line spaced, with each spread numbered and printed on separate sheets of A4.
2 The **first three spreads** worked out as roughs AND finished art.
3 The **subsequent three roughs** worked out.
4 **Preparatory drawings, sketch books and reference material.**

I remove the watercolour paper from the light box and start drawing – not tracing! There's a great difference between the two. I don't slavishly follow the pencil lines, as this would produce a dull, lifeless work. They are merely guides. The trick is to recapture the fresh spontaneity so often found in the rough drawings. I draw mainly with a dip-pen using black Kandahar ink or waterproof coloured inks, but toothbrushes, porcupine quills, goose feathers have all been used achieve certain effects. Once the line work is complete, I paint with Schmincke Horadam Aquarell watercolours.

Masking fluid. Masking fluid is applied over complex objects in the foreground. Background colours and washes can be painted broadly and effortlessly over the masked objects, which is simpler than painting around them. Colourless masking fluid is best applied with silicone brushes (colour shaper) or, for fine details, a dip-pen.

Do you need an agent?

Publishers seem to insist on authors having agents but not so with illustrators. My problem is that agents claim a percentage of your earnings in perpetuity. I do not have an agent.

After nearly 40 years I still love what I do. My aim is always to entice reluctant readers to enjoy the world of books through my illustrations. When I experience this, it's a real pleasure.

Illustrating for children

'That's a magic moment!', as Winnie the Witch would say...

Korky Paul is an award-winning illustrator of picture books, pop-up books, chapter books, educational books and poetry books for children. His bestselling *Winnie the Witch* series began with *Winnie the Witch* (Oxford University Press 1987) which won the Children's Book Award in 1988. Other publications include *Dinner with Fox* (Dial Books for Young Readers 1990), *Professor Puffendorf's Secret Potions* (Checkerboard Press 1992), *The Rascally Cake* (Andersen Press 1994) and *The Fish Who Could Wish* (OUP 2008). The latest in his *Sir Scallywag* series (written by Giles Andraea) is *Sir Scallywag and the Battle for Stinky Bottom* (Puffin 2015). See more at http://www.korkypaul.com/ and http://winnie-the-witch.com.

See also...

- *Picture books for children: the writer's story*, page 255
- *An illustrator's life*, page 267
- *Presenting your portfolio to a publisher*, page 273

Creating graphic novels

Raymond Briggs has created many graphic novels and here he describes his method.

Book writers have such an easy time of it. They sit down, write their book and when they come to the end they send it off to the publisher. It might be long, it might be short, the publisher doesn't mind.

The writer needs no materials or equipment. He can do it all with a pencil and a note pad. Even the typing may be done for him. Unlike the illustrator, he needs no paints, crayons, T-squares, set squares, brushes, dividers, spray cans, handmade paper and mounting boards, light boxes, cutting tables, guillotines, type scales, magnifier lamps, wall-to-wall display boards and masses of space. The writer can scribble it all in bed. (They often do.)

Drawing the book

For the picture book illustrator, when he has finished the writing, that is the easy bit done. His true task then begins.

First he has to design the book. Picture books have to be exactly 32 pages, not 33 or 31. This includes prelims. So the text has to be divided into fewer than 16 spreads. On rare occasions, the publisher may allow 40 pages, or on even rarer occasions 48, though this allowance may contain 'self-ends' which take up eight pages. (This is too technical to explain to book writers.)

Then, the illustrator becomes a typographer. He casts off the manuscript, chooses a suitable font, decides on the type size, the measure and the leading, and has it set. Surprisingly, some writers I have met know nothing about typography. Some don't even know the name of the font their own book is set in! Some have never even set foot in a printer's.

If the book is strip cartoon with speech bubbles, the task is even greater as each speech bubble has to be individually designed. The size and shape of it is part of its expressive quality and once the bubble is finalised the illustrator becomes a hand-lettering expert and letters in, possibly many hundreds of words, trying to maintain a consistent style over many days' work. In America, strip cartoon work is divided amongst several people: writer, pencilling-in artist, inker-in, and letterer. In England we are made of sterner stuff – 'blood, toil, tears and sweat' and we 'graphic novelists' do it all.

The illustrator then makes a dummy (a blank book) with the correct number of pages and of the exact size. If he is well established and commands respect from the publisher, the publisher may have a dummy made for him – but you need to be at least 60 years old to be granted this privilege. (You might have to show them your bus pass.) He then cuts up the type proofs (which used to be called 'galleys') and sticks them onto the dummy, imagining the pictures on the page as he does so. Again, for strip cartoons it is much more complicated – you have to consider not just what text goes on each spread but how many frames the text is to be divided amongst, and what size and shape the frames are to be.

This brings us to the next stage: designing the 'grid', i.e. how many rows of frames per page and the number of frames in each row there are to be. Places where small frames give way to a big picture, either vignetted or bled off, will be determined by the text itself, not only in terms of space but also by the feeling the text is trying to express.

Creating the action

When all this is done, it is time to stop book designing and start making the 'film'. You become the director. Who comes on from the left and who from the right? A slight nuisance is that the character on the left is the one who has to speak first. What are the characters doing and thinking and feeling? We have their words, but is there a subtext? Can this be expressed by body language? Is one of them angrily scrubbing the floor, whilst the other gazes moodily out of the window?

You then become the art director, designing the sets. Where does the scene take place? Indoors or outdoors? In the garden or in the street? What does a 1930s kitchen look like? How big is the room? What is the view from the window?

You also have to be the costume designer and the lighting designer. What would they be wearing at the time? Is it winter or summer? What were overcoats and hats like then? What did they wear on the beach? Should it be daylight or artificial light in this scene? What exactly was the look of gaslight? Does it need a dark ominous light or a happy morning light?

Then as the cameraman you have to decide where to shoot from. Close-up, long shot, or middle distance? Both characters in shot or one off-screen? Perhaps a speech bubble stays in the frame but the speaker is unseen, through a doorway or simply out of shot. Shall it be a high view looking down on the scene or a low angle looking up? It all depends on what the action is trying to convey.

Finally, you have to become the actor and feel yourself inside the character when you're drawing it. This is the essence of good narrative illustration. It is an odd bit of psychology. You have to be mentally in two places at once. One part of you is inside character, feeling what it is like to be huddled and running in the pouring rain, the other part of your brain is detachedly looking at this figure from a certain point of view, taking note of perspective. 'Ah yes, the lower leg will be foreshortened from this angle; we're looking down on the thigh and on the back; we can't see his face as his head is down and his arm is up. Will we see the sole of the shoe that is raised or is it edge on?'

The lucky writer need know nothing about human and animal anatomy, perspective, drawing, line tone or colour. All they have to do is write down some words! It's a doddle. I wish I could do it.

Raymond Briggs is creator of *The Snowman*, *Fungus the Bogeyman*, *Father Christmas* and many other characters and stories for children, and *When the Wind Blows* and *Ethel and Ernest* for adults. His most recent children's book is *The Father Christmas It's a Bloomin' Terrible Joke Book* (Puffin 2013). Since leaving art school in 1957 he has been a writer and illustrator, mainly of children's books. He has written plays for the stage and radio and a few 'adult' books. In 2004 he designed the Christmas stamps for the Royal Mail, and was made a Fellow of the Royal Society of Literature, but his proudest achievement is going on the radio programme *Desert Island Discs*, twice. His fansite is www.toonhound.com/briggs.htm.

See also...

- *Notes from a successful children's author and illustrator*, page 116
- *Finding your own style*, page 270
- *Eight great tips to get your picture book published*, page 276
- *Writing and illustrating picture books*, page 280

Notes from the first Children's Laureate

Quentin Blake was the first Children's Laureate (1999–2001).

I started life – my life as someone who does pictures to appear in print, that is – by doing illustrations and cartoons for magazines. It wasn't so long, however, before I got the idea that I would like to be on my own between two covers; or at least on my own with an author. There were various reasons. One was that I wanted to organise a sequence of images that would follow a narrative; another was to get into a wider range of subject matter, a wider range of mood and atmosphere than was supplied by humorous commentary on current everyday life. I had been trained as a teacher, and I thought it was possible that, as the humour I had to offer was mainly visual, children might appreciate it as much as adults. The prospect of children's books was an attractive one, but I had no idea at all about how to begin. In the event I asked a friend, John Yeoman, if he would write something for me to illustrate. He could read Russian and it was a sample Russian folk-tale that he offered to me, which I illustrated, and which we submitted to Faber and Faber. We fell on our feet. I think perhaps we had hoped for a picture book, but Faber said that if we could find another handful of stories they would publish them – and in due course they became a book called *A Drink of Water*.

So we were very lucky. We were spared the frustrating (and generally unavoidable) round of submissions, and we had something printed. And there is nothing, I suspect, so reassuring to a prospective commissioning editor as seeing drawings actually in print.

Now (50 years later), holding the *Children's Writers' & Artists' Yearbook* in my hand, it's clear to me that, if we hadn't been as lucky as we were, how useful such a volume as this would have been. It has two great virtues. One, of course, is the wealth of information it contains. From their listing in 'Children's book publishers UK and Ireland', for example, we discover that Faber and Faber won't look at unsolicited manuscripts – so we wouldn't have got far with them nowadays.

The other is an impressive raft of notes, comments and advice from practitioners in every aspect of the business. It's as good as a correspondence course in the creation of children's books. And as well as the sage advice of such examples as Raymond Briggs and Tony Ross, there are more recent personal reactions. I was fascinated to read accounts of self-discovery from Lauren Child, David Lucas and Oliver Jeffers. The great advantage of such a personal approach is that the advice you find there is not merely prescriptive. In fact, though there is useful advice to be had, nothing is certain. Conventional wisdom would no doubt say that a readership of eight- and nine-year-olds wouldn't want to be given a heroine years younger than themselves, nor would that age group want to read about a middle-aged bachelor trying to persuade a middle-aged woman to marry him. But Matilda is a huge success, and Esio Trot does pretty well too. The book that you now hold in your hand is a wonderful guidebook, but it's still nice to think that none of us know quite where we may be going.

Quentin Blake CBE has always made his living as an illustrator, as well as teaching for over 20 years at the Royal College of Art, where he was Head of Illustration 1978–86. His first drawings were published in *Punch* when he was 16 and he continued to draw for *Punch*, the *Spectator* and other magazines over many years. He entered the world of children's books with *A Drink of Water* by John Yeoman in 1960 and has since collaborated with other writers such as Russell Hoban, Joan Aiken, Michael Rosen and, most famously, Roald Dahl. He has also illustrated classics such as *Don Quixote* and *Candide*, and created much-loved characters of his own, including Mister Magnolia and Mrs Armitage. Since the 1990s Quentin Blake has curated shows in, among other places, the National Gallery, the British Library and the Musée du Petit Palais in Paris. His work can be seen in the wards and public spaces of several London hospitals and mental health units in England and France. He has been very involved in setting up the House of Illustration (see page 283). His books have won numerous major prizes and awards. In 1999 he was appointed the first ever Children's Laureate. In 2012 he won the Prince Philip Designers Prize. He was knighted in 2013 and in 2014 was appointed a Chevalier of the Légion d'Honneur.

See also...

An illustrator's life

David Lucas describes his journey to creating picture books.

It helps me to think of my life as a river: water is a symbol of creativity, and I want my career to be long, with breadth and depth, and I want my work to be beautiful and useful. And a river is *heading somewhere* – it flows, just like a story flows, always new, yet always recognisably the same, a dynamic whole, like a *life*.

I was born in a dull suburb of an ugly town, and even when I was tiny I was aware of the soullessness of my surroundings: there was something wrong, something missing. I have been in search of *soul* ever since: I want magic, resonance, meaning, beauty, a feeling of connection – it is a spiritual need.

My father worked in the steelworks, my mother was a teacher – but they were both misfits aspiring to a better life and not sure how to get there. I had five brothers, all of us very close and inclined to be inward-looking too, and our parents encouraged us to draw, write and make things – and we had amazing, rambling conversations about *everything*. My father used to describe himself as a 'nature-worshipper', my mother is a devout Catholic. The home developed a strange hothouse atmosphere, fertile but stifling, and we grew up a bit *odd*. But I had no doubt that my life was full of meaning and purpose: I had my own ideas about religion, art and spirituality, my own answers. I read obscure books on magic and mysticism, and I spent most of my time drawing intricate pictures and writing fantastical stories. I was like an underground stream, winding through secret caverns, my work grotesque and dark.

My father applied to art college to study design, and we all moved to London. But he always felt like an outsider; he lacked role models and never saw how he could really fit in. My mother became a head teacher and did ground-breaking work teaching damaged children, but as her career blossomed so my father withdrew from the world, and the marriage fell apart.

That turned me even more inward – I swirled about in darkness. I wrote an illustrated fantasy novel – a terrible book, I'm sure – and the one publisher I dared to send it to sent it straight back with a standard polite note. I began to be aware that the answers, the certainties, I had clung to were restrictive, suffocating and airless; I just hadn't really lived. I was afraid of living. To grow, I needed to leave my 'cave'.

Breaking out

When I went to art college it was as if I had suddenly burst into the open, into the light: the spell of my sealed world was broken and I began to see how much catching up I had to do. I wanted to fit in, to be normal, fashionable, cool. I did my best to forget about magic and fairy tales and spirituality.

Modern artistic culture is liberal, atheist, materialist – doubt and questions are valued above answers and certainty, fragments are valued above wholeness, and any sort of spirituality, any belief in real purpose and meaning, is looked on with suspicion, as if it can't possibly be authentic, as if only doubt and questions are truly authentic. That is the culture I tried to fit in to – and it meant tearing my old self in pieces. So I did.

And it was liberating suddenly to question everything. My watery nature is impressionable. Told that nothing was fixed or stable, I found I was good at being fluid, good at being chaotic. I was like a mountain stream, splashing from rock to rock. My drawing was empty, ugly, fragmented. I had lost faith in stories, in wholeness. I found it very hard to finish anything and I changed my drawing style every few months. My work might have seemed refreshing to some stray traveller in the hills, some similarly lost soul, but it was thin stuff.

After college I got some illustration work. An editor saw potential and I illustrated a picture book by Ted Hughes – in a loose, empty style. I did some work for design companies and worked in greetings cards – my chameleon style changing from job to job. Unable to decide who I was and what I wanted, unable to bring things into focus, I could still convince myself that doubt and questions, fragments and open-endedness were signs of 'seriousness' as an artist. So I drew constantly, often angrily, my whirl of activity never settling into a meaningful whole. I was going nowhere fast. And it was easier to keep going than to stop and *think*.

But years had passed now and tensions, questions that I had been afraid to answer, were becoming impossible to ignore: it was becoming horribly clear that my ceaseless, restless activity itself was a trap. I was heading over a cliff. A waterfall. Everything suddenly turned upside down: for a few months everything seemed to go wrong at once, both in my personal life and in work. All sorts of factors combined to tip me over the edge. I let go. I was sure I had failed. At last, I stopped. I'd never been good at doing *nothing*, but now I was like a reflective pool, no longer flowing, just staring at the sky, the honesty of failure preferable, somehow, to my previous avoidance strategies.

Life beyond the waterfall

I had been keeping a journal for a few years, in a bid to make sense of things, but it was a mess of scrawls. Now I began writing clearly, neatly, in well-formed sentences. I began to try and define who I was. I could see my life as a river – as a *story* – but how did I want it to end, where did I want to go, what did I want to say? Our lives are short, our abilities are limited. Fear of being defined, of admitting both our strengths and limitations, is the fear of death. I tried to imagine how I'd use my time if I knew I had only a short time to live. I knew that, above all, I wanted to be whole, true to myself, I wanted answers not questions, and as an artist I wanted to create wholeness, beauty, something that had real meaning.

I began writing stories again, fairy tales, spiritual fables: children's books. I set myself the simple goal of making the most beautiful books I could in whatever time I'd been given. Creative energy must be channelled, a river without banks is lost. Defining myself, defining my goals, I was learning to channel my energy at last and I began to flow on, deeper, calmer, stronger.

I found inspiration again in the medieval art I had loved as a teenager, in folk art and oriental art: art that is animated by profound spirituality, art that is decorative not just to be beautiful, but because pattern-making is like a sacred ritual, a magic spell of connectedness.

Human nature is the same across every culture and across all of time, our intercon-nectedness is a hard fact, and in discovering the deepest regions of our souls we reach those dark subterranean layers that link us all. The deeper I look into my heart the more I know that we are all the same, we all have very similar problems, each of us is always torn between opposing forces, we have to cope with the same tensions in our lives. Being honest about who I am, speaking from the heart, I could be confident that my work would resonate with others. My first book, *Halibut Jackson*, was about a chameleon-like character, going to great lengths to blend in wherever he is. He makes a mistake, everyone sees him for who he is and he finds the courage to be himself, at last. I've been making picture books ever since. And perhaps I've become something like a grown-up river, at last. But rivers twist and turn, they are *meant* to be turbulent.

I *need* questions. For me, the beginning of a story idea is a swirling current of energy, an inner conflict that I am struggling to resolve. A good picture or satisfying story is an answer to that question, a resolution to the conflict, the discovery of a new, unexpected point of balance, a happy ending. But, as Heraclitus said, *everything flows*. Happy endings aren't forever, balance is only ever temporary (at least from our time-bound, mortal perspective). The ending of one story becomes the beginning of another. An old answer becomes a new question. But good stories, good pictures, show that balance is *possible*, that fulfilment, wholeness and authenticity are achievable. The best art offers neither monolithic certainties, nor a jumble of random fragments, but something fluid, sparkling and richly, miraculously alive. I am still working on picture books, but the more I learn about human nature, and the more I learn about how stories work, the more ambitious I want to be as a writer.

My writing remained hidden, bubbling somewhere deep underground, until that 'waterfall' moment when I saw how to make myself whole. It was a confluence of words and pictures and those two streams have been intertwined ever since. I am often told by publishers that my ideas are too 'sophisticated' for picture books, yet my romantic world-view, my belief in happy endings, makes me a natural children's writer.

I have published one longer story, *The Lying Carpet*, an illustrated fable that is my own mix of words and images – and I have been writing other fables, and a fantasy novel. And if that works out I will have fulfilled those first teenage ambitions. Really it's just a matter of seeing what depth and breadth I can achieve before I reach the sea!

David Lucas was born in Middlesbrough and grew up in Hackney. He studied at the Royal College of Art and is the author and illustrator of 13 picture books. Recent books are *This Is My Rock* (Flying Eye Books 2015), *A Letter for Bear* (Flying Eye Books 2013) and *Grendel* (Walker Books 2013).

See also...

- *Creating graphic novels*, page 263
- *Notes from the first Children's Laureate*, page 265
- *Finding your own style*, page 270
- *Presenting your portfolio to a publisher*, page 273
- *Eight great tips to get your picture book published*, page 276
- *Writing and illustrating picture books*, page 280
- *House of Illustration*, page 283

Finding your own style

The 'style' of a good illustrator shines through no matter what the nature of the artwork is.
Emily Gravett tells the tale of how she found her style.

When I saw that the theme of this article was 'finding your own style' it immediately brought back memories of my days at Brighton University where I studied illustration.

Not because university was the place that I found my own style, but because it was the place where I spent so much time, energy (and tears) searching for it. What I discovered was that, sadly, finding my own style wasn't like supermarket shopping. I couldn't just go to Aisle G and pay £10.99, or 50 sleepless nights, or my firstborn, etc and come away with a nice box of 'Gravett Style' (preferably tastefully packaged … I was an art student after all!).

So this is the story of how I *did* find my style.

I was the child of two talented and arty people. I had grown up with more than one set of coloured pencils and the expectation that I would do my (art-based) A levels and go straight on to art college. Unfortunately (for my parents) teenage rebellion hit me hard, and I didn't even get halfway through my first year of A-levels. I left sixth form, and home, on a sunny day with only a rucksack on my back, a lovely set of dreadlocks and a new and wonderful feeling of complete freedom. I liked the feeling of freedom so much that I spent the next eight years living in a bus as a new age traveller. During those years, thoughts of careers and job fulfilment were the last thing on my mind. The minutiae of living on the road absorbed much of each day. When we weren't being evicted, my partner and I spent our time cooking, cleaning, fetching water and wood, digging holes and a thousand other jobs that living in ancient vehicles with very little money and no plumbing or electricity involve.

I also drew. The big advantage of living in a bus is that the view from the window changes a lot, and so I could sit and draw the world outside from the comfort of my own home with a cup of tea and my slippers on. (So not that different from now!)

Life changed after I gave birth to my daughter. Although being dirty had been somewhat a badge of honour for my partner and me, I wasn't so keen for our daughter to grow up being spat at in public. So after nearly a year of searching we eventually found a small cottage to rent in rural Wales. We parked the bus in the garden and went about setting up the idyllic life. A vegetable plot, cosy fires, and time to play and watch our (lovely clean) daughter grow up. It should have been perfect, but somehow it wasn't.

Horses got in and trampled the vegetables, the fire smoked, and the time to play turned into hours of boredom in an isolated area without the community of travellers we were used to. Living in a house was more expensive than in the bus so my partner started working. I found that the days stretched emptily before me. Our daughter wasn't the content little baby we'd envisaged and cried and cried (and then cried some more). The only thing that seemed to pacify her (and me) was endless readings, and re-readings of her picture books. I spent on average about four hours a day on the sofa with her reading. We had to put up new shelves to house her expanding picture book collection.

She was turning the pages to Jez Alborough's *Where's My Teddy?* long before she could talk. I loved the books, and I loved our hours together on the sofa reading (well … until my voice went – which it did frequently!). It was often the only time when I felt like I was succeeding at being a parent. The more we read, the more I started to really look at the books. I began to notice the way individual authors and illustrators used shape/colour/text and the structure of the book to communicate their ideas, and started to wonder if I could do the same.

About this time my partner brought home a prospectus for the local community college. He'd had enough of working for minimum wage and wanted to train as a plumber. Looking through the prospectus I saw that they had an art foundation course. I applied, got a place, and loved it. Within the first week a fantasy began to shape in my mind, which developed into a 'Master Plan'. We would up-sticks and move somewhere that I could do an illustration degree. I won't bore you with the details of the following year, but it involved a lot of hard work, frustration, sleepless nights and worry sprinkled with large doses of excitement of the type I'd not experienced since the day I left home.

It wasn't easy, but eventually I got myself a place at Brighton University. We packed up our belongings, waved goodbye to the cottage and the bus, and set off to start our new life.

It wasn't what I expected. I had somehow imagined that at university there would be a lot of teaching and that drawing would be central, but I think in common with most universities the course was much more self directed and conceptual. I struggled. The first year was the worst. We were asked to tear down any notion of what we did – or where we were going work-wise. Often tutors would examine the back of artwork, or wax lyrical over a squiggle in a sketchbook rather than the project we'd just spent the previous six weeks slaving over. By the end of the first year I felt totally disillusioned and that my work had lost any merit and individuality it might have once had. I felt I was constantly trying to chase the approval of the tutors, and failing.

But by far the worst parts of my first year at university were the class crits. For anyone lucky enough never to have experienced one, a 'crit' (short for critique) is when the class gets together and looks at each other's work to give constructive criticism with the aim of helping their fellow students' progress. The crits on my foundation year had been frightening (mainly because I knew I'd have to stand up and explain my work in front of the class – public speaking wasn't my strong point), but university crits were frightening in a whole different way. The most positive thing that could be hoped for in a class crit was disinterested disdain, but more often than not it felt like a competition in nastiness. They were HORRIBLE!

At the end of the first year we were set the project of illustrating a selection of letters from Edward Gorey's ABC *The Gashleycrumb Tinies*, an alphabet of children's deaths. I'd never seen Edward Gorey's work before (and avoided looking at it until after the project), but was excited by the narrative. I really enjoyed myself, and eventually finished a piece of work that I was pleased with. It felt like I was heading in the right direction at last. I went to the end-of-project crit scared but hopeful. The crit was an all-day, whole class affair (i.e. the worst kind). They started at ten o'clock in the morning, and didn't finish until after five. Needless to say my project went down like a lead balloon!

The comment that still (quite vividly) sticks in my mind was 'it looks the same as all your other work' to which I retorted that although it was recognisably my 'style' I disagreed that it was like anything else I'd produced that year. This opened the floodgates, and the tutor informed me that developing 'style' too early was dangerous for an illustrator.

After that I'm ashamed to say that I swore, and then cried. To which was added (fairly, I think in this case) the observation that I also don't take criticism well. I went home and stomped and ranted (and cried some more) and vowed never to go back to university again (me, not take criticism well?!). At this point my lovely patient partner who had just moved 300 miles and was struggling to support us by unblocking nasty things from strangers' u-bends produced a set of drain rods, and told me there was always another option.

So of course I went back, but it did make me think long and hard about style, and what it means to me. That crit was a turning point for me at university. It forced me to sit down and examine exactly what I was doing, and I discovered that what I was doing was everything that the tutors asked me to, without considering if it was something that interested me, or was right for me. I'd spent the whole year thinking that if I did exactly what they asked, that my work would improve, but without hearing that all I really was being asked to do was to think. From that day on I listened to all their advice, and I thought about all their advice, but I also thought about what was right for my work and me. I decided to follow the avenues that excited me. I started to spend a lot of time studying the structure of books and how the structure relates to the contents. For example, I made a concertina book about an accordionist, and a cautionary tale of playing with fire inside a box of matches. I was lucky that my university had a well-equipped bookbinding department where we were taught to make books properly. It's something that I still love to do, and often make a few hand-bound copies of my books. I also relaxed my drawing, and let myself draw any way I wanted to. If drawing wasn't right for whatever I was working on I found something that was. I started to gauge the success of a project not by what the tutors thought but what *I* thought, and how much pleasure it had given me.

Looking back, I think I probably misunderstood the tutor on that day of the bad crit. I think that what he meant when he was so derisive about 'style' was purposefully setting out to create a particular 'look' in your work, to follow fashion or to try to be different. I agree that this is a bad thing. Pretending to be something you're not is never going to keep you satisfied for long. When I use the word 'style' I mean it more as a fingerprint that shines through and makes each piece of work recognisably belong to its creator, whether the work is written, painted, or doodled on the back of an envelope with a biro. To me style is a subconscious expression of who you are, rather than what you are trying to be, and is as individual as your own handwriting. I think that an individual's style is just an outward sign of their personality, and personality is shaped by the experiences you've already had in your life, and will continue to develop with every triumph, catastrophe, and evening spent watching *Big Brother* with a cup of tea … .

So that's the story of how I found my style, not after all at university (although that's maybe where I recognised it) but somewhere in the 30 years before that.

I still haven't worked out if all that self doubt and gazing at squiggles was a necessary part of the whole process of becoming an illustrator. I don't think there's any magic formula that must be followed for success. Like style, and the process of discovering your own, I'm sure it's an individual journey. For me the three years spent studying provided the time I needed to think, draw, and develop, and most importantly to realise that I already had my own style. As do you!

Emily Gravett won the Macmillan Prize for Illustration and the CILIP Kate Greenaway Medal with her first book, *Wolves* (Macmillan Children's Books). She has since produced many other highly acclaimed picture books.

Presenting your portfolio to a publisher

Identifying an appropriate publisher for your work is the first step to gaining a commission for illustration. Val Brathwaite outlines how to present your samples and approach a publisher.

The best way to start when deciding how to show your work to publishers is to research the market. Think about the type of illustration you would like to do and the areas of publishing that appeal to you. Take some time to look at the different publishers and the kinds of books they publish and where your work would be suitable. Research the styles of illustration that are selling: visit specialist children's bookshops (see page 94) or bookshops with a good children's department to examine a wide variety of books.

Once you have identified the publishers you feel are most appropriate for your work, make a list of the ones to contact. This *Yearbook* contains pretty much all the contact details you'll need. If a particular listing doesn't include the name of the person to send your submission to, then call the publisher to find out. This could be the Art Director, Art Editor, designers or a specific name. If your work crosses over into both children's and adult publishing, you should send your work to both departments. It is also very important to find out how each publisher prefers samples to be supplied, i.e. by email, CD or colour copies. Always check this because it will vary from publisher to publisher. It really helps if you're able to arrange an appointment to see someone in person, as good advice and feedback on your work will stand you in good stead for future submissions. Whatever you do, don't drop off your folder expecting it to be viewed unless you have made a prior arrangement – chances are it won't be and, even worse, it might get lost. And never spontaneously drop in to a publisher on the off chance there'll be someone willing to see you. It won't happen so always phone or email for an appointment first.

Presenting your work

It might sound obvious but always select the best work from your portfolio. Show the work you feel happy and confident with – not the stuff you don't feel strongly about. And don't include too much – usually 10–15 pieces are sufficient. If you have a variety of styles, show a selection of work. For example, if you work in colour as well as in black and white line then show samples of both, and if your illustration style works for both children's and adult books or you have a different style for older age group books, show this too. It can take some time to break into the children's market so if your work lends itself to adult publishing, editorial and/or advertising, look to cross over into these markets. It all adds to gaining all round experience and further developing your style. Many well-known children's illustrators have started in other areas of illustration.

And it goes without saying, give due thought to how your work is presented – you are an artist after all. Clean and well-presented work shows that you are organised and proud of your work. A good quality portfolio with plastic compartments for each sample looks very neat and is easy to view.

Picture books

If you want to break into the picture book market and think you have a good idea, conduct a thorough research of which houses are publishing the type of book where it would fit. If it is a novelty book, make sure the publishers you approach have a novelty list. There is no point sending in an idea to a publisher which doesn't publish novelty books as they won't start a new list just to accommodate your idea. Don't waste your time making basic mistakes like this – ensure you are targeting the right publishers otherwise it's effort and expense down the drain. When presenting ideas for a picture book, a few sample illustrations are adequate along with the text, which can be printed onto A4 paper. Send jpegs or pdfs by email if that's what the publisher wants. If you have created a full 'book dummy' with illustrations and text in place as a college project or at some other point in your career, be prepared to make some changes to suit a particular publisher. Adapting each presentation to cater to each individual house may be more time consuming, but it will certainly increase your chances of getting a deal.

Each publisher will have a different format in mind as they have their own ways and ideas of making a book a financially viable investment. Also be aware that picture book publishers will be looking to sell co-edition rights and so will be keen to know that potential new books have an international appeal and that the art is as universal as possible.

If you are primarily an illustrator and don't write text to accompany your drawings, pay extra attention to the presentation of your work. And be encouraged as publishers are always on the lookout to find great illustrators for authors and need many different styles of illustration. But there is a downside – picture book publishing is one of the most difficult areas to break into, as there is fierce competition and the chances are that you'll be turned down several times before you get a break. So be prepared to keep trying and be patient. Having lots of experience in researching the market, submitting your work, and talking to publishers and getting feedback will help you to continually develop your work to suit the needs of your target audience.

Preschool books

The preschool market is very diverse, ranging from simple concept board books to pop-up novelty and interactive books. These ideas can come from an illustrator, author or the publisher. Submitting an idea for this category as a rough dummy, and a more finished spread together with the text is adequate.

Young illustrated fiction

Black and white line art is a good way into the book illustration market. Many children's publishers have illustrated fiction lists for young readers which carry very varied styles of illustration, from a fun cartoon look to more delicate or decorative illustrations. If you are able to work in line as well as colour this will help to broaden your prospect of being commissioned by a publisher.

Older fiction and teen fiction

The fiction market for older readers usually requires cover illustrations only. Cover art tends to be one-off commissions, unless you are lucky enough to be asked to illustrate a series. Undertaking cover work is a very good way to build up your contacts and it can allow you to carry out single jobs with several different publishers simultaneously. Again it is important to research the market and be sure to target only those publishers which your work will suit, for example there is no point in presenting illustrations to a publisher which only uses photographs.

Promotional material

Promotional material can be a very good way of introducing yourself, and postcards are a great approach. If the person you send a sample to likes your work, you'll be put on file and hopefully contacted in the future. Or better than that, if your postcard arrives on their desk at the right time, you might get called straightaway! It's a convenient, compact and non-intrusive way of showing an example of your work and leaving a (hopefully) memorable sample along with your contact details when approaching several publishers at once. A website is also an excellent way of showcasing your illustrations and makes it easy for people to view your work. Including the address on any printed samples you send out or emailing a link is helpful.

Follow up

Fingers crossed, when you send your postcards, email your jpegs or conclude your face-to-face meeting with the publisher of your choice, you'll secure a commission/deal. However, it's quite likely that you might not get any response or be waiting for a reply for a long time. If your work was received positively the first time, then follow this up say, six months later with any relevant new work you've produced in the interim. A gentle reminder can help push things along if you're sure your work is right for that publisher. There's every chance that publisher may not have had any suitable work for you the first time you approached them but six months down the line a project may have arisen.

Never be afraid to contact a publisher after a reasonable amount of time (3–4 months) has passed. In-house teams are always busy and constantly working to deadlines and seeing new people all the time, so follow-up is important to increasing your chances of securing work with them. But be sensible and patient about it: don't call right away as the publisher will need time to consider your work, talk to others in the department and see what work they have which will match your talents. A pushy approach can be all it takes for the publisher to dismiss you as a potential freelance illustrator – regardless of the quality of your work. Never forget the degree of competition there is out there and the need for you to be professional, reliable and easy to work with.

And last but by no means least, the main thing is to not give up. If you really want to illustrate for the children's book market and believe your work matches the needs of particular publishers then you must keep trying. It can take a long time to establish yourself but if you're good enough, you'll get there.

Good luck!

Val Brathwaite is the Design Director at Bloomsbury Children's Books.

See also...

Illustrating for children

Eight great tips to get your picture book published

Tony Ross gives some sound advice for illustrators and writers of children's picture books.

I have always had the uncomfortable feeling that if I can get published, anyone can. A belief that being published is something that only happens to other people, holds some very good writers and illustrators back.

Assuming you have drawings – or a story – to offer, there are several ways to go about it. Probably the best way is to have a publishing house in the family! Failing that, all is not lost.

Work can be sent directly to a publisher's office. Most editors receive a good amount of unsolicited work, so be patient with them for a reply. A stamped addressed envelope for the return of postal submissions is always appreciated, bearing in mind that the majority of work submitted is refused. At the beginning of a career, refusal is quite normal and a great deal about yourself and your talent can be gleaned from this experience. Sometimes, advice gained at this stage can change your future.

Starting on a drawing career is an exciting time and I think it's a good idea to get yourself in perspective. Visit the library and some bookshops to look at all the styles that are around. Get a sense for what's out there: you don't want to regurgitate it, but to get a feel for the parameters. You can learn a lot, maybe more than you learned at art school, from looking at great artists such as Edward Ardizzone, E.H. Shepard, Maurice Sendak and Chris Van Allsburg.

Great Tip No 1: Use black and white

There is great appeal in working in full colour but it's good to remember black and white. Sometimes a publisher may have a black and white project waiting for an illustrator, while all of the big interest is going into the colour picture book list. Some of the greatest children's books are illustrated in black and white – A.A. Milne and E.H. Shepard made one of the greatest partnerships with those tiny black ink drawings contributing so much to a great classic. Not a bad place to start, eh?

Ink drawing is simple in the hands of a master but not easy. That unforgiving fluid! Wonder at the uncomplicated, straightforwardness of the Pooh drawings. Consider Toad in *The Wind in the Willows*. When he applied to do the illustrations, Kenneth Graham said to Shepard: 'I have seen many artists who can draw better than you, but you make the animals live.' Can you learn anything from that? Look at Ardizzone's ability to draw mood. He can show both a summer afternoon and a cold November morning simply by using black ink. There is so much to look at, so much to learn from.

Try to include black and white work in your folder. Also include a series of perhaps 30 drawings, such as a fully illustrated story, where you show your ability to be consistent with the characters and the style, without repetition or irrelevance (like the radio programme *Just a Minute*).

It is a duty of an illustrator to be able to read, i.e. to try and understand the writer's aims, and to help them rather than to inflict a totally different angle onto the book (again, think of the Milne and Shepard partnership). Much of this comes down to being sensitive enough to recognise the tone of the writing, and skilful enough to draw in the same tone. So the importance of really taking an interest in the story cannot be overstressed. In the text, there will be either clues, or blatant instructions to help the drawings gel. Be very aware.

Great Tip No 2: Experiment

I have known illustrators who convinced themselves that they couldn't use black ink. Mostly this was because they were using the wrong ink, the wrong pen, and/or the wrong paper. Types of black ink vary: waterproof behaves differently from water soluble. Fine nibs and broad nibs each give a totally different result, as does an old fountain pen or a sharpened stick. Try ten different inks, 50 different nibs, odd sticks and all the papers you can find: tracing, layout, calendered, five different cartridges, smooth and rough watercolour, handmade, wrapping paper, anything at all. It's a case of finding the combination that suits your hand and your intention. Your own genius, unrecognised at art school, could surprise you.

Many of the points I've made about black and white work also apply to colour. The marriage of image to text will be in your hands, but it must work.

Great Tip No 3: Choose the right words

I am hesitant to give advice to writers. After all, there are few rules, and the next J.K. Rowling may read this. My own view is really quite simple, and rather obvious. I write mainly for under eight year-olds, so my stories are as short as I can make them. I feel that it is good to have a magnetic first sentence, and an ending that EXPLODES WITH SURPRISE. I think that the ending is the most important part of the story. The bit in the middle should waft the reader along, remembering that the *sound* of words and sentences can be a useful tool.

I like stories to be either funny or scary. *Very* funny, or *very* scary. To be dull is the worst thing in the world! That sounds so obvious, but it gets overlooked. If you are not excited with your work, maybe nobody else will be either.

A picture book has about 23 pages of text (but this can be flexible). I think those pages should have fewer than 2,000 words; 1,000–1,500 is good. One word per page would be great, if the one word was brilliant. As brilliant as the story. Don't be frightened of editing out surplus words. One brilliant one will work better than a dozen mundane ones.

Don't fall into the mindset that writing for children is easy. It has all the disciplines of writing for adults, with the added problem of understanding a child's mind and world. The great writers have a passport to a child's world – think of Roald Dahl. I have seen many brilliant ideas, with less than brilliant pictures, make wonderful books. I have seen a bad idea saved by wonderful illustrations. So, writing style apart, be your own concept's greatest critic. It is quite natural to be protective of your baby, of your story. But try to remember that there are a lot of good editors out there and it will be in your own interest to consider their advice. So don't be a young fogey: be flexible, listen, understand experienced points of view. This can be a good time to change for the better, and to start a relationship with one publishing house that may serve you for a lifetime.

Great Tip No 4: Choose what you draw

Don't plan huge drawing problems into your submitted roughs. They may be accepted, and the editor will expect the final art to be better than the roughs.

I illustrate my own writing. This appeals to me for all sorts of reasons, few of them noble. Firstly, I get all of the available fee or/and royalty because I don't have to let half or more go to a writer. Secondly, if there is something I don't like to draw, I don't write about it. For instance, most of my stories take place in the summer, because I prefer to handle trees with their leaves on.

Illustrations being worked on to be published is not the place to practise your drawing. *Practise, change, experiment* all the time, but not in a publishing project. Your finished illustrations must be as good as you can make them. I know an illustrator who won't draw feet, always hiding the ends of legs in grass, water, behind rocks, etc. This is okay if the text will allow; a well-drawn puddle is better than a badly drawn foot any day. It is better to think around a drawing problem, than just to go along with it.

Great Tip No 5: Experiment with your main character

Before you start, try drawing your main character (the most important visual element of the story) in all sorts of ways. A day spent doing this can be so valuable. Getting the main character right can indicate ways to proceed with the whole book.

Great Tip No 6: Think global

Remember that editors react well to stories with wide appeal, rather than minority groups. Foreign sales are in everyone's interest, so try to allow your work to travel. Rhyme is sometimes difficult to translate, as are unusual plays on words.

Great Tip No 7: Plan the whole book

Do little mock-up books for yourself to plan what text goes on which page. This helps to get the story right throughout the book. A 32-page children's book (the most common extent for a picture book) includes covers, end papers, title and half-title pages. This leaves you 23–25 pages to play with. These little mock-ups are for your own use, not to be presented as roughs, so they can be quite work-a-day.

By working out what text goes on which page you will get some sort of an idea of which illustrations go where. Just as the drawings are creative, so is their use on the page. If you use a full double-page spread, another can be expected to follow it. But imagine the effect if the next page explodes with huge typography, and tiny pictures? I am not suggesting you do this, only reminding you that pages of a book are there to be turned, and the turning can be unpredictable and adventurous. Book design is important, along with everything else.

Great Tip No 8: Persevere

So much to do, so much to remember. The main thing is, every children's illustrator and writer I know who has kept trying has got there in the end and been published. But I've also seen great talents give up far too early. Remember that rejection is normal: it's only someone's point of view. Some great books have had long hunts for a publisher. Be open to change and always bear in mind that editors have the experience that you may lack and an editor's advice is meant to help you, not choke you off. However, not all of their advice may apply in your case, so try to recognise what applies to you. When I worked in advertising, I had an art director who said: 'Half of what I say is rubbish. Trouble is, I don't know which half.'

And a reminder

Don't waste time by sending work to publishers who don't publish material like yours. Libraries and bookshops are worth exploring to familiarise yourself with which publishing houses favour what types of work. Research of this kind is time well spent.

Try to show your work in person so that you get a chance to talk, and learn. Do not, however, just drop in. Make an appointment first and hope that these busy people have some time available.

There are also agents prepared to represent new talent (see *Illustrators' agents* on page 284). Of course, an agent will take a percentage of the fee for work sold, but as my dad used to say, 'Seventy-five per cent of something is better than 100% of nothing.'

I am troubled by giving advice. I can't help thinking of the young composer who approached the slightly older Mozart and asked, 'Maestro, how should I compose a concerto?' to which Mozart replied, 'You are very young, perhaps you should start with a simple tune'. The young composer frowned and argued: 'But, Maestro, *you* composed a concerto when you were still a child!' 'Ah yes,' said Mozart, 'but I didn't have to ask how'.

Tony Ross is a renowned illustrator of international repute and the creator of such classics as *The Little Princess* and *I Want My Potty*. His first book was published in 1976 and since then he has illustrated between 2,000 and 2,500 books including titles by David Walliams, Astrid Lindgren, Francesca Simon, Roald Dahl and Jeanne Willis.

See also...

- *Notes from a successful children's author and illustrator,* page 116
- *Creating graphic novels,* page 263
- *Writing and illustrating picture books,* page 280
- *On being a storyteller: the illustrator's story,* page 258

Illustrating for children

Writing and illustrating picture books

Debi Gliori tells the story of how she started writing and illustrating children's books.

The prospect of spending your life making children's books has a great deal to recommend it, not least the fact that you will never have to buy those nasty big itchy rolls of rockwool to insulate the walls of your home ever again. Twelve thousand or so volumes will do the job far better. Following the children's books career path will ensure that books will pour into your home, year after year, yours and other people's; foreign editions and large-print versions; pop-ups and boards; collections and anthologies; so many that you might think about studying 'Elementary Bookshelf Building for Beginners and Fumblethumbs' before your piles of books reach to the ceiling. You will also be forced to develop a pronounced and sincerely apologetic grovel each time your postman staggers laden to your door – after all, his sciatica/lower back pain/slipped disc is *entirely your fault.*

Tottering heaps of hardbacks notwithstanding, I can say, with hand-on-heart, that being a children's author and illustrator is the best job in the world. I'm not alone in this opinion. Some years ago, a midwife visited me in the studio I work from in my garden and said, apropos of nothing: 'Eee lass, you've landed with your bum in the butter'.

Unsurprisingly, I looked suitably horrified. (What *was* this, pray? Surely not more indignities to be visited upon my person in the name of childbirth?) Seeing my expression, she hastily explained that what she had *meant* was that I was exceedingly fortunate to be paid to do what I love best. 'Bum in the butter' huh? Takes all sorts. But hey, Gentle Reader, it was not always thus. Back in the mists of that ghastly period of human history known as the Eighties when I set off on this Quest for Publication, I recall that I underwent a long period of major struggle during which many lentils were consumed. This was a lengthy phase which also involved dressing in the morning *in* bed, serious layering of woolly jumpers and, I kid you not, bathrooms so cold that one's toothbrush *froze.*

After graduation from Edinburgh College of Art, I trawled round London publishers with my too-big portfolio and quickly realised that good picture book texts were as rare as talking bears. While illustrators, such as I'd been studying to become, were everywhere in abundance. Encouraging, *not.*

Stubborn is my middle name. That's right, Debi Stubborn Gliori – I know it's weird, but parents … pffff, what can I say? Anyway, stubbornly I decided that there was no way that I was going to take on a badly paid job to 'support' my unpaid non-existent career in children's books. That would be *two* jobs. I mean, get real. Nor did I much fancy the kind of grinding-noble-poverty-consumption-in-a-garret artist's lifestyle afforded by a complete lack of cash. Mercenary little beast that I was, I picked up as many well-paid advertising jobs as possible (illustrating whisky labels and smoked salmon packaging, mainly) and in my spare time hauled myself off to libraries and bookshops and did my research. Who was publishing what? Why were these books published rather than, say, *mine*? What was fashionable and why? Did retellings work? Were books for babies no-brainers? Trust me, it wasn't all that hard for me to see what was required from a good picture book. I won't insult your intelligence by telling you. You know this stuff. Or if you don't, you'll pick it up quickly.

So, armed with a rough idea of what first publishers, then parents and finally, children might want (the order is, sadly, significant), I holed myself up in a 1.2 square metre cupboard and wrote a book which, joy of joys, was picked off the Walker Books slush pile and published. Read my lips: at that point, I had no 'in' in publishing – no contacts, no money and no influence. I was a single parent living in a freezing cold, damp cottage waaaaay out in the sticks in Scotland. And yet, and yet, and yet, I managed to get my book published. The message here is Take Heart. It *can* be done.

Making a picture book the Gliori way

How I go about starting to make a book from scratch is another matter. All of us approach the process of creating picture books from a multitude of different directions. For what it's worth, here's how I go about it. Although I always start with the text, nine times out of ten the initial idea for a book arrives in my head as a couple of images that I know I'd love to paint. Unsurprisingly, I never experience a burning desire to make a book that involves cars or horses, mainly because I cannot draw either. On the other hand, I love landscapes. So, for example, there's a scene in one of my early books called *Mr Bear Babysits* in which Mr Bear is walking home by moonlight through trees, and all around him are baby animals, birds and insects being tucked in for the night. Immediately that image sparks off a series of questions. What season would this be set in? Answer – summer, because then I can draw golden moonlit fields and haystacks. What time is it? Probably after midnight. Why is Mr Bear out so late? Maybe he's having a *liaison dangereux* with Mrs Grizzle-Bear … or then again, perhaps not. Let's imagine he's been babysitting for the Grizzle-Bear cubs. How many? Three. Heavens, poor Grizzle-Bears, they must *really* need a night off. What are the cubs like? Rumbustious. Has Mr Bear got kids of his own? Is he going home? Is this the end or is it the beginning? You can see the process, can't you? By trying to supply answers to my own questions, I am effortlessly beginning to build a framework round which I could start to construct a narrative.

I wouldn't like you to think that it's easy though. Frequently, the entire framework begins to assume the tensile properties of overcooked tagliatelle, at which point I will decide that this is an idea that's not ready to be written yet. I have several of these raw and palely loitering things tucked away in various notebooks, and once in a while I'll drag them out into the unforgiving daylight; poke, prod and play with them until they turn to mush at which point, with deep regret, I'll put them back and try a different tack. Sometimes, to my delight, the poking and prodding succeeds and a picture book text emerges, oozing and flubby in parts, but with a decent story at its heart. Over the course of the next month, I'll return to that text and read it out loud until my ears bleed, because reading out loud is the single best way for me to expose flaws, glitches and bumpy bits before I self-edit in what I blithely imagine to be a ruthlessly incisive fashion.

Afterwards, breathless and pink with the unaccustomed exertion, I type it out and email it to my editor. When I was a beginner, I would assemble a thick envelope in which I included the following items for editor-seduction purposes: one lovingly typed covering letter on headed stationery, one double-spaced (with Tippex blobs) manuscript (both typed and corrected on an ancient manual typewriter bought in a junk shop), a set of thumbnail sketches showing how I anticipated pacing the text and pictures over 32 pages, two hideously expensive colour photocopies of two spreads of artwork and one sae for the return of said hideously expensive samples. And then I would wait … and wait … and wait.

These days, if my editor likes my initial idea, she usually lets me know within a week of me sending an email. This has little to do with talent, and everything to do with expediency. My editor knows my work and she trusts me. From past experience, she is fairly certain that come hell or high water, or even both, simultaneously, along with some obstetric complications thrown in for good measure, three months after she has read and approved my text, I will deliver detailed black and white pencil roughs showing how I intend each spread to look. For her part, she will comment on the roughs, sending them back to me with a tactful and light powdering of Post-it notes. Only *suggestions*, Debi. Put that axe down. Five months afterwards, I will deliver camera-ready artwork.

Proofs and publication

Back when I was starting out, nothing much happened after I delivered a book. There was a lull and then the first proofs arrived – a stage I loved, and still love, because suddenly the whole book appears to fall into focus – it looks like a real book at last and it's one of many identical copies, thus saving me from my illustrator's artwork-related paranoia about someone accidentally dropping a slice of raw tomato onto it. Before you dismiss me as neurotic, Gentle Reader, let me say that this tomato-on-watercolour-artwork-falling-incident really happened. He'll never walk again without a limp, though. After the heady rush of seeing my work in proof form, came the not-so heady rush of publication day, which came … and went, unremarked. Sometimes there would be a wee card in the post, signed by everyone who'd had anything to do with the book; sometimes I'd cook something special for my family, or bake a cake or just sit in my studio and gnaw my fingernails off one by one, wondering just how far we could make 10% of not a lot stretch.

These days, I'm so involved with my next project that I'll have achieved a measure of distance from the book just published. What happens to your book from now on is, by and large, out of your hands. It's the day that unpublished authors dream of: the day you see *your* book in print. Perhaps I'm just an old cynic, but seeing my book in mint condition in bookshops doesn't press any of my buttons whatsoever. No, what *I* want to see is *my* book being read till it *falls to bits*. I want to see the date-stamp page at the front of a library copy of one of my books full to the brim with the inky evidence of many withdrawals. *That's* the whole point. Being *read* – not being published.

But first you have to get published, and that's why we're here; you reading and me attempting to spout wisdom like an illustrator's version of the Delphic Oracle. Did anyone remember to bring me a goat, by the way? Problem is, I'm not an oracle, and nor am I a teacher. All that I know is based my own experience of the business. Your experience will be significantly different. Without sitting down beside you and looking over your text or your portfolio, the best advice I can give is *keep going*. Be stubborn – if you want to be published, you're going to have to be rhinoceros-like in your determination as well as acquiring a rhino-hide to shrug off those slings and arrows of unkind comment. Follow your own star, even if it's a redundant Russian satellite. Er, learn how to put up bookshelves and develop a series of nifty recipes for lentils. And good luck: like all the best things in life, the process of learning how to make picture books is well worth the effort.

Debi Gliori has written and illustrated many picture books and her best-loved titles include *No Matter What* and the *Mr Bear* series. She is also the author of the *Pure Dead…* series of novels for older children and the *Witch Baby and Me* series of books for in-between-picture-books-and-novels children. Her most recent picture books are *Alfie in the Garden* and *Alfie in the Bath* (Bloomsbury 2015). She lives in Scotland and works from her International Shedquarters at the bottom of her garden. Her website is www.debiglioribooks.com.

See also...

• *Notes from a successful children's author and illustrator*, page 116

House of Illustration

The House of Illustration is a vibrant charity, passionate about promoting illustration, the world's most accessible art form, and celebrates the way it touches our lives.

When the doors of its flagship centre in the King's Cross regeneration area opened in July 2014, the House of Illustration became the world's first ever public gallery and education space dedicated exclusively to exhibiting, celebrating and learning about British and international illustration and illustrators.

Further information

House of Illustration
2 Granary Square,
King's Cross London N1C 4BH
020-3696 2020
website www.houseofillustration.org.uk
Includes details of competitions and exhibitions.

From advertising to animation, picture books to political cartoons, and medical drawing to travel and fashion design, the House of Illustration has something for everyone.

Each year there will be major exhibitions showcasing the best of British and international illustration, alongside a changing programme of free exhibitions, Family Days and hands-on workshops. It also provides a pioneering and established schools programme using illustration to enhance literacy and communication skills, an Illustrator-in-Residence programme, talks, events and masterclasses, illustration competitions, and a vibrant online programme including education resources.

The picture so far

• The first Illustrator in Residence in 2014 was Rachel Lillie. Illustrator in Residence for 2015 is David Lemm.

• Previous critically and commercially successful exhibitions include *What are You Like?* at Dulwich Picture Gallery (and now touring the UK) and *Fifty Years of Quentin Blake* at Somerset House, which broke box office records with 28,500 visitors over 15 weeks.

• Sir Quentin Blake has most generously pledged his archive of his lifetime's work to the House of Illustration.

• An annual book illustration competition, working with the Folio Society, searches for the best up-and-coming talent from around the world. See website for details.

• Pioneering education work takes illustrators into schools.

• A series of 'Expert Eye' talks for illustration enthusiasts and partnerships with the Big Draw and Pop Up: Festival of Stories have been formed.

• Partnerships with the Victoria & Albert Museum, the British Museum and the British Library have been established, all of whom have agreed to lend from their collections.

• In partnership with Hodder Children's Books, five 70th anniversary editions of Enid Blyton's *Famous Five* series were published in 2012. The covers were created by Quentin Blake, Emma Chichester Clark, Oliver Jeffers, Helen Oxenbury and Chris Riddell.

Illustrators' agents

Before submitting work, artists are advised to make preliminary enquiries and to ascertain terms of work. Commission varies but averages 25–30%. The Association of Illustrators (see page 393) provides a valuable service for illustrators, agents and clients.

*Member of the Society of Artists Agents †Member of the Association of Illustrators

Advocate Art
56 The Street, Ashtead, Surrey KT21 1AZ
tel 020-8879 1166
email mail@advocate-art.com
website www.advocate-art.com
Director Edward Burns

Has 7 agents representing 300 artists and illustrators. Bespoke Illustration for children's books, greeting cards and fine art publishers, gift and ceramic manufacturers. For illustrators' submission guidelines see website. New: animation, design and original content represented through LaB; Writers and Artists coLLaBorate. Also original art gallery, stock library and website in German, Spanish and French. Founded as a co-operative in 1996.

Allied Artists/Artistic License
tel 07971 111256
email info@allied-artists.net
website www.alliedartists-illustration.com
Contact Gary Mills

Represents over 40 artists specialising in realistic figure, cute and stylised illustrations for children's books, magazines, adult books, plates, prints, cards editorial and advertising. Extensive library of stock illustrations. Commission: 33%. Founded 1983.

Arena*†
Arena Illustration Ltd, 31 Eleanor Road,
London E15 4AB
tel 020-8555 9827
website www.arenaillustration.com
Contact Tamlyn Francis

Represents 26 artists illustrating mostly for book covers, children's books and design groups. Average commission 25%. Founded 1970.

The Art Agency
The Lodge, Cargate Lane, Saxlingham Thorpe,
Norwich NR15 1TU
tel (01508) 471500
email artagency@me.com
website www.the-art-agency.co.uk

Represents more than 40 artists producing top-quality, highly accurate and imaginative illustrations across a wide variety of subjects and for all age groups, both digitally and traditionally. Clients are children's fiction and non-fiction publishers. Include

sae with submissions. Do not email portfolios. Commission: 30%. Founded 1992.

The Artworks*†
12–18 Hoxton Street, London N1 6NG
tel 020-7729 1973
email mail@theartworksinc.com
website www.theartworksinc.com
Contact Lucy Scherer, Stephanie Alexander-Jinks, Alex Gardner

Represents 22 illustrators for design and advertising work as well as for book jackets, illustrated gift books and children's books. Commission: 25% advances, 15% royalties.

Beehive Illustration
42A Cricklade Street, Cirencester, Glos. GL7 1JH
tel (01285) 885149
email contact@beehiveillustration.co.uk
website www.beehiveillustration.co.uk
Contact Paul Beebee

Represents 200 artists specialising in ELT, education and general children's publishing illustration. Commission: 25%. Founded 1989.

The Bright Agency
Studio 102, 250 York Road, London SW11 3SJ
tel 020-7326 9140
email vicki@brightgroupinternational.com
website www.thebrightagencyl.com

Represents artists for children's publishing covering all ages.

Bright Group International
Studio 102, 250 York Road, London SW11 3SJ
tel 020-7326 9140
email amber@brightgroupinternational.com
website www.brightgroupinternational.com

Childrens illustration and content agency focusing on publishing, greetings, licensing and merchandising.

Jenny Brown Associates – see page 240

The Catchpole Agency
53 Cranham Street, Oxford OX2 6DD
tel 07789 588070
email james@thecatchpoleagency.co.uk
email celia@thecatchpoleagency.co.uk

website www.thecatchpoleagency.co.uk
Proprietors James Catchpole, Celia Catchpole

Agents for authors and illustrators of children's books from picture books through to young adult novels. Commission from 10% to 15%. Based in London and Oxford. See website for contact and submissions details. Founded 1996. See also page 240.

The Copyrights Group Ltd
3 Cambridge Court, 210 Shepherd's Bush Road, Hammersmith, London W6 7NJ
tel 020-3714 1181
email enquiries@copyrights.co.uk
website www.copyrights.co.uk
Chairman Nicholas Durbridge, *Creative Director* Linda Pooley *Brand & Marketing Director* Polly Emery, *Licensing Director* Rachel Clarke

A boutique international Licensing Agency representing writers, artists and brand owners. The company focuses on the long-term development of quality merchandise programmes around the world. Properties include *Paddington Bear*, *The Snowman*, *The Country Diary of an Edwardian Lady*, *Bunnies by the Bay*, the artwork of Shinzi Katoh, *Father Christmas* and Greenwich Polo Club.

David Lewis Agency
3 Somali Road, London NW2 3RN
tel 020-7435 7762 *mobile* (07931) 824674
email davidlewis34@hotmail.com
website www.davidlewisillustration.com
Director David Lewis

All kinds of material for all areas of children's publishing, including educational, merchandising and toys. Represents approx. 25 artists, half of whom produce children's material. Also considers complete picture books with text. Send A4 colour or b&w copies of samples with return postage. Commission: 30%. Founded 1974.

Graham-Cameron Illustration
59 Hertford Road, Brighton BN1 7GG
tel (01273) 385890
email enquiry@gciforillustration.com
and Helen Graham-Cameron, Graham-Cameron Illustration, The Art House, Uplands Park, Sheringham, Norfolk NR26 8NE
tel (01263) 821333
website www.gciforillustration.com
Partners Helen Graham-Cameron, Duncan Graham-Cameron

Represents 37+ artists and undertakes all forms of illustration for publishing and communications. Specialises in educational, children's and information books. Telephone before sending A4 sample illustrations with sae or email samples or a link to a website. Do not send MSS. Founded 1985.

David Higham Associates Ltd – see page 243

The Illustration Cupboard
22 Bury Street, London SW1Y 6AL
tel 020-7976 1727
email galleryn@illustrationcupboard.com
website www.illustrationcupboard.com
Chief Executive John Huddy

London art gallery specialising in the exhibition and sale of original book illustration artwork from around the world. It represents over 150 different leading illustrators and displays their work in group and single artist exhibitions; annual catalogue produced in November. Founded 1996.

B.L. Kearley Ltd
16 Chiltern Street, London W1U 7PZ
tel 020-7935 9550
email christine.kearley@kearley.co.uk
website www.kearley.co.uk
Agent C.R. Kearley

Represents over 30 artists and has been supplying top-quality illustrations for over 60 years. Mainly specialises in children's book and educational illustration for the domestic market and overseas. Known for realistic figurative work. Specialises in the sale of original book illustration artwork dating back to the founding of the company. Commission 25%. Founded 1948.

Kids Corner
The Old Candlemakers, West Street, Lewes BN7 2NZ
tel 020-7593 0500
email info@meiklejohn.com
website www.kidscornerillustration.co.uk
Managing Director Claire Meiklejohn

Illustration Agency, representing a collection of highly talented illustrators, from award-winning to emerging artists for children's publishing. Styles include fun, cute, stylised, picture book, young fiction, reference, graphic, traditional, painterly and digital. Established 2015.

LAW (Lucas Alexander Whitley Ltd)
14 Vernon Street, London W14 0RJ
tel 020-7471 7900
website www.lawagency.co.uk
Contacts Philippa Milnes-Smith, Elizabeth Briggs

Illustrations for children's publishing for children 0–16 years. See website for submission requirements. Particular interest in authors/artists creating their own projects. Clients include Doodlemum, Chris Judge, Jane Porter, Philip Reeve and Chris Riddell. Commission: 15% (20% overseas). See also page 244. Founded 1996.

Frances McKay Illustration
17 Church Road, West Mersea, Essex CO5 8QH
tel (01206) 383286
email frances@francesmckay.com
website www.francesmckay.com
Proprietor Frances McKay

Represents Represents 20+ artists for illustration mainly for children's books. For information on submissions please look at website. Submit email low-res scans or colour copies of recent work; sae essential for return of all unsolicited samples. Commission: 25%. Founded 1999.

Monkey Feet Illustration
tel 07760 162374
email enquiries@monkeyfeetillustration.co.uk
website www.monkeyfeetillustration.co.uk
Director Adam Rushton

Presenting portfolios of over 50 artists creating work for children's book publishers, design agencies, greeting cards companies and toy manufacturers. Founded 2002.

NB Illustration
40 Bowling Green Lane, London EC1R 0NE
tel 020-7278 9131
email info@nbillustration.co.uk
website www.nbillustration.co.uk
Directors Joe Najman, Charlotte Dowson, Paul Najman

Represents 50+ artists, of whom 40% produce children's material for picture books and educational publishing. Submit samples either as web link by email or by post with a sae. Commission: 30%. Founded 2000.

The Organisation*
The Basement, 69 Caledonian Road, London N1 9BT
tel 0845 054 8033
email info@organisart.co.uk
website www.organisart.co.uk
Contact Lorraine Owen

Represents 60 artists, 75% of whom produce children's material for all ages. Can supply both traditional and digital illustration for all markets, including the children's and educational book markets. Also produces illustrations for other print markets, advertising, packaging and editorial. Before submitting samples research the website. New artists must not have a similar style to one already represented. Send samples either by email or on a CD by post, or send printed images with sae. Average commission: 30%. Founded 1987.

Plum Pudding Illustration
Park House, 77–81 Bell Street, Reigate, Surrey RH2 7AN
tel (01737) 244095
email letterbox@plumpuddingillustration.com
website www.plumpuddingillustration.com
Director Mark Mills *Associate Director* Hannah Whitty

Represents 80+ artists, producing illustrations for children's publishing, advertising, editorial, greeting cards and packaging. See website for submission procedure. Commission: 30%. Founded 2006.

Sylvie Poggio Artists Agency
36 Haslemere Road, London N8 9RB
tel 020-8341 2722
email sylviepoggio@blueyonder.co.uk
website www.sylviepoggio.com
Directors Sylvie Poggio, Bruno Caurat

Represents 40 artists producing illustrations for publishing and advertising.

Elizabeth Roy Literary Agency
White Cottage, Greatford, Nr Stamford, Lincs. PE9 4PR
tel/fax (01778) 560672
website http://elizabethroy.co.uk

Handles illustrations for children's books. Only interested in exceptional material. Illustrators should research the children's book market before sending samples, which must include figure work. Send by post with return postage; no CD, disk or email submissions. See also page 246. Founded 1990.

Caroline Sheldon Literary Agency Ltd
71 Hillgate Place, London W8 7SS
tel 020-7727 9102
email felicitytrew@carolinesheldon.co.uk
email pennyholroyde@carolinesheldon.co.uk
website www.carolinesheldon.co.uk, www.carolinesheldonillustrators.co.uk
Contacts Caroline Sheldon, Felicity Trew

Represents a select list of leading illustrators working mainly in children's books. Also author/illustrators. Send introductory information about yourself and samples by email only (type Artist's Submission in subject line and attach samples and/or link to your website). Also specialises in the sale of books to TV/film; not interested in non-book-originated merchandised characters. See also page 246. Founded 1985.

Vicki Thomas Associates
195 Tollgate Road, London E6 5JY
tel 020-7511 5767
email vickithomasassociates@yahoo.co.uk
website www.vickithomasassociates.com
Consultant Vicki Thomas

Represents approx. 50 artists, 75% of whom produce children's material for all ages. Specialises in gift products and considers images for publishing, toys, stationery, clothing, decorative accessories. Email sample images, covering letter and CV. Commission: 30%. Founded 1985.

United Agents LLP
12–26 Lexington Street, London W1F 0LE
tel 020-3214 0800
email info@unitedagents.co.uk
website www.unitedagents.co.uk
Agent Jodie Hodges (née Marsh)

Represents illustrators of children's books for all ages (home 15%, USA/translation 20%). See website for submission details. Founded 2008.

Publishing practice
Publishing agreements

Before signing a publisher's agreement, it should be thoroughly checked. Caroline Walsh introduces the key points of this very important contract.

So, you've done the difficult bit and persuaded a publisher to make an offer to publish your book. But how do you know if you're getting a fair deal? And what should you be looking out for in the contract? I would always advise an author or illustrator to engage an agent. An agent will ensure that the contract gives you the best possible chance of maximising your income from a book. Alternatively, the Society of Authors (see page 375) and the Writers' Guild of Great Britain (see page 408) will both check publishing agreements for their members. In addition, there are lawyers who specialise in publishing contracts and for those who prefer to go it alone, there are some useful books on the subject listed at the end of this article.

What follows is a whistle-stop tour around the key points of a publishing contract, especially for those writing for children. To begin, the offer from the publisher should come in writing clearly setting out exactly what rights the publisher wants to license and what they are willing to pay for those rights. A contract is a business agreement for the supply of goods or performance of work at a specified price. Normally, that payment comes as an advance against royalties. Occasionally, a flat fee payment is appropriate, but a royalty allows the author to share in the income from a book throughout its life and is therefore generally preferable. Perhaps the most important point of all is that you make sure you fully understand which rights are being licensed under the contract and aren't seduced merely into worrying about the advance and royalty (tempting though they may be!).

Publishers' agreements often have useful headings for each clause and I've used some of those headings here for ease of reference.

Licence

The very first thing to be clear about is what is being licensed to the publisher. For a new book one expects to grant to the publisher, for the legal term of copyright, the exclusive right to publish and sell the work in certain forms. The standard grant is of 'volume form', which means all book forms (hardback, paperback, other formats). However, the offer or contract may also state other forms, for example serial (newspaper and magazine rights) or audio rights. Some publishers' contracts include all-encompassing wording such as 'all media forms currently in existence and hereinafter invented'. This in effect hands control to the publisher of a wide range of rights, including electronic, dramatic (film, television, radio), merchandising and so on. In such a case, it's likely that the author's share of income from such rights will be less than it would be were the author to reserve those rights and have them handled separately.

Territory

Territory states *where* the publisher has the right to sell or sub-license the book. For picture books of all kinds, fiction and non-fiction, UK publishers generally require world rights as the UK market alone is not large enough to sustain the costs of four-colour printing. US publishers are lucky enough to have a sufficiently large home market to mean they are not reliant on foreign sales and therefore will not always require world rights.

For fiction (i.e. novels) a judgement needs to be made about which territories should be granted to the publisher. English language rights are made up of two large mutually exclusive territories: the UK and Traditional British Commonwealth (including or excluding Canada) on the one hand and the USA, its dependencies and the Philippines on the other. The rest of the world is considered an open market. One could grant Traditional British Commonwealth rights in the English Language to a publisher, thereby reserving US and translation rights to be sold separately. Or one could grant World English Language rights, so the publisher can sell on US rights while translation rights are held in reserve to be sold separately. Or again, one could grant world rights to the originating publisher.

When thinking of granting a wide range of territories to a publisher, it is worth checking out how proactive and successful their foreign rights department is. It may be possible to speak to the foreign rights manager and find out for yourself if they have a good track record. An agent will have an informed view on a publisher's expertise in this area and furthermore, they will probably either be experienced themselves in selling foreign and US rights, or will work with associate agencies in all the different language territories. Publishers will take a 15–30% share on US and foreign sales and, if you have an agent too, their commission will also be deducted before you receive your percentage. Agents will generally charge 15–20% on US and foreign sales.

Advances

We've all read the newspaper headlines about huge advances, but the fact is most children's book advances currently fall within the range of £1,000–£25,000. For books that will be published in the trade (i.e. by a mainstream publishing house and where the book will appear in bookshops) most offers are framed as an advance against royalties. Advances may be paid in one go, on signature, but don't be surprised if the publisher proposes paying half on signature and half on publication, or in thirds (signature, delivery and publication), or even in quarters (signature, delivery, hardback publication, paperback publication), though the latter is more common when the advance offered is substantial.

Royalties

As a very basic rule of thumb, hardbacks attract a 10% base royalty and paperbacks 7.5%. Bear in mind that on picture books these figures will be shared between author and illustrator. Sometimes, children's black and white illustrated fiction titles also bear a small royalty for the illustrator, which will come out of the total royalty. Most novelty books, including board books, work on a smaller royalty, for example 5% or even less because of the high production costs and relatively low retail price.

Ideally, the royalty will escalate to a higher level when a certain number of sales have been achieved and this can prove to be very important if a book becomes a long-running success.

For a trade book the royalties should ideally be based on the recommended retail price for home sales. Export sales and sales to book clubs or book fairs are usually calculated on the publisher's price received (or net receipts). The contract should set out each type of sale and list the appropriate royalty rate. Nowadays, particular attention needs to be paid to 'high discount' clauses in contracts. However good the main home sales royalty is, a disadvantageous high discount clause can mean that disappointingly few of the sales attract the full royalty and consequently revenues will be much reduced. This is especially important now because retailers are pushing publishers hard on discounts. An agent will be used to negotiating carefully on precisely this kind of area to secure the best possible terms.

Co-edition royalties

As previously mentioned, picture books in the UK are very dependent upon publishers selling US and foreign language co-editions. Therefore, it is important to note on the contract what the author's share of any such co-edition deals will be. These generally fall under two categories in the contract:

• If the UK publisher prints for the foreign publisher, the books are usually sold for a fixed price per copy as 'royalty inclusive' and the author's and artist's share will be expressed as a percentage of the publisher's price received. These deals help to get the book published by bringing the unit cost down and they begin the process of earning out the advance.

• US and foreign language sales also fall under the heading of subsidiary rights. In this case, the UK publisher may or may not print the books, but the US or foreign publisher will have agreed to pay an advance and royalty for the right to sell the book in their territory (a 'royalty exclusive' deal). The author's and artist's share in this instance shouldn't be less than 50% and it could be much more. If a book is particularly sought after by foreign or US publishers, such a royalty exclusive deal could mean that the original UK advance is earned out immediately.

Subsidiary rights

Other subsidiary rights include reprint rights (large print, book club, paperback reprint, etc), serial rights (the right to publish in newspapers and magazines), anthology and quotation rights, educational rights, audio rights and so on. There will usually be a percentage listed against each right and that is the author's share of any deal. Generally the author receives at least 50% on these deals and more in the case of serial, US and translation rights. The rights listed in the sub-rights clause should be checked against the opening grant of rights clause to see that they conform.

Delivery and publication

There should be clauses in the contract that state the agreed delivery date of the book and give some indication of what is expected, for example 'a work for children to be written and illustrated by the said author to a length of not more than 25,000 words plus approximately 50 black and white line illustrations'. There should also be an undertaking by the publisher to publish the work within a stated time period, for example 'within 12 months from delivery of the complete typescript and artwork'. There might also be an indication of what the published price will be.

Copyright and moral rights

As you are licensing your work, you should retain copyright and there should be a clause that obliges the publisher to include a copyright line in every edition of the work published or sub-licensed by them. The author's moral rights are also often asserted within the contract.

Production

Though the publishers will generally insist on having the final decision regarding details of production, publication and advertising, they should agree to consult meaningfully with the author over the blurb, catalogue copy, jacket and cover design. There should also be an undertaking to supply the author with proofs for checking and enough time for the author to check those proofs.

Accounts

Publishers usually account to authors twice a year for royalties earned. Even if the advance has not earned out, the publishers should still send a royalty statement. Royalty statements are notoriously enigmatic and vary from publisher to publisher. Mistakes on royalty statements are more common than one might like to think and an agent will be used to checking royalty statements carefully and taking up any anomalies with the publisher.

In addition to the twice-yearly accounting, once the initial advance has been earned out, an agent will be able to ensure that any substantial income from sub-rights deals (e.g. in excess of £100) will be paid immediately.

Electronic or ebook rights

The electronic or ebook market has grown quickly over recent years, with a proliferation of devices and formats for accessing ebooks coming on to the market. Many children's books are now available in ebook format and protocols with online retailers have been established. Ebook development currently encompasses several different forms, the most popular of which are straightforward verbatim text; 'enhanced' ebook, i.e. with added material such as author interviews, or in the case of picture books, simple animations; and as apps for smart phones. Authors should take care to retain the right of approval over every aspect of these enhanced electronic editions.

At the time of writing, standard ebook royalties have settled at around 25% of the publisher's price received, however some ebook specialist publishers pay 50% and some mainstream print publishers will agree to rising royalties for popular authors. These rates are often subject to review after a fixed period to enable both sides to take account of changing practice. As this part of the market is fluid and expanding, it's wise to keep your options open if you can.

Reversion

It's important to ensure that the author can get back the rights to their book if the publisher either fails to stick to the terms of the contract or lets the book go out of print. Historically, if the publisher left a book out of print for 6–9 months after receiving a written request to reprint it, rights would revert. However, ebook and print-on-demand formats mean that standard 'stock level' reversion clauses no longer provide adequate protection and new triggers for reversion need to be agreed. This might be a rate of sale or revenue threshold. It is well worth reclaiming rights to out-of-print books as it may well be possible to re-license them later on.

Assignment

A small but important clause that may need to be added states that the publishers shall not assign the rights granted to them without the author's express written consent. This gives the author at least a degree of control over the book's destiny if the publishing company runs into trouble or is sold.

Educational publishers' contracts

Many children's authors begin as writers for educational publishers and quite a number continue to work in this field alongside producing books for the trade market. Educational publishers usually commission tightly briefed work. Advances are generally modest and the royalties are based on the publishers' price received. However, substantial sums can eventually be earned. Educational publishers usually expect to be granted a very wide range of rights and while it makes sense to grant audio or electronic rights where the publisher has the capacity to produce or license such formats for their market, it may be possible and desirable to reserve, for example, dramatic and merchandising rights. However, discretion is needed here. If, for example, the publisher is commissioning writers to create stories about a given set of characters created by the publisher, then the publisher will rightly expect to control such rights.

That really is a scratching of the surface of publishing agreements. Do take advice if you don't feel confident that the contract presented to you is fair. It seems a very obvious thing to say but always read a publishing agreement carefully before signing it and if anything in it isn't clear, ask for an explanation. Remember, too, that it's a negotiation and that despite publishers' talk of 'standard terms' and 'standard agreements', it is always possible to make amendments to contracts.

Caroline Walsh is a literary agent and a director of David Higham Associates Ltd (www.davidhigham.co.uk). She specialises in the children's book market.

Useful reading

Flint, Michael; Fitzpatrick, Nicholas and Thorne, Clive, *A User's Guide to Copyright*, Bloomsbury Professional, 6th edn, 2006 (7th edn due October 2015)

Jones, Hugh and Benson, Christopher, *Publishing Law*, Routledge, 4th edn, 2011

Owen, Lynette *Clark's Publishing Agreements: A Book of Precedents*, Bloomsbury Professional, 9th edn, 2013

See also...

- *How to get an agent*, page 223
- *Meet the parents: agent, author and the birth of a book*, page 232
- *Do you have to have an agent to succeed?*, page 235
- *Children's literary agents UK and Ireland*, page 239
- *Children's literary agents overseas*, page 249
- *The Society of Authors*, page 375

Publishing practice

Faqs about Isbns

The Nielsen ISBN Agency for UK & Ireland receives a large number of enquiries about the ISBN system. The most frequently asked questions are answered here.

What is an ISBN?

An ISBN (International Standard Book Number) is a product identifier used by publishers, booksellers and libraries for ordering, listing and stock control purposes. It enables them to identify a specific edition of a specific title in a specific format from a particular publisher. The digits are always divided into five parts, separated by spaces or hyphens. The five parts can be of varying length and are as follows:

Contact details

Nielsen ISBN Agency for UK and Ireland
3rd Floor, Midas House, 62 Goldsworth Road, Woking GU21 6LQ
tel (01483) 712215
email isbn.agency@nielsen.com
website www.isbn.nielsenbook.co.uk

• Prefix element – distinguishes the ISBN from other types of product identifier which are used for non-book trade products; three-digit number that is made available by GS1 (Global Standards – required for barcodes). Prefixes that have already been made available by GS1 are 978 and 979, but there may be a further prefix allocation made in the future as required to ensure the continued capacity of the ISBN system.
• Group Identifier – identifies a national, geographic or language grouping of publishers. It tells you which of these groupings the publisher belongs to (not the language of the book).
• Publisher Identifier – identifies a specific publisher or imprint.
• Title Number – identifies a specific edition of a specific title in a specific format.
• Check Digit – this is always and only the final digit which mathematically validates the rest of the number.

Since January 2007 all ISBNs are 13 digits long. The older ten-digit format can be converted to the 13-digit format by adding the 978 EAN (European Article Number, i.e. a 'barcode') prefix and recalculating the check digit.

Do all books need to have an ISBN?

There is no legal requirement for an ISBN in the UK and Ireland and it conveys no form of legal or copyright protection. It is a product identifier.

What can be gained from using an ISBN?

If you wish to sell your publication through major bookselling chains, independent book-shops or internet booksellers, they will require it to have an ISBN to assist their internal processing and ordering systems. The ISBN also provides access to bibliographic databases such as Nielsen Book's bibliographic database and Discovery Services (Nielsen BookData), which are organised using ISBNs as references. These databases are used by the book trade – publishers, booksellers and libraries – for internal purposes, to provide information for customers and to source and order titles. ISBNs are also used by Nielsen Book's Commerce Services (Nielsen BookNet TeleOrdering and Nielsen PubEasy) and Research Services (Nielsen BookScan and Books & Consumers) to monitor book sales. The ISBN therefore provides access to additional marketing opportunities which assist the sales and measurement of books (including ebooks and other digital products).

Where can I get an ISBN?

ISBN prefixes are assigned to publishers in the country where they are based by the national agency for that country. The UK and Republic of Ireland Agency is run by Nielsen. The Agency introduces new publishers to the system, assigns prefixes to new and existing publishers and deals with any queries or problems in using the system. The Nielsen ISBN Agency for UK & Ireland was the first ISBN agency in the world and has been instrumental in the set up and maintenance of the ISBN. Publishers based elsewhere will not be able to get numbers from the UK Agency but may contact them for details of the relevant agency in their market.

Who is eligible for ISBNs?

Any organisation or individual who is publishing a qualifying product for general sale or distribution to the market is eligible (see below, 'Which products do not qualify for ISBNs?').

What is a publisher?

The publisher is generally the person or body which takes the financial risk in making a product available. For example, if a product went on sale and sold no copies at all, the publisher is usually the person or body which loses money. If you get paid anyway, you are likely to be a designer, printer, author or consultant of some kind.

How long does it take to get an ISBN?

In the UK and Ireland the 'Standard' service time is ten working days, the 'Fast Track' service is three working days, and the 'Super Fast Track' service is the same day for applications received before 1pm.

How much does it cost to get an ISBN?

In the UK and Ireland there is a registration fee which is payable by all new publishers. The fees for ISBNs are subject to review so applicants should check with the Agency. A publisher prefix unique to you will be provided and allows for ten ISBNs. Larger allocations are available where appropriate.

ISBNs are only available in blocks. The smallest block is ten numbers. It is not possible to obtain a single ISBN.

Which products do not qualify for ISBNs?

Calendars and diaries (unless they contain additional text or images such that they are not purely for time-management purposes); greetings cards, videos for entertainment; documentaries on video/CD-Rom; computer games; computer application programs; items which are available to a restricted group of people, e.g. a history of a golf club which is only for sale to members or an educational course book only available to those registered as students on the course.

Can I turn my ISBN into a barcode?

Since ISBNs changed to 13 digits in 2007 it has been possible (with the appropriate software) to use the same number to generate a barcode. Information about barcoding for books is available on the Book Industry Communication website (www.bic.org.uk).

What is an ISSN?

An International Standard Serial Number is the numbering system for journals, magazines, periodicals, newspapers and newsletters. It is administered by the British Library, *tel* (01937) 546959.

Vanity publishing

Mainstream publishers invest their own money in the publishing process. In contrast, vanity publishers require an up-front payment from the author to produce a book. Johnathon Clifford highlights the perils of vanity publishing.

My research into vanity publishing began in 1990 when a 12-year-old girl wrote to me stating she had found a publisher willing to publish her work. I telephoned the 'publisher' under the guise of an aspiring author, and this call was all it took for them to agree to publish my work. Their offer was 100 copies of a 38-page book for a fee of £1,900, with no need for them to see my poetry first.

Since then, I have written *Vanity Press & The Proper Poetry Publishers* (1991), a

> ### Definition of vanity publishing
> 'Vanity publishing, also self-styled (often inaccurately) as "subsidy", "joint-venture", "shared-responsibility" or even "self" publishing, is a service whereby authors are charged to have their work published. Vanity publishers generally offer to publish a book for a specific fee, or offer to include short stories, poems or other literary or artistic material in an anthology, which the authors are then invited to buy.'
>
> – Advertising Standards Authority definition of vanity publishing, 1997

book based on feedback I received from vanity publishers, assisted the Advertising Standards Authority, and collaborated in making television and radio programmes. In 1999, I was invited to the House of Lords to talk about the problem of vanity publishing and the need for a change in the law to stop 'rogue traders' in the publishing world. However, it was not until 2008 that the law was suitably changed to enable the authorities to better curb the excesses of rogue vanity publishers, should they wish.

The perils of vanity publishing

'Vanity publisher' is a phrase I coined in the early 1960s when two American companies were advertising widely in the British press offering to publish poems for a payment of £9 and £12 per poem, respectively. Since then the term has extended its meaning to 'any company that charges a client to publish a book'.

Mainstream publishers invest in the marketing and promotion of a book and make their profit from its sales. In contrast, vanity publishers make their money from up-front charges. One of the main drawbacks of being published by a vanity publisher is its lack of credibility within the industry. The majority of booksellers and library suppliers are loath to handle vanity books and few reviewers are willing to consider a book published in this way. The Business Unit Director of one of the UK's biggest booksellers wrote in 1996: 'We do not buy from vanity publishers except in exceptional circumstances. Their books are, with one or two exceptions, badly produced, over-priced, have poor, uncompetitive jackets and usually have no marketing support.'

I have an extensive collection of documentation passed to me from authors who have approached one of the 100-plus vanity publishers operating in the UK. It consists of vanity publishers' initial promotional letters, subsequent written promises, the contracts and letters of complaint from the author, and the vanity publishers' response to those complaints. In recent years, court judgements have found that some vanity publishers are guilty of 'gross misrepresentation of the services they offer' and, as a result, some have been successfully sued and others forced into 'voluntary' liquidation – often only to swiftly reappear under different names.

How vanity publishers operate

Mainstream publishers never advertise for authors and almost never charge a client, whether known or unknown. Vanity publishers place advertisements wherever they possibly can inviting authors to submit manuscripts. Almost without exception, when authors submit work the vanity publisher will reply that they would like to publish the book but that, as an unknown, the author will have to pay towards the cost. Vanity publishers may tell the author they are very selective in the authors they accept and praise the work, but this is false flattery. I have not been able to find one person during the last 22 years who has been turned down by a vanity publisher – however poorly written their book is. The vanity publisher may state that this is the way many famous authors in the past set out, but this is untrue. Some famous, well-respected authors *have* self-published but none of the 'famous authors' they quote started their writing career by paying a vanity publisher. The BBC programme *Southern Eye* reported that many authors had been sent exactly the same 'glowing report', whatever the subject or quality of their book.

Vanity publishers have charged aspiring authors anything from £1,800 up to (in one recorded instance) £20,000 for publishing their book. Many authors have borrowed thousands of pounds on the strength of promised 'returning royalties', as authors are often led to believe that sales through the vanity publisher's marketing department will recoup their outlay.

In December 1997, *Private Eye* ran an article about three authors, one of whom had paid £2,400 and the other two £1,800 each to a vanity publisher, on the basis that their books would command a 'high level of royalties'. These royalties amounted to £16.35, £21.28 and £47.30 respectively. When the authors complained they each received a threatening letter from the vanity publisher's solicitor. The same company's business practices were featured on the BBC programme *Watchdog* in November 2002.

Some vanity publishers ask their clients to pay a 'subvention', the *Collins English Dictionary* definition of which is 'a grant, aid, or subsidy, as from a government', and therefore it is a meaningless term when used in the context of vanity publishing. However the request for payment is worded, it is the author who will bear the full cost of publishing their book. Not a share of, or a subsidy towards, but the whole cost and a healthy profit margin on top.

Few vanity publishers quote for a specific number of copies, leaving the author with little idea what they are paying for. Vanity publishers may simply keep manuscripts 'on file' and only print on demand, making it difficult to deliver copies quickly enough to the outlets which *do* order them. Other companies propose that once book sales have reached a certain 'target' figure, the client's outlay will be refunded. The number of copies required to be sold is always well in excess of a realistic target.

Some companies claim that part of the service they offer is to send copies of books they 'publish' to Nielsen Books, the Copyright Receipt Office and the British Library. In fact, this is a legal requirement for all UK publishers. Other companies claim a 'special' relationship which enables them to supply information on your book to particular outlets on the internet. But Amazon does not support this: 'Books are listed on Amazon.co.uk's website in a number of ways – we take feeds from BookData and Nielsen (who automatically update these details on our website) as well as from several wholesalers'.

Authors using a vanity publisher should be aware that once they have made the final payment, that the vanity publisher doesn't need to sell a single copy of their book.

Self-publishing — another form of vanity publishing?

One way for an author to see their book in print is to self-publish but, since that became more acceptable, some vanity publishers try to pass themselves off as self-publishers. For a book to be genuinely self-published, a name designated by the author as his or her publishing house must appear on the copyright page of the book as 'publisher' and the book's ISBN number must be registered by the ISBN Agency to that author as publisher.

All the copies of a self-published book are the property of the author to dispose of as they wish. If an author does not want to be involved with the sale and distribution of their book, this can be indicated by ensuring that when details of a book are sent to the ISBN Agency before publication they include a section on the form for 'Distributor (if different from Publisher)'.

On the title page of every book there is a paragraph which, in essence, states 'All rights are reserved. No part of this book can be stored on a retrieval system or transmitted in any form or by whatever means without the prior permission in writing from the *publisher*', i.e. not 'the author' who may have been led to believe that their book is '*self*-published'.

Any company which publishes books under its own name or imprint cannot, by definition, claim to help authors to self-publish. If the name of the company, not the author, appears in the book as that of the publisher, not only can the author not claim to have self-published their book, but they have lost all control over it. If, after the initial publication, someone should wish to produce large type copies (for the poorly-sighted), take up film or television rights, reprint the book under their own imprint, or to publish a copy in translation, there are (in some cases very lucrative) fees to be discussed and paid. But it is legally 'to the publisher' that such application must be made and it is legally 'the publisher' not the author who will benefit. *True* self-publishing gives authors much greater control over the production and dissemination of their books.

'But what does it matter?', I hear some of you ask. Where the honest publisher is concerned, not a great deal perhaps; but there have always been so many 'out there' whose intention is to relieve the unwary of their money, and they are aided in their intent by being able to refer to themselves in terms that are misleading.

Johnathon Clifford may be contacted via his website, www.vanitypublishing.info, which was archived by the British Museum Library in 2009. There you will find a free Advice Pack designed to protect aspiring authors.

Public Lending Right

Under the PLR system, payment is made from public funds to authors (writers, translators, illustrators and some editors/compilers) whose books are lent out from public libraries. Payment is made once a year, and the amount authors receive is proportionate to the number of times that their books were borrowed during the previous year (July to June).

How the system works

From the applications received, the PLR office compiles a computerised register of authors and books. A representative sample of book issues is recorded, consisting of all loans from selected public libraries. This is then multiplied in proportion to total library lending to produce, for each book, an estimate of its total annual loans throughout the country. Each year the computer compares the register with the estimated loans to discover how many loans are credited to each registered book for the calculation of PLR payments. This is done using the ISBN printed in the book (see below).

Parliament allocates a sum each year (£6.6 million for 2014/15) for PLR. This fund pays the administrative costs of PLR and reimburses local authorities for recording loans in the sample libraries (see below). The remaining money is then divided by the total registered loan figure in order to work out how much can be paid for each estimated loan of a registered book.

Since July 2014 the UK PLR legislation has been extended to include public library loans of audiobooks ('talking books') and ebooks downloaded to library premises for taking away as loans ('on-site' ebook loans).

Limits on payments

If all the registered interests in an author's books score so few loans that they would earn less than £1 in a year, no payment is due. However, if the books of one registered author score so high that the author's PLR earnings for the year would exceed £6,600, then only £6,600 is paid. (No author can earn more than £6,600 in PLR in any one year.) Money that is not paid out because of these limits belongs to the fund and increases the amounts paid that year to other authors.

The sample

Because it would be expensive and impracticable to attempt to collect loans data from every library authority in the UK, a statistical sampling method is employed instead. The sample represents only public lending libraries – academic, school, private and commercial libraries are not included. Only books which are loaned from public libraries can earn PLR; consultations of books on library premises are excluded.

Further information

Public Lending Right
PLR Office, Richard House, Sorbonne Close, Stockton-on-Tees TS17 6DA
tel (01642) 604699
websites www.bl.uk/plr, www.plr.uk.com, www.plrinternational.com
Contact Head of PLR

The UK PLR scheme is administered by the British Library from its offices in Stockton-on-Tees (the 'PLR office'). The UK PLR office also provides registration for the Irish PLR scheme on behalf of the Irish Public Lending Remuneration office.

Application forms, information and publications are all obtainable from the PLR Office. See website for further information on eligibility for PLR, loans statistics and forthcoming developments.

British Library Advisory Committee for Public Lending Right
Advises the British Library Board and Head of PLR on the operation and future development of the PLR scheme.

The sample consists of the entire loans records for a year from libraries in more than 40 public library authorities spread through England, Scotland, Wales and Northern Ireland. Sample loans represent around 20% of the national total. All the computerised sampling points in an authority contribute loans data ('multi-site' sampling). The aim is to increase the sample without any significant increase in costs. In order to counteract sampling error, libraries in the sample change every three to four years. Loans are totalled every 12 months for the period 1 July–30 June.

An author's entitlement to PLR depends on the loans accrued by his or her books in the sample. This figure is averaged up to produce first regional and then finally national estimated loans.

ISBNs

The PLR system uses ISBNs (International Standard Book Numbers) to identify books lent and correlate loans with entries on the PLR Register so that payments can be made. ISBNs are required for all registrations. Different editions (e.g. first, second, hardback, paperback, large print) of the same book have different ISBNs. See *FAQs about ISBNs* on page 292.

Authorship

In the PLR system the author of a printed book or ebook is the writer, illustrator, translator, compiler, editor or reviser. Authors must be named on the book's title page, or be able to prove authorship by some other means (e.g. receipt of royalties). The ownership of copyright has no bearing on PLR eligibility. Narrators, producers and abridgers are also eligible to apply for PLR shares in audiobooks.

Most borrowed authors and books

- The most borrowed children's author in 2013–14 was Daisy Meadows.
- The most borrowed classic author overall was children's writer Roald Dahl.
- The most borrowed children's title was *Diary of a Wimpy Kid* by Jeff Kinney.

Summary of the 32nd year's results

Registration: authors. When registration closed for the 32nd year (30 June 2014) there were 54,839 authors and assignees.

Eligible loans. Of the 247 million estimated loans from UK libraries, 108 million belong to books on the PLR register. The loans credited to registered books – 44% of all library borrowings – qualify for payment. The remaining 56% of loans relate to books that are ineligible for various reasons, to books written by dead or foreign authors, and to books that have simply not been applied for.

Money and payments. PLR's administrative costs are deducted from the fund allocated to the British Library Board annually by Parliament. Operating the scheme this year cost £622,000, representing some 9.3% of the PLR fund. The Rate per Loan for 2014/15 was 6.66 pence. The amount distributed to authors was just over £6 million. Total government funding for 2014/15 was £6.66 million.

The numbers of authors in various payment categories are as follows:

*281	payments at	£5,000–6,600
359	payments between	£2,500–4,999.99
809	payments between	£1,000–2,499.99
879	payments between	£500–999.99
3,336	payments between	£100–499.99
16,387	payments between	£1–99.99
22,051	TOTAL	

* Includes 190 authors whose book loans reached the maximum threshold

Co-authorship/illustrators. In the PLR system the authors of a book are those writers, translators, editors, compilers and illustrators as defined above. Authors must apply for registration before their books can earn PLR and this can be done via the PLR website. There is no restriction on the number of authors who can register shares in any one book as long as they satisfy the eligibility criteria.

Writers and/or illustrators. At least one must be eligible and they must jointly agree what share of PLR each will take based on contribution. This agreement is necessary even if one or two are ineligible or do not wish to register for PLR. The eligible authors will receive the share(s) specified in the application.

Translators. Translators may apply, without reference to other authors, for a 30% fixed share (to be divided equally between joint translators).

Editors and compilers. An editor or compiler may apply, either with others or without reference to them, to register a 20% share. An editor must have written at least 10% of the book's content or more than ten pages of text in addition to normal editorial work and be named on the title page. Alternatively, editors may register 20% if they have a royalty agreement with the publisher. The share of joint editors/compilers is 20% in total to be divided equally. An application from an editor or compiler to register a greater percentage share must be accompanied by supporting documentary evidence of actual contribution.

Audiobooks. PLR shares in audiobooks are fixed by the UK scheme and may not be varied. *Writers* may register a fixed 60% share in an audiobook, providing that it has not been abridged or translated. In cases where the writer has made an additional contribution (e.g. as narrator), he/she may claim both shares. *Narrators* may register a fixed 20% PLR share in an audiobook. *Producers* may register a fixed 20% share in an audiobook. *Abridgers* (in cases where the writer's original text has been abridged prior to recording as an audiobook) qualify for 12% (20% of the writer's share). *Translators* (in cases where the writer's original text has been translated from another language) qualify for 18% (30% of the writer's share). If there is more than one writer, narrator, etc the appropriate shares should be divided equally. If more than one contribution has been made, e.g. writer and narrator, more than one fixed share may be applied for.

Dead or missing co-authors. Where it is impossible to agree shares with a co-author because that person is dead or untraceable, then the surviving co-author or co-authors

Publishing practice

Most borrowed children's authors

1	Daisy Meadows	11	Jeanne Willis
2	Julia Donaldson	12	Terry Deary
3	Francesca Simon	13	Eric Hill
4	Adam Blade	14	Lucy Cousins
5	Jacqueline Wilson	15	Ian Whybrow
6	Roald Dahl	16	Lauren Child
7	Mick Inkpen	17	Tony Ross
8	Fiona Watt	18	Roderick Hunt
9	Michael Morpurgo	19	Jeff Kinney
10	Enid Blyton	20	Giles Andreae

This list is of the most borrowed authors in UK public libraries. It is based on PLR sample loans in the period July 2013–June 2014. It includes all writers, both registered and unregistered, but not illustrators where the book has a separate writer. Writing names are used; pseudonyms have not been combined.

may submit an application but must name the co-author and provide supporting evidence as to why that co-author has not agreed shares. The living co-author(s) will then be able to register a share in the book which reflects individual contribution. Providing permission is granted, the PLR Office can help to put co-authors (including illustrators) in touch with each other. Help is also available from publishers, writers' organisations and the Association of Illustrators.

Life and death. First applications may not be made by the estate of a deceased author. However, if an author registers during their lifetime the PLR in their books can be transferred to a new owner and continues for up to 70 years after the date of their death. The new owner can apply to register new titles if first published one year before, or up to ten years after, the date of the author's death. New editions of existing registered titles can also be registered posthumously.

Residential qualifications. PLR is open to authors living in the European Economic Area (i.e. EU member states plus Norway, Liechtenstein and Iceland). A resident in these countries (for PLR purposes) must have their only or principal home there.

Most borrowed children's fiction titles

	Author	Title	Publisher	Year
1	Jeff Kinney	*Diary of a Wimpy Kid*	Puffin	2008
2	Jeff Kinney	*Diary of a Wimpy Kid: The Last Straw*	Puffin	2009
3	Jeff Kinney	*Diary of a Wimpy Kid: Dog Days*	Puffin	2010
4	Julia Donaldson (illus. Axel Scheffler)	*The Gruffalo*	Macmillan Children's	1999
5	Jeff Kinney	*Diary of a Wimpy Kid: Rodrick Rules*	Puffin	2008
6	Jeff Kinney	*Diary of a Wimpy Kid: The Third Wheel*	Puffin	2012
7	Jeff Kinney	*Diary of a Wimpy Kid: Cabin Fever*	Puffin	2013
8	Jeff Kinney	*Diary of a Wimpy Kid: The Ugly Truth*	Puffin	2012
9	Claire Freedman and Ben Cort	*Aliens Love Underpants!*	Simon & Schuster	2007
10	Liz Pichon	*The Brilliant World of Tom Gates*	Scholastic	2011
11	David Walliams (illus. Tony Ross)	*Ratburger*	HarperCollins Children's	2012
12	David Walliams (illus. Quentin Blake)	*Mr Stink*	HarperCollins Children's	2010
13	David Walliams (illus. Quentin Blake)	*The Boy in the Dress*	HarperCollins Children's	2009
14	Maurice Sendak	*Where the Wild Things Are*	Red Fox	2000
15	Martin Waddell and Patrick Benson	*Owl Babies*	Walker	1992
16	Julia Donaldson (illus. Axel Scheffler)	*The Snail and the Whale*	Macmillan Children's	2003
17	Julia Donaldson (illus. Axel Scheffler)	*Superworm*	Alison Green	2012
18	David Walliams (illus. Tony Ross)	*Billionaire Boy*	HarperCollins Children's	2011
19	Jeff Kinney	*Diary of a Wimpy Kid: Cabin Fever*	Puffin	2013
20	Michael Rosen (illlus. Helen Oxenbury)	*We're Going on a Bear Hunt*	Walker	1989

Eligible books

In the PLR system each edition of a book is registered and treated as a separate book. A book is eligible for PLR registration provided that:
• it has an eligible author (or co-author);
• it is printed and bound (paperbacks counting as bound);
• it has already been published;
• copies of it have been put on sale, i.e. it is not a free handout;
• the authorship is personal, i.e. not a company or association, and the book is not crown copyright;
• it has an ISBN;
• it is not wholly or mainly a musical score;
• it is not a newspaper, magazine, journal or periodical.

Audiobooks. An audiobook is defined as an 'authored text' or 'a work recorded as a sound recording and consisting mainly of spoken words'. Applications can therefore only be accepted to register audiobooks which meet these requirements and are the equivalent of a printed book. Music, dramatisations and live recordings do not qualify for registration.

Most borrowed classic children's titles

	Author	Title	Publisher	Year
1	Roald Dahl (illus. Quentin Blake)	The BFG	Penguin	2007
2	J.R.R. Tolkien (illus. David Wyatt)	The Hobbit, or There and Back Again	Collins	2012
3	J.R.R. Tolkien	The Hobbit, or There and Back Again	HarperCollins	2012
4	J.R.R. Tolkien (illus. David Wyatt)	The Hobbit, or There and Back Again	Collins	1998
5	C.S. Lewis	The Lion, The Witch and the Wardrobe	HarperCollins	2009
6	J.R.R. Tolkien	The Hobbit: An Unexpected Journey: The Movie Storybook	HarperCollins	2012
7	Enid Blyton	The Secret Seven	Hodder	2006
8	Enid Blyton	Secret Seven Adventure	Hodder	2006
9	Kenneth Grahame (illus. Richard Johnson)	The Wind in the Willows	Usborne	2012
10	Enid Blyton	Secret Seven on the Trail	Hodder	2006
11	Enid Blyton	Well Done, Secret Seven	Hodder	2006
12	J.R.R. Tolkien (illus. David Wenzel)	The Hobbit, or There and Back Again	HarperCollins	2006
13	Enid Blyton	Secret Seven Win Through	Hodder	2006
14	Enid Blyton	Go Ahead Secret Seven	Hodder	2006
15	Roald Dahl	Fantastic Mr Fox	Puffin	2009
16	Michael Bond (illus. Peggy Fortnum)	A Bear Called Paddington	Collins	2003
17	Frank Cottrell Boyce (illus. Joe Berger)	Chitty Chitty Bang Bang and the Race Against Time	Macmillan	2012
18	Shirley Hughes	Hero on a Bicycle	Walker	2012
19	Roald Dahl (illus. Quentin Blake)	The Vicar of Nibbleswicke	Penguin	1992
20	Roald Dahl (illus. Quentin Blake)	George's Marvellous Medicine	Puffin	2011

Publishing practice

To qualify for UK PLR in an audiobook contributors should be named on the case in which the audiobook is held; OR be able to refer to a contract with the publisher; OR be named within the audiobook recording.

Ebooks. Only ebooks downloaded to fixed terminals in library premises and then taken away on loan on portable devices to be read elsewhere qualify for PLR payment. As far as PLR is aware, no public libraries in the UK currently provide on-site ebook lending facilities and public library ebook loans in the UK are made to 'remote' off-site locations (e.g. people's homes). Remote ebook loans are covered by copyright licensing arrangements and a change in copyright legislation would be required for 'remote' loans to be included in the UK PLR scheme. The government is committed to looking at the feasibility of such a change in copyright law. Due to these current restrictions, PLR is recommending that ebooks are NOT registered for PLR at present.

Statements and payment

Authors with an online account may view their statement online. Registered authors who do not have an online account receive a statement posted to their address if a payment is due.

Most borrowed children's non-fiction titles

	Author	Title	Publisher	Year
1	Eric Hill	Spot's Opposites	Frederick Warne	2013
2	Lucy Cousins	Maisy's First Colours	Walker Books	2013
3	Lucy Cousins	Maisy's First 123	Walker Books	2013
4	Eric Hill	Spot's ABC	Penguin	2013
5	Julia Donaldson (illus. Axel Scheffler)	Numbers	Macmillan Children's	2011
6	Julia Donaldson (illus. Axel Scheffler)	Animal Actions	Macmillan Children's	2011
7	Eric Hill	Spot Counts to 10	Frederick Warne	2013
8	Julia Donaldson (illus. Axel Scheffler)	Opposites	Macmillan Children's	2011
9	Julia Donaldson (illus. Axel Scheffler)	Colours	Macmillan Children's	2011
10	Eric Hill	What Can You See, Spot?	Frederick Warne	2012
11	Mick Inkpen	Wibbly Pig has 10 Balloons	Hodder Children's	2012
12	Rod Campbell	Dear Zoo Animal Shapes	Macmillan Children's	2012
13	Mick Inkpen	Wibbly Pig Has 10 Balloons	Hodder Children's	2011
14	Lauren Child	I Absolutely Love Animals	Puffin	2012
15	Julia Donaldson (illus. Axel Scheffler)	Stick Man's First Words	Scholastic	2013
16	Bill Martin (illus. Eric Carle)	Brown Bear, Brown Bear, What Do You See?	Puffin	2007
17	Stella Blackstone (illus. Christopher Corr)	My Granny Went to Market	Barefoot	2006
18	Characters created by Lauren Child	I Completely Know About Guinea Pigs	Puffin	2012
19		Touch and Feel ABC	Dorling Kindersley	2013
20		Touch and Feel Animal Colours	Dorling Kindersley	2013

Sampling arrangements

To help minimise the unfairness that arises inevitably from a sampling system, the scheme specifies the eight regions within which authorities and sampling points have to be designated and includes libraries of varying size. Part of the sample drops out by rotation each year to allow fresh libraries to be included. The following library authorities have been designated for the year beginning 1 July 2014 (all are multi-site authorities). This list is based on the nine government regions for England plus Northern Ireland, Scotland and Wales.

• East – Essex, Southend-on-Sea and Thurrock, Norfolk
• London – Hillingdon, Southwark, Sutton, Triborough Libraries (Hammersmith and Fulham, Kensington and Chelsea, Westminster)
• North East – Gateshead, Middlesbrough, South Tyneside
• North West & Merseyside – Blackpool, Knowsley, Manchester, Salford, Warrington
• South East – East Sussex, Hampshire, Portsmouth
• South West – LibrariesWest (Bath & North East Somerset, Bristol, North Somerset, Somerset, South Gloucestershire)
• West Midlands – Telford and Wrekin
• Yorkshire & The Humber – North Yorkshire
• Northern Ireland – The Northern Ireland Library Authority
• Scotland – Edinburgh, Highland, Midlothian, North Lanarkshire
• Wales – Ceredigion, Vale of Glamorgan, Wrexham.

Participating local authorities are reimbursed on an actual cost basis for additional expenditure incurred in providing loans data to the PLR Office. The extra PLR work mostly consists of modifications to computer programs to accumulate loans data in the local authority computer and to transmit the data to the PLR Office at Stockton-on-Tees.

Reciprocal arrangements

Reciprocal PLR arrangements now exist with the German, Dutch, Austrian and other European PLR schemes. Authors can apply for overseas PLR for most of these countries through the Authors' Licensing and Collecting Society (see page 322). The exception to this rule is Ireland. Authors should now register for Irish PLR through the UK PLR Office. Further information on PLR schemes internationally and recent developments within the EC towards wider recognition of PLR is available from the PLR Office or on the international PLR website.

See also...
● *Book Trust's top 100 books for children*, page 383
● *Prize winners*, page 417

Glossary of publishing terms

The selected terms in this glossary relate to the content of this *Yearbook*.

advance

Money paid by a publisher to an author before a book is published which will be covered by future royalties. A publishing contract often allows an author an advance payment against future royalties; the author will not receive any further royalties until the amount paid in advance has been earned by sales of the book.

advance information (AI) sheet

A document that is put together by a publishing company to provide sales and marketing information about a book before publication and can be sent several months before publication to sales representatives. It can incorporate details of the format and contents of the book, key selling points and information about intended readership, as well as information about promotions and reviews.

backlist

The range of books already published by a publisher that are still in print.

blad (book layout and design)

A pre-publication sales and marketing tool. It is often a printed booklet that contains sample pages, images and front and back covers which acts as a preview for promotional use or for sales teams to show to potential retailers, customers or reviewers.

blurb

A short piece of writing or a paragraph that praises and promotes a book, which usually appears on the back or inside cover of the book and may be used in sales and marketing material.

book club edition

An edition of a book specially printed and bound for a book club for sale to its members.

co-edition

The publication of a book by two publishing companies in different countries, where the first company has originated the work and then sells sheets to the second publisher (or licenses the second publisher to reprint the book locally).

commissioning editor

A person who asks authors to write books for the part of the publisher's list for which he or she is responsible or who takes on an author who

approaches them direct or via an agent with a proposal. Also called acquisitions editor or acquiring editor (more commonly in the USA). A person who signs-up writers (commissions them to write) an article for a magazine or newspaper.

copy-editor

A person whose job is to check material ready for printing for accuracy, clarity of message and writing style and consistency of typeface, punctuation and layout. Sometimes called a desk editor.

copyright

The legal right, which the creator of an original work has, to only allow copying of the work with permission and sometimes on payment of royalties or a copyright fee. An amendment to the Copyright, Designs and Patents Act (1988) states that in the UK most works are protected for 70 years from the creator's death. The 'copyright page' at the start of a book asserts copyright ownership and author identification.

distributor

Acts as a link between the publisher and retailer. The distributor can receive orders from retailers, ship books, invoice, collect revenue and deal with returns. Distributors often handle books from several publishers. Digital distributors handle ebook distribution.

editor

A person in charge of publishing a newspaper or magazine who makes the final decisions about the content and format. A person in book publishing who has responsibility for the content of a book and can be variously a senior person (editor-in-chief) or day-to-day contact for authors (copy-editor, development editor, commissioning editor, etc).

endmatter

Material at the end of the main body of a book which may be useful to the reader, including references, appendices indexes and bibliography. Also called back matter.

extent

The number of pages in a book.

folio

A large sheet of paper folded twice across the middle and trimmed to make four pages of a book. Also a page number.

frontlist

New books just published (generally in their first year of publication) or about to be published by a publisher. Promotion of the frontlist is heavy, and the frontlist carries most of a publisher's investment. On the other hand, a backlist which continues to sell is usually the most profitable part of a publisher's list.

imprint

The publisher's or printer's name which appears on the title page of a book or in the bibliographical details; a brand name under which a book is published within a larger publishing company, usually representing a specialised subject area.

inspection copy

A copy of a publication sent or given with time allowed for a decision to purchase or return it. In academic publishing, lecturers can request inspection copies to decide whether to make a book/textbook recommended reading or adopt it as a core textbook for their course.

ISBN

International Standard Book Number.

ISSN

International Standard Serial Number. An international system used on periodicals, magazines, learned journals, etc. The ISSN is formed of eight digits, which refer to the country in which the magazine is published and the title of the publication.

literary agent

Somebody whose job is to negotiate publishing contracts, involving royalties, advances and rights sales on behalf of an author and who earns commission on the proceeds of the sales they negotiate.

moral right

The right of people such as editors or illustrators to have some say in the publication of a work to which they have contributed, even if they do not own the copyright.

out of print or o.p.

Relating to a book of which the publisher has no copies left and which is not going to be reprinted. Print on demand technology, however, means that a book can be kept 'in print' indefinitely.

packager

A company that creates a finished book for a publisher.

PDF

Portable Document Format. A data file generated from PostScript that is platform-independent, application-independent and font-independent. Acrobat is Adobe's suite of software used to generate, edit and view PDF files.

picture researcher

A person who looks for pictures relevant to a particular topic, so that they can be used as illustrations in, for example, a book, newspaper or TV programme.

prelims

The initial pages of a book, including the title page and table of contents, which precede the main text. Also called front matter.

pre-press

Before a book goes to press.

print on demand or POD

The facility to print and bind a small number of books at short notice, without the need for a large print run, using digital technology. When an order comes through, a digital file of the book can be printed individually and automatically.

production controller

A person in the production department of a publishing company who deals with printers and other suppliers.

proofreader

A person whose job is to proofread texts to check typeset page presentation and text for errors and to mark up corrections.

publisher

A person or company that publishes books, magazines and/or newspapers.

publisher's agreement

A contract between a publisher and the copyright holder, author, agent or another publisher, which lays down the terms under which the publisher will publish the book for the copyright holder.

publishing contract

An agreement between a publisher and an author by which the author grants the publisher the right to publish the work against payment of a fee, usually in the form of a royalty.

reading fee

Money paid to somebody for reading a manuscript and commenting on it.

recto

Relating to the right-hand page of a book, usually given an odd number.

reprint

Copies of a book made from the original, but with a note in the publication details of the date of reprinting and possibly a new title page and cover design.

rights

The legal right to publish something such as a book, picture or extract from a text.

rights manager

A person who negotiates and coordinates rights sales (e.g. for subsidiary, translation or foreign rights). Often travels to book fairs to negotiate rights sales.

royalty

Money paid to a writer for the right to use his or her property, usually a percentage of sales or an agreed amount per sale.

royalty split

The way in which a royalty is divided between several authors or between author and illustrator.

royalty statement

A printed statement from a publisher showing how much royalty is due to an author.

sans serif

A style of printing letters with all lines of equal thickness and no serifs. Sans faces are less easy to read than seriffed faces and they are rarely used for continuous text, although some magazines use them for text matter.

serialisation

Publication of a book in parts in a magazine or newspaper.

serif

A small decorative line added to letters in some fonts; a font that uses serifs, such as Times. The addition of serifs (1) keeps the letters apart while at the same time making it possible to link one letter to the next, and (2) makes the letters distinct, in particular the top parts which the reader recognises when reading.

slush pile

Unsolicited manuscripts which are sent to publishers or agents, and which may never be read.

style sheet

A guide listing all the rules of house style for a publishing company which has to be followed by authors and editors.

sub-editor

A person who corrects and checks articles in a newspaper before they are printed.

subsidiary rights

Rights other than the right to publish a book in its first form, e.g. paperback rights; rights to adapt the book; rights to serialise it in a magazine; film and TV rights; audio, ebook, foreign and translation rights.

territory

Areas of the world that the publisher has the rights to publish or can make foreign rights deals.

trade discount

A reduction in price given to a customer in the same trade, as by a publisher to another publisher or to a bookseller.

trade paperback (B format)

A paperback edition of a book that is superior in production quality to a mass-market paperback edition and is similar to a hardback in size 198 x 129mm.

trim size or trimmed size

The measurements of a page of a book after it has been cut, or of a sheet of paper after it has been cut to size.

typesetter

A person or company that 'sets' text and prepares the final layout of the page for printing. It can also now involve XML tagging for ebook creation.

typographic error or typo

A mistake made when keying text or typesetting.

verso

The left-hand page of a book, usually given an even number.

volume rights

The right to publish the work in hardback or paperback (this can now sometimes include ebook).

XML tagging

Inserting tags into the text that can allow it to be converted for ebooks or for use in electronic formats.

Editing your work

If you have been lucky enough to secure a publisher for your work, a vital component of the process is editing. In this article, Lauren Simpson answers some commonly-asked questions.

What is editing?

Broadly speaking, 'editing' involves the refinement of a piece of writing (manuscript) to make it as near perfect as possible and thus ready to be published. Editing covers a whole range of interventions to a manuscript at different stages in its life, including restructuring, fact checking, copy-editing and proofreading.

Typically, when a manuscript is copy-edited, the editor will pay close attention to every word, reviewing and refining:

• spelling and grammar;
• syntax (the arrangement of words and phrases), structure and layout;
• factual and/or technical accuracy;
• whether the writing has the appropriate tone and content for the intended readership.

Some manuscripts need very little editing, while others need to be heavily edited or, in some cases, almost completely rewritten. It is essential that a manuscript is edited as comprehensively as time and budget allows – the aim being to ensure optimum sense and clarity for the reader. How much editing a particular manuscript will require depends on a number of factors, including:

• the complexity of the subject matter;
• whether or not a publisher's house style has to be imposed upon it;
• the quality of the writing;
• the expertise of the writer.

Should I edit my work before submitting the completed manuscript?

On completion of a manuscript, a diligent author should always go back over their work in order to eliminate spelling and grammatical mistakes ('typos') and to ensure that there are no inconsistencies (for example, in plot, dialogue, characterisation, physical descriptions, dates or sequences of events) or factual inaccuracies.

Before delivering your completed manuscript, you might also want to:

• read through your manuscript as an 'outsider' to identify errors that you may have overlooked while you were writing;
• consider how a reader might think/feel when reading your work, and revise anything they might not like or understand. This is not an easy task, so you might want to ask a trusted friend or colleague to read it through for you and suggest improvements.

Exercising 'good housekeeping' along these lines demonstrates that you are serious about your craft and can help save time and money down the editorial track. However, it is worth pointing out that any editing you undertake won't replace the editing that your publisher will carry out once your manuscript has been delivered, so there is no need to pay for your work to be edited in advance. For a cautionary note on editing your own work, see *Do self-published authors need to pay for an editor?* below.

What happens to my manuscript once it has been submitted?

While processes differ from publisher to publisher, the sequence of events from manuscript to printed copy can be broadly summarised as follows:

• The author (or their agent) delivers the completed manuscript to the publisher. The author should make every effort to submit the manuscript in accordance with the publisher's style guide and format requirements, to avoid the time and expense of revising the material at a later stage.

• The publisher arranges for the manuscript to be copy-edited and any queries arising from this process are passed to the author to be resolved in advance of typesetting/design.

• Copy-edited material is typeset or put through an electronic page layout or design process.

• Page proofs are produced and: (1) first page proofs are proofread by the publisher and the author; (2) corrections are incorporated and revised page proofs are produced; (3) revised page proofs are checked, corrected and signed off.

• The final, edited text is ready to be printed.

What do different types of editor do?

It is important to remember that no two publishing companies are the same and there are many different monikers applied to the editing professionals that you may come across: commissioning editor, copy-editor, managing editor, project editor, desk editor, sub-editor, assistant editor, chief editor … In addition, your work will almost certainly be pored over by one of the most important cogs in the editorial wheel – the proofreader.

Space constraints prevent a description of every editor listed above but an overview of the key editorial staff that you are likely to encounter will give you a good idea of the work they do.

Commissioning (or acquiring) editors identify books to publish in order to build up a publisher's list in a particular area or genre. They commission work by finding authors or responding to book proposals and, for fiction work, acquire most of their books through a literary agent. They are responsible for ensuring that authors deliver manuscripts to specification and on time.

Copy-editors check that content is accurate, clearly and logically expressed, conveys the desired message or tone, and comes together to form a coherent and cohesive whole. Copy-editors must be analytical in their approach and able to weed out factual errors as well as annotate diagrams, cross-check references and apply a publisher's house style to a text. They may also be required to have specialist knowledge of the subject matter, particularly in the case of science, maths and law.

Proofreaders scrutinise content in very fine detail to ensure that errors relating to syntax, spelling, grammar, punctuation, design and format are eliminated. Proofreaders have good technical language skills and an excellent eye for detail. The latter is especially important in order to deal effectively with errors in technical or complex text, or when checking that the copy-editor has applied a style guide correctly.

What are the differences between copy-editing and proofreading?

Copy-editing and proofreading are crucial stages of the publishing process and, while the two can often be confused or referred to interchangeably, there are important differences. The copy-editing function normally takes place when a manuscript is complete but before typesetting or design, allowing substantial revisions to be made at minimal cost. Proofreading, on the other hand, typically takes place after a manuscript has been copy-edited and typeset/designed and serves to 'fine-polish' the text to ensure that it is free from editorial and layout inaccuracies.

Is all editing done electronically?

Traditionally, manuscripts were copy-edited on paper, which was labour-intensive and time-consuming. These days, nearly all copy-editing is carried out electronically, usually using Microsoft Word or a bespoke publishing system. The 'track changes' function allows the copy-editor to make alterations to the manuscript: deletions/additions can be highlighted so that the copy-editor's work can be easily monitored; comments and queries for the author or publisher can be inserted into the margins of the document; and the 'find and replace' function enables inaccuracies and inconsistencies to be corrected globally. Furthermore, tracking changes electronically allows changes to a manuscript to be accepted or rejected on an individual basis, giving them great control over the final version. Another advantage of copy-editing electronically is that an edited manuscript can be emailed – saving time and money.

How is proofreading carried out?

If a manuscript is very 'clean' (i.e. it does not contain many errors), a publisher may insist that the proofreading is carried out electronically. In this case, the proofreader will be sent the manuscript by email, usually in pdf format, and will annotate changes to the document on screen. However, proofreaders will usually receive a manuscript in hard copy and then mark up corrections directly onto the printed page, often using the protocols set down by the British Standards Institution (www.bsigroup.co.uk).

What are proofreading symbols and why do I need to know them?

Proofreading symbols (or marks) are the 'shorthand' that copy-editors and proofreaders use for correcting written material. Typesetters, designers and printers also require this knowledge as part of correcting page layout, style and format.

Mistakes to look out for when editing and proofreading

- Similar words used incorrectly, e.g. effect/affect.
- Phrases used inappropriately, e.g. 'should of' instead of 'should have'.
- Apostrophe misuse, especially in respect of its/it's.
- Words with similar spelling or pronunciation but with different meanings used incorrectly, e.g. their/they're/there.
- References in the text that do not correspond to footnotes.
- Inaccurate or inadequate cross-referencing.
- Index listings which cannot be found on the page given in the index.
- Text inadvertently reordered or cut during the typesetting process.
- Headings formatted as ordinary text.
- Running heads that do not correspond to chapter headings.
- Fonts and font sizes used incorrectly.
- Inconsistent use of abbreviations and acronyms.
- Formatting inconsistencies such as poorly-aligned margins or uneven columns.
- Captions/headings omitted from illustrations, photographs or diagrams.
- Illustrations/photographs/diagrams without appropriate copyright references.
- Missing bullet points or numbers in a sequenced list.
- Word processing errors, e.g. '3' instead of '£'.
- Incorrect layout of names, addresses, telephone numbers and email/web addresses.
- Incorrect use of trademarks, e.g. 'blackberry' instead of 'BlackBerry™'.
- Abbreviations/acronyms that have not been defined in full.
- Widows and orphans, e.g. text which runs over page breaks and leaves a word or a line stranded.
- Past and present tenses mixed within a piece of text.
- Use of plural verb conjugations with single subjects, e.g. 'one in five children are...' instead of 'one in five children is...'.

Marks/symbols for general instructions

INSTRUCTIONS	MARGIN	TEXT
Leave the text in its original state and ignore any marks that have been made, commonly referred to as 'stet'	⊘	____ under the characters to be left as they were
Query for the author/typesetter/ printer/publisher.	⟨?⟩	A circle should be placed around text to be queried
Remove non-textual marks	✕	A circle should be placed around marks to be removed
End of change	/	None

Marks/symbols for inserting, deleting and changing text

INSTRUCTIONS	MARGIN	TEXT
Text to be inserted	New text, followed by ⋏	⋏
Additional text supplied separately	⋏ followed by a letter in a diamond which identifies additional text ◈A	⋏
Delete a character	⌐σ	/ through the character
Delete text	⌐σ	⊢⊣ through text
Delete character and close space	⊂⌐σ	I through the character
Delete text and close space	⊂⌐σ	⊟ through text
Character to replace marked character	New character, followed by /	/ through the character
Text to replace marked text	New text, followed by /	⊢⊣ through text

Marks/symbols for grammar and punctuation

INSTRUCTIONS	MARGIN	TEXT
Full stop	⊙	⋏ at insertion point or / through character /
Comma	،	As above
Semi-colon	;	As above
Colon	⊙	As above
Hyphen	⊢=⊣	As above
Single quote marks	⋎̓ or ⋎̓	As above
Double quote marks	⋎̈ or ⋎̈	As above
Apostrophe	⋎̓	As above
Ellipses or leader dots	⟨•••⟩	As above
Insert/replace dash	⊢1en⊣ Size of dash to be stated between uprights	As above

Marks/symbols for altering the look/style/layout of text

INSTRUCTIONS	MARGIN	TEXT
Put text in italics	⌐⌐⌐	——— under text to be changed
Remove italics, replace with roman text	⌐+⌐	Circle text to be changed
Put text in bold	∿∿∿	∿∿∿ under text to be changed
Remove bold	∿∼∿	Circle text to be changed
Put text in capitals	≡	≡ under text to be changed
Put text in small capitals	=	= under text to be changed
Put text in lower case	≢ or ≠	Circle text to be changed
Change character to superscript	Y under character	/ through character to be changed
Insert a superscript character	Y under character	⋀ at point of insertion
Change character to subscript	⋀ above character	/ through character to be changed
Insert a subscript character	⋀ above character	⋀ at point of insertion
Remove bold and italics	∿∼∿	Circle text to be changed
Paragraph break	⌐	⌐
Remove paragraph break, run on text	∽	∽
Indent text	⊏	⊏
Remove indent	⊐	⊐
Insert or replace space between characters or words	Y	⋀ at relevant point of insertion or / through character
Reduce space between characters or words	⋀	|
Insert space between lines or paragraphs	Mark extends into margin	—(or)—
Reduce space between lines or paragraphs	Mark extends into margin	—→ or ←—
Transpose lines	⊐	⊐
Transpose characters or words	⊔⊓	⊔⊓
Close space between characters	⌒	character ⌒ character
Underline words	(underline)	⌒ circle words
Take over character(s) or word(s) to next line/column/page	Mark extends into margin	⊏
Take back character(s) or word(s) to previous line/column/page	Mark extends into margin	⊐

Once a manuscript has been copy-edited and typeset, authors will be sent a set of page proofs to look at and so it is important that they, too, have at least a basic understanding of proofreading symbols so that they can correct their proofs quickly, uniformly and without any ambiguity.

Proofreading marks/symbols fall into separate categories:

• general instructions;
• inserting, deleting and changing text;
• grammar and punctuation;
• altering the look/style/layout of text.

Depending on the nature of the changes needed, proofreading marks are typically positioned in the margin of the document, with some changes requiring a mark within the text or some additional instructions.

The full set of proofreading marks is defined by the British Standards Institution (BS 5261), however, most authors will be able to mark up proofs using only the most common symbols. The most useful marks can be found on pages 310 and 311.

Are there any handy proofreading tips?

Effective proofreading takes time and practice but by following these tips you'll be able to spot mistakes quickly and accurately in no time.

• Set aside adequate time for proofreading. It requires concentration and should not be rushed.
• Before starting on a proofreading task, make sure you have easy access to a dictionary and thesaurus, and ensure that you have any relevant style guides for language style and format/design.
• If possible, proofread a document several times and concentrate on different aspects each time, e.g. sense/tone, format, grammar/punctuation/use of language.
• Spot typos by reading the text backwards – that way you will not be distracted by the meaning of the text.
• Always double-check scientific, mathematical or medical symbols as they can often be corrupted during the typesetting process. Accented characters and currency symbols can also cause problems.
• If possible, have a version of the copy-edited text to refer to while you proofread – it might help solve minor inaccuracies or inconsistencies more quickly.

Do self-published authors need to pay for an editor?

Self-published authors do not have to obtain or pay for editorial advice, but remember that if you want to sell a book that looks as good and reads as well as a professionally produced one, you should consider how you are going to achieve this. There are a host of individuals and companies available to review or edit your work at all stages in the writing process, from concept to publication. We even offer such editorial services here at Writers & Artists.

If you think a professional eye would enhance your text, be cautious and read the small print. Decide what type of edit your text requires, agree a fair price for the edit and try to employ a professional with a track record and recommendations. Look at the advice, rates and contacts provided by the Society of Editors and Proofreaders (www.sfep.org.uk).

Further resources

All writers and editors need a quality dictionary to hand, such as *The Shorter Oxford English Dictionary* (2 volumes, 6th edn, 2007) or the single-volume *Oxford Dictionary of English* (3rd edn, 2010). Other good dictionaries, available in print, ebook and online are published by Collins and Chambers. See also www.oxforddictionaries.com, www.dictionary.com and www.collinslanguage.com.

Burchfield, R.W., *Fowler's Modern English Usage*, Oxford University Press, re-revised 3rd edn, 2004

Butcher, Judith; Drake, Caroline and Leach, Maureen, *Butcher's Copy-editing: The Cambridge Handbook for Editors, Copy-editors and Proofreaders*, Cambridge University Press, 4th edn, 2006

The Chicago Manual of Style: The Essential Guide for Writers, Editors, and Publishers, University of Chicago Press, 16th edn, 2010

New Oxford Dictionary for Writers and Editors: The Essential A-Z Guide to the Written Word, Oxford University Press, revised edn, 2014

New Hart's Rules: The Oxford Style Guide, Oxford University Press, 2014

Society for Editors and Proofreaders (SfEP), www.sfep.org.uk (see page 405)

The Publishing Training Centre offers courses on editing, proofreading and all aspects of publishing, www.train4publishing.co.uk

Lauren Simpson is a freelance editor, writer and proofreader with 20 years' experience. She has contributed to and developed a wide range of publications covering subjects as diverse as agriculture, local government, marketing, business, English language teaching, boating, law, HR, social work, human rights and counselling & psychotherapy. Lauren also has experience of editing biography and autobiography, as well as manuscripts for self-published authors. In addition, she has been editor of a number of prestigious reference works including *The Municipal Year Book* and *Whitaker's Almanack*.

Publishing practice

Copyright
Copyright questions

Gillian Haggart Davies answers questions to draw out some of the legal issues and explain the basics of how copyright works, or should work, for the benefit of the writer.

What is copyright?

Copyright is a negative right in the sense that it is not a right of possession but is a right of *exclusion*. However, if you know your rights it can be a strong legal tool because copyright law affords remedies in both the civil and criminal courts. Material will automatically be protected by copyright without registration (in the UK) if it is original, i.e. not copied. The onus is on you, the writer, and your publisher to do the work of protecting, policing and enforcing your valuable intellectual property. Copyright is different in every country – registration is not possible in the UK, Japan or the Netherlands; it is optional in the USA (for some works), China and India; and mandatory for some works in other jurisdictions (e.g. for some works in the Kyrgyz Republic, Mauritius and Nepal). Unfortunately, generally speaking, people do not respect copyright and there are ongoing issues to do with copyright, especially online, with large expanses of 'grey areas'.

I am a freelance writer and submitted an article to a magazine editor and heard nothing back. Six months later I read a feature in a Sunday newspaper which looks very similar. Can I sue someone?

Pitching ideas can be fraught with difficulty. In legal terms you do not have any protection under copyright law for 'ideas', but only for 'the expression of those ideas' – for the way in which the ideas have been 'clothed in words' to paraphrase a Learned Judge. It could be argued that in many ways this distinction between ideas and their expression does not work for writing and 'literary works'. But that won't help you in court or get you legal recompense if you are ripped off.

In the situation described, you would need to prove that your work came first in time; that your work was seen by the second writer or publisher; and that the second person copied unlawfully a 'substantial part' of your work (this is qualitative not quantitative), which these days involves a very woolly and subjective judicial comparison of one work weighed against the other. You would also need to be able to counter any claims that the subject matter is not capable of being monopolised by you and show that there is actual language copying. Further, you might then have to fend off counter-arguments from the other party that you did not have copyright in the first place. The other writer can rely on a 'defence' that she has 'incidentally included' the text; or that her use is 'fair dealing' (because she is using it for a permitted purpose, for example of reporting news or current affairs; or that it is for research for non-commercial purposes; or for private use; or for 'criticism or review'; or that it is parody, pastiche or satire. These defences are actually referred to in the legislation as 'exceptions' and are very strict, i.e. they have always been difficult to make out.

In addition, as if all that were not complicated enough, the person doing the 'copying' or publishing could say that she had an 'implied licence' from you to do so; or that she had a common law right under trusts law: this would arise, say, if she and you had been accustomed to dealing with each other in such a way that you commonly gave her original work and she used/copied it.

Avoid these difficulties by taking practical pre-emptive steps: mark your speculative pieces 'in confidence' and add '© Your Name 201X'. Using the © symbol puts people on notice that you are aware of your rights. It would also have an effect later on if it came to litigation evidentially, i.e. if a person sees the copyright sign but nevertheless goes ahead and uses work without permission, the defence of 'innocent dissemination' cannot be relied upon.

You did not have copyright in the first place: if the subject matter is 'out there', i.e. common knowledge, copyright law may not protect the first work. The law is very contradictory in this area, as can be seen in these three cases which went to court: the persistent lifting of facts from another newspaper, even with rewriting, was deemed a copyright infringement; but copyright did protect a detailed sequence of ideas where precise wording was not copied; the fact that an author went to primary sources did not necessarily ensure that he was not copyright-infringing. However, copyright law does weigh heavily in favour of protecting the originator.

If a newspaper pays for an article and I then want to sell the story to a magazine, am I free under the copyright law to do so?

Yes, provided that you have not assigned copyright or licensed exclusive use to the newspaper. When selling your work to newspapers or magazines, make it clear in writing, that you are selling only First or Second Serial Rights, not your copyright.

Does being paid a kill fee affect my copyright in a given piece?

No, provided that you have not assigned or licensed your copyright to the magazine or newspaper. Broadly, never agree to an assignation; it is irreversible. Always license, and those parts of copyright you want to license, for example print-only; UK only; not television rights, etc. Copyright rights are infinitely divisible and negotiable. If you have inadvertently or purposely granted copyright permission to the publisher and the publisher prints the piece, and you have taken a kill fee, don't forget that you can at least also claim 'secondary licence' income from the collective pool of monies collected on behalf of UK authors by both the ALCS (see page 322) and PLR (see page 297) if you are named on the piece. This may amount to only a tiny amount of money but it may take the sting out of the tail.

I am writing an (unauthorised) biography of a novelist. Can I quote her novels – since they are published and 'public domain'?

Using extracts and quotes is a very difficult area and there is no easy answer to this. If the author has definitely been deceased for 70 years or more, you may be fine; the work may have passed into the 'public domain'. However, unpublished works require caution. In general, unpublished works are protected by copyright as soon as they are 'expressed' and copyright belongs to the author until/unless published and rights are transferred to a publisher. Protection for unpublished works lasts for 50 years (usually); Crown copyright lasts for 125 years for unpublished works – it's a legal minefield!

Generally, copyright law requires you to ask permission and (usually) pay a fee for reuse. There is no exact recipe for the amount of money payable or the number of words you can 'take' before you need to pay. A new law passed on 1 October 2014 says, somewhat vaguely, that you can take 'no more than is required for the specific purpose for which it is needed'. To quote from the legislation: 'Copyright in a work is not infringed by the use of a quotation from the work (whether for criticism or review or otherwise) provided that (a) the work has been made available to the public, (b) the use of the quotation is fair dealing with the work, (c) *the extent of the quotation is no more than is required by the specific purpose for which it is used* [emphasis added], and (d) the quotation is accompanied by a sufficient acknowledgement (*unless this would be impossible for reasons of practicality or otherwise* [emphasis added])' [Copyright and Rights in Performances (Quotation and Parody) Regulations 2014, No. 2356 (in force since 1 June 2014)]. But does this help? Is it not a bit woolly? In the biography example here, how much would 'no more than is necessary' be? A line from every work? A paragraph from every work? A page? The entirety of one work but excerpts only of others ... or none at all? What if the biography is authorised, not unauthorised? These are all unanswered questions and untried by case law.

I want to use a quote from another book but don't know who owns the copyright. Can I just put it in quotes and use it?

If you cannot identify the source of the quote, we enter the murky waters of 'orphan works'. A new scheme is now in place whereby you can buy a licence to use an 'orphan work' from the IPO (Intellectual Property Office), for an application fee of £20 (for a single 'work', e.g. book), up to £80 for 30 'works', plus a licence fee, which will depend on the work and what you say about its use on the application form. The licence will last for seven years, which is the window of time allowed for a copyright owner to 'claim' the work (which goes on the IPO orphan works register when it becomes a licensed subject under the scheme).

The IPO will not grant an orphan-use licence if it thinks your use will be 'derogatory' of the copyright work, or if you are unable to show that you have made diligent attempts to trace the copyright owner, so the old rules about making such efforts now apply in statutory form. 'Diligent' efforts to trace the copyright owner could include contacting publishers, searching the WATCH (Writers Artists and their Copyright Holders) database (www.watch-file.com, http://norman.hrc.utexas.edu/watch), and placing an advertisement in the *TLS*, the *Bookseller*, etc). Keep a record of all your efforts in case the copyright question comes back to bite you later, and use a disclaimer on your material. In an ideal world, all content would be tagged with details of what is permissible and how to contact the owner. [See www.alcs.co.uk/wiseup; BPP Legal Advice Clinic www.whatcanIdowiththiscontent.com; IPO orphan works https://www.gov.uk/copyright-orphan-works; and the section above relating to quoting from a novel.]

My publisher has forgotten to assert my copyright on the imprint page. What does that mean for me?

Technically, what is usually asserted on the imprint page is the moral right to be identified as author of the work. This 'paternity right' is lost if it is not 'asserted', so if it is not on the imprint page or anywhere else you lose the right. Moral rights are copyrights, separate to and additional to what we normally refer to as '('economic') copyright': they protect the personal side of creation, in that they are about the integrity of the work and the person/reputation of the creator. Whereas the 'main'/economic copyright protection is there to ensure you get revenues from your work, for example licence fees and royalties. Both economic copyrights and moral rights were conferred by the 1988 UK statute and derive from the Berne Convention. They exist separately, so you can keep moral rights and 'licence away' copyright (economic copyrights). And so in reverse, even if your moral right to be identified as author is lost, your other rights – economic copyright and the moral right to not have your work subjected to 'derogatory treatment' – remain with you. Moral rights cannot be licensed or assigned because they are personal to the author, but they can be 'waived'; for example, a ghostwriter may well waive the right to be identified as author. Moral rights are very flexible and useful, but are not widely used.

I've found an illustration I want to use for the cover of a book that I'm self-publishing. I chose the picture (dated 1928) on purpose because the artist is out of copyright and the picture is in the 'public domain'. Why is the picture library, which holds the image, charging a reproduction fee?

You have to pay a reproduction fee under copyright law because of the separate copyright issue for photography. Because the original artwork was photographed, copyright vests separately in the photograph (of the artwork) as opposed to the artwork itself. It is a controversial area and one where the UK/US legal systems are split. Make sure that standing behind this is a contract with your publishing services provider identifying you as the copyright holder. Do not cede any rights. You should be granting the publisher a non-exclusive licence to publish your book only.

I included someone's work on my blog, but as I blog for free and it's not a money-making exercise, can I be sued for copyright infringement?

Yes you can. If the person alleging copyright infringement can show she has copyright in the work, that you had access to her work, can show you copied the whole of that work or a 'substantial part' of it, and that you did not have permission, you could well be infringing criminal and civil copyright laws. The point of copyright law – the economic as opposed to the moral rights aspect – is to protect the economic interests of the original copyright owner. If she can demonstrate that her position has been undermined by your blog in terms of her market share having diminished and/or that sales have been adversely affected, etc or if she can show that you have not paid her any reuse fee or asked permission or acknowledged her authorship, you are on very thin ice.

I retweeted, edited, two lines from Twitter. I tweet for free and it's not a money-making exercise, can I be sued for copyright infringement?

A similar answer to the above. 'Yes' or at least 'probably yes'. A ruling of the Court of Justice of the European Union (CJEU) interpreting EU copyright law strongly suggests copyright vests in anything that is the original author's creation, and in the EU case in point (*Infopaq*, 2009) that applied to an 11-word extract. This is in spite of the fact that there is a broader general principle in copyright that an 'insubstantial part' of a work does not enjoy copyright protection in the first place, and therefore there could be no breach. If you had a good lawyer she could argue either way as this is a grey area. The situation in the USA may be different but seems certainly arguable. An alternative way of viewing the situation is that this is a 'quote', and therefore 'exceptional', i.e. non-infringing under new legislation introduced in 2014 (see above). But the issues have not been tested in court and again, I would say, are wide open to argument.

My book has been made available by a free book download site but I never agreed to this. What can I do?

Contact your publisher or ask the site direct (if it's a self-published work) to remove it from their website. If they do not act or do not respond, get legal advice: a lawyer will be able to issue a warning followed by a 'take down notice', followed if necessary by a court injunction. However, this is very difficult for cases worth under £10,000. And it is no understatement to say that the present system of access to justice and costs of lawyers and litigation will prove to be a significant hurdle for most writers. Take practical steps to protect copyright in your own works yourself by setting up a Google Alert for every title you own.

First steps legal advice may be available from the Society of Authors (see page 375), the Writers' Guild of Great Britain (see page 408), the National Union of Journalists (NUJ), the Society for Editors and Proofreaders (SfEP, page 405) or your local BusinessLink or an intellectual property specialist adviser like Own-It or Artquest (which deals with the visual arts but carries advice applicable to writers too).

Gillian Haggart Davies MA (Hons), LLB is the author of *Copyright Law for Artists, Designers and Photographers* (A&C Black 2010) and *Copyright Law for Writers, Editors and Publishers* (A&C Black 2011).

See also...

Copyright

The Copyright Licensing Agency Ltd

The Copyright Licensing Agency (CLA) licenses organisations to copy extracts from copyright publications on behalf of the authors, publishers and visual creators it represents.

CLA's licences permit limited copying from print and digital publications. This copying includes photocopying, scanning and emailing of articles and extracts from books, journals and magazines, as well as digital copying from electronic publications, online titles and websites. CLA issues its licences to schools, further and higher education, businesses and government bodies. The money collected is distributed to the copyright owners to ensure that they are fairly rewarded for the use of their intellectual property.

Why was CLA established?

CLA was set up by its owners, the Authors' Licensing and Collecting Society (ALCS, see page 322) and the Publishers Licensing Society (PLS), and has an agency agreement with the Design and Artists Copyright Society (DACS, page 324), which represents visual artists, such as photographers, illustrators and painters. CLA represents creators and publishers by licensing the copying of their work and promoting the role and value of copyright generally. By championing copyright it is helping to sustain creativity and maintain the incentive to produce new work.

> **Further information**
>
> **The Copyright Licensing Agency Ltd**
> Saffron House, 6–10 Kirby Street,
> London EC1N 8TS
> *tel* 020-7400 3100
> *email* cla@cla.co.uk
> *website* www.cla.co.uk

How CLA helps creators and users of copyright work

CLA allows licensed users access to millions of titles worldwide. In return, CLA ensures that creators, artists, photographers and writers, along with publishers, are fairly recompensed by the payment of royalties derived from the licence fees which CLA collects and distributes.

Through this collective licensing system CLA is able to provide users with the simplest and most cost-effective means of obtaining authorisation for the photocopying and scanning of published works, albeit under strict copy limits.

CLA has licences which enable digitisation of existing print material, enabling users to scan and electronically send extracts from print copyright works.

In addition, CLA has launched a series of licences for business and government which allow users to reuse and copy from digital electronic and online publications, including websites. Writers and publishers can benefit further from the increased income generated from these enhanced licences, which operate under the same copy limits as the established photocopying licences.

Who is licensed?

CLA's licences are available to three principal sectors:
- education (schools, further and higher education);
- government (central departments, local authorities, public bodies); and
- business (businesses, industry and the professions).

Copyright

CLA offers licences to meet the specific needs of each sector and user groups within each sector. Depending on the requirement, there are both blanket and transactional licences available. Every licence allows copying from most books, journals, magazines and periodicals published in the UK. Most licences include digital copying permissions granted by copyright owners on an opt-in basis.

International dimension

Many countries have established equivalents to CLA and the number of such agencies is set to grow. Nearly all these agencies, including CLA, are members of the International Federation of Reproduction Rights Organisations (IFRRO).

Through reciprocal arrangements covering 36 overseas territories, including the USA, Canada and most EU countries, CLA's licences allow copying from an expanding list of international publications. CLA receives monies from these territories for the copying of UK material abroad, passing it on to UK rights holders.

Distribution of licence fees

The fees collected from licensees are forwarded to PLS, ALCS and DACS for distribution to publishers, writers and visual artists respectively. The allocation of fees is based on subscriptions, library holdings and detailed surveys of copying activity. CLA has collected and distributed to rights holders over £814 million since 1983. For the year 2013/14, £72.5 million was paid to creators and publishers in the UK and abroad.

Enabling access, protecting creativity

CLA believes it is important to raise awareness of copyright and the need to protect the creativity of artists, authors and publishers. To this end, it organises a range of activities such as copyright workshops in schools, seminars for businesses and institutions and an extensive programme of exhibitions and other events.

CLA believes in working positively together with representative bodies in each sector, meaning legal action is rare. However, organisations – especially in the business sector – are made aware that copyright is a legally enforceable right and not a voluntary option. CLA's compliance arm, Copywatch (www.copywatch.org), is active in these sectors to educate users and seek out illegal copying.

By supporting rights holders in this way, CLA plays an important role in maintaining the value of their work, thereby sustaining creativity and its benefit to all. Through protection of this sort the creative industries in the UK have been able to grow to support millions of jobs and contribute to the economy.

See also...

Copyright

Authors' Licensing and Collecting Society

The Authors' Licensing and Collecting Society is the rights management society for UK writers.

The Authors' Licensing and Collecting Society (ALCS) is the UK collective rights management society for writers. Established in 1977, it represents the interests of all UK writers and aims to ensure that they are fairly compensated for any works that are copied, broadcast or recorded.

A non-profit company, ALCS was set up in the wake of the campaign to establish a Public Lending Right (see page 297) to help writers protect and exploit their collective rights. Today, it is the largest writers' organisation in the UK with a membership of approximately 87,000. In the financial year of 2013/14, over £32 million (gross) in royalties were paid out to almost 70,000 writers.

ALCS is committed to ensuring that the rights of writers, both intellectual property and moral, are fully respected and fairly rewarded. It represents all types of writers and includes educational, research and academic authors drawn from the professions: scriptwriters, adaptors, playwrights, poets, editors and freelance journalists, across the print and broadcast media.

Internationally recognised as a leading authority on copyright matters and authors' interests, ALCS is committed to fostering an awareness of intellectual property issues among the writing community. It maintains a close watching brief on all matters affecting copyright, both in the UK and internationally, and makes regular representations to the UK government and the European Union.

ALCS collects fees that are difficult, time-consuming or legally impossible for writers and their representatives to claim on an individual basis, money that is nonetheless due to them. To date, it has distributed over £380 million in secondary royalties to writers. Over the years, ALCS has developed highly specialised knowledge and sophisticated systems that can track writers and their works against any secondary use for which they are due payment. A network of international contacts and reciprocal agreements with foreign collecting societies also ensures that UK writers are compensated for any similar use overseas.

The primary sources of fees due to writers are secondary royalties from the following:

Membership

Authors' Licensing and Collecting Society Ltd
The Writers' House, 13 Haydon Street,
London EC3N 1DB
tel 020-7264 5700
email alcs@alcs.co.uk
website www.alcs.co.uk
Chief Executive Owen Atkinson

Membership is open to all writers and successors to their estates at a one-off fee of £36 for Ordinary membership. Members of the Society of Authors, the Writers' Guild of Great Britain, National Union of Journalists, Chartered Institute of Journalists and British Association of Journalists have free Ordinary membership of ALCS. Operations are primarily funded through a commission levied on distributions and membership fees. The commission on funds generated for Ordinary members is currently 9.75%. Most writers will find that this, together with a number of other membership benefits, provides good value.

Photocopying

The single largest source of income, this is administered by the Copyright Licensing Agency (CLA, see page 320). Created in 1982 by ALCS and the Publishers Licensing Society (PLS),

CLA grants licences to users for copying books and serials. This includes schools, colleges, universities, central and local government departments, as well as the British Library, businesses and other institutions. Licence fees are based on the number of people who benefit and the number of copies made. The revenue from this is then split between the rights holders: authors, publishers and artists. Money due to authors is transferred to ALCS for distribution. ALCS also receives photocopying payments from foreign sources.

Digitisation
In 1999, CLA launched its licensing scheme for the digitisation of printed texts. It offers licences to organisations for storing and using digital versions of authors' printed works that have been scanned into a computer. Again, the fees are split between authors and publishers.

Foreign Public Lending Right
The Public Lending Right (PLR) system pays authors whose books are borrowed from public libraries. Through reciprocal agreements, ALCS members receive payment whenever their books are borrowed from German, Belgian, Dutch, French, Austrian, Spanish, Estonian and Irish libraries. Please note that ALCS does not administer the UK Public Lending Right; this is managed directly by the UK PLR Office (see page 297).

ALCS also receives other payments from Germany. These cover the loan of academic, scientific and technical titles from academic libraries; extracts of authors' works in textbooks and the press, together with other one-off fees.

Simultaneous cable retransmission
This involves the simultaneous showing of one country's television signals in another country, via a cable network. Cable companies pay a central collecting organisation a percentage of their subscription fees, which must be collectively administered. This sum is then divided by the rights holders. ALCS receives the writers' share for British programmes containing literary and dramatic material and distributes it to them.

Educational recording
ALCS, together with the main broadcasters and rights holders, set up the Educational Recording Agency (ERA) in 1989 to offer licences to educational establishments. ERA collects fees from the licensees and pays ALCS the amount due to writers for their literary works.

Other sources of income include a blank tape levy and small, miscellaneous literary rights.

Tracing authors
ALCS is dedicated to protecting and promoting authors' rights and enabling writers to maximise their income. It is committed to ensuring that royalties due to writers are efficiently collected and speedily distributed to them. One of its greatest challenges is finding some of the writers for whom it holds funds and ensuring that they claim their money.

Any published author or broadcast writer could have some funds held by ALCS for them. It may be a nominal sum or it could run into several thousand pounds. Either call or visit the ALCS website – see box for contact details.

Design and Artists Copyright Society

Established by artists for artists, the Design and Artists Copyright Society (DACS) is the UK's leading visual arts rights management organisation.

As a not-for-profit organisation, DACS translates rights into revenues and recognition for a wide spectrum of visual artists. It offers three rights management services – Payback, Artist's Resale Right and Copyright Licensing – in addition to lobbying, advocacy and legal advice for visual artists.

DACS is part of an international network of rights management organisations. Today DACS represents 80,000 artists and in 2013 it distributed over £14 million in royalties to artists and their beneficiaries. See website for more information about DACS and its services.

Payback

Each year DACS pays a share of royalties to visual artists whose work has been reproduced in UK magazines and books or broadcast on UK television channels. DACS operates this service for situations where it would be impractical or near impossible for an artist to license their rights on an individual basis, for example when a university student wants to photocopy pages from a book that features their work.

Artist's Resale Right

The Artist's Resale Right entitles artists to a royalty each time their work is resold for more than €1,000 by an auction house, gallery or dealer. See website for details of eligibility criteria. DACS ensures artists receive their royalties from qualifying sales not just in the UK but also from other countries in the European Economic Area (EEA). Since 1 January 2012 in the UK, artists' heirs and beneficiaries can now benefit from these royalties.

Copyright Licensing

This service benefits artists and their estates when their work is reproduced for commercial purposes, for example on t-shirts or greetings cards, in a book or on a website. DACS can take care of everything on behalf of the artist, ensuring terms, fees and contractual arrangements are all in order and in their best interests. Artists who use this service are also represented globally through the DACS international network of rights management organisations.

Copyright facts

- Copyright is a right granted to visual artists under law.
- Copyright in all artistic works is established from the moment of creation – the only qualification is that the work must be original.
- There is no registration system in the UK; copyright comes into operation automatically and lasts the lifetime of the visual artist plus a period of 70 years after their death.
- After death, copyright is usually transferred to the visual artist's heirs or beneficiaries. When the 70-year period has expired, the work then enters the public domain and no longer benefits from copyright protection.

• The copyright owner has the exclusive right to authorise the reproduction (or copy) of a work in any medium by any other party.

• Any reproduction can only take place with the copyright owner's consent.

• Permission is usually granted in return for a fee, which enables the visual artist to derive some income from other people using his or her work.

• If a visual artist is commissioned to produce a work, he or she will usually retain the copyright unless an agreement is signed which specifically assigns the copyright. When visual creators are employees and create work during the course of their employment, the employer retains the copyright in those works.

See also...

● *Copyright questions*, page 315
● *The Copyright Licensing Agency Ltd*, page 320

Copyright

Magazines and newspapers
Writing for the teenage market

How can a writer try to please today's teenage audience, who have so many added distractions, demands and pressures on their time? Michelle Garnett sets out some important guidelines, advising you to jettison any preconceptions and to respect the individuality, intelligence and concerns of this complex and fascinating age group.

There's no denying that the reading habits of teenagers have changed dramatically in recent years. Rewind to the 1990s and most likely your average adolescent reader would be sitting quietly, turning the pages of a book or a magazine. Fast forward to the present day and they're scouring their iPhone on the move, or devouring information on their tablet or laptop in bite-sized chunks. It's not surprising, considering 65% of 12–15 year-olds now own smartphones and 95% have access to the internet at home.

But enough of the stats. Times might be a-changing, but teenagers are still the same complex – and fascinating – individuals they ever were. Adolescence is an intense time. Just starting out in the world, teens are attempting to navigate the transition from childhood to adulthood, walking the fine line between feeling invincible and feeling totally lost, while ticking off a rapid succession of firsts: first love, first car, first job, first holiday with their mates ... the list goes on.

They're breaking away from their parents and making their own decisions – and consequently notching up a fair few mistakes along the way. They're also starting to look outward, finding their place in the world and figuring out how their actions affect others. And with the advent of the internet and the rise of social media they're having to grow up faster than ever, with so many distractions and demands on their time.

So with all this in mind, how does a writer even begin to try to please these (demanding, streetwise and fickle) customers?

1. Get to know your readers

If you're going to write for a teen audience you've got to get into their mindset and suss out what makes them tick. Young people are too often made to feel inconsequential and their views are commonly ignored. Talk to them, ask their opinion, find out what their priorities are, what fires their passions, what dreams and ambitions they have. They'll appreciate your interest – and, given the chance to talk, they'll be searingly honest.

You also need to discover how much they already know about your proposed subject, whether you're likely to be challenging any prejudices, and what kind of questions your feature might prompt. By painting a clear picture of your reader in your mind you'll find it so much easier to define your motive. They'll only care how much you know when you show how much you care – and that means showing that you're aware of who they are and what they're about.

2. Lay off the teen slang

If you're talking to teens, you need to use their lingo, right? Wrong. Forget about any attempts to sound cool. Put down that 'yoof' dictionary. You'll struggle to keep up with their ever-evolving language and your efforts will reek of 'Trying Too Hard' – a trait that's a total no-no when it comes to appealing to young people.

'*When adults use text talk or slang it's annoying and embarrassing*', confirms Emily (16). '*Teenagers don't actually say LOL when they're talking.*'

Instead, be direct and informative. Adopt an authoritative tone, but keep it chatty.

3. Offer reassurance

Puberty is a confusing, and sometimes lonely, time. Reach out to your readers by talking about their worries and insecurities. Sure, not all of them are necking vodka in their school lunch break, risking unprotected sex or having panic attacks over their exams but, for many, it's their reality. Whether it's bullying, unwanted pregnancy, peer pressure, drugs, abusive relationships or an uncertain future, it's happening out there all around them and even if your readers aren't directly experiencing these issues, you can bet a classmate, a teen neighbour or a 'friend of a friend' will be.

Teen magazines historically adopted the guiding tone of an older sister. It's a good starting point. Build trust by being frank with your facts and crystal clear with your message. And be sure to let your readers know that they're not alone.

4. Celebrate individuality

The teen years are full of contradictions. Most young people yearn to belong and be part of a community while also testing out their emerging individual attributes and attitudes, and pinpointing what makes them unique. Big up that uniqueness. Let them know it's good to be different.

And avoid making assumptions about what motivates them. They don't all aspire to being permatanned, WAG-wannabes or football fanatics with chiselled six-packs. Goth girl, tech geek, eco-warrior, skater boy ... they're all guises teens adopt as they seek out their true identities.

Jack (14) points out that teens' interests are as far-reaching and diverse as those of adults: '*We don't all listen to R&B, you know. One of my friends listens to opera music!*'

Carla (16) agrees: '*I can't bear it when all teens get tarred with the same brush. Adults assume we're all the same, but very few teenagers are 'yobs', hanging around in parks causing trouble, and we're not all 100% obsessed with social media. We have other interests too.*'

And get this: some teens are well-rounded, untroubled, rational individuals who, contrary to the navel-gazing, introspective stereotype, are (gasp!) capable of showing interest in and empathy with others.

5. Don't underestimate teens ... Ever

Today's teens are far savvier than previous generations. They have the world with all its gritty realism at the swish of a fingertip. What's more, having come to the realisation that their parents don't actually know as much as they initially made out, they have a tendency to mistrust 'Adults Telling Them How It Is'.

So don't lecture them or come across as 'preachy' and condescending. Most teens have a finely tuned, built-in radar that hones in on an author who believes themselves to be superior simply because of their more advanced years. After all, the majority of young people soak up the same TV programmes and websites as adults, and those nearing the end of their teen years are only a short amble from adulthood itself.

As 16-year-old Sam points out, '*I don't think there always needs to be much deviation when writing for teens from how you would write for adults. I'm obviously not speaking for all of teen-kind, but there's so many mind-numbing reality shows and celebrity magazines out there, I actually enjoy having my intellect challenged now and then.*'

Respect their intelligence and integrity.

6. Find your inner teen

You were an adolescent yourself once upon a time (maybe not that long ago in fact), so dredge the deep recesses of your mind for memories of your youth. One word of caution: beware when making references to popular teen culture. Raving on about the finer points of NSYNC's first album or discussing the complex love triangles on *Dawson's Creek* will blow your cover. Remember, most of your readers were still in nappies when Busted bounced onto the pop scene. Gulp…

7. Consider the where and when

Think about where and when your teen readers are likely to be reading your copy. Will you have their full concentration or will they be interacting with other media at the same time (listening to music on their iPod or phone, watching TV, direct messaging their mates)?

Keep the flow of your writing fast-paced. Use shorter, to-the-point sentences and split up long copy with frequent paragraph breaks. Your article will appear less daunting and your readers will have more opportunity to dip in and out as desired. With so many distractions threatening to steal their attention, there's an even greater need than normal to write a punchy opener, use bullet points, lists, sub-heads and box features to create an easily digestible format and create a clear, logical structure.

'*It's easier to read features when they're broken up into chunks. Then you can just choose the bits that are more interesting or apply to you,*' says Clara (16). But as Jack (14) rightly points out, '*It's important to get the correct balance. You want some detail in there so the feature is useful, but if it's too long, it just becomes plain dull.*'

8. Think about your tone

The success of books like *The Hunger Games*, with its themes of warfare, betrayal and sacrifice, and the *Twilight* series which explores vampire-slaying and the old standby of Good versus Evil, is proof of teenagers' craving to read about the deeper, darker side of reality.

What attracts them? Well, adult and teen brains work differently. Adults think with the rational area of their noggins, while teens use the emotional part and they're hungry for gritty, thought-provoking material.

They also have a thirst for humour. With exams, emotional upheavals and friendship issues to contend with, life can be tense. '*Even when I'm reading about a serious subject, I don't want it to be written in a long-winded, serious way,*' says Jack (14).

Entertain them. Make them laugh. Play up to their love of sarcasm and dry wit.

9. Relax the rules of grammar

I'm not suggesting you take an anarchic approach to grammar, dropping punctuation and scrimping on your syntax with every tap of your keyboard, but remember: this is one audience who might appreciate you being a little more informal with your writing. Feel free to allow sentences to end abruptly and prematurely or to double back on themselves. As long as you put your point across clearly, a casual regard of the rules will give your text a more youthful, friendlier feel.

10. Give them what they want

Avoid topics that your audience have had more than enough of from teachers, parents and other scholarly types. '*I like reading things that we don't learn in school – advice that's useful to my age group, like how to travel safely alone,*' says Emily (16).

Put simply, yet another 'How To' guide to studying will provoke immediate boredom. Sure there's already a plethora of features online exploring drugs, self-harm, sexism, eating disorders – but that's why it's your challenge to take on an old issue that affects your audience directly, and to find a new angle to tackle it from. Reading about other teens' lives is also a winner, nine times out of ten, but the stories don't have to be overwhelmingly traumatic and depressing. Choose ones that show the wonderful variety amongst the young individuals out there.

To sum up

Shake off those preconceptions of the stereotypical teen; recognise the demands being placed on their rapidly eroding free time; give young people the respect they deserve – and the credit to handle weighty issues with intelligence and empathy, and offer them reading matter that doesn't just dish out the same old lazy messages, but ignites their enthusiasm, seeks to reassure them, and empowers them to greater thoughts and actions.

Michelle Garnett is an ex-teen magazine editor who now divides her time between copywriting and subbing for various B2B publications, and writing, interviewing and editing at top celebrity weekly, *OK!* magazine.

See also...
- *Teenage fiction*, page 174
- *Writing for a variety of ages*, page 139
- *Writing crime fiction for teenagers*, page 167
- *Writing thrillers for teenagers*, page 170

Magazines and newspapers for children

Listings of magazines about children's literature and education start on page 337.

Adventure Box

Bayard, PO Box 61269, London N17 1DF
tel 0800 055 6686
email contact@bayard-magazines.co.uk
website www.bayard-magazines.co.uk
Editor-in-chief Simona Sideri, *Art Director* Pat Carter
10 p.a. £55 p.a.

Aimed at 6–9 year-old children starting to read on their own. Each issue contains a 44-page illustrated story plus games, a nature/science feature and comic strips. Length: 2,500–3,000 words (stories). Specially commissions most material. Founded 1996.

Animals and You

D.C. Thomson & Co Ltd, 80 Kingsway East,
Dundee DD4 8SL
tel (01382) 575863
email glorimer@dcthomson.co.uk
website www.animalsandyou.co.uk
Editor Graham Lorimer
Every 4 weeks £3.99

Features, stories and posters for girls aged 7–10 who love animals. Founded 1998.

Aquila

Studio 2, 67a Willowfield Road, Eastbourne,
East Sussex BN22 8AP
tel (01323) 431313
email office@aquila.co.uk
website www.aquila.co.uk
Editor Freya Hardy
Monthly £45 p.a.

Dedicated to encouraging children aged 8–13 to reason and create, and to develop a caring nature. Short stories and serials of up to three parts. Occasional features commissioned from writers with specialist knowledge. Approach in writing with ideas and sample of writing style, with sae. Length: 700–800 words (features), 1,000–1,100 words (stories or per episode of a serial). Payment: by arrangement. Founded 1993.

Astonishing Spider-Man

Panini UK, Brockbourne House, 77 Mount Ephraim,
Tunbridge Wells TN4 8AR
tel (01892) 500100
email astonspid@panini.co.uk
website www.paninicomics.co.uk
Editor Brady Webb
Every 2 weeks £3.50, £91 p.a.

76pp of comic strips, including both contemporary and classic stories.

BBC Doctor Who Adventures

Immediate Media Co. Ltd, Vineyard House,
44 Brook Green, London W6 7BT
tel 020-7150 5310
email hello@dwamag.com
website www.dwamag.com
Editor Moray Laing
Weekly £3.99

Magazine for 6–12 year-old fans of *Doctor Who*. Readers are immersed into the world of the Doctor, taking them on an adventure into time and space, with monsters and creatures, excitement, action, adventure and humour. Founded 2006.

BBC Toybox

Immediate Media Co. Ltd, Vineyard House,
44 Brook Green, London W6 7BT
tel 020-7150 5021
email toybox@immediate.co.uk
website www.immediatemedia.co.uk
Editor Steph Cooper
Every 4 weeks £3.99

Magazine for 3–5 year-olds with workbook and stickers, plus free gifts. Contains stories, puzzles, quizzes and colouring-in. Features characters from CBeebies.

The Beano

D.C. Thomson & Co. Ltd, 2 Albert Square,
Dundee DD1 9QJ
email editor@beano.com
185 Fleet Street, London EC4A 2HS
tel 020-7400 1030
Editor Craig Graham
50 p.a. £2.20

Comic strips for children aged 6–12. Series, 8–20 pictures. Artwork and scripts. Payment: on acceptance.

Ben 10 Magazine

Egmont UK Ltd, 1st Floor, The Yellow Building,
London W11 4AN
email info@egmont.co.uk
website www.egmont.co.uk
Every 3 weeks £2.99

The official Ben 10 magazine aimed at 5–8 year-old children. Includes an 8pp comic strip, activities, fact files and posters. Founded 2009.

Bob the Builder

Immediate Media Co. Ltd, Vineyard House,
44 Brook Green, London W6 7BT
tel 020-7150 5021
website www.immediatemedia.co.uk
Editor Andrea Turton
Every 4 weeks £2.50

Stories, puzzles, stickers and activities built around
Bob and his team for children aged 3–5 and their
parents.

Cars

Egmont UK Ltd, The Yellow Building,
1 Nicholas Road, London W11 4AN
tel 020-3220 0400
website www.egmont.co.uk
Editor Julia Millen
Monthly £2.99

Magazine for 3–6 year-old boys. Includes stories,
games, puzzles and colourings as well as a Planes
mini-mag section.

CBeebies Art

Immediate Media Co. Ltd, Vineyard House,
44 Brook Green, London W6 7BT
tel 020-7150 5021
email hello@cbeebiesart.com
Editor Steph Cooper
Every 4 weeks £2.99

Aimed at young children who like art. Linked to
popular CBeebies art brands including Mister Maker
and Get Squiggling.

CBeebies Magazine

Immediate Media Co. Ltd, Vineyard House,
44 Brook Green, London W6 7BT
tel 020-7150 5119
email hello@cbeebiesweekly.com
website www.bbc.co.uk/cbeebies
Editor Steph Cooper
Fortnightly £2.20

Fortnightly preschool magazine with educational
content targeted at $3\frac{1}{2}$-year-olds. Actively promotes
learning through play. Showcases new characters,
presenters and programmes as they appear on the
CBeebies channel. Founded 2006.

Charlie and Lola

Kennedy Publishing, Unit 16, Bath Road, Wick,
Bristol BS30 5RL
tel (0117) 937 3003
email charlieandlola@kennedypublishing.co.uk
website www.kennedypublishing.co.uk
Editor Paul Kennedy
4-weekly £3.50

Interactive arts and crafts magazine for children aged
4–7 years.

Commando

D.C. Thomson & Co. Ltd, 80 Kingway East,
Dundee DD4 8SL

tel (01382) 223131
email editor@commandomag.com
website www.commandocomics.com
Editor Calum Laird
4 per fortnight £2.00

Fictional stories set in time of war told in pictures.
Scripts: about 135 pictures. Synopsis required as an
opener. New writers encouraged; send for details.
Payment: on acceptance. Founded 1961.

Discovery Box

Bayard, PO Box 61269, London N17 1DF
tel (0800) 055 6686
email contact@bayard-magazines.co.uk
website www.bayard-magazines.co.uk
Editor Simona Sideri
10 p.a. £50 p.a.

Voyage of discovery through nature, science and
history for children aged 9–12. Every issue contains:
animal topics, information about important historical
events, articles about the world, DIY activities, comic
strips, games and more. Founded 1996.

Disney & Me

Egmont UK Ltd, The Yellow Building,
1 Nicholas Road, London W11 4AN
tel 020-3220 0400
website www.egmont.co.uk
Editor Julia Millen
Every three weeks £2.75

Magazine for 3–6 year-olds featuring favourite Disney
and Pixar characters, both old and new. Includes
stories, games, puzzles, posters and colouring pages.

Disney Princess

Egmont UK Ltd, The Yellow Building,
1 Nicholas Road, London W11 4AN
tel 020-3220 0400
website www.egmont.co.uk
Editor Rebecca Boxer
Every 2 weeks £2.99

Magazine for 4–7 year-old girls featuring stories,
activities, colouring and crafts all based around
Disney Princesses. Founded 1998.

Disney Tinker Bell

Egmont UK Ltd, The Yellow Building,
1 Nicholas Road, London W11 4AN
tel 020-3220 0400
website www.egmont.co.uk
Editor Julia Millen
Monthly £2.99

Magazine for 4–6 year-old girls. Contains magical
stories, puzzles, colouring activities and content based
on the popular Tinker Bell films. Founded 2006.

Dora the Explorer

Egmont UK Ltd, The Yellow Building,
1 Nicholas Road, London W11 4AN

tel 020-3220 0400
website www.egmont.co.uk
Editor Jane Tarrant
Monthly £3.99

Magazine for preschool children based on the Dora the Explorer character. Content includes puzzles, stories, posters and basic educational elements. Payment: by arrangement.

Eco Kids Planet

Eco Kids Planet, 41 Claremont Road, Barnet, EN4 0HR
tel 0800 639 1365
email hello@ecokidsplanet.co.uk
website www.ecokidsplanet.co.uk
Editors Anya Dimelow, Struan Simpson
11 p.a. £33.90 p.a.

Aimed at 7–11 year-old children. Each issue is dedicated to a different ecosystem and contains facts, photographs, puzzles and projects. The magazine uses fun, fictional characters in a story format to convey facts about nature and the environment. It also provides children with real-world examples of how they can make a difference on the planet. Length: 500–1,200 words (themed articles). Upcoming themes are listed on the website. Requirements: well-researched, up-to-date, informative articles, creative approach, interesting language. Specially commissions most material. Payment: by arrangement. Founded 2014.

Essential X-Men

Panini UK, Brockbourne House, 77 Mount Ephraim, Tunbridge Wells TN4 8AR
tel (01892) 500100
email paninicomics@panini.co.uk
website www.paninicomics.co.uk
Editor Scott Gray
Every 4 weeks £3.50

76pp of graphic stories centred around the Marvel X-Men characters.

Fireman Sam Magazine

Egmont UK Ltd, The Yellow Building, 1 Nicholas Road, London W11 4AN
tel 020-3220 0400
email info@egmont.co.uk
website www.egmont.co.uk
Editor Jane Tarrant
Monthly £2.99

Magazine and stickers for preschool children with a range of activities based around the Fireman Sam characters.

FirstNews

4th Floor, Shand House, 14–20 Shand Street, London SE1 2ES
email newsdesk@firstnews.co.uk
website www.firstnews.co.uk

Editor Nicky Cox, *Cofounder* Piers Morgan
Weekly Fri £1.50

National newspaper and website for 7–14 year-olds with news, sport, showbiz, interviews and in-depth features. It aspires to raise the profile of children's views and opinions in society. Founded 2006.

Fun to Learn Bag-o-Fun

Redan Publishing Ltd, Suite 2, Prospect House, Belle Vue Road, Shrewsbury, Shrops. SY3 7NR
tel (01743) 364433
email info@redan.com
website www.redan.co.uk
8 p.a. £3.99

Magazine, magic painting and colouring books, with at least three gifts, for preschool children and their parents to encourage early educational activities. Uses popular characters, including Mr Men, Peppa Pig, Clifford's Puppy Days, Dora the Explorer, Guess with Jess and many more, to help bring to life stories and activities whilst developing basic educational skills.

Fun to Learn Favourites

Redan Publishing Ltd, Suite 2, Prospect House, Belle Vue Road, Shrewsbury, Shrops. SY3 7NR
tel (01743) 364433
email info@redan.com
website www.redan.co.uk
Every 2 weeks £2.99

Magazine for preschool children comprising stories and activities using popular children's TV characters including Dora the Explorer, Mr Men, Scooby-Doo, Peppa Pig and more. Each issue includes a pull-out workbook with 75 reward stickers, based on one of these characters for parent and child interaction with activities including counting, matching, puzzles and colouring.

Fun to Learn Friends

Redan Publishing Ltd, Suite 2, Prospect House, Belle Vue Road, Shrewsbury, Shrops. SY3 7NR
tel (01743) 364433
email info@redan.com
website www.redan.co.uk
Every 2 weeks £2.35

Magazine for preschool children and their parents to encourage early educational activities. Comprises stories and activities using popular children's TV characters including Ben & Holly's Little Kingdom, Dora the Explorer and Peppa Pig. Includes a 24pp pull-out workbook with 75 reward stickers based on one of these characters for parent and child interaction, with activities including counting, matching, puzzles and colouring. The content supports the National Curriculum's Early Years Foundation Stage.

Fun to Learn Peppa Pig

Redan Publishing Ltd, Suite 2, Prospect House, Belle Vue Road, Shrewsbury, Shrops. SY3 7NR

tel (01743) 364433
email info@redan.com
website www.redan.co.uk
Editor Deb Harrison
Every 2 weeks £1.99

Interactive magazine for girls and boys aged 3–7 with stories, activities and puzzles based on the *Peppa Pig* TV show. Supports the National Curriculum's Early Years Foundation Stage and includes a pull-out workbook with 75 reward stickers.

Girl Talk

Immediate Media Co. Ltd, Vineyard House, 44 Brook Green, London W6 7BT
tel 020-7150 5000
email hello@girltalkmagazine.com
website www.girltalkmagazine.com
Editor Sara Oldham
Fortnightly £2.99

Magazine for children aged 7–12 years old. Contains pop, TV and film celebrity features, personality features, quizzes, fashion, competitions, stories. Length: 500 words (fiction). Payment: £75. All material is specially commissioned. Founded 1997.

Go Girl

Egmont UK Ltd, The Yellow Building, 1 Nicholas Road, London W11 4AN
tel 020-3220 0400
email gogirlmag@euk.egmont.com
website www.gogirlmag.co.uk
Every 3 weeks £2.99

Magazine for 7–11 year-old girls including fashion, beauty, celebrity news and gossip. Payment: by arrangement. Founded 2003.

Guiding Magazine

17–19 Buckingham Palace Road, London SW1W 0PT
tel 020-7834 6242
email guiding@girlguiding.co.uk
website www.girlguiding.co.uk
Editor Jane Yettram
Quarterly Free download

Official magazine of Girlguiding. Articles of interest to women of all ages, with special emphasis on youth work and the Guide Movement. Illustrations: line, half-tone, colour. Payment: £300 per 1,000 words. Please contact editor with proposal in the first instance.

Headliners

Rich Mix, 35–47 Bethnal Green Road, London E1 6LA
tel 020-7749 9360
email enquiries@headliners.org
website www.headliners.org
Director Fiona Wyton

Award-winning news agency charity (does not publish a magazine or newspaper) offering young people aged 8–18 the opportunity to write on issues of importance to them, for newspapers, radio and TV. Founded 1995.

Kids Alive! (The Young Soldier)

The Salvation Army, 101 Newington Causeway, London SE1 6BN
tel 020-7367 4911
email kidsalive@salvationarmy.org.uk
website www.salvationarmy.org.uk/kidsalive
Editor Justin Reeves, *Deputy Editor* Cara Macfarlane
Weekly 50p (£39 p.a.)

Children's magazine: pictures, scripts and artwork for cartoon strips, puzzles, etc; Christian-based with emphasis on education and lifestyle issues. Payment: by arrangement. Illustrations: half-tone, line and 4-colour line, cartoons. Founded 1881.

Marvel Heroes

Panini UK, Brockbourne House, Mount Ephraim, Tunbridge Wells TN4 8BS
tel (01892) 500100
email paninicomics@panini.co.uk
website www.paninicomics.co.uk
Every 4 weeks £3.99

Comic strips, games and news on the Marvel heroes.

Match of the Day

Immediate Media Co. Ltd, Vineyard House, 44 Brook Green, London W6 7BT
tel 020-7150 5000
email shout@motdmag.com
website www.motdmag.com
Weekly £1.99

Aimed at football-mad children with star interviews, match results, gossip and quizzes. Also includes an 8pp pull-out football skills guide.

Octonauts

Immediate Media Co. Ltd, Vineyard House, 44 Brook Green, London W6 7BT
tel 020-7150 5020
email hello@octonautsmagazine.com
website www.bbc.co.uk/cbeebies/octonauts
Editor Sara Oldham
Monthly £2.99

Magazine aimed at 3–6 year-olds, focusing on nature and science and tying in to the accompanying TV series' motto of 'explore, rescue, protect'. Activities and gifts feature in each issue.

The Official Jacqueline Wilson Mag

D.C. Thomson & Co. Ltd, 80 Kingsway East, Dundee DD4 8SL
tel (01382) 223131
email jwmag@dcthomson.co.uk
website www.jw-mag.com
Publisher Maria Welch
Every 3 weeks £3.75

Based on the books and characters of award-winning author, Dame Jacqueline Wilson. For readers aged 7–12, content is tailored to encourage literacy and creativity across a range of reading abilities. Contains interactive features, art and writing projects, recipes and crafts; for less confident readers, educational benefits are presented in a fun and interesting format – e.g. story-starter games and writing prompts, design challenges and word puzzles. Dame Jacqueline contributes photos, stories and writing tips and her illustrator, Nick Sharratt, supplies drawings and art secrets.

PONY Magazine
Marlborough House, Headley Road, Grayshott, Surrey GU26 6LG
tel (01428) 601020
email djm@djmurphy.co.uk
website www.ponymag.com
Editor Janet Rising
13 p.a. £3.49

Lively articles and short stories with a horsey theme aimed at readers aged 8–16. Technical accuracy and young, fresh writing essential. Length: up to 800 words. Payment: by arrangement. Illustrations: drawings (commissioned), photos, cartoons. Founded 1949.

Scooby-Doo
Panini UK, Brockbourne House, 77 Mount Ephraim, Tunbridge Wells TN4 8BS
tel (01892) 500100
email paninicomics@panini.co.uk
website www.paninicomics.co.uk
Monthly £2.99

Shout
D.C. Thomson & Co. Ltd, 80 Kingsway East, Dundee DD4 8SL
tel (01382) 223131
website www.shoutmag.co.uk
Editor Laura Brown
Monthly £3.90

Magazine for 11–15 year-old girls. Includes fashion and beauty; celebrity gossip and interviews; TV and pop content; real-life stories; emotional and advice features with a teen focus. Length of article accepted: up to 1,000 words. Illustrations: links to online portfolios or websites welcome, but illustrations are commissioned on a feature-by-feature basis only. Payment: on acceptance. Founded 1993.

Sparkle World
Redan Publishing Ltd, Canon Court East, Abbey Lawn, Shrewsbury SY2 5DE
tel (01743) 364333
email anita@redan.com
website www.redan.co.uk
Group Editor Anita Cash, *Associate Editor* Helen Rushton

Every 3 weeks £2.99

Magazine aimed at 4–9 year-old girls with stories and activities based on a selection of popular licensed characters, including Care Bears, Littlest Pet Shop and Strawberry Shortcake.

Storybox
Bayard, PO Box 61269, London N17 1DF
tel (0800) 055 6686
email contact@bayard-magazines.co.uk
website www.bayard-magazines.co.uk
Editor-in-Chief Simona Sideri, *Art Director* Pat Carter
10 p.a. £55 p.a.

Aimed at 3–6 year-old children. Stories with rhyme and evocative pictures stimulate children's imagination and introduce them to the delights of reading. Each issue presents a new, full-colour, 24pp story created by teams of internationally acclaimed writers and illustrators for laptime reading. A non-fiction section linked to a theme in the story follows, together with pages of games and craft ideas. Includes games, an animal feature, science and a cartoon. Founded 1996.

Length: 500–1,000 words (stories). Requirements: rhyme, repetition, interesting language. Specially commissions most material. Payment: by arrangement.

Thomas & Friends
Egmont UK Ltd, The Yellow Building, 1 Nicholas Road, London W11 4AN
tel 020-3220 0400
website www.egmont.co.uk
Every 3 weeks £2.75

Magazine for 3–6 year-old children designed to encourage early reading skills and all-round child development using stories and activities involving Thomas and all his friends. Each issue contains posters, colouring pages, competitions and readers' letters and pictures as regular features.

Thomas Express
Egmont UK Ltd, The Yellow Building, 1 Nicholas Road, London W11 4AN
tel 020-3220 0400
website www.egmont.co.uk
Monthly £3.99

Magazine pack for 3–6 year-old children with puzzles, stories, colouring and posters based around Thomas and his friends.

Tom and Jerry
Panini UK, Brockbourne House, 77 Mount Ephraim, Tunbridge Wells TN4 8AR
tel (01892) 500100
email paninicomics@panini.co.uk
website www.paninicomics.co.uk
Monthly £2.99

Activities, stories and cartoons.

Top of the Pops

Immediate Media Co. Ltd, Vineyard House,
44 Brook Green, London W6 7BT
tel 020-7150 5123
email totpmag@totpmag.com
website www.totpmag.com
Editor Peter Hart
Monthly £3.99

Celebrity gossip and news, primarily aimed at girls
aged 10–14. Founded 1995.

Toxic Magazine

Egmont UK Ltd, The Yellow Building,
1 Nicholas Road, London W11 4AN
website www.toxicmag.co.uk
Editor Frank Tennyson
Every 3 weeks £2.99

Topical lifestyle magazine for 8–12 year-old boys.
Includes competitions, pull-out posters, reviews and
jokes. Covers boys' entertainments, sports, video
games, films, TV, music, fashion and toys. Slapstick
humour. Showcases latest products, events and
trends. Payment: by arrangement. Founded 2002.

2000 AD

Riverside House, Osney Mead, Oxford OX2 0ES
email publicrelations@2000adonline.com
website www.2000adonline.com
Editor Matt Smith

Weekly, Wed £2.45

Cult sci-fi and fantasy comic. Founded 1977.

Wolverine and Deadpool

Panini UK, Brockbourne House, 77 Mount Ephraim,
Tunbridge Wells TN4 8AR
tel (01892) 500100
email paninicomics@panini.co.uk
website www.paninicomics.co.uk
Editor Scott Gray
Every 4 weeks £3.50

76pp comic based around the exploits of the
eponymous Marvel heroes.

Young Scot

Rosebery House, 9 Haymarket Terrace,
Edinburgh EH12 5EZ
tel 0131 313 2488
email info@youngscot.org
website www.youngscot.org
Editor Fiona McIntyre
Quarterly Free with *Scottish Daily Record* and at
selected venues

News, features, discounts, and competitions for
young Scots aged 12–26. Offers incentives,
information and opportunities to people in this age
group to help them make informed choices, play a
part in their community and make the most of their
free time and learning.

Magazines about children's literature and education

Listings of magazines and newspapers for children start on page 331.

Armadillo

Louise Ellis-Barrett, c/o St John's School,
Epsom Road, Leatherhead, Surrey KT22 8SP
tel (01372) 385484
email armadilloeditor@gmail.com
website https://sites.google.com/site/
armadillomagazine
Editor Louise Ellis-Barrett
4 p.a. Free

Online children's book review magazine including
reviews, interviews, features, competitions and
profiles. Linked to a blog for weekly children's book
news updates, issues posted March, June, September
and December. New reviewers and writers always
welcome. Founded 1999.

Books for Keeps

Unit 1, Brampton Park Road, London N22 6BG
tel/fax 020-8889 1292
email andrea@booksforkeeps.co.uk
website www.booksforkeeps.co.uk
Editor Ferelith Hordon
Bi-monthly, free online

Features, reviews and news on children's books.
Readership is both professionals and parents.
Founded 1980.

The Bookseller

Ground Floor, Crowne House,
56–58 Southwark Street, London SE1 1UN
tel 020-3358 0365
email felicity.wood@thebookseller.co.uk
website www.thebookseller.com
Editor Philip Jones,
Features Editor Tom Tivnan
Weekly £4.95

Journal of the UK publishing and bookselling trades.
The *Children's Bookseller* supplement is published
regularly and there is news on the children's book
business in the main magazine. Produces the
Children's Buyer's Guide, which previews children's
books to be published in the following six months.
The website holds news on children's books,
comment on the children's sector, author interviews
and children's bestseller charts. Founded 1858.

Carousel – The Guide to Children's Books

Saturn Business Centre, 54–76 Bissell Street,
Birmingham B5 7HP
tel 0121 622 7458
email carousel.guide@virgin.net
website www.carouselguide.co.uk
Editor David Blanch
3 p.a. £4.95

Reviews of fiction, non-fiction and poetry books for
children, plus in-depth articles; profiles of authors
and illustrators. Length: 1,200 words (articles); 150
words (reviews). Illustrations: colour and b&w.
Payment: by arrangement. Founded 1995.

The Caterpillar

Drummullen, Cavan, Co. Cavan, Republic of Ireland
tel +353 49 436 2677
email editor@thecaterpillarmagazine.com
website www.thecaterpillarmagazine.com
Editor Rebecca O'Connor
Quarterly €5, €20 p.a., €40 institutions, libraries and
schools

Arts and literature magazine for children aged 7–11,
featuring original poetry, short fiction and full-colour
artwork. Submissions from adults welcome, but
contributors should familiarise themselves with
magazine content first. Send no more than six poems
or two short stories (max. 1,000 words) by email or
post (sae). Also runs The Caterpillar Poetry Prize
(€1,000 for best poem written for children by an
adult). Founded 2013.

Children's Bookshelf

Publishers Weekly, 71 West 23 Street, Suite 1608,
New York, NY 10010, USA
tel +1 212-377-5500
email chidrensbooks@publishersweekly.com
website www.publishersweekly.com
Editor Diane Roback, Children's Books Editor
Semiweekly, free

E-newsletter about children's and young adult books.
Published under the auspices of *Publishers Weekly*,
which was founded in 1872, *Children's Bookshelf* is
edited by *PW*'s children's book editor Diane Roback.
Children's book news, feature story ideas, new trends
and pitches for author or illustrator interviews should
be sent to Diane Roback. Visit website for PW's
submission guidelines; send news and story pitches to
childrensbooks@publishersweekly.com.

Mary Glasgow Magazines

Scholastic UK Ltd, Westfield Road, Southam,
Warks. CV47 0RA

tel (01926) 815560
email orders@maryglasgowplus.com
website www.maryglasgowplus.com

Publisher of 16 magazines for learners of English, French, German, and Spanish. Also publishes a series of resource books for teachers of English as a foreign language. Wholly owned subsidiary of Scholastic Inc.

Inis – The Children's Books Ireland Magazine

Children's Books Ireland,
17 North Great George Street, Dublin 1,
Republic of Ireland
tel +353 (0)1 8727475
email jenny@childrensbooksireland.ie
website www.childrensbooksireland.ie
Contact Jenny Murray
3 p.a. €5

Wide variety of children's literature articles and features, as well as in-depth reviews of new titles for young people of all ages, from babies to teenagers. Published by Children's Books Ireland. Founded 1989.

Literacy

UK Literacy Association, University of Leicester,
Leicester LE1 7RH
tel 0116 223 1664
email admin@ukla.org
website www.ukla.org, www.blackwellpublishing.com
Editor-in-Chief Dr Jill McClay, Professor Emerita, University of Alberta, 11210 - 87 Ave, Edmonton AB T6G 2G5, Canada. (jill.mcclay@ualberta.ca); *Associate Editor* Dr Clare Dowdall, Lecturer in Language and Literacy Education, Plymouth University, Plymouth, Devon, PL4 8AA (cdowdall@plymouth.ac.uk)
3 p.a. (subscription only)

The official journal of the United Kingdom Literacy Association (see page 407) and is for those interested in the study and development of literacy. Readership comprises practitioners, teachers, educators, researchers, undergraduate and graduate students. It offers educators a forum for debate through scrutinising research evidence, reflecting on analysed accounts of innovative practice and examining recent policy developments. Length: 2,000–6,000 words (articles). Illustrations: b&w prints and artwork. Formerly known as *Reading – Literacy and Language*. Published by Blackwell Publishing. Founded 1966.

Nursery World

MA Education, St Jude's Church, Dulwich Road,
London SE24 0PB
tel 020-8501 6693
email news.nw@markallengroup.com
website www.nurseryworld.co.uk
Editor Liz Roberts
Weekly £2.95

For all grades of primary school, nursery and child-

care staff, nannies, foster parents and all concerned with the care of expectant mothers, babies and young children. Authoritative and informative articles, 800 or 1,300 words, and photos, on all aspects of child welfare and early education, from 0–8 years, in the UK. Practical ideas, policy news and career advice. No short stories. Payment: by arrangement. Illustrations: line, half-tone, colour.

Publishers Weekly

71 West 23 Street, Suite 1608, New York, NY 10010, USA
tel +1 212-377-5500
email childrensbooks@publishersweekly.com
website www.publishersweekly.com
Children's Books Editor Diane Roback

International news magazine for the book industry. Covers all segments involved in the creation, production, marketing and sale of the written word in book, audio, video and electronic formats. In addition to reaching publishers worldwide, it influences all media dealing with the acquisition, sale, distribution and rights of intellectual and cultural properties.

Children's books for review, from pre-school to young adult, should be sent to Diane Roback, Children's Books Editor; note that all reviews are pre-publication. Also send to her story suggestions on children's publishing, new trends, author or illustrator interviews, etc for the semiweekly *Children's Bookshelf* e-newsletter. Diane also edits the listings for new children's books twice a year for the Spring and Fall Children's Announcements issues, as well as the Children's Starred Reviews Annual. See PW's guidelines for the submission of review books at www.publishersweekly.com; send story pitches to childrensbooks@publishersweekly.com. Founded 1872.

Report

ATL, 7 Northumberland Street, London WC2N 5RD
tel 020-7930 6441
email report@atl.org.uk
website www.atl.org.uk/report
Editors Alex Tomlin, Charlotte Tamvakis
9 p.a. Free to members, otherwise £2.50, £15.50 p.a. (UK), £27 p.a. (overseas)

Magazine from the Association of Teachers and Lecturers (ATL). Features, articles, comment, news about nursery, primary, secondary and further education. Payment: minimum £120 per 1,000 words.

Right Start

PO Box 481, Fleet, Hants GU51 9FA
tel 07867 574590
email lynette@rightstartmagazine.co.uk
website www.rightstartmagazine.co.uk
Editor Lynette Lowthian
Bi-monthly £10.90 p.a.

Features on all aspects of preschool and infant

education, child health and behaviour. No unsolicited MSS. Length: 800–1,500 words. Illustrations: colour photos, line. Payment: varies. Founded 1989.

The School Librarian
1 Pine Court, Kembrey Park, Swindon SN2 8AD
tel (01793) 530166
email sleditor@sla.org.uk
website www.sla.org.uk
Editor Steve Hird
Quarterly £85 p.a.

Official journal of the School Library Association. Articles on school library management, use and skills, and on authors and illustrators, literacy, publishing. Reviews of books, CD-Roms, websites and other library resources from preschool to adult. Length: 1,800–3,000 words (articles). Payment: by arrangement. Founded 1937.

The TES
26 Red Lion Square, Holborn WC1R 4HQ
tel 020-3194 3000
email newsdesk@tes.co.uk
email features@tes.co.uk
website www.tes.co.uk
Editor Ann Mroz
Weekly £36.75 p.a. (print)

Education newspaper. Articles on education written with special knowledge or experience; news items; books, arts and equipment reviews. Check with the news or picture editor before submitting material. Outlines of feature ideas should be emailed. Illustrations: suitable photos and drawings of educational interest, cartoons. Payment: standard rates, or by arrangement.

TES Magazine
Weekly Free with TES
Magazine for teachers focusing on their lives, inside and outside the classroom, investigating the key issues of the day and highlighting good practice. Length: 800 words max.

The TESS
tel 07825 033445
email scoted@tess.co.uk
website www.tes.co.uk/scotland
Senior Reporter Henry Hepburn
Weekly £1.95

Education newspaper. Articles on education, preferably 800–1,000 words, written with special knowledge or experience. News items about Scottish educational affairs. Illustrations: line, half-tone. Payment: by arrangement. Founded 1965.

The Times Educational Supplement – see The TES

The Times Educational Supplement Scotland – see The TESS

Under 5
Pre-school Learning Alliance,
The Fitzpatrick Building, 188 York Way,
London N7 9AD
tel 020-7697 2500
email editor.u5@pre-school.org.uk
website www.pre-school.org.uk
Editor Shannon Hawthorne
10 p.a. £38 p.a. (non-members)

Articles on the role of adults, especially parents/ preschool workers, in young children's learning and development, including children from all cultures and those with special needs. Length: 600–1,200 words. Founded 1962.

Television, film and radio
Creating content for multi-platform media

Greg Childs of the Children's Media Conference offers guidelines for writing for children's television and other media outlets.

What are the classic children's television programme titles? *Blue Peter*, of course, *Magpie*, *Bagpuss*, *Grange Hill*, *My Family Are Aliens*, *Art Attack*, *Bob the Builder*, *Teletubbies*, *Spongebob*, *Ben 10*, etc. But ask a child today and they will also include *Moshi Monsters*, *Stampy Longnose* and *Angry Birds*. Children's content embraces a multitude of different kinds of programming, now on a whole variety of platforms, some of which require writers.

Blue Peter clearly isn't the result of a single writer's vision. It has evolved over the years and through various production teams, and its content is written in a semi-journalistic way by its producers. But fundamental to its longevity is its grounding in knowledge of the audience and how that audience has changed over the years. That grounding can come from experience, but more and more nowadays it also comes from research. *Teletubbies*, and more recently *In the Night Garden*, used this approach. Their creator, Anne Wood, spent months researching the target audience and testing ideas before committing to them.

There is nothing new in the drive to understand the audience, but productions are increasingly grounded in developmental/educational research so that their aims fit those of potential international funders – especially in the USA. And more and more productions utilise an understanding of the needs, habits, likes and dislikes of the young audience to ensure that characters, scenarios, storylines and the merchandise which provides a vital funding source, all 'hit the spot'.

Know your audience and your customers

Know your audience and the age range that you are aiming for. Make sure your understanding is based on a representative sample – your own children only account for part of the story. Get to know the schedules, and the wider world of new outlets for children's content. Be aware of the available slots and the kind of programmes which go into them, and study the output and the varying requirements of the different channels and the new 'aggregators' like YouTube or Netflix. Commissioning websites are particularly useful for this, as is the Children's Media Conference which holds 'Meet the Commissioner' sessions each year in Sheffield in early July (and if you can't get there, many of those sessions are made available as podcasts or video on www.thechildrensmediaconference.com). But you might also consider whether your project could find its way to market through other more innovative routes. Companies like Netflix and Amazon are commissioning children's content and run children's services – as do many other smaller video-on-demand providers, such as the UK educational service Hopster.The new tax incentives and Britain's track record in children's content success make Britain an attractive place for world-class content providers to produce their content.

After considering the 'purchasing' landscape, familiarise yourself with the various producers who specialise in the children's market, what their specialisms are and which routes to market they favour. Again, their websites are generally very clear, and they are more often than not your route to the market and your audience.

Intelligence about the landscape you are working in is vital. For example, are you aware that CBeebies upped its age range a few years ago and now caters for 2–6 year-olds, with CBBC picking up the audience around the age of six? Or that CITV has abandoned the preschool audience in favour of those aged 6+? Five caters for preschool only on its Milkshake block and mostly acquires its programmes. Channel 4 does some content for 10–14 year-olds, but currently only one series per year, and BBC Learning mainly delivers its content online. But it's worth thinking about whether your project could be appropriate for their curriculum-focused commissioning.

Nickelodeon, Cartoon Network and Disney all commission in the UK but their approach is to invest in shows which can become big international successes. For example, *The House of Anubis* was made by Nick in the UK but intended for all English-speaking territories including the USA, and *The Amazing World of Gumball* on Cartoon Network was a European production made in London but clearly destined for wide international (and especially US) audiences. So when thinking of the international broadcasters, you need to consider whether your style and approach fits the demands of an audience on the other side of the Atlantic.

And are you aware that Mind Candy, the company behind *Moshi Monsters*, the social/gaming website with its 60 million-plus registered users, have launched a completely new product, PlayJam, which will be a community of creative children, and will provide a platform for the UK creative community too.

Online resources

KidScreen
website http://kidscreen.com
Produces a daily digest of great articles.

The Children's Media Conference
website www.thechildrensmediaconference.com
Sign up for their ebulletin and seriously consider attending the annual conference and other occasional workshops that they organise. They not only offer insights and learning opportunities, but are also very useful occasions to network and build relationships with producers and commissioning executives.

Facebook and LinkedIn
websites
www.facebook.com/groups/237549918203
www.facebook.com/groups/133583286677976
www.linkedin.com/groups?home=&gid=2646350
Join the various children's media groups online such as these to keep up your networking connections and for further tips and insights.

Most broadcasters now take the 360 or 'transmedia' approach to projects. They will certainly ask questions about how the brand – and note the use of the word 'brand' – will manifest itself in apps, online, in social media, as books and music spin-offs, as a live show, and of course as a toy and other product ranges. The exploitation of spin-off revenues through toys and other merchandise is as much a part of the funding equation for some properties (mainly animation or large-scale live action shows such as *Teletubbies*) as conventional broadcasters and distribution companies' advances. It's a fact that most animation series are internationally financed (often by more than one broadcaster, and a distributor) and that without the further advances on merchandising sales, they would not get funded and not be made.

To immerse yourself in this brave new world you should consider subscribing to online trade magazines and exploring other online resources (see box).

Present proposals professionally

Learn how to write proposals and how to pitch them. Commissioners receive hundreds of proposals every year and presentation, clarity and passion are all important. Be ambitious (after all, producers and commissioners are looking for new talent) but also be realistic – consider the likely cost of realising your ideas against the potential sales or funds available.

It's a very competitive world and if you get an opportunity to pitch in person, know how to do it as it may be your only chance to impress. Rehearse, take advice and feedback from people in the know. Have your visual material prepared and presented professionally and don't waffle. Pitches are always about making an emotional connection through characters and story – and that applies equally to factual formats as it does to fiction. Beyond that, you'll have to convince the commissioner that your project has a real USP (unique selling point) and that you can deliver it.

Organisations like the Children's Media Conference offer development and pitching workshops. You can also take projects to courses that focus on development, such as Pixel Labs (http://powertothepixel.com/events-and-training) which focuses on multi-platform approaches.

Commissioning

The children's content sector can be broken down into various genres in terms of television commissioning:

Children's television drama

The BBC is now virtually the only commissioner of children's drama, although Sky has announced a new policy to produce several feature length 'family dramas' each year – on the model of *Skellig* (2009) and *Treasure Island* (2011).

The BBC policy of 'bigger, fewer, better' has resulted in higher budgets and production values, but fewer slots on CBBC. For the most part, it's about tried and tested brands such as *Tracy Beaker* in its various forms, or tried and tested writers, such as Russell T. Davies's series, *Wizards vs Aliens*. There are some opportunities for innovation and the key to entry as a writer is to ally yourself to a major production company so your track record of delivery is evident.

Smaller scale adaptations might be commissioned, especially if they have a long running potential. If you find a book which you think would work for television, you'll have to buy an option before you take it to the producer or commissioner. As a result of the huge success of *Harry Potter*, *Lemony Snicket*, etc the cost of optioning children's books has risen steeply and the potential 'biggies' are generally snapped up before publication. However, there are a number of excellent children's books published every year which could make good television and you might pick up the next 'big thing', so keep an eye on what is happening in the children's publishing world, read the trade magazines and get to know children's publishers. When you are looking at books, consider their potential beyond one book or a limited series. Commissioners are always looking for something which has the possibility to go to more than one series and to become a franchise or brand. Once you have secured your option, write a brief treatment of how you see the television version working and submit it together with the book either to an independent producer, or to a commissioner – remembering the guidelines outlined above.

Animation

Animation is the most prolific and potentially the most financially rewarding children's genre, but it is rather specialised. To get a feel for it, it's well worth studying successful animated series. Remember that this really is a visual medium and often words are minimal – think *Pingu*! An alternative is to start with a book or a series of characters and then approach an animation production house. You don't have to provide the visuals, but you do need to remember that animation requires a minimum of 26 episodes in the first series with the potential to go to 104 episodes or more. Animation also needs to have international appeal as almost all animated series are international co-productions. We are already seeing a resurgence in UK-based animation production due to the new tax incentives introduced in April 2013. For example, during 2013–14 there was a 300% increase in the animation work being carried out in the London area. It's a time of opportunities. Once again, the Children's Media Conference and its spin-off events offer the best methods for keeping in touch with trends and for meeting key people in animation.

Preschool

Considered by many as the heart of children's television worldwide, in the UK the preschool sector offers opportunities for writers in live action and animation. As with other genres, animation is likely to be international in scope, but British writers are highly regarded in preschool and have a real stake in this market. Live-action is commissioned almost entirely at the BBC and is frequently intended purely for the UK audience. Much of it is produced in-house at CBeebies, and they certainly use the skills of writers in many of their programmes.

Comedy and comedy-drama

Comedy and comedy-drama has become an increasingly popular part of children's television output. The success of the *Horrible Histories* franchise is an example. Compared to drama, it's relatively cheap to make and it works well in the schedule. The same comments about longevity and long runs apply and you should always have this in mind – how will your idea extend over multiple episodes?

Having said all this, however, the main thing is to write something that you really care about and you think will work for the audience. There is no substitute for passion and a great story well told.

Greg Childs is the Editorial Director of the Children's Media Conference and Director of the Children's Media Foundation. He worked in the BBC Children's department for over 20 years as a director, producer and executive producer and, as Head of Digital Commissioning, was responsible for the launch of the BBC children's channels in 2002. Subsequently he has been a consultant in children's media strategies, working on the launch of Teachers TV and CITV, and was the UK adviser to the Al Jazeera Children's Channel. He has advised the European Broadcasting Union on children's and youth strategies and is currently Head of Studies at the German Akademie für Kindermedien.

See also...
- *Writing to a brief*, page 352
- *Children's television and radio*, page 355

Children's literature on radio and audio

The technologies for transmitting the spoken word to children are developing rapidly.
Neville Teller describes the fast-changing world of radio and audio, and explores what a writer
for the microphone needs to know and how to break into this market.

'Read me a story' – one of childhood's perennial cries. Until radio arrived, parents found little relief from it (palming it off on grandma or auntie was perhaps the best bet). But from its very beginning, radio included in its schedules stories read aloud for children. So, for part of the time at least, the loudspeaker was able to provide a fair substitute for mummy or daddy by providing literature, specially prepared for performance at the microphone, read by professional actors.

Very early on, actors learned that performing at the microphone was a new skill – the techniques were specialised and quite different from those required on the stage. Writers, too, had to acquire a whole range of new skills in preparing material for radio. Two things quickly became apparent. First, the time taken to read a complete book on the air would be far too long to be acceptable, and in consequence most books would need to be abridged. Secondly, literature simply read aloud from the printed page often failed to 'come across' to a listening audience, because material produced to be scanned by the eye is often basically unsuited to the requirements of the microphone.

Today there are two main outlets in this country for aspiring writers and abridgers for children in the radio/audio sphere: BBC radio and audiobook publishers. How has this market reached its present position?

Radio

Children's radio in the UK has certainly had its ups and downs. It came into existence in December 1922, just a few weeks after the BBC itself was born, and for some 40 years the daily 'Children's Hour' became an established and much-cherished feature of life in the UK.

However, in the 1960s the imminent death of radio was a generally accepted prognostication. Starting in 1961, on the belief that television was children's preferred medium, children's radio was slowly but surely strangled. First the much-loved title Children's Hour was dropped, then the time allotted to programmes 'For the Young' (as it was subsequently called) was cut back. Finally, in March 1964, the programme was put out of its agony.

The demise of children's radio naturally evoked a massive groundswell of protest. In response – although the BBC of the day had clearly lost faith in it – they did grant some sort of reprieve. *Story Time* – a programme of abridged radio readings – started life in the old Children's Hour slot with a strong bias towards children's literature. It was not long, however, before more general literature began to be selected, and finally, in 1982, the programme was dropped. For the next 20 years the only regular children's programme left on BBC radio was *Listen with Mother*, the 15-minute programme for the under-fives.

The comeback started slowly, and then suddenly gathered momentum. Early in the new millennium the BBC – moved, doubtless, by mounting evidence of the undiminished popularity of radio – decided to reintroduce a regular programme for children. All they could offer at the time was a 30-minute programme each Sunday evening on Radio 4 called *Go4It,* a magazine-type show which included a ten-minute reading, and I found myself abridging books for the programme like *The Lion, the Witch and the Wardrobe* by C.S. Lewis and *The Wolves of Willoughby Chase* by Joan Aiken. Unfortunately, this renaissance was typically short lived. *Go4It* was axed on 24 May 2009.

But the door had been pushed ajar, and in the autumn of 2002, when the BBC launched its new digital radio channel, BBC7, its schedules included, as a basic ingredient, daily programmes for children incorporating readings from children's literature, both current and classic. These abridgements were specially prepared for the two daily shows: for older children, *The Big Toe Radio Show* and for the youngsters, *The Little Toe Radio Show.* I prepared a considerable number of books for these programmes, including not only classical children's literature like *Robinson Crusoe* and *The Prince and the Pauper,* but also more general classics like *20,000 Leagues Under the Sea* and *Oliver Twist.* The Big Toe programme also featured up-to-the-moment favourites such as Anthony Horowitz's series about his boy secret agent, Alex Rider, the *Artemis Fowl* novels by Eoin Colfer, Terry Pratchett's *A Hat Full of Sky* and *The Amazing Maurice,* and Jackie French's *Callisto* series. For younger listeners, I abridged books like the *Whizziwig* series by Malorie Blackman, the *Lily Quench* books by Natalie Jane Prior, and Kaye Umansky's *The Silver Spoon of Solomon Snow.*

Children's radio had been re-established and all seemed set fair. But towards the end of 2006 came news of major changes. *The Little Toe Radio Show* was converted into a radio extension of CBeebies, the BBC's digital television channel for the youngest children, while *Big Toe Books* became readings drawn from the programme's extensive archive, including my own abridgements of, among many others, *Bootleg* by Alex Shearer, *Stop the Train* by Geraldine McCaughrean, *Huckleberry Finn* by Mark Twain, *Slaves of the Mastery* and *Firesong* by William Nicholson, *Stig of the Dump* by Clive King, *The BGF* by Roald Dahl, *The Little House on the Prairie* by Laura Ingalls Wilder, *Dream Master* by Theresa Breslin, and *Point Blanc* by Anthony Horowitz.

Nothing lasts for ever, and 2011 saw BBC Radio 7 transformed into BBC Radio 4 Extra. With the transformation came a new shape to children's radio – almost a return to the Children's Hour concept of yesteryear – the *Four O'Clock Show* always including abridged readings of children's literature. Among the specially commissioned readings for the show I have abridged Frank Cottrell Boyce's *Chitty Chitty Bang Bang Flies Again, Wonder* by R.J. Palacio and *Maggot Moon* by Sally Gardner.

Sadly, the *Four O'Clock Show* too has succumbed to the rapidly changing technological needs of its audience. April 30th 2015 saw its final transmission. By then only around 5,900 children were listening to the programme each week, and the BBC Trust concluded 'few children would be affected' by its closure. The axing of this hour of dedicated children's radio means there will no longer be any children's programming on Radio 4 Extra, and its service licence will be amended to remove its commitment to the content.

Explaining the decision, Controller Gwyneth Williams said that as the listening habits of younger audiences was changing, on-demand content was a 'more reliable way' to serve their needs. She said the savings will be reinvested in children's content online and CBeebies Radio, as well as programming for older children. CBeebies Radio is a daily web-based radio show for pre-school children. They can either listen online through the CBeebies

Radio Player or download and keep the podcast, choosing when and where is best for them to listen.

Audiobooks

Audiobooks are literary works of all types, some abridged, some unabridged, read by actors and now generally available as CDs or as downloads from the internet. UK industry statistics are sketchy, but in the USA most recent statistics show that downloads have overtaken CDs as the preferred delivery method, and that audiobooks for children are flourishing. Recent estimates indicate that the UK children's audio market stands at about £45 million per annum. In 2014 Audible, the largest provider of digital audiobooks in the UK, announced that it would in future calculate and pay royalties in line with the standard ACX terms.

Until early 2014 the BBC's audio output was marketed through AudioGo. When the company went out of business, all rights in BBC titles, including the large and flourishing children's backlist, reverted to the BBC, which is now marketing them through other outlets such as Audible and Random House.

Nowadays, it is common for major publishers to launch a fair number of their new books, including books for older children, in printed and audiobook form simultaneously. Publishers of books for younger children often adopt the 'twin pack' concept – packaging book and audiobook together – so that children can read and listen at the same time. This development has mushroomed since 2003, when HM Revenue & Customs decided that such products could be zero-rated for VAT.

In March 2009 ECOFIN (the EU's Economic and Financial Affairs Council) agreed to reduce VAT on audiobooks to 5%. As a result, it was expected that within a reasonable period of time UK audiobook publishers would be able to charge significantly less for both their physical and digital products. However, so far no intention to apply a reduced rate to audiobooks in the UK has been announced.

How children listen

The ways in which children listen to the readings intended especially for them are multiplying at what seems an ever-increasing rate.

The digital radio channel, BBC Radio 4 Extra, which carries the BBC's main children's programme, the *Four O'Clock Show*, is also transmitted online (where it can be heard simul-streamed and also through 'Listen Again', a BBC iPlayer service that gives access to broadcast programmes for a further seven days) and via satellite and cable television.

Audiobooks for children have become available as downloads via a range of other online outlets, including Audible and Apple iTunes. Taken together, these DTO (Download to Own) providers have available an enormous and expanding list of children's books, and stories are proving a popular second-best to music for many children for delivery via their tablets, personal iPods and smartphones. Subscribers pay either a monthly fee for the right to download a specific number of titles or pay for downloads book by book. However, these days a surprising number of websites are offering free downloads of children's stories. One US website lists no less than 62 online sites from which children can download stories at no cost. The UK also has a fair number of such sites.

Amazon has some 30,000 children's audiobooks available to be purchased and downloaded. Users can start listening within seconds, transfer the audiobook to a Kindle, computer, iPod or other device, or burn it to a CD. Other specialist providers of audiobooks for children include Audiobooks for Kids (www.kidsaudiobooks.co.uk), Children's Storybooks On Line (www.magickeys.com/books), Storynory (www.storynory.com) and the Story Home (www.thestoryhome.com). All commission new stories for children.

Young people are increasingly accessing not only their social networks via their smartphones, but also audiobooks. Google, Amazon and Audible are providing access to audiobooks via the mobile phone, and other providers are crowding into the marketplace.

Amazon's ebook reader, the Kindle, and its younger brother, Kindle Fire, which offers a colour touch-screen, have been runaway successes. The Kindle can download a book in about 30 seconds, either to be read on its 6-inch wide screen or to be read aloud to you (albeit in a somewhat robot-like voice).

Other brands of ebook readers (such as the Sony and Kobo) are available, but the Kindle's biggest rival as a non-print reading device is Apple's iPad and iPad Mini (launched at the end of 2012), and its growing number of tablet competitors. All tablets include an ebook application (or app), through which an enormous selection of books can be downloaded speedily.

In-car MP3 playback, via the car radio, now widely available, is becoming increasingly popular as a means of keeping children happy on long journeys. Children's audiobooks are also now part of in-flight entertainment on long-haul flights.

A recent phenomenon is 'podiobooks', or podcast audiobook novels, released on the internet in instalments, and free. They are often made available at the same time in the form of a PDF ebook and are commonly offered together with a range of stickers, ringtones and wallpapers – all designed to appeal to the younger market. The pioneer is Scott Sigler, whose website offers free audio fiction, together with videos, ebooks and blog posts via Google-plus, Twitter, Facebook, YouTube, iTunes, RSS, Flickr and Goodreads. The whole concept is aimed particularly at young people.

The message of all this for writers is that the radio/audio market is mushrooming, and that the burgeoning technological developments and innovations seem designed to appeal particularly to the internet-savvy younger generations. If you are keen to break into the rapidly changing world of children's literature on radio and audio, this seems as favourable and opportune a time to succeed as ever. For contact details for children's radio, see *Children's television and radio* (page 355) or search online for children's audiobook publishers, and offer your services. Do not be discouraged by initial rejection – that is often a writer's early experience. Persevere. As in all professional fields, the tyro is faced with the classic catch-22 situation: radio producers and audio publishers are reluctant to offer commissions to people without a track record, while it is of course impossible to gain a track record without having won a commission or two. The only advice is to keep plugging away, hoping for that elusive lucky break – and the only consolation on offer is that even the most experienced of today's professionals was once a complete novice.

Writing for the microphone

What of the techniques that need to be applied in converting material produced for the printed page into a script that can be performed by an actor with ease at the microphone, and bring real listening pleasure to the child at the other end?

Getting to grips with abridging books for the microphone requires, in the first instance, the application of some simple arithmetic. Take a book of around 70,000 words. Children's radio is currently devoting 10–12 minutes' airtime to its reading slot, and producers usually allow no more than ten episodes for a book. In 12 minutes, an actor can read about 1,800 words. It is clear, therefore, that normally the abridger will be required to reduce the wordage from 70,000 to no more than 18,000 words – in short, to remove 70% or more of the original.

The audio field has different requirements. When dealing with books abridged for CD format, the general rule is that CDs can accommodate some 70 minutes of airtime, which translates to about 10,500 words. So a 140-minute abridgement is presented in the form of two CDs, and will allow the abridger about 21,000 words. These days CD publishers will also make the abridgement available as a download, but increasingly the writer may be called on to abridge specifically for download. In such cases the audiobook publishers will specify the length either in terms of time or wordage. Remember, an actor can normally get through about 2,200 words in 15 minutes.

What makes a good abridgement? To reproduce the sense of an original in fewer words while, in addition and quite as important, to retain the character of the original writing. That demands the capacity to respond sympathetically to the feel of an author's style and to be able to preserve it, even when large chunks of the original are being cut away. Abridging for radio goes beyond even this, for the writer must fulfil his or her commission through the medium of that highly technical artefact, the radio script.

How much liberty is the abridger allowed in translating the printed to the spoken word, while reducing the wordage? Some audiobook producers ask for the minimum of interference with the published text; some radio producers are content for the abridger to adapt the original freely, so as to enhance the actor's performance at the microphone. The different approaches reflect the fact that, in acquiring radio reading rights, the BBC retains editorial independence over the final product, while the granting of abridged audio rights is often conditional on the original writer's approval of the abridged text. So audio producers, reluctant to run the risk of rejection, sometimes allow the abridger very little freedom.

Nevertheless it is an undoubted fact that the requirements of eye and of ear do not always coincide, and that a message easily absorbed from the printed page can become surprisingly garbled if transmitted unamended at the microphone.

In crafting a radio/audio script, the needs of the listener must be one of the prime considerations. The needs of the actor who will read it at the microphone are another. The writer must keep in the forefront of the mind the fact that the script has to be performed. The words must 'flow trippingly on the tongue'. With audio the listener is in control, and can switch on or off whenever convenient. However, a radio script needs shape. On the air, ten minutes on an emotional plateau can be pretty boring. *Crescendi* and *diminuendi* are called for. A good plan is to provide a modest peak of interest about halfway through the script, and work up to a climax at the end, leaving the listener anxious for more of the story.

Principles, principles – what about practice? Let me offer a modest illustration, assuming I'm abridging for radio.

'How are you going?' Harriet said, stifling a yawn.

'The Oxford bus,' returned Pam.

Nothing wrong with that – on the printed page. If faced with it, though, the experienced radio abridger would feel it necessary to present it somewhat along the following lines:

Harriet stifled a yawn.
'How are you going?'
'The Oxford bus,' said Pam.
Why? Let's take the points in order.
Harriet said.

If the speaker's name instantly follows a piece of reported speech, and especially a question, a moment of confusion can arise in the listener's mind. In this instance, it could be unclear for a second whether 'Harriet' is included in, or excluded from, the question. It might be: *'How are you going, Harriet...?'*

The meaning is soon resolved, of course, but impediments to understanding are best eliminated.

'Stifling a yawn' is an indication of the way in which the words were said. If the actor is to provide that indication, he or she needs to know ahead of the speech how it is to be delivered. Moreover, taking the original version, if the actor stifles a yawn while saying Harriet's speech, and then reads 'said Harriet, stifling a yawn,' the passage becomes tautologous.

For this reason it is best to cut back to a bare minimum all indications in the text of how speeches are delivered – 'grimly', 'lugubriously', 'chuckling merrily', and so on. It is better to leave it to the actor and the producer to interpret most of them.

There are no apostrophes on the air. By and large, 'said' is the best radio indicator of speech. An alternative is to precede speech by some description of the speaker, and to insert the words spoken with no further indication of who is speaking. Thus:

Harriet stifled a yawn.
'How are you going?'
It is clearly Harriet speaking.
'The Oxford bus,' returned Pamela.

Two points here. Almost all the literary variants of 'said' ring false through the loudspeaker or headphones – 'cried', 'riposted', 'remarked', 'answered', and so on. For reading purposes, most are best replaced with 'said' (or better, wherever possible, omitted altogether) and the speech in question left to the actor to interpret. In this instance, 'returned' is particularly difficult for the listener – again, for no more than a moment – but is 're-turned' part of the speech? *'The Oxford bus returned...?'* It is surely best to eliminate obstacles to understanding.

This peek into the radio/audio abridger's toolbox might leave one thinking that the business is all gimmick and no heart – noses pressed up so hard against tree trunks that there is no time for the wood. It is certainly necessary in this field, as in any other, for basic techniques to be acquired and then absorbed to the point where they become second nature. Only then can they be applied to ensure that the radio and audio media are used to interpret a writer's intentions as fully and as honestly as possible.

It is, though, equally essential that the abridger of children's books reproduces, as far as possible, the plot, atmosphere and character of the original. The aim must be to leave the listener with as complete a feeling of the original book as possible, given the technical limitations of time and wordage. It is, in short, an essential aspect of the radio/audio writer's craft to keep faith with the author.

Neville Teller MBE has been contributing to BBC radio for over 50 years. He has well over 250 abridgements for radio readings to his credit, some 50 radio dramatisations and over 250 audiobook abridgements. His most recent children's abridgements include *Chitty Chitty Bang Bang Flies Again* by Frank Cottrell Boyce, *Silver* by Andrew Motion, Michael Morpurgo's *A Medal for Leroy*, and *Five Children on the Western Front* by Kate Saunders. Neville Teller is a past chairman of the Society of Authors' Broadcasting Committee and of the Audiobook Publishing Association's Contributors' Committee. He was made an MBE in 2006 'for services to broadcasting and to drama'.

See also...

- *Children's audio publishers*, page 87
- *Writing to a brief*, page 352
- *Children's television and radio*, page 355

Television, film and radio

Writing to a brief

Writing to a brief is an exacting process in which the writer has to produce work to satisfy others as opposed to exploring their own project ideas. The writer may work with others as part of a team when script writing or collaborate with an artistic director when adapting a play. Di Redmond looks at three aspects of writing to a brief for children.

Writing to a brief is enormously varied. I never know what's going to land on my desk – it could be anything: a children's animation series, a series of books, a live action drama script or a stage play. When writing to a brief, you need to have the ability to absorb material very quickly and be disciplined enough to put your own ideas on the back burner. If you twist the commissioner's brief in order to accommodate what you want to write you'll very soon be out of a job!

Animation

The writing team

An animation series is usually commissioned in blocks of 26 or 52 ten-minute episodes. US companies like to have commissioning meetings with large numbers of writers brainstorming for two or three days. UK companies generally prefer smaller groups of writers brainstorming for a day at most. You might be invited to meetings through your agent or through your own personal contact with the animation house or broadcaster. At the initial meeting you will be told the content of the show, after which you'll pitch ideas – or 'thumbnails' as they are often called. If they are approved, you will become one of the writing team.

On a financial note, every stage of the writing process should be covered in your writer's contract, from the writers' meeting where you should receive a full day's fee plus travelling expenses, to separate payments for the Treatment, Draft 1, Draft 2, and the Final Polish Draft. If a contract along these lines isn't offered in advance I'd be extremely wary of attending any meeting.

The writing process

Working from the 'Bible', a document which contains everything the writer needs to know, from character descriptions to locations and props, the writing process begins in earnest. It's a real bonus if the 'Bible' contains a fully executed script as it is the best template to work from: an added bonus would be a promo tape to give you the chance to see the characters and hopefully hear their 'speak'. Hearing Neil Morrisey as Bob the Builder on a promo CD crystalised Bob's character for me and made the writing process so much fun and a lot easier too. Your writing will be hugely affected by the animators' criteria. CGI (computer-generated image) animations like Disney's *Zou* and *Wanda and the Alien* are vastly different from stop frame puppetry animation like *Timmy Time* and *Postman Pat*. It's best to sort out all practical problems with the animators at an early stage so you don't waste time writing scripts that are impossible to execute. For example, if your plot line is about bubbles, make sure the studio can do bubbles; if it's about little boats bobbing in a harbour, check that the animators can do different kinds of water – stormy, misty, calm and choppy. There's nothing more frustrating than getting to Draft 1 stage only to discover that one of the main elements in the story can't be animated. Be bold and ask the practical questions right from the start.

When you finally get the red light to go to Draft 1, remember that behind the dialogue other things are happening simultaneously: action on the set, facial expressions, sound effects and music too. Short phrases like 'Oh, no!' might have camera instructions that cover half a page.

Storylines

To kick-start a series, storylines might be developed when the writing team meet for the first time. Writers may be invited to choose a storyline that grabs them and develop it into a three- or four-page treatment, which is a detailed scene-by-scene breakdown of a ten-minute episode. Further down the line writers develop storylines in their own time, in my case when I'm walking the dog! The first script is without doubt the hardest because no matter how good the 'Bible' is you've still got to familiarise yourself with the characters and their locations, and balance out the A and the B plot. If the script is too long it will be edited down before it's recorded, so make sure that it's the right length before you send it off to the broadcaster. A ten-minute script with opening and closing credits is around 13–15 pages, depending on the font size you use. The commissioners will be looking for scripts that contain humour, warmth, clarity and an understanding of the target audience. If the show is about a builder then a building job will be essential to every plot line; if it's about a postman then he has to do his post round. Most scripts, even if they're only ten minutes long, have an A and a B plot, both of which have to be reconciled by the end of the episode. Some commissionaires prefer a three-act structure, with three underpinning questions – What's the goal? What's the risk? What does the character learn? It's a disciplined writing process which highlights the dramatic peaks in the story.

The script editor

A good script editor coordinates the scripts and makes sure the series has one voice, whether it's a ballerina, an alien, a runaway train or a sailing boat. Writers have different styles, which is why they've been chosen to do the job. The script editor with her overall view of the show will make changes to scripts and she'll also keep an eye on the timing. She has the sensitive task of liaising with the commissioner and the producer on the writers' behalf. Sometimes you *don't* want to see the notes the producer has made: they may be too abrupt or confusing. A good script editor will work on the notes before handing them on to the writers to make the necessary changes.

Stage plays

As well as writing my own stage plays, I've also adapted stage plays from the classics such as *Hard Times* by Charles Dickens and Homer's *The Odyssey*. The Dickens play was commissioned for the Edinburgh Festival with a cast of 30, whilst *The Odyssey* was staged at the Polka Theatre in London with a cast of six. Writers should listen hard to the artistic director's requirements and take on board the limitations of the theatre's budget. If too much is spent on props and costumes it may be at the cost of funding an actor, so be prepared to adapt and compromise.

Adapting from the classics

The two books I adapted couldn't have been more different although the writing process was exactly the same. I read both books until I knew them backwards, after which I felt confident about dramatising them for a young modern audience.

The brief for *The Odyssey* was to write a 90-minute play with a ten-minute interval for 8–12 year-olds. But *The Odyssey* is full of sex and the language of Homer, though hauntingly beautiful, is certainly not pitched at children. The greatest challenge was making the story come alive for a very young audience without destroying the nobility of the original piece. Working closely with the artistic director, I wrote three drafts of the play before I felt I'd got it right, by which time I felt like the gods and heroes of Ancient Greece were part of my extended family! It's a knowledge I've never lost and have since written four books based on classical Greek heroes. That's another great thing about writing: you can transpose a story from one art form to another.

Book series

A book series may be commissioned as a result of a writer pitching an idea to a publisher, or a publisher may have spotted a gap in the market that a writer has been invited to fill. The books vary in length – 2,000–40,000 words – depending on the age range.

I've written book series on football, show jumping, theatre school, a veterinary practice, a drama queen, and a dog. No matter what target age group you're writing for, you have to thoroughly research the subject. For my show-jumping series I virtually lived at the livery yard, trailing the head groom and asking questions. I've been lucky finding professionals who have allowed me into their lives and let me watch them at work, though I have had a few nasty shocks in the process. Once I found myself masked and gloved in an equine operating theatre watching a Newmarket racehorse under the scalpel. You *really* do have to know your subject when you're writing this kind of specialist book. The readers will be highly critical of any inaccuracies, so be careful what you write otherwise you'll get letters of complaint.

Di Redmond is a prolific writer for children's television. She has worked for Disney, Aardman, CBBC, CITV, HIT Entertainment NYC, Milkshake Channel 5, Nikelodeon and Nick Jn. Her credits include *Timmy Time*, *Wanda and the Alien*, *Elias*, *Bob the Builder*, *Postman Pat*, *Roary the Racing Car*, *Tweenies*, *Fifi Forget-me-Not* and *Angelina Ballerina*. She also writes for screen, stage and radio and has published over 100 books, and is a ghostwriter.

See also...

Children's television and radio

The information in this section has been compiled as a general guide for writers, artists, agents and publishers to the major companies and key contacts operating within the children's broadcasting industry. As personnel, corporate structures and commissioning guidelines can change frequently, please check the relevant websites for the most up-to-date information.

REGULATION

Ofcom is the regulator for the communications industries in the UK and has responsibility for TV and radio, as well as telecommunications and wireless services. Advertising is regulated by the Advertising Standards Authority and on-demand TV services are regulated by the Authority for Television On Demand.

Ofcom

Riverside House, 2A Southwark Bridge Road, London SE1 9HA
tel 020-7981 3000, 0300 123 3000
website www.ofcom.org.uk
Chief Executive Sharon White

Ofcom is required to report annually to parliament and exists to: further the interests of consumers by balancing choice and competition with the duty to encourage plurality, protect viewers and listeners, promote diversity in the media and ensure full and fair competition between communications providers.

Advertising Standards Authority

Mid City Place, 71 High Holborn, London WC1V 6QT
tel 020-7492 2222
website www.asa.org.uk
Chief Executive Guy Parker

The Advertising Standards Authority is the UK's independent regulator of advertising across all media. Its work includes acting on complaints and taking action against misleading, harmful or offensive advertisements.

Authority for Television On Demand (ATVOD)

27 Sheet Street, Windsor, Berks. SL4 1BN
tel (01753) 860498
email atvod@atvod.co.uk
website www.atvod.co.uk
Chief Executive Pete Johnson

ATVOD is the independent co-regulator for the editorial content of UK video-on-demand services that fall within the statutory definition of on-demand programme services.

TELEVISION

BabyTV

Baby Network Ltd, 10 Hammersmith Grove, London W6 7AP
email info@babytvchannel.com
website www.babytv.com
Channel Controller Debbie Hunt

BabyTV is the world's leading baby and toddler network from FOX, for children under five and their parents, airing 24 hours a day and completely commercial-free. BabyTV features top quality shows that are created by child development experts and are designed for child and parent to enjoy together. Each hour on BabyTV is an enriching journey full of stories, songs, rhymes and loveable characters.

The BBC

website www.bbc.co.uk
Director, Children's Alice Webb

The BBC is the world's largest broadcasting organisation, with a remit to provide programmes that inform, educate and entertain. Established by Royal Charter, the BBC is a public service broadcaster funded by a licence fee.

The Director, Children's is responsible for the overall direction and management of all of the BBC's services for children, including CBeebies and CBBC channels and their websites. Both channels are self-commissioning and self-scheduling, and proposals may be submitted at any time throughout the year. All submissions for TV and online should be made via Pitch. For further details and commissioning guidelines visit:
www.bbc.co.uk/commissioning/briefs/tv/browse-by-genre/cbeebies
www.bbc.co.uk/commissioning/briefs/tv/browse-by-genre/cbbc/
www.bbc.co.uk/commissioning/tv/articles/pitch

CBeebies

website www.bbc.co.uk/cbeebies
Controller, CBeebies Kay Benbow, *Commissioning* Michael Towner, Catherine McAllister, Sarah Harkins, Mario Dubois

CBeebies offers mixed genre output for TV, online and radio and is specifically produced for a young audience using a variety of formats including live action and animation. Content covers drama,

Television, film and radio

comedy, entertainment and factual, and the target audience is children aged 0–6 years. CBeebies is on air daily from 6am–7pm.

CBBC

website www.bbc.co.uk/cbbc
Controller, CBBC Cheryl Taylor, *Commissioning* Melissa Hardinge, Kez Margrie, Catherine McAllister, Hugh Lawton, Sue Nott, Mario Dubois, Sarah Muller, Sarah Harkins

CBBC offers mixed genre output for TV and online. Content covers drama, factual, comedy, entertainment, animation and news, and the target audience is children aged 6–12 years. CBBC is on air daily from 7am–7pm.

BBC Writersroom

website www.bbc.co.uk/writersroom

BBC Writersroom is the first port of call at the BBC for unsolicited scripts and new writers. It champions writing talent across a range of genres, including children's drama and comedy. Visit the website to discover:
• how and when to submit a script;
• new opportunities for writers;
• writing tips and success stories;
• interviews and top tips from writers;
• competitions and events.

The BBC Writersroom blog provides a wealth of behind-the-scenes commentary from writers and producers who have worked on BBC TV and radio programmes: www.bbc.co.uk/blogs/writersroom.

Boomerang

email contact@cartoonnetwork.co.uk
website www.boomerangtv.co.uk

Boomerang was developed by Cartoon Network to provide fun, entertaining and light educational viewing for children aged 3–7. Online, children can experience a range of games and activities including adventure, sports, puzzles and fun educational games.

Cartoon Network

email contact@cartoonnetwork.co.uk
website www.cartoonnetwork.co.uk

Cartoon entertainment broadcast 24 hours a day. Sister channel Cartoonito (www.cartoonito.co.uk) provides fun, entertaining and light educational viewing for preschoolers. Toonix (www.toonix.com) is an online virtual world for children aged 6–13 in which they create an avatar and where they can play games, take part in challenges, give virtual gifts and collect stickers.

Channel 4

124 Horseferry Road, London SW1P 2TX
tel 020-7396 4444
website www.channel4.com

Channel 4 is a publicly-owned, commercially-funded, not-for-profit public service broadcaster and has a remit to be innovative, experimental and distinctive. Its public ownership and not-for-profit status ensure all profit generated by its commercial activity is directly reinvested back into the delivery of its public service remit. As a publisher-broadcaster, Channel 4 is also required to commission UK content from the independent production sector and currently works with over 400 creative companies across the UK every year. In addition to the main Channel 4 service, its portfolio includes E4, More4, Film4, 4Music, 4Seven, channel4.com and brand new digital service All 4 which presents of all of C4's on-demand content, digital innovations and live linear channel streams in one place online for the first time.

4Talent supports people to build their careers in the media industry across a range of disciplines. Visit http://4talent.channel4.com
Chief Executive David Abraham
Chief Creative Officer Jay Hunt

Commissioning

Information about commissioning and related processes and guidelines can be found at www.channel4.com/info/commissioning.

Channel 5

10 Lower Thames Street, London EC3R 6EN
tel 020-8612 7000
website www.channel5.com

Channel 5 brands include Channel 5, 5* and 5USA, and an on-demand service, Demand 5. Channel 5 broadcasts over 24 hours of children's programmes every week under the Milkshake brand, which is aimed at children aged 2–7 and airs daily from 6–9.15am (10am at weekends). Channel 5 commissions, co-produces and acquires preschool programming through a wide range of deals and arrangements.
Director of Programmes Ben Frow
Head of Children's Jessica Symons
Children's Programmes Coordinator Josie Grierson

Commissioning

Information about commissioning and how to submit an idea can be found at:
http://about.channel5.com/programme-production/commissioning/fives-production-process
http://about.channel5.com/programme-production/commissioning/commissioning-teams/childrens-programming

CITV

The London Television Centre, Upper Ground, London SE1 9LT
tel 0344 881 4150
website www.itv.com/citv

ITV is the UK's largest commercial TV network. In addition to TV broadcasting services, ITV also delivers programming via a number of platforms, including ITV Player. The ITV network is responsible for the commissioning, scheduling and marketing of network programmes on ITV1 and its digital channel portfolio including ITV2, ITV3, ITV4, ITVBe, ITV Encore and CITV, the commercial free-to-air children's channel. CITV commissions and acquires a variety of programmes aimed at children up to age 11.

Commissioning
website www.itv.com/commissioning

See website for information about commissioning and how to submit an idea.
Ceo, ITV Adam Crozier
Head of Programming, CITV Jamila Metran

Disney Channel UK
3 Queen Caroline Street, Hammersmith, London W6 9PE
tel 020-8222 1000
website www.disney.co.uk/disney-tv

A cable and satellite network run by the Walt Disney Company specialising in programming for children from preschoolers to teens. There are 3 channels: Disney Channel, Disney Junior and Disney XD.

Nickelodeon UK
53 Queensway, London W2 4QH
website www.nick.co.uk

Nickelodeon UK comprises three channels with a target audience spanning children aged approximately 2–12: Nickelodeon, NickToons (www.nicktoons.co.uk) aimed at children aged 6–9 and NickJr (www.nickjr.co.uk) aimed at children aged 2–5.

POP
CSC Media Group, PO Box 782425, Golden Square, London W1A 9AR
email info@popfun.co.uk
website www.popfun.co.uk

Cartoons and live action series for boys and girls aged 4–9 with three sister channels:

Pop Girl
website www.popgirl.tv

Live action series, movies and pop music videos for girls aged 7–12.

Tiny Pop
website www.tinypop.com

Cartoons and live action series for children aged 3–7.

Kix!
website www.kixtv.co.uk

Animated and live action series aimed at boys aged 7–12.

Radio Telefis Éireann (RTÉ)
Donnybrook, Dublin 4, Republic of Ireland
website www.rte.ie
Controller and Cross Divisional Head of Children's Content Sheila de Courcy

RTÉ offers a comprehensive range of programmes for children and young people. RTÉjr is aimed at children under 7 and delivers a mix of original and acquired live action and animated content. RTÉ Two offers preschool programming in the mornings. Mixed programming for older children is available in the afternoons and early evenings, and is branded TRTÉ.

Commissioning
website www.rte.ie/commissioning/young_peoples_commissioning.html

See website for information about commissioning and submitting proposals for children and young people.

S4C
Parc Ty Glas, Llanishen, Cardiff CF14 5DU
tel 0870 600 4141
website www.s4c.co.uk

S4C is the world's only Welsh language TV channel, broadcasting programmes on sport, drama, music, factual, entertainment and culture. S4C also provides services for children including: Cyw, for younger viewers (http://cyw.s4c.co.uk/cy) and Stwnsh (www.s4c.cymru/cy/stwnsh/) for older children and teenagers. See website for full details of commissioning and production guidelines and personnel.
Chief Executive Ian Jones
Director of Content Dafydd Rhys

RADIO

CBeebies Radio
website www.bbc.co.uk/cbeebies/radio

CBeebies Radio is aimed at encouraging preschool children to develop their listening skills. Over 30 shows are available and in addition to radio output, the website contains games, songs, make & colour and story-time activities.

BBC School Radio
website www.bbc.co.uk/schoolradio

BBC School Radio provides audio resources for primary schools including podcasts, downloads, audio and video clips, learning resources and teachers' notes that are curriculum-linked to Early Years, Key Stage 1 and Key Stage 2.

Fun Kids
Folder Media, 96A Curtain Road, London EC2A 3AA
tel 020-7739 7880

email contact@foldermedia.co.uk
website www.funkidslive.com

A British children's digital radio station (not national) providing programming to entertain children aged seven to 12 with a mixture of songs, stories, competitions and news. Available to listen via the website or on DAB Digital Radio across London and south east England.
Managing Director, Folder Media Gregory Watson
Creative Director, Folder Media Matt Deegan

ORGANISATIONS CONNECTED TO BROADCASTING

BARB
20 Orange Street, London WC2H 7EF
tel 020-7024 8100
email enquiries@barb.co.uk
website www.barb.co.uk
Chief Executive Justin Sampson

The Broadcasters' Audience Research Board is the official source of viewing figures in the UK.

Ipsos MediaCT (specialist division of Ipsos MORI)
79–81 Borough Road, London SE1 1FY
tel 020-7347 3000
website www.ipsos-mori.com
Managing Director Ipsos MediaCT Liz Landy
Ceo Ipsos MORI Ben Page

Involved in running BARB and RAJAR.

Media UK
website www.mediauk.com

Maintains detailed listings of UK TV and radio providers, newspapers, magazines and media ownership.

Pact (Producers Alliance for Cinema and Television)
3rd Floor, Fitzrovia House, 153–157 Cleveland Street, London W1T 6QW

tel 020-7380 8230
website www.pact.co.uk

Pact is the trade association representing the commercial interests of UK independent TV, film, digital, children's and animation media companies. For details of children's independent TV and film production companies, see the website.

Public Media Alliance
website www.publicmediaalliance.org
Ceo Sally-Ann Wilson

World's largest association of public broadcasters.

The Radio Academy
3rd Floor, 55 New Oxford Street, London WC1A 1BS
tel 020-3174 1180
website www.radioacademy.org
Ceo Paul Robinson

The Radio Academy is a registered charity dedicated to the promotion of excellence in UK radio broadcasting and production. For over 30 years the Radio Academy has run the annual Radio Academy Awards, which celebrate content and creativity in the industry.

RadioCentre
6th Floor, 55 New Oxford Street, London WC1A 1BS
tel 020-7010 0600
email info@radiocentre.org
website www.radiocentre.org
Chief Executive Siobhan Kenny

RadioCentre is the voice of UK commercial radio and works with government, policy makers and regulators, and provides a forum for industry-wide debate and discussion.

RAJAR
6th Floor, 55 New Oxford Street, London WC1A 1BS
tel 020-7395 0630
website www.rajar.co.uk
Chief Executive Jerry Hill

RAJAR – Radio Joint Audience Research – is the official body in charge of measuring radio audiences in the UK. It is jointly owned by the BBC and the RadioCentre on behalf of the commercial sector.

Theatre
Writing for children's theatre

Writing plays for children is not a soft option. David Wood considers children to be the most difficult audience to write for and shares his thoughts here about this challenge.

'Would you write the Christmas play?' These six words, uttered by John Hole, Director of the Swan Theatre, Worcester, unwittingly changed my life, setting me off on a trail I'm still treading over 40 years later. It wasn't a totally mad question, even though I was then cutting my teeth as an 'adult' actor/director – and indeed I have managed to continue these so-called mainstream activities to a limited degree ever since. No, it had already struck me that children's audiences were important and, by doing magic at parties since my teens, I had already developed an aptitude for and delight in entertaining children.

At Worcester I had organised Saturday morning children's theatre, inveigling my fellow repertory actors into helping me tell stories, lead participation songs and perform crazy sketches. And I was still haunted by the memory of seeing, a couple of years earlier, a big commercial panto in

Further information

TYA (Theatre for Young Audiences)
website www.tya-uk.org
TYA is the UK Centre of ASSITEJ (International Association of Theatre for Children and Young People). The website lists most of the companies currently in production. In association with Aurora Metro Press, it publishes *Theatre for Children and Young People* (see 'Further reading'), a comprehensive collection of articles about the development of children's theatre and theatre-in-education in the UK over the last 50 years.

National Theatre Bookshop
National Theatre, South Bank, London SE1 9PX
tel 020-7452 3456
email bookshop@nationaltheatre.org.uk
website www.shop.nationaltheatre.org.uk

French's Theatre Bookshop
52 Fitzroy Street London W1T 5JR
tel 020-7387 9373
email theatre@samuelfrench-london.co.uk
website www.samuelfrench-london.co.uk

which the star comedian cracked an off-colour joke to a matinee house virtually full of children, got an appreciative cackle from a small party of ladies in the stalls, then advanced to the footlights and said, 'Let's get the kids out of here, then we can get started!'. In the dark I blushed and my hackles rose. How dare this man show such disdain for the young audience whose parents' hard-earned cash had contributed towards his doubtless considerable salary? It set me thinking about how few proper plays were then written and performed for children. There were traditional favourites like *Peter Pan* in London, the occasional *Wizard of Oz*, *Toad of Toad Hall* and *Alice in Wonderland* in the regions but that was about it. Nothing new. Later I discovered my assessment had been too sweeping. There were several pioneers out there presenting proper plays for children, including Brian Way (Theatre Centre), Caryl Jenner (Unicorn), John Allen (Glyndebourne Children's Theatre) and John English (Midlands Arts Centre), but their work was not then widely recognised. Their contribution to the development of children's theatre in the UK cannot be overestimated. Also, in 1965, the Belgrade Theatre, Coventry, had created the first theatre-in-education company, touring innovative work into schools; and early in 1967 I had acted in the first production of the TIE Company at the Palace Theatre, Watford.

Theatre

So writing *The Tinder Box* for Christmas 1967 seemed a natural opportunity and, although I don't think it was very good, it paved the way for me to write around 75 (so far) plays that try to trigger the imagination, make children laugh, cry and think, and hopefully lead them towards a love of theatre. The journey hasn't always been easy. It is frustrating that children's theatre is still often perceived as third division theatre; funding for it is less than for its adult counterpart, even though it often costs as much, sometimes more, to put on, and always commands a lower seat price; critics generally ignore it; and most theatre folk seem to think it is only for beginners or failures, a ridiculous belief, since children are the most difficult and honest audience of all – and yet the most rewarding when we get it right.

Let's pause briefly to talk terminology. The phrase 'children's theatre' means different things to different people. Whereas 'youth theatre' clearly implies that young people are taking part in the play, 'children's theatre' can mean not only children performing but also (more correctly, in my view) theatre produced by adults for children to watch. And, although I have occasionally, and enjoyably, written plays for children to perform (*Lady Lollipop*, from Dick King-Smith's book) or for children to take part in alongside adults (*The Lighthouse Keeper's Lunch*, from Ronda and David Armitage's book and *Dinosaurs and All That Rubbish*, from Michael Foreman's book), the vast majority of my plays have been written for professional actors to perform for children. Don't get me wrong. Participation by children is hugely beneficial and worthwhile, but I like to feel my plays might provide the inspiration to encourage them to want to do it themselves. I believe that children respond to exciting examples that inspire them. I also believe that children are more likely to, say, want to learn to play a musical instrument if they see and hear the best professional musicians playing in a concert. They are more likely to want to excel at football if they see – live or on television – the best professional teams displaying dazzling skills.

So any advice I can offer about children's theatre is mainly aimed towards writers who would like to create plays for grown-ups to perform for children. Having said that, it has always surprised me that several of my professionally performed plays have been subsequently put on by schools and youth groups who cope, showing tremendous flair and imagination, with tricky technical demands. I sometimes wish I could write more plays specifically for schools and youth groups, but I think I might be tempted to oversimplify (which would be patronising) or to try to write enough roles for a very large cast, which might dilute the content and fail to provide a satisfying structure.

Encouragingly, the professional children's theatre scene today is much healthier than when I started. There are many more touring companies (see page 370) large and small, producing high-quality work for all ages. There has been an exciting explosion in the amount of work for under-fives. And at last we have two full-time children's theatre buildings – Unicorn and Polka – who put on their own plays as well as receive other companies' work. They are both in London, and the big hope is that there will in the future be many more such beacons in other cities and towns. Children are entitled to their own theatre, and creating theatre buildings especially for them, run by committed professionals, is the best way to improve the quantity, quality and status of the work. Alongside that, our major theatres, including the National and the Royal Shakespeare Company, should be setting an example by making children's theatre an integral part of their programming, rather than occasionally mounting a children's play as an optional extra. And this means more than coming up with an annual Christmas show.

Study the market

Go to see shows. Which companies are doing what? How many cast members can they afford? Are they looking for original plays as well as adaptations of successful books with big titles and box office appeal? Try to meet the artistic directors, to discuss what they might be looking for. What size spaces are the companies playing in? Studios? Large theatres? Do they have facilities for scene changes? Is there flying? Incidentally, restrictions on cast size and staging possibilities are not necessarily a bad thing. Well-defined parameters within which to work can be a help not a hindrance. I was asked to write a play for the Towngate, Basildon, a theatre that had no flying, not much stage depth and virtually no wing space. And I was allowed a cast of only six. At first I despaired but then managed to think positively and wrote *The Gingerbread Man*, which ended up paying the rent for 30 years! The play is set on a giant Welsh dresser. No props or scenery come on or off stage during the show – the basic set is self-contained. And the six characters are joined by the off-stage voices (recorded) of the 'Big Ones', the human owners of the dresser.

It may be putting the cart before the horse to worry about where and how your play might be performed – before you've written it! But it really is foolish to start before finding out what might be practical and realistic. Quite frankly, a cast of 20, or even a dozen, is going to be out of the question for most professional companies, so if your idea demands such numbers, maybe you should approach a school, a youth drama group or an amateur dramatic society instead.

Rather than rely on others, might you be in a position to create your own openings? Many children's theatre practitioners, including myself, have had to start by 'doing it themselves'. I, like Richard Gill, Vicky Ireland and Annie Wood (former artistic directors of the Polka Theatre) not only write but also direct. And Richard Gill, Tim Webb (Oily Cart), Guy Holland (Quicksilver) and I (Whirligig), went as far as to create companies to produce our own work, because we knew we were unlikely to get other companies to put it on. The TYA (Theatre for Young Audiences) website (see box) lists most of the companies currently in production, and is a useful first port of call to see the scope of the work.

What 'works' for children?

A good, satisfying story makes a helpful start, told with theatrical flair. By that I mean that we should use theatrical techniques to spark the imagination of the audience – scenery, costume, sound, lighting, puppetry, magic, circus skills, masks, mime, dancing and music. The physical as well as the verbal can help to retain the attention and interest of children. Page after page of two characters sitting talking are likely to prove a turn-off. It's better to see them do something rather than just talk about it. I try to introduce lots of 'suddenlies' to help keep the audience riveted to their seats, wanting to know what happens next. I've often said that my life's work has been dedicated to stopping children going to the lavatory. Suddenlies – a new character appearing, a sound effect, a lighting change, a surprise twist, a musical sting – can be a huge help. Compare it to the page-turning appeal of a successful children's book.

Play ideas can be found in fairy tales, myths and legends, traditional rhymes and popular stories. Be careful, however, not to waste time adapting books in copyright, unless you have got the necessary permission – no public performances, paid or unpaid, can be given without this. Approach the publisher or the author's agent to discover if the stage rights are available and, if they are, how much it might cost to acquire them for a year or two.

Or you might use an incident from history, a pertinent modern social issue, such as conservation, or the real life of an inspirational or controversial person. Or you could explore a social problem especially relevant to children, like single-parent families or bullying.

In my book *Theatre for Children: A Guide to Writing, Adapting, Directing and Acting*, I identify useful ingredients for children's plays. They are really fairly obvious – things that we know children respond to. They include animals, toys, fantasy, a quest, goodies and baddies, humour, scale (small characters in large environments and *vice versa*), a child at the centre of the story. And justice – think *Cinderella*. Children, like adults, have a strong sense of fairness and will root for the underdog. Roald Dahl's stories, eight of which I have been lucky enough to adapt, all use this. Sophie (in *The BFG*), James (in *James and the Giant Peach*) and Boy (in *The Witches*) are all disadvantaged orphans whose strength of character leads them through immense difficulties to eventual triumph. They are empowered to succeed in an adult-dominated world, and children identify with them.

The use of audience participation is an option much argued about by children's theatre practitioners. Many hate it. For some plays, it would, indeed, be totally inappropriate. But for others it can be exciting and fun. I'm not talking about basic panto participation – 'he's behind you!' – though even this can be used on occasion with integrity. I'm talking about what I call 'positive participation', in which the audience contribute to the action by helping or hindering, by having ideas or by taking part in a 'set piece'. In *The Selfish Shellfish* they create a storm to fool an oil slick. In *The Meg and Mog Show* (for very small children), they make springtime noises and movements to encourage Meg's garden to grow. In *The See-Saw Tree* they vote on whether to save an ancient oak or allow it to be cut down to make way for a children's playground. In *The Gingerbread Man* they help catch the scavenging Sleek the Mouse under an upturned mug. Their contribution is crucial to the development and resolution of the plot. In *The Twits* the audience fools Mr and Mrs Twit by making them think that they, the audience, are upside down. They all remove their shoes, put them on their hands and stretch their arms up while lowering their heads! The sight of a thousand children all doing this, with joy and not a shred of cynicism, is pure magic to me.

I don't believe that a children's play has to have a moral, a self-improving message for the audience. But I do believe a children's play should *be* moral, presenting a positive attitude and an uplifting, hopeful conclusion. And I resent the notion that children's plays should always be written to tie in with the National Curriculum. Many do, but the educationalists shouldn't dictate our agenda – the tail shouldn't wag the dog.

Before you start

I strongly recommend that you create a synopsis, outlining the events in story order. This leads to clarity of storytelling, to the disciplined pursuit of a through-line, with not too many subplots that could end up as time-wasting, irrelevant cul-de-sacs. For myself it would be foolish to think I had the brilliance to start a play with only an initial idea and just let my imagination lead me through uncharted waters. I find it far better to let the juices flow during the synopsis stage and, when it comes to writing the play, to conscientiously follow through my original instincts with not too many diversions.

Good luck with getting your first play produced. Getting it published may need determination. It was a very special day for me when Samuel French accepted (after initial rejections) *The Owl and the Pussycat Went to See…*, my second play, co-written with Sheila

Ruskin. After its first production at Worcester, I beavered away to get it on stage in London and, thanks to several friends helping financially, managed to produce it at the Jeannetta Cochrane Theatre. To save money I directed it myself. We were lucky enough to get two rave reviews. I approached Samuel French again. They came to see it and, hallelujah, offered to publish it. Since then their loyalty has been more than gratifying – they still publish most of my efforts. There are now several specialist children's play publishers, many of whom also act as licensees of amateur performances. The National Theatre Bookshop and French's Theatre Bookshop stock a fair number of plays and, when searching for a publisher, it is worth checking out their shelves. The internet can help too. Tap in the names of successful children's playwrights, like Mike Kenny, Charles Way, Brendan Murray or the late Adrian Mitchell and see what comes up.

I find that the challenge of writing a play for children never gets easier, however many times I go through the process. It certainly isn't a soft option, i.e. easier than writing a play for adults. And it carries, I believe, a big responsibility. I always worry that I haven't the right to fail: the last thing I want to do is write something that might put children off theatre for life. I'm aware that many in the audience will be first-time theatre-goers, some of whom never asked to come! It's so important to get it right, to enthuse them so much they can't wait to return. And this is where the passion comes in. Most children's theatre practitioners are passionate about what they do, with an almost missionary zeal to stimulate and delight their audience. Also, we all know that, unlike adult audiences who tend to sit quietly and clap at the end, even if they've hated the play, our children's audiences won't be (and shouldn't be) so polite. It is palpably obvious when we 'lose' them. We are dedicated to using our experience and instinct to 'hold' them, to help them enjoy the communal experience of a theatre visit and willingly enter the spirit of the performance. The buzz I get from being in an auditorium of children overtly having a great time – listening hard, watching intently, reacting, feeling, letting the play take them on a special, magical, unique journey – is a buzz I constantly strive for. I suppose that's really why I do it.

David Wood OBE has been dubbed 'the national children's dramatist' by *The Times*. His plays are performed regularly on tour, in the West End and all over the world. In 2006, for the Queen's 80th birthday party celebrations, he wrote *The Queen's Handbag*, which was broadcast live from Buckingham Palace Gardens and watched by 8 million viewers on BBC1. In 2011, his adaptation of *The Tiger Who Came to Tea* toured the UK before playing a season at the Vaudeville Theatre in London's West End, and was nominated for an Olivier Award in 2012. David's grown-up musical, *The Go-Between* (co-written with Richard Taylor, adapted from L.P. Hartley's novel), won Best Musical Production in the Theatre Awards UK 2012. His adaptation of Michelle Magorian's novel *Goodnight Mister Tom* won the 2013 Olivier Award for Best Entertainment and Family, following its season at the Phoenix Theatre. In 2014, there were UK tours of his adaptations of *Tom's Midnight Garden* and *George's Marvellous Medicine*. *The Tiger Who Came to Tea* tours throughout 2015, including visits to Sydney Opera House, Hong Kong, Singapore and China, before returning to the West End for a Christmas season. His website is www.davidwood.org.uk.

Further reading

Bennett, Stuart (ed.), *Theatre for Children and Young People,* Aurora Metro Press, 2005

Maguire, Tom and Schuitema, Karian (eds) with foreword by David Wood, *Theatre for Young Audiences: A Critical Handbook*, Institute of Education Press, 2013

Wood, David, with Janet Grant, *Theatre for Children: A Guide to Writing, Adapting, Directing and Acting,* Faber and Faber, 1997

See also...

- *Adapting books for the stage*, page 364

Theatre

Adapting books for the stage

Stephen Briggs ponders the challenges and rewards of dramatising other people's novels.

Why me?

Stephen Briggs? Stephen Briggs? Who on earth is Stephen Briggs to write about adapting novels for the stage?

Well, many years ago I wrote a stage version of *A Christmas Carol* for my amdram group … no, stick with me on this…. *Then*, a few years later I adapted two Tom Sharpe novels (these were for one-off productions and the scripts are now long gone). *However*, my overwhelming – and more recent – experience has been with dramatising the novels of the late Sir Terry Pratchett. I've now adapted 20 of Terry's books – four for Transworld/Doubleday, three for Samuel French, three for Oxford University Press, six for Methuen Drama (now at Bloomsbury) and three to come from Oberon Books. These have been staged by amateur groups in over 20 countries from Zimbabwe to Antarctica (yes, really, Antarctica) and by professional groups in France and the Czech Republic. I also co-scripted the mini-dramatisations used by Sky One to promote their big budget television films of Terry's *Hogfather* and *Colour of Magic*.

I have been involved in amateur theatre since I left school. Not just acting, but also directing, choreography, set design/construction, costume design/construction – even including brewing mulled wine for the audiences in our chilly medieval theatre. None of this makes me an expert, not by any interpretation of the word, but I was the one who had to make my scripts work on stage since I also directed them. I was also able to get useful and honest feedback from the original author. Hopefully I've learned a few lessons along the way, which I'm happy to pass on.

Dialogue

When you watch a film, a lot of screen time is taken up by fancy stuff – Imperial star cruisers roaring through space, ill-fated liners ploughing the waves, swooping pan shots over raddled pirate ships. In a play, you don't get any of that stuff. The dialogue has to drive the action.

The methods used to adapt a novel for the stage are as varied as the authors you try to adapt. Terry Pratchett, like Charles Dickens, wrote very good dialogue and the scenes already leap from the page. Other authors make greater use of narrative which the adapter has to weave into the play as well, if they are to keep to the spirit of the original work. Terry is well known for his use of footnotes and, for some of the plays, I even included the Footnote as a 'character' – a Brechtian alienation device, for those who want a more literary justification.

Keep it simple

Terry Pratchett wrote 'filmically' – his scenes cross-cut and swoop like a screenplay. On the silver screen, you can set a scene visually in a second. On the stage it can take longer, and you have to give the audience a chance to realise where they are if they are to have any possibility of keeping up with the – often quite complex – plot.

It's important to remember that a theatre audience doesn't have the luxury of being able to reread a page, or skip back to check a plot point – they (usually) get to see the play only once. It's vital, therefore, to ensure that important plot points are not lost along the way while one is tempted to keep in other favoured scenes from the much longer novel.

Keep it moving

Novelists are not constrained by budget – they can destroy cities, have characters who are 60-foot long dragons, write vital scenes involving time travel and other difficult concepts. These can initially appear to be a challenge for anyone without the budget of Industrial Light and Magic (www.ilm.com).

When I write, I have the good fortune to be writing for a theatre which has very limited space – on and off stage – and virtually no capacity for scenic effects. This makes staging the plays a nightma…, ahem… a challenge, but the benefit is that my adaptations can be staged virtually anywhere. I don't write them with essential big effects or big set changes. Of course, drama groups with huge budgets can go wild with all that – but the plays can work without it.

Plays which demand massive set changes or pose huge scenic problems are likely to put off many directors working to a tight budget. It's different if you're Alan Ayckbourn, of course … onstage swimming pool, floating river cruiser … no problem.

People say that radio has the best scenery. Allowing the audience to fill in the gaps can not only save on costly wood and canvas but, on occasions, can even be more effective than an expensive but stagey scenic effect. After all, Shakespeare's *Antony and Cleopatra* includes a sea battle between two great navies – all seen by two blokes standing on a hill.

The plays – like the books – have to keep moving. Scenes need to flow fairly seamlessly into one another. Set changes slow things down. I get to see large numbers of productions of my plays and the general rule is that the ones with frequent set-changes are the ones which plod.

Writing for schools

Three of my plays were written specifically for classroom use. I had to bear in mind that the plays were as likely to be used for reading in a classroom as well as for production on a stage. So I tried to keep the number of stage directions to a minimum because I know all too well from reading plays with my own amateur drama group that the need to read through huge chunks of explanatory stuff in italics, interspersed with snippets of uninformative dialogue, is very tedious. Here is an example (not, I hasten to add, an extract from a real play):

> (*As Smithers looks out of the window, Bert rushes downstairs, carrying an aspidistra in a brass bowl. He passes, but fails to notice, the gorilla. He trips and falls, dropping the plant and pot on Smithers' head*)
>
> SMITHERS: Oof!
>
> (*Smithers picks up a broom from the floor and chases after Bert. They run into the kitchen and out again, up the stairs and across the landing. Bert takes a wad of banknotes out of his pocket and throws them at Smithers*)
>
> BERT: Take that!

It was also important to avoid characters with just 'one line and a cough'. Nothing is worse in a read-through than to be given the role of 'King of France' only to find that the character speaks one line on page one and then is silent for the rest of the play. Except, perhaps, being allocated a role meant for someone of the opposite sex and then finding it contains dialogue that will invite ridicule from the rest of the class: 'I fink I've got a beard coming through' or 'Oh la, I feel so pretty; I do love wearing frilly pink underwear'.

I also try to ensure that whatever special effects are mentioned should be either easily achievable or not essential and again, that the plays can be performed with the minimum amount of scenery.

Two of the three plays I wrote for OUP I would not be staging myself. It was really fascinating (and quite gratifying) to see the plays staged by schools and to find that they *worked*.

How do I start?
• **I read the book.** Then I read the book again. I then put it down, leave it for a week and write down all the main plot points I can recall, and a rough list of scenes. That should give me a rough shape for the play. Anything I've forgotten to include can probably go high up on the list of potential material to cut.

• **I write it.** I sit down and write the script. At this stage I don't try to keep to a specific length; I just adapt the book, making mental notes of any scenes that show potential for trimming, cutting or pasting into another as I go along. My overall plan is to keep the play to around two hours. If, when I get to the end, the play is too long, I then go back and look again at each scene and character to ensure they can justify their place in the script.

• **I dump it.** Reducing a 95,000-word novel into a 20,000-word play means that there will have to be an element of trimming. The trick, I suppose, is to ensure that the cuts will not be too glaring to the paying audience ('I reckon if we cut out the Prince of Denmark, we can get *Hamlet* down to an hour and a half, no problem'). Hopefully, there will be subplots, not vital to the main story, which can be excised to keep it all flowing. But even so, occasionally tough decisions have to be made once all the fat's been removed and one is forced to cut into muscle and bone (as it were). It's important to let stuff go – even if it's a favourite scene in the book, or a favourite character.

• **I share it.** It's good then to let someone else read it. It's all too easy to get so far into the wood that you can no longer see the trees. Being challenged on the decisions you made in adapting the book is a very good thing. I'd certainly recommend anyone adapting a book to have the script read by someone who knows the book well, and who can point out any important plot omissions. It is also good to have your script read by someone who does *not* know the book and who can ask the 'what on earth does that mean?' questions.

It's useful for me that many of my drama club are not *Discworld* 'fans'. Their outsider's view of the script is extremely useful. I also then have the luxury of amending the script in rehearsal to tidy up scenes, add in bits and take bits out. This means that the script which is submitted to the publisher is then fully tried and tested.

Some golden rules
It's difficult to be hard and fast about 'rules' for adapting books, but here are a few useful guidelines that I try to stick to:
• **Don't change the principle plot** – there's no point in calling a play *Bram Stoker's Dracula* if you're then going to have Dracula surviving at the end and starting up a flourishing law firm in Whitby.

- **Never sacrifice 'real' scenes in order to add in some of your own** – after all, you've chosen to adapt the author's work because, presumably, you admire their writing. If you think you can improve on their humour/drama/characterisation you should really be writing your own plots and not torturing theirs.
- **Use the author's dialogue whenever possible** – same as the above, really. Also try to attribute it to the right character whenever practicable.
- **Don't add characters** – stick to the ones the author has given you.
- **Don't be afraid to cut material** – after all, you're trying to squeeze a 300-page novel into a two-hour play; you just can't fit everything in, so don't try. Anything which does not advance the main plot should be on your list for potential dumping if your play overruns.
- **If it doesn't *need* changing – don't change it.**

As well as the 20 plays he mentions in his article, **Stephen Briggs** is the co-author, with Terry Pratchett, and illustrator, of *Turtle Recall: The Discworld Companion*, *The Streets of Ankh-Morpork*, *The Wit & Wisdom of Discworld* and a small raft of other publications emanating from Terry Pratchett's *Discworld* books. He reads the unabridged audio versions of Terry's books for Isis, HarperCollins and for Random House (in the USA). In 2005 he won an Audie Award (Audio Publishers Association, USA) for his reading of Terry's *Monstrous Regiment* and in 2013 was nominated for his reading of *Dodger*. He also won the Audible Audio Download Book of the Year 2008 for *Good Omens* and in 2009 received an Odyssey Award for his recording of Terry's *Nation* for Harper Audio. In 2010 he won two awards from *AudioFile* magazine for his recording of *Unseen Academicals*, and in 2014 he won two more for *Raising Steam* and for *The Science of Discworld*. Stephen's website is www.stephenbriggs.com.

See also...

Theatre

Theatre for children

London and regional theatres are listed below; listings of touring companies start on page 370.

LONDON

Chickenshed Theatre
Chase Side, Southgate, London N14 4PE
tel 020-8351 6161
email info@chickenshed.org.uk
website www.chickenshed.org.uk
Managing Director Gill Dodge

Produces theatre for all ages as well as running successful education courses, outreach projects and membership programmes.

The Colour House Theatre
Merton Abbey Mills, Watermill Way,
London SW19 2RD
tel 020-7542 5511
email info@colourhousetheatre.co.uk
website www.colourhousetheatre.co.uk
Director Peter Wallder, *Manager* Charlie Shakespeare

Grade II-listed building seating 50–70 people. The resident children's theatre has now staged over 80 original musical adaptations of famous fairy tales, such as Little Red Riding Hood, and achieved charitable status in 2008. The one-hour shows run for 10 weeks each (July and August excepted) on Saturdays and Sundays at 2pm and 4pm.

Polka Theatre
240 The Broadway, London SW19 1SB
tel 020-8543 8320
email stephen@polkatheatre.com
website www.polkatheatre.com
Artistic Director Peter Glanville

Theatre of new work, with targeted commissions. Exclusively for children aged 0–14, the Main Theatre seats 300 and the Adventure Theatre seats 70. Programmed 18 months–2 years in advance. Founded 1967.

Theatre-Rites
Unit 612, Erlang House, 128 Blackfriars Road,
London SE1 8EQ
tel 020-7928 4875
email info@theatre-rites.co.uk
website www.theatre-rites.co.uk
Artistic Director Sue Buckmaster

Creates devised theatre for family audiences and young people using a mix of performance, installation, puppetry, dance and sound. Working within the UK and internationally, the company creates site-specific and touring productions. Founded 1995.

Unicorn Theatre
147 Tooley Street, London SE1 2HZ
tel 020-7645 0560
email hello@unicorntheatre.com
website www.unicorntheatre.com
Artistic Director Purni Morell, *Executive Director* Anneliese Davidsen

Produces a year-round programme of theatre for children and young people under 21. In-house productions of full-length plays with professional casts are staged across two auditoria, alongside visiting companies and education work. Unicorn rarely commissions plays from writers who are new to it, but it is keen to hear from writers who are interested in working with the theatre in the future.

Do not send unsolicited MSS as Unicorn does not have the resources to read and respond to them in appropriate detail. Send a short statement describing why you would like to write for Unicorn and a CV or a summary of your relevant experience.

Young Vic Theatre Company
66 The Cut, London SE1 8LZ
tel 020-7922 2922
email info@youngvic.org
website www.youngvic.org
Artistic Director David Lan

Leading London producing theatre. Founded 1969.

A Younger Theatre
email jake@ayoungertheatre.com
website www.ayoungertheatre.com
Contact Jake Orr

Voluntary project with teams of reviewers, feature-writers and bloggers who write for free in return for seeing a show or in order to build a portfolio of interviews or promote their own performance work. Content is generally aimed at those 26 and under.

REGIONAL

Chichester Festival Theatre
Oaklands Park, Chichester, West Sussex PO19 6AP
tel (01243) 784437
website www.cft.org.uk
Artistic Director Jonathan Church

Stages annual Summer Festival Season April–Oct in Festival and Minerva Theatres together with a year-round education programme, autumn touring programme and youth theatre Christmas show. Unsolicited scripts are not accepted.

Theatre

Clwyd Theatr Cymru Theatre for Young People

Mold, Flintshire CH7 1YA
tel (01352) 701575
email nerys.edwards@clwyd-theatr-cymru.co.uk
website www.ctctyp.co.uk,
www.clwyd-theatr-cymru.co.uk
Writer & Director Tim Baker, *Producer* Anne
Plenderleith, *Co-ordinator* Jane Meakin,
Administrator Nerys Edwards, *Outreach Worker* Emyr
John

Dedicated to creating arts experiences for children
and young people. Also the home of Clwyd Theatr
Cymru.

Contact Theatre Company

Oxford Road, Manchester M15 6JA
tel 0161 274 0600
website www.contactmcr.com
Artistic Director Matt Fenton, *Head of Creative
Development* Suzie Henderson

Multidisciplinary arts organisation focused on
working with and for young people aged 13–35.

The Edge Theatre and Arts Centre

Manchester Road, Chorlton, Manchester M21 9JG
tel 0161 282 9776
email info@edgetheatre.co.uk
website www.edgetheatre.co.uk
Artistic Director Janine Waters

Produces and presents theatre for all ages, including
families and children. Musical and children's theatre
specialities. 70-seat flexible theatre space and studio
spaces. Also runs classes, courses and workshops in
theatre, dance, music, writing and other creative
genres. Theatre Club for ages 5–8; Edge Youth
Theatre for ages 9–12 and for 13–18. Founded 2011.

The Egg

Sawclose, Bath BA1 1ET
tel (01225) 823409 (reception and administration)
email egg.reception@theatreroyal.org.uk
website www.theatreroyal.org.uk/the-egg

Part of the Theatre Royal Bath. Purpose-built theatre
for young people and their families. Hosts and
produces shows for children and young people
alongside a year-round participation and outreach
programme for people aged 0–21. Opened 2005.

Everyman Theatre

7 Regent Street, Cheltenham, Glos. GL50 1HQ
tel (01242) 512515
email admin@everymantheatre.org.uk
website www.everymantheatre.org.uk
Creative Director Paul Milton

Regional presenting and producing theatre
promoting a wide range of plays. Small-scale
experimental, youth and educational work

encouraged in The Studio Theatre. Contact the
Creative Director before submitting material.

HOME: Theatre

2 Tony Wilson Place, First Street,
Manchester M15 4FN
tel 0161 228 7621
email info@homemcr.org
website www.homemcr.org
Artistic Director Walter Meierjohann

World classic drama, international and new writing,
adaptations and cross-art projects. Produces one
family show a year. Formed following the merger of
Cornerhouse and Library Theatre Company.
HOME's purpose-built centre for international
contemporary art, theatre and film opened in Spring
2015.

Leeds Children's Theatre

c/o The Carriageworks Theatre, The Electric Press,
3 Millennium Square, Leeds LS2 3AD
email emma@leeds-childrens-theatre.co.uk
website www.leeds-childrens-theatre.co.uk

One of the many amateur dramatic societies based at
The Carriageworks Theatre. A member of the Leeds
Civic Arts Guild, Leeds Children's Theatre stages two
shows each year. It is dedicated to the principle of
quality, affordable entertainment in order to
introduce the theatrical experience to young children.
It covers most aspects of theatrical production.
Membership is open to all young people. Workshops
for children of all ages. Adult membership is also
available. Founded 1935.

Norwich Puppet Theatre

St James, Whitefriars, Norwich NR3 1TN
tel (01603) 629921 (box office), (01603) 615564
(admin.)
email info@puppettheatre.co.uk
website www.puppettheatre.co.uk
Director Joy Haynes

Norwich Puppet Theatre is the base for a professional
company which creates and presents its own
productions at the theatre, as well as touring to
schools and venues throughout the UK and to
international venues and festivals. Founded 1979.

Nottingham Playhouse

Nottingham Playhouse Trust Ltd, Wellington Circus,
Nottingham NG1 5AF
tel 0115 947 4361
website www.nottinghamplayhouse.co.uk
Artistic Director Giles Croft

Works closely with communities of Nottingham and
Nottinghamshire. Takes six months to read
unsolicited MSS.

Roundabout is the Theatre in Education company
of Nottingham Playhouse. Produces plays and
workshops for children and young people, and offers

Theatre

training and support for teachers. Since 1973, Roundabout has commissioned and produced nearly 300 new plays for schools, young people and their families. Submissions are accepted for reading as part of an assessment procedure but almost all productions are commissioned. See www.nottinghamplayhouse.co.uk/education.

Queen's Theatre, Hornchurch
(Havering Theatre Trust Ltd)
Billet Lane, Hornchurch, Essex RM11 1QT
tel (01708) 462362
email info@queens-theatre.co.uk
website www.queens-theatre.co.uk
Chair, Havering Theatre Trust Dennis Roycroft

500-seat producing theatre serving outer East London with a permanent company of actors/musicians presenting eight main house and two TIE productions each year. Unsolicited scripts may be returned unread. Also offers writers' groups at various levels.

The Queen's Youth Theatre Programme provides the opportunity for young people aged 7–19 to become involved in drama. There is no selection process on the basis of experience or ability. See website for further details.

Royal Shakespeare Company
The Royal Shakespeare Theatre, Waterside, Stratford-upon-Avon, Warks. CV37 6BB
tel (01789) 296655
email literary@rsc.org.uk
website www.rsc.org.uk
Artistic Director Gregory Doran, *Deputy Artistic Director* Erica Whyman, *Literary Manager* Pippa Hill

Based in Stratford-upon-Avon, the Company produces a core repertoire of Shakespeare alongside modern classics, new plays and the work of Shakespeare's contemporaries. The Company commissions new plays, new translations and new adaptations that illuminate the themes and concerns of Shakespeare and his contemporaries for a modern audience. The Literary department does not accept unsolicited work but rather seeks out writers it wishes to work with or commission, and monitors the work of emerging writers in production in the UK and internationally. Writers are welcome to invite the Literary department to readings, showcases or productions by emailing the address above. The RSC studio theatre, The Other Place, is due to re-open in 2016 with a programme of cutting-edge new work.

Sherman Cymru
Senghennydd Road, Cardiff CF24 4YE
tel 029-2064 6900
email margaret.jones@shermancymru.co.uk
website www.shermancymru.co.uk
Artistic Director Rachel O'Riordan, *Executive Director* Margaret Jones

Produces two Christmas productions (under and over 7s) and actively seeks high-quality work for children and young people as part of its programming. Commissions writers for projects with young people. Participatory work with youth theatres for 5–25 age range. Founded 2007.

TOURING COMPANIES

Arad Goch
Stryd Y Baddon, Aberystwyth, Ceredigion SY23 2NN
tel (01970) 617998
email post@aradgoch.org
website www.aradgoch.org
Artistic Director Jeremy Turner

Performs in Welsh and English and tours nationally throughout Wales, and occasionally abroad. The company is particularly interested in enabling children and young people to recognise and appreciate their own unique cultural identity though theatre. Some of the company's work is based on traditional material and children's literature but it also commissions new work from experienced dramatists and new writers. Arad Goch performs in theatres and other locations, including schools, and also offers seminars/workshops for students and teachers. The company has its own production house in Aberystwyth which is used by other arts and community organisations and where it programmes a variety of participatory activities for young people. It organises the biennial 'Agor Drysau–Opening Doors' Wales International Festival of Performing Arts for Young Audiences (www.agordrysau-openingdoors.org). Founded 1989.

Booster Cushion Theatre
75 How Wood, Park Street, St Albans, Herts. AL2 2RW
tel (01727) 873874
email admin@booster-cushion.co.uk
website www.booster-cushion.co.uk
Director Philip Sherman

Comical theatre company formed especially to re-tell traditional tales to primary-school pupils and their families using surprising Big Books. BCT has performed to over 500,000 people in schools, libraries, museums and theatres across the UK using pop-up books up to 3m tall and concertina books over 5m wide.

All productions are solo performing shows using mime, voice and some sign language. They involve a high level of audience participation. Each show is completely portable and can be performed inside or outside – the technical requirements are minimal. Founded 1989.

Cahoots NI
109–113 Royal Avenue, Belfast BT1 1FF
tel 028-9043 4349
email info@cahootsni.com
website www.cahootsni.com
Artistic Director Paul Bosco McEneaney

Professional children's touring theatre company which concentrates on the visual potential of theatre and capitalises upon the age-old popularity of magic and illusion as an essential ingredient in the art of entertaining. It aims to provide inspiring theatrical experiences for children and to encourage appreciation of the arts in children from all sections of society. Each production is at the centre of a body of outreach work designed to maximise artistic potential, customise the individual theatre experience and extend the imaginative life of the piece beyond the actual event. Founded 2001.

Classworks Theatre

Unit 12, Barnwell Business Park, Barnwell Road, Cambridge CB5 8UY
tel (01223) 210883
email jenny@classworks.org.uk
website www.classworks.org.uk
Artistic Director Jenny Culank

Professional touring company which focuses on new work for and with young people as well as the wider community. Also provides supporting workshops. Tours locally and nationally to small- and mid-scale arts venues. Founded 1983.

Cornelius & Jones

49 Carters Close, Sherington, Newport Pagnell MK16 9NW
tel/fax (01908) 612593
email admin@corneliusjones.com
website www.corneliusjones.com
Co-directors Neil Canham and Sue Leech

Small touring theatre company which performs for children and adults in schools and theatres. The company creates its own productions and commissions scripts and music. Founded 1986.

The Hiss & Boo Company Ltd

1 Nyes Hill, Wineham Lane, Bolney, West Sussex RH17 5SD
tel (01444) 881707
email email@hissboo.co.uk
website www.hissboo.co.uk
Managing Director Ian Liston

Little scope for new plays, but will consider comedy thrillers/chillers and plays/musicals for children. Produces pantomimes. No unsolicited scripts – email first. Plays/synopses will be returned only if accompanied by a sae.

Kazzum Arts Project

Oxford House, Derbyshire Street, London E2 6HG
email hello@kazzum.org
website www.kazzum.org
Artistic Director Daryl Beeton

Creates playful theatrical experiences in unusual places that involve the imaginations of diverse young audiences. A theatre and participative arts company which applies an innovative approach to producing theatre that allows young people to become part of a captivating experience in a safe environment. These aims are achieved through:

• outdoor productions and interactive environments for audiences aged 8 and under, and their families;
• promenade and site-specific work for audiences aged 10 and over;
• 'Pathways', a programme of arts activities for young people across Greater London's refugee and new migrant communities;
• education and outreach work in schools and community settings;
• cultural development opportunities. Founded 1989.

Konflux Theatre in Education

Commer House, Station Road, Tadcaster, Leeds LS24 9JF
tel/fax (01937) 832740
email info@konfluxtheatre.com
website www.konfluxtheatre.com
Artistic Director Anthony Koncsol

Theatre in Education company and accredited Gifted & Talented provider and Arts Award Supporter. Works with 1,000 schools each year, building close working relationships with teachers and other education professionals and ensuring its programmes and their delivery are tailored to the needs of the organisation. Konflux's Play in a Day workshops are designed to build confidence and promote team work. They give pupils the opportunity to learn through drama, increase their acting skills, and present a performance back to peers and parents. Founded 1997.

The Little Angel Theatre

14 Dagmar Passage, London N1 2DN
tel 020-7226 1787
email info@littleangeltheatre.com
website www.littleangeltheatre.com
Interim Director Slavka Jovanovic

Committed to working with children and families through schools, the local community and the wider community through its extensive touring programme. Little Angel Theatre develops innovative projects, implements improved access to their creative work, increases opportunities for participation and provides stimulating learning and creativity for all using puppetry. Termly activities are run for children, families and schools, including INSET training for teachers. Regular introductory and professional development courses are run throughout the year for teenagers and adults.

Productions last approximately an hour and many are toured to theatres, arts centres and festivals around the UK. Little Angel Theatre is committed to its education programme and continues to work with schools, youth groups and Education Authorities.

M6 Theatre Company

Studio Theatre, Hamer C.P. School, Albert Royds Street, Rochdale, Lancs. OL16 2SU

Theatre

tel (01706) 355898
email admin@m6theatre.co.uk
website www.m6theatre.co.uk
Contact Gilly Baskeyfield

Touring theatre company specialising in creating and delivering innovative theatre for young audiences.

Magic Carpet Theatre
18 Church Street, Sutton on Hull,
East Yorkshire HU7 4TS
tel (01482) 709939
email jon@magiccarpettheatre.com
website www.magiccarpettheatre.com
Director Jon Marshall

Touring company which incorporates the traditional skills of variety theatre, the circus and puppets including clown, slapstick and physical theatre to make highly entertaining productions for schools and theatres. Founded 1982.

Moby Duck
12 Reservoir Retreat, Birmingham B16 9EH
tel 0121 242 0400
email guyhutchins@blueyonder.co.uk
website www.moby-duck.com
Contact Guy Hutchins

Produces stimulating, challenging and accessible work for young people and adults that celebrates the common ground between cultures. Tours throughout the UK, presenting new cross-artform, cross-cultural work to young children and adults in small- and middle-scale theatres, arts centres, village halls and schools. Also performs in less conventional venues, e.g. a farm equipment museum, a Crown Court and a three-hole Georgian privy! Performances are storytelling-led and have included live Karnatic music, western jazz, Bharatanatyam dance, masks, mime, puppetry, visual arts, digital media and Eastern and Western cooking. Founded 1999.

Oily Cart
Smallwood School Annexe, Smallwood Road,
London SW17 0TW
tel 020-8672 6329
email oilies@oilycart.org.uk
website www.oilycart.org.uk
Artistic Director Tim Webb

Touring company staging at least two children's productions a year. Multi-sensory, highly interactive work is produced, often in specially constructed installations for three specific audiences: children aged 6 months–2 years, children aged 3–6 years, and young people (3–19) with profound and multiple learning disabilities or autism. Considers scripts from new writers but at present all work is generated from within the company. Founded 1981.

Playtime Theatre Company
18 Bennells Avenue, Whitstable, Kent CT5 2HP
tel (01227) 266272

email playtime@dircon.co.uk
website www.playtimetheatre.co.uk
Writer and Director Nickolas Champion, *Workshop Director* Sara Kettlewell, *Admin* Catherine Dyson

Touring theatre company specialising in theatre for children, performing in schools and theatres nationally and internationally. Has an extensive drama workshop programme, running adjunct to performances or as a bespoke entity. Founded 1983.

Proteus Theatre Company
Proteus Creation Space, Council Road, Basingstoke,
Hants RG21 3DH
tel (01256) 354541
email info@proteustheatre.com
website www.proteustheatre.com
Artistic Director and Chief Executive Mary Swan

Small-scale touring company particularly committed to new writing and new work, education and community collaborations. Produces three touring shows per year plus several community projects. Founded 1979.

Replay Theatre Company
Skainos Square, 239 Newtownards Road,
Belfast BT4 1AF
tel 028-945 4562
email info@replaytheatreco.org
website www.replaytheatreco.org
Artistic Director Anna Newell

Provides professional theatre that entertains, educates and stimulates children and young people. It produces educational theatre performances, activities and accompanying resource materials for primary, secondary and special schools throughout Northern Ireland and the Republic of Ireland. Founded 1988.

Scamp Theatre
44 Church Lane, Arlesey, Beds. SG15 6UX
tel (01462) 734843
email admin@scamptheatre.com
website www.scamptheatre.com
Directors Jennifer Sutherland and Louise Callow

Produces high-quality theatre for audiences of all ages, with an increased focus on the adaptation of children's literature, including works by Julia Donaldson. With productions constantly touring, Scamp has operated in London, on tour and at the world's leading venues and festivals. Does not accept unsolicited manuscripts. Founded 2003.

Sixth Sense Theatre for Young People
c/o The Wyvern Theatre, Theatre Square,
Swindon SN1 1QN
tel (01793) 614864
email info@sixthsensetheatre.com
website www.sixthsensetheatre.com
Artistic Director Mark Powell

Professional theatre company prioritising work with young people. It promotes theatre and helps young people explore issues that are important to them. Each year, the company produces both issue-based and creative theatre productions and performs in schools, theatres and arts centres in Swindon and the South West region. These productions are supported by additional young people-led work, workshops, training sessions and other projects.

Theatr Iolo
Chapter, Market Road, Canton, Cardiff CF14 3HS
tel 029-2061 3782
website www.theatriolo.com
Artistic Director Kevin Lewis, *Producer* John Williams

Aims to produce and programme the best of live theatre, making it widely accessible to children and young people across Wales and beyond.

Theatr Spectacle Theatre
Coleg Morgannwg Rhondda, Llwynypia, Tonypandy, Rhondda Cynon Tâf CF40 2TQ
tel (01443) 430700
email info@spectacletheatre.co.uk
website www.spectacletheatre.co.uk
Artistic Director Steve Davis

Community theatre company. Also offers workshops, training and mentoring.

Theatre Centre
Shoreditch Town Hall, 380 Old Street, London EC1V 9LT
tel 020-7729 3066
email admin@theatre-centre.co.uk
website www.theatre-centre.co.uk
Artistic Director Natalie Wilson

Young people's theatre company producing plays and workshops which tour nationally and internationally. Productions are staged in schools, arts centres and other venues. Recently produced work includes *The Muddy Choir* by Jesse Briton, *Advice for the Young at Heart* by Roy Williams, *The Day the Waters Came* by Lisa Evans, *Under a Foreign Sky* by Paula B Stanic, and *The Littlest Quirky* by Naomi Cortes. Also manages writing awards – see website for details. Keen to hear from writers from ethnic minority groups. Founded 1953.

The Theatre Company Blah Blah Blah
Roundhay Road Resource Centre, 233–237 Roundhay Road, Leeds LS8 4HS
tel 0113 380 5646
email admin@blahs.co.uk
website www.blahs.co.uk
Artistic Director Deborah Pakkar-Hull

Theatre in Education company which specialises in touring theatre for children and young people and residency work in schools. The company will be reconnecting with internationally celebrated playwright Mike Kenny in their thirtieth anniversary year to share in re-imagining Theatre in Education for the twenty-first century, re-working 'Bag Dancing', a classic from the Blahs back catalogue and creating new work for Partition in 2017. Founded 1985.

Theatre Hullabaloo
The Meeting Rooms, 5 Skinnergate, Darlington DL3 7NB
tel (01325) 352004
email info@theatrehullabaloo.org.uk
website www.theatrehullabaloo.org.uk
Creative Producer Miranda Thain

Specialist theatre company in the North East creating and touring work for young audiences. Creates theatre experiences for children and young people which aim to contribute to their emotional, spiritual and social development. Promotes greater awareness of the value of theatre to children and young people by working with teachers and others through courses, events and publications. Tours professional theatre productions to schools and venues within Tees Valley, the North East and nationally. Organiser of the annual Take Off Festival since 1994.

Travelling Light Theatre Company
Barton Hill Settlement, 41–43 Ducie Road, Lawrence Hill, Bristol BS2 0AX
tel 0117 377 3166
email info@travellinglighttheatre.org.uk
website www.travellinglighttheatre.org.uk
Artistic Producer Jude Merrill

Professional theatre company producing work for young audiences. Collaborates with many different arts organisations to create original, cross-artform productions that inspire and engage young people. Tours to theatres and festivals throughout the UK and abroad as well as to local schools. Founded 1984.

Tutti Frutti Productions
Shine, Harehills Road, Harehills, Leeds LS8 5DR
tel 0113 388 0027
email emma@tutti-frutti.org.uk
website www.tutti-frutti.org.uk
Artistic Director Wendy Harris

Professional theatre aimed specifically at family audiences (age 3+ and accompanying adults). Productions are adaptations of children's books and stories or specially commissioned new shows and include original music together with different art forms, i.e. puppetry, dance, movement. Tours nationally and internationally and performs in a host of different small-scale venues, including arts centres, village halls, rural touring schemes and schools, undertaking approx. 200 performances a year. Founded 1991.

Societies, prizes and festivals

The Society of Authors

The Society of Authors is an independent trade union, representing writers' interests in all aspects of the writing profession.

Founded over 100 years ago, the Society now has more than 9,000 members. It has a professional staff, responsible to a Management Committee of 12 authors, and a Council (an advisory body meeting twice a year) consisting of 60 eminent writers.

Specialist groups

Specialist groups within the Society serve particular needs: the Broadcasting Group, the Children's Writers and Illustrators Group (see below), the Educational Writers Group and the Translators Association. There are also groups representing Scotland and the North of England.

The Children's Writers and Illustrators Group

The Children's Writers and Illustrators Group (CWIG) was formed in 1963. Besides furthering the interests of writers and artists and defending them whenever they are threatened, the Group seeks to bring members together professionally and socially, and in general to raise the status of children's books.

The Group has its own Executive Committee with representation on the Management Committee of the Society of Authors. Meetings and socials are held on a regular basis. Speakers have so far included publishers, librarians, booksellers and reviewers, and many distinguished writers and illustrators for children.

The annual subscription to the Society of Authors includes membership of all its groups. Membership of the CWIG is open

Membership

The Society of Authors
84 Drayton Gardens, London SW10 9SB
tel 020-7373 6642
email info@societyofauthors.org,
membership@societyofauthors.org
website www.societyofauthors.org
Chief Executive Nicola Solomon

Membership entitles authors to advice on all aspects of the writing profession and confidential clause-by-clause vetting of any contract offered. Members also receive a quarterly journal, free ALCS membership and a wide range of benefits, including offers on books and professional insurance.

Membership is available to authors who have had a full-length work published, broadcast or performed commercially. Membership is also open to those who have had published or commercially performed an equivalent body of literary work; owners or administrators of a deceased author's estate; those who have been published on a non-traditional basis (e.g. self-published or on a print-on-demand/ebook-only basis) and who meet sales criteria to indicate profit. Those who do not meet the criteria for Membership may apply to become an Associate, for instance if they have been offered a contract for publication or agent's representation.

Both Members and Associates are subject to election, and to the payment of subscription fees. The annual subscription fee (tax deductible) is £95, or £68 for those who are 35 and under and not yet earning a significant income from writing. From the second year of subscription, discounted and quarterly Direct Debit options are available and there are concessionary rates for over 65s who are no longer earning a significant amount of income from writing. See website for full details.

to writers and illustrators who have had at least one book published by a reputable British publisher, five short stories or more than 20 minutes of material broadcast on national radio or television. Election is at the discretion of the Committee.

The Society and members

Through its permanent staff (including a solicitor), the Society is able to give its members a comprehensive personal and professional service covering the business aspects of authorship, including:

> 'It does no harm to repeat, as often as you can, "Without me the literary industry would not exist: the publishers, the agents, the sub-agents, the accountants, the libel lawyers, the departments of literature, the professors, the theses, the books of criticism, the reviewers, the book pages – all this vast and proliferating edifice is because of this small, patronised, put-down and underpaid person."' – *Doris Lessing*

• advising on negotiations, including the individual vetting of contracts, clause by clause, and assessing their terms both financial and otherwise;
• helping with members' queries, major or minor, over any aspect of the business of writing;
• taking up complaints on behalf of members on any issue concerned with the business of authorship;
• pursuing legal actions for breach of contract, copyright infringement, and the non-payment of royalties and fees, when the risk and cost preclude individual action by a member and issues of general concern to the profession are at stake;
• holding conferences, seminars, meetings and social occasions;
• producing a comprehensive range of publications, free of charge to members, including the Society's quarterly journal, the *Author*.

The Society frequently secures improved conditions and better returns for members. It is common for members to report that, through the help and facilities offered, they have saved more, and sometimes substantially more, than their annual subscription.

Further membership benefits include special offers and discounts on books, places to stay, insurance and other products and services, and free membership of the Authors' Licensing and Collecting Society (ALCS; see page 322).

The Society and authors

The Society lobbies Members of Parliament, ministers and government departments on all issues of concern to writers, litigates in matters of importance to authors and campaigns for better terms for writers. It is recognised by the BBC for the purpose of negotiating rates for writers' contributions to radio drama, as well as for the broadcasting of published material. It was instrumental in setting up the ALCS, which collects and distributes fees from reprography and other methods whereby copyright material is exploited without direct payment to the originators.

The Society keeps in close touch with the Association of Authors' Agents, the Booksellers Association and Publishers Association, the British Council, the Department for Culture, Media and Sport, the National Union of Journalists and the Writers' Guild of Great Britain. It is a member of the European Writers Council and the British Copyright Council.

Awards

The following awards are administered:
• the Authors' Foundation and Kathleen Blundell Trust, which give grants to assist authors working on their next book;
• the Francis Head Bequest and the Authors' Contingency Fund, which assist authors who, through physical mishap, are temporarily unable to maintain themselves or their families;

• Travelling Scholarships, which give honorary awards;
• two prizes for first novels: the Betty Trask Awards and the McKitterick Prize;
• the Somerset Maugham Awards for a full-length published work;
• two poetry awards: the Eric Gregory Awards and the Cholmondeley Awards;
• the Tom-Gallon Award for short story writers;
• two radio drama prizes: the Imison Award for a writer new to radio drama and the Tinniswood Award;
• awards for translations from Arabic, Dutch/Flemish, French, German, Greek, Italian, Portuguese, Spanish and Swedish into English;
• educational and medical book awards.

The Alliance of Independent Authors

The ALLi is a professional association of self-publishing writers and advisors.

The Alliance of Independent Authors

The Alliance of Independent Authors (ALLi) is a global collaborative collective of self-publishing writers. It was founded in 2012 at the London Book Fair by former trade published author and literary agent, Orna Ross, in response to her personal experience of self-publishing and she has been named 'One of the 100 most influential people in publishing' for this work.

ALLi has an Advisory Board of world-class authors and educators, bloggers and service providers, all of whom hold the self-publishing choice in high esteem and all with exceptional knowledge and skills. Their contribution is supplemented by ALLi's global ambassadors, who aid writers to create vibrant self-publishing literary communities in their local areas or online.

A rapidly growing organisation, with members all over the world, ALLi invites 'indie' authors to come together in a spirit of mutual cooperation, empowerment and service to the reading and writing community. As well as encouraging ethics and excellence in the writing, printing, formatting and promotion of self-published books, ALLi advances, supports and advocates for the interests of independent, self-publishing authors everywhere. Its Open Up To Indie Authors Campaign promotes the interests of indie authors within the literary and publishing industries – engaging with booksellers, festivals, prize-giving committees, libraries, book clubs and the media.

ALLi's core mission is the democratisation of writing and publishing.

Membership

The Alliance of Independent Authors
Free Word Centre, 60 Farringdon Road, London EC1R 3GA
email press@allianceindependentauthors.org
website http://allianceindependentauthors.org, www.SelfPublishingAdvice.org

At ALLi, 'independent' is an inclusive description, including trade-published, self-published and hybrid authors. There are 4 grades of membership (see website).

Society of Children's Book Writers & Illustrators

The Society of Children's Book Writers & Illustrators (SCBWI) is the only international professional organisation dedicated to serving people who share a vital interest in children's literature, magazines, film, television and/or multimedia.

Whether you are a professional children's writer or illustrator, or a newcomer to the field, SCBWI has plenty to offer you, from local to national to international events, from advice on getting your first deal to help in navigating your career as a writer or illustrator. Established in 1971, SCBWI now has over 22,000 members in 70 regional chapters worldwide. Membership benefits include professional development and networking opportunities, marketing information, events, publications, online profiles, grants and awards.

What does SCBWI British Isles do?

SCBWI British Isles is a dynamic and friendly chapter of 850 members, which aims to support aspiring and published writers and illustrators and provide opportunities for them to network, hone their craft and develop their careers. Events include an annual two-day conference, a fiction and picture book retreat, an annual Agents' Party, the Industry Insiders series (six talks a year in London aimed at professional development on a variety of topics), the Illustrators' series (Saturday workshops with a hands-on craft element), sketch and scrawl crawls, author masterclasses and PULSE events (SCBWI Pulse provides professional development opportunities for published members). A network of regional organisers run local critique groups, workshops and social events across the British Isles.

What SCBWI does for its members

• SCBWI is a professional guild. It speaks as a consolidated global voice for professional children's writers and illustrators. In recent years, SCBWI has successfully lobbied for such issues as new copyright legislation, equitable treatment of authors and artists, and fair contract terms.

• It keeps members up to date with industry developments through the SCBWI PULSE series of events, with opportunities to learn more about the 'business' of writing and illustrating, to do school visits at festivals and to network with librarians and booksellers at exclusive events.

• It offers members invaluable exposure to editors, art directors and agents through one-to-one manuscript or portfolio reviews at the annual conference and retreat, the members-only Agents' Party, and the Slush Pile Challenge and biennial SCBWI Undiscovered Voices (www.undiscoveredvoices.com) competitions.

• It supports professional development for members to hone their craft through the Masterclass series, conference workshops and highly successful critique groups.

• It gives members increased visibility online with a free profile on its website, which is a point of call for agents, art directors and editors.

• It provides support and a network of like-minded people, helping to answer members' queries through a variety of online resources, including an email forum and social networking site.

• It facilitates networking opportunities with professionals worldwide.

• Publications include the *Bulletin*, the SCBWI international magazine, *Words & Pictures* newsletter blog with daily content (www.wordsandpics.org), and resources including the annual publications and market guide.

• Website resources include book launch parties, members' bookshop, discussion boards, illustrator gallery, find-a-speaker search facility, webinars and podcasts.

Further information

Society of Children's Book Writers & Illustrators (SCBWI)
website http://britishisles.scbwi.org
Regional Advisor (Chair) Natascha Biebow
email ra@britishscbwi.org
Membership Coordinator Anita Loughrey
email membership@britishscbwi.org
Membership £50 p.a.

Awards and grants

The SCBWI administers a number of awards and grants:

• The Golden and Crystal Kite Awards are for the most outstanding books published by SCBWI members each year, voted for by SCBWI peers.

• The Sid Fleischman Humour Award is presented to authors whose work exemplifies the excellence of writing in the genre of humour.

• The annual Spark Award recognises excellence in a children's book published through a non-traditional publishing route.

• The Book Launch Award provides authors or illustrators with $2,000 in funds to help the promotion of their newly published work and take the marketing strategy into their own creative hands.

• The Emerging Voices Award fosters the emergence of diverse voices in children's books.

• The Multi-Cultural Work-in-Progress Grant assists writers in the completion of a manuscript featuring a voice traditionally underrepresented in children's books.

• The Magazine Merit Awards are presented for outstanding original magazine work for young people.

• The Sue Alexander Most Promising New Work Award is for the best manuscript submitted for individual critique at the LA conference.

• The Martha Weston Grant encourages authors and illustrators to nurture their creativity in a different genre of children's books.

• The Lee Bennett Hopkins Poetry Award recognises and encourages the publication of an excellent book of poetry or anthology for children or young adults (given every three years).

• The Jane Yolen Mid-List Author Grant honours the contribution of mid-list authors.

• Several Work-in-progress Grants are available each year.

• The Tomie dePaola Illustrator Award for an illustrator of promise is chosen by Tomie himself.

• The Portfolio Award is presented to the best art portfolio on view at the Juried Portfolio Display at the LA conference.

• There are four Student Illustrator Scholarships for full-time graduate and undergraduate students of children's book illustration.

• There are two Student Writer Scholarships to the Summer and Winter conferences for full-time university students in an English or Creative Writing programme.

• There are two Annual Conference Scholarships to attend the annual SCBWI-BI conference.

See also...

- *Book Trust*, page 382
- *Seven Stories – National Centre for Children's Books*, page 385
- *The Children's Book Circle*, page 387
- *Federation of Children's Book Groups*, page 388

Book Trust

Book Trust is the largest literature organisation in the UK.

Book Trust is an independent reading and writing charity that makes a nationwide impact on individuals, families, communities and culture in the UK. Book Trust works to build a literate, connected and creative society by empowering people through reading and writing.

Book Trust runs national bookgifting programmes and campaigns which promote books and reading for all ages. The organisation has gifted over 52 million books to families since 1992. It also administers a number of literary prizes for adults (including the Baileys Women's Prize for Fiction, BBC National Short Story Award and David Cohen Prize for Literature) and for children (see below), as well as promoting books and reading for all ages through various campaigns.

Book Trust and children

• The children's area of the website has a searchable database of more than 5,000 book reviews, resources for teachers, illustrators' galleries, interviews with authors and illustrators, games and puzzles and news about children's book prizes and events happening throughout the UK.

• Book Trust coordinates four national bookgifting programmes. Bookstart offers the gift of free books to all children at two key ages before they start school, to inspire a love of reading that will give children a flying start in life. Booktime promotes reading for pleasure by giving a book pack to children across the UK shortly after they start school. The Bookbuzz programme runs in participating schools to give their students the opportunity to choose their own book to keep from a list of 17 titles suitable for 11-year-olds and selected by a panel of experts. The Letterbox Club provides a parcel of books and other materials for looked after children, every month for six months.

• Book Trust runs the Roald Dahl Funny Prize (see page 412), which aims to celebrate, publicise and honour the funniest books of the year. This is part of a wider campaign to promote and draw attention to humour in children's literature. The Prize is currently on hold.

• Book Trust administers the Blue Peter Book Awards (see page 410).

• Book Trust administers the Waterstones Children's Laureate (Chris Riddell 2015–17); see page 411.

Further information

Book Trust
G8 Battersea Studios, 80 Silverthorne Road, London SW8 3HE
tel 020-7801 8800
email query@booktrust.org.uk
website www.booktrust.org.uk

Top ten children's books

To mark Children's Book Week 2013, Book Trust invited book fans of all ages to pick their ultimate storybook to read before the age of 14 from a list voted as the 100 best children's books from the last century (see page 382). With 24,000 votes cast, the top ten is as follows:

1 *Harry Potter and the Philosopher's Stone* by J.K. Rowling
2 *The Hunger Games* by Suzanne Collins
3 *The BFG* by Roald Dahl, illustrated by Quentin Blake
4 *The Very Hungry Caterpillar* by Eric Carle
5 *Winnie-the-Pooh* by A.A. Milne, illustrated by E.H. Shepherd
6 *The Cat in the Hat* by Dr Seuss
7 *The Fellowship of the Ring* by J.R.R. Tolkien
8 *Charlotte's Web* by E.B. White
9 *Northern Lights* by Philip Pullman
10 *The Lion, the Witch and the Wardrobe* by C.S. Lewis

BOOK TRUST'S TOP 100 BOOKS FOR CHILDREN

To mark Children's Book Week 2013, Book Trust invited book fans of all ages to pick their ultimate storybook to read before the age of 14. This is a list of the top 100 books. See page 382 for the favourite ten books and www.booktrust.org.uk for more information.

12–14 age group

Watership Down Richard Adams
Noughts and Crosses Malorie Blackman
Forever Judy Blume
The Boy in the Striped Pyjamas John Boyne
Junk Melvin Burgess
Looking for JJ Anne Cassidy
The Hunger Games Suzanne Collins
The Graveyard Book Neil Gaiman
Maggot Moon Sally Gardner
The Owl Service Alan Garner
Coram Boy Jamila Gavin
The Curious Incident of the Dog in the Night-Time Mark Haddon
Stormbreaker Anthony Horowitz
The Kite Rider Geraldine McCaughrean
The Knife of Never Letting Go Patrick Ness
Life: An Exploded Diagram Mal Peet
Northern Lights Philip Pullman
The Ruby in the Smoke Philip Pullman
Witch Child Celia Rees
Mortal Engines Philip Reeve
Angus, Thongs and Full-Frontal Snogging Louise Rennison
How I Live Now Meg Rosoff
Revolver Marcus Sedgwick
I Capture the Castle Dodie Smith
The Fellowship of The Ring J.R.R. Tolkien

9–11 age group

The Wolves of Willoughby Chase Joan Aiken
Skellig David Almond
Carrie's War Nina Bawden
Artemis Fowl Eoin Colfer
Millions Frank Cottrell Boyce
The Witches Roald Dahl
Matilda Roald Dahl and Quentin Blake
Flour Babies Anne Fine
Once Morris Gleitzman
The Adventures of Tintin Hergé
Journey to the River Sea Eva Ibbotson
Stig of the Dump by Clive King
The Lion, the Witch and the Wardrobe C.S. Lewis
Goodnight Mister Tom Michelle Magorian
Private Peaceful Michael Morpurgo
A Monster Calls Patrick Ness
The Borrowers Mary Norton
Truckers Terry Pratchett
Swallows and Amazons Arthur Ransome

Harry Potter and the Philosopher's Stone J.K. Rowling
Holes Louis Sachar
The Little Prince Antoine de Saint-Exupery
Ballet Shoes Noel Streatfeild
The Hobbit J.R.R. Tolkien
The Story of Tracy Beaker Jacqueline Wilson

6–8 age group

The Enchanted Wood Enid Blyton
Five on a Treasure Island Enid Blyton
A Bear Called Paddington Michael Bond
The Milly-Molly-Mandy Storybook Joyce Lankester Brisley
Flat Stanley Jeff Brown
Clarice Bean, That's Me Lauren Child
That Rabbit Belongs to Emily Brown Cressida Cowell
The BFG Roald Dahl
The Story of Babar Jean De Brunhoff
My Naughty Little Sister Dorothy Edwards
Asterix the Gaul René Goscinny
Amazing Grace Mary Hoffman and Caroline Binch
Finn Family Moomintroll Tove Jansson
The Queen's Nose Dick King-Smith
The Sheep-Pig Dick King-Smith
Diary of a Wimpy Kid Jeff Kinney
Pippi Longstocking Astrid Lindgren
Winnie-the-Pooh A.A. Milne
The Worst Witch Jill Murphy
The True Story of the Three Little Pigs Jon Scieszka and Lane Smith
Horrid Henry Francesca Simon and Tony Ross
The Arrival Shaun Tan
Charlotte's Web E.B. White
Little House in the Big Woods Laura Ingalls Wilder
Mister Magnolia Quentin Blake

0–5 age group

Each Peach Pear Plum Janet and Allan Ahlberg
The Jolly Postman or Other People's Letters Janet and Allan Ahlberg
The Snowman Raymond Briggs
Gorilla Anthony Browne
Would You Rather? John Burningham
Dear Zoo Rod Campbell
The Very Hungry Caterpillar Eric Carle
I Will Not Ever Never Eat a Tomato Lauren Child
Princess Smartypants Babette Cole
Hairy Maclary from Donaldson's Dairy Lynley Dodd
Room on the Broom Julia Donaldson and Axel Scheffler
Ten Little Fingers and Ten Little Toes Mem Fox and Helen Oxenbury
Little Mouse's Big Book of Fears Emily Gravett

Where's Spot? Eric Hill
Dogger Shirley Hughes
Lost and Found Oliver Jeffers
The Tiger Who Came to Tea Judith Kerr
I Want My Hat Back Jon Klassen
Not Now, Bernard David McKee
Meg and Mog Helen Nicholl and Jan Pienkowski

We're Going on a Bear Hunt Michael Rosen and Helen Oxenbury
I Want My Potty! Tony Ross
Where the Wild Things Are Maurice Sendak
The Cat in the Hat Dr Seuss
The Elephant and the Bad Baby Elfrida Vipont and Raymond Briggs

Seven Stories – National Centre for Children's Books

At Seven Stories the rich heritage of British children's books is collected, explored and celebrated.

seven stories
National Centre for Children's Books

Once upon a time an idea was born on the banks of the Tyne to create a national home for children's literature – a place where the original work of authors and illustrators could be collected, treasured and celebrated. After ten years of pioneering work by founding directors Elizabeth Hammill and Mary Briggs, that dream became a reality. In August 2005 Seven Stories, the Centre for Children's Books, opened in an award-winning converted seven storey Victorian granary in the Ouseburn Valley, a stone's throw from Newcastle's vibrant quayside. Seven Stories is now officially known as the National Centre for Children's Books, following approval by Arts Council England in 2012. It is the only accredited museum in the UK that specialises in children's books.

The collection

At the heart of Seven Stories is a unique and growing collection of manuscripts, artwork and other pre-publication materials. These treasures record the creative process involved in making a children's book and provide illuminating insights into the working lives of modern authors and illustrators. The collection focuses on work created in modern Britain. It already contains thousands of items by authors such as Peter Dickinson, Berlie Doherty, Jan Mark, Philip Pullman, Michael Rosen, Robert Westall and Ursula Moray Williams; illustrators like Edward Ardizzone, Faith Jaques, Harold Jones, Anthony Maitland, Pat Hutchins, Helen Cooper, Jan Ormerod and Jane Ray; and editors and other practitioners such as Kaye Webb. Many more bodies of work are pledged. A catalogue of the collection is available via the Seven Stories website.

Exhibitions

A celebration of creativity underpins the Seven Stories project: its collection documents the creative act, and its exhibitions and programmes interpret this original material in unconventional but meaningful ways. The aim is to cultivate an appreciation of books and their making, and inspire creativity in its audience.

Seven Stories, known during its development as the Centre for the Children's Book, has been mounting exhibitions since 1998 – first in borrowed venues and now in its own home. Here it provides the only exhibition space in the UK wholly dedicated to showcasing the incomparable legacy of British writing and illustrating for children. Its current exhibition is *Moving Stories – Children's Books from Page to Screen*, which showcases innovative and influential film and television adaptations inspired by children's books These include *Through the Magic Mirror, The World of Anthony Browne, Daydreams and Diaries, the Story of Jacqueline Wilson* and *A Squash and a Squeeze, Sharing Stories with Julia Donaldson*.

Throughout its seven storeys – from the Creation Station to the bookshop and café to the Artist's Attic, visitors of all ages are invited to engage in a unique, interactive exploration of creativity, literature and art. In this ever changing literary playground and landscape for the imagination, they can become writers, artists, explorers, designers, storytellers, readers or collectors, in the company of storytellers, authors, illustrators and Seven Stories' own facilitators and education team.

Seven Stories aims to place children, young people and their books at the heart of the UK's national literary culture. An independent educational charity, it is committed to access for all and has initiated several innovative participation projects. The centre has developed close links with the Newcastle and regional communities, and is working with the Children's Literature Unit in the Department of English Literature, Language and Linguistics at Newcastle University to develop the Seven Stories collection and maximise its potential for research and display.

Seven Stories is dedicated to the celebration of children's literature and was the 2010 winner of the Eleanor Farjeon Award. It is supported by Arts Council England and Newcastle City Council.

Further information

Seven Stories – National Centre for Children's Books
30 Lime Street, Ouseburn Valley, Newcastle upon Tyne NE1 2PQ
tel (0845) 271 0777
email info@sevenstories.org.uk
website www.sevenstories.org.uk
Registered Charity No 1056812.
Public opening hours Mon–Sat 10am–5pm, Sun 10am–4pm
Admission charges Adult (17 and over) £7; child (4-15)/concession £6; child (12 months-4 years) £2.50; Family £21; under 12 months: free. Annual passes available.

See also...
- *Society of Children's Book Writers & Illustrators*, page 379
- *Book Trust*, page 382
- *The Children's Book Circle*, page 387
- *Federation of Children's Book Groups*, page 388

The Children's Book Circle

The Children's Book Circle is open to anyone who has a passion for children's books and the activities of the organisation are introduced here.

Are you passionate about children's books? The Children's Book Circle (CBC) provides an exciting forum where you can develop your interest, build your contacts and get involved in lively debate on important issues in the children's book world. The CBC's membership consists of publishers, librarians, authors, illustrators, agents, teachers, booksellers and anyone with an active interest in the field. If you're an aspiring author or illustrator, you'll already know how important it is to become as knowledgeable as possible about the current marketplace for children's books. The CBC is the ideal place to broaden your knowledge. It's not the place to try for a publishing contract, but it will give you the forum to take part in discussions with people from the industry in an informal and enjoyable context.

> ### Further information
>
> **The Children's Book Circle**
> *website* www.childrensbookcircle.org.uk
> *Membership* £25 p.a. Corporate membership (up to five staff covered) £100 p.a. Membership includes free or discounted entry to all events. Non-member tickets can also be purchased for individual events from the website.

The CBC meets regularly at venues in central London. At the meetings, invited guest speakers debate key issues relating to the world of children's books. Recent and upcoming events include hearing about the experiences of three extraordinary publishers who have built publishing houses from scratch, a panel discussion about the changing role of the author in the digital age and 'Meet and Critique' evenings, where aspiring authors can meet with industry experts and discuss their plot ideas and writing concerns one to one. Social drinks are fast becoming part of the CBC calendar and are a great chance to catch up with industry contacts and make new ones.

The CBC is also the proud host of the annual Eleanor Farjeon Award (generously sponsored by the estate of Eleanor Farjeon) and the Patrick Hardy Lecture. The Eleanor Farjeon Award recognises an outstanding contribution to the world of children's books. Recent winners include illustrator Quentin Blake, The Federation of Children's Book Groups, Seven Stories, and authors Philip Pullman and Jacqueline Wilson. The Patrick Hardy Lecture is delivered each year by a distinguished speaker on a relevant topic of their choice. Past speakers include Jonathan Stroud, Cathy Cassidy, Jeremy Strong, Verna Wilkins (founder of Tamarind Books) and Michael Rosen.

Another highlight of the CBC calendar is the annual quiz, which offers members a chance to show off their children's book knowledge.

See also...
- *Society of Children's Book Writers & Illustrators*, page 379
- *Book Trust*, page 382
- *Seven Stories – National Centre for Children's Books*, page 385
- *Federation of Children's Book Groups*, page 388

Federation of Children's Book Groups

Julia Miller, Chair, introduces the Federation of Children's Book Groups.

'The Federation of Children's Book Groups, has, in its own quiet, single-minded way, done more for reading than almost anyone else' – Anthony Horowitz, March 2011.

The achievements of the Federation of Children's Book Groups were publicly recognised in 2011 when it was nominated for and subsequently won the Eleanor Farjeon Award (see page 412). Its aim is simple: to bring children and books together, promote children's books and inspire a love of reading through its national and local events. If you are a parent, carer, author, illustrator or professional with a passion for encouraging children to read, the Federation will be of interest to you.

Federation history

The Federation of Children's Book Groups was formed in 1968 by Anne Wood to co-ordinate the work of the many different children's book groups already in existence across the country.

In 1981 we inaugurated the Children's Book Award, the only national award voted for entirely by children. Throughout the year Federation Testing Groups read and vote on new fiction generously supplied by publishers. A shortlist (Top Ten) is drawn up with four picture books in the Younger Children category, three shorter novels for Younger Readers, and three novels for Older Readers, with children from all over the UK voting in their groups or online. The Award has a track record of identifying future bestsellers: the first Overall Winner was *Mr Magnolia* by Quentin Blake; other winners include *The Hunger Games*, and the *Harry Potter* and *Percy Jackson* books. For over ten years the Award has been supported by Red House and their financial commitment has enabled the Award to go from strength to strength. In February 2012 the Award Ceremony moved to the Queen Elizabeth Hall, Southbank in London as part of the Imagine Children's Festival (see page 421), with over 800 adults and children celebrating as our 2011 Winner, Michael Morpurgo, handed the trophy to Patrick Ness for *A Monster Calls*.

In 1976 National Tell-A-Story-Week was established and it has now grown into National Share-A-Story-Month (NSSM), which takes place each May. It enables groups to focus on the power of story and to hold events which celebrate all forms of storytelling. In 2012 NSSM was sponsored by Templar Publishing and groups held Storyworld events nationwide.

In 1977, the first Federation anthology was published, and since then we have compiled booklists covering the whole age range from picture books to the latest teen and young adult novels; these are available on request free of charge via the website. *It's a fact* covers quality non-fiction books.

In 2010 the Federation created National Non-Fiction Day to celebrate the quality and variety of information books available for children; this takes place on the first Thursday of each November, with a host of events focused on non-fiction.

Societies, prizes and festivals

Each year the Federation holds a conference: three days of author and illustrator events, panel discussions and seminars enable group and individual members, publishers, authors, illustrators, teachers, librarians and booksellers to meet and exchange ideas. Delegates are inspired by meeting others who share their passion. Venues range across the country: 'Books and Beyond' in 2014 was held at Worth Abbey, West Sussex, and we were delighted to host Meg Rosoff, Jonathan Stroud, Cressida Cowell, Philip Reeve, Justin Somper and many others. The 2015 conference called 'Inspire' took place at Marston near Grantham, Lincolnshire, on 10–12 April and speakers included Frank Cottrell Boyce, Philip Ardagh, Sarah Crossan, Jonathan Stroud, Nicola Morgan and Kjartan Poskitt.

The Children's Book Groups

Federation Book Groups exist throughout the UK: from Plymouth to Dundee, from Grantham to St David's and from Harrogate to Lewes. Their activities are as varied and diverse as the groups themselves, serving their own community's needs, includ-

Further information

Federation of Children's Book Groups
tel 0300 102 1559
email info@fcbg.org.uk
website www.fcbg.org.uk
Registered Charity No 268289

ing author and illustrator visits, bonfire parties, museum and library events, book swaps and parties. But, above all, we are passionate about children's books, bringing together ordinary book-loving families, empowering parents, grandparents, carers and children to become enthusiastic and excited about all kinds of good books. Some book groups are based around schools run by enthusiastic librarians and teachers. You can still be a member of the Federation if there is no book group near you. Individual and professional membership enables everyone to participate in sharing their passion for children's books.

See also...
- *Society of Children's Book Writers & Illustrators*, page 379
- *Book Trust*, page 382
- *Seven Stories – National Centre for Children's Books*, page 385
- *The Children's Book Circle*, page 387

National Literacy Trust

The Trust is the only national charity dedicated to raising literacy levels in the UK.

The National Literacy Trust is an independent charity that transforms lives through literacy. One person in six in the UK is held back by poor literacy skills which compromise employability, health, confidence and happiness.

The National Literacy Trust improves reading, writing, speaking and listening skills in communities where poverty is on the increase and where literacy levels are low. Its research and analysis make it the leading authority on literacy and drive the interventions.

The National Literacy Trust campaigns to make literacy a priority for politicians and parents and provides schools with resources to transform their literacy teaching. The charity's work is focused on the critical moments in literacy development where the greatest impact. In the last year:

• the charity worked with staff in 120 early years settings to mentor 550 families in supporting their child's home learning, and trained 155 early years staff and 675 volunteers to help;

• 365,000 mums and dads were reached with tips and resources;

• the charity worked with 61,060 children from 1,950 schools, and trained and supported 4,700 teachers to improve literacy outcomes in 3,650 schools;

• 40,350 children discovered reading for enjoyment and 30,000 books were given away;

• 35,000 children and young people took part in its annual literacy survey;

• the charity worked with more than 4,000 children and 200 teachers and teaching assistants in Middlesbrough, and set foundations for new literacy hubs in Peterborough and Bradford.

The National Literacy Trust needs help to raise literacy levels in the UK and donations to support its work may be made via the website.

Further information

National Literacy Trust
68 South Lambeth Road, London SW8 1RL
tel 020-7587 1842
email contact@literacytrust.org.uk
website www.literacytrust.org.uk

Societies, associations and organisations

The societies and associations listed here include appreciation societies devoted to specific authors, professional bodies and national institutions. Some also offer prizes and awards (see page 409).

AccessArt

6 West Street, Comberton, Cambridge CB23 7DS
tel (01223) 262134
email info@accessart.org.uk
website www.accessart.org.uk

AccessArt is a UK Charity which aims to inspire and enable high quality visual arts teaching, learning and practice. The AccessArt website features over 500 unique resources to inspire practice, plus online courses in drawing and sketchbooks.

Action for Children's Arts

PO Box 2620, Purley CR8 3WA
email admin@childrensarts.org.uk
website www.childrensarts.org.uk
Membership £30 p.a. individuals; see website for organisation rates

A membership charity organisation that values children, childhood and the arts. It embraces the UN Convention on the Rights of the Child:

• by campaigning for the right of all children in the UK to experience high-quality arts experiences as an integral part of their childhood;
• by connecting people within and across the cultural and education sectors, across art-forms and across the regions and nations of the UK;
• by celebrating achievement, dedication and best practice in artistic activity for and with children. The J.M. Barrie Award is given annually to a children's arts practitioner or organisation whose work, in the view of ACA, will stand the test of time. Winners: Dick King-Smith (2005), Judith Kerr (2006), Oliver Postgate and Peter Firmin (2007), Quentin Blake (2008), Roger McGough (2009), Shirley Hughes (2010), Lyndie Wright (2011), Baroness Floella Benjamin (2012), Lynne Reid Banks and Lyn Gardner (2013), Bernard Cribbins and Northern Ballet (2014). Founded 1998.

Louisa May Alcott Memorial Association

Orchard House, 399 Lexington Road, PO Box 343, Concord, MA 01742–0343, USA
tel +1 978-369-4118
email info@louisamayalcott.org
website www.louisamayalcott.org

A private, not-for-profit association that provides the financial and human resources required to conduct public tours, special programmes, exhibitions and the curatorial work which continues the tradition of the Alcotts, a unique 19th century family. Founded 1911.

Alliance of Independent Authors – see page 378

American Society of Composers, Authors and Publishers

website www.ascap.com

An organisation owned and run by its members, it is the leading performance rights organisation representing over 450,000 songwriters, composers and music publishers.

Arab Children's Book Publisher's Forum

email acbpf@yahoo.com
website www.acbpub.org

Aims to improve the level and quality of children's book publishing and reinforce the mission of Arab children's book publishers.

Arts Council England

tel 0845 300 6200
email enquiries@artscouncil.org.uk
website www.artscouncil.org.uk

The national development agency for the arts in England, distributing public money from Government and the National Lottery. Arts Council England's main funding programme is Grants for the Arts, which is open to individuals, arts organisations, national touring companies and other people who use the arts in their work. Founded 1946.

East

Eastbrook, Shaftesbury Road, Cambridge CB2 8BF
tel 0845 300 6200

East Midlands

Room 005-005A, Arkwright Building, Nottingham Trent University, Burton Street, Nottingham NG1 4BU
tel 0845 300 6200

London

21 Bloomsbury Street, London WC1B 3HF
tel 0845 300 6200

North East

Central Square, Forth Street, Newcastle upon Tyne NE1 3PJ
tel 0845 300 6200

North West
The Hive, 49 Lever Street, Manchester M1 1FN
tel 0845 300 6200

South East
Sovereign House, Church Street, Brighton BN1 1RA
tel 0845 300 6200

South West
Third Floor, St Thomas Court, Thomas Lane, Bristol
BS1 6JG
tel 0845 300 6200

West Midlands
82 Granville Street, Birmingham B1 2LH
tel 0845 300 6200

Yorkshire
21 Bond Street, Dewsbury, West Yorkshire
WF13 1AX
tel 0845 300 6200

Arts Council/An Chomhairle Ealaíon

70 Merrion Square, Dublin 2, Republic of Ireland
tel +353 (0)1 6180200
website www.artscouncil.ie
Arts Directors Liz Meaney, Stephanie O'Callaghan,
Acting Head of Literature Liz Powell, *Head of Visual
Arts* Claire Doyle

The national development agency for the arts in
Ireland. Founded 1951.

Arts Council of Northern Ireland

77 Malone Road, Belfast BT9 6AQ
tel 028-9038 5200
email info@artscouncil-ni.org
website www.artscouncil-ni.org
Chief Executive Roisín McDonough, *Head of Drama
& Literature* Damian Smyth, *Head of Visual Arts*
Suzanne Lyle

Promotes and encourages the arts throughout
Northern Ireland. Artists in drama, dance, music and
jazz, literature, the visual arts, traditional arts and
community arts can apply for support for specific
schemes and projects. The value of the grant will be
set according to the aims of the application. Artists of
all disciplines and in all types of working practice,
who have made a contribution to artistic activities in
Northern Ireland for a minimum period of one year
within the last five years, are eligible.

Arts Council of Wales

Bute Place, Cardiff CF10 5AL
tel 0845 873 4900
email info@artscouncilofwales.org.uk
website www.artswales.org.uk

National organisation with specific responsibility for
the funding and development of the arts in Wales.
Arts Council of Wales receives funding from the
Welsh Government and also distributes National
Lottery funds for the arts in Wales. From these

resources, Arts Council of Wales makes grants to
support arts activities and facilities. Some of the
funds are allocated in the form of annual revenue
grants to full-time arts organisations such as
Literature Wales. It also operates schemes which
provide financial and other forms of support for
individual artists or projects. Arts Council of Wales
undertakes this work in both the English and Welsh
languages. Wales Arts International is the unique
partnership between the Arts Council of Wales and
British Council Wales, which works to promote
knowledge about contemporary arts and culture from
Wales and encourages international exchange and
collaboration.

North Wales Regional Office
Princes Park II, Princes Drive, Colwyn Bay LL29 8PL
tel (01492) 533440

Mid and West Wales Regional Office
4–6 Gardd Llydaw, Jackson Lane, Carmarthen
SA31 1QD
tel 0845 873 4900

South Wales Office
Bute Place, Cardiff CF10 5AL
tel 0845 873 4900

Association for Library Service to Children

American Library Association, 50 East Huron Street,
Chicago, IL 60611–2795, USA
tel +1 800-545-2433 ext. 2163
email alsc@ala.org
website www.ala.org/alsc

Develops and supports the profession of children's
librarianship by enabling and encouraging its
practitioners to provide the best library service to US
children.

Association for Scottish Literary Studies (ASLS)

c/o Dept of Scottish Literature, 7 University Gardens,
University of Glasgow G12 8QH
tel 0141 330 5309
email office@asls.org.uk
website www.asls.org.uk
President Ian Brown, *Secretary* Ronnie Young,
Director Duncan Jones
Membership £47 p.a. individuals; £12 UK students;
£75 corporate

Promotes the study, teaching and writing of Scottish
literature and furthers the study of the languages of
Scotland. Publishes annually *New Writing Scotland*,
an anthology of new Scottish writing; an edited text
of Scottish literature; a series of academic journals;
and a newsletter (two p.a.) Also publishes *Scotnotes*
(comprehensive study guides to major Scottish
writers), literary texts and commentary CDs designed
to assist the classroom teacher, and a series of

occasional papers. Organises three conferences a year. Founded 1970.

Association of American Publishers

71 Fifth Avenue, 2nd Floor, New York,
NY 10003-3004,
USA and 455 Massachusetts Avenue NW, Suite 700,
Washington, DC 20001, USA
tel +1 212-255-0200 (NY); +1 202-347-3375 (DC)
email info@publishers.org
website www.publishers.org
President & Ceo Tom Allen

AAP is the largest trade association for US books and journal publishers, providing advocacy and communications on behalf of the industry and its priorities nationally and worldwide. Founded 1970.

Association of Authors' Representatives Inc.

302A West 12th Street, #122, New York, NY 10014,
USA
email administrator@aaronline.org
website www.aaronline.org
Administrative Secretary Jody Kahn

A professional organisation of over 400 agents who work with book authors and playwrights.

Founded 1991.

Association of Canadian Publishers

174 Spadina Avenue, Suite 306, Toronto,
Ontario M5T 2C2, Canada
tel +1 416-487-6116
email admin@canbook.org
website www.publishers.ca
Executive Director Carolyn Wood

Represents approximately 135 Canadian-owned and controlled book publishers from across the country. Founded 1976.

The Association of Illustrators

Somerset House, Strand, London WC2R 1LA
tel 020-7759 1010
email info@theaoi.com
website www.theaoi.com
Contact Membership Coordinator

Trade association which supports illustrators, promotes illustration and encourages professional standards in the industry. Publishes *Varoom* magazine (four p.a.); presents an annual programme of events; annual competition, exhibition and tour of the World Illustration Awards in partnership with the Directory of Illustration (www.theaoi.com/awards). Founded 1973.

Australia Council

PO Box 788, Strawberry Hills, NSW 2012, Australia
located at 372 Elizabeth Street, Surry Hills,
NSW 2010, Australia
tel +61 (0)2 9215 9000
email mail@australiacouncil.gov.au
website www.australiacouncil.gov.au
Ceo Tony Grybowski

Provides a broad range of support for the arts in Australia, embracing music, theatre, literature, visual arts, crafts, Aboriginal arts, community and new media arts. It has an office of the Chief Executive and five divisions.

Australian Copyright Council

PO Box 1986, Strawberry Hills, NSW 2012, Australia
tel +61 (0)2 8815 9777
email info@copyright.org.au
website www.copyright.org.au
Executive Director Fiona Phillips

The Australian Copyright Council is an independent, non-profit organisation. It represents the peak bodies for professional artists and content creators working in Australia's creative industries and Australia's major copyright collecting societies. The Council comprises 24 organisations or associations of owners and creators of copyright material, including the Australian Society of Authors, the Australian Writers' Guild and the Australian Publishers Association.

The Council acts as an advocate for the contribution of creators to Australia's culture and economy; the importance of copyright for the common good. Works to promote the understanding of copyright law and its application, lobbies for appropriate law reform and fosters collaboration between content creators and consumers. Provides easily accessible and affordable practical, user-friendly information, legal advice, education and forums on Australian copyright law for content creators and consumers. Founded 1968.

Australian Publishers Association (APA)

60–89 Jones Street, Ultimo, NSW 2007, Australia
email office@publishers.asn.au
website www.publishers.asn.au
Ceo Maree McCaskill

The Australian Publishers Association is the peak industry body for Australian book, journal and electronic publishers. Founded 1948.

Australian Writers' Guild (AWG)

5 Blackfriars Street, Chippendale, NSW 2008
tel +61 (0)2 9319 0339
email admin@awg.com.au
website www.awg.com.au
Executive Director Jacqueline Elaine

The professional association for all performance writers, i.e. writers for film, TV, radio, theatre, video and new media. The AWG is recognised throughout the industry in Australia as being the voice of performance writers. Founded 1962.

Authors Aloud UK

72 Castle Road, St Albans, Herts AL1 5DG
tel (01727) 893992

email info@authorsalouduk.co.uk
website www.authorsalouduk.co.uk
Partners Anne Marley, Naomi Cooper, Annie Everall

Authors Aloud UK is an author booking agency which brings together authors, illustrators, poets, storytellers and trainers with schools, libraries and festivals to promote enthusiasm for reading, both for enjoyment and information. Authors Aloud UK is happy to take on new speakers, published by mainstream children's publishers, who meet the relevant criteria and guidelines. Keen to work with new and debut authors who wish to visit schools and libraries.

Authors' Licensing and Collecting Society Ltd – see page 322

Beanstalk

(formerly Volunteer Reading Help)
Beanstalk Central Office, Third Floor,
6 Middle Street, London EC1A 7JA
tel 020-7729 4087
email info@beanstalkcharity.org.uk
website www.beanstalkcharity.org.uk

Beanstalk is a national charity that gives one-to-one literacy support to children in primary schools in the most deprived areas of England. Beanstalk's vision is a nation of confident children who can read and grow up to lead successful lives.

Enid Blyton Society

email tony@enidblytonsociety.co.uk
website www.enidblytonsociety.co.uk

To provide a focal point for collectors and enthusiasts of Enid Blyton through its magazine *The Enid Blyton Society Journal* (three p.a.) and the annual Society Day which attracts in excess of a hundred members each year. Founded 1995.

Book Marketing Society

5th Floor, Endeavour House,
189 Shaftesbury Avenue, London WC2H 8JR
email jo@bookmarketingsociety.co.uk
website www.bookmarketingsociety.co.uk
Executive Jo Henry

The Book Marketing Society was launched with the objective of becoming the representative body of marketing within the book industry. As such, it champions marketing professionalism with the ultimate goal of expanding the UK book market. Anyone who works for a book publisher, book retailer or book wholesaler is eligible for membership, including those working in associated areas of the publishing and book retailing industry. Founded 2004.

The Booksellers Association of the United Kingdom & Ireland Ltd

6 Bell Yard, London WC2A 2JR
tel 020-7421 4640

email mail@booksellers.org.uk
website www.booksellers.org.uk
Chief Executive T.E. Godfray

A membership organisation for all booksellers in the UK and Ireland, representing over 95% of bookshops. Key services include National Book Tokens and World Book Day. Founded 1895.

Book Trust – see page 382

The British Council

10 Spring Gardens, London SW1A 2BN
email general.enquiries@britishcouncil.org
website www.britishcouncil.org
Chair Sir Vernon Ellis, *Chief Executive* Ciarán Devane, *Director of Arts* Graham Sheffield

The British Council connects people worldwide with learning opportunities and creative ideas from the UK, and builds lasting relationships between the UK and other countries. It has 6,000 staff in offices, teaching centres, libraries and information and resource centres in the UK and 110 countries and territories worldwide.

Working in close collaboration with book trade associations, British Council offices participate in major international book fairs.

The British Council is an authority on teaching English as a second or foreign language. It also gives advice and information on curriculum, methodology, materials and testing.

The British Council Literature Department works with hundreds of writers and literature partners in the UK and collaborates with offices overseas to broker relationships and create activities which link thousands of artists and cultural institutions around the world, drawing them into a closer relationship with the UK. The Department works with writers, publishers, producers, translators and other sector professionals across literature, publishing and education. With them they develop innovative, high-quality programmes and collaborations that provide opportunities for cultural exchange with the UK.

The Visual Arts Department promotes the UK's visual arts sector internationally. It stages and supports contemporary art projects in areas of the developing world via exhibitions, training and development, professional study visits and the management of the British Pavilion at the Venice Biennale and an expansive collection of 20th- and 21st-century British art.

British Museum

Great Russell Street, London WC1B 3DG
tel 020-7323 8000/8299
website www.britishmuseum.org

Young Explorers

website www.britishmuseum.org/explore/young_explorers1.aspx

An online opportunity for children to discover world cultures using games and activities.

Randolph Caldecott Society

Secretary Kenn Oultram, Blue Grass Cottage,
Clatterwick Lane, Little Leigh, Northwich,
Cheshire CW8 4RJ
tel (01606) 891303 (office), (01606) 781731 (evening)
website www.randolphcaldecott.org.uk
Membership £12.50 p.a. individual; £17.50 p.a.
families/corporate

Aims to encourage an interest in the life and works of
Randolph Caldecott (1846–86), the Victorian artist,
illustrator and sculptor. Caldecott produced 16
picture books, each based on the words of a nursery
rhyme or well-known nonsense verse. Meetings held
in Chester. Liaises with the American Caldecott
Society. Founded 1983.

Canadian Authors Association

6 West Street North, Suite 203, Orillia,
Ontario L3V 5B8
tel +1 705-325-3926
email admin@canadianauthors.org
website www.canadianauthors.org
President Matthew Bin, *Executive Director* Anita
Purcell

Provides writers with a wide variety of programmes,
services and resources to help them develop their
skills in both the craft and the business of writing. A
membership-based organisation for writers in all
areas of the profession. Branches across Canada.
Founded 1921.

The Canadian Children's Book Centre (CCBC)

Suite 217, 40 Orchard View Blvd, Toronto,
Ontario M4R 1B9, Canada
tel +1 416-975-0010
email info@bookcentre.ca
website www.bookcentre.ca

A national, not-for-profit organisation, founded in
1976, that is dedicated to encouraging, promoting
and supporting the reading, writing, illustrating and
publishing of Canadian books for young readers.
 CCBC programs, publications and resources help
teachers, librarians, booksellers and parents select the
very best for young readers.

Canadian Publishers' Council

250 Merton Street, Suite 203, Toronto,
Ontario M4S 1B1, Canada
tel +1 416-322-7011
website www.pubcouncil.ca
Executive Director Jacqueline Hushion

Represents the interests of Canadian publishing
companies that publish books and other media for
schools, colleges and universities, professional and
reference markets, the retail and library sectors.
Founded 1910.

CANSCAIP (Canadian Society of Children's Authors, Illustrators & Performers)

720 Bathurst Street, Suite 501, Toronto,
Ontario M5S 2R4, Canada
tel +1 416-515-1559
email office@canscaip.org
website www.canscaip.org
Administrative Director Helena Aalto
Membership $85 p.a.

A non-profit support network for children's artists.
Promotes children's literature and performances
throughout Canada and internationally. Founded
1977.

Careers Writers' Association

email reedwendy@btinternet.com
website www.parentalguidance.org.uk
Membership £40 p.a.

Society for established writers and editors of print
and web-based materials on all careers-related issues,
including study options, career choice and change,
labour market information and specific vocational
areas. Runs a careers website for parents to help them
advise young people in their care. Details of
members' publications and specific expertise are
available on the website. Holds twice-yearly meetings.
Founded 1979.

The Lewis Carroll Society

6 Chilton Street, London E2 6DZ
email membership@lewiscarrollsociety.org.uk
website www.lewiscarrollsociety.org.uk
Membership £20 p.a. UK; £23 Europe; £26 elsewhere.
Special rates for institutions

Aims to promote interest in the life and works of
Lewis Carroll (Revd Charles Lutwidge Dodgson)
(1832–98) and to encourage research. Activities
include regular meetings, exhibitions, and a
publishing programme that includes the first
annotated, unexpurgated edition of his diaries in nine
volumes, the Society's journal *The Carrollian* (two
p.a.), a newsletter, *Bandersnatch* (quarterly) and the
Lewis Carroll Review (occasional). Founded 1969.

Lewis Carroll Society (Daresbury)

Secretary Kenn Oultram, Blue Grass Cottage,
Clatterwick Lane, Little Leigh, Northwich,
Cheshire CW8 4RJ
tel (01606) 891303 (office), (01606) 781731 (evening)
Membership £7 p.a.; £10 families/corporate

Aims to encourage an interest in the life and works of
Lewis Carroll (1832–98), author of *Alice's Adventures*.
Meetings take place at Carroll's birth village
(Daresbury, Cheshire). Founded 1970.

Lewis Carroll Society of North America (LCSNA)

PO Box 197, Annandale, VA 22003
email secretary@lewiscarroll.org
website www.lewiscarroll.org
President Stephanie Lovett, *Secretary* Sandra Lee
Parker
Membership $35 p.a. USA; $50 elsewhere

An organisation of Carroll admirers of all ages and interests. It is dedicated to furthering Carroll studies, increasing accessibility of research material, and maintaining public awareness of Carroll's contributions to society. The Society has a worldwide membership and meets twice a year. The Society maintains an active publication programme and members receive copies of the Society's magazine *Knight Letter*. An interest in Lewis Carroll, a simple love for Alice (or the Snark for that matter) qualifies for membership. Founded in 1974.

The Center for Children's Books (CCB)

Graduate School of Library and Information Science, University of Illinois at Urbana–Champaign, 501 East Daniel Street, Champaign, IL 61820, USA
tel +1 217-244-9331
email ccb@uiuc.edu
website http://ccb.lis.illinois.edu

CCB houses a non-circulating collection of more than 16,000 recent and historically significant trade books for children, plus review copies of nearly all trade books published in the USA in the current year.

There are over 1,000 professional and reference books on the history and criticism of literature for youth, literature-based library and classroom programming, and storytelling. Although the collection is non-circulating, it is available for examination by scholars, teachers, librarians, students and other educators.

Centre for Literacy in Primary Education (CLPE)

Webber Street, London SE1 8QW
tel 020-7401 3382/3
email info@clpe.co.uk
website www.clpe.co.uk

A centre for children's language, literacy, literature and educational assessment which provides in-service training for teachers, consultancy to educational establishments and publishers, and courses for parents. It contains a reference library of children's books plus teachers' resources. CLPE publishes teaching resources relating to literacy in the primary classroom. Book recommendations online at www.corebooks.org.uk. CLPE is the National Centre for Poetry in Primary Schools, see www.poetryline.org.uk.

The Children's Book Circle – see page 387

The Children's Book Council (CBC)

54 West 39th Street, 14th Floor, New York, NY 10018, USA
tel +1 212-966-1990
email cbc.info@cbcbooks.org
website www.cbcbooks.org

The non-profit trade association of publishers and packagers of trade books and related materials for children and young adults. The goals of the CBC are to make the reading and enjoyment of children's books an essential part of the USA's educational and social goals; to enhance public perception of the importance of reading by disseminating information about books and related materials for young people and information about children's book publishing; and to create materials to support literacy and reading encouragement programmes and to encourage the annual observance of National Children's Book Week.

The Children's Book Council of Australia

PO Box 3174, West Hobart, TAS
email inquiries@cbca.org.au
website www.cbca.org.au

Aims to foster children's enjoyment of books through managing the Children's Book of the Year Awards; providing information on and encouragement to authors and illustrators; organising exhibitions and activities during Children's Book Week; supporting children's library services; and promoting high standards in book reviewing, along with promoting greater equity of access to reading through community projects.

The Children's Book Guild of Washington DC

email theguild@childrensbookguild.org
website www.childrensbookguild.org
President Fred Bowen

A regional association of writers, artists, librarians and other specialists dedicated to the field of children's literature. Its aims are to uphold and stimulate high standards of writing and illustrating for children; to increase knowledge and use of better books for children in the community; and to cooperate with other groups having similar purposes. Founded 1945.

Children's Books Ireland

17 North Great George's Street, Dublin 1, Republic of Ireland
tel +353 (0)1 8727475
email info@childrensbooksireland.com
website www.childrensbooksireland.ie
Director Elaina Ryan, *Publications and Communications Manager* Jenny Murray, *Programme Manager* Aoife Murray

Children's Books Ireland (CBI) is the national children's books resource organisation of Ireland. Its mission is to make books part of every child's life.

Champions and celebrates the importance of authors and illustrators and works in partnership with the people and organisations who enhance children's lives through books. Core projects include: the CBI Annual Conference; the CBI Book of the Year Awards and its shadowing scheme for school groups and book clubs; the annual nationwide reading campaign which promotes books and reading and which coincides with the publication of Recommended Reads, a guide to the best books of the year; nationwide Book Clinics and *Inis* magazine in print and online, a forum for discussion, debate and critique of Irish and international books. CBI administers the Laureate na nÓg project on behalf of the Arts Council and runs live literature events throughout the year. Founded 1996.

Children's Literature Association (ChLA)
1301 West 22nd Street, Suite 202, Oak Brook, IL 60523, USA
tel +1 630-571-4520
email info@childlitassn.org
website www.childlitassn.org
Membership Membership open to both individuals and institutions. Individual membership $80 (USA), $96 (Mexico/Canada), $110 (outside North America. Institutional membership $165 (USA), $181 (Mexico/Canada), $195 (outside North America)

An organisation encouraging high standards of criticism, scholarship, research and teaching in children's literature. Members receive the *ChLA Quarterly* and the annual volume of *Children's Literature*.

Children's Literature Centre (CLC)
Martynas Mazvydas National Library of Lithuania, Gedimino pr. 51, LT–01504, Vilnius, Lithuania
tel +370 5 249 7023
email biblio@lnb.lt
website www.lnb.lt

Accumulates, processes and stores children's literature, both original and in translation, as well as works on history, theory and literary criticism, informative and reference publications from various countries related to children's literature. Its aim is to acquire, as fully as possible, earlier Lithuanian and translated children's books and books published by Lithuanian exiles.

CLC organises children's reading research and analyses book popularity, design, illustrations and quality of translations. It arranges international children's book exhibitions, seminars and conferences on children's books and reading. Presentation of new books, meetings with authors, publishers and designers are regularly carried out. CLC is the coordination and monitoring centre of children's libraries in Lithuania. Founded 1994.

Comhairle nan Leabhraichean/The Gaelic Books Council
32 Mansfield Street, Glasgow G11 5QP
tel 0141 337 6211
email rosemary@gaelicbooks.org
website www.gaelicbooks.org
Director Rosemary Ward

Stimulates Scottish Gaelic publishing by awarding publication grants for new books, commissions new works from established and emerging authors and provides editorial advice and guidance to Gaelic writers and publishers. Has a bookshop in Glasgow that stocks all Gaelic and Gaelic-related books in print. All stock is listed on the website and a paper catalogue is also available. Founded 1968.

Creative Scotland
Waverley Gate, 2–4 Waterloo Place, Edinburgh EH1 3EG
tel 0330 333 2000
email enquiries@creativescotland.com
website www.creativescotland.com

Creative Scotland is the public body that supports the arts, screen and creative industries across all parts of Scotland on behalf of everyone who lives, works or visits there. Through distributing funding from the Scottish Government and the National Lottery, Creative Scotland enables people and organisations to work in and experience the arts, screen and creative industries in Scotland by helping others to develop great ideas and bring them to life.

Cwlwm Cyhoeddwyr Cymru
Bethan Mair, Y Berth, 29 Coed Bach, Portarddulais, Abertawe, Swansea SA4 8RB
tel 07779 102224
email geiriau@gmail.com
website www.bedwen.com

Represents and promotes Welsh-language publishers and organises Bedwen Lyfrau, the only national Welsh-language book festival, held annually in May. Founded 2002.

Roald Dahl's Marvellous Children's Charity
81A High Street, Great Missenden, Bucks. HP16 0AL
tel (01494) 890465
website www.roalddahlcharity.org
website www.roalddahl.com

This charity supports seriously ill and disabled children in the UK, continuing Roald Dahl's charitable work by helping children with neurological and blood conditions.

The websites are illustrated with the artworks of Quentin Blake, Roald Dahl's principal illustrator and President of the charity, and include full information about the author, his life and his works. The charity website includes details of the children's Dahlicious Dress Up Day event and the Roald Dahl website includes a free online club for children and the online magazine *Dahl-y Telegraph*.

The Roald Dahl Museum and Story Centre
81–83 High Street, Great Missenden, Bucks. HP16 0AL
tel (01494) 892192

website www.roalddahlmuseum.org
Housing Roald Dahl's unique archive, the Roald Dahl Museum and Story Centre has two biographical galleries and a hands-on Story Centre that inspires visitors to write creatively.

Walter de la Mare Society
3 Hazelwood Close, New River Crescent, Palmers Green, London N13 5RE
website www.walterdelamare.co.uk
Hon. Secretary and Treasurer Frances Guthrie
Membership £15 p.a.

To promote the study and deepen the appreciation of the works of Walter de la Mare (1873–1956) through a magazine, talks, discussions and other activities. Founded 1997.

Discover Children's Story Centre
383–387 High Street, Stratford, London E15 4QZ
tel 020-8536 5555
email bookings@discover.org.uk
website www.discover.org.uk

Discover Children's Story Centre is the UK's first hands-on creative literacy centre for children aged 0–11 years and their families, carers and teachers. Its mission is to spark children's and adults' imagination, curiosity and creativity in a magical and stimulating environment through creative play. It offers a variety of programmes including schools workshops, family art activities, a literature programme led by children's writers and illustrators, community and education projects, artist residencies in schools and training for professionals that work with children and families. Artists are commissioned to create multisensory installations and exhibitions. Registered charity.

The Arthur Conan Doyle Society
PO Box 1360, Ashcroft, BC V0K 1A0, Canada
tel +1 250-453-2045
email sirhenry@telus.net
website www.ash-tree.bc.ca/acdsocy.html

Promotes the study of the life and works of Sir Arthur Conan Doyle (1859–1930). Publishes *ACD* journal (bi-annual) and occasional reprints of Conan Doyle material. Occasional conventions. Founded 1989.

Editors' and Proofreaders' Alliance of Northern Ireland (EPANI)
tel 07875 857278
email info@epani.org.uk
website www.epani.org.uk
Manager Averill Buchanan

Aims to establish and maintain high professional standards in editorial skills in Northern Ireland. Membership is free, but a small fee is charged for inclusion in EPANI's online directory. Full details can be found on the website. Founded 2011.

Educational Publishers Council
The Publishers Association, 29B Montague Street, London WC1B 5BW

tel 020-7691 9191
email mail@publishers.org.uk
website www.publishers.org.uk

Provides a forum for publishers of printed and electronic learning resources for the school and college markets. It runs events and meetings for its members and provides an information service. It also promotes the industry through the media.

English Association
University of Leicester, University Road, Leicester LE1 7RH
tel 0116 229 7622
email engassoc@leicester.ac.uk
website www.le.ac.uk/engassoc
Chair Martin Halliwell, *Chief Executive* Helen Lucas

Aims to further knowledge, understanding and enjoyment of English literature and the English language, by working towards a fuller recognition of English as an essential element in education and in the community at large; by encouraging the study of English literature and language by means of conferences, lectures and publications; and by fostering the discussion of methods of teaching English of all kinds.

Federation of Children's Book Groups – see page 388

Federation of European Publishers
Rue Montoyer 31 Bte 8, B–1000 Brussels, Belgium
tel +32 2-7701110
email info@fep-fee.eu
website www.fep-fee.eu
President Pierre Dutilleul, *Director General* Anne Bergman-Tahon

Represents the interests of European publishers on EU affairs; informs members on the development of EU policies which could affect the publishing industry. Founded 1967.

Federation of Spanish Publishers' Association
(Federación de Gremios de Editores de España)
email fgee@fge.es
website www.federacioneditores.org
President Daniel Fernández

A non-profit, private professional association created to represent, manage, enhance and defend the general common interests of Spanish publishers on a national, European and international level. Founded 1978.

French Publishers' Association
(Syndicat National de l'Édition)
115 Blvd St Germain, 75006 Paris, France
tel +33 (0)1 4441 4050
website www.sne.fr

The French Publishers' Association is France's trade association of book publishers. It represents approximately 660 member companies whose combined business endeavours account for the bulk of French publishing.

The Gaelic Books Council – see Comhairle nan Leabhraichean/The Gaelic Books Council

The Greeting Card Association

United House, North Road, London N7 9DP
tel 020-7619 0396
website www.greetingcardassociation.org.uk
Chief Executive Sharon Little

The trade association for greeting card publishers. See website for information, including teachers' resources, lesson plans and card-making projects for children of all ages. Official magazine: *Progressive Greetings Worldwide*. Founded 1919.

Guernsey Arts Commission

North Esplanade, St Peter Port Guernsey GY1 2LQ
tel (01481) 709747
email info@arts.gg

The Commission's aim is to help promote, develop and support the arts in Guernsey through exhibitions, a community arts programme and public events.

Hayward Gallery

Southbank Centre, Belvedere Road, London SE1 8XX
tel 020-7960 4200
email customer@southbankcentre.co.uk
website www.southbankcentre.co.uk/visualarts

IBBY UK

2 Goodison Close, Fair Oak, Hants. SO50 7LE
email info@ibby.org.uk
website www.ibby.org.uk

IBBY (the International Board on Books for Young People) is a unique international alliance of everyone interested in children's literature including academics, librarians, publishers, booksellers, writers, illustrators, teachers, literacy workers, parents and others.

Imaginate

Summerhall, 1 Summerhall, Edinburgh EH9 1PL
tel 0131 225 8050
email info@imaginate.org.uk
website www.imaginate.org.uk
Director Tony Reekie, *General Manager* Tessa Rennie

Imaginate is a unique organisation in Scotland, leading in the promotion and development of the performing arts for children and young people. It is Imaginate's goal to ensure that children and young people in Scotland have regular access to high quality performing arts experiences. Imaginate's vision is driven by the belief that inspiring young people is essential not only to their individual development but to the development of Scotland, its economy and its place in the world. To achieve this ambition, Imaginate delivers an annual programme of art-form development and creative learning alongside the world renowned Imaginate Festival.

Imperial War Museums

Lambeth Road, London SE1 6HZ
tel 020-7416 5000
email publishing@iwm.org.uk
website www.iwm.org.uk
Contact Caitlin Flynn

Imperial War Museums tell the stories of people who have lived, fought and died in conflicts involving Britain and the Commonwealth since 1914. Drawing on unique collections, Imperial War Museums publish a large range of books linked to its exhibitions and archives. Books are produced both in-house and in partnership with other publishers.

Independent Publishers Guild

PO Box 12, Llain, Login SA34 0WU
tel (01437) 563335
email info@ipg.uk.com
website www.ipg.uk.com
Chair Oliver Gadsby
Membership Open to new and established publishers and book packagers

Provides an information and contact network for independent publishers. Also voices concerns of member companies within the book trade. Founded 1962.

Independent Theatre Council (ITC)

The Albany, Douglas Way, London SE8 4AG
tel 020-7403 1727
email admin@itc-arts.org
website www.itc-arts.org
Membership Rates start at £175 + vat

The Independent Theatre Council exists to enable the creation of high quality professional performing arts by supporting, representing and developing the people who manage and produce it. It has around 500 members from a wide range of companies, venues and individuals in the fields of drama, dance, opera, musical theatre, puppetry, mixed media, mime, physical theatre and circus. Founded 1974.

International Board on Books for Young People (IBBY)

Nonnenweg 12, Postfach CH–4009–Basel, Switzerland
tel +41 61-272 2917
email ibby@ibby.org
British Section 2 Goodison Close, Fair Oak, Hants SO50 7LE
email j.f.dunne@btinternet.com
website www.ibby.org
Secretary John Dunne

A non-profit organisation which represents an international network of people from all over the world who are committed to bringing books and children together. Its aims are:

• to promote international understanding through children's books;
• to give children everywhere the opportunity to have access to books with high literary and artistic standards;
• to encourage the publication and distribution of quality children's books, especially in developing countries;
• to provide support and training for those involved with children and children's literature;
• to stimulate research and scholarly works in the field of children's literature.

IBBY is composed of more than 75 National Sections all over the world and represents countries with well-developed book publishing and literacy programmes, and other countries with only a few dedicated professionals who are doing pioneer work in children's book publishing and promotion. Founded in Zurich, Switzerland in 1953.

International Publishers Association

23 avenue de France, 1202 Geneva, Switzerland
tel +41 22-704 1820
email secretariat@internationalpublishers.org
website www.internationalpublishers.org
President Richard Charkin, *Secretary-General* Jens Bammel

A federation of national, regional and specialist publishers' associations. Its membership comprises more than 60 organisations from more than 50 countries worldwide. Founded 1896.

Irish Writers' Centre

19 Parnell Square, Dublin 1, Republic of Ireland
tel +353 (0)1 872 1302
email info@writerscentre.ie
website www.writerscentre.ie
Director Valerie Bistany

The national resource centre for Irish writers. It runs workshops, seminars and events related to the art of writing, hosts professional developments seminars for writers, provides space for writers, writing groups and other literary organisations. It also provides information to writers and the general public.

The Kipling Society

Hon. Secretary John Lambert, 31 Brookside, Billericay, Essex CM11 1DT
email john.lambert1@btinternet.com
website www.kipling.org.uk
Membership £24 p.a.; £12 under age 23

Aims to encourage discussion and study of the work and life of Rudyard Kipling (1865–1936), to assist in the study of his writings, to hold discussion meetings, to publish a quarterly journal and website, with a Readers' Guide to Kipling's work, and to maintain a Kipling Library in London.

The Learning Hub

University of Reading, 4 Redlands Road, London Road Campus, Reading RG1 5EX
tel 0118-378 2702
email ncll@reading.ac.uk
website www.ncll.org.uk
Membership from £50 p.a.

The Learning Hub, which incorporates the National Centre for Language and Literacy (NCLL) and a Teaching Resource Base (TRB) offers many advantages for teachers, but a huge benefit to members is the ability to go and look at books and sets of teaching resources at the Hub, and get professional advice from staff, before they decide to invest in teaching materials for their school. Investing in materials is a big step – not only financially but also because decisions have a big impact on how literacy is taught. Membership of the Hub also entitles members to support in the form of materials for loan.

The C.S. Lewis Society (New York)

Secretary Clare Sarrocco, 84–23, 77th Avenue, Glendle, NY 11385–7706, USA
email subscribe@nycslsociety.com
email csarrocco@aol.com
website www.nycslsociety.com

The oldest society for the appreciation and discussion of C.S. Lewis (1898–1963). Founded 1969.

Literature Wales

Literature Wales, 4th Floor, Cambrian Buildings, Mount Stuart Square, Cardiff CF10 5FL
tel 029-2047 2266
email post@literaturewales.org
North West Wales Office: Tŷ Newydd, Llanystumdwy, Criceith, Gwynedd LL52 0LW
tel (01766) 522811
email tynewydd@literaturewales.org
website www.literaturewales.org
Chief Executive Lleucu Siencyn

The national company responsible for developing and promoting literature in Wales. Its activities include Wales Book of the Year, the National Poet of Wales, Writers on Tour funding scheme, Young People's Laureate for Wales, Bardd Plant Cymru, residential writing courses at Tŷ Newydd, funding and advice for writers, the Dinefwr Literature Festival, Young People's Writing Squads and an annual Literary Tourism events programme.

Literature Wales represents the interests of Welsh writers in all genres and languages, both inside Wales and internationally. It offers advice, support, bursaries, mentoring and opportunities to meet other writers. It works with the support of the Arts Council of Wales and the Welsh Government. It is one of the resident organisations of the Wales Millennium Centre, where it runs the Glyn Jones Centre.

Little Theatre Guild of Great Britain
Guild Secretary Caroline Chapman, Satley House, Satley, near Bishop Auckland,
Co. Durham DL13 4HU
tel (01388) 730042
website www.littletheatreguild.org

Aims to promote closer cooperation amongst the little theatres constituting its membership; to act as a coordinating and representative body on behalf of the little theatres; to maintain and advance the highest standards in the art of theatre; and to assist in encouraging the establishment of other little theatres.

Llyfrau Amgueddfa Cymru – National Museum Wales Books
Cathays Park, Cardiff CF10 3NP
tel 029-2057 3248
website www.museumwales.ac.uk
Head of Publishing Mari Gordon

Books based on the collections and research of Amgueddfa Cymru for adults, schools and children, in both Welsh and English. Founded 1907.

Magazines Canada (Canadian Magazine Publishers Association)
425 Adelaide Street West, Suite 700, Toronto, Ontario M5V 3C1, Canada
tel +1 416-504-0274
email info@magazinescanada.ca
website www.magazinescanada.ca
Chief Executive Officer Mark Jamison

The national trade association representing Canadian-owned, Canadian-content consumer, cultural, speciality, professional and business media magazines.

L.M. Montgomery Heritage Society
L.M. Montgomery Institute,
University of Prince Edward Island,
550 University Avenue, Charlottetown,
Prince Edward Island, Canada C1A 4P3
tel +1 902-628-4346
email lmmi@upei.ca
website www.lmmontgomery.ca

Dedicated to protecting L.M. Montgomery's (1874–1942) Prince Edward Island literary and historic legacy for the benefit, education and enjoyment of the public. The Society is a non-profit organisation made up of representatives from Island heritage sites and groups with a mutual interest in preserving and promoting Montgomery's Island home. The Society holds events honouring the life and times of Montgomery, including an annual birthday celebration held each November and the L.M. Montgomery Festival held each August. L.M.

Montgomery is the author of *Anne of Green Gables* and *Emily of New Moon*. Founded 1994.

Museum of London
150 London Wall, London EC2Y 5HN
tel 020-7001 9844
email info@museumoflondon.org.uk
website www.museumoflondon.org.uk

The Mythopoeic Society
Corresponding Secretary Edith Crowe,
The Mythopoeic Society, PO Box 6707, Altadena, CA 91003-6707, USA
email correspondence@mythsoc.org
website www.mythsoc.org
Membership with electronic *Mythprint* $12 p.a. (USA)

A non-profit international literary and educational organisation for the study, discussion and enjoyment of fantastic and mythic literature, especially the works of Tolkien, C.S. Lewis and Charles Williams. The word 'mythopoeic' (myth-oh-PAY-ik or myth-oh-PEE-ic), meaning 'mythmaking' or 'productive of myth', aptly describes much of the fictional work of the three authors who were also prominent members of an informal Oxford literary circle (1930s–1950s) known as the Inklings. Membership is open to all scholars, writers and readers of these literatures. The Society sponsors three periodicals: *Mythprint* (a bulletin of book reviews, articles and events), *Mythlore* (scholarly articles on mythic and fantastic literature), and *Mythic Circle* (a literary annual of original poetry and short stories). Each summer the Society holds an annual conference. Founded 1967.

National Art Library
Victoria & Albert Museum, South Kensington, London SW7 2RL
tel 020-7942 2000
website www.vam.ac.uk/page/n/national-art-library

The National Art Library is a public reference library of fine and decorative arts housed within the V&A. It contains books and documents from many different countries and periods. The Library is open to the public on Tuesday, Wednesday, Thursday and Saturday: 10.00–17.30 and on Friday 10.00–18.30.

National Association for the Teaching of English (NATE)
50 Broadfield Road, Sheffield S8 0XJ
tel 0114 255 5419
email info@nate.org.uk
website www.nate.org.uk
Membership £6.50 p.m. (individuals), £99 p.a. (schools/institutions)

The professional association for all those working in English education in the UK. NATE provides information about current developments, publications and resource materials. It also conducts research, in-service training and holds annual and regional conferences. Annual membership gives members termly copies of *Teaching English* (the Association's professional journal which includes practical teaching strategies and resources for both primary and secondary teachers as well as curriculum and pedagogy updates); *English in Education* (the Association's internationally-benchmarked academic journal); Resource Watch (a monthly email highlighting quality-assured resources, most of them available for free); *NATE News* (a monthly newsletter with national and Association updates); and access to the members' area of the website, which contains exclusive resources free to members. Membership also gives discounts on publications, courses and conferences. In addition, NATE runs a bespoke consultancy service for schools, providing tailored support for individual English departments and groups of schools. See website for details of how to join.

National Association of Writers' Groups (NAWG)

email chris.huck@ymail.com
website www.nawg.co.uk
Secretary Chris Huck
Membership £40 p.a. per group; £20 Associates (individuals)

Aims 'to advance the education of the general public throughout the UK, including the Channel Islands, by promoting the study and art of writing in all its aspects'. Publishes *LNK,* a bi-monthly magazine. Festival of Writing held annually in August/ September. New members always welcome. Founded 1995.

National Association of Writers in Education (NAWE)

PO Box 1, Sheriff Hutton, York YO60 7YU
tel (01653) 618429
email p.johnston@nawe.co.uk (general enquiries)
email clare@nawe.co.uk (membership enquiries)
website www.nawe.co.uk
Deputy Director Anne Caldwell

Membership organisation which represents and supports writers, teachers and all those involved in the development of creative writing in education. Professional membership benefits include public liability insurance cover and processing of CRB checks. The NAWE Professional Directory includes details of writers who work in schools and communities.

National Centre for Research in Children's Literature (NCRCL)

Department of English and Creative Writing, Digby Stuart College, Roehampton University, Roehampton Lane, London SW15 5PH
email l.sainsbury@roehampton.ac.uk
website www.ncrcl.ac.uk

NCRCL promotes research excellence in the field of children's literature, primarily through thriving MA programmes (which include academic and creative writing modules), doctoral research, conferences and staff publications. The NCRCL is based at Roehampton University, which houses a children's literature collection and a number of archives (including the Richmal Crompton archive) and special collections in the library. The website provides information on resources, activities and children's literature-related events. Professorial Fellow, Dame Jacqueline Wilson works closely with the NCRCL as does Research Fellow, Melvin Burgess.

National Galleries of Scotland

National Gallery Complex, The Mound, Edinburgh EH2 2EL
tel 0131 624 6200, 0131 624 6332 (press office)
email pressinfo@nationalgalleries.org
Scottish National Portrait Gallery, 1 Queen Street, Edinburgh EH2 1JD
Scottish National Gallery of Modern Art, Belford Road, Edinburgh EH4 3DR
The Dean Gallery, Belford Road, Edinburgh EH4 3DS
website www.nationalgalleries.org

National Gallery

Information Department, Trafalgar Square, London WC2N 5DN
tel 020-7747 2885
email information@ng-london.org.uk
website www.nationalgallery.org.uk

National Literacy Trust – see page 390

National Museum Wales – see Llyfrau Amgueddfa Cymru – National Museum Wales Books

National Museums Liverpool

127 Dale Street, Liverpool L2 2JH
tel 0151 207 0001
website www.liverpoolmuseums.org.uk

Venues: World Museum, Walker Art Gallery, Merseyside Maritime Museum, International Slavery Museum, Lady Lever Art Gallery, Sudley House, Museum of Liverpool.

National Museums Scotland

Chambers Street, Edinburgh EH1 1JF
tel 0300 123 6789
website www.nms.ac.uk

National Portrait Gallery

St Martin's Place, London WC2H 0HE
tel 020-7306 0055
website www.npg.org.uk

National Society for Education in Art and Design

3 Mason's Wharf, Potley Lane, Corsham, Wilts. SN13 9FY

tel (01225) 810134
email info@nsead.org
website www.nsead.org
General Secretary Lesley Butterworth, *Assistant General Secretary* Sophie Leach

The leading national authority concerned with art, craft and design across all phases of education in the UK. Offers the benefits of membership of a professional association, a learned society and a trade union. Has representatives on national and regional committees concerned with art and design education. Publishes *International Journal of Art and Design Education* online (three p.a.; Wiley Blackwell) and *AD* magazine for teachers. Founded 1888.

Natural History Museum
Cromwell Road, London SW7 5BD
tel 020-7942 5000
website www.nhm.ac.uk

The Edith Nesbit Society
21 Churchfields, West Malling, Kent ME19 6RJ
email edithnesbit@googlemail.com
website www.edithnesbit.co.uk
Membership £8 p.a. (single); £10 p.a. (joint); £15 (organisations/overseas)

Aims to promote an interest in the life and works of Edith Nesbit (1858–1924) by means of talks, a regular newsletter and other publications, and visits to relevant places. Founded 1996.

New Writing North
PO Box 1277, Newcastle upon Tyne NE99 5BP
email office@newwritingnorth.com
website www.newwritingnorth.com

The literature development agency for the North of England. Specialises in developing writers and acts as a broker between writers, producers, publishers and broadcasters. Flagship projects include Northern Writers' Awards, Gordon Burn Prize and Durham Book Festival.

New Zealand Association of Literary Agents
PO Box 46-031, Park Avenue, Lower Hutt 5044, New Zealand
email tfs@elseware.co.nz
website www.elseware.co.nz

Set up to establish standards and guidelines for literary agents operating in New Zealand. All members subscribe to a code of ethics which includes working on commission and not charging upfront fees for promotion or manuscript reading.

Newcastle University Library
Robinson Library, Newcastle University, Newcastle upon Tyne NE2 4HQ
tel 0191 208 7662
email libraryhelp@ncl.ac.uk
website www.ncl.ac.uk/library

A modern academic library with multi-disciplinary collections, including historical children's books.

The Special Collections
tel 0191 208 5146
email lib-speceng@ncl.ac.uk
website www.ncl.ac.uk/library/special-collections

Has over 100 collections. These range in date from the late-thirteenth century to the present day and include children's literature and many other subjects. The collection includes the internationally important Robert White Collection. Special collections of children's books include the Chorley Collection of over 200 books published in the 19th and early 20th centuries; the Meade Collection of 184 books written by the children's author L.T. Meade (1854–1914); the Joan Butler Collection of about 5,000 children's books published up to the mid-20th century (uncatalogued). Other collections include the Wallis Collection which contains material designed for the instruction of children; the Crawhall Collection which includes items such as the children's ABC books illustrated with woodcuts by Joseph Crawhall; the Bradshaw-Bewick Collection which contains several books designed for children and illustrated with woodcuts by Thomas Bewick. It also holds collections built up by schools from North-East England since the 16th century.

Special Collections at the Robinson Library is working in close collaboration with Seven Stories to collect and preserve neglected collections of historical children's books.

Office for Standards in Education (OFSTED)
Piccadilly Gate, Store Street, Manchester M1 2WD
tel 0300 123 1231
email enquiries@ofsted.gov.uk
website www.ofsted.gov.uk

A non-ministerial government department established under the Education (Schools Act) 1992. OFSTED is responsible for inspecting all educational provision for 16–19 year-olds to establish and monitor an independent inspection system for maintained schools in England. Its inspection role also includes the inspection of local educational authorities, teacher training institutions and youth work.

The Poetry Book Society – see page 217

The Poetry Society – see page 217

Poetry Society Education – see page 221

The Beatrix Potter Society
c/o The Lodge, Salisbury Avenue, Harpenden, Herts. AL5 2PS

tel (01582) 769755
email beatrixpottersociety@tiscali.co.uk
website www.beatrixpottersociety.org.uk
Membership £25 p.a. UK (£31 overseas); £30/£36 commercial/institutional

Promotes the study and appreciation of the life and works of Beatrix Potter (1866–1943) as author, artist, diarist, farmer and conservationist. Regular lecture meetings, conferences and events in the UK and USA. Quarterly newsletter. Small publishing programme. Founded 1980.

The Publishers Association
29ʙ Montague Street, London WC1B 5BW
tel 020-7691 9191
email mail@publishers.org.uk
website www.publishers.org.uk
Ceo Richard Mollet, *President* Dominic Knight, *Director of Publisher Relations* Emma House, *Operations Director* Mark Wharton, *Director of Policy and Communications* Susie Winter

The leading representative voice for books, journal, audio and electronic publishers in the UK. The Association has over 100 members and its role is to support publishers in their political, media and industry stakeholder communications. Founded 1896.

Publishers Association of New Zealand (PANZ)
B3, 72 Apollo Drive, Rosedale, Auckland 0632, New Zealand
tel +64 (0)9 280 3212
email anne@publishers.org.nz
website www.publishers.org.nz
Association Director Anne de Lautour

PANZ represents book, educational and digital publishers in New Zealand. Members include both the largest international publishers and companies in the independent publishing community.

Publishing Ireland – Foilsiú Éireann
25 Denzille Lane Dublin 2, Republic of Ireland
tel +353 (0)1 6394868
email info@publishingireland.com
website www.publishingireland.com
President Michael McLoughlin

Publishing Scotland
(formerly Scottish Publishers Association)
Scott House, 10 South St Andrew Street, Edinburgh EH2 2AZ
tel 0131 228 6866
email enquiries@publishingscotland.org
website www.publishingscotland.org
Chief Executive Marion Sinclair

A network for trade, training and development in the Scottish publishing industry. Founded 1973.

The Arthur Ransome Society Ltd (TARS)
Abbott Hall Museum, Kendal, Cumbria LA9 5AL
website www.arthur-ransome.org
President Gabriel Woolf

To celebrate the life, promote the works, and diffuse the ideas of Arthur Ransome (1884–1967), author of the world-famous *Swallows and Amazons* series of books for children. The Society seeks in particular to encourage children and others to engage, with due regard to safety, in adventurous pursuits; educate the public generally about Ransome and his work; sponsor research in relevant areas; be a communications link for those interested in any aspect of Arthur Ransome's life and works. Founded 1990.

ReadWell
26 Nailsworth Mills, Avening Road, Nailsworth, Glos. GL6 0BS
tel 0870 240 1124
email reading@readathon.org
website www.readwell.org.uk

In consultation with hospital and education staff in several children's hospitals, ReadWell was established in 2010 to help children in hospital through the therapeutic powers of reading. ReadWell brings books and storytellers to hospitalised children to help take their minds off their situation, ease their worries and entertain them. Carefully-chosen books are also available to help ensure that children don't suffer educationally by falling behind at school. ReadWell currently provides services to children's hospitals in Bristol, Birmingham and Oxford, with ambitions to expand the service across all UK children's hospitals and children's wards over the coming months and years.

RNIB National Library Service
RNIB HQ, 105 Judd Street, London WC1H 9NE
tel 0303 123 9999
email library@rnib.org.uk
website www.rnib.org.uk/library

The largest specialist library for readers with sight loss in the UK. It offers a comprehensive range of books and accessible information for children and adults in a range of formats including braille, large print and unabridged audio. Members have access to a free bi-annual magazine, an online library catalogue and a reader services team.

The Malcolm Saville Society
5 Churchfield, Harpenden, Herts. AL5 1LJ
email mystery@witchend.com
website www.witchend.com
Membership £15 p.a. (£17.50 Europe; £21 elsewhere)

Aims to remember and promote interest in the work of Malcolm Saville (1901–82), children's author. Regular social activities, library, contact directory and magazine (four p.a.). Founded 1994.

Scattered Authors' Society
email membership@scatteredauthors.org
website www.scatteredauthors.org

Aims to provide a forum for informal discussion, contact and support for professional writers in children's fiction. Founded 1998.

School Library Association

1 Pine Court, Kembrey Park, Swindon SN2 8AD
tel (01793) 530166
email info@sla.org.uk
website www.sla.org.uk

Promotes the development of school libraries and information literacy as central to the curriculum. It publishes book lists and guidelines for library and resource centres, a quarterly journal and provides training and an information service.

Science Museum

Exhibition Road, London SW7 2DD
tel 0870 870 4868
website www.sciencemuseum.org.uk

Scottish Book Trust (SBT)

Sandeman House, Trunk's Close, 55 High Street, Edinburgh EH1 1SR
tel 0131 524 0160
email info@scottishbooktrust.com
website www.scottishbooktrust.com

Scottish Book Trust (SBT) is Scotland's national agency for the promotion of reading, writing and literature. Programmes include: Bookbug, a free universal book-gifting programme which encourages families to read with their children from birth; an ambitious school's programme including national tours, the virtual events programme Authors Live and the Scottish Children's Book Awards; the Live Literature funding programme, a national initiative enabling Scottish citizens to engage with authors, playwrights, poets, storytellers and illustrators; a writer development programme, offering mentoring and professional development for emerging and established writers; and a readership development programme featuring a national writing campaign as well as Book Week Scotland during last week in November. SBT also has a website full of information for readers and writers, including writing tips, booklists, podcasts, competitions and blogs for all ages.

The Scottish Storytelling Forum

The Scottish Storytelling Centre, 43–45 High Street, Edinburgh EH1 1SR
tel 0131 556 9579
email reception@scottishstorytellingcentre.com
website www.scottishstorytellingcentre.co.uk
Membership Network members annual subscription £15 (£12 concession), for updates, discounts and opportunities

Scotland's national charity for oral storytelling, established to encourage and support the telling and sharing of stories across all ages and all sectors of society, in particular those who, for reasons of poverty or disability, were excluded from artistic experiences. The Scottish Storytelling Centre is the Forum's resource and training centre which also presents a year-round programme of storytelling and traditional arts events, as well as training workshop opportunities. The Storytelling Network has over 100 professional storytellers across Scotland. Founded 1992.

Seven Stories – National Centre for Children's Books – see page 385

Society for Editors and Proofreaders (SfEP)

Apsley House, 176 Upper Richmond Road, London SW15 2SH
tel 020-8785 6155
email administrator@sfep.org.uk
website www.sfep.org.uk

Works to promote high editorial standards and achieve recognition of its members' professional status, through local and national meetings, an annual conference, discussion forums and a regular e-magazine. The Society publishes an online directory of ordinary and advanced members. It also runs a programme of reasonably priced open and in-house workshops/training days, which help newcomers to acquire basic editorial skills, and enable experienced editors and proofreaders to update their skills or broaden their competence. Training also covers aspects of professional practice or business for the self-employed. The Society supports moves towards recognised standards of training and accreditation for editors and proofreaders and has developed its own Accreditation in Proofreading qualification. It has close links with the Publishing Training Centre and the Society of Indexers, is represented on the BSI Technical Committee dealing with copy preparation and proof correction (BS 5261), and works to foster good relations with all relevant bodies and organisations in the UK and worldwide. Founded 1988.

Society for Storytelling (SfS)

The Morgan Library, Aston Street, Wem, Shrops. SY4 5AU
tel 07534 578386
email admin@sfs.org.uk
website www.sfs.org.uk

A registered charity providing information on oral storytelling, events, storytellers and traditional stories. SfS volunteers have specialist knowledge of storytelling in education, health, therapy and business settings. To increase public awareness of the art it promotes National Storytelling Week, which takes place in the first week of February. The SfS provides a network for anyone interested in the art of oral storytelling whether they are full-time storytellers, use storytelling in their work, tell for the love of it or just want to listen. It holds an annual conference each Spring and produces a quarterly newsletter, a *Directory of Storytellers* and a variety of books and fact sheets. Unsolicited ideas or manuscripts are welcome if thoroughly researched and relevant. Founded 1993.

Society of Artists Agents
website www.saahub.com

Formed to promote professionalism in the illustration industry and to forge closer links between clients and artists through an agreed set of guidelines. The Society believes in an ethical approach through proper terms and conditions, thereby protecting the interests of the artists and clients. Founded 1992.

The Society of Authors – see page 375

Society of Children's Book Writers and Illustrators (SCBWI) – see page 379

Society of Editors
Director Bob Satchwell, University Centre, Granta Place, Mill Lane, Cambridge CB2 1RU
tel (01223) 304080
email office@societyofeditors.org
website www.societyofeditors.org
Membership £230 p.a. depending on category

Formed from the merger of the Guild of Editors and the Association of British Editors, the Society has more than 400 members in national, regional and local newspapers, magazines, broadcasting and digital media, journalism education and media law. It campaigns for media freedom, self regulation, the public's right to know and the maintenance of standards in journalism. Founded 1999.

Society of Young Publishers
The Secretary, c/o The Publishers Association, 29ʙ Montague Street, London WC1B 5BW
email sypchair@thesyp.org.uk
website www.thesyp.org.uk
Membership Open to anyone employed in publishing or hoping to be soon; £30 p.a. standard; £24 student/unwaged

Organises monthly events which offer the chance to network and hear senior figures talk on topics of key importance to the publishing industry. Runs a job database advertising the latest vacancies and internships as well as a blog, PressForward, and a print magazine, *InPrint*. Also has branches in Oxford, Scotland and the North. Founded 1949.

Speaking of Books
46ʙ Vanbrugh Park, London SE3 7JQ
tel 020-8858 6616
email jan@speakingofbooks.co.uk
website www.speakingofbooks.co.uk

Arranges school visits by writers, illustrators and storytellers. Also in-service training days relating to literacy.

Spread the Word
The Albany, Douglas Way, London SE8 4AG
tel 020-8692 0231 extension 249
email info@spreadtheword.org.uk
website www.spreadtheword.org.uk

Spread the Word is London's writer development agency. Provides advice, information, craft and career support for the writers of London. Works with writers at all stages of development from those beginning to engage with writing to those who are professional career writers, across all forms and genres. Spread the Word is a national portfolio organisation of Arts Council England. Founded 1995.

The Robert Louis Stevenson Club
Secretary John W.S. Macfie, 17 Heriot Row, Edinburgh EH3 6HP
tel 0131 556 1896
email mail@stevenson-house.co.uk
Membership £25 p.a.; £180 for 10 years

Aims to foster interest in Robert Louis Stevenson's life (1850–94) and works through various events and its newsletter. Founded 1920.

The Story Museum
42 Pembroke Street, Oxford OX1 1BP
tel (01865) 790050
email onceuponatime@storymuseum.org.uk
website www.storymuseum.org.uk

The Story Museum celebrates story in all forms and explores their enduring power to teach and delight. In April 2014 the Story Museum opened a building in central Oxford as a centre to inspire present and future generations by providing great ways of engaging with great stories. Also runs an active education and outreach programme alongside an exhibition and events programme.

The Swedish Institute for Children's Books (Svenska barnboksinstitutet)
Odengatan 61, SE–113 22 Stockholm, Sweden
tel +46 8-54542050
email info@sbi.kb.se
website www.sbi.kb.se

A special library open to the public and an information centre for children's and young people's literature. The aim is to promote this kind of literature in Sweden as well as Swedish children's and young people's literature abroad. Founded 1965.

Tate
Tate Britain, Millbank, London SW1P 4RG
tel 020-7887 8888
email visiting.britain@tate.org.uk
Tate Modern, Bankside, London SE1 9TG
tel 020-7887 8888
email visiting.modern@tate.org.uk
Tate Liverpool, Albert Dock, Liverpool L3 4BB
tel 0151 702 7400

email visiting.liverpool@tate.org.uk
Tate St Ives, Porthmeor Beach, St Ives, Cornwall TR26 1TG
tel (01736) 796226
email visiting.stives@tate.org.uk
website www.tate.org.uk

Tate is a family of four galleries which hold the national collection of British art from 1500 to the present day and international modern and contemporary art. The collection embraces all media, from painting, drawing, sculpture and prints to photography, video and film, installation and performance. It is on display at the four galleries and around the world in temporary and long-term exhibitions, via loans.

Teenage Magazine Arbitration Panel (TMAP)

35–38 New Bridge Street, London EC4V 6BW
tel 020-7404 4166
website www.tmap.org.uk

The magazine industry's self-regulatory body which ensures that the sexual content of teenage magazines is presented in a responsible and appropriate manner.

The Tolkien Society

email membership@tolkiensociety.org
website www.tolkiensociety.org
Membership £30 p.a.; £2 p.a. (Entings (under 16s))

United Kingdom Literacy Association (UKLA)

University of Leicester, Leicester LE1 7RH
tel 0116 223 1664
email admin@ukla.org
website www.ukla.org

UKLA is a registered charity, which has as its sole object the advancement of education in literacy. It is committed to promoting good practice nationally and internationally in literacy and language teaching and research. Its activities include:

• a conference programme of international, national and local conferences reflecting language and literacy interests;
• an active publications committee. Members are kept up to date via UKLA journals and website. Members receive a copy of the newsletter, *UKLA News* (three p.a.), and the journal *Literacy* (see page 338). For an additional subscription, members can receive the *Journal of Research in Reading*. Both of the UKLA journals are refereed and include research reports, both qualitative and quantitative research, and critiques of current policy and practice as well as discussions and debates about current issues. UKLA also produces a range of books, written mainly with teachers and students in mind. In addition UKLA offers *English 4–11* published jointly with the English Association;
• regular responses to national consultations, including those organised through the DfES or QCA.

Consequently, the UKLA often seeks information and responses from its members, as well as establishing a UKLA response to particular issues;
• promoting and disseminating research. UKLA provides support and small grants for literacy research;
• networking – UKLA helps its members to network both in the UK and through its worldwide contacts. UKLA's affiliation to the International Reading Association enables it to keep members in touch with events and ideas in other parts of the world. UKLA is also involved in specific international projects such as Project Connect, for which it provides some support for literacy education in Zanzibar and Malawi. Founded in 1963, renamed in 2003.

V&A Museum of Childhood

Cambridge Heath Road, London E2 9PA
tel 020-8983 5200
email moc@vam.ac.uk
website www.museumofchildhood.org.uk

Holds one of the largest and oldest collections of toys and childhood artefacts in the world. As well as its permanent displays, the museum has temporary exhibitions, workshops and activities for all.

V&A Publishing

Victoria and Albert Museum, South Kensington, London SW7 2RL
tel 020-7942 2966
email vapubs@vam.ac.uk
website www.vandapublishing.com
Publisher Mark Eastment, *PR and Marketing* Julie Chan, *Sales* Susannah Priede, *Rights* Nina Jacobson

Popular and scholarly books on fine and decorative arts, architecture, contemporary design, fashion and photography. Founded 1980.

Voice of the Listener & Viewer Ltd (VLV)

The Old Rectory Business Centre, Springhead Road, Northfleet DA11 8HN
tel (01474) 338716
email info@vlv.org.uk
website www.vlv.org.uk
Administrator Sue Washbrook

An independent, non-profit-making membership association, free from political, commercial and sectarian affiliations, working for quality and diversity in British broadcasting. VLV represents the interests of listeners and viewers as citizens and consumers across the full range of broadcasting issues. VLV is concerned with the structures, regulation, funding and institutions that underpin the British broadcasting system but also takes note of developments in Europe and the wider world. It holds regular conferences and seminars and publishes The Bulletin and an e-newsletter. VLV is a charitable company limited by guarantee. Founded 1983.

Welsh Books Council/Cyngor Llyfrau Cymru

Castell Brychan, Aberystwyth, Ceredigion SY23 2JB
tel (01970) 624151
email castellbrychan@cllc.org.uk
website www.cllc.org.uk
website www.gwales.com
Ceo Elwyn Jones

A national body funded directly by the Welsh Government which provides a focus for the publishing industry in Wales. Awards grants for publishing in Welsh and English. Provides services to the trade in the fields of editing, design, marketing and distribution. The Council is a key enabling institution in the world of books and provides services and information in this field to all who are associated with it. Founded 1961.

The Henry Williamson Society

General Secretary Sue Cumming, 7 Monmouth Road, Dorchester, Dorset DT1 2DE
tel (01305) 264092
email zseagull@aol.com
Membership Secretary Margaret Murphy, 16 Doran Drive, Redhill, Surrey RH1 6AX
tel (01737) 763228
email mm@misterman.freeserve.co.uk
website www.henrywilliamson.co.uk
Chairman Will Harris
Membership £15 p.a.

Aims to encourage a wider readership and greater understanding of the literary heritage left by Henry Williamson (1895–1977). Two meetings annually; also weekend activities. Publishes an annual journal. Founded 1980.

Writers Advice Centre for Children's Books

Shakespeare House, 168 Lavender Hill, London SW11 5TG
tel 020-7801 6300
email info@writersadvice.co.uk
website www.writersadvice.co.uk
Managing Editor Louise Jordan

Dedicated to helping new and published children's writers by offering both editorial advice and tips on how to get published. The Centre also runs an online children's writing correspondence course and publishes a small list of its own under the name of Wacky Bee Books (www.wackybeebooks.com). Founded 1994.

The Writers' Guild of Great Britain

First Floor, 134 Tooley Street, London SE1 2TU
tel 020-7833 0777
email admin@writersguild.org.uk
website www.writersguild.org.uk
General Secretary Bernie Corbett

Membership Full, Candidate and Affiliate membership available

A trade union for professional and aspiring writers in TV, radio, film, theatre, books and games with 2,000 members; affiliated to the Trades Union Congress. The Guild negotiates collective minimum terms agreements with the main broadcasters and trade bodies for film and TV producers and subsidised theatre – these cover fees, advances, royalties, residuals, pension contributions, rights, credits and other matters. Guild members have access to free contract vetting, legal advice and representation in work-related disputes, and the Writers' Guild Welfare Fund gives emergency assistance to members in financial trouble. Also offered are professional, cultural and social activities to help provide writers with a sense of community, making writing a less isolated occupation. Members receive a weekly email bulletin containing news and work opportunities. The Writers' Guild Awards are presented every year.

Young at Art

Cotton Court, 30–42 Waring Street, Belfast BT1 2ED
tel 028-9023 0660
email admin@youngatart.co.uk
website www.youngatart.co.uk

Coordinates the annual Belfast Children's Festival as well as a wide variety of projects that encourage children and young people under 18 to enjoy the arts, develop awareness of its impact on their lives, and have a say in what their arts provision should be. These include workshop programmes, commissions, regional touring, seminars, training, research, publications and online resources. Founded 2000.

Youth Libraries Group (YLG)

c/o Sue Polchow, Literacy & Library Adviser, MLS, Arden House, Shepley Lane, Hawk Green, Marple, Stockport, Cheshire SK6 7JW
tel 07919 001003
email sue@microlib.co.uk
website www.cilip.org.uk/about/special-interest-groups/youth-libraries-group
Secretary Sue Polchow

YLG is open to all members of the Chartered Institute for Library and Information Professionals (CILIP) who are interested in children's work. At a national level its aims are:

• to influence the provision of library services for children and the provision of quality literature;
• to inspire and support all librarians working with children and young people;
• to liaise with other national professional organisations in pursuit of such aims.

At a local level, the YLG organises regular training courses, supports professional development and provides opportunities to meet colleagues. It holds an annual conference and judges the CILIP Carnegie and Kate Greenaway Awards (see page 411).

Children's book and illustration prizes and awards

This list provides details of prizes, competitions and awards relevant to children's writers and artists.

ALCS Educational Writers' Award

The Society of Authors, 84 Drayton Gardens, London SW10 9SB
tel 020-7373 6642
email info@societyofauthors.org
website www.societyofauthors.org/education-book-prize

This is an annual award alternating each year between books in the 5–11 and 11–18 year age groups. It is given to an outstanding example of traditionally published non-fiction (with or without illustrations) that stimulates and enhances learning. The work must have been first published in the UK, in the English language, within the previous two calendar years. Deadline 30 June.

The Hans Christian Andersen Awards

International Board on Books for Young People, Nonnenweg 12, Postfach CH–4009 Basel, Switzerland
tel +41 61-272 2917
email ibby@ibby.org
website www.ibby.org

The Medals are awarded every two years to a living author and an illustrator who by the outstanding value of their work are judged to have made a lasting contribution to literature for children and young people. *2014 winners*: Nahoko Uehashi (author), Roger Mello (illustrator).

Arts Council England, London

Arts Council England, 21 Bloomsbury Street, London WC1B 3HF
tel 0845 300 6200
email enquiries@artscouncil.org.uk
website www.artscouncil.org.uk

Arts Council England, London is the regional office for the capital, covering 33 boroughs and the City of London. Grants are available through the 'Grants for the Arts' scheme throughout the year to support a variety of projects.
    Contact the Literature Unit for more information, or see website for an application form.

Arts Council site YouWriteOn.com Book Awards

tel 07948 392634
email edward@youwriteon.com
website www.youwriteon.com

Arts Council-funded site publishing awards for new fiction writers. Random House and Orion, the publishers of authors such as Dan Brown and Terry Pratchett, provide free professional critiques for the highest rated new writers' opening chapters and short stories on YouWriteOn.com each month. The highest rated writers of the year are then published, three in each of the adult and children's categories, through YouWriteOn's free paperback publishing service for writers. The novel publishing awards total £1,000. Writers can enter at any time throughout the year: closing date is 31 December each year. Join YouWriteOn.com to participate. Previous YouWriteOn.com winners have been published by mainstream publishers such as Random House, Orion, Penguin and Hodder including Channel 4 TV Book Club winner and bestseller *The Legacy* by Katherine Webb. Founded 2005.

Association for Library Service to Children Awards

American Library Association, 50 East Huron Street, Chicago, IL 60611, USA
tel +1 800-545-2433 ext. 2163
email alscawards@ala.org
website www.ala.org/alsc

The following awards are administered by ALSC:
• The Caldecott Medal (named in honour of the 19th-century English illustrator Randolph Caldecott) is awarded annually to the artist of the most distinguished US picture book for children.
• The Newbery Medal (named after the 18th-century British bookseller John Newbery) is awarded annually to the author of the most distinguished contribution to US literature for children.
• The Theodor Seuss Geisel Award (named after the world-renowned children's author a.k.a. Dr Seuss) is given annually to the author(s) and illustrator(s) of the most distinguished contribution to the body of children's literature known as beginning reader books published in the USA during the preceding year.
• The Robert F. Sibert Informational Book Award is given annually to the author of the most distinguished informational book published in English during the preceding year.
• The Wilder Medal, a bronze medal, honours an author or illustrator whose books, published in the USA, have made, over a period of years, a substantial and lasting contribution to literature for children.

• The Batchelder Award is awarded annually to an outstanding children's book translated from a language other than English and originally published in a country other than the United States.

• The Pura Belpré Awards are presented annually to a Latino/Latina writer and illustrator whose work best portrays, affirms and celebrates the Latino cultural experience, co-sponsored with REFORMA.

• The Odyssey Award is given for the best audio book produced for children and/or young adults. Co-administered with YALSH and sponsored by Book list.

Bardd Plant Cymru (Welsh-Language Children's Poet Laureate)
Welsh Books Council, Castell Brychan, Aberystwyth, Ceredigion SY23 2JB
tel (01970) 624151
email castellbrychan@wbc.org.uk
website www.cllc.org.uk

The main aim is to raise the profile of poetry amongst children and to encourage them to compose and enjoy poetry. During his/her term of office the bard will visit schools as well as helping children to create poetry through electronic workshops.

The scheme's partner organisations are: S4C, the Welsh Books Council, Urdd Gobaith Cymru and Literature Wales.

The Bath Children's Novel Award
12 Great Pulteney Street, Bath BA2 4BR
email bathnovelaward@gmail.com
website www.bathnovelaward.co.uk
Founder Caroline Ambrose

International competition for unpublished and indie novelists writing for children. Any genre of chapter books, middle grade and young adult. No picture books. 1st prize £1,000. Submission guidelines: first 5,000 words and synopsis. £20 entry fee. Closing date: 11 October 2015. For full details see the website.

Blue Peter Book Awards
Book Trust, G8 Battersea Studios,
80 Silverthorne Road, London SW8 3HE
tel 020-7801 8800
email bluepeter@booktrust.org.uk
website www.booktrust.org.uk
Contact Katherine Woodfine

Awarded annually, winners are shortlisted by a panel of expert adult judges, then a group of young *Blue Peter* viewers judge the two categories, which are: the Best Story and the Best Book with Facts. Winning books are announced on *Blue Peter* in March. Established 2000.

2015 winners: Pamela Butchart (illustrated by Thomas Flintham) for *The Spy Who Loved School Dinners* and Andy Seed (illustrated by Scott Garrett) for *The Silly Book of Side-Splitting Stuff*.

Bologna Children's Book Fair International Award for Illustration
email bookfair@bolognafiere.it
website www.bolognachildrensbookfair.com

The aim of the award is to support the illustration work of young artists, the special quality of whose work has yet to be acknowledged. Established in 2009, this annual award is granted to one of the young illustrators selected each year from the Bologna Children's Book Fair Illustrators Exhibition.

BolognaRagazzi Award
Piazza Costituzione 6, 40128 Bologna, Italy
tel +39 051-282111
email bolognaragazziaward@bolognafiere.it
website www.bolognachildrensbookfair.com
Takes place March

Prizes are given to encourage excellence in children's publishing in the categories of fiction, non-fiction, new horizons and Opera Prima, which is devoted to new authors and illustrators and aims to acknowledge publishers' efforts at finding new talent. The Digital Award recognises innovation and excellence in global digital children's publishing.

The Branford Boase Award
8 Bolderwood Close, Bishopstoke, Eastleigh, Hants SO50 8PG
tel 023-8060 0439
email anne.marley@tiscali.co.uk
website www.branfordboaseaward.org.uk

An annual award of £1,000 is made to a first-time writer of a full-length children's novel (age 7+) published in the preceding year; the editor is also recognised. Its aim is to encourage new writers for children and to recognise the role of perceptive editors in developing new talent. The Award was set up in memory of the outstanding children's writer Henrietta Branford and the gifted editor and publisher Wendy Boase who both died in 1999. Closing date for nominations: end of December.

Carnegie Medal – see The CILIP Carnegie and Kate Greenaway Awards

The CBI Book of the Year Awards
Children's Books Ireland,
17 North Great George's Street, Dublin 1,
Republic of Ireland
tel +353 (0)1 8727475
email info@childrensbooksireland.ie
website www.childrensbooksireland.ie

These awards are made annually to authors and illustrators born or resident in Ireland and are open to books written in Irish or English. The awards are: CBI Book of the Year, the Eilis Dillon Award (for a first children's book), the Honour Award for Fiction, the Honour Award for Illustration, the Special Judges' Award and the Children's Choice Award. Schools and reading groups nationwide take part in a shadowing scheme: each group reads the shortlisted books and engages with them using the suggested questions and activities in the CBI shadowing packs.

Each group then votes for their favourite book, the results of which form the basis for the Children's Choice Award. Closing date: December for work published between 1 January and 31 December of an awards year. Winners announced in May. Founded 1990.

Cheltenham Illustration Awards

email cheltillustrationawards@glos.ac.uk
website www.cheltenham-illustration-awards.com

Exhibition and Annual submissions are invited and can be freely interpreted in a narrative context. Submissions of work are free and open to all students, emerging and established illustrators and graphic novelists. A selection panel will assess entries.

The selected work will be showcased in an exhibition and published in the Cheltenham Illustration Awards Annual, which will be distributed to education institutions and publishers. Deadline for submissions: June. See website for further information.

The Children's Laureate

Book Trust, Studio G8, Battersea Studios,
80 Silverthorne Road, London SW8 3HE
tel 020-7801 8800
email childrenslaureate@booktrust.org.uk
website www.childrenslaureate.org.uk
Contact Katherine Woodfine

The idea for the Children's Laureate originated from a conversation between (the then) Poet Laureate Ted Hughes and children's writer Michael Morpurgo. The post was established in 1999 to celebrate exceptional children's authors and illustrators and to acknowledge their importance in creating the readers of tomorrow. Quentin Blake was the first Children's Laureate (1999–2001), followed by Anne Fine (2001–2003), Michael Morpurgo (2003–2005), Jacqueline Wilson (2005–2007), Michael Rosen (2007–2009), Anthony Browne (2009–2011), Julia Donaldson (2011–2013), Malorie Blackman (2013–2015) and Chris Riddell (2015–2017).

The CILIP Carnegie and Kate Greenaway Awards

CILIP, 7 Ridgmount Street, London WC1E 7AE
tel 020-7255 0650
email ckg@cilip.org.uk
website www.carnegiegreenaway.org.uk

Recommendations for the following two awards are invited from members of CILIP (the Chartered Institute of Library and Information Professionals), who are asked to submit a preliminary list of not more than two titles for each award, accompanied by a 50-word appraisal justifying the recommendation of each book. The awards are selected by the Youth Libraries Group of CILIP.

Carnegie Medal

Awarded annually for an outstanding book for children (fiction or non-fiction) written in English and first published in the UK during the preceding year or co-published elsewhere within a three-month time lapse.

Kate Greenaway Medal

Awarded annually for an outstanding illustrated book for children first published in the UK during the preceding year or co-published elsewhere within a three-month time lapse. Books intended for older as well as younger children are included, and reproduction will be taken into account. The Colin Mears Award (£5,000) is awarded annually to the winner of the Kate Greenaway Medal.

The CLPE Poetry Award

CLPE, Webber Street, London SE1 8QW
tel 020-7401 3382/3
email ann@clpe.co.uk
website www.clpe.co.uk

An award that aims to honour excellence in children's poetry. Organised by the Centre for Literacy in Primary Education, it is presented annually in July for a book of poetry published in the preceding year. The book can be a single-poet collection or an anthology. Submissions deadline: end of February. *2014 winner*: *Wayland* by Tony Mitton, illustrated by John Lawrence (David Fickling Books).

Commonword Diversity Writing for Children Prize

6 Mount Street, Manchester M2 5NS
tel 0161 832 3777
email admin@cultureword.org.uk
website www.cultureword.org.uk
website www.ihaveadream.org.uk

Commonword is a valuable resource for poets and writers in the North West. It provides support, training and publishing opportunities for new writers. The Commonword Diversity Writing for Children Prize is awarded annually by Commonword in conjunction with Puffin Books and Catherine Pellegrino & Associates. The Prize welcomes submissions from unpublished children's authors whose writing embraces ethnic diversity either through their own ethnicity and culture and/or in their writing. The winning writer receives £500, professional mentoring and £100 of Puffin books.

Costa Book Awards

(formerly the Whitbread Book Awards)
The Booksellers Association, 6 Bell Yard,
London WC2A 2JR
tel 020-7421 4640
email naomi.gane@booksellers.org.uk
website www.costabookawards.com
Contact Naomi Gane

The awards celebrate and promote the most enjoyable contemporary British writing. There are five categories: Novel, First Novel, Biography, Poetry and Children's. Each category is judged by a panel of three judges and the winner in each category receives £5,000. Nine final judges then choose the Costa Book of the Year from the five category winners. The overall winner receives £30,000. Authors of submitted books must have been resident in the UK or Ireland for over six months of each of the previous three years (although UK or Irish nationality is not essential). Books must have been first published in the UK or Ireland between 1 November of the previous year and 31 October of the current year. Books previously published elsewhere are not eligible. Submissions must be received from publishers. Closing date: end of June.

Creative Scotland

tel 0330 333 2000
email enquiries@creativescotland.com
website www.creativescotland.com

Support is offered to writers, playwrights and publishers through Open Project Funding. See www.creativescotland.com for details. See also Scottish Children's Book Awards (page 415).

The Roald Dahl Funny Prize

Book Trust, G8 Battersea Studios,
80 Silverthorne Road, London SW8 3HE
tel 020-7801 8800
email prizes@booktrust.org.uk
website www.booktrust.org.uk
Contact Claire Shanahan

Founded by Michael Rosen, Children's Laureate (2007–9), this prize is unique in its aim to honour the funniest children's books of the year. This is part of the wider objective of promoting and drawing attention to humour in children's literature. The winners of the two categories, the Funniest Book for Children Aged 6 and Under and the Funniest Book for Children Aged 7–14, are awarded £2,500 each, as well as both receiving a bottle of wine from the Dahl family's wine cellar. Fiction, non-fiction and poetry are welcomed in each category. The Prize is currently on hold.

East Sussex Children's Book Award

website www.eastsussex.gov.uk/libraries/
childrenslibrary/goodreads/reviews/bookaward

Each year children in East Sussex can vote for their favourite read from five fiction paperbacks. Participating schools read and discuss shortlisted books and the winner is announced in June.

Etisalat Award for Arabic Children's Literature

email info@uaebby.org.ae
website www.etisalataward.ae

The prize of one million dirhams (about £79,000) is open only to children's books written in Arabic.

Translated titles are not eligible. Organised by The UAE Board on Books for Young People.

Evening Standard Oscar's First Book Prize

Oscar's First Book Prize, Evening Standard,
Room 121, 2 Derry Street, London W8 5TT
website www.standard.co.uk

Launched in 2013 in memory of Oscar Ashton, son of Evening Standard's Executive Editor James Ashton, this £5,000 prize sponsored by Waitrose is awarded to the pre-school book (published during the previous year) the judges consider to be the best.

Publishers may enter up to three books per imprint. Collections and anthologies are not eligible. Books must be first published in the UK between 1 January and 31 December. Previously published books, self-published books and ebooks are not eligible. Full terms and conditions and a downloadable entry form are available on the website.

The Eleanor Farjeon Award

website www.childrensbookcircle.org.uk

An annual award which may be given to an individual or an organisation. Librarians, authors, publishers, teachers, reviewers and others who have given exceptional service to the children's book industry are eligible for nomination. It was instituted in 1965 by the Children's Book Circle (page 387) for distinguished services to children's books and named after the much-loved children's writer Eleanor Farjeon.

Foyle Young Poets of the Year Award – see page 222

Grampian Children's Book Award

website www.aberdeenshire.gov.uk/libraries/
young_people

This award is for best fiction book, judged solely by pupils in participating secondary schools in Aberdeen City, Aberdeenshire and Moray and children in Aberdeen Central Children's Library. The award is given to a children's book published in paperback between July and June of the previous year.

Kate Greenaway Medal – see The CILIP Carnegie and Kate Greenaway Awards

The Guardian Children's Fiction Prize

email childrensprize@guardian.co.uk
website www.guardian.co.uk/books/
guardianchildrensfictionprize

The *Guardian's* annual prize is for a work of fiction for children published by a British or Commonwealth writer. See website for eligibility, submission guidelines and closing dates.

Kelpies Prize

Floris Books, 15 Harrison Gardens,
Edinburgh EH11 1SH
tel 0131 337 2372
email floris@florisbooks.co.uk
website www.florisbooks.co.uk/kelpiesprize

An annual prize open to writers of fiction suitable for both boys and girls. Entries can be submitted in three categories: Young Kelpies (6–8 year olds), Kelpies (8–11 year olds) and Kelpies Teen (11–14 year olds). Stories must be set wholly, or mainly, in Scotland and must not have been previously commercially published. The winner receives £2,000 and their book will be published in the Kelpies range of Scottish fiction by Floris Books. Closing date: end February. Winner announced August. 2014 winner: *The Mixed-up Summer of Lily McLean* by Lindsay Littleson. See website for full details.

Lancashire Book of the Year Award

tel 0845 053000
email enquiries@lancashire.gov.uk
website www.lancashire.gov.uk

A prize of £1,000 is awarded to the best work of fiction for children aged 12–14 years, written by a UK author and first published between 1 September and 31 August of the previous year. The winner is announced in May. *2014 winner*: *Undone* by Cat Clarke.

The Astrid Lindgren Memorial Award

Swedish Arts Council, PO Box 27215,
SE–102 53 Stockholm, Sweden
tel +46 8-51926400
email literatureaward@alma.se
website www.alma.se

An award to honour the memory of Astrid Lindgren, Sweden's favourite author, and to promote children's and youth literature around the world. The award is five million Swedish kronas, the world's largest for children's and youth literature, and the second-largest literature prize in the world. It is awarded annually to one or more recipients, regardless of language or nationality.

Authors, illustrators, storytellers and promoters of reading are eligible. The award is for life-long work or artistry rather than for individual pieces. The prize can only be awarded to living people. The body of work must uphold the highest artistic quality and evoke the deeply humanistic spirit of Astrid Lindgren.

The winner is selected by a jury based on nominations for outstanding achievement from selected nominating bodies around the world. The jury has the right to suggest nominees of their own. Neither individuals nor organisations may nominate themselves. *2015 winner*: PRAESA, the Project for the Study of Alternative Education in South Africa. The Astrid Lindgren Memorial Award is administered by the Swedish Arts Council. Founded 2002.

The Macmillan Prize for Children's Picture Book Illustration

Macmillan Children's Books, 20 New Wharf Road,
London N1 9RR
email macmillanprize@macmillan.co.uk

Four prizes are awarded annually for unpublished children's book illustrations by art students in higher education establishments in the UK. Prizes: £1,000 (1st), £500 (2nd), £250 (3rd) and the Lara Jones award for the entrant that shows most promise as an illustrator of books for babies and very young children (£500).

Marsh Award for Children's Literature in Translation

Administered by The English-Speaking Union (on behalf of the Marsh Christian Trust),
Dartmouth House, 37 Charles Street,
London W1J 5ED
tel 020-7529 1590
email education@esu.org
website www.esu.org/marsh

This biennial award of £3,000 is given to the translator of a book for children (aged 4–16) from a foreign language into English and published in the UK by a British publisher. The award celebrates the high quality and diversity of translated literature for young readers. Ebooks, encyclopedias and other reference books are not eligible. Next award: January 2017 (entries accepted from Spring 2016).

The Mythopoeic Fantasy Award for Children's Literature

Award Administrator, The Mythopoeic Society,
PO Box 6707, Altadena, CA 91003-6707, USA
email correspondence@mythsoc.org
website www.mythsoc.org

This award honours books for younger readers (from young adults to picture books for beginning readers), in the tradition of *The Hobbit* or *The Chronicles of Narnia*.

Specsavers National Book Awards

c/o Agile Marketing, Magnolia House,
172 Winsley Road, Bradford-on-Avon,
Wilts. BA15 1NY
tel (01225) 865776
email cath@agileuklimited.com
website www.nationalbookawards.co.uk

The National Book Awards showcases the best of British writing and publishing whilst celebrating books with wide popular appeal, critical acclaim and commercial success. *Award categories* include: Children's Book of the Year.

National Short Story Week Young Writer Competition

email competition@shortstoryweek.org.uk
website www.nationalshortstoryweek.org.uk

Takes place 16–22 November 2015

An annual short story competition for UK schoolchildren in years 7 and 8. Judged by children's authors. Winning stories are published in a print and ebook anthology, with all royalties going to Teenage Cancer Trust. The competition opens each National Short Story Week, with the deadline in the following January. Schools must email in advance to register for the competition.

New Zealand Post Book Awards for Children and Young Adults

c/o Booksellers New Zealand, 16–20 Willis Street, Wellington 6011, New Zealand
tel +64 (0)4 472 1908
email awards@bookawardstrust.org.nz
website www.bookawardstrust.org.nz

Annual awards to celebrate excellence in, and provide recognition for, the best books for children and young adults published annually in New Zealand. Awards are presented in four categories: non-fiction, picture book, junior fiction and young adult fiction. The winner of each category wins $7,000. One category winner is chosen as the *New Zealand Post Margaret Mahy Book of the Year* and receives an additional $7,500. Check the website for full eligibility criteria, as submissions dates occasionally change. Founded 1990. Subsidiary Awards: Maori Language Award, for books wholly in Te Reo Maori. The winner receives $1,000. First books are eligible for the Best First Book Award, the winner receives $2,000.

North East Book Award

Eileen Armstrong, Cramlington Learning Village, Cramlington, Northumberland NE23 6BN
tel (01670) 712311
email earmstrong@cramlingtonlv.co.uk
website http://northeastbookaward.wordpress.com

Awarded to a book written by a UK resident author and first published in paperback the previous year. The shortlist is selected by school librarians, teachers and the previous year's student judges. The final winner is decided entirely by the student judges (Year 7/8) and is announced in May. *2014 winner*: *Frost Hollow Hall* by Emma Carroll (Faber).

North East Teen Book Award

Eileen Armstrong, Cramlington Learning Village, Cramlington, Northumberland NE23 6BN
tel (01670) 712311
email earmstrong@cramlingtonlv.co.uk
website http://
northeastteenagebookaward.wordpress.com

Awarded to a book written by a UK resident author and first published in paperback during the previous year. The shortlist is selected by school librarians, teachers and the previous year's student judges. The final winner is decided entirely by the teenage student judges (Year 9+). Winner announced in January.

2014 winner: *Say Her Name* by James Dawson (Hot Key).

Nottingham Children's Book Awards

Nottingham City Libraries and Information Service, Sneinton Library, Sneinton Boulevard, Nottingham NG2 4FD
tel 0115 876 1934
email sandra.edis@nottinghamcity.gov.uk
website www.mynottingham.gov.uk/ncba
Contact Sandra Edis

Nottingham children aged 2–4 years choose their favourite picture books from books published the previous year. The shortlist of titles is drawn up by the end of November with the help of local nurseries and children's centres. Voting takes place in under-5 settings and libraries in spring, with the winner announced on the website at the end of May. The book award focuses on children's literature for different ages, this year concentrating on preschool children. Launched 1999.

The People's Book Prize

23 Berkeley Square, London W1J 6HE
tel 020-7665 6605
email thepeoplesbkpr@aol.com
website www.peoplesbookprize.com
Founder and Prize Administrator Tatiana Wilson, *Patron* Frederick Forsyth OBE, *Founding Patron* Dame Beryl Bainbridge DBE

The People's Book Prize awards prizes in five categories: fiction, non-fiction, children's, first time author (the Beryl Bainbridge First Time Author Award), and best achievement. Titles must be submitted by publishers, with a limit of one title per category. For entry rules and submission guidelines, see the website.

Phoenix Award

Children's Literature Association,
1301 West 22nd Street, Suite 202, Oak Brook, IL 60523, USA
tel +1 630-571-4520
email info@childlitassn.org
website www.childlitassn.org

This Award is presented by the Children's Literature Association (ChLA) for the most outstanding book for children originally published in the English language 20 years earlier which did not receive a major award at the time of publication. It is intended to recognise books of high literary merit. *2015 winner*: *One Bird* by Kyoko Mori (Henry Holt & Company, 1995). Founded 1985.

The Red House Children's Book Award

123 Frederick Road, Cheam, Sutton, Surrey SM1 2HT
website www.redhousechildrensbookaward.co.uk

This award is given annually to authors of works of fiction for children published in the UK. Children participate in the judging of the award. Awards are made in the following categories: Books for Younger Children, Books for Young Readers and Books for Older Readers. Founded in 1980 by the Federation of Children's Book Groups.

The Royal Society Young People's Book Prize

The Royal Society, 6–9 Carlton House Terrace, London SW1Y 5AG
tel 020-7451 2254
email sciencebooks@royalsociety.org
website https://royalsociety.org/awards/young-people
Events Officer, Public Engagement David Chapman

This prize is open to books for under-14s that have science as a substantial part of their content, narrative or theme. An expert adult panel choose the shortlist, but the winner is chosen by groups of young people in judging panels across the UK. The winning entry receives £10,000 and shortlisted entries receive £1,000.

Entries open in November each year. Pure reference works including encyclopedias, educational textbooks, and descriptive books are not eligible. The Prize is offered thanks to the generosity of an anonymous donor. Founded 1988.

RSPCA Young Photographer Awards (YPA)

Brand Marketing and Content Department Department, RSPCA, Wilberforce Way, Southwater, Horsham, West Sussex RH13 9RS
email ypa@rspca.org.uk
website www.rspca.org.uk/ypa

Annual awards are open to anyone aged 18 or under. The aim of the competition is to encourage young people's interest in photography and to show their appreciation and understanding of the animals around them. See website for a full list of categories and submission guidelines. Founded 1990.

Scottish Children's Book Awards

Scottish Book Trust, Sandeman House, Trunk's Close, 55 High Street, Edinburgh EH1 1SR
tel 0131 524 0160
website www.scottishbooktrust.com/scba

Scotland's largest book awards for children and young people. Awards totalling £12,000 are given to new and established authors of published books in recognition of high standards of writing for children in three age group categories: Bookbug Readers (3–7 years), Younger Readers (8–11 years) and Older Readers (12–16 years). A shortlist is drawn up by a panel of children's book experts and then a winner in each category is decided by children and young people by voting for their favourites in schools and libraries across Scotland. An award of £3,000 is made for the winner in each category and £500 for runners-up. Books published in the preceding calendar year

are eligible. Authors must be resident in Scotland. Guidelines available on request. Closing date: 31 March. Award presented: February. Administered by Scottish Book Trust, in partnership with Creative Scotland.

Sheffield Children's Book Award

Schools & Young People's Library Service, Stadia Technology Park, 60 Shirland Lane, Sheffield S9 3SP
tel 0114 250 6844
email jennifer.wilson@sheffield.gov.uk
website www.sheffield.gov.uk/libraries
website http://sheffieldchildrensbookaward.blogspot.co.uk/

Presented annually in November to the book chosen as the most enjoyable by the children of Sheffield. In 2014 there were five category winners and an overall winner. Baby Book Award: *Fish Food* by A Mansfield; Picture Book: *Spider Sandwiches* by Claire Freedman & Sue Hendra (and Overall Winner); Shorter/Longer Novel *Fluff the Farting Fish* by Michael Rosen & Tony Ross; Young Adult: *The 5th Wave* by Rick Yancy; Special Category, Poetry Books: *The Monster Sale* by Brian Moses

The Times/Chicken House Children's Fiction Competition

Chicken House, 2 Palmer Street, Frome, Somerset BA11 IDS
tel (01373) 454488
email chickenhouse@doublecluck.com
website www.doublecluck.com
Contact Kesia Lupo

This annual competition is open to unpublished writers of a full-length children's novel (age 7–18). Entrants must be over 18 and novels must not exceed 80,000 words in length. The winner will be announced in *The Times* and will receive a worldwide publishing contract with Chicken House with a royalty advance of £10,000. The winner is selected by a panel of judges which includes children's authors, journalists, publishers, librarians and other key figures from the world of children's literature.

Submissions are invited between April and October, with a shortlist announced the following February and the winner chosen at Easter. See website for further details.

Tir na n-Og Awards

Welsh Books Council, Castell Brychan, Aberystwyth, Ceredigion SY23 2JB
tel (01970) 624151
email wbc.children@wbc.org.uk
website www.wbc.org.uk

The Tir na n-Og Awards were established with the intention of raising the standard of children's and young people's books in Wales. Three awards are presented annually by the Welsh Books Council and are sponsored by the Chartered Institute of Library and Information Professionals Cymru/Wales and Cymdeithas Lyfrau Ceredigion:

• The best English-language book of the year with an authentic Welsh background. Fiction and factual books originally in English are eligible; translations from Welsh or any other language are not eligible. Prize: £1,000.
• The best original Welsh-language book aimed at the primary school sector. Prize: £1,000.
• The best original Welsh-language book aimed at the secondary school sector. Prize: £1,000.
  Founded 1976.

Christopher Tower Poetry Prize – see
page 222

UKLA Book Awards
General Manager, UKLA, University of Leicester, University Road, Leicester LE1 7RH
email admin@ukla.org
website www.ukla.org

The UKLA Book Award is a national, annual award judged by teachers. There are three categories: 3–6, 7–11 and 12–16+. Teachers are looking for books which evocatively express ideas and offer layered meanings through the use of language, imaginative expression and rich illustration/graphics. Detailed submission criteria can be found on the website. Publishers are asked to submit titles in June (of books published between 1 June of the preceding year and 31 May). The award ceremony is at the UKLA International Conference in July the following year. *2014 winners*: (3–6) *This is not my Hat* by Jon Klassen (Walker Books); (7–11) *The Story of the Blue Planet* by Andri Snær Magnason, Julian Meldon D'Arcy (translator), Áslaug Jónsdóttir (illustrator) (Pushkin Press); (12–16) *Now is the Time for Running* by Michael Williams (Tamarind Monkey).

The V&A Illustration Awards
Victoria & Albert Museum, London SW7 2RL
email villa@vam.ac.uk
website www.vam.ac.uk/illustrationawards

These annual awards are given to practising book and magazine illustrators living or publishing in the UK for work first published during the 12 months preceding the closing date of the awards. Awards are made in the following categories: book cover, book illustration and editorial illustration.

Waterstones Children's Book Prize
Waterstones, 203–206 Piccadilly, London W1J 9HD
tel 020-7071 6300
email childrensbookprize@waterstones.com
website www.waterstones.com

The aim of the Prize is to reward and champion new and emerging children's writers, voted for by booksellers. For the 2016 prize, books must be new

during 2015. There are three categories, Best Illustrated Book, Best Younger Fiction and Best Book for Teenagers. Submission criteria:

Illustrated books. Illustrated books authored and illustrated by the same person: The author/illustrator may not have previously published more than one title of any fiction genre worldwide (educational titles are exempt). Author/illustrator partnerships: Neither the author nor illustrator may have previously solely published more than one title of any fiction genre (which includes picture books) worldwide (educational titles are exempt). Author/illustrator partnerships may not have previously published more than two titles together.

Younger Fiction and Teen. No more than one previously published title of any fiction genre worldwide (educational titles are exempt). The title must make sense as a standalone novel. 2016 shortlist announced February 2016. Winners announced March 2016. Publishers to declare any titles written under another name including series fiction. Writing and concept must be solely the work of the author. Titles must have been published in 2015. There will be one winner in each category. There will be an overall winner receiving an additional prize. Prize and submission criteria may be subject to change. All dates subject to change at the discretion of the organiser.

Winchester Writers' Festival Competitions and Scholarships
University of Winchester, Winchester, Hants SO22 4NR
tel (01962) 827238
email judith.heneghan@winchester.ac.uk
website www.writersfestival.co.uk
Festival Director Judith Heneghan

Ten writing competitions are attached to this major international festival of writing, which takes place in June. Entrants do not have to attend the Festival and can opt to receive a written adjudication. Categories are First Three Pages of a Novel, Poetry, Short Stories, Flash Fiction, Children's Picture Book, Children's Funny Fiction, Memoir, Writing Can Be Murder, Young Writers' Poetry Competition and Pitch a TV Drama. Deadline for entries: mid May. Fee £7 without written adjudication; £12 with written adjudication. Prizes include editorial consultations, writing software, writing courses and books. First place winning entries and their adjudications will be published in the Festival anthology. The Festival also offers ten scholarships for young writers aged 18–25 to attend the Festival for free.

World Illustration Awards
Association of Illustrators, Somerset House, Strand, London WC2R 1LA
tel 020-7759 1012
email awards@theaoi.com
website www.theaoi.com/awards/
Awards Manager Sabine Reimer

The World Illustration Awards, in partnership with the Directory of Illustration, is an awards programme that sets out to celebrate contemporary illustration across the globe. A panel of international judges create a shortlist, which is displayed at an exhibition in Somerset House and subsequently tours the UK.

An accompanying publication of a selection of shortlisted work is distributed to commissioners worldwide. Entries can be submitted by practising illustrators or students from around the world, created in any medium into one of eight categories. Two awards are given for Best in each category and to one overall winner of Professional and New Talent respectively. Call for entries: November 2015 to February 2016; shortlist announced late April 2016; exhibition and publication October 2016; UK tour for one year thereafter.

YouWriteOn.com – see Arts Council site
YouWriteOn.com Book Awards

PRIZE WINNERS

This is a selection of high-profile literary prize winners from the last year presented chronologically. Entries for many of these prizes are included in the *Yearbook*, starting on page 409.

May 2014
CBI Book of the Year Award
Hagwitch by Marie-Louise Fitzpatrick
Nottingham Children's Book Award
Ten Little Pirates by Mike Brownlow and Simon Rickerty
The Macmillan Prize for Children's Picture Book Illustration
Bethan Woollvin for *Little Red Riding Hood*
Tir na n-Og Awards
Welsh Cakes and Custard by Wendy White (English)
Cwmwl Dros y Cwm by Gareth F. Williams, and *Diffodd y Ser* by Haf Llewelyn (Welsh)

June
The CILIP Carnegie Medal
The Bunker Diary by Kevin Brooks
The CILIP Kate Greenaway Medal
This is Not My Hat by Jon Klassen
The V&A Illustration Awards
Helen Musselwhite Illustrations for *Ten Myths of Creativity* by Audrey Niffenegger, in *Dance Gazette*, 1 Feb. 2013 (Editorial Illustration Award & Overall Winner); Anne-Marie Jones for cover for *Sons and Lovers* by D.H. Lawrence (Folio Society 2013) (Book Cover Illustration); Yasmeen Ismail for illustrations for *Time for Bed, Fred!* by Yasmeen Ismail (Bloomsbury Children's Books 2013) (Book Illustration); Grace Russell for illustrations based on scenes from *The Wild Places* by Robert MacFarlane (Student Illustrator of the Year)

East Sussex Children's Book Awards
Osbert the Avenger by Christopher William Hill
Lancashire Book of the Year Award
Undone by Cat Clarke
North East Book Award
Frost Hollow Hall by Emma Carroll

July
UKLA Book Awards
This is Not My Hat by Jon Klassen (3–6 years); *The Story of the Blue Planet* by Andri Snær Magnason, translated by Julian Meldon D'Arcy (7–11 years); *Now is the Time for Running* by Michael Williams (12–16 years); *Open Very Carefully* by Nick Bromley (Highly Recommended, 3–6 years)
CLPE Poetry Award
Wayland by Tony Mitton
Branford Boase Award
Infinite Sky by C.J. (Chelsey) Flood (and her editor Venetia Gosling, joint winners)

August
Mythopoeic Fantasy Award for Children's Literature (USA)
Doll Bones by Holly Black
Kelpies Prize
The Mixed-Up Summer of Lily McLean by Lindsay Littleson

November
The Guardian Children's Fiction Prize
The Dark Wild by Piers Torday
Eleanor Farjeon Award
Polka Theatre, Wimbledon
Sheffield Children's Book Award
Spider Sandwiches by Claire Freedman and Sue Hendra (Overall winner and Picture Book); *Fluff the Farting Fish* by Michael Rosen, illustrated by Tony Ross (Shorter & Longer Novel); *The 5th Wave* by Rick Yancey (Young Adult); *Fish Food* by Andy Mansfield and Henning Lohlein (Baby Book); *The Monster Sale* by Brian Moses (Poetry)

December
Specsavers National Book Awards
The Miniaturist by Jessie Burton (Book of the Year); *Awful Auntie* by David Walliams (Children's Book of the Year)

January 2015
Marsh Award for Children's Literature in Translation

Margaret Jull Costa for translation from the original Basque text of *The Adventures of Shola* by Bernardo Atxaga
Costa Book of the Year
Five Children on the Western Front by Kate Saunders (Costa Children's Book of the Year)

February
Red House Children's Book Award
The Day the Crayons Quit by Drew Daywalt and Oliver Jeffers (Younger Children); *Demon Dentist* by

David Walliams (Younger Readers); *Split Second* by Sophie McKenzie (Older Readers)
North East Teenage Book Award
Say Her Name by James Dawson

March
Blue Peter Book Awards
*The Spy Who Loved School Dinners*by Pamela Butchart, illustrated by Thomas Flintham (Best Story); *The Silly Book of Side-Splitting Stuff* by Andy Seed, illustrated by Scott Garrett (Best Book with Facts)
BolognaRagazzi Award
Flashlight, text and illustrations by Lizi Boyd (Fiction); *Avant Après*, text by Anne-Margot Ramstein, illustrations by Matthias Aregui (Non-fiction); *Abecedario*, text by Ruth Kaufman and Raquel Franco, illustrations by Diego Bianki (New Horizons); *Lá Fora*, text by Maria Ana Peixe Dias and Inęs Teixeira do Rosário, illustrations by Bernardo P. Carvalho (Opera Prima)

International Award for Illustration Bologna Children's Book Fair
Maisie Shearring
Scottish Children's Book Awards
Robot Rumpus by Sean Taylor, illustrated by Ross Collins (Bookbug Readers Award, readers aged 3–7); *Attack of the Giant Robot Chickens* by Alex McCall (Younger Readers, aged 8–11); *Mosi's War* by Cathy MacPhail (Older Readers, aged 12–16)

April
Waterstones Children's Book Prize
Blown Away by Rob Biddulph (Best Picture Book and Overall Winner); *Murder Most Unladylike* by Robin Stevens (Best Younger Fiction); *Half Bad* by Sally Green (Best Book for Teenagers)

May
Grampian Children's Book Award
Say Her Name by James Dawson
Angus Book Award
Cross My Heart by Carmen Reid

Children's literature festivals and trade fairs

Some of the literature festivals in this section are specifically related to children's books and others are general arts festivals which include literature events for children.

Aspects Irish Literature Festival

email info@aspectsfestival.com
website www.apectsfestival.com

An annual celebration of contemporary Irish writing with novelists, poets and playwrights. Includes writers' visits to schools and Young Aspects Showcase, where young people are given the opportunity to publicly read their own work.

Bath Children's Literature Festival

Bath Festivals, Abbey Chambers, Kingston Buildings, Bath BA1 1NT
tel (01225) 462231
email info@bathfestivals.co.uk
website www.bathfestivals.org.uk/literature
25 September–4 October 2015

Staged in association with the *Daily Telegraph*, the *Sunday Telegraph* and Waterstones, the Bath Festival of Children's Literature was established in 2007. It is the largest dedicated children's book festival in the UK and presents over 80 public, ticketed events and an extensive programme of events in schools. The Festival regularly attracts some of the biggest children's authors and illustrators from the UK and internationally. Past contributors have included: Jacqueline Wilson, Michael Morpurgo, Anthony Horowitz, Lauren Child, Shirley Hughes, Julia Donaldson, Michael Rosen, Terry Deary, Cornelia Funke, Eoin Colfer, Darren Shan, Neil Gaiman, Anthony Browne, Francesca Simon and Malorie Blackman.

The ethos of the festival is simple: to entertain children and to enthuse them about reading. The Festival aims to create a friendly, family atmosphere in which young book fans can attend events and meet their favourite authors and book characters. Events regularly feature much humour and book readings as well as craft activities, quizzes and games.

Beyond the Border: The Wales International Storytelling Festival

St Donats Castle, Nr Llantwit Major, Vale of Glamorgan CF61 1WF
tel (01656) 890289
email davidambrose@beyondtheborder.com
website www.beyondtheborder.com
Programme Director David Ambrose
Takes place 1–3 July 2016

A biennial international festival celebrating oral tradition and bringing together storytellers, poets and musicians from around the world. This is the largest event of its type in the UK. On the last day there is a competition for young storytellers aged 10–20 to be BTB Young Storyteller of the Year.

Bologna Children's Book Fair

Piazza Costituzione 6, 40128 Bologna, Italy
tel +39 051-282111
email bookfair@bolognafiere.it
website www.bolognachildrensbookfair.com
Takes place Spring

Held annually, the Bologna Children's Book Fair is the leading children's publishing event. Publishers, authors and illustrators, literary agents, licensors and licensees, and many other members of the children's publishing community meet in Bologna to buy and sell copyrights, establish new contacts and strengthen their professional relationships, discover new illustrators, develop new business opportunities, learn about the latest trends and developments and explore children's educational materials, including new media products. Approximately 5,000 professionals active in children's publishing attend from 70 countries, along with 7,000 Italian visitors. Entry is restricted to those in the publishing trade.

Selected by a jury, the Bologna Illustrators' Exhibition showcases fiction and non-fiction children's book illustrators, both new and established, from all over the world. Many illustrators also visit the Fair to show their latest portfolios to publishers.

Winners of the BolognaRagazzi Award are displayed. Prizes are given to encourage excellence in children's publishing in the categories of fiction, non-fiction, new horizons (books from emerging countries) and Opera Prima (works by authors or illustrators being published for the first time), and books are judged on the basis of their creativity, educational value and artistic design. The Hans Christian Andersen Award and the Astrid Lindgren Memorial Award are announced at the Fair.

Borders Book Festival

Harmony House, St Mary's Road, Melrose TD6 9LJ
tel (01896) 822644
email info@bordersbookfestival.org
website www.bordersbookfestival.org
Directors Alistair Moffat, Paula Ogilvie
Takes place June

An annual festival with a programme of events

featuring high-profile and bestselling writers. Winner of the Walter Scott Prize for Historical Fiction is announced during the festival. Founded 2004.

Cardiff Children's Literature Festival

Cardiff Council Events Team, Motorpoint Arena, Mary Ann Street, Cardiff CF10 2EQ
email h.a.brown@cardiff.gov.uk
website www.childrenslitfest.com
Festival Organiser Heather Brown
Takes place March

The Cardiff Children's Literature Festival is an annual event aimed at youngsters who appreciate the magic of books and grown-ups who want to write them. The festival includes events with local and national contemporary authors and comprises a number of educational sessions for schools. The 2015 programme included Martin Brown, Emma Dodd, Lydia Monks and Jonathan Meres.

The Times and The Sunday Times Cheltenham Literature Festival

109–111 Bath Road, Cheltenham, Glos. GL53 7LS
tel (01242) 511211
website www.cheltenhamfestivals.com
Takes place 2–11 October 2015

This annual festival is the largest of its kind in Europe. Events include talks and lectures, poetry readings, novelists in conversation, exhibitions, discussions, workshops and two large bookshops. *Book It!* is a festival for children within the main festival with an extensive programme of events. Brochures are available in August. Founded 1949.

Chester Literature Festival

website www.chesterliteraturefestival.co.uk
Takes place October

A leading literature festival, grown in stature and scale in recent years, with scores of events spread over a fortnight featuring writers from the internationally acclaimed to emerging local talent. The festival incorporates GobbleDeeBook, an annual week-long children's literature festival with workshops, plays and parties as well as events featuring dozens of children's authors.

Children's Book Week

Book Trust, G8 Battersea Studios, 80 Silverthorne Road, London SW8 3HE
tel 020-7801 8800
email cbw@booktrust.org.uk
website www.booktrust.org.uk

An annual celebration of reading for pleasure for children of primary school age. Free teachers' packs are sent to schools, libraries and teacher training institutions in England, and during the week schools, libraries and other venues hold a range of events and activities. Check the Book Trust website for more details and event timings.

Dinefwr Literature Festival

Literature Wales, 4th Floor, Cambrian Buildings, Mount Stuart Square, Cardiff CF10 5FL
tel 029-2047 2266
email post@literaturewales.org
website www.dinefwrliteraturefestival.co.uk
Takes place June

Dinefwr Literature Festival takes place at the beautiful Dinefwr Park and Castle in Carmarthenshire. The bilingual (Welsh/English) festival features an eclectic mix of literature, music, comedy, children's activities and nature walks. The line-up includes award-winning novelists, performance poets, children's authors, singer-songwriters and scriptwriters, plus fringe acts appealing to children and adults alike. The festival is organised by Literature Wales in partnership with National Trust, Cadw and University of Wales Trinity Saint David, and is supported by Arts Council of Wales.

Edinburgh International Book Festival

5A Charlotte Square, Edinburgh EH2 4DR
tel 0131 718 5666
email admin@edbookfest.co.uk
website www.edbookfest.co.uk
Director Nick Barley
Takes place August

Europe's largest public celebration of books and reading. In addition to a unique independent bookselling operation, more than 800 UK and international writers appear in over 750 events for adults and children. Programme details available in June.

Essex Poetry Festival

Flat 3, 1 Clifton Terrace, Southend-on-Sea, Essex SS1 1DT
email adrian@essex-poetry-festival.co.uk
website www.essex-poetry-festival.co.uk
Contact Adrian Green
Takes place October

A poetry festival across Essex. Also includes the Young Essex Poet of the Year Competition.

The Festival of Writing

The Writers' Workshop, The Studio, Sheep Street, Charlbury OX7 3RR
tel 0345 459 9560
email info@writersworkshop.co.uk
website www.writersworkshop.co.uk
Events Director Laura Wilkins
Takes place in York 4–6 September 2015

A festival for aspiring writers providing the opportunity to meet literary agents, publishers, professional authors and book doctors. Keynote speakers from across the industry. Also workshops, competitions, networking events, Q&A panels and the chance to pitch work directly to literary agents.

Folkestone Book Festival

tel (01303) 760740
email info@folkestonebookfest.com
website www.folkestonebookfest.com

Takes place 20–29 November 2015

An annual festival with over 40 events, including a Children's Day.

The Hay Festival

Festival Office, The Drill Hall, 25 Lion Street, Hay-on-Wye HR3 5AD
tel (01497) 822620 (admin)
email admin@hayfestival.org
website www.hayfestival.org
Takes place May/June

This annual festival of literature and the arts in Hay-on-Wye, Wales, brings together writers, musicians, film-makers, historians, politicians, environmentalists and scientists from around the world to communicate challenging ideas. More than 700 events over ten days. Within the annual festival is a festival for families and children, Hay Fever, which introduces children, from toddlers to teenagers, to their favourite authors and holds workshops to entertain and educate. Programme published April.

Hoo's Kids Book Fest

Luton Hoo Estate, Luton, Beds LU1 3TQ
tel (01582) 879089
website www.lutonhooestate.co.uk
Takes place 8–10 July 2016. Autumn Evening 30 October 2015.

Lord Bute, the founder of Luton Hoo Estate's walled garden, had a passion for learning and amassed a vast collection of books on all subjects, in order to enrich his life. The Hoo's Kids Book Fest was launched to bring the world of books alive for children in order to inspire them to follow Lord Bute's example and discover a love of learning.

The festival includes visits from authors, illustrators and comic artists, a full programme of events and entertainment, books sales and signings and activities for schools.

Ilkley Literature Festival

9 The Grove, Ilkley LS29 9LW
tel (01943) 601210
email admin@ilkleyliteraturefestival.org.uk
website www.ilkleyliteraturefestival.org.uk
Festival Director Rachel Feldberg, *Festival Manager* Gail Price, *Administrator* Laura Beddows
Takes place 2–18 October 2015

The north of England's oldest, largest and most prestigious literature festival with over 250 events, from author discussions to workshops, readings, literary walks, children's events and a festival fringe. Founded 1973.

The Imaginate Festival

Summerhall, 1 Summerhall, Edinburgh EH9 1PL
tel 0131 225 8050
email info@imaginate.org.uk
website www.imaginate.org.uk

Takes place May

As one of the UK's largest performing arts festivals for children and young people, this annual festival provides the opportunity for school children and their teachers, families and industry professionals to see the best theatre the world has to offer. Produced by Imaginate (page 399), the festival's aim is that children and young people aged up to 18 have regular access to a diverse range of high-quality performing arts activities, from home and abroad, that will entertain, enrich, teach and inspire them. Each year the festival presents around 15 national and international productions attracting an audience of over 10,000, and tours to both rural and urban areas throughout Scotland. Founded 1990.

Imagine: Writers and Writing for Children

South Bank Centre, London SE1 8XX
tel 020-7960 4200
website www.southbankcentre.co.uk/whatson/festivals-series/imagine-childrens-festival-1
Takes place February

An annual festival celebrating writing for children. Three days featuring a selection of poets, storytellers and illustrators.

Independent Bookshop Week

website www.independentbooksellersweek.org.uk
Takes place June

Independent Bookshop Week is an annual celebration of independent bookshops and is part of the IndieBound campaign (www.indiebound.org.uk) to promote independent bookshops, strong reading communities and the idea of shopping locally and sustainably. Independent Bookshop Week brings together bookshops, publishers and consumers through events such as National Reading Group Day, author visits and storytime sessions, and offers from publishers.

Jewish Book Week

Jewish Book Council, ORT House, 126 Albert Street, London NW1 7NE
tel 020-7446 8771
email info@jewishbookweek.com
website www.jewishbookweek.com
Festival Coordinator Sarah Fairbairn
Takes place Feb/March

A festival of Jewish writing, with contributors from around the world and sessions in London and nationwide. Includes events for children and teenagers.

Laureate na nÓg

Children's Books Ireland,
17 North Great George's Street, Dublin 1, Ireland
tel +353 (0)18 727475
email info@childrenslaureate.ie
email info@childrensbooksireland.ie
website www.childrenslaureate.ie

This is a project recognising the role and importance of literature for children in Ireland. This unique honour was awarded for the first time in 2010. The position is held for a period of two years. The laureate participates in selected events and activities around Ireland and internationally during their term.

The laureate is chosen in recognition of their widely recognised high-quality children's writing or illustration and the considerably positive impact they have had on readers as well as other writers and illustrators. Laureate na nÓg 2014–2016: Eoin Colfer. The 2016–2018 Laureate na nÓg will be announced in May 2016.

Ledbury Poetry Festival

Church Street, Ledbury HR8 1DH
email director@poetry-festival.co.uk
website www.poetry-festival.co.uk
Festival Director Chloe Garner
Takes place July and throughout the year

Ledbury Poetry Festival runs a year-round programme during which it sends poets into primary and secondary schools in the region. It also runs poetry events for children during the ten-day summer festival, which is held during the first two weeks of July.

London Literature Festival

Southbank Centre, Belvedere Road, London SE1 8XX
tel 020-7960 4200
email customer@southbankcentre.co.uk
website www.southbankcentre.co.uk/whatson/
festivals-series/london-literature-festival
Takes place October

A two-week festival featuring international and prize-winning authors, historians, poets, performers and artists, children's events, specially commissioned work, debate and discussion, interactive and improvised writing and performance. Founded 2007.

Lowdham Book Festival

c/o The Bookcase, 50 Main Street,
Lowdham NG14 7BE
tel 0115-966 4143
email info@fiveleaves.co.uk
website www.lowdhambookfestival.co.uk
Contact Jane Streeter
Takes place June

An annual ten-day festival of literature events for adults and children, with a daily programme of high-profile national and local writers. The last day always features dozens of free events and a large book fair.

Manchester Children's Book Festival

The Manchester Writing School at MMU,
Dept of English,
Manchester Metropolitan University,
Rosamond Street West, Off Oxford Road,
Manchester M15 6LL
tel 0161 247 2424
email mcbf@mmu.ac.uk
website www.mcbf.org.uk
Festival Directors Carol Ann Duffy (Creative Director), James Draper (Director: Marketing & Development), Kaye Tew (Director: Education & Partnerships)
Takes place 24 June–3 July 2016

An annual festival celebrating the very best writing for children, inspiring young people to engage with literature and creativity across the curriculum, and offering extended projects and training to ensure the event has an impact and legacy in classrooms.

May Festival

Events Team, University of Aberdeen,
King's College, Aberdeen AB24 3FX
tel (01224) 273233
email festival@abdn.ac.uk
website www.abdn.ac.uk/mayfestival
Takes place May

The May Festival programme aims to engage people of all ages and backgrounds, providing a culturally-enriching experience of the North East, Scotland and beyond. It aims to build on the success of research projects and past and present activities such as Word, Director's Cut, the British Science Festival and the music concert series. Events include debates, lectures, readings, workshops and concerts spanning areas such as literature, science, music, film, Gaelic, food and nutrition.

Off the Shelf Festival of Words Sheffield

Room 311, Town Hall, Pinstone Street,
Sheffield S1 2HH
tel 0114 273 4716
email offtheshelf@sheffield.gov.uk
website www.offtheshelf.org.uk
Takes place 10–31 October 2015

A diverse and exciting literature festival with more than 150 events including well-known author talks, writing workshops, poetry, family activities, debates, competitions and exhibitions.

Oundle Festival of Literature

email oundlelitfest@hotmail.co.uk
website www.oundlelitfest.org.uk
Festival Manager Helen Shair
Takes place March and throughout the year

Featuring a full programme of author events, poetry, philosophy, politics, storytelling, biography, illustrators and novelists for young and old. Includes events for children.

FT Weekend Oxford Literary Festival

Registered office, Greyfriars Court, Paradise Square,
Oxford OX1 1BE
email info@oxfordliteraryfestival.org
website www.oxfordliteraryfestival.org

Festival Director Sally Dunsmore
Takes place March/April

An annual festival for both adults and children. Presents topical debates, fiction and non-fiction discussion panels, and adult and children's authors who have recently published books. Topics range from contemporary fiction to discussions on politics, history, science, gardening, food, poetry, philosophy, art and crime fiction.

Readathon

Read for Good, 26 Nailsworth Mills, Avening Road, Nailsworth, Glos. GL6 0BS
tel 0845 606 1151
email reading@readathon.org
website www.readathon.org

Readathon is the UK-wide sponsored reading event for schools, encouraging children of all ages to read for pleasure, motivated by the knowledge that the money they raise will help seriously ill children via Readathon's partner charities. Readathon may be run at any time of year to suit each school's preference. Pupils choose their own reading material, which needn't just be books. Pre-readers may listen to stories or share picture books. Each school receives book vouchers worth 20% of its sponsorship total. Founded 1984.

Richmond upon Thames Literature Festival, Arts Service

Orleans House Gallery, Riverside, Twickenham TW1 3DJ
tel 020-8831 6000
email artsinfo@richmond.gov.uk
website www.richmondliterature.com
Takes place Throughout November

An annual literature festival featuring a diverse programme of authors in venues across the borough. The festival includes an exciting programme of author events for children and families as well as opportunities to explore creativity in literature through workshops and interactive sessions.

Scottish International Storytelling Festival

43–45 High Street, Edinburgh EH1 1SR
tel 0131 556 9579
email reception@scottishstorytellingcentre.com
website www.scottishstorytellingcentre.co.uk
Festival Director Donald Smith
Takes place 23 October–1 November 2015

A celebration of Scottish storytelling set in its international context, complemented by music, ballad and song. The main theme of the 2015 Festival will be 'Stories without Borders'. Takes place at the Scottish Storytelling Centre and partner venues across Edinburgh and the Lothians.

StAnza: Scotland's International Poetry Festival

tel (01334) 475000 (box office), (01334) 474610 (programmes)

email info@stanzapoetry.org
website www.stanzapoetry.org
Festival Director Eleanor Livingstone
Takes place March

The festival engages with all forms of poetry: read and spoken verse, poetry in exhibition, performance poetry, cross-media collaboration, schools work, book launches and poetry workshops, with numerous UK and international guests and weekend children's events. Founded 1997.

Stratford-upon-Avon Poetry Festival

Shakespeare Centre, Henley Street, Stratford-upon-Avon CV37 6QW
tel (01789) 204016
email info@shakespeare.org.uk
website www.shakespeare.org.uk
Takes place June/July

An annual festival to celebrate poetry past and present with special reference to the works of Shakespeare. Events include: evenings of children's verse, a Poetry Mass and a local poets' evening. Sponsored by The Shakespeare Birthplace Trust.

Wigtown Book Festival

Wigtown Festival Company, County Buildings, Wigtown, Dumfries & Galloway DG8 9JH
tel (01988) 402036
email mail@wigtownbookfestival.com
website www.wigtownbookfestival.com
Festival Manager Anne Barclay
Takes place 25 September–4 October 2015

An annual celebration of literature and the arts in Scotland's National Book Town. Over 180 events including author events, theatre, music, film and children's and young people's programmes.

The Winchester Writers' Festival

University of Winchester, Winchester, Hants SO22 4NR
tel (01962) 827238
email judith.heneghan@winchester.ac.uk
email sara.gangai@winchester.ac.uk
website www.writersfestival.co.uk
Festival Director Judith Heneghan, *Events Manager* Sara Gangai
Takes place University of Winchester, third weekend in June

This festival of writing, celebrating its 35th year in 2015, attracts emerging writers from the UK and around the world who come for one-day masters' courses, talks, workshops and over 750 one-to-one appointments with 60 internationally renowned authors, poets, playwrights, literary agents and commissioning editors to help them harness their creativity and develop their writing, editing and marketing skills. Ten writing competitions, including Poetry, Short Stories, First Three Pages of the Novel, Flash Fiction, Children's Picture Books, Children's

Funny Fiction, Memoir, Young Writers' Poetry Competition, Writing Can Be Murder and Pitch a TV Drama are open to all with prizes including editorial consultations. All first place winners are published in the annual Festival anthology. For information and registration, visit the website.

World Book Day

6 Bell Yard, London WC2A 2JR
tel 0906 265 0004 (helpline)
email wbd@education.co.uk
website www.worldbookday.com

Takes place first Thursday in March

An annual celebration of books and reading aimed at promoting their value and creating the readers of the future. Every schoolchild in full-time education receives a £1 (€1.50) book token and events take place all over the UK and Ireland in schools, bookshops and libraries. World Book Day was designated by UNESCO as a worldwide celebration of books and reading and is marked in over 30 countries. It is a partnership of publishers, National Book Tokens, booksellers and interested parties who work together to promote books and reading for the personal enrichment and enjoyment of all.

Children's writing courses and conferences

Anyone wishing to participate in a writing course should first satisfy themselves as to its content and quality. Contact your local library, college or university, or consult one of the various internet course listings databases for further information.

Arvon

Arvon, Free Word Centre, 60 Farringdon Road, London EC1R 3GA
tel 020-7324 2554
email national@arvon.org
website www.arvon.org
Contacts Suzie Jones, Joe Bibby
Centres:
Lumb Bank – The Ted Hughes Arvon Centre, Heptonstall, Hebden Bridge, West Yorkshire HX7 6DF
tel (01422) 843714
email lumbbank@arvon.org
Contact Becky Liddell
Totleigh Barton, Sheepwash, Beaworthy, Devon EX21 5NS
tel (01409) 231338
email totleighbarton@arvon.org
Contact Sue Walker
The Hurst – The John Osborne Arvon Centre
Clunton, Craven Arms, Shrops. SY7 0JA
tel (01588) 640658
email thehurst@arvon.org
Contact Dan Pavitt

Residential creative writing courses and retreats in beautiful rural locations, led by highly respected authors. A powerful mix of workshops, individual tutorials and time and space to write. Grants are available to help with course fees. Founded 1968.

Blue Elephant Storyshaping

email hello@blueelephantstoryshaping.com
website www.blueelephantstoryshaping.com
Contact Natascha Biebow (Editor, Coach and Mentor)

Cook Up a Picture Book online courses offer picture book coaching with an experienced editor. Two courses available: Online Picture Book Course for beginner and intermediate level authors and illustrators, who would like a more structured coaching experience; and Small-Group Coaching Course for those who have begun writing picture books and wish to fine-tune their work, plus illustrators who would like to write and illustrate.

These six-week-long courses feature weekly, one-to-one detailed editorial feedback and top tips on key aspects of picture book craft and publishing. The aim is to create at least one marketable picture book at the end of six weeks. There is the opportunity to submit to an editor or agent at the end of the Small-Group Coaching Course. Please see website for full details.

The Federation of Children's Book Groups Conference

Karen Hellewell, 10 St Laurence Road, Bradford on Avon BA15 1JG
tel 0300 102 1559
email info@fcbg.org.uk
website www.fcbg.org.uk
Takes place April

Held annually, guest speakers include well-known children's authors as well as experts and publishers in the field of children's books. Publishers also exhibit their newest books and resources.

IBBY Congress

Nonnenweg 12, Postfach CH-4003-Basel, Switzerland
tel +41 61-272 2917
email ibby@ibby.org
website www.ibbycongress2016.org

A biennial international congress for IBBY (International Board on Books for Young People) members and other people involved in children's books and reading development. Every other year a different National Section of IBBY hosts the congress and several hundred people from all over the world attend the professional programme.

The 2016 Congress is to be held on 18–21 August in Auckland, New Zealand on the theme of Literature in a Multi-literate World. See also page 399.

NCRCL British IBBY Conference

Department of English and Creative Writing, Roehampton University, London SW15 5PU
tel 020-8392 3000
email enquiries@roehampton.ac.uk
email l.sainsbury@roehampton.ac.uk
website www.roehampton.ac.uk/Research-Centres/National-Centre-for-Research-in-Childrens-Literature/Conference
Contact Dr Lisa Sainsbury

Conference held annually in November on a specific theme.

Oxford University Day and Weekend Schools

Day & Weekend Programme Administrator, Oxford University Department of Continuing

Education, Rewley House, 1 Wellington Square, Oxford OX1 2JA
tel (01865) 270368
email ppdayweek@conted.ox.ac.uk
website www.conted.ox.ac.uk
Contact Day School Administrator

Effective Writing: a series of three-day accredited courses for creative writing. Topics vary from year to year. Courses always held on Fridays. See website for further courses on creative writing.

SCBWI-BI Annual Conference

University of Winchester, Winchester SO22 4NR
email conference@britishscbwi.org
website www.britishisles.scbwi.org/events
Regional Adviser (Chair) Natascha Biebow

The SCBWI-BI annual conference offers a mix of inspiration, networking and fun for writers and illustrators, both published and unpublished. An exclusive PULSE track for published authors and illustrators aims to offer opportunities to meet librarians and booksellers and market your books. Features a faculty of award-winning authors, illustrators and other industry professionals. Discover more about the secrets behind fiction, picture books, social media, book promotion and building a career through practical workshops.

One-to-one manuscript and portfolio reviews offer an opportunity to receive personalised feedback from editors, agents and art directors. Illustrators may submit to the juried portfolio exhibition and all attendees will have the chance to liaise with industry professionals at the exclusive mass book launch party. Two scholarships offered.

Swanwick, The Writers' Summer School

Hayes Conference Centre, Swanwick, Derbyshire DE55 1AU
tel 07765 890733
email secretary@swanwickwritersschool.org.uk
website www.swanwickwritersschool.org.uk
Takes place 8–14 August 2015 / 6–12 August 2016

A week-long programme for writers of all ages, abilities and genres featuring courses, talks, workshops, panels and one-to-one sessions, all run by expert tutors. Attracts top speakers such as Simon Brett, Alex Gray, Peter James, Helen Lederer, Deborah Moggach and other best-selling authors, playwrights, screenwriters and comedy writers plus the literary agents and publishers who represent them. Full-board accommodation available on site; day tickets also available. Founded 1949.

Tŷ Newydd Writers' Centre

Tŷ Newydd, Llanystumdwy, Cricieth, Gwynedd LL52 0LW
tel (01766) 522811
email tynewydd@literaturewales.org
website www.literaturewales.org

Tŷ Newydd, the former home of Prime Minister David Lloyd George, has hosted residential creative writing courses for writers of all abilities for over 25 years. Whether you're interested in a poetry masterclass, writing for the theatre, developing a novel for young adults or conquering the popular fiction market, there'll be a course in our programme suitable for you. Courses are open to everyone over the age of 16 and no qualifications are necessary. Literature Wales staff based at Tŷ Newydd can advise on the suitability of courses, and further details about each individual course can be obtained by visiting the website, or contacting the team by phone or email.

Writers Advice Centre for Children's Books – see page 408

The Writers' Workshop

The Studio, Sheep Street, Charlbury, Oxon OX7 3RR
tel 0345 459 9560
email info@writersworkshop.co.uk
website www.writersworkshop.co.uk
Contacts Harry Bingham, Laura Wilkins, Nikki Holt

Runs courses for every range of experience, all tutored by professional authors, including: How to Write a Novel, Screenwriting, Writing for Children, Writing Picture Books, Writing from Life, Self-editing your Novel, Creative Writing Flying Start and the Complete Novel Writing Course. Plus events, editorial critiques, mentoring and the Festival of Writing. See website for full details.

POSTGRADUATE COURSES

Bath Spa University

Dept of Creative Writing and Publishing, School of Humanities and Cultural Industries, Bath Spa University, Newton Park, Newton St Loe, Bath BA2 9BN
tel (01225) 875875
email b.soyinka@bathspa.ac.uk
website www.bathspa.ac.uk

MA in Writing for Young People. Also MA in Creative Writing and PhD in Creative Writing.

University of Bolton

University of Bolton, Deane Road Campus, Bolton BL3 5AB
tel (01204) 903903
website www.bolton.ac.uk
Contact Programme Leader, Creative Writing

MA in Children's Literature & Culture, MPhil/PhD in Creative Writing Specialisms.

University of Central Lancashire

School of Art, Design and Performance, University of Central Lancashire, Preston PR1 2HE
tel (01772) 892400

email cenquiries@uclan.ac.uk
website www.uclan.ac.uk/courses/
ma_childrens_book_illustration.php
Course Leader, MA Children's Book Illustration Steve Wilkin

The emphasis of this course is on the practice of illustration for children's picture books and story books. The course is designed to encourage pursuit of a unique and personal line of enquiry within a chosen area of children's book illustration. It is hoped that this will lead to publication or continuing research. The course was founded in 2005.

University of London, Goldsmiths College

New Cross, London SE14 6NW
email course-info@gold.ac.uk
website www.gold.ac.uk
Contact Dr Clare Kelly

MA in Children's Literature.

The Manchester Writing School at Manchester Metropolitan University

Department of English, Rosamond Street West, Off Oxford Road, Manchester M15 6LL
tel 0161 247 1787
email writingschool@mmu.ac.uk
website www.manchesterwritingschool.co.uk
Contact (admission and generic enquiries) James Draper, Manager: The Manchester Writing School at MMU

MA in Creative Writing: Writing for Children. Home of the Manchester Children's Book Festival.

Nottingham Trent University

School of Arts and Humanities,
Nottingham Trent University, Clifton Lane,
Nottingham NG11 8NS
tel 0115 848 4200
email rory.waterman@ntu.ac.uk
email hum.enquiries@ntu.ac.uk
website www.ntu.ac.uk/creativewriting
Contact Dr Rory Waterman, Programme Leader

MA in Creative Writing. One of the longest-established programmes of its kind in the UK, with many highly successful graduate writers. Diverse options include: Children's and Young Adult Fiction; Fiction; Poetry; Writing for Stage, Radio and Screen.

University of Roehampton

Department of English and Creative Writing,
Digby Stuart College, Roehampton Lane,
London SW15 5PU
email enquiries@roehampton.ac.uk
website www.roehampton.ac.uk
Contact Dr Lisa Sainsbury

MA/PGDip in Children's Literature.

University of Winchester

Winchester SO22 4NR
tel (01962) 827234
email course.enquiries@winchester.ac.uk
website www.winchester.ac.uk
Contact Course Enquiries & Applications

MA Writing for Children.

Finance for writers and artists
FAQs for writers

Peter Vaines, a chartered accountant and barrister, addresses some frequently asked questions.

What can a working writer claim against tax?

A working writer is carrying on a business and can therefore claim all the expenses which are incurred wholly and exclusively for the purposes of that business. A list showing most of the usual expenses can be found in the article on *Income tax* (see page 431) but there will be other expenses that can be allowed in special circumstances.

Strictly, only expenses which are incurred for the sole purpose of the business can be claimed; there must be no 'duality of purpose' so an item of expenditure cannot be divided into private and business parts. However, HM Revenue & Customs are now able to allow all reasonable expenses (including apportioned sums) where the amounts can be commercially justified.

Allowances can also be claimed for the cost of business assets such as a car, personal computers, fax, copying machines and all other equipment (including books) which may be used by the writer. An allowance of 100% of the cost can now be claimed for most assets except cars, for which a lower allowance can be claimed. See the article on *Income tax* for further details of the deductions available in respect of capital expenditure.

Can I request interest on fees owed to me beyond 30 days of my invoice?

Yes. A writer is like any other person carrying on a business and is entitled to charge interest at a rate of 8% over bank base rate on any debt outstanding for more than 30 days – although the period of credit can be varied by agreement between the parties. It is not compulsory to claim the interest; it is your decision whether to enforce the right.

What can I do about bad debts?

A writer is in exactly the same position as anybody else carrying on a business over the payment of his or her invoices. It is generally not commercially sensible to insist on payment in advance but where the work involved is substantial (e.g. a book), it is usual to receive one third of the fee on signature, one third on delivery of the manuscript and the remaining one third on publication. On other assignments, perhaps not as substantial as a book, it could be worthwhile seeking 50% of the fee on signature and the other 50% on delivery. This would provide a degree of protection in case of cancellation of the assignment because of changes of policy or personnel at the publisher.

What financial disputes can I take to the Small Claims Court?

If somebody owes you money you can take them to the Small Claims section of your local County Court, which deals with financial disputes up to £10,000. It is much less formal than normal court proceedings and involves little expense. It is not necessary to have a solicitor. You fill in some forms, turn up and explain why you are owed the money (see www.gov.uk/make-court-claim-for-money/overview).

If I receive an advance, can I divide it between two tax years?

Yes. There is a system known as 'averaging'. This enables writers (and others engaged in the creation of literary or dramatic works or designs) to average the profits of two or more consecutive years if the profits for one year are less than 75% of the profits for the highest year. This relief can apply even if the work takes less than 12 months to create and it allows the writer to avoid the higher rates of tax which might arise if the income in respect of a number of years' work were all to be concentrated in a single year.

How do I make sure I am taxed as a self-employed person so that tax and National Insurance contributions are not deducted at source?

To be taxed as a self-employed person you have to make sure that the contract for the writing cannot be regarded as a contract of employment. This is unlikely to be the case with a professional author. The subject is highly complex but one of the most important features is that the publisher must not be in a position to direct or control the author's work. Where any doubt exists, the author might find the publisher deducting tax and National Insurance contributions as a precaution and that would clearly be highly disadvantageous. The author would be well advised to discuss the position with the publisher before the contract is signed to agree that he or she should be treated as self-employed and that no tax or National Insurance contributions will be deducted from any payments. If such agreement cannot be reached, professional advice should immediately be sought so that the detailed technical position can be explained to the publisher.

Is it a good idea to operate through a limited company?

It can be a good idea for a self-employed writer to operate through a company but generally only where the income is quite large. The costs of operating a company can outweigh any benefit if the writer is paying tax only at the basic rate. Where the writer is paying tax at the higher rate of 40% (or 45%), being able to retain some of the income in a company at a tax rate of only 20% is obviously attractive. However, this will be entirely ineffective if the writer's contract with the publisher would otherwise be an employment. The whole subject of operating through a company is complex and professional advice is essential.

When does it become necessary to register for VAT?

Where the writer's self-employed income (from all sources, not only writing) exceeds £82,000 in the previous 12 months or is expected to do so in the next 30 days, he or she must register for VAT and add VAT to all his/her fees. The publisher will pay the VAT to the writer, who must pay the VAT over to HM Revenue & Customs each quarter. Any VAT the writer has paid on business expenses and on the purchase of business assets can be deducted. It is possible for some authors to take advantage of the simplified system for VAT payments which applies to small businesses. This involves a flat rate payment of VAT without any need to keep records of VAT on expenses.

If I make a loss from my writing can I get any tax back?

Where a writer makes a loss, HM Revenue & Customs may suggest that the writing is only a hobby and not a professional activity, thereby denying any relief or tax deduction for the loss. However, providing the writing is carried out on a sensible commercial basis with an expectation of profits, any resulting loss can be offset against any other income the writer may have for the same or the previous year.

Income tax

Despite attempts by successive governments to simplify our taxation system, the subject has become increasingly complicated. Peter Vaines, a chartered accountant and barrister, gives a broad outline of taxation from the point of view of writers and other creative professionals. The proposals in the March 2015 Budget are broadly reflected in this article.

How income is taxed

Generally

Authors are usually treated for tax purposes as carrying on a profession and are taxed in a similar fashion to other self-employed professionals. This article is directed to self-employed persons only, because if a writer is employed he or she will be subject to the much less advantageous rules which apply to employment income.

Employed persons may try to shake off the status of 'employee' to attain 'freelance' status so as to qualify for the tax advantages, but such attempts meet with varying degrees of success. The problems involved in making this transition are considerable and space does not permit a detailed explanation to be made here – individual advice is necessary if difficulties are to be avoided.

Particular attention has been paid by HM Revenue & Customs (HMRC) to journalists and to those engaged in the entertainment industry with a view to reclassifying them as employees so that PAYE is deducted from their earnings. This blanket treatment has been extended to other areas and, although it is obviously open to challenge by individual taxpayers, it is always difficult to persuade HMRC to change its views.

There is no reason why employed people cannot carry on a freelance business in their spare time. Indeed, aspiring authors, artists, musicians, etc often derive so little income from their craft that the financial security of an employment, perhaps in a different sphere of activity, is necessary. The existence of the employment is irrelevant to the taxation of the freelance earnings, although it is most important not to confuse the income or expenditure of the employment with that of the self-employed activity. HMRC is aware of the advantages which can be derived by an individual having 'freelance' income from an organisation of which he or she is also an employee, and where such circumstances are contrived, it can be extremely difficult to convince an Inspector of Taxes that a genuine freelance activity is being carried on. Where the individual operates through a company or partnership providing services personally to a particular client, and would be regarded as an employee if the services were supplied directly by the individual, additional problems arise from the notorious IR35 legislation and professional advice is essential.

For those starting in business or commencing work on a freelance basis there is a useful section called 'Working for yourself' on the GOV.UK website (www.gov.uk/working-for-yourself/overview).

Income

For income to be taxable it need not be substantial, nor even the author's only source of income; earnings from casual writing are also taxable but this can be an advantage because occasional writers do not often make a profit from their writing. The expenses incurred in connection with writing may well exceed any income receivable and the resultant loss may then be used to reclaim tax paid on other income. Certain allowable expenses and capital allowances may be deducted from the income, and these are set out in more detail below. The possibility of a loss being used as a basis for a tax repayment is fully appreciated by HMRC, which sometimes attempts to treat casual writing as a hobby so that any losses incurred cannot be used to reclaim tax; of course by the same token any income receivable would not be chargeable to tax. This treatment may sound attractive but it should be resisted vigorously because HMRC does not hesitate to change its mind when profits begin to arise. In the case of exceptional or non-recurring writing, such as the autobiography of a sports personality or the memoirs of a politician, it could be better to be treated as pursuing a hobby and not as a professional author. Sales of copyright cannot be charged to income tax unless the recipient is a professional author. However, the proceeds of sale of copyright may be charged to capital gains tax, even by an individual who is not a professional author.

Royalties

Where the recipient is a professional author, the proceeds of sale of copyright are taxable as income and not as capital receipts. Similarly, lump sums on account of, or in advance of royalties are also taxable as income in the year of receipt, subject to a claim for averaging relief (see below).

Copyright royalties are generally paid without deduction of income tax. However, if royalties are paid to a person who normally lives abroad, tax must be deducted by the

Arts Council awards

Arts Council category A awards

- Direct or indirect musical, design or choreographic commissions and direct or indirect commission of sculpture and paintings for public sites.
- The Royalty Supplement Guarantee Scheme.
- The Contract Writers' Scheme.
- Jazz bursaries.
- Translators' grants.
- Photographic awards and bursaries.
- Film and video awards and bursaries.
- Performance Art Awards.
- Art Publishing Grants.
- Grants to assist with a specific project or projects (such as the writing of a book) or to meet specific professional expenses such as a contribution towards copying expenses made to a composer or to an artist's studio expenses.

Arts Council category B awards

- Bursaries to trainee directors.
- Bursaries for associate directors.
- Bursaries to people attending full-time courses in arts administration (the practical training course).
- In-service bursaries to theatre designers and bursaries to trainees on the theatre designers' scheme.
- In-service bursaries for administrators.
- Bursaries for actors and actresses.
- Bursaries for technicians and stage managers.
- Bursaries made to students attending the City University Arts Administration courses.
- Awards, known as the Buying Time Awards, made not to assist with a specific project or professional expenses but to maintain the recipient to enable him or her to take time off to develop his or her personal talents. These include the awards and bursaries known as the Theatre Writing Bursaries, awards and bursaries to composers, awards and bursaries to painters, sculptors and print makers, literature awards and bursaries.

payer or his agent at the time the payment is made unless arrangements are made with HMRC for payments to be made gross under the terms of a Double Taxation Agreement with the other country.

Grants, prizes and awards

Persons in receipt of grants from the Arts Council or similar bodies will be concerned whether or not such grants are liable to income tax. Many years ago HMRC issued a Statement of Practice after detailed discussions with the Arts Council regarding the tax treatment of the awards. Grants and other receipts of a similar nature were divided into two categories (see box) – those which were to be treated by HMRC as chargeable to tax and those which were not. Category A awards were considered to be taxable; awards made under category B were not chargeable to tax.

The Statement of Practice has not been withdrawn but it is no longer publicly available – although there is nothing to suggest that the treatment of awards in these categories will not continue to be treated in this way. In any event, the statement had no legal force and was merely and expression of the view of HMRC. It remains open to anybody in receipt of a grant or award to challenge the HMRC view on the merits of their own case.

The tax position of persons in receipt of literary prizes will generally follow a decision by the Special Commissioners in connection with the Whitbread Book Awards (now called the Costa Book Awards). In that case it was decided that the prize was not part of the author's professional income and accordingly not chargeable to tax. The precise details are not available because decisions of the Special Commissioners were not, at that time, reported unless an appeal was made to the High Court; HMRC chose not to appeal against this decision. Details of the many literary awards that are given each year start on page 409, and this decision is of considerable significance to the winners of these prizes. It would be unwise to assume that all such awards will be free of tax as the precise facts which were present in the case of the Whitbread awards may not be repeated in another case; however, it is clear that an author winning a prize has some very powerful arguments in his or her favour, should HMRC seek to charge tax on the award.

Allowable expenses

To qualify as an allowable business expense, expenditure has to be laid out wholly and exclusively for business purposes. Strictly there must be no 'duality of purpose', which means that expenditure cannot be apportioned to reflect private and business usage, for example food, clothing, telephone, travelling expenses, etc. However, HMRC will usually allow all reasonable expenses (including apportioned sums) where the amounts can be commercially justified.

It should be noted carefully that the expenditure does not have to be 'necessary', it merely has to be incurred 'wholly and exclusively' for business purposes. Naturally, however, expenditure of an outrageous and wholly unnecessary character might well give rise to a presumption that it was not really for business purposes. As with all things, some expenses are unquestionably allowable and some expenses are equally unquestionably not allowable – it is the grey area in between which gives rise to all the difficulties and the outcome invariably depends on negotiation with HMRC.

Great care should be taken when claiming a deduction for items where there may be a duality of purpose and negotiations should be conducted with more than usual care and

Finance for writers and artists

courtesy – if provoked, the Inspector of Taxes may well choose to allow nothing. An appeal is always possible although unlikely to succeed as a string of cases in the Courts has clearly demonstrated. An example is the case of *Caillebotte* v. *Quinn* where the taxpayer (who normally had lunch at home) sought to claim the excess cost of meals incurred because he was working a long way from his home. The taxpayer's arguments failed because he did not eat only in order to work, one of the reasons for his eating was in order to sustain his life; a duality of purpose therefore existed and no tax relief was due.

Other cases have shown that expenditure on clothing can also be disallowed if it is the kind of clothing which is in everyday use, because clothing is worn not only to assist the pursuit of one's profession but also to accord with public decency. This duality of purpose may be sufficient to deny relief – even where the particular type of clothing is of a kind not otherwise worn by the taxpayer. In the case of *Mallalieu* v. *Drummond* a barrister failed to obtain a tax deduction for items of sombre clothing that she purchased specifically for wearing in Court. The House of Lords decided that a duality of purpose existed because clothing represented part of her needs as a human being.

Allowances

Despite the above, Inspectors of Taxes are not usually inflexible and the following list of expenses are among those generally allowed.

(a) Cost of all materials used up in the course of the work's preparation.

(b) Cost of typewriting and secretarial assistance, etc; if this or other help is obtained from one's spouse then it is entirely proper for a deduction to be claimed for the amounts paid for the work. The amounts claimed must actually be paid to the spouse and should be at the market rate, although some uplift can be made for unsocial hours, etc. Payments to a spouse are of course taxable in their hands and should therefore be most carefully considered. The spouse's earnings may also be liable for National Insurance contributions and it is important to take care because otherwise you may find that these contributions outweigh the tax savings. The impact of the National Minimum Wage should also be considered.

(c) All expenditure on normal business items such as postage, stationery, telephone, email, fax and answering machines, agent's fees, accountancy charges, photography, subscriptions, periodicals, magazines, etc may be claimed. The cost of daily papers should not be overlooked if these form part of research material. Visits to theatres, cinemas, etc for research purposes may also be permissible (but not the costs relating to guests). Unfortunately, expenditure on all types of business entertaining is specifically denied tax relief.

(d) If work is conducted at home, a deduction for 'use of home' is usually allowed providing the amount claimed is reasonable. If the claim is based on an appropriate proportion of the total costs of rent, light and heat, cleaning and maintenance, insurance, etc (but not the Council Tax), care should be taken to ensure that no single room is used 'exclusively' for business purposes, because this may result in the Capital Gains Tax exemption on the house as the only or main residence being partially forfeited. However, it would be a strange household where one room was in fact used exclusively for business purposes and for no other purpose whatsoever (e.g. storing personal bank statements and other private papers); the usual formula is to claim a deduction on the basis that most or all of the rooms in the house are used at one time or another for business purposes, thereby avoiding any suggestion that any part was used exclusively for business purposes.

(e) The appropriate business proportion of motor running expenses may also be claimed although what is the appropriate proportion will naturally depend on the particular circumstances of each case. It should be appreciated that the well-known scale of benefits, whereby employees are taxed according to the size of the car's CO_2 emissions, do not apply to self-employed persons.

(f) It has been long established that the cost of travelling from home to work (whether employed or self-employed) is not an allowable expense. However, if home is one's place of work then no expenditure under this heading is likely to be incurred and difficulties are unlikely to arise.

(g) Travelling and hotel expenses incurred for business purposes will normally be allowed but if any part could be construed as disguised holiday or pleasure expenditure, considerable thought would need to be given to the commercial reasons for the journey in order to justify the claim. The principle of 'duality of purpose' will always be a difficult hurdle in this connection – although not insurmountable.

(h) If a separate business bank account is maintained, any overdraft interest thereon will be an allowable expense. This is the only circumstance in which overdraft interest is allowed for tax purposes.

(i) Where capital allowances (see below) are claimed for a personal computer, laptop, iPad, fax machine, mobile phone, television, CD or DVD player, etc used for business purposes, the costs of maintenance and repair of the equipment may also be claimed.

Clearly many other allowable items may be claimed in addition to those listed. Wherever there is any reasonable business motive for some expenditure it should be claimed as a deduction although it is necessary to preserve all records relating to the expense. It is sensible to avoid an excess of imagination as this would naturally cause the Inspector of Taxes to doubt the genuineness of other expenses claimed.

The question is often raised whether the whole amount of an expense may be deducted or whether the VAT content must be excluded. Where VAT is reclaimed from HMRC by someone who is registered for VAT, the VAT element of the expense cannot be treated as an allowable deduction. Where the VAT is not reclaimed, the whole expense (inclusive of VAT) is allowable for income tax purposes.

Capital allowances

Where expenditure of a capital nature is incurred, it cannot be deducted from income as an expense – a separate and sometimes more valuable capital allowance being available instead. Capital allowances are given for many different types of expenditure, but authors and similar professional people are likely to claim only for 'plant and machinery'; this is a very wide expression which may include cars, personal computers, laptops, iPads, fax machines, televisions, CD and DVD players used for business purposes. Plant and machinery will normally qualify for an allowance of 100%.

The reason capital allowances can be more valuable than allowable expenses is that they may be wholly or partly disclaimed in any year that full benefit cannot be obtained – ordinary business expenses cannot be similarly disclaimed. Where, for example, the income of an author is not large enough to bring him above the tax threshold, he would not be liable to tax and a claim for capital allowances would be wasted. If the capital allowances were to be disclaimed their benefit would be carried forward for use in subsequent years. This would also be advantageous where the income is likely to be taxable at the higher rate of 40% (or the 45% rate) in a subsequent year. Careful planning with claims for capital allowances is therefore essential if maximum benefit is to be obtained.

As an alternative to capital allowances, claims can be made on the 'renewals' basis whereby all renewals are treated as allowable deductions in the year; no allowance is obtained for the initial purchase, but the cost of replacement (excluding any improvement element) is allowed in full. This basis is no longer widely used, as it is considerably less advantageous than claiming capital allowances as described above.

Leasing is a popular method of acquiring fixed assets, and where cash is not available to enable an outright purchase to be made, assets may be leased over a period of time. Whilst leasing may have financial benefits in certain circumstances, in normal cases there is likely to be no tax advantage in leasing an asset where the alternative of outright purchase is available.

Books

The question of whether the cost of books is eligible for tax relief has long been a source of difficulty. The annual cost of replacing books used for the purposes of one's professional activities (e.g. the cost of a new *Children's Writers' & Artists' Yearbook* each year) has always been an allowable expense; the difficulty arose because the initial cost of reference books, etc (e.g. when commencing one's profession) was treated as capital expenditure but no allowances were due as the books were not considered to be 'plant'. However, the matter was clarified by the case of *Munby* v. *Furlong* in which the Court of Appeal decided that the initial cost of law books purchased by a barrister was expenditure on 'plant' and eligible for capital allowances. This is clearly a most important decision, particularly relevant to any person who uses expensive books in the course of exercising his or her profession.

Pension contributions

Where a self-employed person makes contributions to a pension scheme, those contributions are usually deductible.

These arrangements are generally advantageous in providing for a pension as contributions are usually paid when the income is high (and the tax relief is also high) and the pension (taxed as earned income when received) usually arises when the income is low and a lower rate of tax may be payable. There is also the opportunity to take part of the pension entitlement as a tax-free lump sum. It is necessary to take into account the possibility that the tax advantages could go into reverse. When the pension is paid it could, if rates rise again, be taxed at a higher rate than the rate of tax relief at the moment.

Each individual has a lifetime allowance (reduced this year to £1 million and when benefits crystallise, which will generally be when a pension begins to be paid, this is measured against the individual's lifetime allowance; any excess will be taxed at the individual's marginal rate.

Each individual also has an annual allowance for contributions to the pension fund, which was £40,000 for 2014/15 but may change in later years. If the annual increase in an individual's rights under all registered schemes of which he is a member exceeds the annual allowance, the excess is chargeable to tax.

For many writers and artists this means that they can contribute a large part of their earnings to a pension scheme (if they can afford to do so) without any of the previous complications. It is still necessary to be careful where there is other income giving rise to a pension because the whole of the pension entitlement has to be taken into account.

Flexible retirement is possible allowing members of occupational pension schemes to continue working while also drawing retirement benefits.

Class 4 National Insurance contributions

Allied to pensions is the payment of Class 4 National Insurance contributions, although no pension or other benefit is obtained by the contributions; the Class 4 contributions are designed solely to extract additional amounts from self-employed persons and are payable in addition to the normal Class 2 (self-employed) contributions. The rates are changed each year and for 2015/16 self-employed persons will be obliged to contribute 9% of their profits between the range £8,060–£42,385 per annum plus 2% on earnings above £42,385. This amount is collected in conjunction with the annual income tax liability.

Averaging relief

Relief for copyright payments

Professional authors and artists engaged in the creation of literary or dramatic works or designs may claim to average the profits of two or more consecutive years if the profits for one year are less than 75% of the profits for the highest year. This relief can apply even if the work took less than 12 months to create and is available to people who create works in partnership with others. It enables the creative artist to utilise their allowances fully and to avoid the higher rates of tax which might apply if all the income were to arise in a single year.

Collection of tax: self-assessment

Under 'self-assessment' you submit your tax return and work out your tax liability for yourself. If you get it wrong, or if you are late with your tax return or the payment of tax, interest and penalties will be charged. Completing a tax return is a daunting task but the term 'self-assessment' is not intended to imply that individuals have to do it themselves; they can (and often will) engage professional help. The term is only intended to convey that it is the taxpayer, and not HMRC, who is responsible for getting the tax liability right and for it to be paid on time.

The deadline for filing your tax return is 31 January following the end of the tax year. You must now file online; a paper tax return cannot be filed in most cases.

Income tax on self-employed earnings remains payable in two instalments on 31 January and 31 July each year. Because the accurate figures may not necessarily be known, these payments in January and July will therefore be only payments on account based on the previous year's liability. The final balancing figure will be paid the following 31 January together with the first instalment of the liability for the following year.

When HMRC receives the self-assessment tax return, it is checked to see if there is anything obviously wrong; if there is, a letter will be sent to you immediately. Otherwise, HMRC has 12 months from the filing date in which to make further enquiries; if it doesn't, it will have no further opportunity to do so and your tax liabilities are final – unless there is an error or an omission. In that event, HMRC can raise an assessment later to collect any extra tax together with appropriate penalties. It is essential that all records relevant to your tax return are retained for at least 12 months after the filing date in case they are needed by HMRC. For the self-employed, the record-keeping requirement is much more onerous because the records need to be kept for nearly six years. If you claim a tax deduction for an expense, it will be necessary to have a receipt or other document proving that the expenditure has been made. Because the existence of the underlying records is so important to the operation of self-assessment, HMRC will treat them very seriously and there are penalties for a failure to keep adequate records.

Interest

Interest is chargeable on overdue tax at a variable rate, which is presently 3% per annum. It does not rank for any tax relief, which can make HMRC an expensive source of credit.

However, HMRC can also be obliged to pay interest (known as repayment supplement) tax-free where repayments are delayed. The rules relating to repayment supplement are less beneficial and even more complicated than the rules for interest payable but they do exist and can be very welcome if a large repayment has been delayed for a long time. Unfortunately, the rate of repayment supplement is only 0.5% and is always less than the rate charged by HMRC on overdue tax.

Value added tax

The activities of writers, painters, composers, etc are all 'taxable supplies' within the scope of VAT and chargeable at the standard rate. (Zero rating which applies to publishers, booksellers, etc on the supply of books does not extend to the work performed by writers.) Accordingly, authors are obliged to register for VAT if their income for the past 12 months exceeds £82,000 or if their income for the coming month will exceed that figure.

Delay in registering can be a most serious matter because if registration is not effected at the proper time, HMRC can (and invariably do) claim VAT from all the income received since the date on which registration should have been made. As no VAT would have been included in the amounts received during this period the amount claimed by HMRC must inevitably come straight from the pocket of the author.

The author may be entitled to seek reimbursement of the VAT from those whom he or she ought to have charged VAT but this is obviously a matter of some difficulty and may indeed damage his or her commercial relationships. Apart from these disadvantages there is also a penalty for late registration. The rules are extremely harsh and are imposed automatically even in cases of innocent error. It is therefore extremely important to monitor the income very carefully because if in any period of 12 months the income exceeds the £82,000 limit, the Customs and Excise must be notified within 30 days of the end of the period. Failure to do so will give rise to an automatic penalty. It should be emphasised that this is a penalty for failing to submit a form and has nothing to do with any real or potential loss of tax. Furthermore, whether the failure was innocent or deliberate will not matter. Only the existence of a 'reasonable excuse' will be a defence to the penalty. However, a reasonable excuse does not include ignorance, error, a lack of funds or reliance on any third party.

However, it is possible to regard VAT registration as a privilege and not a penalty, because only VAT registered persons can reclaim VAT paid on their expenses such as stationery, telephone, professional fees, etc and even computers and other plant and machinery (excluding cars). However, many find that the administrative inconvenience – the cost of maintaining the necessary records and completing the necessary forms – more than outweighs the benefits to be gained from registration and prefer to stay outside the scope of VAT for as long as possible.

Overseas matters

The general observation may be made that self-employed persons resident and domiciled in the UK are not well treated with regard to their overseas work, being taxable on their worldwide income. It is important to emphasise that if fees are earned abroad, no tax saving can be achieved merely by keeping the money outside the country. Although exchange control regulations no longer exist to require repatriation of foreign earnings, such income remains taxable in the UK and must be disclosed to HMRC; the same applies to interest or other income arising on any investment of these earnings overseas. Accordingly, whenever foreign earnings are likely to become substantial, prompt and effective action is required to limit the impact of UK and foreign taxation. In the case of non-resident authors it is important that arrangements concerning writing for publication in the UK, for example in newspapers, are undertaken with great care. A case concerning the wife of one of the great train robbers who provided detailed information for a series of articles published in a Sunday newspaper is most instructive. Although she was acknowledged to be resident in Canada for all the relevant years, the income from the articles was treated as arising in this country and fully chargeable to UK tax.

The UK has double taxation agreements with many other countries and these agreements are designed to ensure that income arising in a foreign country is taxed either in that country or in the UK. Where a withholding tax is deducted from payments received from another country (or where tax is paid in full in the absence of a double taxation agreement), the amount of foreign tax paid can usually be set off against the related UK tax liability.

Many successful authors can be found living in Eire because of the complete exemption from tax which attaches to works of cultural or artistic merit by persons who are resident there. However, such a step should only be contemplated having careful regard to all the other domestic and commercial considerations and specialist advice is essential if the exemption is to be obtained and kept; a careless breach of the conditions could cause the exemption to be withdrawn with catastrophic consequences. Consult the Revenue Commissioners in Dublin (www.revenue.ie) for further information concerning the precise conditions to be satisfied for exemption from tax in the Republic of Ireland.

Companies

When authors become successful the prospect of paying tax at high rates may drive them to take hasty action, such as the formation of a company, which may not always be to their advantage. Indeed some authors seeing the exodus into tax exile of their more successful colleagues even form companies in low tax areas in the hope of saving large amounts of tax. HMRC is fully aware of these possibilities and has extensive powers to charge tax and combat avoidance. Accordingly, such action is just as likely to increase tax liabilities and generate other costs and should never be contemplated without expert advice; some very expensive mistakes are often made in this area which are not always able to be remedied.

To conduct one's business through the medium of a company can be a very effective method of mitigating tax liabilities, and providing it is done at the right time and under the right circumstances very substantial advantages can be derived. However, if done without due care and attention the intended advantages will simply evaporate. At the very least it is essential to ensure that the company's business is genuine and conducted properly with regard to the realities of the situation. If the author continues his/her activities unchanged, simply paying all the receipts from his/her work into a company's bank account, he/she cannot expect to persuade HMRC that it is the company and not himself who is entitled to, and should be assessed to tax on, that income.

It must be strongly emphasised that many pitfalls exist which can easily eliminate all the tax benefits expected to arise by the formation of the company. For example, company directors are employees of the company and will be liable to pay much higher National Insurance contributions; the company must also pay the employer's proportion of the contribution and a total liability of nearly 26% of gross salary may arise. This compares most unfavourably with the position of a self-employed person. Moreover, on the commencement of the company's business the individual's profession will cease and the possibility of revisions being made by HMRC to earlier tax liabilities means that the timing of a change has to be considered very carefully.

The tax return

No mention has been made above of personal reliefs and allowances; this is because these allowances and the rates of tax are subject to constant change and are always set out in detail in the explanatory notes which accompany the tax return. The annual tax return is an important document and should be completed promptly with extreme care. If filling in the tax return is a source of difficulty or anxiety, *Money Which? – Tax Saving Guide* (Consumer Association, annual, March) is very helpful.

Peter Vaines FCA, CTA, barrister, is a partner in the international law firm of Squire Patton Boggs (UK) LLP and writes and speaks widely on tax matters. He is on the Editorial Board of *Personal Tax Planning Review*, tax columnist of the *New Law Journal* and author of a number of books on taxation.

See also...
- *FAQs for writers,* page 429
- *National Insurance contributions and social security benefits,* page 441

National Insurance contributions and social security benefits

Most people who work in Great Britain either as an employee or as a self-employed person are liable to pay National Insurance contributions. The law governing this subject is complex and Peter Arrowsmith FCA (with updates by Sarah Bradford) has summarised it here for the benefit of writers and artists. This article also contains an outline of the benefits system and should be regarded as a general guide only.

All contributions are payable in respect of years ending on 5 April. See box (below) for the classes of contributions.

Employed or self-employed?

Employed earners pay Class 1 contributions and self-employed earners pay Class 2 and Class 4 contributions. It is therefore essential to know the status of a worker to ensure that the correct class of contribution is paid. The question as to whether a person is employed under a contract *of* service and is thereby an employee liable to Class 1 contributions, or performs services (either solely or in partnership) under a contract *for* service and is thereby self-employed and liable to Class 2 and Class 4 contributions, often has to be decided in practice. One of the best guides can be found in the case of *Market Investigations Ltd* v. *Minister of Social Security* (1969 2 WLR 1) when Cooke J. remarked:

Classes of contributions

Class 1 Payable by employees (primary contributions) and their employers (secondary contributions), based on earnings.

Class 1A Payable only by employers in respect of all taxable benefits in kind.

Class 1B Payable only by employers in respect of PAYE Settlement Agreements entered into by them.

Class 2 Weekly flat rate contributions payable by the self-employed.

Class 3 Weekly flat rate contributions, payable on a voluntary basis in order to provide, or make up entitlement to, certain social security benefits.

Class 3A Voluntary contributions payable from 12 October 2015 by those reaching state pension age before 6 April 2016. Amount depends on age.

Class 4 Payable by the self-employed in respect of their trading or professional income, based on earnings.

'…the fundamental test to be applied is this: "Is the person who has engaged himself to perform these services performing them as a person in business on his own account?" If the answer to that question is "yes", then the contract is a contract for services. If the answer is "no", then the contract is a contract of service. No exhaustive list has been compiled and perhaps no exhaustive list can be compiled of the considerations which are relevant in determining that question, nor can strict rules be laid down as to the relative weight which the various considerations should carry in particular cases. The most that can be said is that control will no doubt always have to be considered, although it can no longer be regarded as the sole determining factor; and that factors which may be of importance are such matters as:

• whether the man performing the services provides his own equipment,
• whether he hires his own helpers,
• what degree of financial risk he takes,
• what degree of responsibility for investment and management he has, and

Finance for writers and artists

• whether and how far he has an opportunity of profiting from sound management in the performance of his task.'

The above case has often been considered subsequently in Tribunal cases, but there are many factors to take into account. An indication of employment status can be obtained on the GOV.UK website (www.gov.uk/employment-status).

Exceptions

There are exceptions to the above rules, those most relevant to artists and writers being:
• The employment of a wife by her husband, or vice versa, is disregarded for National Insurance purposes unless it is for the purposes of a trade or profession (e.g. the employment of his wife by an author would not be disregarded and would result in a liability for contributions if her salary reached the minimum levels). The same provisions also apply to civil partners from 5 December 2005.
• The employment of certain relatives in a private dwelling house in which both employee and employer reside is disregarded for social security purposes provided the employment is not for the purposes of a trade or business carried out at those premises by the employer. This would cover the employment of a relative (as defined) as a housekeeper in a private residence.

Personal service companies

Since 6 April 2000, those who have control of their own 'one-man service companies' are subject to special rules (commonly referred to as IR35). If the work carried out by the owner of the company for the company's customers would be – but for the one-man company – considered as an employment of that individual (i.e. rather than self-employment), a deemed salary may arise. If it does, then some or all of the company's income will be treated as salary liable to PAYE and National Insurance contributions (NICs). This will be the case whether or not such salary is actually paid by the company. The same situation may arise where the worker owns as little as 5% of a company's share capital.

The calculations required by HMRC are complicated and have to be done very quickly at the end of each tax year (even if the company's year-end does not coincide). It is essential that affected businesses seek detailed professional advice about these rules which may also, in certain circumstances, apply to partnerships.

The rules have attracted much criticism. In April 2014 the House of Lords Select Committee published the findings of their review into the personal service company rules and made a number of recommendations. Although various changes were made to the rules, the Government is committed to retaining IR35.

In order to escape the application of the IR35 rules, a number of workers have arranged their engagements through 'managed service companies', etc where the promoter is heavily involved in all the company management to the exclusion of the workers themselves. Such companies are now subject to similar, but different, rules, which apply from 6 April 2007 for tax and 6 August 2007 for NICs.

For further information, see www.gov.uk/business-tax/ir35.

State pension age

Workers, both employed and self-employed, stop paying NICs once they reach state pension age. However, employers must continue to pay secondary Class 1 contributions in respect of earnings paid to employees who have reached state pension age.

The current state pension age for men is 65. The state pension age for women is gradually being increased so as to equalise it with that for men. The state pension age for women is being increased gradually from 6 April 2010 and will reach age 65 on 6 November 2018. From that date, the state pension age for both men and women will rise to 66 to achieve a state pension age of 66 on 6 September 2020. The state pension age will be further increased from 66 to 67 between 2026 and 2028 and will rise from 67 to 68 between 2044 and 2046. Provisions included in the Pensions Act 2014 provide for the state pension age to be reviewed every 5 years.

In 2015/16 women will reach state pension age on the following dates depending on their date of birth. Men will reach state pension age at age 65.

Date of birth	Date state pension age reached
6 October 1952 to 5 November 1952	6 May 2015
6 November 1952 to 5 December 1952	6 July 2015
6 December 1952 to 5 January 1953	6 September 2015
6 January 1953 to 5 February 1953	6 November 2015
6 February 1953 to 5 March 1953	6 January 2016
6 March 1953 to 5 April 1953	6 March 2016

Class 1 contributions

Primary Class 1 contributions are payable by employed earners and secondary Class 1 contributions are payable by self-employed workers by reference to their earnings. Where an employee contracts out of the second state pension (S2P), a rebate is payable in respect of both employee and employer contributions, which effectively reduces the contributions rate on earnings within a certain band. Since 6 April 2012, it is only possible to contract-out by means of a defined benefit (salary-related) scheme. Contracting out for money purchase schemes (COMPS) came to an end on 5 April 2012. Contracting out for salary-related schemes will come to an end on 5 April 2016 consequent on the introduction of the single-tier state pension payable to those who reach state pension age on or after that date.

Contributions are payable by employees on earnings that exceed the primary threshold (£155 per week for 2015/16) and by employers on earnings that exceed the secondary threshold (£156 per week for 2015/16). However, where the employee is under the age of 21, employer contributions are only payable on earnings that exceed the upper secondary threshold for under 21s. For 2015/16 this is set at £815 per week (the same as the upper earnings limit). Contributions are normally collected via the PAYE tax deduction machinery, and there are penalties for late submission of returns and for errors therein and also for PAYE and NICs paid late on more than one occasion in the tax year. Interest is charged automatically on PAYE and social security contributions paid late.

Employees' liability to pay

Contributions are payable by any employee who is aged 16 years and over (even though they may still be at school) and who is paid an amount equal to, or exceeding, the primary earnings threshold (£155 per week for 2015/16). Where the employee has earnings between the lower earnings limit and the primary threshold, contributions are payable at a notional zero rate. This preserves the employee's contributions record and entitlement to the state pension and contributory benefits. Nationality is irrelevant for contribution purposes and, subject to special rules covering employees not normally resident in Great Britain, Northern Ireland or the Isle of Man, or resident in EEA countries or those with which there are reciprocal agreements, contributions must be paid whether the employee concerned is a British subject or not provided he/she is gainfully employed in Great Britain.

Persons over state pension age are exempt from liability to pay primary contributions, even if they have not retired. However, the fact that an employee may be exempt from liability does not relieve an employer from liability to pay secondary contributions in respect of that employee.

Employees' (primary) contributions

From 6 April 2015, the rate of employees' contributions on earnings from the employee earnings threshold (£155 per week) to the upper earnings limit (£815 per week) is 12%. Contributions are payable at a rate of 2% on earnings above the upper earnings limit. A rebate of 1.4% is payable to contracted-out employees on earnings between the lower earnings limit and the upper accruals point (£770 per week) (meaning that the effective rate between the primary earnings threshold and upper accruals point is 10.6% rather than 12%). Certain married women who made appropriate elections before 12 May 1977 may be entitled to pay a reduced rate of 5.85%. However, they have no entitlement to benefits in respect of these contributions.

Employers' (secondary) contributions

All employers are liable to pay contributions on the gross earnings of employees above the age of 16 where their earnings exceed the secondary earnings threshold (£156 per week for 2015/16). However, from 6 April 2015 where the employee is under 21, employer contributions are only payable on earnings in excess of the upper secondary threshold for under 21s (£815 per week for 2015/16). As mentioned above, an employer's liability is not reduced as a result of employees being exempted from contributions, or being liable to pay only the reduced rate (5.85%) of contributions.

For earnings paid on or after 6 April 2015, employers are liable at a rate of 13.8% on earnings paid above the secondary earnings threshold (or, where the employee is under 21). Where the employee is in a contracted-out employment, the employer receives a rebate of 3.4% on earnings between the lower earnings limit and the upper accruals point. Most employers are entitled to an annual employment allowance of £2,000, which is offset against their secondary Class 1 liability. The allowance is claimed through the employer's real time information (RTI) software.

The employer is responsible for the payment of both employees' and employer's contributions, but is entitled to deduct the employees' contributions from the earnings on which they are calculated. Effectively, therefore, the employee suffers a deduction in respect of his or her social security contributions in arriving at his weekly or monthly wage or salary. Special rules apply to company directors and persons employed through agencies.

Items included in, or excluded from, earnings

Contributions are calculated on the basis of a person's gross earnings from their employment. This will normally be the figure shown on the deduction working sheet or computer equivalent record, except where the employee pays superannuation contributions and, from 6 April 1987, charitable gifts under payroll giving – these must be added back for the purposes of calculating Class 1 liability.

Earnings include salary, wages, overtime pay, commissions, bonuses, holiday pay, payments made while the employee is sick or absent from work, payments to cover travel between home and office, and payments under the statutory sick pay, statutory maternity pay, statutory paternity pay and statutory adoption pay schemes.

However, certain payments, some of which may be regarded as taxable income for income tax purposes, are ignored for Class 1 purposes. These include:
- certain gratuities paid other than by the employer;
- redundancy payments and some payments in lieu of notice;
- certain payments in kind;
- reimbursement of specific expenses incurred in the carrying out of the employment;
- benefits given on an individual basis for personal reasons (e.g. birthday presents);
- compensation for loss of office.

Booklet CWG 2 (2015 edition) gives a list of items to include in or exclude from earnings for Class 1 contribution purposes (available from www.gov.uk). Some such items may, however, be liable to Class 1A (employer-only) contributions.

Class 1A and Class 1B contributions

Class 1A contributions are employer-only contributions payable in respect of most taxable benefits provided to employees earning at a rate of at least £8,500 a year and to directors, as reported on form P11D. Class 1A contributions are payable at a rate of 13.8%.

Class 1B contributions are payable by employers using PAYE Settlement Agreements in respect of small and/or irregular expense payments and benefits, etc. This rate is also 13.8%.

Upper accrual point

The upper accrual point (UAP) was introduced from 6 April 2009 and is the rate from which entitlement to benefit (principally earnings-related state pension) ceases, even though main rate Class 1 contributions continue to be due. This impacts on contracted-out employees in particular. The UAP is fixed at a constant cash amount of £770 per week, the original intention being that it would gradually erode the earnings related element of the state pension. However, the current two-tier state pension is being replaced by a single-

Rates of Class 1 contributions and earnings limits from 6 April 2015

Earnings per week	Rates payable on earnings in each band			
	Not contracted out		Contracted out	
	Employee	Employer	Employee	Employer
£	%	%	%	%
Below 112.00	–	–	–	–
112.00–154.99	0**	–	-1.4%*	-3.4%*
155.00–155.99	12	–	10.6	-3.4%*
156.00–769.99	12	13.8***	10.6	10.4***
770.00–810.00	12	13.8***	12	13.8***
Over 810.00	2	13.8	2	13.8

* Special rebates deductible in respect of this band of earnings (contracted-out salary-related schemes only).

** Contributions payable at a notional zero rate.

*** No employer contributions where employee is under 21.

tier state pension for those who reach state pension age on or after 6 April 2016. Contracting out will come to an end as a result.

Class 2 contributions

Class 2 contributions are payable at the weekly rate of £2.80 as from 6 April 2015. Certain persons are exempt from Class 2 liability as follows:

• A person over state pension age.
• A person who has not attained the age of 16.
• A married woman or, in certain cases, a widow, either of whom elected prior to 12 May 1977 not to pay Class 2 contributions.
• Persons with earnings below the small profits threshold (see below).
• Persons not ordinarily self-employed (see below).

Small profits threshold

From 6 April 2015 no liability to Class 2 contributions arises unless earnings from self-employment exceed the small profits threshold, which is set at £5,965 for 2015/16. The small profits threshold replaced the small earnings exception which applied for 2014/15 and earlier years.

• for the year of application are expected to be less than a specified limit (£5,885 in the 2014/15 tax year); or
• for the year preceding the application were less than the limit specified for that year (£5,725 for 2013/14) and there has been no material change of circumstances.

Certificates of exception must be renewed in accordance with the instructions stated thereon. At the discretion of HMRC, the certificate may commence up to 13 weeks before the date on which the application is made. Despite a certificate of exception being in force, a person who is self-employed is still entitled to pay Class 2 contributions if they wish, in order to maintain entitlement to social security benefits.

Persons not ordinarily self-employed

Part-time self-employed activities (including as a writer or artist) are disregarded for contribution purposes if the person concerned is not ordinarily employed in such activities and has a full-time job as an employee. There is no definition of 'ordinarily employed' for this purpose. Persons qualifying for this relief do not require certificates of exception but are well advised to apply for one nonetheless.

Payment of contributions

For 2015/16 onwards, Class 2 contributions are payable via the self-assessment system with income tax and Class 4 contributions. Class 2 contributions for 2015/16 are due by 31 January 2017.

Class 3 and Class 3A contributions

Class 3 contributions are payable voluntarily, at the weekly rate of £14.40 per week from 6 April 2015, by persons aged 16 or over with a view to enabling them to qualify for a limited range of benefits if their contribution record is not otherwise sufficient. In general, Class 3 contributions can be paid by employees, the self-employed and the non-employed.

Broadly speaking, no more than 52 Class 3 contributions are payable for any one tax year, and contributions cannot be paid in respect of tax years after the one in which the individual concerned reaches state pension age. Class 3 contributions may be paid by monthly direct debit, quarterly bill or by annual cheque in arrears.

A new class of voluntary contribution, Class 3A, is to be introduced from October 2015 to provide those who reach state pension age before 6 April 2016 with an opportunity to top up their state pension. The amount of the Class 3A contribution will depend on the contributor's age.

Class 4 contributions

In addition to Class 2 contributions, self-employed persons are liable to pay Class 4 contributions. These are calculated at the rate of 9% on the amount of profits or gains chargeable to income tax which exceed the lower profits limit (£8,060 per annum for 2015/16) but which do not exceed the upper profits limit (£42,385 per annum for 2015/16). Profits above the upper limit of £42,385 (2015/16) attract a Class 4 charge at the rate of 2%. The income tax profit on which Class 4 contributions are calculated is after deducting capital allowances and losses, but before deducting personal tax allowances or retirement annuity or personal pension or stakeholder pension plan premiums.

Class 4 contributions produce no additional benefits, but were introduced to ensure that self-employed persons as a whole pay a fair share of the cost of pensions and other social security benefits, yet without those who make only small profits having to pay excessively high flat rate contributions.

Payment of contributions

In general, Class 4 contributions are self-assessed and paid to HMRC together with the income tax as a result of the self-assessment income tax return, and accordingly the contributions are due and payable at the same time as the income tax liability on the relevant profits. Under self-assessment, payments on account of Class 4 contributions are payable at the same time as interim payments of tax.

Class 4 exemptions

The following persons are exempt from Class 4 contributions:
• Persons over state pension age at the commencement of the year of assessment (i.e. on 6 April).
• An individual not resident in the UK for income tax purposes in the year of assessment.
• Persons whose earnings are not 'immediately derived' from carrying on a trade, profession or vocation.
• A person under 16 years old on 6 April of the year of assessment.
• Persons not ordinarily self-employed.

Married persons and partnerships

Under independent taxation, each spouse is responsible for his or her own Class 4 liability.

In partnerships, each partner's liability is calculated separately. If a partner also carries on another trade or profession, the profits of all such businesses are aggregated for the purposes of calculating their Class 4 liability.

When an assessment has become final and conclusive for the purposes of income tax, it is also final and conclusive for the purposes of calculating Class 4 liability.

Maximum contributions

There is a form of limit to the total liability for social security contributions payable by a person who is employed in more than one employment, or is also self-employed or a partner. Where a person would otherwise pay more than the permitted maximum it may be possible to defer some contributions. The calculations are complex and guidance on the permitted maximum and deferment can be found on the GOV.UK website (see www.gov.uk/defer-self-employed-national-insurance).

Social security benefits

Benefits may be contributory (i.e. dependent upon set levels of social security contributions and/or NIC-able earnings arising in all or part of one or more tax years) or means-tested (i.e. subject to a full assessment of the income and capital of the claimant and their partner). Child benefit is one of a handful falling outside either category being neither contributory nor means-tested, although the high income child benefit tax charge claws back child benefit where anyone in the household has taxable income over £50,000 per annum. The benefit is clawed back at a rate of 1% for each £100 of income over £50,000 such that the tax is equal to the child benefit received where income is £60,000 or above.

Most benefits are administered by the Department for Work and Pensions and its agencies (such as Jobcentre Plus and The Pension Service). Some are administered wholly or partly by HMRC and the latter are marked with an asterisk in the following lists.

Universal Credit is replacing a number of benefits and is in the process of being phased in.

Universal benefits

• Child Benefit*
• Carer's Allowance (for those looking after a severely disabled person)
• Disability Living Allowance (DLA) – progressively being replaced by Personal Independence Payment (PIP) during 2013
• Personal Independence Payment (PIP) (help with some of the extra costs caused by long-term ill-health or disability for those aged 16–64)

Contributory benefits

• State Pension – basic and earnings-related
• Bereavement benefits
• Contribution-based Jobseeker's Allowance (JSA) (time limited, i.e. unemployment)
• Contribution-based Employment and Support Allowance (ESA) (time limited for some, i.e. sickness and incapacity)
• Statutory Sick Pay* (SSP) (for employees only, paid by the employer)
• Statutory Maternity Pay* (SMP) (for employees only, paid by the employer)
• Maternity Allowance (for self-employed and others meeting the conditions)
• Statutory Paternity Pay* (SPP) (for employees only, paid by the employer)
• Shared Parental Pay* (ShPP) (for employees only, paid by the employer)
• Statutory Adoption Pay* (SAP) (for employees only, paid by the employer)
• Guardian's Allowance*

Means-tested benefits

• Income-based Jobseeker's Allowance (JSA) (i.e. unemployment)
• Income-based Employment and Support Allowance (ESA) (i.e. sickness and incapacity)
• Income Support (low-income top up for those of working age, not working but neither unemployed nor sick/incapacitated)
• Working Tax Credits* (WTC) (low-income top up for those of working age)
• Child Tax Credit* (low-income top up for those of working age with children, in addition to Working Tax Credit if applicable)
• Disabled Person's Tax Credits* (DPTC) (low-income top up for disabled people)
• Pension Credit (low-income top up for those of pension age)
• Social Fund grants (one-off assistance for low-income household with unexpected, emergency expenditure)

In addition, help with rent and rates is available on a means-tested basis from local authorities.

Many of the working age benefits are in the process of being replaced with 'Universal Credit', starting with new claimants. Universal Credit will eventually replace Income-based Jobseeker's Allowance, Income-related Employment and Support Allowance, Income Support, Working Tax Credit, Child Tax Credit and Housing Benefit.

Peter Arrowsmith FCA is a former sole practitioner specialising in National Insurance matters, and member and former chairman of the Employment Taxes and National Insurance Committee of the Institute of Chartered Accountants in England and Wales. **Sarah Bradford** BA (Hons), ACA CTA (Fellow) is the director of Writetax Ltd and the author of *National Insurance Contributions 2015/16* (and earlier editions) published by Bloomsbury Professional. She writes widely on tax and National Insurance contributions and provides tax consultancy services.

Finance for writers and artists

INDEX

Index

Writing Children's Fiction
A Writers'&Artists' Companion
By Yvonne Coppard & Linda Newbery

"...*filled to the brim with so many new insights and hidden ancient wisdom about writing that I myself will be reaching for its guidance and its pleasures.*"

– David Fickling

Full of both inspirational and practical advice, *Writing Children's Fiction* is an essential guide to writing for some of the most difficult and demanding readers of all: children and young people.

· **Part 1** explores the nature, history and challenges of children's literature, and the amazing variety of genres available for children from those learning to read to young adults.

· **Part 2** includes tips by bestselling authors such as David Almond, Malorie Blackman, Meg Rosoff and Michael Morpurgo.

· **Part 3** contains practical advice - from shaping plots and creating characters to knowing your readers, handling difficult subjects and how to find an agent and publisher when your book or story is complete.

Aug 2013 | 9781408156872| PB | 272 pp | £14.99

About the series: *Writers' & Artists' Companions* are practical guides to various writing genres and narrative forms, which include tips from big-name authors and provide exercises, examples and advice for aspiring writers in a non-prescriptive and encouraging way. These inspiring companions are essential reading for anyone who is truly serious about becoming a writer.

Series Editors: Carole Angier & Sally Cline

www.bloomsbury.com/series/writers-and-artists-companions

BLOOMSBURY